Third Edition

Accounting Systems

PROCEDURES AND METHODS

Cecil Gillespie, M.B.A., C.P.A.

Professor of Accounting
and Information Systems
Northwestern University

PRENTICE-HALL, INC., Englewood Cliffs, N.J.

Printed in the United States of America

ISBN: 0-13-001933-X

Library of Congress Catalog Card Number: 71-158195

10 9 8 7 6 5 4 3

PRENTICE-HALL INTERNATIONAL, INC., *London*
PRENTICE-HALL OF AUSTRALIA, PTY. LTD., *Sydney*
PRENTICE-HALL OF CANADA, LTD., *Toronto*
PRENTICE-HALL OF INDIA PRIVATE LTD., *New Delhi*
PRENTICE-HALL OF JAPAN, INC., *Tokyo*

Preface

Accounting Systems: Procedures and Methods explains how to make the survey of the business, select the methods to be used, design the system or procedure, and prepare the systems report or manual. It is based upon extensive experience in systems and procedures work, and the various survey techniques and basic procedures described have been amply tested in practice. This book comprises a complete systems methodology which will be a useful guide to the practitioner who designs and installs complete systems or procedures. It will also be useful to the office manager or accountant who wants to improve the procedures in operation in his office or reduce clerical cost.

The material is arranged in the following sections, each comprising one or more chapters:

(1) Survey and design techniques
(2) Methods
(3) Systems and procedures
(4) Cost systems
(5) Reports
(6) Punched-card accounting
(7) Electronic data-processing
(8) Time sharing
(9) Management information systems

The first section explains how a survey is made and a new system designed, using an actual distributing business as the basis for the illustrations.

A thorough treatment of the systems problems of small businesses is presented in the first two sections. The former section presents complete plans of journalizing, using standard forms which may be purchased from form stationers. The requirements of one-man businesses as well as those of businesses which employ full-time bookkeepers are covered. In the second section, special attention is given to the internal check problems of businesses in which it is difficult to achieve dispersion of clerical activities. Operation of control through use of autographic registers and cash registers is explained.

The methods chapters explain recent developments whose basic concepts are changing the character of systems work, even in small companies. The recent development of an entire new generation of writing machines, bookkeeping machines, and desk size computers is treated exhaustively. Electronic equipment for the accounting system and its sub-systems is described and illustrated and new ways of using it are explained along with the latest developments in mechanically actuated equipment. Electronic operation is now a feature of even some of the "smaller" units. Fully explored are the uses of automatic writing machines with calculating and memory capability, computer terminals as standalone writing machines, electronic printing calculators, and machines used for what are basically posting operations (which used to be called bookkeeping machines). The machines in this class are keyboard machines, but their new capabilities vastly change their potentials.

Uses of the new generation of cash registers, the new window machines used in financial and other service organizations, and point-of-transaction recorders designed for in-plant use are described. The use of machines for combined cash control and inventory control is likewise covered.

The various aspects of storage and retrieval are given proper recognition and treatment. Subjects in this area include microfilm systems, information retrieval (transmitter and monitor), and computer output microfilming. The new mechanized files and power files are introduced.

These chapters precede the systems and procedures chapters in order that a proper foundation may be laid for the study of procedures. It is recognized that in systems work a working knowledge of all the fundamental manual and machine methods of doing work in an office is absolutely necessary. The treatment of the methods phase of systems work is a special feature of this book.

The systems and procedures section covers all the basic procedures in a business. These chapters explain what information management gets from each of the basic procedures of a business and how the procedures operate in today's accounting.

Each of these chapters embraces, in general, the following topics:

(1) Function served by the procedure.
(2) Organization: what departments or sections operate the procedure and what departments benefit from the operation of the procedure.
(3) Management information provided by the records, and classifications used.

(4) Typical forms.

(5) Typical list of clerical operations.

(6) Methods applicable to this procedure.

(7) Accounting control and internal check.

The aim of each chapter is to show how to design a procedure for any of a variety of types and sizes of business, and to present forms and methods plans which the designer can use in solving the problem on which he is working. The systems and procedures section includes a new chapter on cost accounting systems which deals with the design problems peculiar to this specialized type of system. The basic design of a complete cost sysem is illustrated.

Chapters on punched-card accounting and electronic data-processing present a balanced treatment of these two important areas. The new punch card accounting machinery is discussed in a separate chapter in the series of chapters on punched card accounting.

The chapter on electronic data processing explains what it is **and** how it works (in non-technical language), including current developments in input-output units (among others, optical character reading and visual display), storage (memory) with consideration of cost and the related factors, number systems and the structural relationship to memory, and data transmission. The section on optical character reading explains the types of reader, the design and use of turnaround documents, field documents, and in-house documents, and the potential for cost saving. The appendix to this chapter includes an elementary discussion of programming, for the non-professional programmer, with an illustration of flow charting of computer logic and a short illustrative program.

The data transmission system is the network which ties the accounting system and all of its sub-systems together. It is the linkage among input, processing, storage and output and it is the visible structure of the operating system and the management information system. This book explains the function of various units which make up the data transmission system and describes briefly how an actual nation-wide transmission system works and the uses made of it.

The chapter on time sharing tells what it is, how it works and what it is being used for. This chapter, completely new in this edition, has been focused on the systems and procedures chapters. It points out the systems and procedures applications to which time sharing is being applied and with what success. Pros and cons to be considered by the systems man are set out in this chapter.

The management information systems chapter explains the relationship of the management information system to the accounting system and the operating system with due regard to internal information and external information, the management information system to the decision structure, and the maturing information system to the evolutionary organization structure.

The same chapter discusses traditional information systems and contemporary information systems, program budgeting and the information system, and the movement toward a total information system. Each of the segments or modules that makes up the contemporary information system is discussed.

Accounting Systems: Procedures and Methods has been popular as a textbook for systems courses in colleges and universities for many years. As the text for the Systems course, it provides the basis for lecture, field trip, and practice method of instruction. In field trips, the classes visit display rooms of business machine companies and the offices of private businesses. In some cases, a field trip is devoted to the demonstration of a particular machine or line of machines, and in other cases the trip is devoted to combination demonstrations of a particular procedure and a particular machine or method.

The practice work includes three multiple-assignment problems, two involving the design of a complete accounting system for non-manufacturing businesses and the other the design of a cost accounting system for a manufacturing business.

Single assignment problems include a number of procedures assignments in which actual forms and facts relating to an existing, unsatisfactory procedure are presented, with the instructions necessary for the student to redesign the procedure. This approach to systems work through examination of the old forms is a practical one which provides maximum reality. The problem and question material is adequate in quantity and coverage to provide for varying time allotments and other instructional needs. As indicated above, this text can be used effectively as the basis for a course which is mainly a field trip course, or a practice (laboratory) course, or a combination course consisting of lectures, field trips, and practice.

Theory problems and questions are also included to focus attention upon the mathematical and other factors affecting the solution of systems problems. Particular attention is paid to the factors that affect determination of the most economical method of performing clerical operations.

The author gratefully acknowledges the assistance of Mr. Eugene Delves of Arthur Andersen and Company and Professor Gardner Jones of Michigan State University who read the manuscript and offered expert suggestions. The chapter on Time Sharing was written by Edward A. Kennedy of Arthur Anderson and Company.

CECIL GILLESPIE

Chicago, Illinois

Contents

METHODS

Flow of Posting Media to the Machine; Handling Media at the Machine, *159*. Posting Sales Tickets to Customers' Accounts, *160*. Stuffing the Ledger, *161*. Posting Expense Invoices to Expense Accounts, *161*. Mixed Media; Random Posting, *162*. Exhaust Method, *162*. Summary: Unit Media; Mixed Media; Methods of Posting, *163*.

8. *Files and Records Housing; Microfilm Systems*   165

Records Management—A Resumé, *165*. Sorting Equipment and Devices, *166*. The Sorting Operation in the Flow of Accounting Papers, *166*. Sorting Operations Classified According to Equipment Used, *167*. Files and Other Record Housing Equipment, *168*. Types of Record Housing Equipment, *168*. Loose Leaf Binders, *168*. Vertical Filing Cabinets, *170*. Visible Record Equipment (for Reference and Posting), *170*. Visible Index Reference Equipment (for Reference to Lists), *176*. Mechanized Files; Power Files, *177*. Ledger Trays for Machine-Posting Applications, *179*. Binders for Filing Summary Strips, *179*. Transfer Cases and Binders, *179*. Microfilm Systems, *180*. Microfilm, *180*. Information Retrieval (Diebold SD-550), *180*. Computer Output Microfilming, *181*. Some Uses (and Users) of COM, *185*. Estimates of Future Developments, *185*.

9. *Internal Check and Accounting Control: Introduction*   187

Definition; Scope of This Chapter, *187*. Systems Design to Prevent Fraud and Error, *188*. Characteristics of a Satisfactory System of Internal Control, *189*. Organization Chart, *189*. Details of Protection Provided by Internal Check and Accounting Control, *191*. Control Devices and Methods, *192*. Internal Check and Accounting Control Procedures Illustrated, *194*.

10. *Autographic Registers; Cash Registers; Internal Check in Small Trading Concerns*   199

Autographic Registers, *199*. Source Record Punch for Source Data Collection, *200*. Writing Boards, *201*. Cash Registers, *205*. Central Cashier; Tube Cashier, *206*. Features of Some of the Earlier Models, *208*. Illustrations, *210*. National Cash Register Class 24, *210*. National Cash Register Class 5, *213*. National Retail On-Line Electronic Terminal Class 280, *215*. Cash Register (Class 5) with Automatic Drink Dispenser, *217*. Internal Check in the Small Store, *217*.

SYSTEMS AND PROCEDURES

11. *Order Procedures; Billing Procedures— Data-Processing Illustrated*   223

The Order Function; The Billing Function, *223*. Organization, *224*. Managerial Information, *224*. Shipping Order and Related Forms, *225*. Customer's Own Written Order as Shipping Order, *226*. Invoice and Related Forms, *228*. Combination of Order Procedures and Billing Procedures, *229*. Combinations Named, *229*. Separate Order and Billing Procedure. *230*. Conditions for Use of Separate Order and Billing Procedure, *230*. Illustration: Separate Order and Billing Procedures; Steel Warehousing, *232*. Illustration: Invoices Prepared on Writing Machines with Arithmetic and Memory Capability, *234*. Integrated Data-Processing for Sales and Cash-Collecting, *236*. Complete Pre-Billing, *238*. Incomplete Pre-Billing, *238*. Incomplete Pre-Billing: Actual Weight for Billing Determined in Shipping Department, *239*. Incomplete Pre-Billing; Actual Shipping Quantities Determined in Shipping Room; Manufacturer of Medical and Dental Equipment, *239*. Unit Shipping Order Procedures, *242*. Unit Shipping Order Procedures in General, *242*. Pre-Printed Unit Shipping Orders, *242*. Cur-

COST SYSTEMS

19. *Cost Systems*   433

REPORTS

20. *Systems and Procedure Reports*   463

PUNCHED-CARD ACCOUNTING

21. *Principles of Punched-Card Accounting*   489

22. *Equipment for Punched-Card Accounting*   504

1

The Field of
Systems and Procedures Work

Everyone who is familiar with modern business has at some time reflected upon the part that accounting forms and papers play in its operation. In some businesses, such as insurance companies and banks, a great many of the employees are inside employees, and most of them spend almost all their time in writing or otherwise handling business papers. In other businesses, such as department stores, there are great numbers of employees (sales persons, for instance) who spend a significant amount of their time writing and handling papers. In still other businesses, such as manufacturing concerns, utilities, and mail-order houses, although the number of clerical employees is not the majority factor in the total number employed, still it is an important minority. One has only to see the Order department of a mail-order house, for instance, to realize that handling order forms is as much a part of operations as handling goods is in the warehouse departments.

The Function of Accounting Forms and Papers in Business

In general, the function of accounting forms and papers, and of the reports prepared from them, is fourfold:

(1) *To determine the results of operations.* This function involves: (a) what in systems work is known as *distribution* (meaning abstracting quantity and dollar information from business papers) and (b) the production of reports for the management.

(2) *To keep track of assets and liabilities of the business.* This function involves keeping accounts of various kinds: cash, accounts with customers, accounts with creditors, accounts for equipment, accounts with proprietors, and so forth.

(3) *To get things done:* To purchase materials or goods for resale, to instruct the factory to produce, to instruct the warehouse employees to fill orders and the shipping clerks to ship them, and so forth. In this connection, the various order procedures in a business come to mind.

(4) *To facilitate planning of business activities, follow-up of performance, and adjustment of plans.* Thus, (a) production planning and production order procedures are operated to tell the factory what to produce and when to produce it, (b) actual production is compared with planned production and (c) adjusted production schedules are made in the light of current and expected factory performance, inventories, unfilled customers' orders, and expected sales.

Some of the paper work, notably that involved in certain order procedures, is often done outside the Accounting department. Other such work, for instance keeping track of assets and liabilities, is done inside the Accounting department. A large part of the record work is done partly in the Accounting department and partly in the operating departments.

Systems and Procedures

Definitions of systems and procedures written by different authors vary in scope. Some definitions and systems emphasize managerial aspects and problem solving; others emphasize paper work structure and the flow of information. Neuschel defines systems and procedures:

> A *system* is a network of related procedures developed according to one integrated scheme for performing a major activity of the business.[1]

> A *procedure* . . . is a sequence of clerical operations, usually involving several people in one or more departments, established to ensure uniform handling of a recurring transaction of the business.[2]

This book deals with the design and installation of various basic systems used in businesses and with the selection of methods for performing clerical operations. The systems and their related procedures are listed in Table 1-1. It will be seen by scanning the list that each system is a set of related procedures that together provide an integrated structure for carrying out a basic objective of the business, such as selling, buying, or manufacturing. Any business consists of some combination of these

---

[1] Richard F. Neuschel, *Management by Systems,* Second Edition (New York: McGraw-Hill, 1960), page 10. The same definition appears in W. Gerald Cole's paper, "What Is Your Company's Integrated Data Potential?" *National Association of Accountants Bulletin* (May 1958), pages 21–22.

[2] Neuschel, op. cit., page 9. A similar definition appears in Cole's paper (see footnote 1).

Table 1-1

THE ACCOUNTING SYSTEM AND RELATED PROCEDURES

The Accounting System Proper
   Classifications of Accounts:
      Financial and Operating Statements
   Ledgers
   Journals
   Business Papers (most of which are produced in the various procedures below)
Sales and Cash-Collecting System
   Sales order, shipping order, and billing
   Sales distribution
   Accounts receivable
   Cash receiving and credit control
Purchase and Payment System
   Purchase order and receiving report
   Purchase and expense distribution
   Vouchers payable; accounts payable
   Cash paying procedure
Timekeeping and Payroll System
   Employment
   Timekeeping
   Payroll
   Labor distribution
Production and Cost System
   Production order
   Inventory control
   Cost accounting

---

basic objectives, and in any business there are therefore combinations of systems that correspond to the basic objects. Thus:

   (1) In a personal service business, the basic systems are:
      (a) The accounting system proper, which is supported by
      (b) The sales and cash-collecting system, and
      (c) The timekeeping, payroll, and cash disbursements system.
   (2) In a retail or wholesale business, the basic systems are:
      (a) The accounting system proper, which is supported by
      (b) The sales and cash-collecting system,
      (c) The purchase and payment system, and
      (d) The timekeeping and payroll system.
   (3) In a manufacturing business, the basic systems are:
      (a) The accounting system proper, which is supported by
      (b) The sales and cash-collecting system,
      (c) The purchase and payment system,
      (d) The timekeeping and payroll system, and
      (e) The production and manufacturing cost system.

Figure 1-1 is a diagram of the accounting system and related procedures for a manufacturing concern. It shows how the basic procedures are tied into the General ledger.

A procedure is considered (in this book) as a group of closely related clerical operations which comprise a subfunction of the sales and cash-collecting system or some other system.[3] Thus, the procedures that comprise the sales and cash-collecting system, with brief descriptions in terms of familiar pen-and-ink methods, are:

(1) The sales order procedure, by which the salesman writes the sales order and sends it to the order department.

(2) The shipping order procedure, by which the order department writes the shipping order instructing the warehouse to pull the product items and the shipping department to pack and ship them.

(3) The billing procedure, by which the invoice and its copies are produced and dispatched.

(4) The sales distribution procedure, by which the various sales reports are prepared from the distribution copies of invoices and the journal entry is prepared for recording sales.

(5) The accounts receivable procedure, by which an account is maintained for the customer. This account is charged for sales made to him and credited for payments received from him.

(6) The cash receipts procedure, by which cash is received, recorded, and deposited in the bank.

It will be noted that the procedures that make up a system are so closely interrelated that it is sometimes impossible for the systems man to study one of them for the purpose of making recommendations without also considering the effect upon one or more of the other procedures in the system. It is possible, for instance, that proposed changes in the sales order procedure might affect all the other procedures. A system is a more nearly complete entity for investigation and recommendation than a procedure, since it represents the complete cycle in the activities involved in the performance of a distinct function. Even in the case of a system, however, it is necessary to consider the effect upon some other system in making recommendations that concern one system primarily. Thus, a recommendation affecting the shipping order procedure in the sales and cash-collecting system may affect (or be affected by) the production control procedure in the production and cost system.

In some cases, when integrated data-processing is being considered, it may be proposed eventually to absorb all the systems of the business into the new processing system. When an information system is being con-

---

[3] In this book, *written instructions* for operating a procedure are called *standard practice instructions*.

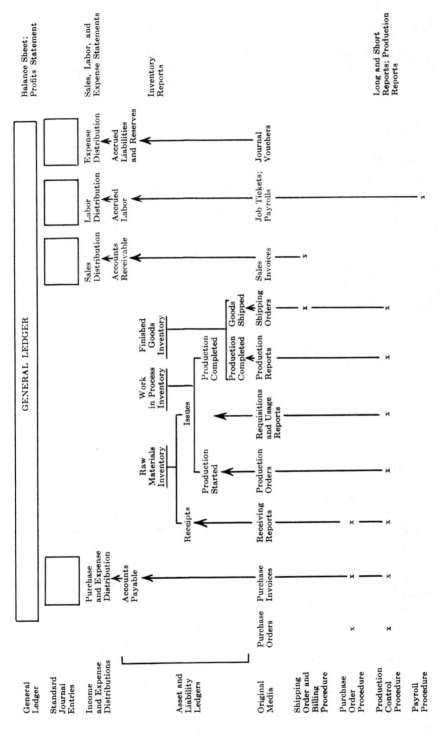

Figure 1-1. The Accounting System and Related Procedures: Manufacturing Concern

sidered (see page 617), it may be proposed to absorb and integrate the distribution procedures of all systems of the business, as well as other information collecting and summarizing procedures.

Clerical Operations

In many of the procedures listed in Table 1-1, there is a single major form, the production, reproduction, and handling of which actually comprise the procedure. Examples of such procedures and their major forms are (1) the sales order form used in the sales order procedure, (2) the shipping order form in the shipping order procedure, and (3) the invoice form in the billing procedure. In some procedures there is a single major form and one or more minor forms from which entries are made to the major form or to which entries are made from the major form.

Methods men describe an operation in general terms as that which occurs "when something is being changed or created or added to." In systems and procedures work, certain readily identifiable clerical work actions or groups of integrated work actions are designated as operations. Examples of clerical operations that may be performed in the processing of forms in a procedure are:

(1) Writing	(5) Posting
(2) Reproducing	(6) Listing
(3) Coding	(7) Sorting
(4) Calculating	(8) Matching

These are examples of what systems men call "do" operations. Note that most of these operations can be performed either manually or by machine. Where the volume of work is significant, it is important that the systems man give adequate consideration to the method by which the operation can be performed most economically.[4] Where the volume of work is large, a major part of a systems or procedures assignment may consist of determining the most economical methods of performing the operations. In fact, the methods and machines selected may have a determining effect upon the design of the steps of the procedure and the managerial information that can be provided by the procedure.

It goes almost without saying that the quantitative factor is important in the study of clerical operations for determining the most economical method of performing the operations. For this reason, the systems man

---

[4] Neuschel (op. cit., page 9) defines *methods* as "the manual or mechanical means by which individual clerical operations are performed. Thus 'methods' have to do with *how* work is performed, not with what work is to be done, or who will do it." Separate chapters in this book are devoted to particular methods.

selects quantitative units, such as papers handled, line items typed, items posted, and so forth, and determines the volume of work for which he must select methods. One of the chief factors in determining the feasibility of machine methods including, of course, electronic data-processing, is volume.

In addition to the "do" operations, systems men may identify the following operations separately:

(1) Transportation, since it makes a difference how many times papers are moved during a procedure and how far they are moved (how many feet if within the same office, or where moved if to another geographic location).
(2) Storage, which may mean temporary holding for action or filing.
(3) Inspection, which means checking or performing a proof operation.

Process

A process, in systems parlance, is a procedure or a set of operations comprising part of a procedure which the systems man selects for study with a view to recommendation and possible re-design. Thus, the entire sales order procedure comprising the operations of writing and processing the sales order might be considered a process for study. Or, the accounts receivable procedure might be studied as two main processes, one concerned with the charges arising from sales and the other with credits arising from cash collections. Each of the processes would involve sorting, posting, filing, and proof operations, but there would be certain differences between them that would warrant separate studies.

General Aims of Systems and Methods Work

The general aims of systems and methods work are:

(1) To improve the information provided by the system, in quality, timeliness, or structure of the information.
(2) To improve the accounting control and internal check, that is, to improve the dependability of accounting information and to provide complete records of accountability for the protection of the assets of the business.
(3) To decrease the clerical cost of keeping the records.

Some systems assignments appear to involve mainly a single aim, at least in the thinking of the client or the employer who authorizes the assignment. A number of companies are either actively working on or at least contemplating what are called information systems. This type of assignment involves improving the structure, quality, and possibly the quantity of information provided the management for decision-making and planning. It involves not only information collected internally in the business but also information collected externally.[5]

As the diagram in Figure 1-2 indicates, however, the three aims of ac-

IMPROVED INFORMATION

REDUCED CLERICAL   IMPROVED
COST   INTERNAL CHECK

Figure 1-2.   General Aims of Systems and Methods Work

counting systems and methods work may be thought of as a triangle, with each of the three aims representing one angle of the triangle. The systems man cannot pursue an assignment involving one aim without at least considering the other two aims. He cannot work on improving the quantity or quality of information without considering the accuracy and the cost of the information. He cannot tighten the clerical controls without considering the clerical cost of the new controls and whether the information is at the same time improved or not. This is not to say, of course, that improvement in the quantity or quality of information necessarily involves an increase in clerical cost; if the systems man is skilled, the improvement may involve a decrease in clerical cost. What is meant, then, is that attention must be paid to all three aims in any assignment. Each of the procedures presented in this book is treated from the standpoint of all three aims of effective systems and methods work.

Typical Systems and Procedures Assignments Described

Systems and procedures assignments range all the way from the design of complete systems from the General ledger down (called "general assignments") to special assignments like designing an order and billing system or finding the most economical way to do a large volume accounts receivable operation. Following are descriptions of five assignments which

---

[5] For an overview of this important type of assignment, see Chapter 26.

are typical of the work done by management engineering firms and the management service departments of public accounting firms:

(1) A complete accounting and profit-planning system for the distributors organization of a large manufacturer of major household appliances. The manufacturer has approximately 100 distributors located in all major cities of the United States, some of them separate corporations owned by the manufacturer, but most of them independent wholesalers who hold franchises with the manufacturer. The system is a standard system used by all distributors.

The "end product" of this assignment was the manual which is used by all the distributors. The list of sections of the manual is interesting because it shows not only the scope of the assignment but the order in which the parts were designed by the systems man. The sections are:

FINANCIAL ACCOUNTING

(a) *Monthly financial statements and reports.* These are presented first because they are what the management is most interested in. They are what the management will get out of the new system. In this case, they are the complete set of reports which the management uses to measure its performance and determine its financial position at the end of a month. They show monthly figures and year-to-date figures. For distributors who have operating budgets for profit-planning (described later), they show comparisons of actual performance with budget.

(b) *Classification of accounts.* These are the accounts which each distributor must keep to produce the statements described in (a). The classification is a complete list of General ledger and Expense ledger accounts, arranged in balance sheet and profit and loss statement order and numbered according to a formal numeric coding scheme.

(c) *Description of debits and credits.* In this section, the possible debits and credits to each account are described and the source of each entry (that is, the journal from which each entry comes) is indicated. Possible debits to each expense account, for instance, are carefully spelled out so that the clerks who operate the system will charge the proper items to each account.

(d) *Journals.* This section contains a complete set of journals used to operate the system—one to a page, reduced in size—with a brief explanation of the use of each journal. Following the blank forms is another set of the more complicated forms filled in to illustrate types of entries and their flow.

(e) *Papers for collecting transactions for entry in the journals.* The forms are illustrated and their use is described.

PROFIT-PLANNING SYSTEM

(f) *Budget worksheets.* This section contains an explanation of the advantages to the distributor in using a budget as the vehicle of his profit-planning, together with illustrations of a set of worksheets which can be used for setting up the plan. The worksheets in this section are blank, being intended to provide a quick look at a budget system.

(g) *Budget worksheets with illustrative entries.* This section explains where budget information comes from and, step by step, how to put the budget together.

EXPENSE ALLOCATIONS

(h) *The expense allocation.* This section explains how to allocate expenses between lines of products to determine whether each of them is profitable. (Many distributors handle not only the line of products with which the manual is identified but also a line of noncompeting goods. Thus, a distributor may handle a line of kitchen appliances and laundry appliances and a line of radios and television sets.)

After the system was designed and the manual written, accountants from the distributor companies were brought to the manufacturer's headquarters where they were taught the main features of the new system. Each distributor did his own installation work.

(2) A complete factory accounting and cost accounting system for a company which operates a large number of relatively small manufacturing plants which produce similar products. The end product of this assignment, like the previous one, is the manual which each factory uses to operate its accounting and cost accounting, although the original assignment included installing the system in a number of the plants.

The first part of this design job was similar to the first part of the one described above. It involved setting up the statements and reports, the classifications of accounts, and the description of debits and credits in the accounts. The second part of the assignment involved designing detailed procedures for the paper work performed at the factories and writing instructions for their operation. These procedures included:

(a) Receiving, shipping, and production procedures
(b) Purchasing procedures
(c) Payroll and labor cost analysis procedures. The factories used a fairly complicated incentive pay plan, and designing the procedures, writing the applicable section of the manual, and teaching the payroll clerks to operate it were a considerable part of the systems man's assignment.

(3) A comparative procedures and methods assignment: Designing an order and billing procedure for a company which was changing its distribution plan from sales to wholesalers and jobbers to sales to retailers. In this assignment, the systems man could not simply make a survey of the present order and billing system and design a better one for the present situation. He had to make a survey of the present system and design one which would take care of a new set of conditions, all of which he had to establish in his survey.

Among the new conditions were an expected increase in the number of customers (and, of course, customers' accounts) and an increase in the number of salesmen for whom sales and commission statistics would have to be kept. There would be a large increase in the number of orders and invoices processed per week. These orders would be smaller than the ones placed by wholesalers and jobbers, and whereas the orders placed by wholesalers and jobbers were mostly future delivery, many of the orders placed by retailers would call for immediate shipment. This would mean that production scheduling would have to be changed from predominantly manufacturing to order to manufacturing for stock. Larger inventories would have to be carried and more people would have to be provided in the warehouse and in the shipping room.

As it turned out, the systems man designed in skeleton form two systems: one which could be installed and used with the production control system without basic change in that system and one which could be used with an improved production control system based upon manufacturing for stock. In the course of this assignment, the systems man made detailed flow charts of the present system from the point where the order came in to the point where the invoice went out and the cash came in, and he time-studied all of the 55 operations. Then he set up comparable operation lists for each of the two proposed systems and estimated the individual operation times per order for each of those systems. Each of the proposed systems could be operated for less minutes per order than the present system. A change in the methods and machines for producing the orders and invoices was indicated. The proposed systems were of course based upon estimates of the volume of each type of paper which would have to be handled.

As would be expected, the report by which the systems man conveyed his recommendations in this assignment was different from that prepared for the general assignment described above. For the initial consideration of the client management, it contained a chart comparing what the proposed systems would provide that the present one did not (facility for immediate shipments, clerical economy, and so forth) and another one comparing the major steps of the proposed systems with the comparable steps of the old system.

Next, the report presented an operation write-up for each of the two proposed systems. This was not merely an operation *list*, but a description in sufficient detail to permit the reader to understand how the operations were to be done. Next, there was a complete set of time study data for all the operations of the old system and all the operations of each of the proposed systems. And finally, there were actual size masters of all the forms to be used in the new systems. These masters were not only the illustrations for the report but the copy from which an offset printer could produce the forms to be used in the systems.

The usefulness, in fact the necessity, of time studies of the old system and estimated times for the proposed systems should be pointed out. In many procedures assignments, it is necessary to make a time comparison of the proposed systems with the old one in order to determine that the proposed systems are really more economical to operate than the old one. In many cases, one proposed system looks better than another until it is timed. It is easy to become intrigued with certain features of a proposed procedure and to convince one's self that it is "the answer," but only timing and costing will settle the matter of true clerical economy.

(4) Clerical work loading. This type of assignment involves determining how many clerical hours of time in each occupational classification and in total should be allowed to operate a system or a department. After an order and billing system is designed for a seasonal business, for instance, it may be desirable to estimate the clerical hours to operate the system (a) at low volume and (b) at high volume. One purpose is to determine how many clerks in each category will be required. (The author recalls a case in which the required personnel ranged from 12 at low volume to 72 at peak volume.) Another purpose is to spread the work equitably among the employees. It is difficult to do this without careful time estimates and statistics on volumes of work load. And finally, clerical work loadings make it possible to compare actual clerical labor paid for with allowed time for the current load to determine operating efficiency.

A clerical work loading report may contain the following sections which themselves show what was involved in doing the loading assignment:

(a) *List of forms used in the system and description of the operations.* The descriptions are detailed enough to eliminate any question of where an operation starts, what the operator does, and where the operation ends. For the operation times to be meaningful, these definitions must be precise.

(b) *Clerical loading tables which provide a list of the operations (in the left-hand column of the table) and time columns for each of the occupational categories such as order writers, calculator operators, billers, file clerks, and so forth.* There is one set of tables for the low volume (which is stated in number of documents of particular categories to be handled) and one table for the high volume. The columns of course show the time allowances for each occupation for each operation which is pertinent.

(c) *Basic time study data.* Where the loading tables are based upon actual time studies of selected batches of work, the times are shown in this section of the report.

(d) *Unmeasured operations.* This section enumerates the operations or activities which it was not feasible to time-study in terms of paper work production units because small amounts of time were involved and the workload was sporadic. Blanket allowances are made in the work loading tables for these operations and activities.

(5) *Feasibility studies for office automation.* Studies of this type are made to determine what areas of paper work and data-collecting should be absorbed into an integrated data-processing system, what type of system is recommended, what hardware will be required and what it will cost, and the advantages of integrated data-processing in the way of clerical cost reduction and improved information. On the question of application areas, R. Hunt Brown says:

> The first step in making a system survey is to determine which application areas are to be covered by the survey team. Often, these are selected or determined by top management. The normal reaction by management is to review the so-called "bread and butter" data processing areas where the greatest number of clerical operations are found. These applications are usually concerned with customer relations (orders, invoices, accounts receivable, statistics, etc.), employee relations (payroll and personnel records), inventory and production control, and cost accounting. However, these are sometimes interrelated and often provide the basis for scientific management activities as well. Thus, operations research and the new automatic decision making techniques may well prove to be important areas for review.[6]

Who Does Systems Work?

Systems and methods work is being done by the following individuals and groups:

(1) Line supervisors (usually accounting supervisors)

These people do the systems work that is done in small companies in which there is no procedures man or staff. They also do systems work in some larger organizations, taking care of the improvement phases and the instructional phases of the systems function which have not been assigned to the regular procedures staff. Thus, in some companies one or more of the line supervisors are part-time procedures staff men.

---

[6] R. Hunt Brown, "The Feasibility Study for Office Automation," *Systems and Procedures* (February 1959), pages 12–13.

(2) Systems groups in private businesses

Numerous companies have regular procedures staffs, and some companies have large staffs. The Association for Systems Management publication, "Profile of a Systems Man," which is the report on a survey of the professional activities of a sample of its membership, gives some interesting statistical information about systems and procedures staffs in private businesses. Among other things, the report shows something about the types of work done by these departments, to whom the groups report, how large the groups are, and the occupations within these groups. Some of the information based upon 3,535 questionnaires returned by members and published in the 1970 report is presented below.[7]

"Activities of Systems Unit" (Table 1-2) lists eleven activities of systems units. Note that "methods and systems analysis" work is done in 3,509 out of 3,535 firms represented by the questionnaires.

Table 1-2

ACTIVITIES OF SYSTEMS UNIT

	No. of Firms	% to Total			
		1969	1965	1959	1955
Methods and Systems Analysis	3254	93%	94%		
Organization Analysis and Planning	1813	52%	57%	52%	56%
Work Measurement, Standards, Incentives, Simp., etc.	1371	39%	53%	79%	33%
Policy and Procedure Manuals	2576	73%	79%	84%	82%
Forms, Records, & Reports Control and Management	2676	76%	83%	83%	84%
Space and Facilities Planning and Utilization	1279	36%	44%	49%	46%
Equipment Evaluation & Selection Standardization	2462	70%	70%	61%	60%
Data Processing—Electro-Mechanical: Analysis, Wiring or Management	436	12%	58%	74%	
Data Processing—Electronic: Analysis, Programming or Management	2725	78%	69%	57%	48%
Management Sciences—Operations Research, etc.	1056	30%	26%	17%	
Management Consulting	1265	36%	32%	25%	31%
Total	3509				
No Reply	26				
Total Questionnaires	3535				

Source: Association for Systems Management.

[7] Association for Systems Management, "Profile of a Systems Man" (Cleveland, Ohio, 1970).

"To Whom Does the Systems Group Report" (Table 1-3) indicates that 738 systems groups out of 3,466 represented report to the activity vice president and 636 report to the president or vice president.

Table 1-3

TO WHOM DOES SYSTEMS GROUP REPORT

	No. of Firms	% to Total				
		1969	1965		1959	1955
President or Executive Vice President	636	18%	14% }	30%	24%	24%
Activity Vice President	738	21%	16% }			
Treasurer or Assistant	251	7%	9% }	44%	55%	47%
Controller or Assistant	705	21%	35% }			
General Manager or Assistant	225	7%	6% }	14%	12%	10%
Department Head	532	15%	8% }			
Other	379	11%	12%		9%	19%
Total	3466	100%	100%		100%	100%
No Reply	69					
Total Questionnaires	3535					

Source: Association for Systems Management.

"Size of Systems Unit" (Table 1-4) indicates that, of 3,484 companies represented, 1,486 or 42 per cent consist of up to 4 employees in the Systems Unit (in other words 42 per cent of the units are small, and at the other end of the scale 248 companies or 7 per cent consist of 50 or more employees). It is a reasonable assumption that in the larger departments,

Table 1-4

SIZE OF SYSTEMS UNIT

No. of Employees	No. of Firms	% to Total			
		1969	1965	1959	1955
0 to 4	1486	42%	48%	3%	8%
1 to 3				47%	47%
5 to 9	859	25%	24%		
4 to 6				20%	23%
7 and over				30%	22%
10 to 19	546	16%	15%		
20 to 49	345	10%	8%		
50 and over	248	7%	5%		
Total	3484	100%	100%	100%	100%
No Reply	51				
Total Quest.	3535				

Source: Association for Systems Management.

actual operation of data-processing is included as well as systems design. This assumption is supported by another table, "Occupations Supervised," which includes systems and/or data-processing analysts (the most numerous group) and also programmers, machine operators, key punch operators, and others.

According to Irene Place, who made an earlier survey of the place and function of systems groups in business, there appear to be "distinct types of systems groups."

In a few instances, the title of the group or the position of the person to whom it reported was reflected in the type or level of work assigned to it. . . . And, emphasis in interpretation appeared also to be affected by whether the organization was clerical or manufacturing oriented.

The following generalizations were drawn by Mrs. Place:

1. Those systems groups that were associated with office services tended to see the job of the systems analyst as primarily concerned with clerical procedures, clerical standards, office layout, and records retention programs.

2. Those groups that reported to a controller and that were staffed mostly by personnel from the accounting department tended to see the job of the systems analyst as primarily an extension of accounting control and standard operating procedures. They seemed to emphasize the writing of standard practice procedures.

3. Those groups that reported directly to a president, secretary, or vice president in charge of operations saw the job of the systems analyst as a management planning, top-level policy and procedure review activity. Particularly outstanding among those were young graduates of the better schools of business, where they had received a general basic training in business administration.

4. Those groups that were concerned primarily with electronic data processing were likely to include analysts with engineering, mathematical, or accounting background and to be concerned primarily with equipment applications.[8]

(3) Public accounting firms and management engineering firms

Most public accounting firms do systems and procedures work for their clients. Some of this work involves the correction of deficiencies in internal check and some of it involves other phases of systems work, business surveys, and advisory service designated collectively as "management services." Likewise, management engineering firms do systems work along with management services. Some public accounting firms and management engineering firms are staffed to assist clients in feasibility studies for electronic data-processing and in the design (including programming) and installation of such systems. Some firms also do information systems assignments (pages 614–638).

---

[8] Irene Place, "Administrative Systems Analysis" (University of Michigan, 1957), page 69. A footnote on page 17 of Mrs. Place's report, quoting a thesis by G. Randolph Jenks, states: "Clerically oriented companies have paper work as their main product. So, it is not unreasonable to assume that the systems staff would get into top organization planning."

(4) Accounting forms and machines salesmen

These people do a great deal of procedures and methods work in connection with the sale (and, in some cases, rental) of their product. In some cases, they work directly with the businessman and his accounting people. In other cases, they work with the procedures staff man in a private business or the systems staff man in a professional accounting or engineering firm.

Organization of Procedures Staffs in Private Business

The organization of procedures staffs in private businesses depends upon such factors as the nature of the assignments that the staff is set up to handle, the number of men on the staff, and the qualifications and experience of the staff members. In a small staff, there is likely to be little specialization among members, except as governed by the qualifications and experience of the individual members. The supervisor will assign a job to the available staff man who is best qualified to handle it.

In larger staffs, a distinct pattern of organization is often discernible within the procedures staff. In one procedures staff, the staff ranks were (1) supervisor, (2) designer, (3) installation man, (4) junior, and (5) trainee. In this staff, the designer has full responsibility for a complete systems or procedures assignment. He makes the survey and designs the new system or procedure. He is assisted by the installation man, who works with him in the later phases of the designing, so that he may learn all the features of the system. The installation man remains on the job during the installation period. Juniors assist in incidental survey and design tasks.

In another private procedures staff, which operates in an organization with diversified subsidiaries, most of the procedures men handle entire assignments, but they specialize in particular types of business in which the subsidiaries are engaged.

In one large manufacturing organization comprising numerous plants and commercial offices and staffs, there is a manager—corporation systems who reports to the comptroller. The duties of the former are enumerated in the upper section of Figure 1-3. Note that procedures in this company includes mathematical and engineering procedures and also the coordination of service centers and other accounting groups. Service centers provide what are indicated (not on the chart) as data-processing and clerical services.

At the plant locations there are supervisors—systems and procedures whose duties are enumerated in the bottom part of the chart. As would be expected, "designs, develops and installs integrated data systems" and other systems is shown in no. 1; also, training local personnel in the operation of new or revised procedures is shown specifically.

Figure 1-3. Functional Organization Charts

Service Center

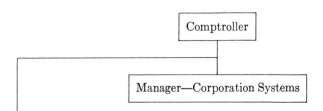

Comptroller

Manager—Corporation Systems

Manage & Direct: (1) design, develop, implement, control, and evaluation of uniform Corporation procedures, including mathematical and engineering procedures; and (2) coordination of Service Center and other Accounting Groups to develop and install uniform systems to effect an integrated Corporate System.

Manager—Regional Procedures

Manage & Direct: (1) administrative responsibility for the installation of applicable Corporate Systems as well as the design, development, and installation of Plant Operating Systems; (2) coordinate Plant and Division systems installations with Corporate uniform systems; (3) maintain these systems and provide for improvements; (4) continuous evaluation of the adequacy and economical output capacity of data-processing and communication equipment at the various plant locations; (5) counsel to plant personnel concerning systems and data-processing principles as related to problem solving; and (6) effective utilization of Systems Personnel at the Plant and Division locations essentially on a priority basis recognizing cost reduction, service to management, and customer service requirements.

Plant Location

Supervisor—Systems & Procedures

Direction for: (1) designs, develops, and installs integrated data-processing and other systems at the plant level; (2) maintain close coordination with plant management in order to be knowledgeable of systems requirements;

(3) assist in training local personnel in the operation of new or revised procedures; (4) adapt local systems to meet requirements of uniform procedures; (5) review and propose revisions to procedures as required for maximum efficiency; (6) assist in developing and implementing an effective Cost Reduction Program; (7) conduct necessary training to develop efficient personnel; and (8) efficient utilization of all assigned Systems personnel.

2

Survey Methods:
Recording the Survey

Recording the Details of the Survey

The success of any systems assignment depends substantially upon the thoroughness and skill with which the survey is made. If some essential point or condition has been overlooked by the systems man, it is quite likely that the new system will not do what it is supposed to do. And by the same token, the details of a survey must be carefully recorded according to a logical plan so that they will be accessible and understandable during the survey and later, and so that they can be analyzed and interpreted.

Although it is necessary to use some form of recording for all surveys, it can be said that the need for formal recording increases as the size of the assignment increases. The author recalls procedures surveys which have required fifteen man-months (which is not uncommon), exclusive of design and installation time. In such surveys, it is obviously impossible to rely on memory in designing the new system. All the facts required for design must come from the record of the survey. Where the new system is to be designed in the consultant's office instead of the client's office, it is obviously necessary to design it from recorded information.

Uses of Notes, Charts, and Worksheets in Systems Assignments

Notes, charts, and worksheets in systems assignments are useful:

(1) to the analyst himself, as a means of organizing the data as it is gathered, controlling it so that the analyst can be certain that all parts tie together and that no parts of the data are missing. Interestingly enough, a well-organized recording plan tends to eliminate the likelihood of gathering more information than needed to solve the problem, as well as gathering insufficient information.

(2) to the analyst's supervisor or to the designer if he is someone other than the analyst. Obviously, formal methods of recording must be used when the data are to be reviewed by other people than the analyst. In some cases, more than one person is involved in designing the new system. Accounting machine or computer experts, for instance, may be consulted by the systems man.

(3) in presenting the report to the client. In some cases, the systems man may find it useful to have his charts at hand when he presents his report to the client, since questions may come up as to particular details of the old system and the reasons for changing them. The use of charts can be very helpful in presenting proposals, because they make it easy to focus on specific points.

(4) as a permanent file of the assignment to use as a record of work done and as the starting point of future assignments. Frequently, some time after a system has been designed and installed, the systems man is consulted about changes that appear to be desirable because of changing operating conditions. In many such cases, it it impossible to make a recommendation without looking up the file.

On the use of charts, Schlosser says:

> . . . systems analysts attack both data flow and data handling simultaneously. They commonly utilize a single flow chart which depicts both the data processing operations and the flow of data from one part of the system to another in applying this technique. Clients are often skeptical when viewing this technique being performed but it is axiomatic that an improved design can rarely result unless the existing operations and data flow are understood by the analyst. . . .
>
> An alternative method of applying this technique would be to use narrative descriptions of the data flow and data handling in the procedure under review. In relatively uncomplicated situations, they would be a recommended method. The data flow and data handling in an involved procedure or procedure group rarely lend themselves to narrative-type analysis. The charting method accompanied by narrative explanations seems to be the most effective method of applying this technique. . . .
>
> Due to the complexity of the accounting system, even in a small company, it is rarely possible to develop a single flow chart for the entire system. Normally, charting is directed at procedures or, in some instances, procedure groups. The evaluated procedure charts must be suitably coordinated so that the flow charts can assist the analyst effectively.[1]

Notes, Charts, and Worksheets Grouped by Function

The parts of a survey are covered in a particular order which is carefully planned in advance. Surveys for general assignments, for instance,

---

[1] Robert E. Schlosser, "Accounting Systems Review Techniques," *The Journal of Accountancy* (December 1962), pages 45–48.

are made from general information to detailed information or "from the top down." This order of events makes it possible for the analyst or supervisor to case the situation quickly and to obtain basic information necessary to start the detail survey.

Survey tools can be grouped according to their place in the survey program and the function which they serve:

    (1) Items of general use assembled at the beginning of a complete systems assignment, such as
        Organization charts
        Product lists
        Classifications of accounts and major financial and operating statements
        Plant layouts

These items are described in Chapter 3 in connection with the description of a general systems assignment.

    (2) Procedures operation lists and charts:
        Skeleton flow charts
        Operation lists
        Forms distribution charts
        Forms charts

These lists and charts are illustrated and explained on pages 22–27. They are used in the surveys of general assignments (except the simpler ones), and they are also used in procedures surveys such as the re-design of an order and billing procedure.

    (3) Process charts and operation time worksheets for clerical cost reduction and control, illustrated and explained on pages 27–31.

Preparing Procedures Notes and Charts in a General Assignment, with Typical Set of Charts Described

In manufacturing concerns, general assignments frequently involve a survey of some of the old procedures, such as sales order, production order, and billing procedures, and payroll and labor cost procedures. This was true, for instance, in the assignment "Financial and Cost Accounting System" for the sixteen branch factories of a manufacturing concern described on page 10. In such an assignment, the existing procedures will be surveyed in detail to provide the basis for re-design.

In making the survey of a particular procedure, the interviewing naturally starts with the supervisor, since clearance has to be obtained before interviewing any of the clerks. Often, the supervisor explains a substantial part of the details from his knowledge of them, and then arranges for the analyst to interview the clerks who work on the form(s) under survey.

The analyst asks the interviewee(s) to explain the steps in order, and makes notes as the interview proceeds. Where multiple copy forms are involved, it is necessary to find out what happens to each of the copies. In the actual interviewing, the analyst takes notes in a fashion complete enough to make them intelligible to him when he gets back to his own desk, but still rapidly and informally enough to avoid holding up the clerk. He shows the name of the interviewee and the date on each set of notes, so that he can come back to the interviewee for further amplification, if ncessary.

Figure 2-1, a skeleton flow chart, is probably the simplest form of

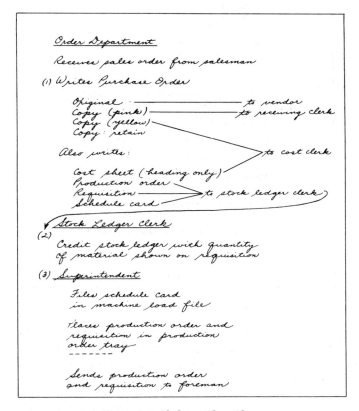

Figure 2-1. Skeleton Flow Chart

chart for recording a procedure. Such a chart would be prepared from the notes described above. A more formal "Operation List" (similar to Figure 2-2) might be prepared. As stated before, charts are prepared so that (1) the analyst can determine as he proceeds whether he has covered all the points and (2) the record will be in permanent form for later use.

```
                                               Date   August 14, 19--

     Subject:  Writing Production Orders and Related Forms

     Sequence                    Description of Clerical Operation

                     ORDER DEPARTMENT

        1.           Receives sales order from salesman and writes-

                          Purchase order
                             Original - vendor
                             Copy (pink) - receiving clerk
                             Copy (yellow) - attached to cost sheet
                                and sent to cost clerk
                             Copy (retain)
                          Cost sheet (heading only)
                          Production Order
                          Requisition
                          Schedule Card

                     Dispatches purchase order and copies.  Sends production
                        order, requisition, and schedule card to stock ledger
                        clerk.

        2.           Stock ledger clerk.  Credit stock ledger with quantity
                        of material shown on requisition.  Sends production
                        order, requisition, and schedule card to superintendent.

                     SUPERINTENDENT

        3.           Receives production order, requisition, and schedule card
                        from order department.  Examines to determine that pro-
                        duction details are correct.

                     Files schedule card in machine load file to keep track of
                        work ahead.

        4.           Places production order and requisition in production
                        order tray

        5.           On date machine capacity is available marks date and
                        time on schedule card.

        6.           Sends production order and requisition to foreman.

                     (Remaining part of the list omitted from illustration)
```

Figure 2-2. Simple Operation List

Where the procedure being surveyed comprises a number of forms with copies, the problem of "nailing down" all the forms and all the copies as he goes along may be of some concern to the analyst. In such a case, the analyst may prepare a forms distribution chart, instead of, say, the skeleton flow chart, directly from his notes. A simple forms distribution chart is illustrated in Figure 2-3. This form of chart is essentially an operation list to which has been added a column for each form and copy. The purpose of the forms columns is to provide for keying (o) the forms that are used in each operation described in the particulars column. The act of preparing a chart of this kind tends to insure that the analyst will find every operation which is performed on every copy of every form.

Where *what is on the form* and the flow of entries from form to form

Production Order	Schedule Card	Requisition	Purchase Order				Cost Sheet	Operation	Descriptions of Operations
			Original	Copy (Pink)	Copy (Yellow)	Copy			
o	o	o	o	o	o	o	o	1	ORDER DEPARTMENT Write purchase order, cost sheet, production order, requisition, and schedule card
o	o	o						2	Credit stock record with quantity of materials shown by requisition. Send to superintendent.
									SUPERINTENDENT
o	o	o						3	File schedule card in machine load file to keep track of work ahead
o		o						4	Place production order and requisition in production order tray.
	o							5	On date machine capacity is available, mark date and time on schedule card.
o		o						6	Send production order and requisition to foreman.
									COST CLERK
					o		o	7	Receive cost sheet and copy (yellow) of purchase order.
									RECEIVING CLERK
				o				8	Receive copy (pink) of purchase order

Figure 2-3. Forms Distribution Chart: Single Description Column
Forms distribution charts are used when it is desired to tie down each copy of each form used in a procedure. This type of chart provides a description of each operation.

are complicated, a forms chart, such as that illustrated in Figure 2-4, may be prepared. Preparing such a chart tends to insure that the analyst has covered the types of entry and their flow. (Production control procedures and incentive payroll and labor analysis plans, for instance, are sometimes complicated. Such procedures may require a forms chart as well as a forms distribution chart.)

A forms chart is prepared by mounting copies of the actual forms on a sheet of paper, with illustrative entries on the forms. Lines are then drawn on the paper to indicate the movement of entries from one form to another. The individual forms are prepared first, with the desired illustrative entries, and these forms are photostated with a reduction of one-half if necessary, to keep the size of the chart down to manageable dimensions. The photostats are mounted on the large paper. If the writing on the original forms is legible and not smaller than the usual handwriting, it will be readable in the final reduced photostat. Note that ordinarily each form is used only once on the chart, even though the form is worked upon in several operations in the procedure. For a multiple copy form, the original and each copy may be shown unless a copy is merely filed, in which case an explanatory note will suffice.

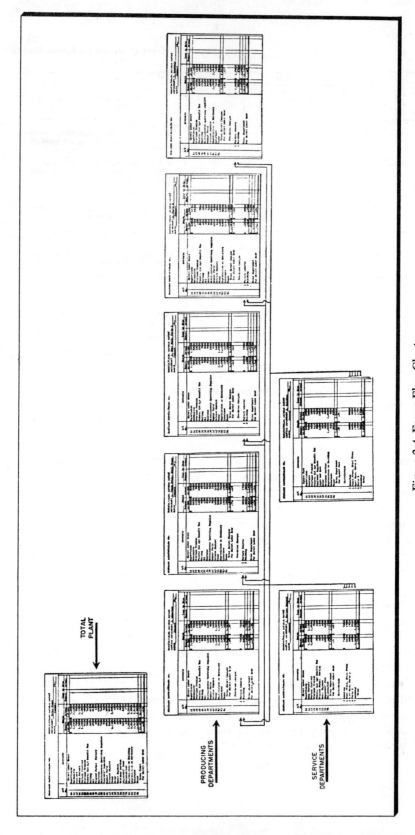

TOTAL PLANT

PRODUCING DEPARTMENTS

SERVICE DEPARTMENTS

Figure 2-4. Forms Flow Chart

Copies of forms with illustrative entries are mounted to make the forms flow chart.

The fact that each form is shown only once on the chart sometimes introduces complications. If, in the actual procedure, entries are made at several different times and from several other forms, the lines on the chart may become confusing to the reader. If the chart is carefully prepared, however, it does "nail down" the types of entries as no other type of chart does. In many cases, it is feasible to use actual transactions to illustrate the use of the forms. One or two transactions can be used on an original paper and wavy lines can be drawn in to show the omission of other (presumably similar) transactions which it is not desired to show. The use of actual transactions is time-consuming, but in complicated procedures, it sometimes brings to light important information which had previously been overlooked.

Usually, the analyst finds in making a forms chart that some of the entries as originally made do not tie through. Upon investigation, he finds that certain details of the actual procedure being followed are different from the ones which he has picked up, due to recent changes in procedure, someone's faulty memory, and so forth. When this occurs, the interviewee can then be asked to assist in locating the discrepancy and correcting it. The office people usually show considerable interest in seeing the finished charts of the procedures on which they work, and it is not difficult to enlist their aid.

As indicated above, for some complicated procedures, it is desirable to prepare both a forms distribution chart and a forms chart. This combination almost insures that every detail of the old procedure is tied down. Moreover, they are so complete that the systems man can design his new procedure, including all the forms, directly from the charts.

Facsimile Forms Chart

An alternative type of chart should be illustrated at this point, for use in recording procedures which are not complicated enough to justify using the forms distribution chart or the forms chart. Figure 2-5 is a facsimile forms chart of a general type which has great popularity. It is prepared by using squares and rectangles to represent the actual forms. It shows operation descriptions and the flow of the papers from operation to operation, but it does not show amounts. Being a graphic picture of a procedure it is suitable for display to clients or employees, and it can be readily absorbed by the reader. This type of chart can also be prepared reasonably quickly.

Process Charts and Worksheets for Procedures Assignments

The previous sections of this chapter have described and illustrated survey tools which can be used for general assignments (systems complete

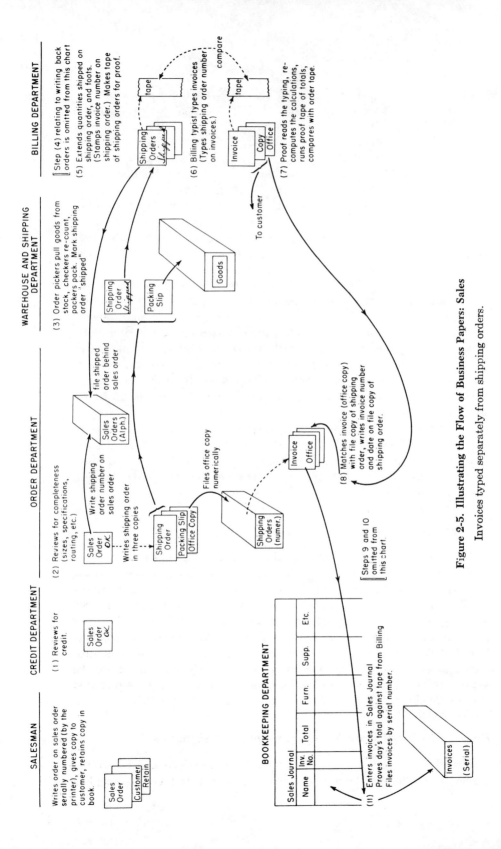

Figure 2-5. Illustrating the Flow of Business Papers: Sales

Invoices typed separately from shipping orders.

from the General ledger down). These tools include forms distribution charts and forms charts which can obviously be used in procedures assignments. In addition to these charts, *process charts* and worksheets for assembling operation times may be used in procedures assignments where the main purpose is likely to be cost reduction or cost control.

The process chart is a visual aid in the study of flow of work and the sequence of operations. It was used first in factories for the study of production methods, and for such use it was described in "Flow Process Charts" by F. B. and L. M. Gilbreth.[2] It is now widely used by procedures and methods men who work with accounting systems and office procedures. The distinguishing feature of the process chart is the use of symbols which make it possible:

(a) in preparing the chart, to classify the operations according to their fundamental mechanical nature, and

(b) in using the chart after it has been completed, to pick out immediately the particular types of operation which it is desired to study.

In the preparation of process charts for factory operations, a large number of symbols are sometimes used to identify significant changes in the nature, position, or location of a product in process. In the preparation of such charts for clerical procedures, however, sometimes as few as

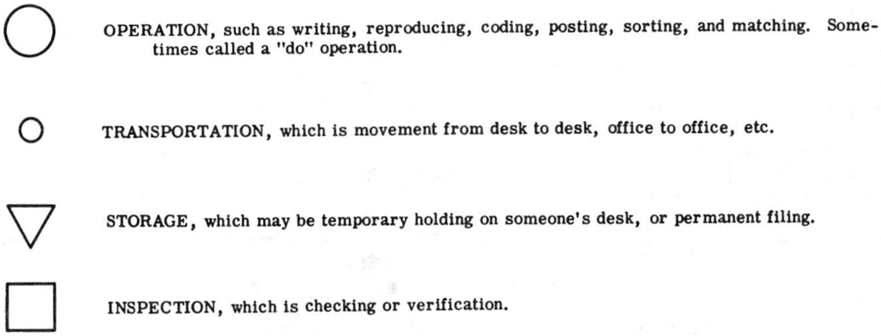

◯ OPERATION, such as writing, reproducing, coding, posting, sorting, and matching. Sometimes called a "do" operation.

○ TRANSPORTATION, which is movement from desk to desk, office to office, etc.

▽ STORAGE, which may be temporary holding on someone's desk, or permanent filing.

☐ INSPECTION, which is checking or verification.

Figure 2-6. Symbols Used in Process Charts (Office Procedures)

four symbols, illustrated and described in Figure 2-6, are used. (Figure 2-7 is a diagram of a process chart template, a plastic ruler in which holes are placed to use as guides in drawing the symbols.) When these

Figure 2-7. Process Chart Template

———————

[2] *Paper No. 1818* (American Society of Mechanical Engineers, 1921).

(PRESENT / PROPOSED) GENERAL WORK ACTIONS	HANDLING	"DO" OPERATION	TRANSPORTATION	INSPECTION	TEMP. STORAGE	PERM STORAGE	DISTANCE IN FEET	NOTES
	○	●	○	□	△	△		
	○	●	○	□	△	△		
	○	●	○	□	△	△		
	○	●	∪	□	△	△		
	○	●	○	□	△	△		
	○	●	○	□	△	△		
	○	●	○	□	△	△		
	○	●	○	□	△	△		
	○	●	○	□	△	△		
	○	●	∪	□	△	△		
	○	●	○	□	△	△		
	○	●	∪	□	△	△		
	○	●	○	□	△	△		
	○	●	○	□	△	△		
	○	●	○	□	△	△		
	○	●	○	□	△	△		
	○	●	○	□	△	△		
	○	●	○	□	△	△		
	○	●	○	□	△	△		
	○	●	○	□	△	△		
	○	●	○	□	△	△		
	○	●	○	□	△	△		

SUMMARY				DEPARTMENT:
METHOD	PRESENT	PROPOSED	SAVINGS	
NO. OF HANDLINGS				DEPT. HEAD:
NO. OF "DO" OPERATIONS				
NO. OF TRANSPORTATIONS				RECORD APPLICATION:
NO. OF INSPECTIONS				
NO. OF TEMP. STORAGE				
NO. OF PERM. STORAGE				
DISTANCE TRAVELED				ANALYST: DATE:

Diebold, Inc.

Figure 2-8. Process Chart: Single Column with Pre-Printed Operation Symbols

four symbols are used, the "do" operations are identified by the large circle, and they thus become separated from transportation, storage, and inspection, each of which has its own symbol. The analyst is interested not merely in the total number of operations required to process certain forms, and the duplications in entering certain details on the various forms in a procedure, but also the number of "do" operations, the number of times they are checked or verified, and so forth. Sometimes, part of or all the same information is written (not reproduced) on each of several successive forms in a procedure, and the question of combining some of the forms to reduce the amount of writing suggests itself. Sometimes, a large number of checking or verification operations have been introduced over a period of time, each with the idea of preventing the recurrence of some error that slipped through; the result may be an overlap in the checking operations.

Some analysts use printed process chart forms on which the four symbols are pre-printed on each operation line. Such a form is illustrated in Figure 2-8. Sometimes a two-part form is used, each part of which is printed identically. The left part can be used to chart the *old* procedure and the right side the *proposed* procedure.

Worksheets for Collecting Operation Times

In many procedures assignments, it is necessary to determine operation times for the old procedure and for the proposed procedure to determine that the latter does promise a saving in clerical labor over the former. Often, the systems man cannot be certain which of several refinements he has in mind is the best until he figures the times and compares them with the times for the present procedure. And furthermore, it is usually necessary to make an estimate of time savings when recommending a new procedure to a client or employer.

This was the case, for instance, in the comparative procedures study described in Chapter 1 (pages 11–12). The report included a tabulation of actual operation times for the existing procedure and for two alternative procedures, one of which could be installed immediately and the other after certain changes were made in the production control procedure.

Sometimes the operation time figures used are estimates made by the systems man or by the clerks doing the operations, and sometimes they are based upon time studies made by the systems man observing actual batches of work in process. Figure 2-9[3] is a worksheet used to summarize actual operation times for an order and billing procedure. The times are

---

[3] Cecil Gillespie, *Cost Accounting and Control* (Englewood Cliffs, N.J.: Prentice-Hall, Inc., 1957), pages 521–522.

Operation Times—Selected Batches in Actual Production

Opera-tion No.	Operation Description	Form Handled (Operator)	Quantity in Sample (Date)	Start: Finish	Minutes Elapsed	Minutes per Form
1	Enter order on production schedule by product code number, promised shipping period, and quantity	Customer Orders (B. Smith)	200 7/2/—	8:00 A 5:00 P	480	2.40
2	Write shipping order and enter on order register	Shipping Orders (J. Thomas)	200 7/3/—	8:00 A 3:00 P	360	1.80
3	File shipping orders in open shipping file according to shipping date	Shipping Order	200 7/3/— 7/4/—	3:00 P 5:00 P 8:00 A 9:00 A	180	.90
4	File customers orders in customers' order file alphabetically by city and customer's name	Customers Orders (A. Morgan)	200 7/4/—	9:00 A 10:30 A	90	.45
5	Each day, pull shipping orders to be released that day from the open shipping order file	Shipping Orders (A. Morgan)	Not timed	Fixed daily allowance 10 min.		
6	Pick goods from stock; enter quantities picked in Shipped column of Shipping Orders. Pack	Shipping Department	Not timed			
7	Write bills of lading	Shipping Department	Not timed			
8	Prove total quantity shipped against total count shown by order packers' control sheet	Shipping Orders (F. Lord)	320 7/2/—	4:22 P 5:00 P	38	.12
9	Enter customer contract number and contract price on shipping order	Shipping Orders (T. Lombard)	320 7/3/—	2:00 P 4:40 P	160	.50
10	Check quantity tallies made on shipping orders by order pickers. Extend shipping orders (——— calculator). Enter house cancellations and back orders on shipping orders	Shipping Orders (E. North)	320 7/3/—	8:00 A 5:00 P	480	1.50
11	Sort shipping orders for later operations	Shipping Orders (F. Lord)	320 7/4/—	8:00 A 8:57 A	57	.18
12	Prepare dollar control of invoices, with subtotals for later use	Invoices (E. North)	320 7/5/—	9:20 A 10:30 A	70	.22
13	Put (invoice) serial number and date on shipping orders. (Numbering stamp)	Shipping Orders (F. Lord)	320 7/4/—	8:57 A 9:19 A	22	.07
14	Type and extend invoices (——— Computing billing machine)	Invoices (E. North)	129 7/4/—	9:19 A 1:45 P	206	1.60
15	Take office copies of invoices to sales department	Invoices (E. North)	Not timed	Fixed daily allowance 10 min.		
16	Check prices on office copies of invoices	Sales Department	Not timed			
17	Separate original bills of lading from copies. Match original bills of lading with original invoices. Staple original bills to original invoices. Mail invoices.	B/L Use Invoices (E. North)	320 7/4/—	2:00 P 4:40 P	160	.5
18	File copies of bills of lading	B/L Use Invoices (E. North)	320 7/5/—	8:00 A 9:20 A	80	.25
19	Post invoices to customers accounts (——— bookkeeping machine)	Invoices (P. Schultz)	320 7/5/—	10:30 A 1:51 P	141	.44
20	Prove dollars posted to customers account (per bookkeeping machine proof sheet) against billing dollar control (Operation 12).	Not timed				
21	Post sales totals (from Operation 12) to sales distribution	Tape (J. Ward)			10/day	
22	Make distribution of shipments by product number	Invoices (J. Ward)	320 7/5/—	3:00 P 4:20 P	80	.25
23	Enter invoices in commission record. Send salesmens copies to salesmen.	Invoices (A. Morgan)	320 7/5/—	4:20 P 4:52 P	32	.10
24	File invoices by invoice serial number.	Invoices (A. Morgan)	320 7/5/—	4:52 P 5:00 P	8	—
25	Enter shipment dates (or completions) on order register	Shipping Orders (B. Smith)	320 7/5/— 7/6/—	2:00 P 5:00 P 8:00 A 9:00 A	240	.75
26	File completed shipping orders in completed shipping order file	Shipping Orders (A. Morgan)	200 7/6/—	9:00 A 10:30 A	90	.45
27	File uncompleted shipping orders in open shipping order file	Shipping Orders (A. Morgan)	120 7/6/—	10:30 A 1:18 P	108	.90

Figure 2-9

fictitious, but the worksheet is based upon actual situations. Note that the worksheet provides spaces for:

Quantity in the sample and date
Operation no.   Start and finish time
Operation description   Minutes elapsed
Form handled and operator   Minutes per form

Clerical Work Loading

Clerical work loading consists in setting up a budget in hours of the time allowed for each clerical occupation in a department to perform a specified work load. Systems men frequently set up such loading tables after designing or changing procedures to determine the new personnel requirements. Sometimes clerical loading studies are made for control purposes where no systems changes are contemplated. It may be found that some occupations have too much to do and others too little, and the purpose of the loading is to set up a reasonable time budget. A clerical work loading project is described in Chapter 1 (pages 12–13).

Table 2-1 is a clerical work loading table[4] which was set up from the time studies in Figure 2-9, assuming a work load of 1,000 orders and 500 invoices a week. For this load 154 clerk hours a week must be provided. A similar loading table was made for a work load of 500 orders and 1,000 invoices a week, and it was found that 172.6 hours must be provided. As was stated before, these figures are fictitious.

---

[4] Ibid., pages 522–533.

Table 2-1

LOADING—MEASURED WORK—BASED UPON ACTUAL OPERATION TIMES

(Period—One Week)

Work-load week: 1,000 orders; 500 invoices

Position	Operation No.	Operation Description	Orders	Minutes per Order	Total Minutes Week	Total Hours Week
Production Schedule Clerk	1	Enter order on production schedule	1,000	2.40	2,400	40
	Total				2,400	40
Order Clerk	2	Write shipping order and enter on order register	1,000	1.80	1,800	
	8	Prove total quantity shipped	500	.12	60	
	9	Enter customer contract number and contract price on shipping order	500	.5	250	
	10	Check quantity tallies on shipping orders	500	1.5	750	
	11	Enter house cancellations and back orders	500	.18	90	
	12	Sort shipping orders for later operation	200	.22	44	
		Prepare control of invoices				
	25	Enter shipment dates (or completions) on order register	500	.75	375	
	Total				3,369	56.2

Position	Operation No.	Operation Description	Invoices	Minutes per Invoice	Total Minutes Week	Total Hours Week
Biller	13	Put serial numbers and date on shipping orders	500	.07	35	
	14	Type and extend invoices (computing billing machine)	500	1.6	800	
	15	Take office copies of invoices to sales department	500	10/day	50	
	17	Separate bills of lading. Match with invoices and staple. Mail	500	.5	250	
	Total				1,135	18.9

		Papers	Minutes per Paper		
Accounts Receivable Operator					
19	Post invoices to customer accounts	500	.44	220	
Total				220	3.7
Distribution Clerk					
21	Post sales totals to sales distribution sheets	500	10/day	50	
22	Make distribution of shipments by product number	500	.25	125	
23	Enter invoices in commission record. Send salesmen's copy to salesmen.	500	.10	50	
Total				225	3.7
File Clerk					
3	File shipping orders in open shipping order file	1,000	.9	900	
4	File customer's order in customers' order file	1,000	.45	450	
5	Pull shipping orders from file for release	500	10/day	50	
18	File copies of bills of lading	500	.25	125	
24	File invoices by serial number	500	10/day	50	
26	File completed shipping orders in completed shipping order file	300	.45	135	
27	File uncompleted shipping orders in open shipping order file	200	.9	180	
Total				1,890	31.5
	TOTAL MINUTES			9,239	
	TOTAL HOURS				154.0

Operations Not Timed

6	Pick goods from stock; pack (warehouse).
7	Write bills of lading (warehouse).
16	Check prices on office copies of invoices.
20	Prove dollars posted to customers accounts.

3

Designing General Ledger Classifications and Statements

A general assignment was described in Chapter 1 as an assignment "complete from the General ledger down to the business papers on which transactions are recorded." It includes all major reports which management uses to operate the business as well as the systems and procedures by which they are produced. Two such assignments were described in Chapter 1:

(1) An accounting system for the distributing organization of a manufacturing concern (pages 8-9).
(2) A financial accounting and cost accounting system for a manufacturing concern (page 10).

The steps in a general assignment may be grouped under the following headings:

(1) Preliminary work
(2) Detailed survey and report
(3) Designing the system
(4) Installing the system

The first two steps and the design of classifications and statements are described in this chapter. Steps 3 and 4 are described in later chapters.

Preliminary Work

Preliminary work includes the following steps:

(1) Discuss the problem with the client to determine the nature of the problem and what the client wants accomplished. This step involves conferences with the client and with the personnel whom he makes available, and it involves getting information on what they consider the

shortcomings of the old system and what they consider to be desirable changes. Frequently the client (the person who is consulting the systems man and who has authority for engaging him) is not an accountant, and his views are those of a person who uses rather than produces the accounting information. He often states the information he needs but is not getting out of the old system, with some comment on the dependability and clerical cost of the information he is now getting. He may call in his accountant for conference, and the latter may explain some of the reports produced by the old system and some of the accounting problems involved as he sees them.

(2) If necessary, make a preliminary survey to gather information required to define the limits of the assignment and to estimate the probable time required to make a complete survey and to design and install the new system. In some cases, a systems man can tell the client what he can do and how much time will be required on the basis of what he learns in the conferences described in the previous paragraph. This is likely to be the case when he has done similar systems in similar lines of business. In other cases, a survey of several days or several weeks may be necessary. Such a survey would involve examining product, plant, and organization structure, and studying the present reports and procedures to determine what is good and can be retained, what will have to be changed, and what will have to be added.

(3) Make a report to the client, stating the scope of the assignment, the estimated consulting time, and the estimated cost. Even though no preliminary survey time is involved, it is a good plan to set out the description of the assignment in writing to avoid any later misunderstanding. Frequently, the oral exchanges of early conferences do not represent complete meeting of minds and a written proposal will tend to crystallize an agreement. Furthermore, clients may expand the assignment in their enthusiasm as the survey gets under way, without realizing that such expansion will require more consulting time than originally planned. Misunderstandings may be eliminated by the use of written proposals.

Detailed Survey and Report

After the assignment has been authorized by the client, the detailed survey is begun. In a general assignment, it is usual to proceed from the top down or from the general to the detailed. This approach is likely to accomplish a maximum amount of coverage with a minimum of disturbance to the client's personnel.

Gather information on the following subjects. Usually it is already in some state of organization that will be useful to the systems man.

(1) The organization chart.

Find out how the company is organized and who is responsible for the various functions and activities. For the accounting divisions of the business (that is, the divisions directly concerned with the old system and the new one to be designed and installed), obtain the number of people in each occupational category under each supervisor. This information will give some clue as to the location and nature of the large work loads.

(2) The financial and operating statements.

Get a complete set of statements. Find out who receives the various copies and what use is made of them.

(3) Classifications of accounts.

Get a copy of the General ledger classification of accounts and such supporting classifications as the expense classification and the sales classification.

(4) Product classification, or nature of the service if the business is not merchandising or manufacturing.

If the company is a manufacturing concern, determine what products it manufactures and the sales volume of the various products or main product groups. Often it is feasible to get this information by studying sales reports, price lists, catalogues, and in some cases, formal product classifications.

(5) Manufacturing plant and facilities.

The extent of the investigation of the manufacturing plant and facilities depends upon the complexity of the product structure and the manufacturing facilities, and the type of cost system that the systems man anticipates designing. In some cases, the survey of the manufacturing processes can be done fairly rapidly, particularly if the systems man is familiar with the industry. In other cases, it is necessary to prepare floor plan charts and to determine and chart such factors as

(a) the departmental lines and the main machine centers,

(b) the flow of production through the plant,

(c) inventory storage spaces for raw materials and finished goods and processed inventory storage points,

(d) machine groupings as affecting the selection of a burden rate structure, and

(e) locations of indirect labor occupational groups (although this information is sometimes obtained by listing from the payroll).

(6) Any procedures manual or standard practice instructions in existence relating to the areas covered in the survey. Of course, before using these items, the systems man must ascertain whether they are up to date.

(7) Account forms and journal forms.

Get a copy of each of these forms and make notes concerning any types of entries that are not immediately explainable by studying printed captions on the forms.

(8) Original business papers.

Get a copy (or a set, if multiple-copy form) of each form that has a bearing on the collection of information for the accounting system. Determine whether the printed captions do indicate what information is entered on the form. If any of the columns or spaces are not used, cross them out. If certain information is added (not indicated by the printing on the form), write a sample entry on the survey copy.

The preceding paragraphs indicate parcels of information, each of which must be studied minutely. Note that, as suggested at the beginning of this section, by starting at the top (organization chart, financial statements, and product lists) and proceeding to the bottom (journal forms and business papers) the systems man learns a great deal about the business before he gets to the journals and business papers. When he gets down to the forms he asks specific questions about the forms and not general questions about the business.

In some cases, it is possible to proceed with the design of a new accounting system on the basis of the parcels of information described above. This might be true in small businesses when no complicated procedures are involved. When the paths to the General ledger are complicated, however, it is necessary to prepare flow charts of the various procedures which lead to the General ledger. These flow charts are then useful in designing the new flow of data into the General ledger. Types of flow charts and their uses are explained on pages 22 to 30.

Designing the Classifications and Statements

Just as the survey is made from the top down, so is the new accounting system designed from the classification of accounts and statements down to the business papers which are used to record transactions. The steps are:

(1) Design a rough classification of accounts and a set of operating statements.
(2) Present the statements to the management, explain them, and get any requests for changes they may have.
(3) Prepare a smooth classification and set of statements and get the approval of the management.
(4) After getting approval of the statements and classifications, prepare the plan of journalizing and business papers, in that order.

The actual construction of the new classification of accounts is often a tedious task, and it may take days or weeks, even in a small business. The exact length of time will depend upon such factors as how good the client's classification was to begin with, the nature of the management controls to be set up, and the skill and thoroughness applied in making the survey.

The systems man will formulate a basic plan of grouping for the classification proper and the general structure of the statements, and he will select a coding plan for the classification that will permit ready addition and removal of accounts within the basic plan. For this plan, the systems man must take the sole responsibility.

After the systems man has put together what he recommends as a satisfactory classification of accounts and a set of statements (containing the exact accounts he believes necessary), he presents them to the client's management. It is expected that they will have convictions of their own as to information they want and do not want. Since accounting information is a tool, it must be fitted to the requirements of the user. Where the ideas are good, they should be noted for inclusion in the designs. If the basic plan is sound and sufficiently flexible, the systems man can make the changes that the client's management asks for, and thus make the statements a tool for the people who are going to use them.

After the statement conferences have been completed, and not until then, the systems man proceeds to design the plan of journalizing. Drafting the formal plan of journalizing is explained in Chapter 4.

Classifications Illustrated

The Household Appliance Corporation (fictitious name) is the wholesale distributor organization through which a large national manufacturer of household appliances distributes its products. The organization includes approximately 100 wholesalers, each separately incorporated, who sell to retailers. Six of these corporations are owned by the manufacturer, and the others are independent franchise holders. The latter agree, according to the terms of the franchise, to handle only the kitchen and laundry appliances made by the manufacturer with whom they have signed. All of them are permitted to (and do) handle noncompeting lines such as radios and television sets. Each franchise holder is given a quota annually, which is worked out by the market research department of the manufacturer. In return for being granted an exclusive franchise in a specified territory, a wholesaler is expected to meet his quota. The classification of accounts shown in this chapter is a modified illustration of the complete one used by each of the wholesalers. It was designed by the manufacturer to provide the wholesalers with all the accounting information which they need to operate their businesses. The manufacturer also provided financial management and profit-planning assistance to the wholesalers.

The typical wholesalers organization (Figure 3-1) comprises a president, vice president in charge of sales and service, secretary and treasurer, purchasing agent, controller, warehouse and delivery manager, service manager, and certain other supervisors. The Sales department includes house salesmen who work only in the warehouse display room and outside salesmen who travel territories and call on retailers. House salesmen are paid salaries and outside salesmen are paid salaries and commissions. The wholesaler sells in several states.

ORGANIZATION CHART

HOUSEHOLD APPLIANCE CORPORATION

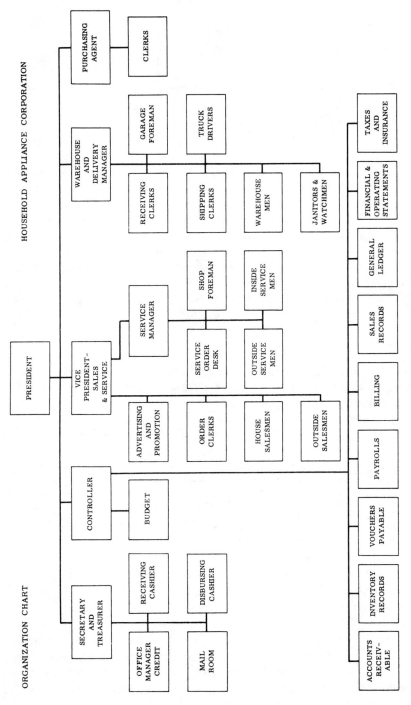

Figure 3-1. Organization Chart—Household Appliance Corporation

The wholesaler maintains a complete service department for repairing appliances. It consists of a crew of outside service men, each provided with a small service truck, who answer service calls and make repairs and replace parts on the customers' premises. All service and repair men are highly trained by the company, whose management realizes that continued product sales depends to some extent upon the quality of repair service that customers receive.

Most of the work of the service department is done on a call or job basis, but the wholesaler also offers service contracts to customers of large installations of appliances. Under these contracts, the wholesaler will provide all repair labor required during a contract year, and not covered by warranties, for a fee. Warranties covering defective parts are given on all appliance sales. Under these warranties, any parts which prove defective under normal use are replaced at no charge to the customer.

The wholesaler does not handle any second-hand parts. Any trade-ins which the retailers make are handled by them alone.

General Ledger Classification

The General ledger classification which was designed for the wholesalers described above appears in Table 3-1. The account numbering scheme is an example of group classification:

Account Groups	Accounts
100	Balance Sheet
200	Sales and Purchase
300	Administrative Expense
400	Selling Expense
500	Receiving, Warehousing, & Shipping Expense
600	Occupancy Expense
700	Service Department—Inside
800	Service Department—Outside
900	Other Income and Expense

The left-hand digit identifies the group and the two right-hand digits the accounts within the group.

The Balance Sheet group (100) comprises familiar accounts for the most part. The investment in fixed assets is significant, and separate asset and allowance for depreciation accounts are maintained for building, warehouse and delivery equipment, and service shop equipment and trucks. A rather detailed classification of current liabilities is kept for accounts, notes, and loans payable, accrued interest, accrued payroll, and accrued taxes of several types.

The Reserve for Warranty account (189) is a contingent reserve. It is credited for a predetermined percentage of sales to provide for the cost of replacing parts under the warranty contracts. Warranty Expense (490) is charged. Actual warranty costs are charged to the Reserve account.

Sales and Purchases group (200) includes the debit and credit accounts needed (along with the inventory accounts) to determine gross profit on kitchen appliances and parts, laundry appliances and parts, and other appliances. It also includes Service Income—Inside account (214) and Service Income—Outside account (215) from which Service Expense —Inside (700 group) and Service Expense—Outside (800 group) can be deducted on the income statement. (It is expected that each class of service will pay its own way.) Finally, there is an income account (216) and an expense account (217) for service contracts to make it possible to show the profit or loss on service contracts.

There is a complete group of expense accounts for each of the functional responsibilities of the business: administrative; selling; receiving, warehousing and shipping; occupancy; service—inside; service—outside; and financial. The group names are descriptive, but it may be noted that the occupancy group includes all building maintenance and fixed charges.

Each of the groups (except the financial) comprises accounts which are grouped by object classes. Thus, for administrative expense, the object groups are as follows:

Object Group	Accounts
310	Labor (3 accounts)
320	Payroll Reserves (2 accounts)
330	Supplies (1 account)
340	Repairs (1 account)
360	Purchased Services (5 accounts)
370	Travel
380	Unclassified
390	Fixed Charges (4 accounts)

The second digit represents object class, and the right-hand digit identifies the object account. Following is a discussion of significant features of the object classification.

In the Labor group (310), there is an account for each indirect labor occupation which involves significant expenditure.

Payroll Reserves and Insurance (320) includes separate accounts for F.I.C.A. Tax and Unemployment Insurance Tax.

The Operating Supplies group (330) is charged with items that are physical or inventoriable in nature. (Accounts in the Purchased Services group (360) are accordingly used for items which are not inventoriable.)

The Fixed Charges group (390) includes Depreciation, Insurance, Taxes, and similar accounts.

There are several advantages in grouping expense accounts as illustrated:

(a) Where there are numerous accounts, the grouping facilitates reading the expense statements prepared from the classification. The reader can get an over-all picture by reading first the eight object group totals (shown above) before proceeding to any necessary examination of the individual account totals.

(b) It facilitates managerial action because accounts are grouped according to the type of remedial action which is possible. Thus, all the labor accounts within each major expense group (over which the manager has some measure of control) are grouped together. Fixed charges, over which the manager has no day-to-day control, are a separate group.

(c) The division of expenses into fixed and variable classes within each major expense group facilitates making the cost calculations of the effect of volume of operations on cost.

A complete set of financial and operating statements prepared from the account classification described above appears in Chapter 20.

Table 3-1

HOUSEHOLD APPLIANCE CORPORATION

CLASSIFICATION OF ACCOUNTS

BALANCE SHEET ACCOUNTS

CURRENT ASSETS

101	Petty Cash
102	Cash in Bank
111	Accounts Receivable—Customers
111A	Allowance for Uncollectible Accounts
112	Accounts Receivable—Officers and Employees
113	Salesmen's Drawing Accounts
114	Notes Receivable
114D	Notes Receivable Discounted
115	Accrued Interest Receivable
120	Merchandise Inventories
121	Kitchen Appliances
122	Laundry Appliances
123	Other Appliances
131	Prepaid Rent—Outside Warehousing
132	Prepaid Insurance
140	Supplies Inventories
141	Office Supplies
142	Warehouse and Shop Supplies
143	Advertising Supplies

FIXED ASSETS

150	Land
161	Building
161A	Allowance for Depreciation—Building
162	Warehouse Equipment
162A	Allowance for Depreciation—Warehouse Equipment
163	Delivery Trucks
163A	Allowance for Depreciation—Delivery Trucks

164	Service Shop Equipment
164A	Allowance for Depreciation—Service Shop Equipment
165	Service Trucks
165A	Allowance for Depreciation—Service Trucks
166	Office Furniture and Fixtures
166A	Allowance for Depreciation—Office Furniture and Fixtures

CURRENT LIABILITIES

171	Vouchers Payable—Appliance Suppliers
172	Vouchers Payable—Other
173	Accrued Payroll
175	Notes Payable
176	Bank Loans
177	Accrued Interest Payable
178	Dividends Payable
181	Accrued Payroll Taxes
182	Withholding Tax Deducted
183	Federal Income Tax Accrued
184	Accrued Real Estate Taxes
185	Accrued Personal Property Taxes
186	Accrued Sales Tax—Illinois
187	Accrued Sales Tax—Other

RESERVES

189	Reserve for Warranty

LONG-TERM LIABILITIES

190	Mortgage Payable

NET WORTH

195	Capital Stock
196	Retained Earnings
199	Profit and Loss

PROFIT AND LOSS ACCOUNTS

SALES AND PURCHASES

210	Sales and Service Income
211	Sales of Kitchen Appliances and Parts
212	Sales of Laundry Appliances and Parts
213	Sales of Other Appliances
214	Service Income—Inside
215	Service Income—Outside
216	Service Contracts
217	Labor used on Service Contracts (debit)
220	Sales Returns and Allowances
221	Kitchen Appliances and Parts
222	Laundry Appliances and Parts
223	Other Appliances
230	Purchases
231	Kitchen Appliances and Parts
232	Laundry Appliances and Parts
233	Other Appliances
240	Freight In
241	Kitchen Appliances and Parts
242	Laundry Appliances and Parts
243	Other Appliances
250	Purchase Returns and Allowances
251	Kitchen Appliances and Parts
252	Laundry Appliances and Parts
253	Other Appliances

ADMINISTRATIVE EXPENSES

300	Administrative Expenses Control
311	Administrative Salaries
312	Office Salaries
319	Overtime Premium
321	F.I.C.A. Tax Expense
322	Unemployment Insurance Expense
331	Stationery and Office Supplies
341	Repairs to Office Furniture and Equipment
361	Postage
362	Telephone and Telegraph
363	Association Dues
364	Professional Services
365	Donations
370	Travel
380	Unclassified
391	Rentals of Office Equipment
392	Depreciation—Office Furniture and Equipment
393	Insurance—Office Furniture and Equipment
394	Taxes—Office Furniture and Equipment

SELLING EXPENSES

400	Selling Expenses Control
411	Sales Supervisory Salaries
412	Inside Salesmen
413	Outside Salesmen
414	Commissions
421	F.I.C.A. Tax Expense
422	Unemployment Insurance Expense
431	Stationery and Office Supplies
451	Newspaper and Magazine Advertising
452	Dealer Aids
453	Convention Expense
454	Advertising Allowances to Dealers
461	Association Dues
462	Professional Services
463	Freight Out
471	Automobile Expense
472	Other Travel and Entertainment
480	Unclassified Expense
490	Warranty Expense

RECEIVING, WAREHOUSING AND SHIPPING EXPENSES

500	Receiving, Warehousing, and Shipping Expenses Control
511	Supervisory Salaries
512	Warehousemen
513	Truck Drivers and Helpers
519	Overtime Premium
521	F.I.C.A. Tax Expense
522	Unemployment Insurance Expense
531	Packing Supplies
541	Repairs to Warehouse Equipment
542	Repairs to Trucks
543	Gasoline and Oil
580	Unclassified
591	Rent—Outside Warehousing
592	Depreciation—Warehouse Equipment
593	Depreciation—Trucks

594   Insurance—Warehouse Equipment
595   Insurance—Inventories
596   Insurance—Trucks
597   Taxes—Warehouse Equipment
598   Taxes—Inventories
599   Taxes and Licenses—Trucks

OCCUPANCY EXPENSES

600   Occupancy Expenses Control
611   Supervisory Salaries
612   Janitors and Watchmen
619   Overtime Premium
621   F.I.C.A. Tax Expense
622   Unemployment Insurance Expense
641   Janitor Supplies
642   Repairs to Building
661   Heat, Light, and Air Conditioning
691   Depreciation—Building
692   Insurance—Building
693   Taxes—Building

SERVICE DEPARTMENT—INSIDE EXPENSES

700   Service Department—Inside Expenses Control
711   Supervisory Salaries
712   Repairmen
719   Overtime Premium
721   F.I.C.A. Tax Expense
722   Unemployment Insurance Expense
730   Operating Supplies
761   Power
791   Depreciation—Service Shop Equipment
792   Insurance—Service Shop Equipment
793   Taxes—Service Shop Equipment
799   Labor used on Service Contracts (Credit)

SERVICE DEPARTMENT—OUTSIDE EXPENSES

800   Service Department—Outside Expenses Control
811   Service Men
821   F.I.C.A. Tax Expense
822   Unemployment Insurance
830   Operating Supplies
841   Repairs to Service Trucks
842   Gasoline and Oil—Service Trucks
880   Unclassified
891   Depreciation—Service Trucks
892   Insurance—Service Trucks
893   Taxes and Licenses—Service Trucks
899   Labor used on Service Contracts (Credit)

OTHER INCOME AND EXPENSE

911   Purchases Discounts
912   Interest Income
951   Sales Discounts
952   Interest Expense
953   Warranty Expense (Labor and Parts)
954   Bad Debts

CODES

Uses of Codes

A code is a plan by which numbers or letters of the alphabet (or a combination of numbers and letters) can be assigned to a previously arranged classification. Codes are a convenient device for identifying and distinguishing the items in a classification. In a machine age (now) coding is almost unavoidable, and *consistent* coding is necessary to have mechanical (including computer) extraction of a particular category of data from among a wide range of accounts.

In accounting systems work, codes are frequently used in connection with the following classifications:

(1) Classification of accounts for financial statements: balance sheet and operating statements.
(2) Sales classifications by product class, territory, customer or customer group, salesman, and so forth for sales statistics purposes.
(3) Expense classifications: by object of expense, by department or responsibility, or both.
(4) Materials classifications and product classifications for purposes of the purchase order system and the production order system.
(5) Employee classifications for payroll purposes.
(6) Burden center classifications, production order classifications, and others for use in the cost system.

In designing a complete accounting system for a manufacturing concern, some of the classifications will be primarily General ledger classifications and supporting report classifications. Others will be primarily order system classifications. Still others will be independent classifications.

Use of account numbers instead of names (or in addition to names) may speed the locating of accounts in the posting operation. In some cases, as in designating accounts to charge on purchase invoices (or accounts to charge on distribution vouchers), account numbers may be used instead of account names to save time that would be required to write the names.

In order systems, such as the production order system, code numbers are used not only to save writing time but to provide for positive identification of the specifications intended. In some technical lines, such as optical goods, codes provide the only convenient means of indicating all the technical characteristics of the product item or part.

Coding is often considered as a preparatory operation to sorting. For mechanical sorting (Keysort cards, tabulating cards), coding is a necessary preparation. Even for manual sorting, it is desirable to consider coding as a preparatory operation. In some cases the systems man has to decide whether to sort the media alphabetically (on the written names) or to apply a numeric code to the media so that the media can be sorted numerically.

Two commonly used coding plans are explained in the following sections: block code and group classification code.[1]

Block Code

Block coding consists in assigning numbers in such manner that a specified series is reserved for one designated class of names. In the original application of the code, a few blank numbers are left in each series to provide for later additions.

Table 3-2

BLOCK CODE: BALANCE SHEET ACCOUNTS

1	Wilson National Bank
2	Acheson National Bank
3	Petty Cash
6	Accounts Receivable
7	Allowance for Bad Debts
8	Notes Receivable
9	Inventories
21	Factory Supplies
22	Office Supplies
23	Prepaid Insurance
30	Land
31	Building
32	Allowance for Depreciation—Building
33	Office Furniture and Fixtures
34	Allowance for Depreciation—Office Furniture & Fixtures
35	Machinery
36	Allowance for Depreciation—Machinery
37	Delivery Equipment
38	Allowance for Depreciation—Delivery Equipment
50	Accounts Payable
51	Accrued Payroll
52	Accrued F.I.C.A. Tax—Employees' Share
53	Accrued F.I.C.A. Tax—Company's Share
54	Notes Payable
60	Capital Stock
61	Surplus
62	Profit and Loss

Table 3-2 illustrates a block code applied to a balance sheet classification. Note that the numbers 1 to 19 are used for current assets, 21 to 29 for prepaid expenses, and so on.

---

[1] For an excellent treatise on coding, see National Association of Accountants, *Research Report 34*, "Classification and Coding Techniques to Facilitate Accounting Operations" (1959).

This method of coding provides in a measure for memorizing, since certain blocks are reserved for certain classes. Also, it will be noted that block codes do not require as many digits for their expression as the more complicated code explained in the following section. They make some slight provision for expansion (that is, to the extent of blank numbers in the original list).

Group Classification

The main characteristics of group classification codes are: (1) digit position has significance; the extreme left-hand digits identify major classes and the right-hand digits the sub-classes; (2) a group classification code number is always limited to a predetermined number of digits (6 in the illustration which follows); (3) the same number of digits is used for any code number; and (4) addition of main groups to the classification is provided for by leaving gaps in the original assignment of left-hand digits.

Table 3-3

GROUP CLASSIFICATION

Symbol	Description
070000	#7 Wagon, complete
070100	Top assembly
070101	sides (2 for each assembly)
070102	bottom
070103	brake
070200	Front bolster assembly
070201	front axle
070202	front bolster
070203	front bolster brace
070204	front wheel (2)
070205	tongue
070206	tongue strap (2)
070207	center pin
070208	handle
070300	Rear bolster assembly
070301	rear axle
070302	rear bolster
070303	rear bolster brace
070304	rear wheel (2)

Table 3-3 is a group classification code applied to the subassemblies and parts of a wagon. Note the group significance of the digits:

First two	07	= Major assembly	complete wagon
Second two	01	= Minor assembly	top
Third two	01	= Part	side
Thus,	070101	= Side for a number 7 wagon	

A group classification code applied to expense account classification is described on pages 43-44. In this illustration a three-digit account number is used. In a four-digit account number, object and department might be identified:

First two	01	= Object	(say, Indirect labor)
Second two	01	= Department	(say, Assembly)
Thus,	0101	= Indirect labor, Assembly Department	

Some very large businesses use group classification codes which involve income and expense accounts (General ledger), departments, and sub-accounts. To illustrate:

First three	330	= Expense Account	(say, Supplies)
Second two	11	= Department	(say, Garage)
Third two	11	= Subaccount	(say, Gasoline)

Note that the subaccounts are a breakdown of the General ledger expense accounts. The subaccounts for the service department Garage might be Gasoline, Oil, Repair Parts, Outside Labor, and so forth. Subaccounts for the Service department Power (which includes refrigeration) might be Coal, Oil, Ammonia, Gas, Electricity, and so forth. Each service department might have a different list of subaccounts, while the General ledger list might be relatively short.

The following points may be made concerning group classification codes:

(1) They aid memory of the user to some extent because users quickly learn the significance of digit position in the code.

(2) Group classification codes tend to comprise more digits than block or sequence codes, but fewer than certain other codes.

(3) Group classification codes provide for expansion of main classes by leaving unassigned numbers in the original list. They do not provide for infinite subdivision since the number of digit positions is definitely fixed.

(4) They identify each item in the code with all superior groups to which the item belongs. Thus, an expense account number will show not only the nature of the expense but also the department which incurred it.

Group classification codes are frequently used on accounting media which are to be sorted (especially by machine). Since each digit position represents a specific set of classes or subclasses, it is easy to sort out specific desired classes.

Need for a Formal Manual of Accounts

It is obvious to the systems man, but not always obvious to the client or the manager of the smaller business, that a formal classification of accounts is necessary even in small businesses. It is also desirable, except in the smallest business, to write up in considerable detail the types of items that are intended to be charged and credited to each account. If the charges and credits are not clearly defined, a bookkeeper is likely to charge what appears to him to be a debatable item to one account at one time and to another account at another time, and the comparability of successive statements is impaired. Another reason for preparing a formal manual of accounts is that it serves a training function in case of turnover among the accounting employees. In the larger business, of course, the classification must be formalized for distribution to the numerous clerks and executives who have a hand in originating, approving, and coding accounting documents.

An illustration of the method of setting up a formal manual of accounts appears in Chapter 20, which deals with systems reports of various kinds.

Uniform Classifications of Accounts Developed by Trade Associations and Other Industry Groups

Numerous trade associations and other industry groups have developed and published classifications of accounts for the businesses of the particular industry. The fundamental purpose of such classifications is to encourage the members of the industry to practice good accounting. In some cases, the members submit expense and other statistics to the association on the basis of the uniform classification, and comparative statistics are distributed to the membership, without disclosing the identity of particular contributors. Each member uses the association report to determine how his performance compares with other members of the group.

The systems man should be familiar with some of these classifications because of the general ideas which they will suggest and because of their applicability to a particular business in which the systems man may be interested.

Organizational Structure of the Ledgers

Figure 3-2 "Organizational Structure of the Ledgers" is a progressive illustration showing five typical ledger arrangements, proceeding from one that might be used for the smallest business which has formal double-entry bookkeeping to one that is typical of the largest businesses. The stages illustrated are briefly described as follows:

(a) In the smallest business, all accounts may be kept in the General ledger. One bookkeeper, possibly the proprietor or a part-time clerk, may do all the ledger work. Conventional T accounts or some modification of them may be used.

(b) In this stage, only one bookkeeper is required to handle the ledger work, but the number of accounts in particular groups is so large as to make it impractical to keep all the accounts in the General ledger. Certain subsidiary ledgers, such as Accounts Receivable, Accounts Payable, and Expenses are set up for the convenience of the bookkeeper. The use of columnar accounts in the General ledger for related groups of accounts, such as expense groups, may be considered.

(c) In this stage, the number of accounts and the volume of posting

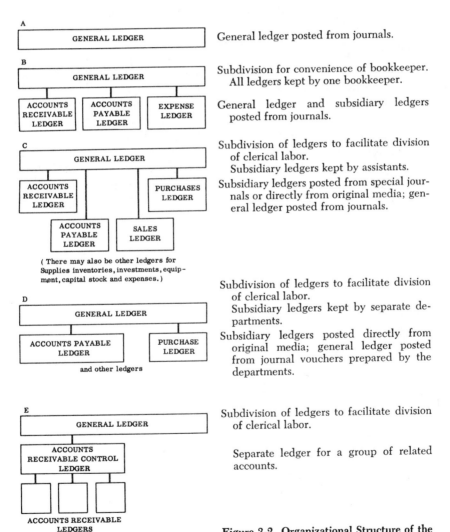

General ledger posted from journals.

Subdivision for convenience of bookkeeper. All ledgers kept by one bookkeeper.

General ledger and subsidiary ledgers posted from journals.

Subdivision of ledgers to facilitate division of clerical labor. Subsidiary ledgers kept by assistants.

Subsidiary ledgers posted from special journals or directly from original media; general ledger posted from journals.

Subdivision of ledgers to facilitate division of clerical labor. Subsidiary ledgers kept by separate departments.

Subsidiary ledgers posted directly from original media; general ledger posted from journal vouchers prepared by the departments.

Subdivision of ledgers to facilitate division of clerical labor.

Separate ledger for a group of related accounts.

Figure 3-2. Organizational Structure of the Ledgers (Evolution of the General Ledger)

is too large for one bookkeeper to handle, and one or more of the subsidiary ledgers are turned over to an assistant. The subsidiary ledgers may be posted from special journals or directly from the original media which would then be summarized in journals.

(d) In this stage, the volume of transactions is assumed to be larger than in the previous stage, and the subsidiary ledgers (which are numerous) are kept by separate departments, such as the Accounts Payable department. The subsidiary ledgers are posted directly from original media, such as purchase invoices. Each type of media moves to the proper ledger in batches accompanied by a listing machine tape of the items totaled to provide a control figure. The General ledger is posted from journal vouchers prepared by the departments that operate the subsidiary records.

(e) This stage is similar to Stage (d), except that particular groups of accounts, such as Accounts Receivable, are extremely large. A certain large department store, which is typical, has 50,000 customers' accounts in 140 ledgers. The control accounts for the subsidiary ledgers are kept in a separate control ledger for the group, which is in turn controlled by a single control account in the General ledger. The subsidiary ledgers are posted from original media and the General ledger is posted entirely from journal vouchers. In the ultimate stage, the General ledger may be almost entirely a book of control accounts.

4

Pen-and-Ink Journals

Basic Plans of Journalizing

The previous chapters have explained how to make the survey and how to design the classification of accounts and the financial and operating statements. After the statements have been approved by the management and the classification of accounts smoothed off to provide all the necessary accounts, the plan of journalizing transactions can be considered.

The basic plans of journalizing and posting are:

(1) Entering business papers in journal (s) and posting to ledgers by pen and ink. The journals may be:
    (a) Specially designed and printed to order (pages 58 to 61).
    (b) Ready printed (pages 62 to 68).
(2) Posting business papers directly to subsidiary ledger accounts and obtaining the journal as a carbon copy. This can be done by:
    (a) Pen and ink, with the use of a writing board (Chapter 6).
    (b) Bookkeeping machine (Chapter 10).
(3) Sorting or filing instead of posting (summary strip accounting or ledgerless bookkeeping).

Factors to Consider in Selecting a Plan of Journalizing

Some factors to consider in selecting a plan of summarizing transactions:

(1) Organization of the accounting function from a personnel stand-point. Obviously, the detailed design of the plan of summarizing is likely to be different in each of the following situations:
    (a) The business is a one-man business and the proprietor does all the summarizing himself. (He may understand double-entry bookkeeping, or he may not. The design of summary

55

records will have to reflect consideration of that fact in either case.)

(b) The business has a bookkeeper, qualified in double-entry bookkeeping, who does all the bookkeeping work.

(c) The business has a bookkeeper and one or more clerical assistants. The bookkeeper is qualified in accounting, but the clerks are qualified or can be trained for specialized-entry or posting work. All accounting people are located in the same office.

(d) The business has some degree of departmentalization in the accounting function. There may be separate departments for each of the following: Accounts Receivable, Accounts Payable, Sales Accounts, and Expense Accounts. Each of these departments comprises a group of clerks who work upon a single type of record. Note that in a large business, there may be departmentalization of asset and liability ledger posting (say accounts receivable, accounts payable, and other groups) or there may be departmentalization of the income and expense accounting. In the largest businesses, there may be departmentalization of both the balance sheet accounts and the profit and loss accounts.

(2) The number of accounts in the new classification:

(a) The number of control accounts and the number of accounts under each control, which in turn leads to consideration of:

(b) Which groups of accounts will be kept in the General ledger and which groups in subsidiary ledgers.

(c) Which ledgers will be posted in detail (separate posting for each transaction, with, say, date, description, and amount), and which ones will be posted with summarized totals, say, once a month.

(3) The types of transaction and the number of each type.

The Detail Plan of Journalizing, Including Adjusting Entries; Standard (Recurring) Journal Entries

Where the accounting system is complicated, the systems man may find it useful to draft the plan of recurring entries that would be made in the General ledger in simple debit and credit form. There would be a pro-forma entry for each of the journals which the systems man contemplates having, and one for each of the adjusting entries for accruals and deferrals that would be made in the General ledger periodically. Collectively, these entries would show how every common debit and credit would enter the ledger. Where pen-and-ink journals are to be used, setting down these debits and credits is a good way to formalize one's thinking on what types of transactions are to be entered in each journal and what debit and credit columns will be most useful. After the systems man is satisfied with his set of "standard journal entries," as they are called, he will design his journals directly from them, or turn them over to an assistant who will do the drafting.

Although the standard journal entries are first of all a tool of systems designing, it is often desirable to include them in the formal manual that is written for the guidance of the people who will operate the new system. This is particularly true where the new system (for instance, a standard cost system) comprises groups of accounts the operation of which will be unfamiliar to the client's personnel. The standard journal entries provide a quick picture of all the entries that have to be made in order to produce the monthly statements.

In large accounting departments, there is a further reason for formalizing the entries by which the books are closed and the statements prepared. Each of the entries is likely to come to the General ledger department from a separate section of the Accounting department, and in the largest organizations, each of the entries will be written on a journal voucher form for transmission. These entries will follow the model of the original standard journal entries, and they will be scheduled through the days of the closing procedure to make certain that the books are closed and the statements prepared on time. The file of standard journal entries is part and parcel of the task of planning the closing procedure and following up each monthly closing.

Standard Journal Entries Illustrated

Table 4-2 (at the end of the chapter) illustrates the 22 standard journal entries which were drafted for the Household Appliance Corporation whose classification of accounts is illustrated in Table 3-1. These journal entries were composed by the systems man after he had designed operating statements and the classification of accounts.

The entries show the results of a number of decisions made by the systems man. Examples:

Journal Entry No. 1 is the plan of the sales entry:

111	Accounts Receivable—Customers
112	Accounts Receivable—Officers and Employees
185	Accrued Sales Tax—Illinois
186	Accrued Sales Tax—Other
211	Sales of Kitchen Appliances and Parts
212	Sales of Laundry Appliances and Parts
213	Sales of Other Appliances
214	Service Income—Inside
215	Service Income—Outside
216	Service Contracts
463	Freight Out

To record sales for month, per sales invoices

This entry indicates that a six-account distribution of sales is to be picked up in the sales journal from the invoices, together with the liability for accrued sales tax in two states and a credit for freight-billed customers.

Sample entry from an invoice:

Dr. 111	Accounts Receivable (Wilson)		$110.00	
Cr. 185	Accrued Sales Tax—Illinois			$ 2.00
211	Sales of Kitchen Appliances and Parts			100.00
463	Freight Out			8.00

Note that the amounts of freight billed are recorded as separate credits to Freight Out through the sales journal to keep freight out of the sales accounts. When the carrier is paid, a voucher register entry is made debiting Freight Out and crediting Vouchers Payable. The balance of the Freight Out account represents any freight paid that has not been billed.

Journal Entry No. 6 indicates that it has been decided to have a voucher system, with the debit distribution for disbursements passed through the voucher register. Note that an expense control column has been provided for each of the six expense control groups. Each control column combines space for folio and amount. (Columnar accounts are to be used in the General ledger, one for each expense control.)

The footnotes to Journal Entry No. 6 outline the complete plan of setting up accruals and deferrals, setting up these accounts in such manner that no reversing or post closing entries will be required. (The footnotes are typical of those that are made by the systems man while he is designing a plan of journalizing.) The plan provides that:

(1) All journals will be recapped at the end of the month so that there will be not more than one debit or credit each month to each income and expense account from each journal. This reduces the number of postings to those accounts to the absolute minimum. Recapping at the source also increases the accuracy of source items posted (since the debits and credits of each journal are balanced by crossfooting). This factor tends to reduce the possibility of trial balance trouble.

(2) All post closing or reversing entries are eliminated by a process of building up accruals.

Designing the Journal Forms

After the standard journal entries—the master plan of journalizing—are thought through and formalized, the journals can be quickly designed. They are drafted directly from the standard journal entries; in fact, they can be set up by an assistant to the designer.

Figures 4-1 through 4-7 are sketches of the journals which are designed from the standard journal entries in Table 4-2, as follows:

Figure No.	Journal	Designed from Standard Journal Entry No.
4-1	Sales Journal	1
4-2	Sales Returns and Allowances Journal	2
4-3	Voucher Register	6
4-4	Cash Receipts Journal	20
4-5	Cash Payments Journal	21
4-6	General Journal	
4-7	Standard Journal	

The actual journals would be drawn to scale for the printer.

Note that the sales journal (Figure 4-1) provides money columns for the two classes of accounts receivable debits, three columns for sales of appliances and parts, three columns for service income, three for accrued sales tax, and one column for credits to the Freight Out account for freight-billed customers.

The voucher register (Figure 4-3) includes, among other columns, one column for Vouchers Payable—Appliance Suppliers and one for Vouchers Payable—Other. The former are all payable to the single manufacturer with whom the wholesaler buys on franchise. It is planned to pay the manufacturer on the 10th, 20th, and last day of the month. Only one voucher will be open at any time. Invoices approved, for instance, between the first and the 10th of the month will be entered on one voucher which will be closed and paid on the tenth of the month.

The voucher register and the general journal (Figure 4-6) each include a column with folio for each of the expense control accounts.

The standard journal (Figure 4-7) is used for recording accruals and deferrals and other recurring entries:

S.J.E. 7 Company's share of F.I.C.A. tax
8 Unemployment insurance expense
9 Depreciation
10 Insurance expired
11 Real estate taxes accrued
12 Personal property taxes accrued
13 Provision for uncollectible accounts
14 Provision for warranty expense
15 Labor used on service contracts
16 Supplies used from stores

A single particulars column is provided together with a number of pairs of debit and credit columns—one for each month. Use of this journal saves the rewriting of account names every month.

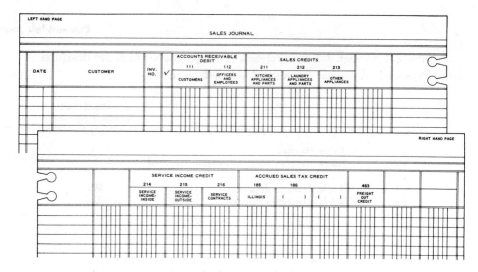

Figure 4-1. Sales Journal

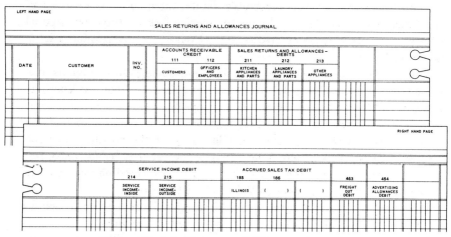

Figure 4-2. Sales Returns and Allowances Journal

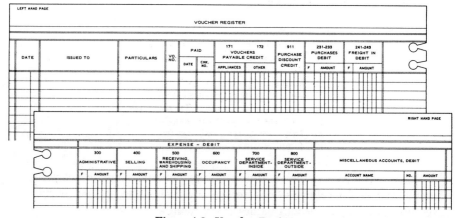

Figure 4-3. Voucher Register

CASH RECEIPTS JOURNAL

| DATE | ACCOUNT | PARTICULARS | GENERAL LEDGER CREDIT | | ACCOUNTS RECEIVABLE CREDIT | | 951 SALES DISCOUNT DEBIT | 102 CASH IN BANK DEBIT |
			A/C NO.	AMOUNT	111 CUSTOMERS	112 OFFICERS AND EMPLOYEES		

Figure 4-4. Cash Receipts Journal

CASH PAYMENTS JOURNAL

| DATE | ISSUED TO | CHK. NO. | VO. NO. | VOUCHERS PAYABLE DEBIT | | 102 CASH IN BANK CREDIT |
				171 APPLIANCES	172 OTHER	

Figure 4-5. Cash Payments Journal

GENERAL JOURNAL

| DATE | PARTICULARS | MISCELLANEOUS ACCOUNTS | | | EXPENSE – DEBIT | | | | | | | | | | | |
| | | F | DEBITS | CREDITS | 300 ADMINISTRATIVE | | 400 SELLING | | 500 RECEIVING, WAREHOUSING AND SHIPPING | | 600 OCCUPANCY | | 700 SERVICE DEPARTMENT-INSIDE | | 800 SERVICE DEPARTMENT-OUTSIDE | |
					F	AMOUNT	F	AMOUNT	F	AMOUNT	F	AMOUNT	F	AMOUNT	F	AMOUNT

Figure 4-6. General Journal

STANDARD JOURNAL

| DATE | PARTICULARS | MONTH: | | | MONTH: | | | MONTH: | | |
		A/C NO.	DEBITS	CREDITS	A/C NO.	DEBITS	CREDITS	A/C NO.	DEBITS	CREDITS

Figure 4-7. Standard Journal

READY-PRINTED JOURNAL FORMS

Typical Sets of Columnar Journals (Table 4-1)

Where the journals are not especially complicated, it may be feasible to buy ready-printed journal forms with certain blank column headings which can be filled in with pen and ink. Table 4-1 lists a number of typical sets of ready-printed journals. The set designated (*) is intended for double entry with current recording on a cash basis and periodic adjustments to accrual basis, and the others are used under full accrual basis. The various sets are discussed and some of the forms are illustrated in the following sections.

One Journal for All Transactions: Two-Column Journal

The familiar two-column journal (not illustrated) is used in practice where the number of transactions is very small. The entire "set of books" may comprise a check book, the two-column journal, and a General ledger. Probably most textbooks on general accounting present the two-column journal as the one that is used when the business is being started. After transactions become numerous, special journals are added. This perennial example is a good one since many ventures, particularly part-time ventures of a businessman, remain small in number of transactions per month. In some cases there may be only 20 or 30 transactions per month.

One Journal for All Transactions: Cash Journal
   (Figure 4-8)

The cash journal is a multiple-column book of original entry designed to accommodate the entry of all classes of transaction. (See Figure 4-8.) In addition to the "General ledger" or "miscellaneous" charges and credits columns, there are special columns for cash received and paid out, sales credits, accounts receivable charges and credits, purchases charges, accounts payable charges and credits, and so on. Use of these special columns reduces the number of postings to the General ledger, if the special columns are posted in total at the end of the month.

The cash journal is designed for use either where all accounts are kept in a General ledger or where some of the accounts are kept in subsidiary ledgers. Thus, if there is an Accounts Receivable ledger, sales invoices may be entered in detail in the Accounts Receivable charges column and the Sales credits column, and the debits in the former column posted to the accounts in the Accounts Receivable ledger. Or, daily totals of sales could be entered in the cash journal and the invoices could be posted in detail to the Accounts Receivable ledger.

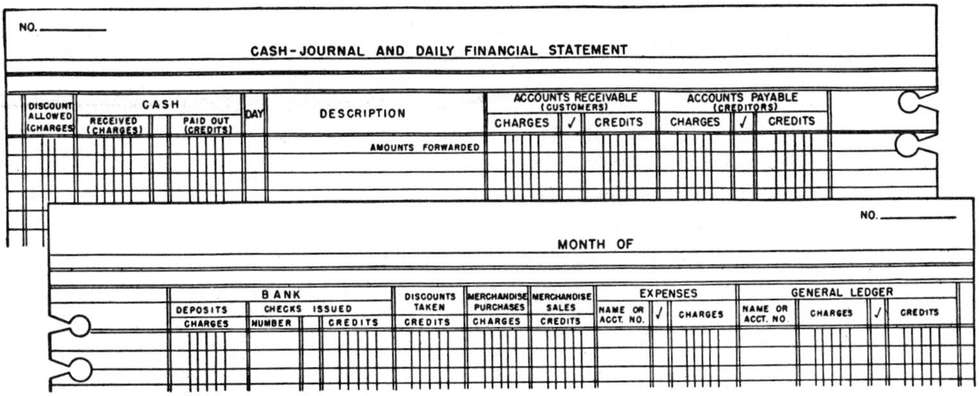

Figure 4-8. Cash Journal

Wilson-Jones

Table 4-1

TYPICAL SETS OF COLUMNAR JOURNALS:

SUBDIVISION AND SPECIALIZATION OF THE GENERAL JOURNAL

(Use of special journals (a) reduces the work of entering and posting and (b) makes it possible to assign the handling of particular types of transactions to clerical assistants.)

One Journal
    Two-Column General Journal
One Journal
    Cash Journal; multiple column journal for all transactions
Two Journals
    Cash Receipts and Sales Journal
    Cash Disbursements and Purchases Journal
*Three Journals
    Cash Receipts Journal
    Cash Disbursements Journal
    General Journal
Five Journals: Accounts Receivable—Accounts Payable
    Cash Receipts Journal
    Cash Payments Journal
    Sales Journal
    Purchases Journal
    General Journal
        and other special journals for particular types of transactions
Five Journals: Accounts Receivable—Vouchers Payable
    Cash Receipts Journal
    Cash Payments Journal
    Sales Journal
    Voucher Register
    General Journal
        and other special journals for particular types of transactions

---

* Double entry with current recording on a cash basis and periodic adjustments to accrual basis. Others: full accrual basis.

Use of the cash journal is suggested where one bookkeeper does all the clerical work, but its use should be questioned if the entries in one or a few of the columns would be very numerous. If the entries for sales on account, for instance, are much more numerous than entries of other types, a separate sales journal and other journals should be considered. Otherwise, much of the space in the cash journal (which is a fifteen-column spread) will be taken up by transactions that could be entered in a one- or two-column spread. The use of the cash journal is most reasonable where the variety of transactions is fairly evenly distributed over the classes.

By the way of objection to the cash journal, some accountants point out that it is more difficult to enter transactions correctly in a cash journal designed for transactions of all classes than it is to enter a transaction in a special journal designed for that class of transaction (illustrated in the following sections). Auditors also state that is difficult to audit a cash journal because if the journal does not balance, it may be necessary to

Figure 4-9. Two-Journal Set

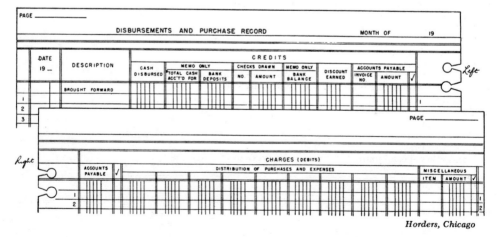

Horders, Chicago

check numerous transactions in detail to see that each was entered in the right column.

Two-Journal Set (Figure 4-9)

Where greater analysis through the journal is desired than can be provided by the cash journal, two journals can be used, with certain classes of transactions in each journal. In the set illustrated in Figure 4-9, the two journals are set up respectively for (1) disbursements and purchases, and (2) receipts and sales. This is often a logical "split" between the classes. The disbursements and purchases journal has 10 analysis columns for debits, which is adequate for the analysis of merchandise and expenses in many small businesses. The sales and cash receipts journal has the same number of columns for the analysis of credits. In most small businesses, these analysis columns will be used for a simple departmental analysis.

Use of the two-journal set makes possible some division of labor. If the volume of transactions warrants, the cash receipts and sales journal can be assigned to one clerk for entry of the sales invoices say, while the cash payments and purchases journal is assigned to another person.

Three-Journal Set; Current Cash Basis; Periodic Adjustment to Accrual Basis (Figure 4-10)

A three-journal set may consist of:
(1) Cash receipts journal with distribution columns for cash sales.
(2) Cash disbursements journal with distribution columns for merchandise purchases and expenses.
(3) General journal.

This journal arrangement is useful where the business sells for cash only and buys for cash and on account. The distribution of cash sales may be recorded as the sales are entered in the cash receipts journal. Merchandise purchases and expenses can be entered in the cash disbursements journal as and when paid, and the debit distribution obtained through the cash disbursements journal. No entry is made for any purchase or expense invoice until it is paid. The invoices are simply filed until payment, thus saving the current entries for recording the liability for the invoice.

At the end of the period, any unpaid invoices in the unpaid file can be summarized and distributed to debit accounts, and a general journal entry can be made to record the liability for unpaid invoices. This entry would be reversed at the beginning of the next period.

Note that a considerable amount of bookkeeping may be saved by using this method of recording merchandise and expense purchases. The saving is made at the sacrifice of formal records of current liabilities, which may not be serious in a small business.

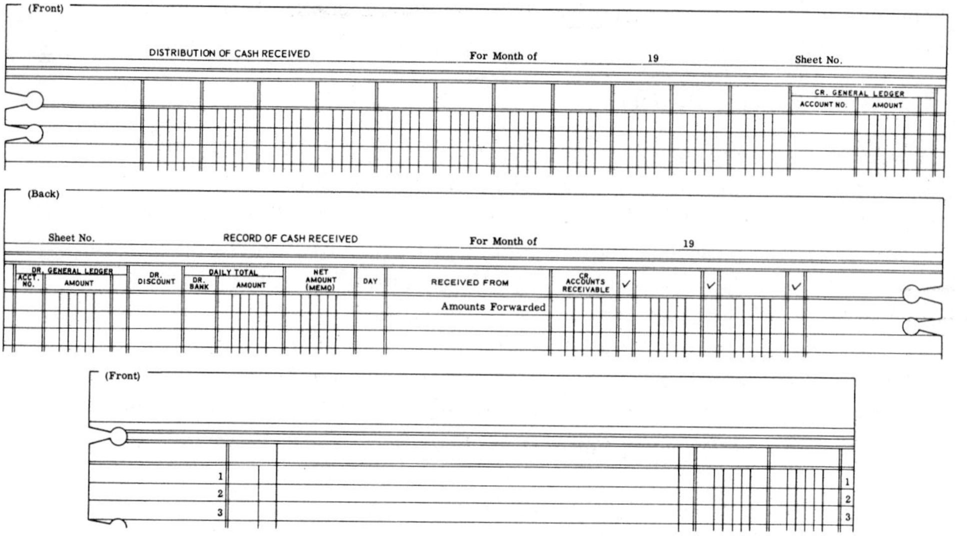

Figure 4-10. Three-Journal Set

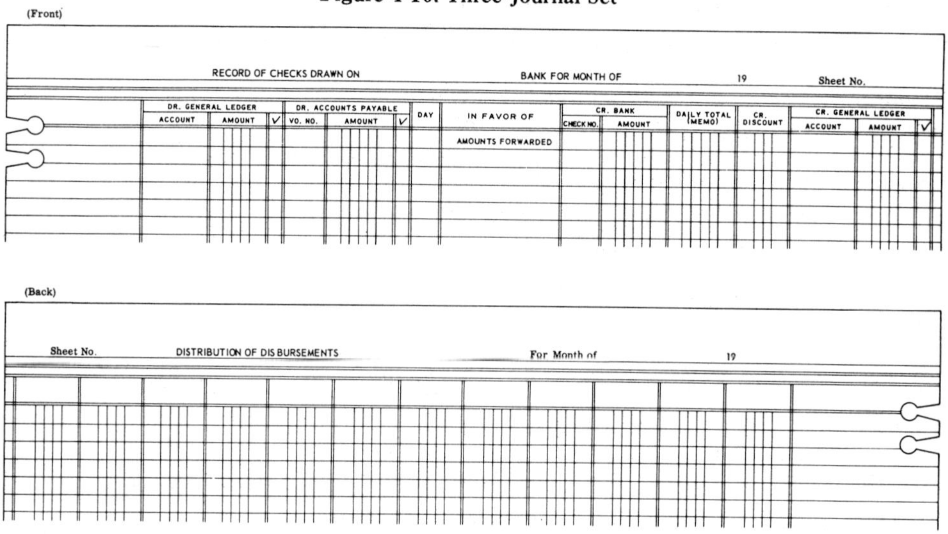

National

Five-Journal Set: Accounts Receivable; Accounts Payable

In a small business selling for cash and on account, the following arrangement of ready-printed special journals might be useful:

(1) Cash receipts journal (no distribution of sales).
(2) Cash disbursements journal (major debit distribution to expenses).
(3) Purchase invoice journal (major debit distribution of merchandise purchases).
(4) Sales journal (distribution of both charge and cash sales).
(5) General journal.

Such a set (not illustrated) can be obtained from accounting forms stationers. It can provide a larger number of distribution columns for sales, purchases, and expense than the previous sets. A five-journal set can be used in a one-bookkeeper business if the number of each type of transaction warrants the use of that many journals. In a larger business, each journal can be assigned to a different clerk.

Note that in this set-up, expense purchases are not recorded until paid, but merchandise purchases are recorded as the invoices are received to provide formal current records of liabilities.

Note also that cash sales are recorded in both the cash receipts journal and in the sales journal so that (1) the former record will include all cash receipts and (2) the distribution columns provided by the sales journal can be used to distribute not only charge sales but cash sales as well. This is done by providing a Cash Sales account which is merely a clearing account. Through the use of this account, cash sales are entered in daily totals in the cash receipts journal by the entry, debit Cash and credit Cash Sales. and then in the sales journal by the entry debit Cash Sales and credit (various) sales accounts.

Five-Journal Set: Accounts Receivable; Vouchers Payable

This arrangement consists of:

(1) Cash receipts journal.
(2) Check register (no distribution of purchases or expense debits).
(3) Sales journal (with major distribution of sales, both charge and cash).
(4) Voucher register (with distribution of merchandise purchases, expense purchases, and the debit distribution controls for all other disbursements).
(5) General journal (with expense debit distribution for journal charges).

This journal combination (not illustrated) is the same as the one described in the previous section, except for the handling of the purchase and expense distributions and the recording of disbursements. This journal arrangement is based upon the voucher system, and all liabilities, whether to be paid immediately or at the end of a credit period, are recorded in the voucher register. The voucher register accordingly combines the expense and purchase and other distributions that would otherwise be in a purchase journal and the cash disbursements journal. Note that a purchase discount column can be provided in the voucher register, thus reducing the cash disbursements journal to a list of checks written.

The general journal provides a folio and a debit amount column for each expense control account. This journal is used to record accruals, deferrals, and corrections, and any transactions for which special journals have not been provided.

Other Columnar Journal Forms; Other Special Journals

Columnar sheets for post binders may be classified in general as (1) stock forms with some or all headings ready printed (illustrated in the previous sections) and (2) stock forms with blank headings. Some of the standardized columnar forms are set up with columns for control accounts (that is with each money column accompanied by a folio or reference column). The systems man can select the class of form which best fits his classification of accounts. Examples of other registers which may be bought at forms stationers are a notes receivable register and an insurance record.

Table 4-2

HOUSEHOLD APPLIANCE CORPORATION

STANDARD JOURNAL ENTRIES

Journal Entry No. 1　　　　　　　(Sales Journal)　　　　　　　Monthly

111	Accounts Receivable—Customers
112	Accounts Receivable—Officers and Employees
186	Accrued Sales Tax—Illinois
187	Accrued Sales Tax—Other
211	Sales of Kitchen Appliances and Parts
212	Sales of Laundry Appliances and Parts
213	Sales of Other Appliances
214	Service Income—Inside
215	Service Income—Outside
216	Service Contracts
463	Freight Out

To record sales for month, per sales invoices

Journal Entry No. 2　　(Sales Returns and Allowances Journal)　　Monthly

186	Accrued Sales Tax—Illinois
187	Accrued Sales Tax—Other
214	Service Income—Inside
215	Service Income—Outside
221	Sales Returns and Allowances—Kitchen Appliances and Parts
222	Sales Returns and Allowances—Laundry Appliances and Parts
223	Sales Returns and Allowances—Other Appliances
454	Advertising Allowances to Dealers
463	Freight Out
111	Accounts Receivable—Customers
112	Accounts Receivable—Officers and Employees

To record sales returns and allowances and advertising allowances for month, per credit memoranda

Journal Entry No. 3   (General Journal)   Monthly

414	Commissions
113	Salesmen's Drawing Accounts
181	Accrued Payroll Taxes
182	Withholding Tax Deducted

To record commissions earned for month

Journal Entry No. 4   (General Journal)   Weekly

*500	Receiving, Warehousing and Shipping Expenses Control
511	Supervisory Salaries
512	Warehousemen
513	Truck Drivers and Helpers
519	Overtime Premium
*600	Occupancy Expenses Control
611	Supervisory Salaries
612	Janitors and Watchmen
619	Overtime Premium
*700	Service Department—Inside Expenses Control
711	Supervisory Salaries
712	Repairmen
719	Overtime Premium
*800	Service Department—Outside Expenses Control
811	Service Men
112	Accounts Receivable—Officers and Employees
173	Accrued Payroll
181	Accrued Payroll Taxes
182	Witholding Tax Deducted

To record warehouse and service payroll for week

NOTE: (1) When the month ends on a day other than Friday, Saturday, or Sunday, the payroll will be split for distribution purposes at the end of the month and two distribution entries will be recorded: one covering the charges to the old month (before the trial balance is taken) and one at the end of the week covering charges to the new month.

(2) The credit to Accounts Receivable—Officers and Employees represents payroll deduction for goods sold to employees and charged to their accounts.

Journal Entry No. 5   (General Journal)   Monthly

*300	Administrative Expenses Control
311	Adminstrative Salaries
312	Office Salaries
319	Overtime Premium
*400	Selling Expenses Control
411	Sales Supervisory Salaries
412	Inside Salesmen
413	Outside Salesmen
173	Accrued Payroll
181	Accrued Payroll Taxes
182	Withholding Tax Deducted

To record office and selling payroll for month

---

* Charge expense control account for total of group following.

Journal Entry No. 6   (Voucher Register)   Monthly

113	Salesmen's Drawing Accounts
131	Prepaid Rent—Outside Warehousing
132	Prepaid Insurance
141	Office Supplies Inventory
142	Warehouse and Shop Supplies Inventory
143	Advertising Supplies Inventory
150	Land
161	Building
162	Warehouse Equipment
163	Delivery Trucks
164	Service Shop Equipment
165	Service Trucks
171	Vouchers Payable—Appliance Suppliers
172	Vouchers Payable—Other
173	Accrued Payroll
175	Notes Payable
176	Bank Loans
177	Accrued Interest Payable
178	Dividends Payable
181	Accrued Payroll Taxes
182	Withholding Tax Deducted
183	Federal Income Tax Accrued
184	Accrued Real Estate Taxes
185	Accrued Personal Property Taxes
186	Accrued Sales Tax—Illinois
187	Accrued Sales Tax—Others
189	Reserve for Warranty
190	Mortgage Payable
231	Purchases—Kitchen Appliances and Parts
232	Purchases—Laundry Appliances and Parts
233	Purchases—Other Appliances
241	Freight In—Kitchen Appliances and Parts
242	Freight In—Laundry Appliances and Parts
243	Freight In—Other Appliances
*300	Adminstrative Expense Control
331	Stationery and Offices Supplies
341	Repairs to Office Furniture and Equipment
361	Postage
362	Telephone and Telegraph
363	Association Dues
364	Professional Services
365	Donations
370	Travel
380	Unclassified
391	Rentals of Office Equipment
*400	Selling Expenses Control
431	Stationery and Office Supplies
451	Newspaper and Magazine Advertising
452	Dealer Aids
453	Convention Expense
461	Association Dues
462	Professional Services
463	Freight Out
471	Automobile Expense
472	Other Travel and Entertainment
480	Unclassified Expense

*500	Receiving, Warehousing, and Shipping Expenses Control	
531	Packing Supplies	
541	Repairs to Warehouse Equipment	
542	Repairs to Trucks	
543	Gasoline and Oil	
580	Unclassified	
*600	Occupancy Expenses Control	
641	Janitor Supplies	
642	Repairs to Building	
661	Heat, Light, and Air Conditioning	
*700	Service Department—Inside Expenses Control	
730	Operating Supplies	
761	Power	
*800	Service Department—Outside Expenses Control	
830	Operating Supplies	
841	Repairs to Service Trucks	
842	Gasoline and Oil	
880	Unclassified	
952	Interest Expense	
171	Vouchers Payable—Appliance Suppliers	
172	Vouchers Payable—Other	
251	Purchase Returns and Allowances—Kitchen Appliances and Parts	
252	Purchase Returns and Allowances—Laundry Appliances and Parts	
253	Purchase Returns and Allowances—Other Appliances	
911	Purchase Discounts	

To record vouchers payable for month

NOTE: (1) No disbursements will be made except against a voucher previously recorded in the voucher register. The above entry includes the most common debits.

(2) Expense invoices chargeable to a single month in total (that is, those which do not have to be split between two months) will be entered in the voucher register of the month which is to be charged with the expense. This applies to most of the accounts listed above under 300, 400, 500, 600, 700, and 800. Necessary effort will be made to secure invoices from creditors in time for a prompt closing.

(3) Expense invoices which represent a prepayment of an expense applying to several months (example, 132 Prepaid Insurance) will be charged to an appropriate prepaid expense account through the voucher register, and the monthly debit to expense will be made through the standard journal.

(4) All expenses ordinarily paid at the end of an accrual period of more than one month (example, taxes) will be accrued at the end of each month in the standard journal. When the accrual is paid, the appropriate accrual account (and in some cases, an expense account) will be debited in the voucher register. (Note the debits to accrual accounts in Journal Entry No. 6.) To illustrate, assume the case of a note payable on which the interest is paid at maturity of the note. Assume that $20 interest expense was accrued (and recorded) at the end of the previous month, and $10 was accrued (but not yet recorded) during the present month, when the note is due. The entry for a voucher to pay off the note and interest would be (split-entry method):

Debit	Accrued Interest Payable	$ 20.00	
	Interest Expense	10.00	
	Notes Payable	1,000.00	
	Credit Vouchers Payable		$1,030.00

(5) Any expense supply ordered by a department head that is not a supply regularly carried in stores will be vouchered and charged to expense in the month when the invoice and the goods are received.

(6) Commission Expense will be debited (and Salesmen's Drawings credited) in month sales are billed, through the general journal. Salesmen's Drawings will be debited in the voucher register as salesmen make drawings.

(7) At the end of each month, the expense debits in the voucher register will be recapped so that there will be one debit to each active expense account, and the general journal and standard journals will be similarly recapped. Accordingly, there will be not more than one debit to each expense account from each source journal each month.

Journal Entry No. 7   (Standard Journal)   Monthly

321	F.I.C.A. Tax Expense
421	F.I.C.A. Tax Expense
521	F.I.C.A. Tax Expense
621	F.I.C.A. Tax Expense
721	F.I.C.A. Tax Expense
181	Accrued Payroll Taxes

To record company's share of F.I.C.A. tax for month

Journal Entry No. 8   (Standard Journal)   Monthly

322	Unemployment Insurance Expense
422	Unemployment Insurance Expense
522	Unemployment Insurance Expense
622	Unemployment Insurance Expense
722	Unemployment Insurance Expense
181	Accrued Payroll Taxes

To record unemployment insurance expense accrued for month

Journal Entry No. 9   (Standard Journal)   Monthly

392	Depreciation—Office Furniture and Equipment
592	Depreciation—Warehouse Equipment
593	Depreciation—Trucks
691	Depreciation—Building
791	Depreciation—Service Shop Equipment
891	Depreciation—Service Trucks
161A	Allowance for Depreciation—Building
162A	Allowance for Depreciation—Warehouse Equipment
163A	Allowance for Depreciation—Delivery Trucks
164A	Allowance for Depreciation—Service Shop Equipment
165A	Allowance for Depreciation—Service Trucks
166A	Allowance for Depreciation—Office Furniture and Fixtures

To record allowance for depreciation for month

Journal Entry No. 10   (Standard Journal)   Monthly

393	Insurance—Office Furniture and Equipment
594	Insurance—Warehouse Equipment
595	Insurance—Inventories
596	Insurance—Trucks
692	Insurance—Building
792	Insurance—Service Shop Equipment
892	Insurance—Service Trucks
132	Prepaid Insurance

To record insurance expense for month

Journal Entry No. 11   (Standard Journal)   Monthly

693	Taxes—Building
184	Accrued Real Estate Taxes

       To record real estate taxes for month

Journal Entry No. 12   (Standard Journal)   Monthly

394	Taxes—Office Furniture and Equipment
597	Taxes—Warehouse Equipment
598	Taxes—Inventories
599	Taxes and Licenses—Trucks
793	Taxes—Service Shop Equipment
893	Taxes and Licenses—Service Trucks
185	Accrued Personal Property Taxes

       To record personal property taxes for month

Journal Entry No. 13   (Standard Journal)   Monthly

954	Bad Debts
111A	Allowance for Uncollectible Accounts

       To record provision for uncollectible accounts for month

Journal Entry No. 14   (Standard Journal)   Monthly

490	Warranty Expense
189	Reserve for Warranty

       To record provision for warranty on appliances sold for month

NOTE: Entry No. 14 is set up to provide for expenditures that may have to be made on warranties given on appliances sold. It is based upon the wholesalers' experience percentage applied to sales. Replacement parts issued under warranty are recorded by Journal Entry No. 19.

Journal Entry No. 15   (Standard Journal)   Monthly

217	Labor Used on Service Contracts
799	Labor Used on Service Contracts
899	Labor Used on Service Contracts

       To record summary of labor used on service contracts

NOTE: *All* service labor is initially charged to Accounts 712 and 811 to provide total figures on the monthly expense statements. Labor used on service contracts is summarized on job tickets and recorded by Journal Entry No. 15. Account 217 is deducted from Account 216 Service Contracts Income to determine profit or loss on service contracts.

Journal Entry No. 16   (Standard Journal)   Monthly

331	Stationery and Office Supplies
431	Stationery and Office Supplies
531	Packing Supplies
641	Janitor Supplies
730	Operating Supplies—Inside Service
830	Operating Supplies—Outside Service
141	Office Supplies Inventory
142	Warehouse and Shop Supplies Inventory
143	Advertising Supplies Inventory

       To record supplies used out of stores

Journal Entry No. 17   (General Journal)   Monthly

| 115 | Accrued Interest Receivable |
| 912 | Interest Income |

To record interest accrued on notes receivable for month

Journal Entry No. 18   (General Journal)   Monthly

| 952 | Interest Expense |
| 177 | Accrued Interest Payable |

To record interest accrued on notes payable for month

Journal Entry No. 19   (General Journal)   As Occurring

189	Reserve for Warranty
231	Purchases—Kitchen Appliances and Parts
232	Purchases—Laundry Appliances and Parts

To record cost of replacement parts issued against warranties

Journal Entry No. 20   (Cash Receipts Journal)   Monthly

102	Cash in Bank
951	Sales Discounts
111	Accounts Receivable—Customers
112	Accounts Receivable—Officers and Employees
	Miscellaneous

To record cash receipts for month

Journal Entry No. 21   (Cash Payments Journal)   Monthly

171	Vouchers Payable—Appliance Suppliers
172	Vouchers Payable—Other
102	Cash in Bank

To record cash disbursements for month

5

Account Forms
and Business Papers

Ready-Printed Account Forms

After the classification of accounts and the standard journal entries have been designed, as explained in the previous chapters, the account forms and business papers are selected or designed.

For the Household Appliance Corporation, on which the data for the previous chapters was based, it was decided to use ready-printed account forms rather than specially designed forms. The following paragraphs illustrate and discuss the forms selected and indicate alternative forms. Many manufacturers produce the forms illustrated or similar ones, together with the alternatives which are named but not illustrated.

(1) For the General ledger, the Debit, Credit, Debit Balance, and Credit Balance form (Figure 5-2). This form was selected because it eliminates several potential disadvantages of the conventional T-account form, Figure 5-1 (identified by forms manufacturers as the Regular ledger form): (a) It is sometimes a confusing task to take off a trial balance from accounts kept on Regular ledger account forms. Where there are a number of debits and a number of credits, with pencil balances on both sides, it may not be quickly apparent whether the last debit balance or the last credit balance is to be picked up. (b) The chronological sequence of debits and credits may not be readily apparent. This is likely to be important when it is desired to prepare an analysis of an account. Note that the form illustrated in Figure 5-2 provides for one series of dates, rather than separate series for debits and credits.

(2) For the Customers ledger, the Debit, Credit, and Balance ledger form (Figure 5-3). This form is similar to the one selected for the General ledger, except that it provides a single balance column. A column for identifying debit or credit balance is also provided.

(3) For the inventory of kitchen appliances, laundry appliances, and

other appliances, the Inventory account illustrated in Figure 5-4. There are numerous types of supplies inventory accounts, but the one illustrated provides vertical sections for goods received, goods issued or used, and balance on hand. One account is used for each model of appliance, and it

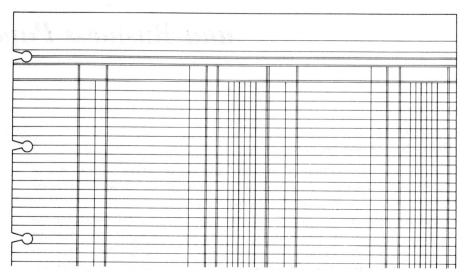

Figure 5-1. Regular Ledger (without Headings)

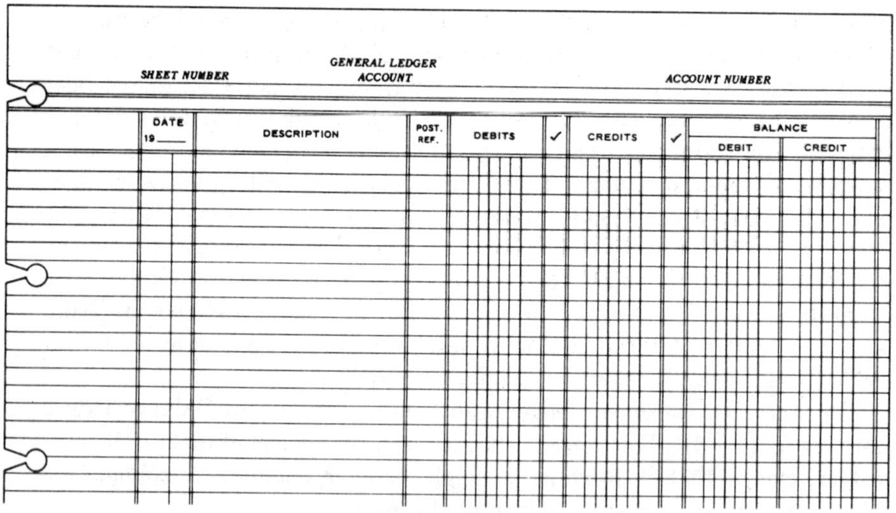

Figure 5-2. Debit, Credit, Debit Balance, and Credit Balance Ledger

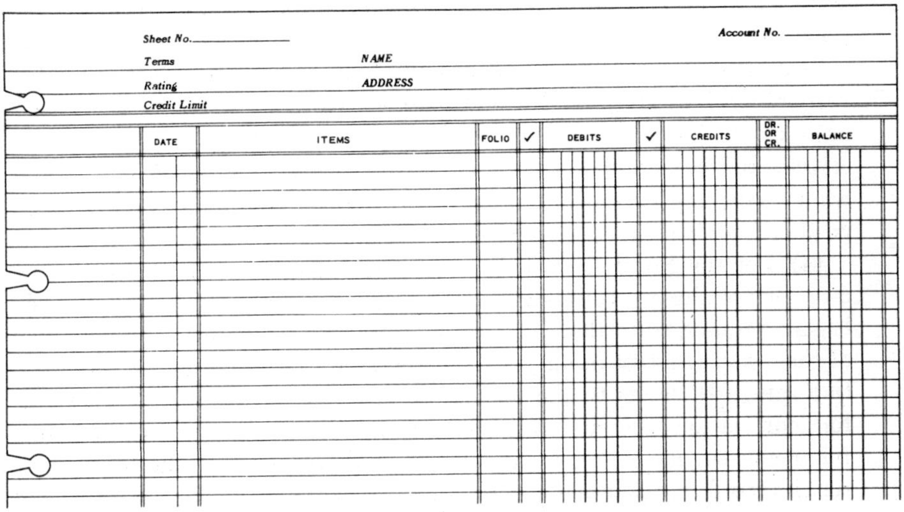

Sheet No._____						Account No. _____			
Terms		NAME							
Rating		ADDRESS							
Credit Limit									

DATE	ITEMS	FOLIO	✓	DEBITS	✓	CREDITS	DR. OR CR.	BALANCE

Figure 5-3. Debit, Credit, and Balance Ledger

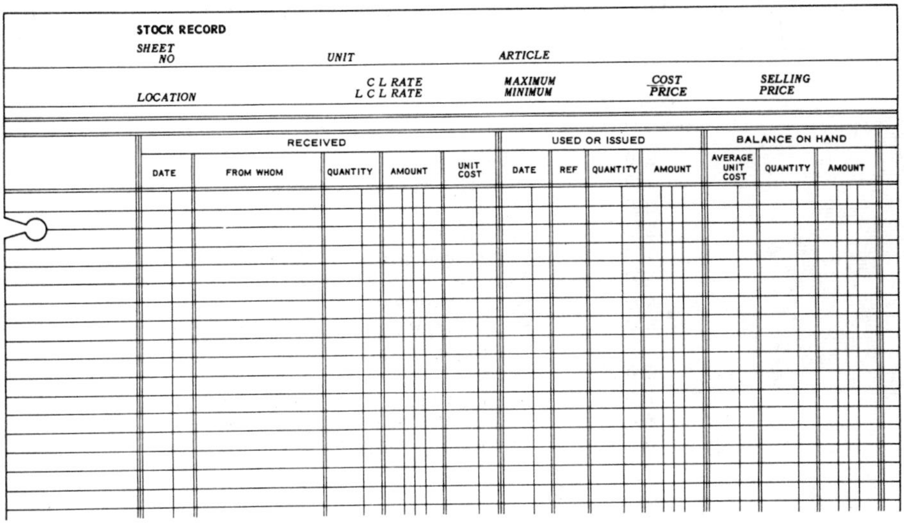

STOCK RECORD

SHEET NO		UNIT		ARTICLE				
LOCATION		C L RATE L C L RATE		MAXIMUM MINIMUM		COST PRICE		SELLING PRICE

	RECEIVED				USED OR ISSUED				BALANCE ON HAND		
DATE	FROM WHOM	QUANTITY	AMOUNT	UNIT COST	DATE	REF	QUANTITY	AMOUNT	AVERAGE UNIT COST	QUANTITY	AMOUNT

Figure 5-4. Supplies Inventory Account

is charged (from the purchase invoice) for goods received and credited for goods sold (from the sale invoice). The form illustrated provides for quantities and values; other forms provide for quantities only.

In manufacturing concerns, perpetual inventory accounts are frequently kept for materials and finished goods. The form illustrated in the previous section may be used to provide a record of goods put into inventory and goods taken out of inventory.

In addition to the basic sections illustrated, sometimes certain other vertical sections are provided on the materials account form. There may be a section for goods on order to show what quantities are due to be received, and a section for reserved or appropriated inventories to show what quantities have been set aside to meet the requirements of finished goods scheduled for manufacture.

(4) For the Fixed Asset ledger, the Fixed Asset account form, Figure 5-5. One of these accounts is used for each fixed asset unit (truck, desk, typewriter, and so forth). Note that it provides space for (a) description of the asset, (b) cost data, (c) data for the computation of the depreciation rate, (d) debits to the plant accounts and credits to the allowance for depreciation accounts. A special feature of the account is the provision for memo entries of the repair charges incurred against the asset. The repair records of machines are important since the question of replacement is often decided partly upon that factor. Some standard forms (not illustrated) provide spaces for recording *revised* depreciation charges.

(5) Columnar account for sales and expenses, Figure 15-12. One of these accounts will be used for each of the following groups of accounts:

Control Account No.	*Name*
210	Sales
220	Sales Returns and Allowances
230	Purchases
240	Freight In
250	Purchase Returns and Allowances
300	Administrative Expenses
400	Selling Expenses
500	Receiving, Warehousing, and Shipping Expense
600	Occupancy Expense
700	Service Department—Inside Expense
800	Service Department—Outside Expense
900	Other Income and Expense

One columnar account (double spread if necessary) will be kept for each control account group. Each columnar account will provide a column for each account in the group, as shown by the classification of accounts, Table 3-1. Thus, the columnar account for 300 Administrative Expense would have 19 money columns (one for total and one for each of 18 accounts). Each journal affecting an expense account would be recapped to provide a single posting to each active column in each columnar account. (The method of posting is illustrated in Figures 15-10 and 15-12.)

ASSET RECORD

Sheet No. _____

Description of Asset

Asset Number

Class Number

Made by

Purchased from

Identification Data—Maker's

Purchase Guarantee

Plant

Building

Floor

Department

Net Price $

Freight $

Cartage $

Setting Up $

Total Cost $

Total Cost $

Ultim. Value $

Total to Depreciate $

Date Received

Date Betterment

Estimated Life

Estimated Life

Depreciation

% per or

$

Location

Connected with

Ultimate Disposition

Remarks

ASSET COST, BETTERMENTS, Etc.(Black Ink)				REPAIRS, Etc.—MEMO ONLY(Red Ink)				DEPRECIATION RESERVE			NET ASSET VALUE
MO.	DAY	YR.	CHARGES	CREDITS	BALANCE	MO.	DAY	YR.	CHARGES	CREDITS	BALANCE	CHARGES	CREDITS	BALANCE	

ASSET RECORD

Sheet No. _____

Description of Asset

Asset Number

ASSET COST, BETTERMENTS, Etc.(Black Ink)				REPAIRS, Etc.—MEMO ONLY(Red Ink)				DEPRECIATION RESERVE			NET ASSET VALUE
MO.	DAY	YR.	CHARGES	CREDITS	BALANCE	MO.	DAY	YR.	CHARGES	CREDITS	BALANCE	CHARGES	CREDITS	BALANCE	

Figure 5-5. Fixed Asset Account

Ledger Sheet Sizes

Ready-printed ledger sheets are available in a variety of sizes, as indicated in the table below, which is reproduced from the catalog of an accounting forms stationer. Popular sizes are $9\frac{1}{4}''$ x $11\frac{7}{8}''$ and $11''$ x $14''$.

Ledger Sheet Sizes
(inches)

$7\frac{1}{2}$ x $10\frac{3}{8}$	11 x 14
$8\frac{1}{4}$ x $10\frac{7}{8}$	11 x 17
$9\frac{1}{4}$ x $11\frac{7}{8}$	$11\frac{1}{4}$ x $11\frac{7}{8}$

Forms in these sizes are small enough to permit easy handling. On the other hand, they are not so small that carryover from one completely filled account to another becomes a nuisance. (The usual $9\frac{1}{4}''$ x $11\frac{7}{8}''$ ledger sheet has 30 lines and the usual $11''$ x $14''$ sheet has 36 or 40 lines.) Note also that a large variety of ready-printed forms can be obtained in the sizes named, together with standard binders for them. It is often advisable to standardize on one form size for various account forms. Sometimes all or several of the ledgers in a small business are kept in one binder, with appropriate dividers to separate the various ledgers.

Other Ledger Forms

Other specialized ledger forms for pen and ink kept in stock by many accounting forms stationers are Installment Ledger account, Investment Ledger account, and Stockholders Ledger account. Also, certain forms stationers carry forms which are specialized by type of business, such as hospitals and hotels. These forms are not illustrated in this book.

Account forms for machine posting are illustrated in Chapter 7.

Business Papers

Business papers are the papers used for making the first record of any transaction. They include (a) all the forms produced inside the business to get a record of each transaction at the source, and (b) incoming papers that can be used as evidence of transactions.

The business papers that would have to be designed for the Household Appliance Corporation are:

(1) Sales and cash collecting: sales order, shipping order, invoice, cash receipts voucher, debit memorandum, credit memorandum.

(2) Purchasing and cash-paying function: request for purchase, request for quotation, purchase order, receiving report, disbursement voucher-check, petty cash voucher. In addition, the purchase invoice which comes from the creditor would be used as a business paper.

(3) Employment and payroll function: application for employment, authorization to place on payroll, separation report, attendance time cards, shop time cards, paycheck or envelope, pay stub or employees earnings statement.

Designing Printed Forms

Features to consider in designing printed forms may be classified as follows:

(1) Form layout, which has to do with what is *on* the form: the columnar arrangement, spacing, and text.
(2) Mechanical features of the forms themselves, such as paper specifications (kind, grade, weight, and color) size of form, spot carbon, punching, and so forth. These features are affected by methods of writing, reproducing, stamping, sorting, binding, and filing the forms.
(3) The possibilities of *eliminating separate writings*. The elimination is done by cutting out forms in some cases and by using copies in other cases.

It should be noted that, whereas some forms are used in small quantities by various people in the organization spending an incidental amount of time on them, other forms are used in very large quantities by operators who spend all their working day producing them. Order and billing forms, for instance, often come in the latter category. These forms, especially, should be designed for efficient writing.

Purpose of the Layout

A layout is the plan of a printed form. It may be a formal drawing done by a draftsman from a sketch made by the systems man, or it may be a written or Vari-typed copy—with various sizes and faces of type. (Layouts produced on the Vari-typer can be used as masters for offset printing after they have been approved by the client or the supervisor.) In large systems assignments, it is usually necessary for the systems man to have drafting or typing assistance in making layouts because layout is extremely time-consuming.

In the case of forms that have not been printed previously, the layout should be an actual size projection of the proposed form, complete in every detail. If particular type faces are used as standard by the organization, the faces and sizes should be indicated. If the form has been used before, but is to be changed somewhat, it is sometimes feasible to show the changes on the old form. In any case, the purpose is to present the proposed designs so clearly that the prospective user of the form or the systems man can approve it or ask for changes in it before it goes to the printer. Of course, changes must be indicated clearly so that the printer can understand exactly what is wanted.

Making the Layout (Account Forms and Business Papers)

The steps to be followed in making layouts for account forms and business papers are:

(1) Determine the exact purpose of the form and assign it a name which will clearly indicate its function.

(2) List the points of information to be shown on the form and indicate the source of the data (that is, where the user of the form will obtain the information he writes on the form). The systems man gets the points mainly from his survey notes and procedures charts, but he is probably also guided to some extent by referring to sample forms which he has accumulated from similar assignments and from illustrations of forms in this book.

(3) Make note of the writing, reproducing, stamping, sorting, binding, and filing equipment which will be involved in the use of the form, so that the design of the form can meet any equipment requirements.

(4) Consider the sizes of form which can be cut from standard sheets of paper without waste. For example: 8½″ x 11″ forms can be cut without waste from the standard 17″ x 22″ sheets, since four sheets can be cut even. Forms 11″ x 17″ can be cut from the same size sheet, since two sheets come out even.

(5) Determine the features of text and composition of the form which will be affected by the equipment to be used. Examples are the margin and spacing requirements of typewriters, duplicating machines, addressing machines, bookkeeping machines, time stamps, and so on.

(6) In the case of multiple copy forms to be reproduced by carbon copy or duplicating methods, determine the fixed text (to appear on all copies of the set) and the variable text (to appear on one or some copies), and any blockouts, short forms, and narrow forms required for the elimination of written information from certain copies. Determine the method of controlling the copies (printed serial numbers, tissue copies bound in the book, and so forth).

(7) Make a rough sketch of the form to determine the proper arrangement of spacing and information. Where the form is to be written on a typewriter or other machine, forms layout sheets may be used to facilitate measurement. These sheets are ruled in light-colored ink, say 10 vertical

guide lines to the inch (for that number of typed characters per inch) and say six horizontal lines per inch (for that particular spacing).

(8) Make a smooth copy of the layout for the printer.

Rules of Spacing for Forms to Be Used on Typewriter

If the form is to be used on the typewriter, the designer must remember the following rules:

(1) Horizontal lines must be spaced one pica ($\frac{1}{6}$ of an inch) apart, or some multiple of one pica. Vertical lines should be set with reference to the style of type in the machine to be used. Large type (pica) has 10 spaces to the inch, and small type has 12 spaces to the inch. It is a good plan when designing such forms to set the layout in the typewriter and type of a vertical line and a horizontal line of periods to assist in making the layout.

(2) Measure the space from the top of the form to the first line to be used for typing. The vertical distance should represent a number of even picas. This precaution is necessary to avoid turning out a form that will require undue alignment in the machine after insertion.

(3) In laying out money columns, anticipate the maximum number of digits to be required, and allow space according to style of type in the typewriter to be used.

(4) Provide for tab stops. The tab stops on a typewriter are devices used to cause the carriage to stop automatically at previously selected positions. The devices so function that the operator can move the carriage of the machine from any particular position to the next tab stop by depressing the tab stop key. Thus, when the typist is typing invoices, the tab stop keys may be so set that the carriage will tab automatically to the quantity column, the description column, the price column, and so forth.

In designing invoice forms for use of tab stops, the same "starting places" (tab stops), should be used for the heading of the invoice as for the listing or description section. For instance, the name and address block in the heading can be placed on the same margin as the quantity or the description margin. This feature of design will reduce the number of times the typist must use the tab stop in typing an invoice. The same rule should be followed for all forms that will require the use of tab stops.

Illustration of Form Layout

Figure 5-6 is a form layout of the invoice copy of an order and invoice set. The complete set consists of the following copies:

Invoice copies:
  Invoice
  Duplicate invoice
  Accounts receivable
  Distribution
Shipping copies:
  Production
  Shipping
  Labels
  Packing slip
  Acknowledgment

This set was designed to eliminate separate writing of the shipping order copies, the packing slip, the labels and the invoice—all on different forms. The invoice layout shown in Figure 5-6 is the basic layout for all the copies, although some of the copies have their own minor variable printing. Separate layouts were prepared for these copies.

Meaning of Form Standardization; Savings Possible in Large Companies

Standardization of printed forms is a systematic procedure for the elimination of unnecessary sizes and other elements in printed forms to effect the greatest economies in the purchase and use of forms. There are five aspects of standardization of printed forms:

(1) Standardization by function, involving classifying the printed forms by title in order to bring together all forms that have the same title, and then determining whether any of those forms that have the same title but which were designed for use of different departments can be combined into one form.

(2) Standardization by size of form, involving the selection of the particular sizes of forms that shall be considered as standard and the formulation of lists of sizes for the guidance of the layout men.

(3) Standardization of production methods and typography, involving selection of the method of production to be used for each of the various classes of forms and selection of type faces and other elements of typography to be used.

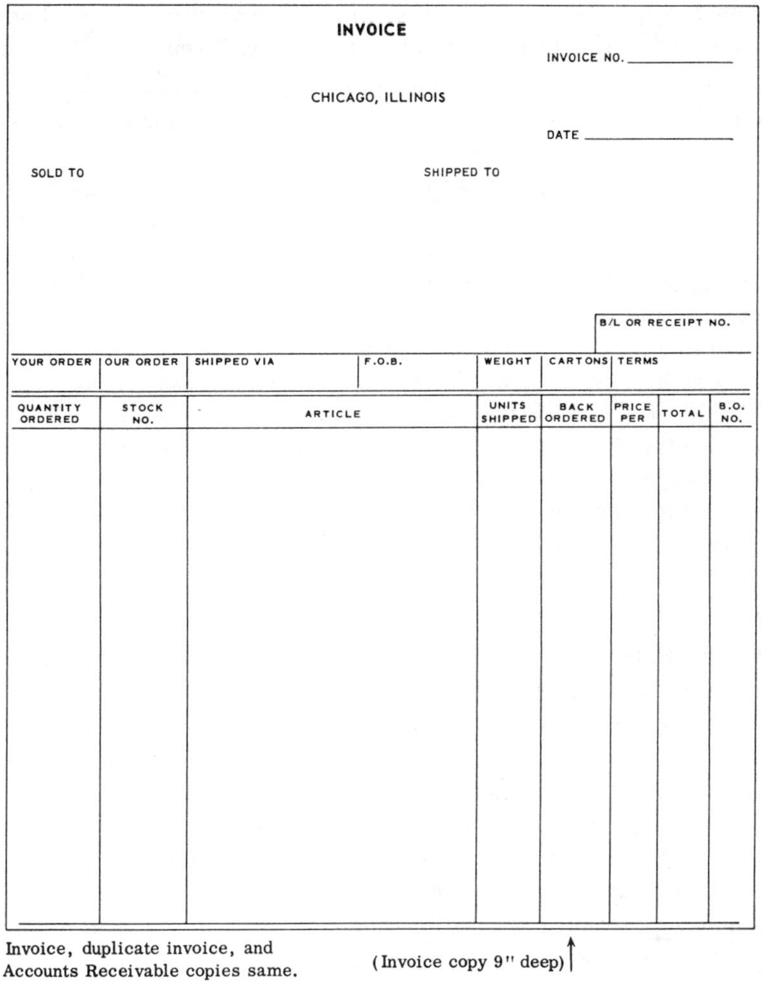

INVOICE

INVOICE NO. _____

CHICAGO, ILLINOIS

DATE _____

SOLD TO

SHIPPED TO

B/L OR RECEIPT NO.

YOUR ORDER	OUR ORDER	SHIPPED VIA	F.O.B.	WEIGHT	CARTONS	TERMS

QUANTITY ORDERED	STOCK NO.	ARTICLE	UNITS SHIPPED	BACK ORDERED	PRICE PER	TOTAL	B.O. NO.

Invoice, duplicate invoice, and
Accounts Receivable copies same.   (Invoice copy 9" deep) ↑

Figure 5-6. Form Layout

(4) Standardization by paper stock, involving the selection of the minimum number of classes of paper (finish, formation, weight, and color) that will fill the requirements of all forms used in the organization, and specification of the most economical class for each form.

(5) Standardization of releases to the printer, involving (a) specification of economical purchase quantities and (b) arrangement of orders into groups of the same class of printing. Grouping in this fashion may make it possible for the printer to print several forms

on a large press at the same time, to save press costs. Forms grouped in this fashion are known as "gang layouts."

Each of these features of standardization of printed forms will be discussed in the following pages. It may be noted as a preliminary point that most businesses which use a significant quantity of printed forms practice one or a few of the methods of form standardization, but comparatively few concerns practice all of them. In some cases, systems men or other members of the accounting departments of private business have undertaken programs of standardization. In other cases, professional systems men and printing engineers have been engaged to do the work. Frequently, a considerable saving in the cost of printed forms has been effected. One concern which prints its own forms saved about $15,000 on an annual printing bill of about $65,000, and several other concerns saved $50,000 each on printing bills of about $250,000 a year. Printing engineers will not accept engagements to standardize forms for smaller businesses, but the work can often be undertaken privately with assurance that the results will justify the cost.

Standardization by Function

It was stated in the section on layout that each form should bear a title which will describe accurately its function, and that one purpose of naming forms is to make it possible to file a sample of each form by function. Thus, as requests for new forms are received, the files can be consulted to ascertain whether any existing form can be used. The need for this step of standardization will be seen when it is realized that some of the larger businesses use thousands of different forms.

To facilitate filing the forms by function, a form numbering scheme which includes a set of digits for function may be used. One concern uses a six-digit numbering scheme as follows:

Division (as Corporate Office)		Office (as Treasurer)		Function (as Daily Bank Balance)
00	–	00	–	00

When forms are numbered and filed according to this numbering scheme, it is possible to find immediately all forms bearing the same function number to see if it is feasible to combine them into a single form that may be used by the several departments.

A second advantage of the numbering scheme illustrated lies in the fact that it brings together all the forms used by each office and likewise all the forms used by each division. This segregation is useful because systems men have occasion to work on specific routines of certain offices and consequently may require files arranged by office.

Standardization by Size of Form

It is desirable to standardize on those sizes that (a) will use standard filing equipment and (b) can be cut out of standard stock without waste. This is important whether the business sends forms to the printer singly or in groups for gang layouts, because in either case, the customer pays for the waste. Furthermore, in the latter case—where groups of forms are sent to the printer—standard sizes of forms facilitate the work of the layout man. It is obviously easier for the printer to fit $8\frac{1}{2}''$ x $11''$ and $11''$ x $17''$ forms into a sheet $34''$ x $44''$ than it is to fit odd sizes into that sheet.

Standardization by Class of Printing; Printing Economies

The first step in standardization by class of printing is the classification of existing forms according to a schedule similar to the following:

Code	Class of Printing
A	One side, one color ink, white paper
B	Two sides, one color ink, white paper
C	One side, one color ink, colored paper
D	Two sides, one color ink, colored paper
E	Printed and ruled, one side
F	Printed and ruled, two sides
G	Two colors ink
H	Multiple forms
	And so forth

The code may be further expanded to include class of paper, where several weights, grades, and colors of paper are used within a single class of printing. To accomplish such an expansion it would only be necessary to assign code letters to the various classes of stock and to combine the printing class code letter with the paper class code letter. Thus, one-side, one-color ink forms printed on 15# white sulphite might be coded "Aa."

In some organizations a file of forms classified by class of printing and paper stock is kept in addition to the file by function explained in the previous section. Classification of forms by class of printing serves two purposes:

(1) It assists the systems man to study the forms in each class to apply the economies feasible *for that class of printing.*

(2) When it includes classification by paper stock, it facilitates the preparation of gang layouts by the printer. (Each form to be included in a gang layout must be of the same class of paper.)

Sometimes economies may be effected by:

(1) Converting printed and ruled forms to printed forms.

(2) Making two-sided forms one-sided. In some cases, it may be found that forms are printed on only a small portion of the back and that it is feasible to redesign the form to include that matter on the front of the form. This is frequently the case where brief contract clauses appear on the back of shipping documents and invoices.

(3) Eliminating color work and other "fancy work." It will be argued that much of the color work on forms and office printing is useful for its attention value, as directed either to the employees or to the customers. The real productivity of such color work should be questioned.

(4) Eliminating "special" operations such as machine perforating where possible. Note that perforating may be done as a separate (special) operation, or if the form is designed properly, by the press. The latter class of perforating is cheaper, although it is said to be of a quality inferior to press perforating.

Standardization of Paper

As was indicated before, standardization of paper means reducing the classes, grades, colors, and weights of paper used in the forms of a business to the smallest number of different items. There are three reasons for standardizing on paper:

(1) To secure the cheapest paper consistent with the requirements of use. Sometimes significant economies are realized through this type of standardization. One concern whose annual printing bill was $65,000 effected a saving of $10,000 in paper by this method.

(2) To make possible the greatest use of gang layouts by the printer.

(3) To make it possible to secure the lowest prices due to quantity discounts. This reason for standardization is chiefly of interest to companies which operate their own printing plants and to those whose requirements are large enough to justify purchasing their own paper.

The exact procedure of standardization depends upon the quantity of paper the business uses per year since the savings possible are governed by that factor. Relatively small users may simply make their selections from sample books of the paper merchants. Larger organizations may send a sample of every form they use to a paper-testing laboratory for analysis and recommendation of an economical paper stock for the purpose. Some of the paper merchants in the larger cities maintain their own laboratories where the service is rendered free of charge.

One company which uses about $200,000 in printed forms each year has standardized on about 18 paper items. Another company, using about $50,000 worth, has standardized on the following:

(1) 16# and 20# sulphite #4—white
(2) 16# 50 per cent rag bond, smooth finish, 20-year life
(3) 9# and 12# "cockle" bond, 50 per cent rag—cheaper grade than (2)
(4) 16# sulphite bond in colors

Buying Own Paper and Delivering to the Printer

Some of the larger users of printed forms, notably the public utilities and the railroads, buy their own paper in large quantities, store it in their own warehouses, and deliver it to the printers as required when jobs are let. Such a program of course is based upon standardization of paper stocks, but is usually profitable only to users of large quantities of forms. The quantity prices may be very tempting, but in any case when purchase is contemplated, the following factors should be considered:

(1) The cost of storing the paper in own warehouse, and delivering it in relatively small lots to the printer.
(2) Interest on investment in paper.
(3) The handling charge made by the printer for moving the paper through his plant.
(4) Deterioration of stock. Where the lots of forms submitted to the printer are of such size that no broken cases of paper need be handled, this factor may not be serious.
(5) Changes in market prices of paper.

Ordering and Inventory Control

The inventory control and ordering system should be so organized that rush orders are avoided and further, the maximum number of items of the same class can be ordered from the printer at the same time. It should be recalled that a "class of printing" means printing produced in the same way with the same color or colors on the same kind of paper. As indicated above, releasing printing orders in large groups at the same time may make it possible for the printer to give a lower price.

To give effect to these principles, it is necessary to have a good system of inventory control and to know what is the monthly use of each form.

In one concern, perpetual inventory cards for forms are kept by the order department. All forms are ordered as of the tenth of each month, and each order consists of a three-months supply. A one-month supply is the minimum for each item to be kept on hand. Between the first and the tenth of each month, the order clerk scans all the perpetual inventory accounts and makes a list of all items that will apparently run below the minimum during the month. These items are combined into printing classes so far as possible and released on the tenth of the month. When forms are ordered, proper notation is made on the inventory card to prevent a duplicate order being released between the time the original order is sent and the goods received.

Multiple Copy Forms; Automatic Writing and Reproducing Equipment

Multiple Forms: Padded; Unit Sets; Continuous Forms

Multiple forms are forms related in function and information and designed to be filled out partially or completely in a single writing through the use of carbon paper or other reproduction methods. The object, of course, is to save separate and repetitive writing of common information appearing on a number of related forms. An example is the shipping order and invoice set (Figure 6-1), which consists of invoice, office copy, shipping copy, and packing slip. (The illustration is diagrammatic and is not intended to illustrate the actual construction of the forms.)

Multiple forms may be purchased from the printer (a) unassembled, (b) in pads, (c) as sales book type filler, (d) in unit sets, (e) in continuous sets, or (f) collated and assembled but not padded. These types of assembly are explained in general terms in the following paragraphs. (There are a number of manufacturers of unit sets and continuous forms. Particular features vary among manufacturers.)

(1) Unassembled forms might be considered if the number of copies in each set is small (or if the copies are to be duplicated, as described on pages 97–100). Thus, the purchase might be 500 copies of the invoice form and a similar number of the invoice—office copy. The typist using the forms would assemble her own sets and insert carbon paper for typing.

(2) Padded multiple forms are assemblies of 25 or more sets (depending upon the number of copies to the set) glued at the top or the side by the printer. When the typist requires a set, she inserts the carbon paper, detaches the set from the pad, and puts the set in the typewriter.

(3) Sales book fillers are assemblies of a number of sets arranged for

insertion in the familiar sales book used by retail sales persons. The filler includes carbon paper, which is used until all the sets in the filler are written.

(4) Unit sets (Figure 6-1) are multiple forms made in separate sets of one complete assortment (say, one complete order and invoice group or one complete invoice group) to a set with one-time carbon paper pre-inserted by the manufacturer. (One-time carbon paper is a grade of paper suitable for use to get one clear impression. It is removed from the set and discarded after the form is completed.) The sets are written on a standard typewriter (no

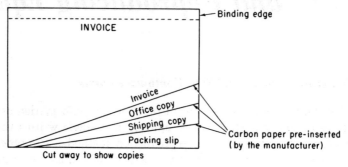

Figure 6-1.   Unit Set (Diagrammatic Sketch)

A carbon interleaved shipping order set which may be typed in a standard correspondence typewriter. The copies are pulled loose from the binding edge after the typing has been completed, and the carbon paper is removed simultaneously in this operation. Use of unit sets saves most of the carbon paper handling time.

special attachment being necessary) or by hand. The carbon paper sheets may be narrow, short, die-cut, or strip-coated when it is not desired to reproduce all parts of the writing or typing on the copies. Where the unit set combines forms which are to be completed at different times (for instance a shipping order set and the related invoice set), the unit set can be manufactured so that one group of forms (the shipping order forms, in this example) can be detached from the other set (the invoice forms).

In the manufacture of unit sets, a binding edge (Figure 6-1) is placed at the top or the side of the set. The forms proper are tied to this binding edge along a perforated line, and the carbon paper is fastened to it. The length of the carbon paper is slightly less than the length of the forms. After the writing operation is completed, the carbon paper may be removed from the set by grasping the binding edge and the opposite edge of the forms in the set and then pulling the binding edge loose. The carbon paper will come out with the binding edge.

The advantage of unit sets over the combinations described above is that handling time of carbon paper is saved. (Note that the larger the number of forms in a set, the larger the proportion of carbon-paper handling time compared to "productive" time.)

(5) A continuous form is a single form printed repetitively on a strip of paper. The successive forms on the strip are separated by perforated lines. The strip can be fed into a typewriter or billing machine, and the forms typed one after another. Labels (for example) may be obtained in continuous strips.

Continuous multiple forms are sets of related forms printed on webs or strips of paper in such manner that the copies (invoice, office copy, and so on) are collated and ready for typing. (See Figure 6-2.) The structure of continuous forms makes it possible to feed successive sets of forms into the typewriter or billing machine rapidly. Where billing, for instance, is a volume job, and where it is not necessary to load and unload the ma-

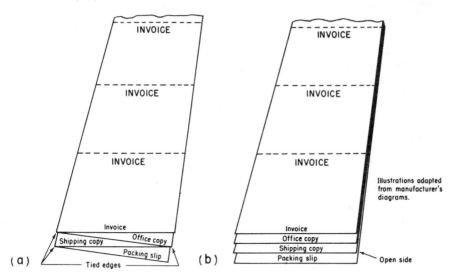

Figure 6-2.   Continuous Forms (Diagrammatic Sketch)

Two types: (a) *fanfold* is a set manufactured with tied edges (actually printed front and back on a web of paper which is folded accordion-fashion to produce the collated set); (b) *open web* is a set manufactured with open sides. (Each copy is printed on a separate strip of paper, and the strips are then collated in the manufacturing process.) Continuous forms may be obtained interleaved with carbon paper or non-interleaved (illustrated in the diagram). Interleaved continuous forms may be used in standard typewriters. Non-interleaved continuous forms are used in standard typewriters or billing machines equipped with devices for handling the carbon paper. Use of continuous forms saves most of the carbon paper handling time which would otherwise be required to get separate sets of forms in and out of the typewriter.

chine with a number of different sets of billing forms, the saving in form-handling made possible by the use of continuous forms over, say, unit sets is considerable.

Continuous forms may be classified from a structural standpoint, as illustrated in Figure 6-2:

(a) Tied-edge forms (of which fanfold forms are an example). In the manufacture of these forms, a single wide web of paper is printed front and back, and folded accordion fashion to produce the finished collated sets. Since the edges are secure, the forms are held in perfect register in the typing or billing machine.

(b) Open-side forms. In the manufacture of these forms, each copy is produced on a separate strip of paper. The various parts of the set are not joined together and are kept in alignment by a device in the machine in which the forms are used.

Non-interleaved forms (that is, no pre-inserted carbon paper) are illustrated in Figure 6-2. The typewriter or billing machine in which the forms are used is equipped to handle the carbon paper. Continuous forms interleaved with one-time carbon paper are also manufactured. Interleaved continuous forms can be used in a standard typewriter, and in certain makes the carbon paper is die-cut to form a tongue which may be grasped by the typist for quick extraction. Note that the factory order can be separated from the invoice set, leaving the latter intact for later completion.

Before passing from carbon-paper methods to duplicating methods, note that in the manufacture of unit sets or interleaved continuous forms special carbon paper may be inserted in the set so that one of the copies can be used as a duplicating master. (See Duplicating Methods, pages 97–100.)

(6) Multiple forms collated and assembled but not padded may be purchased for use in duplicating machines.

Carbonless Paper

The National Cash Register Company distributes a chemically treated paper which produces copies without the use of carbon paper. A unit set may consist, for example, of an order and all copies—with no carbon paper in the set. Writing on the original sheet produces an impression on the sheets underneath. Carbonless paper costs a little more than noncarbonless paper, but it saves disposal of carbons, carbon pulling, reloading billing machines, and so forth.

Writing Machines and Registers for Handling Continuous Forms

Writing machines and registers for handling continuous forms may be classified as follows:

(1) Billing machines with cylindrical platens (that is, conventional carriage). These machines resemble correspondence typewriters except that they have special features for handling the forms. Figure 6-3 is an IBM Model C Formswriter showing the attach-

Figure 6-3.   IBM Model C Formswriter

ment for handling continuous forms. Carbon paper is suspended from the blades between the forms strips on the carbon carrier at the right of the illustration.

(2) Correspondence typewriters equipped with attachments for handling continuous forms (not illustrated).

(3) Autographic registers, which are devices for holding and feeding continuous forms and for positioning them for writing by hand. Use of autograph register is explained on pages 199–200 and illustrated in Figure 10-1.

(4) Automatic typewriters which can type information from punched cards or punched paper tape or from memory. Examples with

differing capabilities are IBM 6400 (Figure 6-19), Victor Terminal Computer 820/03 (Figure 6-25), and the Burroughs Electronic Billing Computer Series L2000 (Figure 6-26a).

Methods of Handling Carbon Paper in Billing Machines

Two methods of handling carbon paper in billing machines (when non-interleaved forms are used) are:

(1) Carbon paper rolls, suspended between the forms. Obsolete. Carbon paper rolls are still on the market for previously installed billing machines manufactured for their use, but the billing machines are no longer manufactured.

(2) Carbon paper packs, illustrated and described in Figure 6-4.

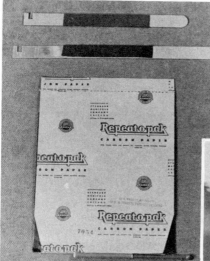

Figure 6-4a. Carbon Pack Suspended from Blade in Forms Holder of Billing Machine

One pack is used for each form.

Standard Manifold Co.

Standard Manifold Co.

Figure 6-4b.   Inside the Pack

The pack consists of one sheet of carbon paper 10 feet long, zig-zag folded and held in place with a tape. The end of the tape is wound around a stick. A fold of carbon paper is released by winding the tape on the stick.

Duplicating Methods

Duplicating consists in producing copies by transferring impressions from a specially prepared master (the original writing) to the copies. Two methods of duplicating used in systems work are:

(1) Direct process by which, as the name states, the impression is transferred directly from the master to the copies. Under this method, the master is produced by writing or typing on a piece of paper behind which is a piece of special carbon paper placed in reverse (Figure 6-5). As the

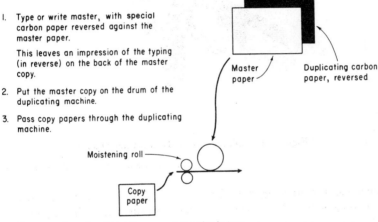

I. Type or write master, with special carbon paper reversed against the master paper.

This leaves an impression of the typing (in reverse) on the back of the master copy.

2. Put the master copy on the drum of the duplicating machine.

3. Pass copy papers through the duplicating machine.

Master paper

Duplicating carbon paper, reversed

Moistening roll

Copy paper

The moistening roll moistens the copy paper which in turn absorbs dye from the master paper on drum.

Figure 6-5. Direct Process Duplicating

master is typed, a dye impression is left in reverse on the back of the master. This impression is utilized in reproduction by placing the master on a drum against which the copy papers are pressed, after being slightly moistened by the machine. Some of the dye comes off the master onto each copy. A direct-process master may be filed for later use and used a number of times until the dye is consumed. About 300 copies can be made from a master. Figure 6-6 is an illustration of a direct-process duplicating machine.

In direct-process duplicating, several masters may be used to produce various copies of a set. Thus, a fixed master containing the information which is identical as between the order copies and the invoice copies would be used alone to produce the order copies. Then, after all or part of the goods are shipped, a variable master showing quantities shipped,

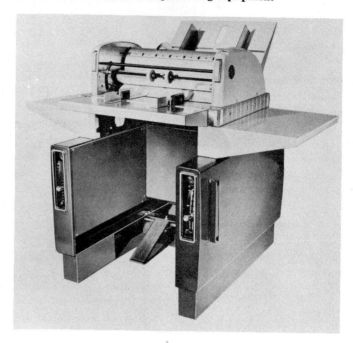

Figure 6-6. Direct-Process Duplicating Machine

Ditto Division of Bell & Howell Company

extensions, and footings would be used *with* the fixed master to produce the invoice copies. The forms and steps are illustrated in Figure 6-7.

Copies can be of various sizes, and various block-out methods can be used for eliminating information shown on the master from particular copies. Packing slips (narrow), bills of lading, and shipping tags and labels can all be produced from the same order master, through proper design of the forms.

If there were several shipments on the same order, the same fixed master would be used for all invoice sets, but a new variable master would be used for each invoice set.[1]

(2) Offset process, by which a positive impression is transferred from the master to the copy in two stages in the duplicating machine. The offset master may be either paper, plastic, or metal, and it may be prepared by writing, typing, drafting, photographing, or printing. Writing or typing is done in the regular manner on the face of the master with reproducing pencil or ink or reproducing paper ribbon. The image is

---

[1] The discussion of order and invoice procedures in this chapter is intended to be incidental to the explanation of writing and reproducing methods. It is included to clarify the explanation of methods. For a complete explanation of order and billing procedures, see Chapter 11.

| ORDER NUMBER ▶ 7071 | DATE ENTERED 4-24 | CUSTOMER'S ORDER NO. 2184 | DATE 4-23 | SALESMAN 4021 |

| SOLD TO | Harrington, Janes & Co.
41 Broad Street
Graves Electrical Supply Co. |
| SHIP TO | Graves Electrical Supply Co.
1431 Broadway
Newark, N. J. |

| F O B | OUR FACTORY X | DESTINATION | REQUESTED ROUTING Acme Fast Freight | PPD. | COL. X |

ITEM NUMBER	QUANTITY ORDERED	OUR NUMBER	DESCRIPTION	UNIT PRICE
1	200	344-D	2-Blade Safety Switch	3.00
2	100	155-C	AC Buzzers 24 V.	2.00
3	100	CR106	Starting Switches	6.00
4				

| ORDER NUMBER ▶ | DATE ENTERED | CUSTOMER'S ORDER NO. | DATE | SALESMAN | | 52,817 ◀ INVOICE NUMBER |
| | | | | | | INVOICE DATE 4-30 |

SOLD TO	
SHIP TO						WEIGHT 71#	NO. OF PKGS 2
	F O B	OUR FACTORY	DESTINATION	REQUESTED ROUTING	PPD.	COL.	SHIPPED VIA Acme

ITEM NUMBER	QUANTITY ORDERED	OUR NUMBER	DESCRIPTION	UNIT PRICE	QUANTITY TO BE SHIPPED	QUANTITY SHIPPED	AMOUNT
1					70	130	390.00
2					60	40	80.00
3					40	60	360.00
4							830.00

Ditto Division of Bell & Howell Company

Figure 6-7. Fixed Master and Variable Master: Direct Process Duplicating

1. The order master (a fixed master) is typed from the sales order. The shipping order set is reproduced from this master.
2. When the shipping order comes back from the shipping room, the billing master (a variable master) is written on the basis of actual shipments.
3. The order master and the billing master are placed in the duplicating machine (with order master behind the billing master) to reproduce the invoice copies. The dye which makes the impression is on the back of these masters. Back-order copies are produced from the same combination of masters.

therefore positive. The reproducing agent contains oil, and this fact is significant in the processing method.

In the offset duplicating machine, the master is moistened slightly and put on a drum so that when the drum revolves, the master presses against a rubber-covered cylinder. Ink which contains oil adheres to the image on the master copy, and it is transferred to the rubber where it appears in reverse. This image is in turn transferred to the copy paper (on which it will appear as positive) on a third cylinder from which it is released into a stacker.

In the offset process, a master can be created from a master. Thus, after the original master is typed from a customer's order, for instance, the order copies and *an invoice master* can be produced from that order master. The order copies are distributed and the invoice master is filed. When goods are shipped, the invoice master is pulled from file, priced, extended and footed, and used to produce invoice copies. Several types of master paper are available to meet various copying needs: short-run, medium-run, and long-run.

Copying

Copying consists in producing copies from the original papers themselves instead of from specially prepared masters (as in duplicating). Under one of the methods of copying known as the *diazo* process, a transluscent master and a sensitized copy paper are used. The master copy must be on transluscent paper, but ordinary pencil, ink, typewriter ribbon, or printing can be used on the master. Prints are produced in a contact printer (see Figure 6-8) by placing the face of the copy paper against the back of the master and passing them through the machine.

In the copying operation, the master together with a sheet of sensitized copy paper is passed over a revolving glass cylinder in which there is a

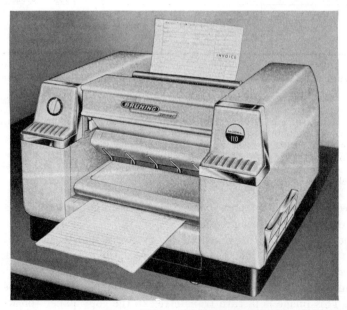

Bruning Division of Addressograph Multigraph Company
Figure 6-8. Copying Machine (Diazo)

mercury arc lamp. The light erodes the coating on the copy paper in those areas not covered by the images on the master. At this stage of the processing, the master is ejected, and the copy paper is passed through a developer to bring out a positive image on the paper. The printing as well as entries and other images on the master will appear on the copy. The developer used in one make of machine is a liquid; that used in another is ammonia vapor.

The translucent paper may be printed as separate sheets or as one copy in a unit set. In the first case, the master is written with pen or ink, or typed, and the required copies are made in the copying machine. For example, a single master may be used to produce order copies in the copying machine. After goods are shipped, the master is priced, extended, and footed, and invoice copies are produced in the copying machine.

When the translucent master is one sheet in a carbon interleaved set, the master can be used for "extra" or "later" copies. Thus, in an order and invoice procedure, the carbon copies may be used for the order set and the master, later priced and extended, may be used to produce invoice copies.

Under the electrostatic transfer or xerography method, almost any kind of paper can be used for the original and almost any kind of paper can be used for the copies. (It is not necessary to use special paper for either.) One process (the "transfer" method as distinguished from the "direct" method) is described as follows in Xerox Corporation literature and diagrammed in Figure 6-9:

> How Xerography Works: One of the simplest illustrations of the xerographic process is the 914 copier.
> The core of this remarkable machine is a rotating, aluminum drum coated with a thin, glasslike film of selenium. The document to be copied is scanned by a moving light source. Light is reflected from the page and sent through a lens onto the surface of the drum as it rotates. The light striking the drum releases the electrostatic charge on the drum in a pattern corresponding to the original document. The drum retains a positive charge in areas that correspond to the black or printed portions of the page. The drum now bears a latent image of the original.
> Xerox copiers and copier/duplicators use three different methods of exposing the original document's image to the xerographic drum. . . . The desktop machines in the 813 [illustrated in Figure 6-10] and 660 family keep the optical system stationary and move the document past it.
> To make this image visible, powdered ink called toner is cascaded over the drum. The toner particles are themselves negatively charged and adhere to the positively charged areas of the selenium surface, forming a visible image on it. The image is transferred by bringing a sheet of paper against the drum and delivering a positive charge to the back of the sheet. This attracts the particles away from the drum surface to the paper. The image is then fixed on the copy by heat.[2]

---

[2] "How Xerography Works" (Communications Services, Xerox Corporation, Rochester, New York).

Multiple Copy Forms; Automatic Writing and Reproducing Equipment

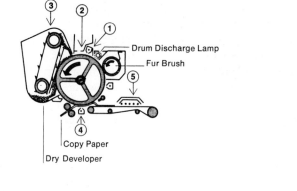

Drum Discharge Lamp

Fur Brush

Copy Paper

Dry Developer

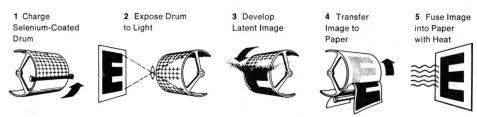

1 Charge
Selenium-Coated
Drum

2 Expose Drum
to Light

3 Develop
Latent Image

4 Transfer
Image to
Paper

5 Fuse Image
into Paper
with Heat

Figure 6-9.   How Xerography Works

Figure 6-10.   Xerox 813 Copier

Combination of Copying and Duplicating

It may be repeated at this point that duplicating consists in producing copies from a specially prepared master whereas copying consists in producing copies from a paper that was not specially prepared for the purpose. Sometimes it is desired to produce a relatively large number of copies of a paper not specially prepared. Some copying machines are built to produce duplicating masters from unprepared copy. These duplicating masters can be used in the usual way in a duplicating machine, producing the required number of copies.

The Ditto Masterfax (Figure 6-11) is a machine which will produce

Figure 6-11. Ditto Masterfax

single copies (i.e., copies one at a time) from unprepared paper or a duplicating master which can in turn be used in a duplicating machine (a separate machine) to produce a large number of copies. The same company produces a combination copying machine and duplicating machine (not illustrated). The copying machine is on the bottom of the unit and the duplicating machine on the top. A company representative says that 3 to 5 copies is the break-even point between the copying operation and the duplicating operation. If more than 3 to 5 copies are required, a spirit duplicating master may be produced and used in the duplicating machine to produce the copies.

Use of Duplicating and Copying Machines for Copies of Reports

In the previous sections, the production of order copies by means of duplicating and copying machines has been explained. Another general use of duplicating and copying machines is the production of copies of reports, for example, financial reports and operating schedules. This use has wide application. The accountant who prepares the report enters his figures directly on a master form on which all captions are pre-printed. (In the duplicating methods described above masters can be printed in duplicating ink so that the captions will reproduce on the copies.) Unprinted copy paper is used, and the reproducing process turns out both the captions and the entries. In some cases, one master is used progressively, with a new column of figures added this month to the columns of figures which were put on the forms in previous months. Some companies which formerly used typed statements and reports now use these copies of the accountant's papers.

Unit Tickets; Line-Picking

In some systems applications involving the use of duplicating machines, it is desirable to obtain a separate card or ticket for each line item on the master, with the particular line of the master reproduced on the edge of the card. In the sales distribution, for instance, tickets for the line items on invoices may be sorted by products and the tickets for each product totaled to obtain product sales reports. Or in a production control procedure, a ticket produced from each line item on a master bill of materials may be used as a requisition. From a systems standpoint, the tickets are known as *unit tickets*. The systems man contemplating using unit tickets would have to consider, among other things, the form of the tickets and the machine on which the tickets are produced.

When unit tickets are to be produced on a duplicating machine, the tickets may be in the form of (a) sets of unit tickets, each set being designed to provide for one ticket for each line item on an invoice (or other master), (b) tabulating cards (Figure 21-1) or Keysort cards (Figure 12-26).

Unit tickets prepared from a duplicating master are illustrated in Figures 6-12a, b, and c. After the master for an invoice (A) has been put

BLANK COMPANY

DATE REQUESTED

CUSTOMER'S ORDER NO.	1238
DATE	Oct. 1, 19—
CUSTOMER'S REQ'N. NO.	
SALES DISTRICT	Illinois

OUR ORDER NO. 6248 — SHIP'T NO.
DATE OF ORDER Oct. 3, 19—

INVOICE NO. 2218
DATE OF INVOICE Oct. 14, 19—
DATE SHIPPED Oct. 13, 19—
VIA our truck
W/B OR B/L NO.
NO. OF PKGS. 1   WEIGHT 28#
SHIP WITH ORDER

SOLD TO Mr. William Smith
935 Main Street
Brownsville, Illinois

SHIP TO Mr. William Smith
935 Main Street
Brownsville, Illinois

TERMS 2/10 n/30
F. O. B.

FORM IND-529

ITEM NO.	ORIGINAL QUANTITY ORDERED	MODEL OR PART NO.	PRODUCT CLASS	DESCRIPTION	UNIT PRICE	QUANTITY BACK-ORDERED	SHIPPED	AMOUNT
1	20		A	Steel	$2.00		20	$ 40.00
2	8		B	Iron	1.00		8	8.00
3	40		C	Copper	.50		40	20.00
4				Total				$ 68.00
5								
6								

1-46 71393 ® Ditto Form-Master   DITTO MASTER   TYPED BY ● BILLED BY

(A)

BLANK COMPANY

DATE REQUESTED

CUSTOMER'S ORDER NO.	1238
DATE	Oct. 1, 19—
CUSTOMER'S REQ'N. NO.	
SALES DISTRICT	Illinois

SALES ANALYSIS
OUR ORDER NO. 6248 — SHIP'T NO.
DATE OF ORDER Oct. 3, 19—

2218
Oct. 14, 19—
Oct. 13, 19—
our truck
1   28#

SOLD TO Mr. William Smith
935 Main Street
Brownsville, Illinois

SHIP TO Mr. William Smith
935 Main Street
Brownsville, Illinois

TERMS 2/10 n/30
F. O. B.

FORM IND-333

ITEM NO.	ORIGINAL QUANTITY ORDERED	MODEL OR PART NO.	PRODUCT CLASS	DESCRIPTION	UNIT PRICE	QUANTITY BACK-ORDERED	SHIPPED	AMOUNT
1	20		A	Steel	$2.00		20	$ 40.00
2	8		B	Iron	1.00		8	8.00
3	40		C	Copper	.50		40	20.00

(B)

Ditto Division of Bell & Howell Company

Figures 6-12a and b. Unit Tickets Prepared from Duplicating Master

(A) is the master, used for reproducing the regular order-invoice set. (B) is the gang of unit tickets, held together through the first run through the duplicating machine by the binding strip at the right. (C) is the three tickets, separated. Name and address were imprinted on the top ticket when the unseparated gang (B) was put through the duplicating machine. Name and address were imprinted on the second and third tickets by putting them through the duplicating machine a second time with the "description" section of the master masked out.

Form 1 (top)

BLANK COMPANY

DATE REQUESTED

CUSTOMER'S ORDER NO. 1238
DATE Oct. 1, 19—
CUSTOMER'S REQ'N. NO.

SALES ANALYSIS

OUR ORDER NO. 6248   SHIP'T NO.
DATE OF ORDER Oct. 3, 19—

2218

SALES DISTRICT Illinois

Oct. 14, 19—
Oct. 13, 19—

SOLD TO   Mr. William Smith
935 Main Street
Brownsville, Illinois

our truck

SHIP TO   Mr. William Smith
935 Main Street
Brownsville, Illinois

1   28#

FORM IND-333

TERMS 2/10 n/30
F.O.B.

ITEM NO.	ORIGINAL QUANTITY ORDERED	MODEL OR PART NO.	PRODUCT CLASS	DESCRIPTION	UNIT PRICE	BACK-ORDERED	SHIPPED	AMOUNT
1	20		A	Steel	$2.00		20	$ 40.00

Form 2 (middle)

BLANK COMPANY

DATE REQUESTED

CUSTOMER'S ORDER NO. 1238
DATE Oct. 1, 19—
CUSTOMER'S REQ'N. NO.

SALES ANALYSIS

OUR ORDER NO. 6248   SHIP'T NO.
DATE OF ORDER Oct. 3, 19—

2218

SALES DISTRICT Illinois

Oct. 14, 19—
Oct. 13, 19—

SOLD TO   Mr. William Smith
935 Main Street
Brownsville, Illinois

our truck

SHIP TO   Mr. William Smith
935 Main Street
Brownsville, Illinois

1   28#

FORM IND-333

TERMS 2/10 n/30
F.O.B.

ITEM NO.	ORIGINAL QUANTITY ORDERED	MODEL OR PART NO.	PRODUCT CLASS	DESCRIPTION	UNIT PRICE	BACK-ORDERED	SHIPPED	AMOUNT
2	8		B	Iron	1.00		8	8.00

Form 3 (bottom)

BLANK COMPANY

DATE REQUESTED

CUSTOMER'S ORDER NO. 1238
DATE Oct. 1, 19—
CUSTOMER'S REQ'N. NO.

SALES ANALYSIS

OUR ORDER NO. 6248   SHIP'T NO.
DATE OF ORDER Oct. 3, 19—

2218

SALES DISTRICT Illinois

Oct. 14, 19—
Oct. 13, 19—

SOLD TO   Mr. William Smith
935 Main Street
Brownsville, Illinois

our truck

SHIP TO   Mr. William Smith
935 Main Street
Brownsville, Illinois

1   28#

FORM IND-333

TERMS 2/10 n/30
F.O.B.

ITEM NO.	ORIGINAL QUANTITY ORDERED	MODEL OR PART NO.	PRODUCT CLASS	DESCRIPTION	UNIT PRICE	BACK-ORDERED	SHIPPED	AMOUNT
3	40		C	Copper	.50		40	20.00

(C)

Figure 6-12c.

in the duplicating machine, a set of unit tickets (B) is run through, and it comes off the machine with a separate ticket for each line item. The tickets are separated from the set by pulling off the binding edge. The separate unit tickets (C) are shown in Figure 6-12c.

Line-picking may be done on a direct-process duplicating machine by equipping it with a line-picking attachment which moves the card feed one line for each revolution of the drum and at the same time includes heading information on the ticket.

A duplicating machine with the line-picking feature built in is illustrated in Figure 6-13. This machine is a direct-process duplicating machine with which full or partial copies can be produced as described above. The controls at the right are used to produce on each ticket, say, the heading of an invoice master and one line item. Each ticket is produced by one pass through the machine, and the machine automatically picks the line items in succession.

The company which manufactures the line-picking duplicator illustrated in Figure 6-13 produces a more advanced model which will supply copies consisting of the heading and any desired selection of items from the master. Selection is controlled from a keyboard.

Ormig

Figure 6-13. Duplicating Machine–Selective Data Printer

This machine is equipped to print unit tickets in one pass through the machine.

Addressing Methods

Addressing consists in transferring name and address or other information from a file of metal plates, stencils, or duplicating masters to correspondence forms, such as envelopes and form letters, or to accounting systems forms, such as customers statements and accounts and employee clock cards, pay checks, earnings statements, and quarterly earnings records. In an accounts receivable system, a plate would be kept in file for each customer; in a payroll system, a plate would be kept for each employee.

Alphabetic and numeric information in the form of raised images are put on the plates by means of an embossing machine. The plates can be bought in any of several forms. One form has a removable-section construction whereby name and address can be put on one section and variable information such as salary and certain deductions, on another section. The variable sections can be re-done as the information changes. Tabs can be affixed to the plates to identify each one according to a particular classification. Also, plates can be provided with index or reference cards for identification and entry purposes, respectively.

In the use of addressing plates, the file drawer containing the plates is unloaded into the plate feed and then put into position under the table of the machine, to receive each plate as it is discharged by the machine. The machine may be used to imprint each plate on a separate form, as in the case of clock cards, or to imprint successive plates on successive lines on one sheet, as with a payroll form. If it is not desired to print all information shown on the plate, certain information can be masked out.

Addressing Plate Combined with Tabulating Card

Figure 6-14 is an addressing plate combined with a tabulating card.[3] When plates of this type are used, any desired classification can be sorted

Figure 6-14. Addressing Plate Combined with Tabulating Card

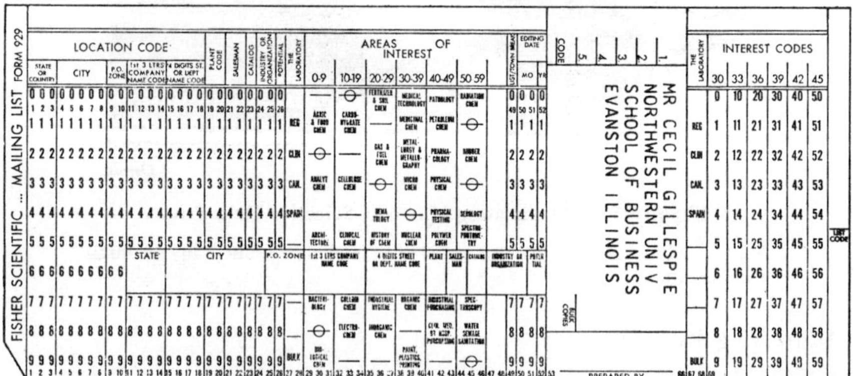

Selectomatic

---

[3] Tabulating cards, sorters, and collators are explained in Chapter 21.

out of the file for use in the addressing machine. Thus, if the file is arranged geographically and it is desired to print a list of some particular class of customers, that class could be sorted out by means of a sorter. This would eliminate hand picking of plates. After use, they can be merged into the file by means of a collator.

AUTOMATIC WRITING (AND CALCULATING) EQUIPMENT

Some Particulars of Automatic Writing (and Calculating) Equipment

Automatic writing (and calculating) equipment may be classified according to the number and types of the automatic features. The basic unit could be a standard electric typewriter and the automatic features could be a computing unit which performs calculations and transmits them to the typewriter and a card or tape *input* which causes the typewriter to type customer names and addresses, product descriptions, and so on. Note that a computer unit coupled to the typewriter makes it possible to do a complete billing job (involving extensions, footings, and so forth), payroll, and other applications involving calculations on the typewriter. In some systems, an *output* punch is coupled to the typewriter to capture on units tickets (tabulating cards) or tapes either all information which is typed by the typewriter or selected information according to program. The purpose of capturing all information on an order form being typed could be to produce an invoice after the order is shipped. The purpose of capturing information on an invoice being typed (customer number, salesman numbers, and products shipped with quantities, prices, and extensions) might be to provide input for a sales analysis procedure.

The automatic writing equipment described in this chapter is sometimes called computer equipment, since it comprises or is coupled to, a computer unit which will do the basic calculating operations and which has memory capacity. The machines in this chapter are really operator attended and computer assisted. A major point made by the manufacturers of this equipment is that it can be handled by the "girl in your office" and it does not require an especially trained computer operator. The terms "computer" and "computer system" can also apply to large installations which have programs that provide for a great degree of automatic operations. (See Chapters 24–26.)

A number of systems of automatic writing equipment are described and illustrated on the following pages.

Computing Typewriter (Dura Model 1041)

The Dura Model 1041 computing typewriter (Figure 6-15) is a combination typewriter and calculator unit. It can handle the preparation

Figure 6-15. Computing Typewriter (Dura Model 1041)

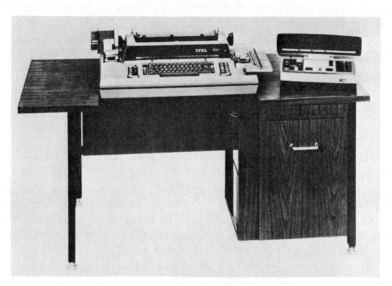

of invoices and other documents; type form letters using information stored on punched tape; or type regular correspondence. Computing and typing operations can be handled as individual operations when desired.

IBM 633

The IBM Billing Typewriter Type 633 (illustrated in Figure 6-16) introduced in January, 1968 is an updated version of the 632. It consists basically of:

(1) A standard IBM electric typewriter. Among other features, the typewriter can be equipped with a split platen on which two different forms (say, an invoice set and a customer's account) can be put on the platen side by side and spaced independently. Or it can be equipped with automatic form feed which controls the spacing of continuous forms in the machine. A pin feed arrangement can be provided for controlling the alignment of continuous forms on the platen.

(2) A card punch and calculating unit. The card punch may be used in a billing installation to punch product line item cards from invoices being typed and invoice total cards for accounts receivable purposes. (There is no input unit for cards or tape. The system is designed for keyboard input.) The calculating unit adds, subtracts, multiplies, rounds off, and column shifts. It can be pro-

IBM

Figure 6-16.   Billing Typewriter Type 633

grammed to accumulate control totals during a run to use for proof purposes.

(3) A ten-key keyboard, which is used for access to the calculating unit. This keyboard is also equipped with a few command keys which the operator uses to cause the machine to perform certain actions. The system is programmed by a plastic tape positioned in the typewriter unit parallel to the carriage.

An invoice prepared on the IBM 633 is illustrated in Figure 6-17, and the two line item cards together with the total invoice card for the invoice are illustrated in Figure 6-18.

Two types of billing can be done on the IBM 633:

(1) Produce a complete invoice. This is either complete pre-billing, meaning that the invoice is typed from the sales order before the goods are shipped, or complete post billing, meaning that the invoice is typed from the shipping order after the goods have been shipped.

(2) Produce an invoice set with shipping ticket before the goods have been shipped, but completing it after the goods have been shipped. After the first typing, the set is removed from the machine and the shipping ticket is removed from the set and sent to the warehouse. When the "shipped" shipping ticket comes back from the ware-

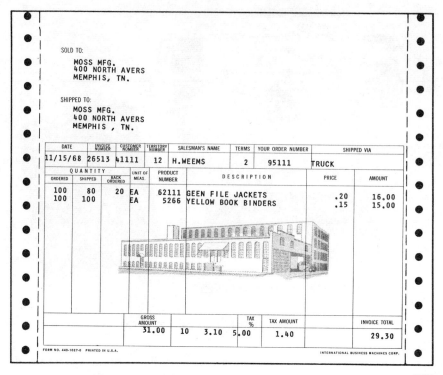

| | | SOLD TO: |
MOSS MFG.
400 NORTH AVERS
MEMPHIS, TN.

SHIPPED TO:
MOSS MFG.
400 NORTH AVERS
MEMPHIS , TN.

DATE	INVOICE NUMBER	CUSTOMER NUMBER	TERRITORY NUMBER	SALESMAN'S NAME	TERMS	YOUR ORDER NUMBER	SHIPPED VIA
11/15/68	26513	41111	12	H.WEEMS	2	95111	TRUCK

QUANTITY			UNIT OF MEAS.	PRODUCT NUMBER	DESCRIPTION	PRICE	AMOUNT
ORDERED	SHIPPED	BACK ORDERED					
100	80	20	EA	62111	GEEN FILE JACKETS	.20	16.00
100	100		EA	5266	YELLOW BOOK BINDERS	.15	15.00

	GROSS AMOUNT			TAX %	TAX AMOUNT		INVOICE TOTAL
	31.00	10	3.10	5.00	1.40		29.30

FORM NO. 440-1027-0 PRINTED IN U.S.A.

INTERNATIONAL BUSINESS MACHINES CORP.

IBM

Figure 6-17. Invoice Prepared on Billing Typewriter Type 633

house, the invoice set is put back into the machine and completed. The latter operation involves entering the quantities shipped and extending them, calculating discounts and sales taxes, adding shipping charges, and determining and entering the total invoice.

IBM 6400

The IBM Accounting Machine System Type 6400 (Figure 6-19) has a central unit which includes a typewriter and a computer which will add, subtract, multiply, divide, round figures, and column shift and which will perform elementary decisions through the use of decision tables.

The 6400 is programmed from a wiring panel (page 498). There are also tape guides, one of which guides the print head and the other the vertical travel of the form on the platen, both of which are directed from the panel. The memory capacity is 38 words of ten digits each. Since the machine is equipped with a panel which takes care of much of the programming of the machine, the memory is used only for certain operations

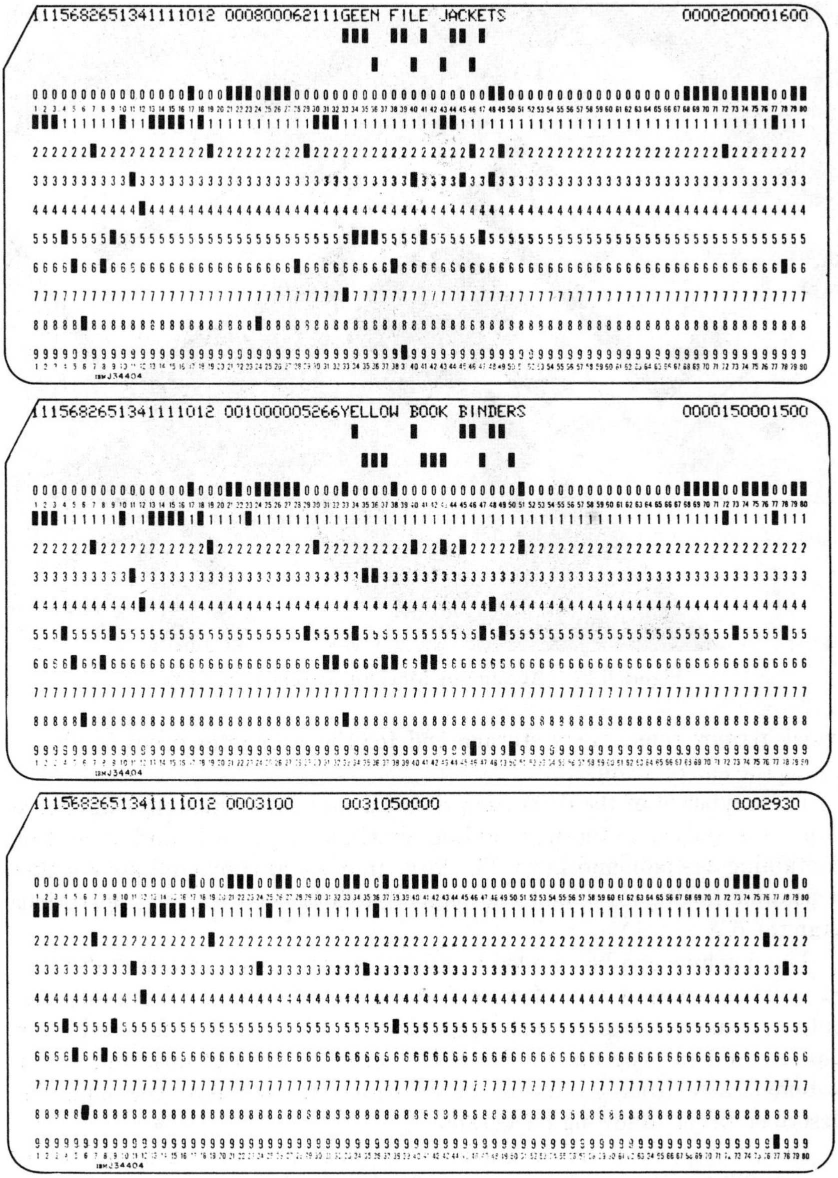

IBM

Figure 6-18. Tabulating Cards Punched as By-Product of Invoice Preparation—
Type 633

IBM

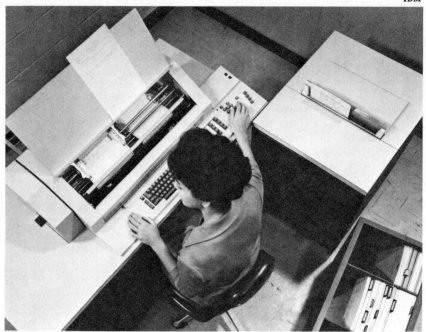

Figure 6-19.   Accounting Machine System Type 6400

which require momentary storage and for the storage of proof totals for use at the end of a run.

The keyboard of the 6400 comprises the standard typewriter keyboard (for caps only), a ten-key adding machine keyboard, and a section containing 24 command keys. The large number of command keys makes it possible for the machine to accommodate a larger variety of operations than the 633.

The machine can be coupled to a card or tape input unit and also to a card or tape output unit. Figure 6-20 is a card input reader (left) and output card unit (right rear) coupled to an IBM 6400. The card input unit is used to type names, addresses, product descriptions, and so on, automatically from tabulating cards which are fed into the input, as described in the following paragraph.

Tabulating cards can be fed into the input unit one at a time or in groups. The cards are kept in a tub file beside the control unit. To type information from the cards, the operator pulls cards from the tub and inserts them in the input unit. After the typewriter types the information read from the cards, they are released through the card stacker. The operator then returns the cards to the file.

Output Card Punch for the IBM 6400

Figure 6-20 (right rear) is a card punch which can be coupled to the 6400 unit to capture selected information from the invoices as they are being prepared on the 6400. The output cards for the 6400 are similar to those of the 633, illustrated in Figure 6-18.

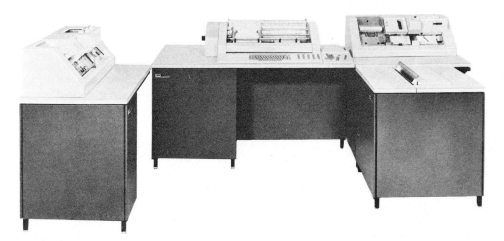

IBM

Figure 6-20.   Card Input Reader and Output Card Punch Coupled to IBM 6400

The output tape punch is not illustrated. An eight-channel tape is illustrated in Figure 6-21. (Other channel widths are also in use.) Tapes, like cards, can be punched for alphabetic, numeric, and function codes. The latter are control punchings for the machines in which the tapes are

Figure 6-21.   Eight-Channel Punched-Paper Tape

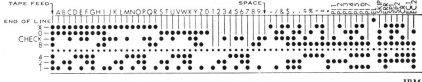

IBM

used. These tapes, which are sometimes called by-product tapes, can be either cumulative—showing all the information on the invoice—or selective—showing only particular information which later may be punched on cards from tapes.

One feature of tapes is that they can be readily transmitted. A tape could be sent to a headquarters office of the company or to an outside service bureau where cards can be punched from the tape on a tape-to-card converter (Figure 22-20, page 526). Five-channel tape can be turned over to a telegraph service for transmission over its wires. Other uses of tapes are discussed on pages 525–527.

Using Both the Input Unit and Output Unit to Produce Shipping Order Sets and Invoice Sets

The input and output units may both be used in an order and billing application. Assume that only the order set is to be produced before the goods are shipped and that the invoice set priced and extended is to be produced after the goods are shipped. To produce the shipping order set, customer cards and product cards may be pulled from file on the basis of the sales order written by the salesman, and put into the input unit of the 6400. The operator writes quantities to be shipped and other variable information, using the keyboard, and the 6400 produces the order and its copies, at the same time producing a tape on the output punch. This shipping order tape is filed, and the shipping order is sent to the warehouse and shipping room. After the goods have been shipped, the shipping order tape is pulled from file and used as an input tape in the 6400. This time, the operator types quantities actually shipped, and any other variable information, using the keyboard, and the 6400 produces the priced, extended, and footed invoice set.

The same kind of operation can of course be done with other machines equipped with both input and output units, described on the following pages. Various combinations of tabulating cards, edge-punched cards, and tapes can be used in the system.

Flexowriter

The Flexowriter automatic writing machine (Figure 6-22) is a typewriter that can be equipped for input from punched tape, described in the previous section, or edge-punched cards, illustrated in Figure 6-23, or tabulating cards. It is equipped with a keyboard on which the operator can type information manually. At the same time, a Flexowriter can produce by-product or output tapes or cards. There are various models of Flexowriter, having differing capabilities. Model 2201 is illustrated in Figure 6-22.

Figure 6-22.   2201 Flexowriter

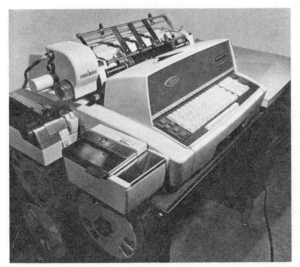

Friden

Outline of the Steps in an Actual Order and Billing Procedure

Illustration of the use of an automatic typewriter may be provided by reference to an order and billing procedure in a company which has 15,000 customers and 15,000 product items. The main office processes 8,000 to 10,000 orders a month.

The procedure in skeleton outline is:

(1) Orders are sent to the registry file after editing and pricing. The registry file contains a file folder which is both a register of the orders received from the customer and a jacket for the customer-heading cards in the file. The customer-heading cards are edge-punched cards (Figure 6-23), showing, in addition to name and

Figure 6-23.   Edge-Punched Card—Name and Address

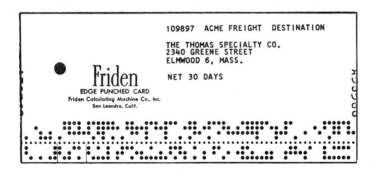

address, any other constant information which should be transmitted to the warehouse and other departments handling the order. At this point a number is assigned to the order, and it is entered in the register, together with the customer's purchase order number. A heading card is pulled from the file jacket, and it is sent to the next operation with the order.

(2) A calculator operator extends and foots the order.

(3) The typewriter operator inserts the heading card in the machine, and the machine automatically types the heading information on the order set. The operator types the product-line items manually. (In some applications, product-line items are typed automatically from edge-punched cards kept in the product card file.)

The typewriter produces a by-product tape, which is used later to produce the invoice set. This tape is placed in an envelope attached to the file copy of the order.

(4) When the order comes back from the shipping room, showing quantities actually shipped, it is referred to the order file where the order and the invoice tape are pulled. The tape is used to produce the invoice on the typewriter. The operator scans the shipping order which shows quantities shipped; if an item was shipped short, she types the item shipped, using keyboard control. Otherwise, the machine types the item, quantity, and extension from the tape.

(5) When an item was shipped short, the typist prepares another shipping order set in the same manner as she prepared the original shipping order set, except that the second order set is for only the items back-ordered. Likewise, when *that* order comes back from the shipping room, she prepares an invoice in the same manner as for the original shipment on the order.

(6) When an invoice is prepared on the typewriter, the machine prepares a tape which is used in turn in a tape-to-card converter to punch tabulating cards. These cards are used for sales analysis and accounts receivable.

IBM 2740 Communications Terminal

This terminal (Figure 6-24) is designed to provide more effective communications between a central computer and widely-separated business locations. When not being used for communicating, it can serve as a regular electric typewriter. It can be used, for instance, in an office, a warehouse (illustrated) or in an engineering laboratory to exchange data with IBM's System/360 (Figure 24-17a) and other 2740 terminals, and serve as a sending and receiving station in a computer-controlled com-

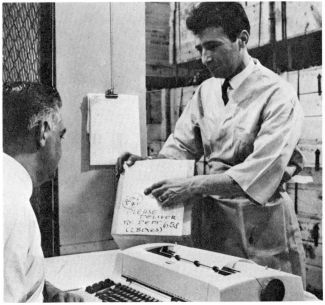

IBM

Figure 6-24. Communications Terminal Type 2740

munications network. Any person with typing ability can "talk" to a
computer.

The Terminal Computer (Victor 820/03) as a Writing Machine

A terminal computer (Figure 6-25) is a unit which combines the
features and capabilities of an input–output terminal for a computer
system and those of a computer. As a terminal, it includes keyboards—
alpha-numeric and numeric ten-key keyboards—with a serial printer
equipped with a ball or "head" printer on which sixty-six type characters
are mounted. (A serial printer is one which delivers a single type impression at a time, as distinguished from a line at a time, as in certain models
of punched-card tabulators.) The head traverses the line of impression
horizontally. This printer operates at 930 characters a minute printing
speed and 200 positions a second when skipping. It also comprises forms
handling equipment for holding continuous multiple forms in register
and spacing them under program control and a front feed chute for ac-
commodating ledgers and other noncontinuous forms.

Figure 6-25.   Terminal Computer Class 820/03

Victor

As a computer, the terminal computer comprises (among others) facilities for arithmetic and logic operations, storage or memory, and control. As a part of the computer control mechanism, there is a program selector and operator's control keyboard.[4]

The terminal computer can be used as a free standing (off-line) writing machine with arithmetic and logic capabilities and memory capabilities. As such it can do billing, statement and accounts receivable, payroll, and other business applications which involve writing, computing, and memory. Figure 11-7 (on page 235) is an invoice form produced complete on a Victor 820/03 from the shipping order (not priced and extended). For this application, customers' names and addresses (indexed by customer number) and product descriptions with unit selling prices and cost prices (indexed by product number) are stored in memory.

There is a minimum of keyboard operation. The operator inserts blank billing forms and the customer account form (from file) in the chute. By indexing customer's number on the keyboard, the customer name and address are called from memory and printed automatically. By indexing each product number, the appropriate product description and prices are likewise printed automatically. Extensions, footings, and commissions are computed by the computer and typed automatically.

If the entire customer's name and address list and the entire product

---

[4] Further description of the Victor terminal computer appears in Chapter 24, pages 587-589.

list are too extensive to be stored in memory, only certain specified customers' groups (say, geographic or trade class) or the most active names may be so stored and the other names may be stored off-line, say on punched cards. The cards may be pulled from file as needed and read into the terminal computer by a card reader. Names not in memory or off-line file (and *any* other special information such as freight charges calculated in the shipping room) can be typed on the keyboard by the operator.

As a telecommunications terminal, the 820/03 can be coupled to a cassette, which under program control takes a record of the day's billing and communicates it when requested to a central computer. In this situation, the central computer may perform inventory record and control functions.

Burroughs Electronic Billing Computer Series L2000

Figure 6-26a is a Burroughs Electronic Billing Computer Series L2000 and Figure 6-26b is the keyboard of the same machine. This machine has writing (keyboard and automatic), computing and logic, and memory capability. The keyboard includes an alpha-numeric keyboard, a ten-key numeric keyboard and (above the former keyboard) 16 program select keys. The programs are stored in memory. Input capability can be pro-

Figure 6-26a.   Electronic Billing Computer (Series L2000)

Burroughs

Burroughs

Figure 6-26b.   Keyboard of Electronic Billing Computer

vided by a punched-card reader, or a punched-paper tape/edge-punched-card reader. Output capability can likewise be provided by an 80-column card punch or tape punch/edge-punched-card punch.

Variable forms set-ups are available including single continuous forms and dual continuous forms (side by side) with the two forms moving independently of each other. Movement of the forms is program controlled from the program in memory. This control is based upon "absolute" commands and "space to" commands (for instance, space to the top of the next form). Printing is by a "ball" printer.

Memory is magnetic disc which can accommodate a total of 1024 words which in turn can be variably divided between user's programs, stored data, and micro-instructions. Mathematical operations are performed electronically under control of micro-instructions. Programs are written in English (COBOL). They can be assembled (converted from man-readable to machine-readable language) on the L2000 or on a large Burroughs computer. Programs are recorded on punched-paper tape which can be fed into the L2000 by the punched-paper tape reader.

AUXILIARY EQUIPMENT

Calculators

Machines which combine writing capability with calculating capability, and in some cases with other capabilities, were illustrated and discussed on pages 109–122. It is not necessary to point out that in many systems involving writing and calculating, the writing machine operations and the calculating machine or operation are separate. In a billing system, for instance, the shipped shipping order may be priced, extended, and footed in one operation and the invoice typed in another operation. In a payroll system, the attendance time cards may be totaled for regular time and overtime, rated, and extended in one operation, and the paychecks (with quarterly earnings records and payroll register) produced in what is essentially a posting operation. Desk calculators are very widely used in both of the calculating operations described above. And of course, desk calculators are widely used in general accounting, cost accounting, and production departments, not to mention the great use made by engineers and engineering designers.

Figure 6-27 is a SONY ICC-2500W electronic programmable calculator

Sony

Figure 6-27. Electronic Programmable Calculator
(Model ICC-2500W)

built for complicated calculations. It is designed, according to the manufacturers, to fill the gap between large computers and limited desk top calculators. It is engineered with 9 memories to handle a wide range of complex general business and commercial problems. Up to 111 program steps are provided for. Program instructions are entered through the keyboard without special symbols or codes, and problems are performed by just depressing one control key. A number of other models are available.

Collator

A collator is a mechanical device used for assembling forms into sets, for instance, before a duplicating operation is to be performed. In the operation of this machine for collating an order set, the order forms, acknowledgment forms, and so forth, would be placed in separate pockets of the machine, which would collate them in separate sets, ready for the duplicating machine.

Burster

Continuous forms are frequently used on various phases of mechanized payroll work, on such forms as pay checks and employees earnings statements. These forms must be separated at the perforations. This operation is known as "bursting." There are several excellent bursters on the market, with varying capacities up to more than 20,000 an hour. Auxiliary equipment may be used on the burster for dating, consecutive numbering, signing (for example, pay checks) and the like. Note that at these very high speeds, the executive responsible for a signature plate can personnally supervise the signing of, say, 5,000 checks in 15 minutes.

7

Account Posting
by Machine Methods:
Common-Language Concept

Account Posting by Machine, in General

Posting an account consists basically of only two operations: (1) writing a date, a reference number or description, and an amount on a piece of paper and (2) adding or subtracting. Where the volume of posting is small, the systems man may give little thought to these operations as such. The bookkeeper may have so little posting to do each day that it is not a significant factor in the day's work. On the other hand, where the volume of posting is large and a considerable amount of time is required to write dates, references, and amounts, and to add and subtract the amounts, the systems man may consider using a machine to perform these two operations.

A study of account posting by machine logically begins with the listing–adding machine, which in its original form would do only these two things: print an amount on a tape each time the operator depressed the keys and pressed the motor bar, and accumulate these amounts to arrive at a total. The present chapter explains the use of listing–adding machines and introduces more complicated types of machines commonly known as bookkeeping machines.

Uses of Listing–Adding Machines

Listing–adding machines are used in accounting for such functions as:

(1) Making lists (tapes) of invoices and other accounting media to provide a formal record of the amounts, together with the totals. In large volume accounting operations, various accounting papers such as invoices are often dispatched in batches accompanied by such a tape, which is called a "pre-list tape."

(2) Making deposit slips.

(3) Posting accounts in simpler installations.

The Full-Keyboard, Single-Register Listing–Adding Machine

There are two general types of listing–adding machines. They are known as: full-keyboard machines (described in this section) and ten-key machines (described in a later section). Both terms refer to the number of keys on the keyboard for recording amounts.

Figure 7-1 is a picture of one of Burroughs' full-keyboard listing–add-

Burroughs

Figure 7-1. Full Visible Keyboard Listing–Adding Machine (Series P1000)

ing machines. The main distinguishing feature of the full keyboard is that one vertical row of nine keys (numbered 1 to 9) is provided for each digit of the amount. Thus, to record the amount of $800.00, the operator would depress the *8* key in the fifth column (the key which is circled below), and depress the *plus* motor bar, which controls the motive power and causes the machine to add.

To record $28.00, the operator would depress the *2* key and the *8* key as follows:

```
9        9        9        9        9
8        8        8        8        8
7        7        7        7        7
6        6        6        6        6
5        5        5        5        5
4        4        4        4        4
3        3        3        3        3
2        2        2        2        2
1        1        1        1        1
```

and depress the *plus* motor bar. Note that there are no cipher keys to depress; the ciphers print automatically.

Listing–Adding Machine Tapes

Figure 7-2 illustrates tapes prepared on a listing–adding machine. The first tape illustrates the addition of two amounts. It was prepared by recording the $800.00 and the $28.00 as described above to print the amounts on the tape and accumulate them in the machine. The total is printed on the tape by depressing the *total* key and the *plus* motor bar. (In some models, it is necessary to press only the *total* key.) Note the asterisk (*) printed beside the total amount. This asterisk indicates that

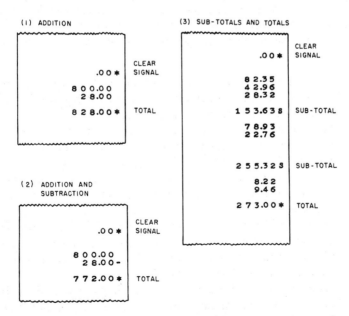

**Figure 7-2. Tapes Produced on Listing-Adding Machine Equipped
for Direct Subtraction**

the accumulated amounts in the machine have been cleared out of the machine.

The second tape illustrates subtraction. Subtraction of the $28.00 is caused by depressing the amount keys and the *minus* motor bar. Note also that, when starting to prepare these tapes, the operator printed a clear signal on the tape. This is done by simply depressing the *total* key and the *plus* motor bar. The purpose is to determine that there is no amount already in the machine—the result of inadvertently striking the amount keys at some previous time. (A clear signal should appear at the beginning of each tape.)

Symbols are: total (*); subtotal (S); and amount subtracted (−). A total "clears the machine." A subtotal does not clear the machine.

The clear signal at the beginning of each tape is printed to demonstrate that the machine contains no amount from previous operations.

The third tape illustrates what is known as a "subtotal." This is a total printed on the tape without clearing the total out of the machine. After a subtotal has been printed on the tape, the machine continues to add the new amounts recorded in the machine to those already accumulated.

Amount Keys and Function Keys

From the previous description of how to prepare a tape, it appears that there are two general kinds of keys on a listing–adding machine keyboard: *amount* keys (the vertical rows of keys) and *function* keys, which are used to cause the machine to perform particular operations. Typical function keys are:

(a) The *total* key. When this key (in some models with the *plus* motor bar) is depressed, the machine will print the balance in the register and clear the register to a zero balance.

(b) The *subtotal* key (in some models in conjunction with the *plus* motor bar) will cause the machine to print the balance in the register but will not clear the balance from the register.

(c) The *error* key will restore to neutral any key on the keyboard that has been depressed, assuming that the motor bar has not also been depressed.

(d) The *non-add* key, used in conjunction with the motor bar, will cause the machine to print the amount of the keys depressed, but will not accumulate in the register. Non-added amounts are identified on the tape with the symbol #.

(e) The *repeat* key will hold the amount keys depressed in the keyboard so that the amount accumulates in the register and prints once each time the motor bar is pressed.

The machine illustrated is described as a "single-register machine." The register is the accumulating device inside the machine that performs the basic function of adding and subtracting. Certain listing–adding machines, described later, are equipped with several registers. Use of such machines would permit accumulating several classes of items at the same time in the machine.

Ten-Key Printing Calculator

Figure 7-3 is an illustration of a ten-key printing calculator. The fundamental difference between this machine and the full visible keyboard machine (illustrated previously) lies in the *amount* keys. The arrangement of amount keys is compared as follows:

Full visible keyboard					Ten-Key		
9	9	9	9	9	7	8	9
8	8	8	8	8	4	5	6
7	7	7	7	7	1	2	3
6	6	6	6	6	0	00	000
5	5	5	5	5			
4	4	4	4	4			
3	3	3	3	3			
2	2	2	2	2			
1	1	1	1	1			

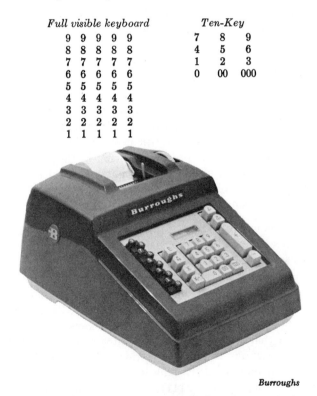

Burroughs

Figure 7-3.   Ten-Key Printing Calculator (Series J700)

On a ten-key machine, the operator strikes the keys one after the other in the order in which he would write them. It is necessary to strike a cipher key to print a cipher. There are three cipher keys (bottom row) : 0, 00, and

000. Thus, to print the amount $800.00 on the tape and to record it in the machine, the operator strikes the following keys successively: 8,0,0,0,0, and then depresses the motor bar. The machine will print 800.00, punctuating automatically. *Multiplication* is accomplished by using the multiplier keys (the vertical columns of keys at the left of the keyboard). The J700 performs shortcut multiplication automatically.

Function keys on the ten-key machine are similar to those on the full visible keyboard machine, with a few exceptions. Both machines are totaled or subtotaled in the same manner.

Posting an Account on Listing–Adding Machine; Principle

The Burroughs listing–adding machine may be equipped with a wide, *movable* carriage to make it possible to post account forms on the carriage of the machine.

Figures 7-4 and 7-5 illustrate account forms that might be posted by a single-register listing–adding machine. Note that the account form carries a running balance. (Many accounts receivable and accounts payable forms designed for machine posting provide running balance columns.) The first illustration shows a debit posting of $28.00 on the 4th of January, and the second illustration shows a credit posting of the same amount on the same date. (There was one previous posting in the account, $800.00, recorded the previous day. Note the balance in the account.)

Posting an account on a listing–adding machine consists of five distinct operations. The operations are:

(1) Pull the account to be posted from the ledger or tray and read the old balance, that is, the balance of the account as it stands after its previous posting ($800.00).

(2) Put the account in the carriage of the machine and move the carriage so that the machine will print in the left-hand column of the account (called the "old balance" column). Record the amount of the old balance by striking the amount keys and the *plus* motor bar. (Note that the amount is now printed on the account.)

(3) Move the carriage to the description column position and print date and invoice number. This is done by depressing date keys (Jan. 4), amount keys (2111), and the number key (a function key) and striking the motor bar. This will cause the machine to print the date and number but prevent it from adding the number in the register. (The number key is really a *non-add* key.)

(4) Move the carriage to the debit column position and record the amount of the debit ($28.00). (Amount keys and *plus* motor bar.)

```
                          LEDGER

NAME    A. B. JONES                        SHEET NO.



 OLD BALANCE      DATE    FOLIO      CHARGES      CREDITS      BALANCE
                                                                           0
                JAN  3    2 0.33 #   8 0 0.0 0                8 0 0.0 0 S₁
    8 0 0.0 0   JAN  4    2 1.1 1 #     2 8.0 0              8 2 8.0 0 S₂
                                                                           3
                                                                           4
                                                                           5
                                                                           6
                                                                           7
                                                                           8
```

Figure 7-4. Debit Postings by Machine

The account carries running balances, which are computed by the machine.

```
                          LEDGER

NAME   A. B. JONES                         SHEET NO.



 OLD BALANCE      DATE    FOLIO      CHARGES      CREDITS      BALANCE
                                                                           0
                JAN  3    2 0.33 #   8 0 0.0 0                8 0 0.0 0 *₁
    8 0 0.0 0   JAN  4     1.0 8 #               2 8.0 0 -   7 7 2.0 0 *₂
                                                                           3
                                                                           4
                                                                           5
                                                                           6
                                                                           7
```

Figure 7-5. Posting a Credit

The machine subtracts the credit to arrive at a new balance.

Now the register has accumulated the total of the two amounts ($828.00). (Total key and *plus* motor bar.)

(5) Move the carriage to the column at the extreme right (called the "new balance" column) and print the amount of the new balance ($828.00). (Total key and *plus* motor bar.)

Note that mathematically the operation of posting a debit is simply the addition of two amounts by the listing–adding machine, with the printing done on a horizontal line on the account. The operation of posting a credit consists in subtracting (*minus* motor bar) the amount of the posting from the amount of the old balance.

Two new terms appear in the above paragraphs: *old balance* and *new balance*. They should be noted particularly because they are in constant use in machine-posting applications. They are defined with reference to a specific posting (for instance, the posting of January 4).

Old balance is the starting amount for the present posting. It is always the balance standing in the account after the previous posting.

New balance is the balance of the account immediately after the present posting has been made. Usually, it is printed as the last amount on the right-hand side, as illustrated in Figures **7-4** and **7-5**.

The Posting Cycle; Register Operation Diagrammed

The term "posting cycle" refers to the sequence of positions of the carriage in posting an account. In the simple posting operation illustrated previously, the posting cycle begins with the "old balance" column. The posting cycle can accordingly be diagrammed as illustrated in Figure **7-6**.

Old Balance	Date	Description	Debits	Credits	New Balance
-	Jan. 3		800.00		800.00*
800.00	Jan. 4	2111	28.00		828.00*
Register operation → Add		Non-Add	Add		Total, Clear
Posting Cycle → (1)		(2)	(3)		(4)

Figure 7-6. Posting Cycle: Register Operation Diagram

In this diagram, the operation sequence is identified by numbers. The number (1) indicates the starting point. (Although the posting cycle in Figure **7-6** started at the extreme left column, this is not the case in certain more complicated operations.)

Note that the diagram also indicates the sequence of register operation. Systems men frequently use diagrams of this kind as a blueprint of a proposed machine operation.

Figure **7-7** is the register operation diagram of posting a credit. Note that, in the register, the credit is subtracted from the old balance.

Figure 7-7.   Register Action: Posting a Credit

Old Balance	Date	Description	Debits	Credits	Now Balance
	Jan. 3		800.00		800.00
800.00	Jan. 4	2111		28.00	772.00
Register action → Add		Non-add		Subtract	Total (Clear)
Posting cycle → (1)		(2)		(3)	(4)

Automatic Tabulation; Automatic Carriage Return

In the previous illustration of posting an account, the operator moved the carriage from position to position by hand. Movement of the carriage to the *left* (so that the machine can print in successive columns of the account) is known as "tabulating." Thus, in the diagram in the previous section, the carriage tabulates from position #1 to #2, #2 to #3, #3 to #4.

Movement of the carriage to the *right*, so that the machine is ready to print in the extreme left side of the account, is known as "carriage return."

Listing–adding machines can be equipped with automatic tabulation and carriage return. Thus, when the operator enters the old balance and strikes the motor bar (at position #1), the machine will print the amount on the account and tabulate automatically to position #2. Likewise after the new balance has been printed (in position #4), the carriage will return automatically.

Some adding–listing machines are equipped with (1) a tab key and (2) a carriage return key on the keyboard. Striking the tab key will cause the machine to tabulate the carriage to the next column position. Tab stops are placed on a control bar on the carriage of the listing–adding machine in the same way as they would be placed on the carriage of a typewriter to set up the various column positions. When the carriage return key is struck, the carriage moves to the extreme right so that the machine is ready to print in position #1 on the form.

Proof of Posting; Illustrative Pre-List Tape

Concurrent with the development of listing–adding machines for posting accounts, there has been a development of methods for proving the accuracy of the posting operation.

In order to understand the operation of these proofs, certain conditions of the posting operation must be understood. Assume that accounts receivable are being posted by machine. In the first place, the accounts are posted directly from the invoices (unlike the frequent practice in pen-and-ink posting). In the second place, the invoices usually come to the machine operator in quantities representing, say, a half day's billing (constituting what is known as a "batch" or "packet"). And in the third place, the batch may be accompanied by a pre-list tape, which is a listing machine tape showing the amount of each invoice and the total amount of the batch. As will be seen, the total of the pre-list tape is used by the operator in applying the proof of posting.

As a basis for the following illustrations, assume that a batch comprises three invoices (although actually, of course, it would comprise a larger number), as follows:

Customer	Amount of Invoice
Jones	$952
White	367
Williams	28

The pre-list tape would show:

The Control Account

The use of control accounts in machine posting is basically similar to the use of control accounts in pen posting. The relationship between the Control account and the subsidiary accounts is diagrammed in Figure 7-8.

Figure 7-8.   Control Account

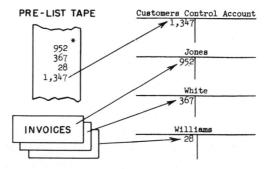

The principle is that the Control account should be charged with totals of items charged in detail to the subsidiary accounts and credited with the total of items credited in detail to the subsidiary accounts. In the diagram, the Control account has been charged with the total shown by the pre-list tape. (It would, of course, be charged with the pre-list tapes of all the batches of media passed to the posting-machine operator during the month.) It follows that the sum of balances in a subsidiary ledger should agree with the balance of the Control account.

In small organizations the Control account may be kept in the General ledger. In larger organizations where the large number of accounts requires several ledgers, there may be a Control account for each ledger, and the control accounts may be kept by a control clerk.

End-of-the-Month Trial Balances

The use of an end-of-the-month trial balance in machine posting is the same as its use in pen-and-ink posting. At the end of the month, a trial balance is taken of the balances in the subsidiary ledger, and the total of the balances is compared with the balance of the Control account. If the total does not agree, it is necessary to locate the error in posting.

How Many Accounts Shall Be Kept Under One Control Account?

In machine-posting operations, where the number of accounts is large (and sometimes it runs into tens of thousands), it is necessary to decide how many accounts shall be kept under one Control account. A number of factors, such as activity (the number of postings per account per day), have to be considered, but one generalization can be made at this point: the fewer the number of accounts placed under each Control account, the fewer the number of accounts there will be to look through in case the subsidiary ledger does not balance with its Control account. At the same time, however, the fewer the number of accounts there are under each Control account, the more Control accounts required and the greater the amount of clerical work in keeping the controls. It is necessary for the systems man to strike a balance between the probable time that will be spent hunting errors on the one hand, and the actual time taken to operate a relatively large number of Control accounts on the other. Of course this statement is a very general one, but it is one which the systems man must keep in mind in connection with the whole subject of proof of posting.

Need for Proof More Frequent Than End-of-the-Month Proof

In machine posting, it is usually considered necessary to operate, in addition to the end-of-the-month trial balance, some daily or weekly proof. Under machine conditions, the number of postings is likely to be so large that the operator cannot afford to wait until the end of the month to demonstrate whether the accounts are in balance.

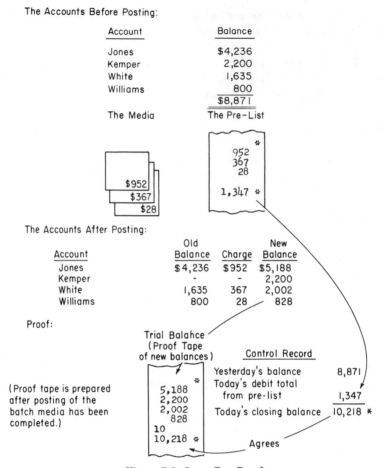

Figure 7-9. Long-Run Proof

Examples of early methods of proof, all of which are in use today, are:

(1) Long-run proof
(2) The old and new balance proof
(3) Direct proof

These proofs are explained and illustrated in the following sections. All of them are based upon use of a machine equipped with a single register.

Long-Run Proof; Trial Balance Proof; Single-Register Machine

What is known as "long-run proof" or "trial balance proof" in systems parlance is simply the practice of taking trial balances more frequently than once a month and comparing the total of the trial balance with the balance of the Control account. Of course, the Control account has to be kept up to date, but this is easy to do if the Control account is posted with totals from pre-list tapes.

Long-run proof is illustrated in Figure 7-9. It consists in:

(1) Posting the total of amounts to be posted to subsidiary accounts from the pre-list tape to the Control account and bringing up a new balance in the Control account ($10,218).

(2) After the media have been posted to the subsidiary accounts, taking a trial balance of the entire subsidiary ledger and comparing the sum balance of that trial balance ($10,218) with the balance of the Control account.

Old and New Balance Proof

This proof, like the previous one, is performed after posting of the batch of media has been completed. It requires a proof tape prepared after completing posting the batch, as well as a pre-list tape prepared before posting the batch. The proof tape is taken by listing the old balances and the new balances of only the accounts which have been posted, adding the new balances and subtracting the old balances (see Figure 7-10). The net balance of the proof tape should agree with the total on the pre-list tape.

When this proof is to be used, the operator must be careful during the posting operation to set aside all the accounts which are posted during the run, so that they will all be at hand when the proof tape is to be run. This is sometimes done by (a) taking the accounts out of the ledger and keeping them together until the proof tape is run, then returning them to the ledger, or (b) "offsetting" each account in the ledger after it has been posted. This means simply setting the account out in the binder so that the edge protrudes a little beyond the rest of the accounts in the binder. Sometimes special binders are used to accommodate offsetting. The backs of such binders are wider than the conventional ones to provide for the offsetting space.

The old and new balance proof should not be used if more than one-half of the accounts in the ledger are active during a typical posting run. In that case less time would be required to prepare a long-run proof tape (a list of all balances in the ledger) than to prepare an old and new balance proof tape because the latter tape would require both the old balance and new balance for each account posted.

What Do the Proofs Prove?

Different kinds of machine proofs are designed to prove different factors of the work. For this reason, it is necessary for the systems man to know just what the different methods of proof really do prove.

The Accounts Before Posting:

Account	Balance
Jones	$4,236
White	1,635
Williams	800

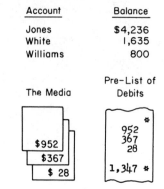

The Media

Pre-List of Debits

The Accounts After Posting:

Account	Old Balance	Charge	New Balance
Jones	$4,236	$952	$5,188
White	1,635	367	2,002
Williams	800	28	828

Proof:

(Proof Tape)
List of Old and New Balances

Pre-List of Charges

```
  -  4,236
  +  5,188
  -  1,635
  +  2,002
  -    800
  +    828
     1,347  *
```

```
     952
     367
      28
   1,347  *
```

agrees

Figure 7-10. Old and New Balance Proof

The long-run proof and the old and new balance proof are each designed to prove:

(1) That the debits (or the credits) have been posted in correct amounts from the media to the accounts.

(2) That the old balances have been picked up correctly and posted to the accounts.

In other words, if the operator has made an error in posting an amount to an account or in picking up an old balance and posting it to an account, either of these proofs will disclose the fact. The total of the proof tape (old and new balance proof), for instance, will not agree with the total of the pre-list tape. These proofs will not, however, disclose the fact of posting to the wrong account. If the operator inadvertently posts an amount to R. F. Jones's account instead of to R. B. Jones's account, this error will not prevent the proof tape from agreeing in total with the pre-list tape.

Localizing the Error to the Account

Direct proof was developed (a) to disclose the existence of an error in the same way as the previous proofs (such existence being indicated by lack of agreement between totals) and (b) to make it possible to find the error without having to look through the accounts which were posted. (Under the previous proofs, if an error is made, it is necessary to look through the posted accounts to find it.)

Direct proof requires the use of a listing–adding machine equipped with a split platen (the platen is the cylinder in the carriage on which the account is placed). The account is inserted at the left side of the platen and a tape at the right side. Since a split platen is really two platens (one an extension of the other), the account moves on one of the two platens and the tape on the other. Thus, it is possible to insert and remove successive accounts without disturbing the tape at the other side of the carriage.

The essential mechanical feature of direct proof is that during the posting operation, certain information posted to each account is also carried to the tape. To find an error after the batch has been posted, the operator compares the media one by one with the tape and not with the accounts. It is obviously faster to compare the media with the items on the tape than it is to locate each account in the ledger and compare the medium with the posting to the account.

Posting Accounts on a Single-Register Machine: Direct Proof

The operations of posting with direct proof are similar to the operations described previously, except that two steps are added to the posting cycle:

(1) Read the old balance of the account ($800.00) (same as in previous illustrations).

(2) Insert the account in the machine and post the old balance to the Old Balance column (same).

(3) Tabulate to the Description column, date and print the number of the invoice (2111) (same).

(4) Tabulate to the Debit column and post the debit ($28.00). The register now contains $828.00 (same).

(5) Tabulate to the New Balance column and strike the subtotal key (not the total key). The amount of $828.00 is printed in the New Balance column, but it is not cleared from the register. (This step is different from the final step under the previous illustrations.)

Account						Tape	
Old Balance	Date	Description	Debits	Credits	New Balance		
800.00	Jan. 3 Jan. 4	2111	800.00 28.00		800.00 S 828.00 S	4,236.00- 952.00* 1,635.00- 367.00* 800.00- 28.00*	

Register action	Add (1)		Non-add (2)	Add (3)		Sub-total (4)	Subtract (5)	Total (6)

Figure 7-11. Posting Cycle: Direct Proof

Illustrated in Figure 7-11 are the two additional steps which distinguish direct proof from the previous methods:

(6) Tabulate to the first position on the tape and post the amount of the old balance, striking the *minus* motor bar. With this step, the old balance is deducted from the register and printed on the tape ($800.00—). The balance in the register is now $28.00.

(7) Tabulate to the second position on the tape and strike the *total* key and the *plus* motor bar. This will print the $28.00 and clear the register to zero.

The complete posting cycle for posting debits is diagrammed in Figure 7-11.

Note that the tape at the right shows the amount of the old balance pickup negative. This step is called the "second pickup of the old balance." It also shows the amount that was cleared onto the tape ($28.00). The previous amounts on the tape represent the proof of previous postings from the present batch of invoices.

Note that if the operator had posted the debit incorrectly (say, $38.00 instead of $28.00), the amount cleared onto the tape in the last step above would not agree with the amount of the invoice posted. In this case, it would be $38.00 instead of the correct $28.00.

Also, if the operator had picked up the old balance incorrectly (say, $900.00 instead of the correct $800.00), the amount cleared onto the tape would not agree with the amount of the invoice. Since the amount of the old balance pickup was $100 too large, the amount cleared onto the tape would likewise be $100 too large.

There is one type of error which direct proof will not disclose. If the operator makes an error (say $900) in posting the old balance to the account and makes the same error ($900) in posting the second pickup of old balance to the proof tape, this error will not be shown by the amounts cleared on the proof tape. The amount cleared onto the proof tape ($28.00) would be the correct amount even though the old balance was posted incorrectly.

Direct Proof Diagrammed

Figure 7-12 summarizes the previous two sections by diagramming the whole procedure of posting a batch of invoices by direct proof method, from the time the pre-list tape is taken until the accounts are posted and the proof tape taken out of the machine.

Figure 7-12.   Direct Proof

The Accounts Before Posting:

Account	Balance
Jones	$4,236
White	1,635
Williams	800

The Media   Pre-List of Debits

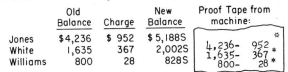

The Accounts After Posting:

	Old Balance	Charge	New Balance	Proof Tape from machine:
Jones	$4,236	$ 952	$ 5,188S	
White	1,635	367	2,002S	
Williams	800	28	828S	

Proof:

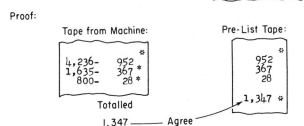

Note that after the proof tape is taken from the machine at the end of the posting operation, it must be added by a separate operation. This total of the proof tape should agree with the total of the pre-list tape. To look for an error, the pre-list tape would have to be compared item for item with the proof tape.

Account Posting and Proof with a Two-Register Machine

A disadvantage of direct proof on a single-register machine (as illustrated in the previous section) is that, after the proof tape is taken out of the machine at the end of the posting run, it has to be added by a separate operation. To avoid this extra operation, a listing–adding machine equipped with two registers may be used. The machine may be mechanically the same in almost all respects as the one illustrated previously except for the extra register in the machine. Moreover, the operator proceeds in exactly the same way as with a one-register machine.

Figure 7-13 diagrams the posting cycle of account posting and proof with a two-register machine. The first register is used in the same way as the one in a single-register machine. The second register automatically accumulates the amounts printed on the right-hand column of the tape, and at the end of the posting run, this register contains the total of those amounts. This total ($1,347.00 in this case) should agree with the total of the pre-list tape. Thus, the use of a second register saves a separate totaling operation at the end of the posting run.

Automatic Control of Registers in a Two-Register Machine

Control of a register refers to causing it to add, subtract, subtotal, total, and so forth. In the previous illustrations relating to single-register machines, the register is controlled by function keys (subtotal, total, and so forth) and motor bars (plus and minus). In these machines the operator actually controls the register each step of the way. Some machines, and particularly multiple-register machines, are equipped with automatic control of registers as well as with function keys and motor bars. Under automatic control, the operation of the register may be controlled by the position of the carriage. Thus, when the carriage is in position for printing in the first (old balance) column, register #1 will automatically add whatever amount is recorded on the keyboard. It also automatically adds when the carriage is in position to print in the debit column of the account form. When the carriage is in the new balance position, register #1 will subtotal, and when it is in the fifth position (tape), the register will subtract whatever amount is recorded on the keyboard.

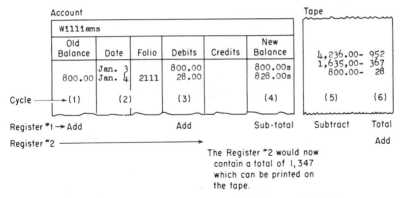

Figure 7-13. Posting: Direct Proof (Two-Register Machine)

Note that register #2 is not engaged (that is, does nothing at all) until the carriage is in position to record in the last column on the tape.

Automatic control makes it unnecessary for the operator consciously to do one or more control operations at each step of posting an account.

When Is a Register Called a Cross-Footer?

The term "cross-footer" is often applied to that register which is used for adding (or subtracting) an account horizontally (old balance plus debit equals new balance). An obviously descriptive term, it is used in connection with multiple-register machines to distinguish the register used to add horizontally from the other register(s) used for other functions in the machine.

In the single-register machine applications illustrated previously, the register was really being used as a cross-footer and might be designated as one. The real need for identifying a register as a cross-footer arises, however, when there are several registers in a machine.

Front-Feed Carriage: Automatic Line-Finding and Ejection

To aid in putting accounts in a listing–adding machine, the front-feed carriage was developed. Figure 7-14 is a bookkeeping machine with a front-feed carriage equipped to provide for ledger form and statement form side by side. (Both forms are original postings; the statement form is an automatic repeat print of the ledger posting.) Basically the operation is: (1) open the feed, (2) insert form(s) to be posted, and (3) close the feed. When the feed is open, the account form moves freely; when it

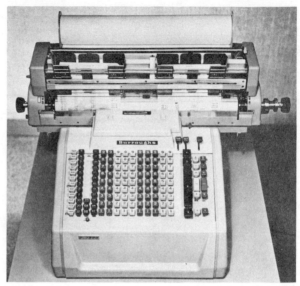

Burroughs

Figure 7-14. Front-Feed Carriage

is closed, the form is held securely for posting. Note that as the operator inserts the account, the front of the account is facing her and is right side up so that she can see the line with which to align the account in the machine.

Some models of bookkeeping machines are equipped with automatic alignment: When an account form is inserted in the feed, the machine automatically finds the line on the account to which the new item is to be posted. The line-finding feature is built in either of two ways. In one construction, the account form is perforated minutely at the edge as a posting is made and when the account form is inserted for a new posting, a device senses the last perforation and positions the account accordingly. The other method involves magnetic strips on the back of the account form. This method is described on page 153. Under either method, automatic ejection is a related feature. When the posting of an item is completed, the carriage returns to the new posting position, the feed opens automatically, and the account form is ejected by rotation of the platen.

Proof Sheet

Another feature of the front-feed carriage in Figure 7-14 is the use of a proof sheet instead of the proof tape described previously. Whereas the proof tape was intended mainly to provide a record of amounts posted to aid in proof, the proof sheet is intended to provide a carbon copy of all entries during the posting run. Old balances, dates, folio numbers, new balances—everything appears on the proof sheet. The proof sheet may be simply a large sheet of paper from a roll which is as wide as the platen of the machine. A length of this paper is put on the platen and covered with a sheet of carbon paper fastened securely over the proof sheet. Proof sheet and carbon paper remain on the platen through the posting run, and therefore the proof sheet is imprinted with a record of everything that was posted to the accounts during the run.

The Accounts After Posting   Proof Sheet Removed from Machine
at End of Posting Batch:

Jones			
O.B	Dr.	Cr.	N.B.
4,236	4,236 952		4,236s 5,188s

White			
O.B.	Dr.	Cr.	N.B.
1,635	1,635 367		1,635s 2,002s

Williams			
O.B.	Dr.	Cr.	N.B.
800	800 28		800s 828s

(O.B.)	(Dr.)(Cr.)	(N.B.)	(Second Pick up of O.B Minus)	
4,236	952	5,188s	4,236–	952
1,635	367	2,002s	1,635–	367
800	28	828s	800–	28
				1,347 *
(1)	(2)	(3)	(4)	(5)

Figure 7-15. Direct Proof, Using Proof Sheet

Figure 7-15 shows a proof sheet, used in an accounts receivable application, as it appears after three debits have been posted to as many accounts. One reason for using a proof sheet instead of a proof tape is that it may be easier to find errors in posting (old balances, say). Also, proof sheets are sometimes used to take the place of pen-kept journals.

Note that the machine on which the proof sheet was prepared was a two-register machine, set up for direct proof. The steps of the posting cycle are the same as in the previous diagram relating to direct proof (Figure 7-13).

Machine-Posted Columnar Journals; Line Proof

Machine-posted columnar journals may be classified as:

(1) Journals prepared in conjunction with a posting operation.
(2) Journals prepared by a separate posting operation.

Figure 7-16 is a general diagram of the operation of posting customers' accounts and distributing sales to the columns on the proof sheet. It is

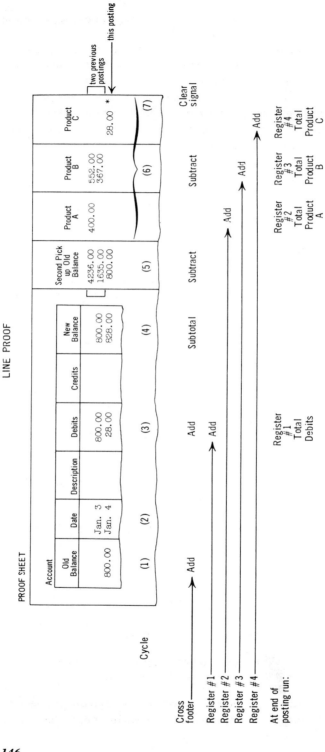

Figure 7-16. Posting Accounts Receivable and Distributing Sales: Columnar Distribution (Posting Cycle Diagrammed)
Machine equipped with crossfooter and four registers.

146

based upon the use of a machine equipped with one cross-footer and four registers. The columnar journal is the proof sheet which remains on the platen of the machine through the posting run. The left side of the journal is covered with carbon paper, so that the journal receives a carbon copy of all postings to the accounts.

The posting cycle illustrated in Figure 7-16 is:

(1) Put the customer's account on the platen and type the old balance ($800.00).

(2) Print the date (Jan. 4).

(3) Post the debit ($28.00).

(4) Tabulate to the new balance position and print the amount in the cross-footer ($828.00). This is a subtotal and the amount is not cleared from the cross-footer.

(5) Make the second pickup of the old balance, negative ($800.00). This leaves the amount of the invoice ($28.00) in the cross-footer.

(6) Since this is a single-item invoice, tabulate to the column for the product class. Post the amount of the item in Product C column. The postings to the distribution columns are negative, subtracting from the cross-footer. If the operations have been correct, the cross-footer will be clear (zero).

(7) Print the clear signal (*) by pressing a *clear-signal* key. The key will not yield if there is any amount in the cross-footer. If the register is not cleared, an error has been made in the posting or the distribution operation.

The proof illustrated in Figure 7-16 is known as a line proof, indicating that each line of the posting and distribution is proved out separately. Figure 7-17 is a diagram of all steps of the posting operation, showing (a) how each line is proved out, and (b) the proofs operated at the end of the posting run. Note that the totals of the distribution columns equal the total debits posted, and the total debits equal the total of the pre-list tape.

As indicated above, machine-posted journals can also be produced by separate operation (that is, not in conjunction with the accounts receivable posting operation). No illustration of this operation is given because of the general similarity to the one described above.

Package Proof

The package proof is designed for use where several old balances are to be picked up on one account; its purpose is to prove that the old balances were picked up correctly. In a payroll application, for instance, in posting employees' earnings records the old balance pickups may be gross

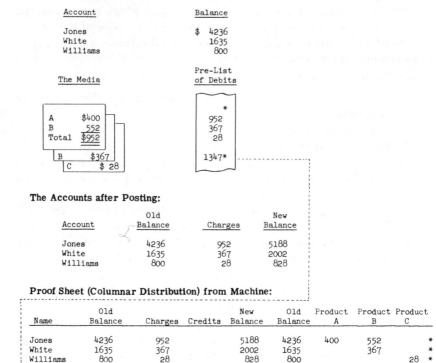

The Accounts before Posting:

Account	Balance
Jones	$ 4236
White	1635
Williams	800

The Media

Pre-List of Debits

A	$400
B	552
Total	$952

B	$367
C	$ 28

```
        *
      952
      367
       28

    1347*
```

The Accounts after Posting:

Account	Old Balance	Charges	New Balance
Jones	4236	952	5188
White	1635	367	2002
Williams	800	28	828

Proof Sheet (Columnar Distribution) from Machine:

Name	Old Balance	Charges	Credits	New Balance	Old Balance	Product A	Product B	Product C
Jones	4236	952		5188	4236	400	552	*
White	1635	367		2002	1635		367	*
Williams	800	28		828	800			28 *
		1347	agree			400	919	28
					agree			

Figure 7-17. Line Proof

earnings to date and payroll taxes deducted to date. Operation of the package proof for these pickups is illustrated in Chapter 17.

Multiple-Register Bookkeeping Machine: Right-Angle Printer

Figure 7-18 is a numeric bookkeeping machine described as a right-angle printer. The machine is equipped with a flat platen, and the forms are inserted for printing in a line at right angles to the keyboard. The machine illustrated is a hotel front-office machine used for posting guests' accounts.

Figure 7-19a is an illustration of a National Class 42 window machine which is a later model than the Class 2000 shown in Figure 7-18. The Class 42 window machine (Figure 7-19b shows keyboard) has 10 or 20 totals and can print a limited number of fixed words (i.e., not typed). It

Figure 7-18. Numeric Keyboard Multiple-Register Bookkeeping Machine (Class 2000 Right-Angle Printer)

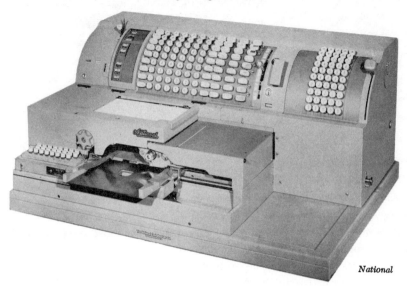

National

is used primarily for window posting and it is custom built for the customer functions. The Class 42, like the Class 2000, features mechanically enforced cash controls required for a cashier operation. The Class 42 can print up to four forms at one time. Examples of applications are accounts receivable for hotels and motels, installment loan accounts, savings and loan association accounts, and the accounts with customers of automobile

Figure 7-19a. Window Machine (Class 42)

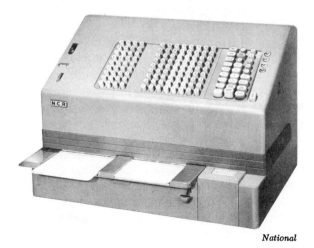

National

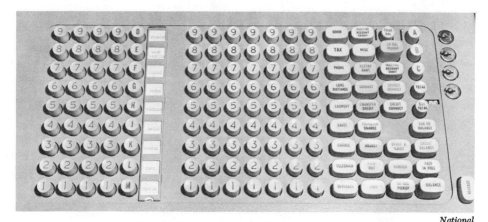

National

Figure 7-19b.   Keyboard: Window Machine (Class 42)

dealers and furniture dealers. Class 42 machines are also used by savings and loan associations, on-line with a computer in a service bureau.

The Class 42 can also be equipped to produce a tape that can be read by an optical scanner. Some of the applications of the machine so equipped are accounts receivable, inventory control, and sales analysis (for a more extensive analysis than can be accommodated by the registers in the machine). Tapes are taken to a service bureau which reads them and processes reports on computers, or they are used as input for an in-house computer.

Alpha-Numeric Bookkeeping Machines

In some cases, it is desired to type descriptive information as a part of the posting procedure. In department store accounts receivable procedures, for instance, a description of the item may be typed on an account or statement form at the time the amount of a charge is posted. For this purpose, an alpha-numeric bookkeeping machine may be used. The National Cash Register Company and the Burroughs Corporation manufacture machines that are equipped to type as well as to post accounts. The National 36 is illustrated in Figure 7-20 and the Burroughs F9000 typewriter bookkeeping machine in Figure 7-21.

The National Class 36 (Figure 7-20) is an alpha-numeric machine equipped with a 26″ front-feed carriage which can handle multiple forms, and with registers for accumulating 6 to 21 totals. The machine is of modular construction permitting various features (registers and other features) to be changed after the initial purchase and installation of the machine. The posting operation is controlled by a program bar. For dis-

National

Figure 7-20.   Alpha-Numeric Bookkeeping Machine
(Class 36)

Burroughs

Figure 7-21.   Alpha-Numeric Bookkeeping Machine (F9000)

tribution, the machine is equipped for key selection. Thus, if the form in the machine comprises six columns, register selection for accumulation of totals in those positions is automatic. Amounts can be put in some other register by the operator, using register selection keys.

Either the National Class 36 or the Burroughs F9000 can be coupled to a key punch to punch tabulating cards as a by-product of the main operation of the machine. Or either can be coupled to a tape perforator similarly to perforate a tape. Figure 7-21 illustrates a tape perforator coupled to the Burroughs F9000. In either case the punch or perforator operation is programmed to pick up the desired classifications of information. Punched cards or perforated tape can then be used as input for a computer operation. When the machines are thus equipped, their range of application can include the preparation of shipping orders and invoices, the preparation of payrolls, pay checks, and earnings statements, and other applications, as well as the "account posting" operations illustrated in the previous pages of this chapter. The Class 36 is not equipped for punched-card or perforated-tape input.

Bookkeeping Machines with Computing Features

The National Class 400 (Figure 7-22) is an electronic (transistorizer) alpha-numeric machine equipped with 26″ carriage with a continuous

Figure 7-22. Electronic Accounting Machine (Class 400)

National

forms handling device and magnetic disk memory which can accumulate 20 to 200 totals (in steps of 20, according to the specified requirements of the customer). It can perform the mathematical operations required for business applications. The Class 400 can accommodate either conventional ledger accounts or magnetic ledger accounts. The magnetic ledger accounts are imprinted on the back with magnetic strips which can store 6, 12, or 20 words of 13 digits each, again as ordered by the customer. Use of customers' accounts with magnetic strip storage is described in the following section of this chapter, and use of the employee's quarterly earnings statement with magnetic strip storage is described in Chapter 17.

The National Class 400 is programmed by tapes which are read by a photoelectric reader. A separate tape is provided for each application.

Methods of input for the Class 400 are (1) keyboard (typewriter, numeric), (2) magnetic tape, (3) punched cards, and (4) programmed tape. Methods of output are (1) printed forms, (2) punched cards, (3) punched paper tape, and (4) magnetic ledger cards.

Magnetic Ledger; Automatic Line Finding

A magnetic ledger form for a stock accounting record is illustrated in Figure 7-23 (front). This form is used with a National Class 400 machine. The distinguishing feature of the statement form is the magnetic strips on the back. The strips store, among other details, account number and account balance. Assuming that the *posting media* show account number, the posting operation will include a proof of account number, i.e., a proof of posting to the right account. (The NCR 400 will store only numeric information, but the NCR 500 can be programmed to store alphabetic characters as well.) The posting operation for the familiar customers account (or depositors account in a bank) would be as follows:

(1) The operator indexes the account number on the keyboard of the machine, reading it from the posting ticket.
(2) The operator selects the account in the tray, identifying it by name and address (not by number).
(3) The operator inserts the account in the machine. The line finder will automatically position it for posting to the next line. If the account number on the strip and the account number indexed on the keyboard are the same, the machine will accept the account. (The operator has read and indexed correctly the account number for Customer Brown and she has pulled Customer Brown's account and inserted it in the machine.) If the numbers do not agree, the machine will reject the statement.

National

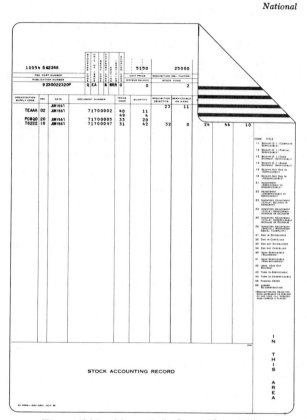

Figure 7-23.   Magnetic Ledger (Class 400)

(4) The machine will electronically pick up the old balance, reading from the magnetic strip.

(5) The operator indexes the amount to be posted on the keyboard of the machine, reading from the posting ticket, and depresses the new balance key. The machine prints the amount posted and the new balance on the front of the statement, at the same time registering the new balance in the strip on the back. While the machine is cycling, the operator looks up the next ticket to be posted and indexes the account number on the keyboard.

Automatic Ledger Reader: Preparing Trial Balance

An Automatic Ledger Reader can be used to prepare a trial balance automatically from magnetic strip ledger forms posted as described and illustrated above. Figure 7-24 illustrates the National Ledger Reader, and

National

Figure 7-24. Automatic Ledger Reader

Figure 7-25 is the Burroughs Automatic Ledger Reader. In a trial balance operation, the ledger forms are fed into the reader which reads the account number and new balance from the strips on each form, listing them to produce the trial balance.

The reader also accumulates the total and prints it on the trial balance at the end of the run.

Which Bookkeeping Machine Proof Shall Be Used?

It is not possible or even desirable to present in this book the details of all proof methods in use in bookkeeping machines. The subject of bookkeeping machines has been outlined in the previous sections, however, to impress upon the reader that:

(1) At least an elementary knowledge of proofs is necessary in order to understand how a bookkeeping machine operates and how it can be used to post accounts.

(2) Some knowledge of machine proofs is necessary to appreciate internal check in a machine system.

(3) The specific proof used in connection with (or built into) a bookkeeping machine affects the clerical economy of the posting job. Thus, the proof method may affect:

(a) The amount of time necessary to prepare the media for posting. This point involves the preparation of pre-list tapes and the like.

Burroughs

Figure 7-25. Automatic Ledger Reader (Series A4000)

(b) The speed of the posting operation itself. Posting operations that require a second pickup of the old balance each time an account is posted are slower than those that do not require such a pickup, other things being equal.

(c) Time required to perform the proof at the end of the posting run. Old and new balance proof may require a great deal of time; direct proof on a two-register machine, very little time.

(d) Time required to locate errors after the proof discloses the existence of an error.

(e) The cost of the machine itself.

Of course, the proof method is only one factor in the clerical economy of a machine-posting operation. Usually, the systems man will ask the accounting machine company for recommendations as to proof-method because the proof is, in a real sense, a feature of the machine. The systems man will then decide whether the machine and its recommended proof will do the job he has in mind.

The Common-Language Concept

Common-language machines are accounting and office machines compatible to a single, basic plan of receiving, processing, and transmitting data. The fundamental principle is that data should be captured in the original writing in such form as will permit automatic re-use as required. Application of the principle involves the use of one code or an integrated set of codes by which one machine can communicate with another machine, transmitting instructions to control the machine (function codes) and information (information codes). Through the use of this principle, successive manual recording of identical information is avoided.

To quote H. F. Van Gorder of United States Steel Corporation, a pioneer in the development and application of the common-language principle:

> To distinguish this solution from the conventional approach, let us emphasize three points of difference:
>
> (1) *Original* data are recorded *at their point of origin* in a mechanical form.
> (2) Once in mechanical form, data are processed exclusively in a mechanical manner.
> (3) All processing of data is integrated so that original data in mechanical form serve all subsequent applications.[1]

Theoretically, all the basic information in a business could be reduced to a single set of codes from which orders could be issued and advices transmitted, asset or liability accounts operated, and distributions made for report purposes. The end result would be a complete system of integrated data-processing. In practice, the plan may be implemented in stages with, say, the sales and cash-collecting function being integrated first, the purchase and payment function second, the payroll and labor distribution function third, and the inventory and cost function fourth. This approach to integration would be followed as a matter of convenience and not because the four functions operate entirely independently of each other. Several of the same codes (for instance, the product code) would be used in several of the functional systems.

The use of eight-channel tape as a means of capturing data in the original writing was explained in Chapter 6 in connection with automatic writing and reproducing machines. A possible extension of the common-language concept appears in this chapter in connection with account posting. Figure 7-26 is a bookkeeping machine coupled with a tape perforator and Figure 7-27 is a bookkeeping machine coupled with a card punch. These illustrations represent an application of the common-language concept. (The products of two manufacturers are illustrated. Either manufacturer can supply either configuration.)

Checklist

Some of the points that should be considered when selecting a bookkeeping machine are listed in Chapter 17. The points in the list refer particularly to bookkeeping machines for payroll applications, but many

---

[1] H. F. Van Gorder, "Integrated Data Processing: The Fundamentals" (American Management Association, 1954), page 9.

Burroughs

Figure 7-26. Bookkeeping Machine Coupled with Tape Perforator

of them are significant when considered in connection with other applications.

HANDLING POSTING MEDIA IN A MACHINE-POSTING APPLICATION

How Machine Posting Differs from Pen-and-Ink Posting

In laying out a procedure for posting accounts by machine, the systems man must keep in mind the particulars in which machine posting differs from pen-and-ink posting. In the first place, the volume of work which is a condition precedent to machine posting usually means that machine posting is a specialized job. The operator posts one kind (or just a few kinds) of media for relatively long periods of time. Media (such as sales invoices) come to her in batches, and she may post complete batches at one sitting. Media may move from one operator to another under batch control, which may mean that they are accompanied by a pre-list tape to which the operators prove.

In the second place, the media are likely to be posted directly to the accounts, contrary to the common pen-kept procedure in which they may be entered in the journal first and then posted to the accounts.

National

Figure 7-27. Bookkeeping Machine Coupled with Card Punch

In the third place, the journal, as found in pen-kept bookkeeping, may be dispensed with and the file of posting media (invoices, say) may be used as the chronological record of transactions. Sometimes, however, a proof sheet prepared as a by-product of posting the accounts is used as a formal journal. If a typewriter bookkeeping machine is required for the account posting, names can also be typed on the proof sheet.

And finally, the machine is used to perform the mathematical operations of posting and balancing, and the proof sheet or proof tape is used to locate errors.

Flow of Posting Media to the Machine; Handling Media at the Machine

Since the quantity of posting media involved in a machine-posting job is often large, it will usually pay the systems man to study the flow of media to the machine and the method of handling the media in the posting operation. Just as flow of work is important in a factory, so may it be important in a machine-posting operation. Some of the factors to consider are:

(1) the form of the papers from which the posting is to be done (the posting media).

    (2) the arrangement of the posted media when received for posting (whether sorted or not).

    (3) how the media shall be sorted or otherwise prepared for posting to the accounts.

    (4) the form of the account

    (5) the form of proof sheet or proof tape   considered in previous

    (6) the posting operation   sections.

    (7) proofs of posting

Two illustrations of account posting procedure will indicate the nature of the problem of handling posting media: (1) posting sales tickets to customers' accounts, and (2) posting incoming invoices for expense purchases to the expense accounts.

Posting Sales Tickets to Customers' Accounts

The procedure for posting sales tickets to customers' accounts in a certain retail store is as follows:

    (1) As charge sales are made to customers, sales tickets are written out by the sales persons. A carbon copy is given to the customer and the original to the bookkeeping department (by way of the clerk who looks up the customer's credit). The tickets are received by the bookeeping-machine operator in unsorted batches.

    (2) The operator sorts the tickets alphabetically and prepares a listing–adding machine tape to determine the total of the batch to be posted. Sorting the tickets alphabetically helps the operator to locate the accounts in the ledger during the posting operation, because it enables her to proceed directly through the ledger.

    (3) The operator posts the tickets direct to the customers' accounts on a four-register typewriter bookkeeping machine, and produces a proof sheet at the same time.

Where there are several tickets (say three tickets) to be charged to the same account, the posting procedure is:

    (a) Pull the account from the ledger and insert it in the machine.

    (b) Post the old balance in the Old Balance column.

    (c) Post first ticket, second ticket, third ticket, keeping the carriage in the debit position all the time.

    (d) Tabulate to the new balance position and print the new balance.

    (e) Remove the account from the machine and put it back in the tray.

    (4) At the end of the posting run, the operator foots the columns on the proof sheet and proves the totals against the pre-list total.

The proof sheet is used as a sales journal. At the end of the month, the sales journal is totaled and the total of charge sales for the month is posted to the General ledger by the entry:

Accounts Receivable	$xx.xx	
Sales		$xx.xx
To record the total of charge		
sales for the month		

Stuffing the Ledger

As a variation of the above procedure, sometimes the operator (or an assistant) sorts the posting media alphabetically and "stuffs the ledger" (as a preliminary step to posting). "Stuffing" means simply placing each ticket in front of the account to be posted. Part of each ticket is allowed to protrude slightly so that as the machine operator goes through the ledger, posting the accounts, she can immediately locate the next account to be posted.

Stuffing is sometimes done by a subordinate clerk in order to save the machine operator's time. It may also be done as a precaution against posting to the wrong account, the theory being that if the stuffer locates the account and then the machine operator verifies the location before proceeding to post the account, there is little likelihood that the ticket will be posted to the wrong account.

Posting Expense Invoices to Expense Accounts

For the purpose of this illustration, assume that incoming invoices for expense purchases are posted by machine to accounts in the Expense ledger.

The flow of expense invoices is as follows:

(1) The accounts payable clerk verifies each invoice as it comes in and indicates on the face of each invoice, the expense account(s) to be charged:

Expense Account No.	Amount
183	$34.65
214	16.22
235	13.45
Total Invoice	$64.32

(2) The machine operator records the invoices in the Accounts Payable ledger, preparing a proof sheet or proof tape. (This step is similar to the posting of sales invoices to customers' accounts.)

(3) The operator records the invoices in the Expense ledger, debiting the various accounts affected by invoices. In this case, the posting operation is more complicated than posting to customers' accounts because, in many cases, a single ticket has to be posted to several expense accounts. The methods that might be used are explained in the following sections.

Mixed Media; Random Posting

An invoice that comprises more than one debit (such as the expense invoices now considered) is known as a "split invoice" or a "mixed invoice." One process of posting mixed media is known as "random posting." Under random posting, the media are not stuffed in the ledger but are simply placed on the posting table beside the operator. The operator takes the first invoice from the pile and proceeds to post each debit on the invoice, just as they come:

Expense Account No.	Amount
183	$34.65
214	16.22
235	13.45
Total Invoice	$64.32

A good deal of work is involved in posting this invoice to the Expense ledger by random posting. The operator reaches for account #183, reads the old balance, posts the old balance, posts the debit ($34.65), prints the new balance, and then returns the account to the ledger. Then she repeats the operation for account #214 and again for account #235. In random posting, an account has to be pulled and posted for each item on a medium. Pulling accounts and picking up old balances are the factors that take time under this method.

Exhaust Method

Another basic method of handling mixed media is known as the "exhaust method." Under this method, any specific account is placed in the machine only once during the posting of the entire batch of media. Thus, when account #183 is in the machine, the operator will post every debit to that account which appears on any medium in the batch. This method, of course, may require that each invoice having more than one distributable item be handled by the operator a number of times. There are two different ways of handling the media under the exhaust method:

(1) *Exhaust method combined with a stuffing operation.* Stuffing is, of course, the preliminary operation and exhausting, the main operation. Before posting, the media are stuffed in the ledger, according to the lowest account number indicated on each medium. (The invoice indicated in the previous section would first be stuffed in account #183.) Then the operator posts the first item on the first medium stuffed in the ledger ($34.65 to #183). After she posts an item, she stuffs the medium in front of the next account to be posted from that medium (A/c #214 in this case). She checks each item as she posts it, and when all the debits on an invoice have been posted, the invoice is taken out of the ledger and put in the completed file.

(2) *Exhaust method without benefit of stuffing.* The operator places the invoices on the table beside her machine. She leafs through the media a number of times, picking out debits to one particular account as she goes through. As in the previous method, the operator checks off each debit as she posts it and puts each completely posted invoice in the completed file.

In the second case, care must be taken in deciding the order in which to exhaust the items on the media. Obviously, it is desirable to exhaust the most frequent debit during the first run through the media, then the second most frequent debit, and so on. (Thus, if charges to Expense Account #214 appear on the media more often than charges to any other account, the charges to #214 should be posted in the first run through the media.) If this is done, most of the media will be completely exhausted in the early runs and will not have to be handled many times. To determine the relative activity of the accounts in batches of media, it is necessary to make test tallies of representative batches, counting the number of times each account appears.

Summary: Unit Media; Mixed Media; Methods of Posting

The following principles with reference to the form of posting media and the methods of handling have been explained in the previous sections:

(1) Unit media are media that comprise a single debit per medium to one account. The best example of unit media is sales tickets in a retail store, each of which comprises a debit to one customer's account.

(2) Unit media may be sorted according to the account classification (alphabetically, in the case illustrated) to facilitate posting to the

accounts. When this is done, all the debits to the same account can be posted at one time.

(3) Mixed media are media that comprise an average of more than one debit (or credit) per medium. Some media in a typical batch will comprise, say, three or four debits.

(4) Mixed media may be handled by either of two methods:

   (a) *Random posting,* which involves posting each medium in a batch just as it comes, going straight through the batch a single time. Under this method, there tends to be a minimum of handling the media and a maximum of handling the accounts—locating them, putting them in the machine, posting them, and returning them to the ledger.

   (b) *Exhaust method,* which involves putting each active account in the machine only once and posting to that account every debit which appears in the batch of media. This method tends to require a minimum of account handling and a maximum of media handling.

It should be obvious that the flow of media to the bookkeeping machine and the method of handling the media at the machine must be given careful consideration by the systems man.

8

Files and Records Housing Equipment; Microfilm Systems

Records Management—A Resumé

It should be obvious from the previous chapters that the systems man may be concerned with the design and installation of the forms not only in an accounting system but also in the whole area of records management from the time the forms are initiated and authorized until they are finally filed or destroyed. In the larger sense, records management includes:

(1) Determining whether a proposed form is actually necessary or whether it is to some extent a duplication of an existing form. (This aspect of records management is known as "forms standardization and control," and was described in Chapter 5.)

(2) Designing forms to serve such basic purposes as order forms, advice forms, and so on, and to provide for efficient use in writing, sorting, filing, and other operations. Where forms are to be used on a machine, records management includes laying out the form for the most efficient use of that machine.

(3) Designing forms that can be printed economically. This involves determining the most economical paper and printing for each form in view of:
   (a) Roughness of use
   (b) Whether the form is an inside form or an outside form
   (c) Length of life, and so forth.
   It must also be determined whether the form will be produced by the company's duplicating facilities; whether the form, if sent outside, will be printed by letterpress or offset printing; whether it will be typed and ruled, pen-and-ink ruled, and so forth.

(4) Classifying forms according to printing characteristics (class of printing) and combining orders for forms of the same class. This enables the printer to make the most efficient combination of runs on his presses and other equipment. Thus, if orders for four different forms—8½″ x 11″, one color, printed on one side, on sulphite paper of the same weight—were sent at one time, the printer might combine them into a single *gang layout* 17″ x 22″ and print them in a single press run, cutting them apart after printing. Some large printing buyers actually combine their printing orders into gang layouts for the printer. This practice calls for a knowledge of press sizes and operating costs.

(5) Controlling of purchase quantities and inventories to prevent overstocking forms and at the same time to provide for the most economical combination of orders (as described in 4).

(6) Setting up a forms retention program to control the length of time each form shall be kept (some are kept permanently), when a form shall be microfilmed and destroyed, and when a form shall be destroyed.

(7) Determining which types of sorting and filing equipment to use and the capacities required both in live storage for ready accessibility and in dead storage.

SORTING EQUIPMENT AND DEVICES

The Sorting Operation in the Flow of Accounting Papers

Sorting consists of arranging the papers in a batch or packet according to some classification or code appearing on the papers. A few of the numerous examples of sorting operations in this book are:

(1) Sorting invoices alphabetically by customer's name to facilitate the posting of customers' accounts (Machine posting: Chapter 7).

(2) Sorting unit tickets created from sales invoices by product class number as a preliminary step to determining total sales by product class (Sales distribution: Chapter 12). In some distribution operations (sales distribution, purchase distribution, payroll distribution, and so forth), the media are sorted and re-sorted a number of times (on a number of different classifications) to obtain various reports.

(3) Sorting customers' orders and correspondence alphabetically for filing. (Filing equipment and devices are explained and illustrated later in this chapter.)

In laying out the flow of work for a procedure, the systems man must determine what sorting operations are necessary and what sorting equipment and devices should be used. In some cases, it will be possible to eliminate or simplify a sorting operation in one department by rearranging the operations in previous departments, at a net saving in the whole flow of work.

Sorting Operations Classified According to Equipment Used

Sorting operations may be classified according to the equipment used as follows:

(1) *Table sort.* In this operation, the papers are sorted into piles on the top of the table. To guide the sorting operation, a sheet of paper for each pile may be placed on the table, and on each sheet may be written the classification group (A-C, D-F, and so on). The classification group should be at the edge of the sheet, so that it will not be covered by the papers being sorted.

(2) *Box sort or pigeon hole sort.* The media are sorted into racks or boxes built in tiers and labeled for alphabetical or numerical groups. Such racks may be placed on the top of a table.

(3) *Leaf sort* (Figure 8-1). Hinged leaves are mounted on a circular base which the operator can rotate by hand. Each leaf is labeled with a classification group, visible to the operator. In the sorting

Figure 8-1. Leaf-Sorting Service

Remington Rand

operation, the operator locates the proper leaf, lifts it with her left hand, and places the paper under the leaf with her right hand.

(4) *Needle sort.* An example of needle sort is the Keysort, described on pages 246–252. This method of sorting requires specially designed cards which are punched to make the sorting operation possible.

(5) *Machine sort.* Examples of machine sorting are found in connection with punched-card accounting, using International Business Machines Corporation equipment or Remington Rand equipment. The principles of punched-card accounting are discussed in Chapter 21. That chapter also describes and illustrates the basic units of equipment.

FILES AND OTHER RECORD HOUSING EQUIPMENT

Types of Record Housing Equipment

Since almost all general systems assignments and many procedures assignments involve the use of filing equipment, the systems man must be familiar with the types of record housing equipment available. Table 8-1 is a list of the major types of record housing equipment, with examples of each type. The major types are discussed in the following sections.

(a) Loose leaf binders
(b) Vertical filing cabinets
(c) Visible record equipment (for reference and posting)
(d) Visible index reference equipment (for reference to lists)
(e) Mechanized files
(f) Ledger trays for machine posting
(g) Files for punched paper tape
(h) Binders for filing summary strips
(i) Transfer cases and binders

A discussion of features to be considered in the selection of record housing equipment appears in this chapter.

Loose Leaf Binders (Figures 8-2 and 8-3)

Loose leaf binders are frequently used for pen-kept journals and ledgers. The main distinguishing features in loose leaf binders are the coverings and the mechanical device for holding and releasing the sheets. Covers are canvas, corduroy, imitation leather, or leather. Two devices for holding the sheets are described:

(1) Sectional post (Figure 8-2). In this type of binder, the front cover

Table 8-1

RECORD HOUSING EQUIPMENT CLASSIFIED

(A) Loose leaf binders
    (1) Sectional post (Figure 8-2)
    (2) Nylon post (Figure 8-3)
    (3) Ring and others
(B) Vertical filing cabinets
    (1) Letter file cabinets
    (2) Card cabinets
(C) Visible record equipment (for reference and posting)
    (1) Boards and ticket holders;
        (a) Boards and ticket holders for filing copies of production orders, job tickets, move tickets, etc.
        (b) Cabinets and ticket holders
        (c) Credit file—accounts receivable file for filing sales checks
    (2) Visible index equipment
        (a) Basic units (Remington Rand Kardex illustrated) (Figure 8-4)
        Record card
        Card pocket
        Pocket slide
        Signals
        (b) Housing equipment
        Cabinet
        Floor model units
        Cabinet equipped with automatic electric elevator (Figure 8-5)
    (3) Visible margin equipment (Account form: Figure 8-6; Cabinet: Figure 8-7)
    (4) Binders: loose leaf visible
(D) Visible index reference equipment (for reference to lists)
    (1) Basic unit: frames containing insert strips (one for each name or other reference item) (Figure 8-8)
    (2) Housings
    Desk stands
    Rotaries
        Single tier
        Double tier
    Wall brackets
    and others
(E) Mechanized files (Figure 8-9); Power files (Figure 8-10)
(F) Ledger trays for machine posting
(G) Binders for filing summary strips
    (1) Working binders
    (2) Report binders
(H) Tranfer cases

is fastened to the back cover by means of posts attached vertically to the back. The top cover latches to these posts and may be removed (by means of a fastener) to permit insertion of a quantity of ledger sheets over the posts. Post binders may be expanded by screwing additional post sections to the base post section. When the binder is not filled to the capacity of the posts, the posts may protrude through the top of the binder.

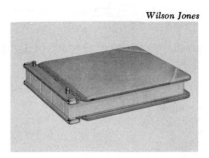

Wilson Jones

Figure 8-2.   Sectional Post Binder

The ledger sheets are punched in this manner:

Edge of sheet

This punching permits the withdrawal of one or several sheets without taking the top off the binder.

(2) Nylon post binders for marginal punched sheets (Figure 8-3). In this class of binder, the flexible nylon posts take the place of the sectional posts described in the previous paragraph. Figure 8-3a is the assembled binder, empty. Flexible posts of any of a variety of lengths may be used. Figure 8-3b illustrates the loading operation and Figure 8-3c the binder loaded and open. All numbers at the binding edge of the form can be read.

(3) The familiar ring binder (not illustrated) also has many uses in an office.

Vertical Filing Cabinets

Two types of filing cabinets are:

(1) Letter file cabinets, which are used for correspondence, office copies of forms, catalogues, and other material filed, say, by customer or creditor name or by subject.

(2) Card cabinets, which are used for checks, job tickets, requisitions, and other tickets or cards in small sizes.

Visible Record Equipment (for Reference and Posting)

This equipment is intended to house written or posted records, being specially designed for speedy location of accounts or names. Some types

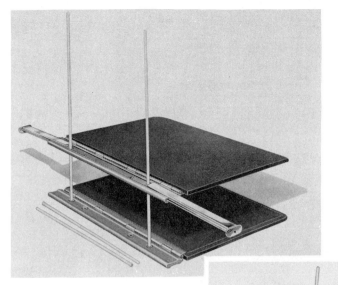

(a) Assembled

(b) Loading

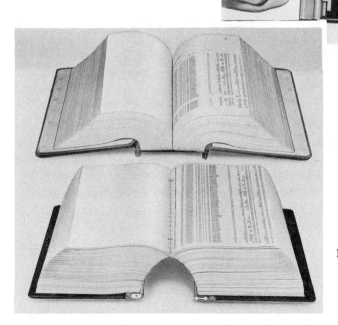

(c) Loaded

Wilson-Jones
Figure 8-3. Nylon Post Binder

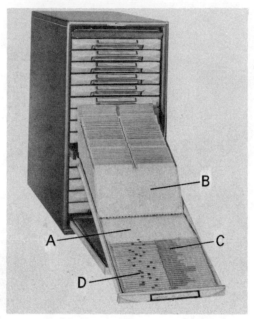

Remington Rand

Figure 8-4. Basic Units of Visible
Index Equipment: (a) Record
Card, (b) Card Pocket, (c) Pocket
Slide, (d) Signal

are also designed for use of signals (Figure 8-4) which facilitate follow-up. The types illustrated are:

(1) Boards and ticket holders which are designed to house copies of production orders, job tickets, move tickets, and so forth (not illustrated). This type of housing provides complete visibility of the last order or ticket filed in a ticket holder, since the spring clip on the holder does not cover any appreciable part of the ticket. Names, items, and running balances (if carried forward from one ticket to the next) are visible.

The same principle is also used in accounts receivable-credit files (not illustrated). Such files serve as both a credit file and Accounts Receivable ledger. They provide a holder for each active customer. Sales slips representing charges to customers' accounts are filed in the appropriate holders.

(2) Visible *index* equipment is designed to house account forms or other summary forms to which postings must be made, and as the name of the equipment indicates, to provide visibility of the index

Figure 8-5.   Elevator File for Visible Index Records

classification (customer name, salesman name, product name, and
so on).

Figure 8-4 illustrates the basic units, in addition to the housing
proper, of the equipment. These units are:

(a) the record card (a stock record card is illustrated),
(b) the card pocket in which the record card fits,
(c) the pocket slide, a tray designed to carry a number of card
pockets in filing position with the index edges exposed, and
(d) the signal.

Note the signal that is placed at the index edge of the card pocket. The purpose of the signal is to identify an account that requires follow-up or action of some kind. Thus in accounts receivable procedures, the signals may identify overdue accounts, and in inventory control procedures, they may identify accounts with low balances.

In some applications, several record cards or inserts may be used in each pocket. One may be used for current posting to an account and the other for summaries of the account. Or in a stock control and purchasing application, one insert may be used for current postings to an inventory account (receipts, issues, and balances) and the other for carrying the information required by the purchasing department to order the goods. The latter card is actually a request for purchase form. When an order point has been reached, it is pulled from the file and sent to the purchasing department.

Three types of housing for visible index equipment are: cabinet (illustrated in Figure 8-4), floor model unit, and elevator model (illustrated in Figure 8-5). This last model is equipped with an automatic electric elevator, which places any tray of cards in position for posting when the appropriate switch is depressed.

(3) Visible margin equipment is housing in which the margins of accounts or other forms are exposed for visibility. Accounts or forms

Figure 8-6. Account Form for Visible Margin

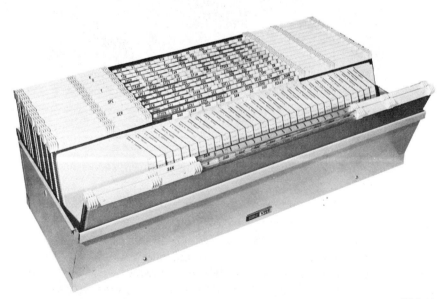

Diebold

may be so designed that the current balance (a running balance) appears in the exposed margin. Figure 8-6 illustrates such account forms in a tray. Special housing units are provided by the manufacturer. See Figure 8-7.

(4) Loose leaf visible binders are those in which the accounts or other forms are filed in tiers so that the index edge of each account is exposed for visibility.

Figure 8-7.   Cabinet for Visible Margin Records

Diebold

Visible Index Reference Equipment (for Reference to Lists)

This type of equipment is considered where frequent looking up of names and related information is required, and particularly where the list of names and related information change frequently. As the name indicates, the equipment is designed to accommodate lists and not current postings to accounts. Customers' lists used by the credit department and materials and parts lists used in planning and production control departments are examples. Either may contain thousands or (in the former case) hundreds of thousands of names.

The basic unit of this type of equipment is a frame comprised of insert strips—one for each name or line item in the list, as illustrated in Figure 8-8. Note that, as the list changes, names can be struck from the list by

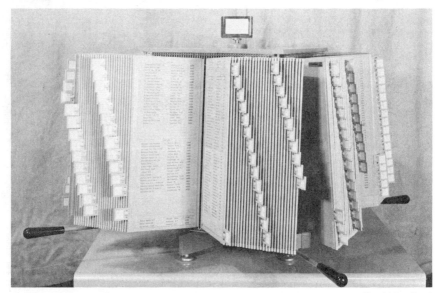

Remington Rand

Figure 8-8. Frames Containing Insert Strips: Visible Reference Equipment

removing the strips, and names can be added by inserting strips on which names and other data have been typed. The strips are purchased in gangs from the manufacturer, to permit continuous typing of the new names.

Where the frames are subjected to rough usage, as they may be in factory departments, tube inserts are recommended. The method of creating and using the inserts is the same as that described above, except that the typist places each insert in a transparent tube before mounting it in the frame.

A number of different housings for visible reference are available. Desk stands, single-tier rotaries, double-tier rotaries, wall brackets, and other types of housing can be obtained.

Mechanized Files; Power Files

In mechanized files (Figure 8-9), horizontal rows of trays are put successively into position in the front of the file for easy access by the operator. The various rows are suspended in a rotating framework which is

Diebold

Figure 8-9. Mechanized File (Series 6600)

similar in principle to a ferris wheel, with the various rows appearing in order in front of the operator who controls the movement by pressing buttons. (The frame work is not a circle; actually the rows of trays move vertically up the front and down the back of the cabinet.) After a button is pressed, the mechanism will move the desired row of trays into work position following the shortest route (forward or reverse). There is also a supervisor button, by which the supervisor can get access to the row he desires. After he relinquishes control, the mechanism—remembering what row of trays the operator was working on—will return that row automatically to working position.

Diebold

Figure 8-10. Power File

Figure 8-10 is a file described by the manufacturer as a power file. It is larger than the one illustrated on Figure 8-9 and it is built to accommodate file folders. It operates electrically in the same way as the previously illustrated one.

Ledger Trays for Machine-Posting Applications

For machine-posting applications, the account forms are frequently kept in trays instead of in the typical binders identified with pen-and-ink bookkeeping. When the tray is placed beside the machine operator, it holds the accounts in nearly upright position so that they can be pulled easily from the tray and returned easily to the tray after being posted.

Trays are also designed to provide for or to facilitate certain operations auxiliary to the machine-posting operation. In some posting operations, for instance, the media in a posting batch are stuffed into the tray before the posting operation is started (each medium being placed in front of the account to which it is to be posted). Likewise in some posting operations, each account posted, when returned to the tray, is placed in an offset position slightly to the right of normal filing position. This may be done to facilitate later action.

Binders for Filing Summary Strips

An illustration of summary strips and a general description of their use appear on pages 263 to 268. In the operation of summary strips, the strips may be assembled on peg strips or peg boards, as indicated in that section, or they may be assembled as they are created in a working binder (not illustrated). In a production summary plan, for instance, where the daily production reports are in the form of summary strips, a tier in the binder can be provided for each department. The daily strips are then filed as they come in, with the quantity columns exposed for visibility. At the end of the week or other period which the binder accommodates, it is necessary only to add the strips across to obtain the totals for the period.

Summary strip report binders are designed in size and appearance to be kept on an executive's desk. Where the operating statements are issued monthly, say in summary strip form, they can be filed in such manner as to provide useful comparisons.

Transfer Cases and Binders

Transfer cases and binders are used to house inactive records. As a class of equipment, they are constructed for storage purposes rather than for frequent reference or posting. No illustrations of this class of housing are presented in this book. Illustrations and descriptive literature may be obtained from manufacturers of filing equipment.

MICROFILM SYSTEMS

Microfilm

Microfilming is a photographic process in which a lens is used to produce copies on a sensitized film, and it may be considered under the headings of both reproducing and filing. It is a method of storing miniature copies of forms.

A set of microfilming equipment includes the microfilmer, which takes the pictures of the original documents, the processor, which develops the pictures and processes them in one of five forms (magazine, roll, jacket, tab card, or microfilm), and the magna print, in which the microfilm may be viewed, enlarged, or converted to hard copy. Particular characteristics of some of the forms of microfilm are described on page 184. Developing can be done by an outside service, if desired. The reels of negatives are filed as such, at a great saving in space over the requirements for filing the papers.

Banks may microfilm checks before they return them to depositors along with bank statements. Department stores using cycle billing microfilm customers' sales checks before they return them with statements to customers. The system is described on pages 299–300. Some companies operate forms-retention programs in which, according to time schedules set for various types of documents, they keep certain documents in their original form, microfilm other documents and destroy the originals, and destroy still other documents without keeping any copies.

Information Retrieval (Diebold SD-550)

The Diebold SD-550 information-retrieval system is a system designed to read information from a data bank when it is stored in microform (microfiche, micro packets, aperture cards) and to transmit it to remote display station(s) in which it is man-readable. The information bank could be stored for fast access in a mechanized file of the type illustrated in Figure 8-11 (background). Figure 8-11 shows the transmitter (foreground), and Figure 8-12 is the display terminal which is a 17" television monitor with a keyboard control assembly. One transmitter can be connected (by coaxial cable) to one or more display terminals. Each terminal is located on or beside the desk of a person who requires—and is authorized to receive—information from the data bank. Diebold literature states that average time from request to viewing at a remote display terminal is 15 seconds or less.

In operation, the request is transmitted by phone or otherwise to the

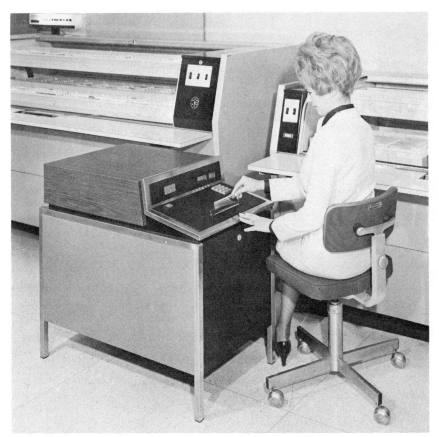

Diebold

Figure 8-11.   Transmitter for Information-Retrieval System (SD-550)

Microforms are filed in the mechanized files.

data bank file clerk who gets the microform from file, puts it in the slot of the transmitter, and indexes the number(s) of the receiving terminals. The terminal numbers "light up" on the transmitter, confirming that the connection has been made. The person receiving can control the image shown on this terminal by using the proper keys. When finished, he can so signal the transmitter.

Computer Output Microfilming

Computer output microfilming (COM) is the production of microfilm from magnetic tape.[1] Under the method used by the Stromberg Division of

---

[1] Magnetic tape as computer output is described on page 573.

Diebold

Figure 8-12. Monitor for Information-Retrieval System (SD-550)

General Dynamics Corporation (the pioneer), magnetic tape from the computer is read by a recorder, or microfilm printer (Figure 8-13, upper center), and is processed in a film processor (same illustration, upper right). In the recorder operation the cathode ray tube converts machine language into man-readable language on the face of the tube, which is in turn photographed by a camera to produce microfilm. The tube contains a disc on which the letters of the alphabet and the arabic numerals are etched; in the operation of the tube, an electronic beam is directed through these characters onto the face of the tube. Form headings, pictures, and so forth can be picked up and registered with the images captured from the magnetic tape so that the microfilm copies will show forms together with information. Film can be marked with retrieval marks for fast retrieval of information.

Microfilm comes in three widths: 16, 32, and 105 millimeter. The Datagraphix 4360 recorder can handle any of these sizes, at the option of the operator, and the output can be printed on roll film or microfiche, depending upon the job application. Roll film can be assembled into cartridges (200 feet to a cartridge) for ready use in a viewer (discussed below). Microfiche consists of separate thin slides, each of which can contain the

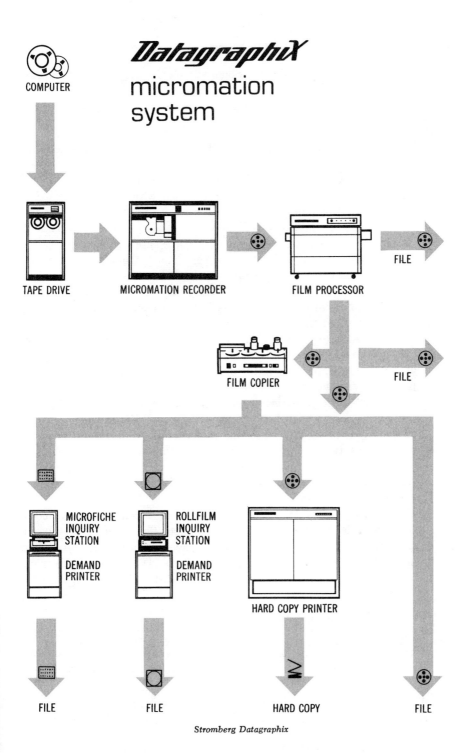

Stromberg Datagraphix

Figure 8-13.   Computer Output Microfilming (COM)

images of 200 pages of a catalog. Some standard sizes of microfiche are $3'' \times 5''$, $4'' \times 6''$, $3\frac{1}{4}'' \times 7\frac{3}{8}''$.

Stromberg units include, in addition to the recorder and the processor described above:

- *A film copier,* which does roll to roll reproduction, making a copy of an entire tape. The duplicate rolls can be used for archive purposes and to provide copies required in a number of locations.
- *Roll film inquiry station,* used for locating frame(s) or pages and viewing on a screen. A tape can comprise up to 12,000 pages of information. The unit consists basically of the screen, at the base of which the film cartridge is inserted (the tape is self-threading), and a control panel at the base of the screen. The buttons on the control panel are used to speed the tape to the frame desired. Information can be retrieved by page number. The image from the tape frame is projected and blown up to $11'' \times 14''$ on the screen. It can be read in a normally lighted room.
- *Microfiche inquiry station.* Microfiche slides are put into the viewer one at a time, at the base of the unit. An indexing device is arranged on an X-Y axis, permitting the operator to locate the page to be projected for viewing.
- *A demand (hard copy) printer* may be used with either a roll film inquiry station or a microfiche inquiry station to produce a paper copy of the image being viewed on the screen of the inquiry station. The demand printer (see Figure 8-13) is positioned underneath the inquiry station, serving as its base, and it is connected electrically to the inquiry station. The demand printer is actuated by pressing a button.
- *Hard copy production printer,* used to print a continuous and consecutive series of printed pages from a tape. The input is the tape in the form of 400-foot reels of positive-image microfilm and the output is fan-folded paper in widths from $8\frac{1}{2}''$ to $14\frac{7}{8}''$ and lengths from $8\frac{1}{2}''$ to $11''$. The basic reason for using COM as the connecting link to produce hard copy is speed.

Business Week (May 9, 1970) says:

[The microfilm camera] is still the starting point for almost every maker of COM equipment. One derivative prints over 50,000 computer-generated lines a minute compared to about 1,500 for the fastest electromechanical line printer.[2]

This is to say that the microfilm method of producing hard copy comes closer to keeping up with the computer than does the impact printer.

---

2 "The Race for Microfilm," *Business Week* (May 9, 1970), page 53.

It should be noted that if filing computer output for later random reference is the objective, retrieval from microfilm is faster than retrieval from magnetic tape. Microfilm can be read by humans when projected in a viewer, whereas magnetic tape cannot be read by humans. It has to be processed into some other medium before it can be so read. Likewise, producing microfilm copies is cheaper than producing paper copies, and microfilm copies, as stated before, require less filing space than paper copies. Microfilm may require as little as 2 per cent of the space required for hard copy.

Some Uses (and Users) of COM

As to uses (and users) of COM, *Business Week* (June 8, 1968) says:

> J. C. Penney is one of a rapidly growing number of companies putting COM systems to work. The thousands of mail orders and customer names and addresses that used to fill 22 volumes of computer forms daily now go on microfilm that Penney's order clerks can easily call for specific information.
>
> Seaboard Coast Line Railroad is microfilming more than half a million pages of data a month, ranging from weekly revenue accounts to daily listings of up to 1,200 pages on interchange cars and contents. . . .
>
> This month, International Harvester Company will start printing its parts inventory on microfilm, using equipment built by 3M.[3]

Business Week (May 9, 1970) says:

> Hundreds or even thousands of pages are stored on one 4″ by 6″ "microfiche." Union Carbide's payroll department, for example, puts monthly payroll records for 22,000 employees on fewer than 100 such pages, and payroll clerks equipped with microfiche readers can answer most questions about a worker's records in only a few seconds.[4]

The same issue states:

> So far, [COM] converts have been slow to line up. Microfilming, users have found, involves extra steps, and microfilm printers are as much as five times as costly as impact printers. . . . But now microfilm appears to be gaining acceptance. At least 100 additional machines went into service last year, and another 30 or so are being shipped every month.

Estimates of Future Developments

Says Duffy (Citibank, New York):

> Someday we will recognize that specialized OCR readers may enable microfilm itself to be used as input to the computer—thus completing the cycle from computer output to microfilm and back to input. This is not a commercial reality now, but the technology exists.[5]

---

[3] "Computer Gets Faster Running Mate," *Business Week* (June 8, 1968).
[4] "The Race for Microfilm," *Business Week* (May 9, 1970), page 53.
[5] "Computer-Microfilm Links By-Pass Paper Printout, Speed Processing," *Bank Equipment News* (February 1969).

Business Week (May 9, 1970):

One shadow hanging over the fast moving industry is whether IBM will move into the microfilm business. Its strategy now, says [one informed source], is that there's not going to be any microfilm—that people are going to use on-line terminals instead. The leaders in COM dispute this contention.[6]

---

[6] Computers and the use of on-line terminals are explained in Chapters 24–26.

9

Internal Check
and Accounting Control:
Introduction

Definition; Scope of This Chapter

It was stated in Chapter 1 that systems assignments are aimed variously toward:

(1) the improvement of managerial information

(2) the improvement of internal check and accounting control

(3) the reduction of clerical expense

Since some systems assignments are mainly internal check and accounting control assignments, and since most assignments involve internal check and accounting control to some extent, it is useful to consider definitions of the term. A study of writings on the subject shows an interesting evolution. Internal check was defined in a bulletin of the American Institute of Accountants (now known as the American Institute of Certified Public Accountants) in 1931 as

> . . . an accounting device whereby a proof of the accuracy of figures can be obtained through the expedient of having different persons arrive independently at the same result.[1]

In 1936, use of the term, "internal check and control" was discussed in the following language:

> The term "internal check and control" is used to describe those measures and methods adopted within the organization itself to safeguard the cash and other assets of the company as well as to check the clerical accuracy of the bookkeeping.[2]

---

[1] *Accounting Terminology* (American Institute Publishing Co., 1931), page 37.
[2] *Examination of Financial Statements* (American Institute Publishing Co., 1936), page 8.

The most recent definition, that published by the Committee of Auditing Procedure, is:

> Internal control comprises the plan of organization and all of the coordinate methods and measures adopted within a business to safeguard its assets, check the accuracy and reliability of its accounting data, promote operational efficiency, and encourage adherence to prescribed managerial policies. . . .
>
> Such a system might include budgetary control, standard costs, periodic operating reports, statistical analyses and the dissemination thereof, a training program designed to aid personnel in meeting their responsibilities, and an internal audit staff to provide additional assurance to management as to the adequacy of its outlined procedures and the extent to which they are being effectively carried out.[3]

Note that in the narrow sense internal checks are "measures and methods" built into an accounting system to check the accuracy of accounting and safeguard the assets of the company. In the broader sense, internal checks and accounting controls include the plan of organization itself and control devices other than those that are purely bookkeeping.

Note also that although the phrase "system of internal check and accounting control" is used, internal check and accounting control does not in fact constitute a distinct system, but rather measures and methods that are an integral part of, say, an order and billing procedure or a vouchers payable procedure or a payroll procedure. When a systems man is asked to design an order and billing procedure, he first determines what paper work is necessary to get the goods out of the warehouse and to produce an invoice. He then reviews the contemplated procedure to determine whether it includes measures and methods that will safeguard the inventory against improper release of goods and that will control the accuracy of the various paper-work operations.

This chapter explains, in general, certain measures and methods of internal check and accounting control and illustrates an effective chart for the examination of internal check and accounting control. Each of the groups of procedures chapters in this book contains a section on internal check and accounting control for the procedure. An internal check review chart is presented in each group.

Systems Design to Prevent Fraud and Error

American business losses due to employee dishonesty are estimated by surety companies at more than $500,000,000 annually. Many accountants have been very much embarrassed, or have even lost clients, because fraud or error resulted in a major loss to a client. Invariably, accounting texts, teachers and manuals stress the need for the accountant to review internal control and recommend such revisions as are required to prevent fraud and

---

[3] Committee on Auditing Procedure, *Internal Control* (American Institute Publishing Co., 1949), page 6. This is the latest edition as of the time this book was prepared.

error. However, systems men often become so intrigued with mechanization and clerical savings that they forget to build control into their systems. Usually, such controls can be obtained at either no cost or an almost insignificant cost.

Other deterrents to the installation of systems which will prevent fraud and error are:

(1) Improper presentation to management (and thus lack of interest by management):
   (a) Danger of major losses through embezzlement or error
   (b) Small cost of proper controls
   (c) Trusted employee is the one who usually embezzles
(2) Lack of interest on part of accountant or systems man:
   (a) Lack of knowledge
   (b) Improper emphasis
   (c) Lack of ability to sell proper controls to management[4]

Characteristics of a Satisfactory System of Internal Control

According to the bulletin *Accounting Control*, the characteristics of a satisfactory system of internal control would include:

A plan of organization which provides appropriate segregation of functional responsibilities.
A system of authorization and record procedures adequate to provide reasonable control over assets, liabilities, revenues and expenses.
Sound practices to be followed in the performance of duties and functions of each of the organizational departments, and
A degree of quality of personnel commensurate with responsibilities.[5]

Organization Chart

Figure 9-1 (Figure 3-1 repeated) is an organization chart which shows how functional responsibilities are segregated in the Household Appliance Corporation. Each of the blocks on the chart represents one or more employees, and the organization is large enough to provide organizational dispersion of responsibilities. No department keeps the final control records of the functions and activities for which the department is responsible. Custodianship of cash and inventories is separated from record control of those assets. Note:

(1) Accounting control of all functions and activities is kept by the controller. In addition to being responsible for the budget, General ledger, and the financial and operating statements, which are the top controls, he is responsible for the detail procedures and records of accounts receivable, inventories, vouchers payable, payrolls, billing, and sales records.

---

[4] From *Prevention of Fraud and Error: An Integral Part of Systems Design*, a technical release to the Chicago Chapter, Systems and Procedures Association of America, by Arthur Weiss, pp. 1-2.
[5] Committee on Auditing Procedure, *op. cit.*, page 6.

ORGANIZATION CHART

HOUSEHOLD APPLIANCE CORPORATION

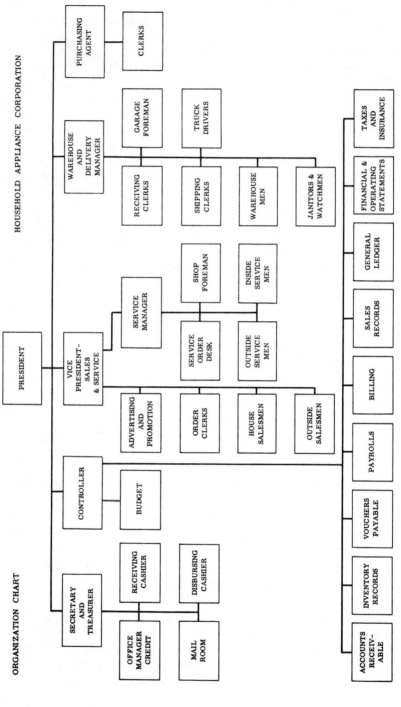

Figure 9-1. Organization Chart: Household Appliance Corporation (Figure 3-1 repeated)

(2) Custodial responsibility for cash is in the hands of the secretary and treasurer. (This feature of the chart is taken directly from the chart in the case study in the bulletin *Internal Control*.) The disbursing cashier is permitted to pay cash only on an approved voucher from the voucher clerk in the controller's division. The receiving cashier receives and deposits all cash, but the cash controls and accounts receivable records are kept by the controller's division.

(3) Custodial responsibility for goods is in the hands of the warehouse and delivery manager. He is responsible for the warehousing and physical control of the goods. His receiving clerks receive goods which have been ordered by the purchasing agent, and they issue receiving reports to the purchasing agent and the controller's division. Similarly, his shipping clerks ship goods out of stock upon proper shipping orders issued in the sales and service division.

Details of Protection Provided by Internal Check and Accounting Control

An accounting system should provide, among others, the following details of protection:

(1) That all transactions are recorded.

(2) That the original recording is verified in the largest practical measure by someone inside the organization other than the one who recorded it. In some cases it may also be verified in some measure by someone outside the organization such as a bank.

(3) That transactions were approved and were performed by authorized persons.

(4) That prices or values are verified.

(5) That assets are under proper custody and that physical control against theft or misappropriation is adequate.

(6) That assets are released to outsiders and taken off the books only on proper authority.

(7) That extensions, discounts, footings, and other mathematical particulars are correct.

(8) That all transactions recorded did get into the books of account.

(9) That the original document or recording was entered in the books (a) in the correct amount and (b) in the correct account.

(10) That the balances of the accounts are correctly computed.

(11) That the balances of accounts are verified (a) by physical inventory or (b) by comparison with records maintained by some outside party.

(12) That proper clerical controls are maintained over journals and other summaries, the ledgers, and the statements and reports prepared for managerial use.

It will be noted that the manner in which these details are effectuated varies among types of transactions. The structure of control procedures varies among sales, accounts receivable, cash receipts, purchases, cash disbursements, and payroll procedures. Specific control and internal check procedures are accordingly illustrated in this book in connection with the particular type of transaction. An abbreviated procedure for sales is presented in Figure 9-2 to introduce the subject of controls and to illustrate the general significance of the details listed above.

Control Devices and Methods

Control devices and methods may be classified as follows:
General:
(1) The formal classification of accounts, with description of debits and credits to each account. One purpose of the formal classification from a control standpoint is to guard against clerks' charging or crediting those transactions that appear to be borderline transactions to one account at one time and to another account at another time, thus upsetting the comparability of the particular account balances on statements issued at different dates.
(2) Organization charts and procedures manuals showing who is responsible for originating and approving various kinds of accounting documents, how the forms are written, and how the various subsequent operations involving the forms are to be done.

Devices aiding in the control of the original recording of transactions:
(1) The original forms themselves are one of the primary devices for getting the proper information at the source of the transaction, and getting it set down in the best arrangement for the operations to follow. (For this reason, the design of the forms required for a control must be considered carefully, whether or not they are to be used in connection with registers or other control devices.) In this connection, note that the serial numbering for forms by the printer is a method of making it possible to determine that all the copies that should have come to a given operation have actually reached that operation.
(2) Autographic registers (Chapter 10) are devices used for containing continuous forms in position for writing the original record of a transaction. Multiple forms are used, and the registers for handling multiple forms are so designed that an audit copy is retained in the machine for withdrawal by the auditor for his purposes.
(3) Cash registers (Chapter 10) are devices used for getting a record of cash receipts and (in some machines) cash paid out. They may be used with or without a written original record of the transaction, such as a sales slip.

(4) Time stamps and time recorders (Chapter 16) which are used for getting a record of employees' time for payroll and cost purposes.

(5) Recording scales, which are used to imprint on an original document the weight (or other measure) of the goods handled. (In this connection the various counters and meters for measuring production and flow should be noted, as devices for assisting in the control of the original information.)

(6) Perforators, similar to those used for cancelling checks, to cancel *all* the documents which support a disbursement voucher—to prevent them being used a second time for fraudulent payment. On this point, Weiss says:

> One of the commonest examples of the failure of a supposed system was exemplified in the case of the embezzlement by the voucher-clerk described earlier in this report. A system was supposedly in effect whereby each invoice and each paper supporting an invoice or other disbursement was cancelled by individually stamping each paper. As nearly always occurs when such a procedure is attempted, the cumbersome nature of the task is such, when contending with some voucher bundles that may be supported by 10, 15, or 20 pages, that the specified procedure is never followed for long. It seems to be just a question of time before the clerical workers who are supposed to be cancelling every page by stamp revert to stamping each bundle only once. Many systems men have recommended the procedure of cancelling each page of voucher bundles, have been assured by management that this was being done, and subsequently have had an auditor point out that the paid file was full of uncancelled items. In the particular case described in this report an inexpensive perforator would have assured the cancellation of all papers in each bundle as a regular procedure and would have prevented the frauds that occurred.[6]

(7) Devices aiding in the control of posting and summarizing: proof lists and proof totals, bookkeeping machine proofs (described in Chapter 7), control accounts, and trial balances.

Miscellaneous special controls:

(1) Quantity controls such as are operated in connection with process cost systems for the control of inventories, and quantity controls for the control of piece-rate wage payments (in which the quantities reported for piece-rate payment are reconciled with the manufactured inventory controls).

(2) Procedures and forms designed for matching related transactions and accounts. Examples: in the insurance register (not illustrated), the left-hand page of the form may be designed for recording premiums paid (the asset, unexpired insurance) and the right-hand page designed for recording insurance expired by month. The design facilitates not only the computation of the insurance expired but also the verification thereof, since it "automatically" matches

---

[6] Weiss, *op. cit.*, page 3.

the expense element with the asset element. Similar examples are the notes receivable register in which the notes proper (assets) are recorded on the left side and the income due is computed and entered on the right side, and the Plant Ledger account on which the asset value and the current depreciation charges are both recorded.

Internal Check and Accounting Control Procedures Illustrated

Figure 9-2 is a chart illustrating the flow of business papers in the recording of sales transactions. This chart is based upon the order and billing procedure explained in Chapter 11. Since the purpose of the present chapter is to explain some of the basic principles of accounting control and internal check, no attempt is made at this point to set out the principles of order and billing procedures as such, or to illustrate the most economical method of writing and reproducing. The chart presented in this chapter represents only one of the several methods of order and billing (the one known as separate order writing and billing), and some of the features of the complete system explained in Chapter 11 have been omitted to keep the present discussion in focus. The back order procedure and the steps involved in handling bills of lading, for instance, have been omitted.

In the procedure illustrated, the salesman takes the customer's order in the customer's presence and writes it on a sales order form consisting of three copies. The salesman gives one copy to the customer, sends the original writing to his home office, and keeps a copy in his order book.

The order department at the home office writes a shipping order form, the purpose of which is to instruct the warehouse to fill the order and the shipping department to ship the goods. The shipping order is written in three copies: the shipping order proper, which goes to the Warehouse and Shipping department; the packing slip, which is enclosed in the package with the goods; and the office copy, which remains in the Order department.

When the goods are shipped, the shipping clerk marks the shipping order "shipped" and the date, and sends it to the Billing department. The Billing department types the invoice from the shipping order, producing three copies: the original, one for the customer, and one for use as the office copy. The office copy of the invoice is checked against the file copy of the shipping order (to make certain that all shipping orders have actually been invoiced) and then sent to the Bookkeeping department where it is recorded in the sales journal and filed in serial number order.

(It is suggested that the reader refer to Figure 9-2 and check through the various steps, from the writing of the sales order to the filing of the office copy of the invoice.)

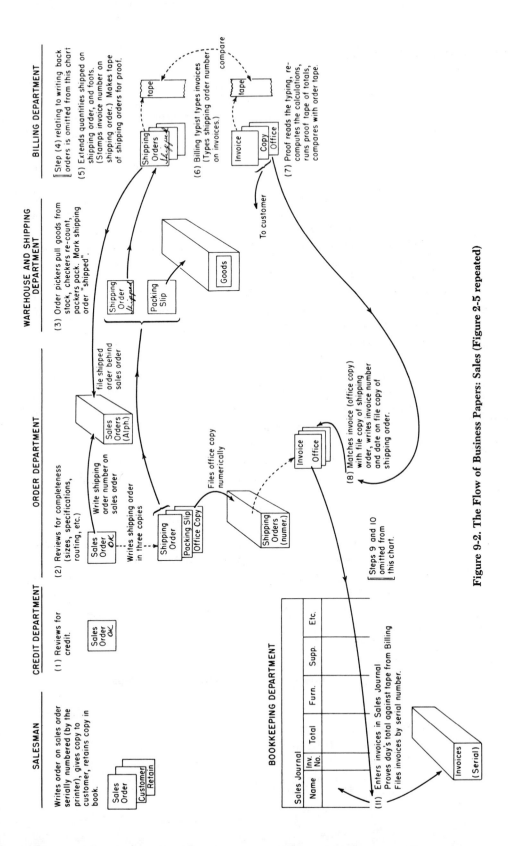

Figure 9-2. The Flow of Business Papers: Sales (Figure 2-5 repeated)

The internal check and accounting control features of the procedure illustrated in Figure 9-2 are tabulated in Figure 9-3. This tabulation provides (at the left) a list of internal check features incorporated in the procedure, and a column for each person or department that has a part in the performance of the internal check function. The internal check operation which each person performs is described in that person's column.

Note the advantage of this type of charting in connection with the review of an internal check procedure: Where only one person is involved in performing a function, the fact is evident because there are no entries in the columns for other persons. Likewise, where several persons perform a function and check each other, all those collateral operations are shown in a single horizontal area. The effect is accordingly an automatic matching of all related internal check features in a procedure. The numbers in parentheses are the operation numbers in the original flow of work. In making an internal check chart, care must be taken to include all factors on which protection is necessary.

The internal check features, and brief comments, follow:

(a) All sales transactions are actually recorded.

    The salesman writes the order in the customer's presence, using a regular sales order form, with serial numbers pre-printed (by the printer). Each day the Order department determines that the sequence of serial numbers received is unbroken to make certain that it does receive all orders that were written. (Note that the shipping orders are serially numbered, as are the invoices. The three sets of numbers are not identical, however, and the documents issued in each series have to be checked against the documents from which they were written.)

(b) The original writing is (or may be) verified by the customer.

    The salesman gives the customer a copy of the order. (In some order systems, a copy of the shipping order is sent to the customer. In such cases, the customer can see what details have been added by the Order department in the procedure of editing and adding the instructions for the Warehouse and Shipping department.)

(c) The sale is approved for credit by the Credit department for technical details.

(d) Prices are verified.

    The salesman prices the order and the Order department verifies the prices.

(e) Goods are kept under proper custody and are shipped (only under proper approval) in the correct quantity.

    Goods are kept in a warehouse under the custody of the warehouse foreman, and order pickers and packers are permitted to release goods only on a proper shipping order issued by the Order

Factor / Person or department	Salesman	Customer	Credit Department	Order Department	Warehouse	Shipping Department	Billing Department	Billing Proof Readers	Bookkeeping Department
All sales transactions are recorded.	Salesman writes order on sales order form (serially numbered by the printer).			Order Department checks serial numbers for missing orders (2).					
The original writing is (or may be) verified by the customer.	Salesman gives copy to customer.	Customer may review order.							
The sale was approved for credit and for technical details.			Credit Department reviews the order for credit (1).	Order Department reviews the order for completeness (sizes, specifications, routing, etc.) and for availability of stock (2).					
Prices are verified.	Salesman prices the order.			Order Department checks prices (2).					
Goods are kept under proper custody and are shipped (only under proper approval) in the correct quantity.		Customer receives goods.		Order Department writes shipping order (2).	Order pickers pick goods from shipping orders written by Order Department (3).	Checkers re-count goods and check against shipping order. Packers put packing slip in package and mark shipping order "shipped" and date (3).			
Extensions, discounts, footings, and other mathematical particulars are correct.		Customer receives invoice.					Extends quantities shipped on shipping order, and foots. Makes tape of shipping orders (5).	Proofreads the invoices, re-computes the calculations, runs proof tape of totals, compares with order tape (7).	
All transactions recorded did get into the books.				Matches invoice (office copy) with file copy of shipping order, writes invoice number and date on file copy of shipping order (8).			Makes tape of shipping orders for proof (5).	Runs tape of invoices, compares with tape of orders (7).	Enters invoices in Sales Journal (for columnar distribution). Proves day's total against tape from Billing. Files invoices by serial number.

Figure 9-3. Internal Check Chart: Sales Order, Shipping Order, Invoice Procedure

Numbers in parentheses refer to operations in the operation chart, Figure 9-2.

department. Also, checkers recount the goods on each order picked by the order pickers, to determine that the quantity is correct.

(f) Extensions, discounts, footings, and other mathematical particulars are correct.

Proofreaders read the invoices, recompute the calculations, and run tapes of totals, which tapes are compared with tapes of the previously computed shipping orders.

(g) All transactions recorded on shipping orders did get into the general books.

The invoices (office copies) come to the Order department in batches with the invoices in serial number order, accompanied by pre-list tape. The Order department matches the invoices with the file copies of shipping orders to make certain that all shipping orders have been billed, and then sends the invoices to the Bookkeeping department. The Bookkeeping department enters the invoices in the sales journal (for columnar sales distribution), proves the day's total against the tape from the Billing department, and files the invoices by serial number.

10

Autographic Registers;
Cash Registers;
Internal Check
in Small Trading Concerns

Autographic Registers

An autographic register (Figure 10-1) is a device for holding and feeding continuous forms and for positioning them for writing by hand. One form (Figure 10-2) may be designed for use in recording all the following types of transactions:

Cash receipts: cash sales
Cash received on account
Paid outs
Charge sales
Credits for returns and allowances on charge sales

The form illustrated provides boxes in which the person who writes the slip can indicate the type of transaction. Three copies of each slip are written, as follows:

Original—office (working) copy
Duplicate—customer (or person receiving cash)
Triplicate—audit copy, which remains in the register

The audit copy, which can be removed only with the proprietor's or the auditor's key, is the control copy. Its purpose is to make it possible to determine whether working copies have been destroyed or changed after the original was released, and of course, to discourage destroying or changing copies.

Figure 10-3 is a diagram of the method of summarizing the various slips. During the day, as the slips are written, the working copies of all kinds are kept in the till. At the end of the day, the slips are sorted by type of transaction and totaled on an adding machine for the daily entry in the Summary of Sales, Cash Receipts, and Cash Paid Out.

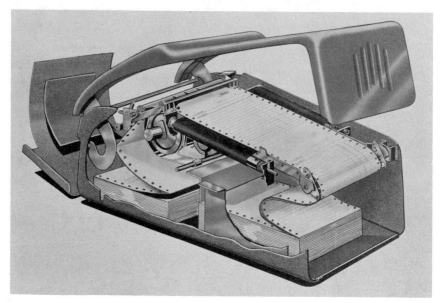

Standard Register Co.

Figure 10-1.   Autographic Register

A device used for holding and feeding continuous strip forms and positioning them for writing. Cutaway shows how the audit copy is retained in the register after the other copies have been written and removed from the register. The audit copy can be removed only by use of the proprietor's or auditor's key. Figure 10-2 illustrates a form printed for use in this register.

Source Record Punch for Source Data Collection

Figure 10-4 is a source record punch for source data collection and Figure 10-5 is a copy of the tabulating card and action copies that are produced by the punch. The punches are point of transaction recorders located at strategic points in the plant and offices. Input to the punches is by master card (a tabulating card), slides (preset inside the machine), badge readers, clocks, and the keyboard of the punch. (The badge for each man is punched with the man's number.) The keyboard is used for variable information; the operator indexes this information manually.

The tabulating card illustrated in Figure 10-5 is used for in-plant recording in a manufacturing plant. Instructions for operating the punch are shown at the bottom of the form. The operator fills in the center blocks of the form manually, inserts the appropriate fixed inputs (named above) in the punch, and inserts the tabulating card (Figure 10-5) and completes it by operation of the keyboard. After completion, the tabulating cards are sent to the computer and the action copies released for their intended use.

Figure 10-2. Continuous Strip Form Used for Autographic Register

Standard Register Co.

Used in the register illustrated in Figure 10-1. This form can be used to record cash receipts, cash sales, cash received on account, paid outs (cash paid out of the till), charge sales, and credits for returns and allowances on charge sales. The appropriate box is checked to identify the type of transaction. This is a three-copy form: original—office (working copy); copy—to customer or person receiving cash; copy—(audit) remains in machine under control of proprietor or auditor.

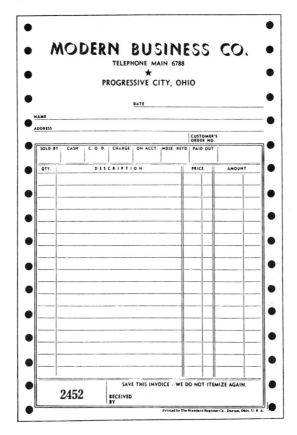

Writing Boards

Writing boards are devices used to produce journals as a carbon copy by-product of manual postings to accounts. The operation is similar to the machine operation of posting to an account and producing a proof sheet which is a journal, except that it is performed by hand.

SUMMARY OF SALES, CASH RECEIVED, AND CASH PAID OUT

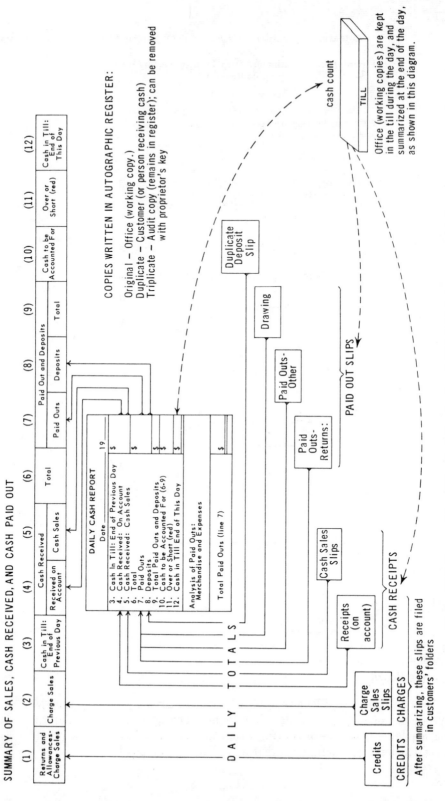

Figure 10-3. Summarizing Sales, Cash Received, and Cash Paid Out: Autographic Register

Standard Register Co.

Figure 10-4.   Source   Record   Punch   for   Source   Data
Collection

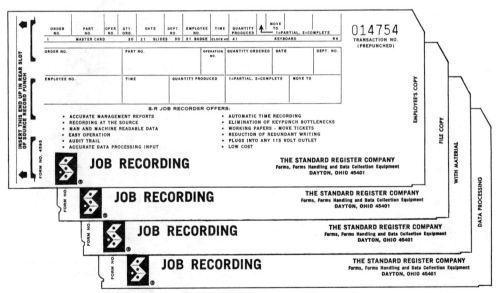

Standard Register Co.

Figure 10-5.   Tabulating Card with Action Copies, Punched and Interpreted in
Source Record Punch (Figure 10-4)

Figure 10-6 is a set of three forms—sales journal, statement, and account—collated for use on an accounting board. Figure 10-7 is an illustration of the board.

The statements and accounts are kept in a file, with each statement in front of its account. (The statement form folds over the account form on the perforated line at the left.) In the posting operation, the statement and account are pulled from the posting binder and placed on the left side of the board, by positioning on the page. A transverse carbon is placed on the board over the sales journal so that it covers the left side of the sales journal, and the journal receives a carbon copy of all postings to the accounts. Date, reference or description, debit, and new balance are

Figure 10-6. Proof Journal, Statement, Accounts Receivable Ledger—Manufactured for Use on an Accounting Pegboard

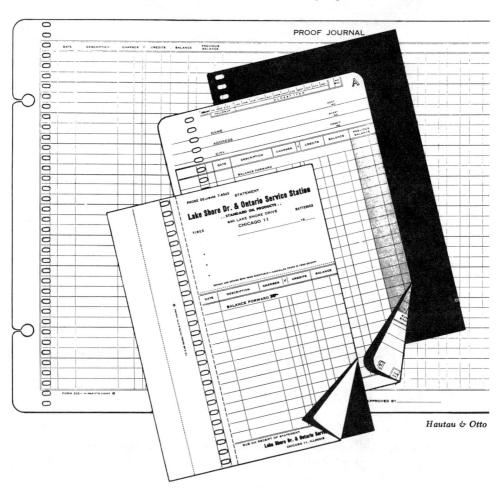

Hautau & Otto

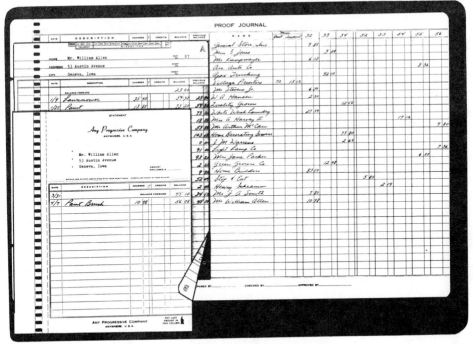

Hautau & Otto

Figure 10-7. Accounting Board—Pegboard

posted, and the distribution of sales is entered at the right of the journal form.

As each journal page is filled, the columns are footed and proved. The sum of the Distribution columns should agree with the total of the Debit column. The total of the Previous Balance column plus the total of the debits should agree with the total of the (new) Balance column. (The latter procedure proves that the new balances equal the old balances picked up plus the debits, but not that the old balances were picked up correctly.)

Cash receipts are posted in the same manner as sales. The same printed form is used for sales journal, cash receipts journal, purchases journal, and cash payments journal. The column headings are filled in by the bookkeeper to suit the use which is to be made of each form.

Cash Registers

A cash register is a machine for recording transactions relating to cash (receipts from cash sales, receipts on accounts receivable, cash paid outs) at the point where the transactions occur, with provision for accumulating totals and for enforcing the accuracy of the recording. Some cash registers are also designed to record and control charge sales. Control categories and the method of control vary among classes of cash registers.

Sales books may be used in connection with some types of registers (with the register certifying the recording and accumulating totals) to get a written record of cash sales, where it is necessary or desirable to get the customer's name and address, cash received on account, charge sales, and credits for returns and allowances—charge sales. The machines become the control over the usual sales book recording. (Note, however, that some registers are built to eliminate some of the sales book recording, as illustrated later.)

Just what transactions will be passed through a particular cash register (and consequently the design of the register) depends upon how the cashiering function is organized in the business. In some stores that sell over the counter for cash, there may be a number of registers located in the sales department, each of which registers and accumulates cash sales and possibly cash paid out for authorized returns of merchandise by customers. Such a register might be a single-register machine. On the other hand, a register in a store selling for cash on account may handle all the types of transactions named above, and the register may be built to accumulate the various classes of total.

In some retail places (soda fountains and lunch counters, for instance) registers known as "printers" are used to issue checks to customers as they are served. The customers pay the cashier who rings up the cash sale on her machine. A printer may be a small model machine, without a cash drawer, but equipped with what is technically known as a receipt printer.

Figure 10-8 diagrams the summarizing procedure for a cash register that is equipped to accumulate one total (and which is used to accumulate cash sales). When the latter is used, the cash register may be used at the end of the day to total the slips for transactions other than cash sales.

Central Cashier; Tube Cashier

Central cashiers are sometimes used where the volume of transactions is great enough to make it possible to use a full-time cashier. In the smaller stores, the cashier may be located at the door, and the customers may present their cash sales checks and cash to the cashier as they leave the store.

In the larger retail stores that are departmentalized to some extent, the central cashier may be located at some distance from the sales persons, and the latter may send their sales checks and cash to the central cashier through pneumatic tubes. Where tubes are used, the cashier is often known as the "tube cashier," particularly where it is necessary to distinguish her from the other cashiers, such as the accounts receivable cashier or the general cashier.

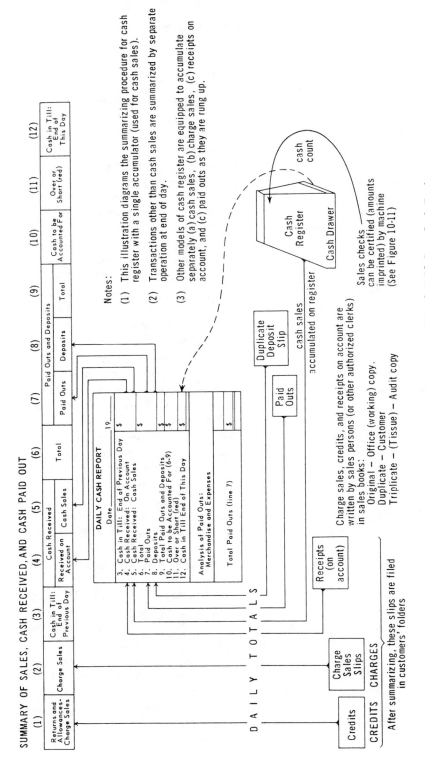

Figure 10-8. Summarizing Sales, Cash Received, and Cash Paid Out: Cash Register

Features of Some of the Earlier Models

The following paragraphs describe in the order of their introduction some of the early models of cash registers and some of their main features. The history of the features is interesting because each feature was devised to solve a problem and because almost all the features except the very earliest ones have been retained, at least in general form, to this day. This information was obtained from literature of the National Cash Register Company, and the chronology relates to developments of various features by that company. The list is not intended to indicate what features might be exclusive in any model or with the manufacturer.

The first cash register was built in 1878 and was called a "Dial Register." The dial showed the amount of the sale, and thus called the customer's attention to the fact that the sale was "recorded." The Dial Register was merely an indication machine, and it provided no mechanism for accumulating the amounts of the sales. It was not practical, but it did start the development of the cash register as it is known today.

The "Paper Roll Machine" was the first machine that provided a real control over the cash taken in by the clerk. There was a roll of paper in the machine comprising a printed column (lengthwise on the roll) for each key on the keyboard. When a key was struck, a hole was punched in the related column of the roll. At the end of the day, the proprietor would remove the roll and determine the total cash receipts by counting the holes, multiplying the number of holes by the appropriate figure to get a total for the key, and adding the totals for the various keys to get the grand total. The roll with its punched holes was soon abandoned in favor of adders, but the principle of proving out the cash at the end of the day, as an integral feature of the register procedure, was established.

The first models of this machine did not have a cash drawer. Later models had a manually operated cash drawer, and still later models had automatic drawers. This feature provided the protection of cash which the merchant desired by making it impossible to open the drawer without calling attention to the fact.

"Detail adders"—one for each key—replaced the paper roll. Each detail adder would accumulate the amounts represented by striking a particular key. Thus, if the 40¢ key was struck three times, the adder would show 120. To obtain the grand total amount registered, it was necessary to read the detail adders, list the totals, and add them. The "total adder," marketed in 1890, replaced the detail adder. It accumulated the amounts put into the machine on all keys and showed the grand total in one figure. The accumulation of totals is one of the features of all registers today.

The model of machine in which the first total adders appeared was a "Press-Down-Key" type: the pressure on the keys by the operator was the actuating force which caused the machine to operate. The next year (1891), a "Handle-Operated Register" was introduced. In using this machine, the operator would press the proper amount keys and turn the handle to provide the actuating force. In addition to press-down-key and handle-operated machines, there are today motor-bar-operated and drawer-operated machines. In the latter type, the closing of the cash drawer by the operator provides the actuating force.

The detail audit strip was introduced after the total adder. It was a tape on which was printed the amount of the transaction and other identifying information. This audit strip, being a formal record of the day's sales, made it possible for the proprietor or other authorized person to determine whether some transaction about which he had information was actually recorded by the sales person, and if so whether it was properly recorded. Likewise, the audit strips, filed by date, provided formal support for certain control figures that appeared in the financial records. The detail audit strip was actually a detail cash receipts journal.

The receipt printer was introduced in 1892. With this device, the machine automatically produced a receipt for the customer. This feature provided the receipt which the customer desired for his own protection. (When the customer wishes to return merchandise bought for cash, it becomes necessary to establish, first, the fact that the merchandise was actually bought at the store, and second, the price he paid for it.) It also strengthened the possibility of customer supervision of the recording, and it was a speedier operation than writing a sales slip.

The receipt printer was the forerunner of the triple printer. In machines equipped with the latter device, each transaction is printed on the audit strip (described above) and also, as desired by the operator, either on a printed receipt produced by the machine or on both the original sales slip and the duplicate sales slip inserted in the machine. Thus:

(a) For cash-take transactions, a machine-printed receipt would be produced unless it was desirable to write a sales check for some special reason.

(b) For charge transactions, where it is necessary to get the customer's name and address and certain other details, a sales check would be written. The original printing (machine certification of amount, etc.) on both the store copy and the customer's copy of the sales slip insured that the recorded amounts on both were identical.

Multiple cash drawers came in 1899, and each clerk was provided with his own drawer. At first, the registers comprised only one total accumulation. The various clerks accordingly wrote reports of their cash receipts.

These reports were combined, and the grand total was compared with the amount shown by the register. This use of multiple drawers did encourage the clerks to keep their hands out of other clerks' cash, but it did not provide the necessary localization of responsibility.

Multiple counters were introduced to make it possible to keep track of each clerk's transactions separately, thus placing the responsibility for cash discrepancies where more than one clerk was involved. This development opened the way to counters for accumulating not only dollars by salesmen, but also dollars for each of several transaction controls, such as cash sales, charge sales, receipts on account, paid outs, and so on. At the same time, there were transaction counters in which were accumulated the number of transactions, such as cash sales, charge sales, receipts on accounts, and paid outs. This was an important development because statistics on the number of transactions were useful for management purposes, providing the basis for computing average amounts per cash sale, average amounts of sales per sales person, and so on.

Item-adding, which is in the same category as receipt-printing, makes it possible to produce a receipt for the customer showing the items purchased and the total purchase, as well as such other details as date, consecutive number, and initial of the cashier. This feature provides machine addition of the items in multiple purchases (thus reducing the possibility of errors by the clerk); it also provides the customer with a list of the amounts for which he was charged. The receipt with stub, which can be produced on some machines, should be mentioned at this point. The main portion of the receipt is given to the customer, and the stub, showing the total amount, date, consecutive number, and clerk's initial, is retained by the clerk.

Illustrations

A number of models of cash registers are illustrated in this chapter (Figures 10-9 to 10-12). Each illustration includes a picture of the machine and a diagram of the keyboard. The descriptive comment accompanying each illustration names some of the features of the machine. It will be noted that various combinations of features are built into the different machines to provide various types and amounts of information for the management and the customer, and to provide for use of the machine under various operating conditions with reference to organization and control.

National Cash Register Class 24

Some of the features of the NCR Class 24 (Figure 10-9) found in various (and not necessarily all) series of that model are described in the following paragraphs. Some of the features are alternates to others.

National

Figure 10-9.   Cash Register (Class 24) and Keyboard

Itemized tape. This is a paper tape on which the machine imprints a record of each entry recorded on the machine. The entries are numbered serially by the machine, and the numbers become a control over the completeness of the record. They are also an approximate indicator of the time of day when the transaction was recorded. They establish an audit trail. The tape can be used by the proprietor or supervisor to inspect the recording of a transaction about which he has knowledge. Each entry on the tape is identified by the keyboard symbol which describes the entry. It is possible for the proprietor or supervisor to pick out particular types of entry and to accumulate separate totals, say at the end of the day, using the register as an adding machine.

Receipt printing. Machines equipped with this feature are used at checkout counters of grocery stores and other retail stores. The receipt given the customer shows the sales amount of each item purchased, total sales value, tax, and total amount. The customer can check the items purchased against the receipt to verify the recording.

Slip printing. Used where sales checks are written by the salesmen. The salesman or the register cashier inserts the sales slip in a slot in the machine which imprints the total amount on the check, as it is rung up on the machine. This imprinting is a certification that the check has been included in the machine total(s) and it discourages manipulation of the check after the customer's copy has been given to the customer.

Print keys for salesman or department identification. This is an optional feature of most Class 24 Series 100 models. Nine keys are provided for printing (but not accumulating totals).

Two total receipt printer. The machine accumulates two totals, one for sales amounts and one for tax. This totalizing makes it unnecessary for the operator or bookkeeper to accumulate the tax totals by separate operation. There also is a two total slip printer, built to certify sales checks and accumulate separate totals for sales and tax.

Push button change dispensing. With a machine so equipped, the operator records the sale and depresses the proper change key (change from 25¢, change from 50¢, or other), and the dispenser drops the change in the cup in the dispenser. Note that the operator must record the sale correctly, or the change will not be correct.

Features of the NCR Class 24 Series 200 and 300 are described in the following paragraphs. Some features of the 100 series are available on the 200-300 series, but are not repeated below.

Salesmen or department totals. Four to eight totals can be provided. A control key is provided for each salesman (or department). The machine will accumulate the total sales dollars for each control.

Autographic sales journal. This journal is the "itemization" tape described above, except that this one can be spaced by the operator to allow entry of descriptive or identifying words by the operator. Control totals are normally cleared onto the tape by the manager or the supervisor who has his own key.

Activity counters. These counters show the number of sales in any one department and, separately, a true customer count. The item counts are picked up from certain keys on the register and the customer counts, from other keys. In certain applications, a counter shows how many charge sales checks must be accounted for at the end of the day.

The reset counter advances each time a control total is reset. It prevents unauthorized resetting of control totals.

Change computation. After recording the sale in the usual way, the operator records amount received from the customer, depressing also the Amount Tendered and the Change keys. The machine will indicate the correct amount of change to be given the customer.

Flash reports. These reports are concerned with certain totals, significant for management purposes. They are produced by inserting the printed report form in the machine and printing the control totals. This may be done at any time during the business day. Certain models can be programmed to suppress certain control totals from the journal while allowing them to print on the flash report.

Credit key. Provides direct subtraction from the sales amount for refunds, bottle returns, and so forth.

Some features of the NCR Class 24 Series 500:

Five-position lock slide. Used by the proprietor or supervisor, using his own key. With it he can put the machine in normal operation or in Read or Reset.

Separate cash drawers for several operators, with a separate control key for each operator. By removing her control key from the register, an operator can prevent access to the cash drawer for which she is responsible and likewise prevent the recording of sales through her register, for which she would be responsible.

National Cash Register Class 5

The NCR Class 5 (Figure 10-10) can be coupled to a paper tape punch (not illustrated). The tape can be sent to a computer service bureau to produce a variety of management reports relating to sales, such as inventories and accounts receivable, all within the basic accounting classification of the business. Keys for 999 merchandise numbers are provided on the keyboard. Of this number, 780 are used for merchandise and the remainder for non-merchandise items and General ledger account numbers. It is possible to expand this classification by the addition of another column of digits (eight places). The National Cash Register Company provides pre-packaged computer programs to be used in producing the management reports from the tapes. The NCR 5 simultaneously records the sale on the register journal tape, on the itemized receipt given the cus-

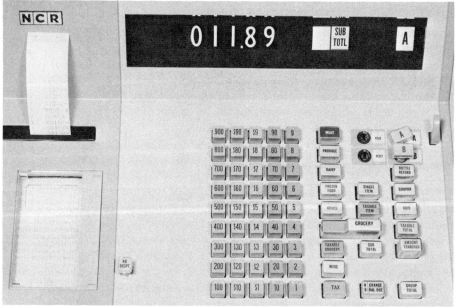

National

Figure 10-10.   Cash Register (Class 5) and Keyboard

tomer, on the inserted form in the machine, and on the paper tape to be used for data-processing.

The NCR 5 can produce an itemized receipt or it can write itemized sales checks. For a charge sale the operator puts a blank sales check in the machine, and the machine writes all pertinent information on the sales check: code number, price of the item, sales tax, salesman's number, total amount of the sale, date, consecutive number, account number, and tracer number. Product code numbers are explained by a legend which appears on the back of the sales check. When a charge sale is recorded, the machine compels the salesman to record an account number. Putting the account number in the machine opens the way to accounts receivable control.

Accounts receivable control can be accomplished in either of two ways. The first way is to put onto the tape all the information necessary for monthly statements, which are produced from the tape by the computer. Note that the product code number is printed on the sales check (as indicated above). When the statement is produced by the computer, a merchandise description related to the product code number can be printed if desired on the statement. The descriptions are stored in memory of the computer. A Type 1 statement provides a description of every item charged or credited. On a Type 2 statement, all "like items" are grouped for an appropriate description. A Type 3 statement is nondescriptive. The second way is to post the customer's monthly statement in the NCR 5, picking up the old balance and adding the sale (or subtracting the cash received on account) to arrive at the new balance—which the machine will post to the statement. The accounts receivable file is kept at the machine.

National Retail On-Line Electronic Terminal Class 280

The NCR Class 280 (Figure 10-11) is a point of transaction recorder designed, among other things, to provide for controlling inventories at a variety of levels. This means that the machine can be built for a unit control over merchandise or for some particular group control, as desired by the management. (The management might desire unit control for garments and for certain classes of furniture, for instance, and group control for certain food inventories.) For unit control, the price tag taken from the merchandise item when the sales is made is one of the inputs to the cash register. It shows such details as product classification number, size, and price, both in machine-readable language and man-readable language. The size of the tags varies according to the amount of information desired for input to the system. Some tags might be produced on a tag-making machine in the store. Other tags might be produced by the manufacturer of the goods and affixed to the goods by the manufacturer. The

National

Figure 10-11. Retail On-Line Electronic Terminal (Class 280)

code number of the product is based upon the particulars required for control of merchandise and it also distinguishes taxable from nontaxable items so that separate totals can be accumulated automatically.

When a sale is made in the store, the merchandise tag is detached from the merchandise and given to the register operator who inputs the machine-readable language into the register by means of a "light" pen. She also picks up the salesman's number from his identification check, which shows his number, likewise in machine-readable language. And if the sale is a charge sale, the customer presents her charge plate which is similarly read into the register with the light pen.

The NCR 280 is equipped with a programmed instruction display panel which tells the operator what she still needs to put into the keyboard. It will instruct her, for instance, to put in the department number or the price. Information which is not put into the register with the light pen can be put in manually through the keyboard. The programmed instructions accordingly provide a control over the completeness of the recording of a transaction.

The 280 can be hooked up to a computer to transmit data at the end of the day, and the computer produces sales and inventory reports in the frequency necessary for good merchandise control. (Note that a sophisticated basic plan of exception reporting is needed.) Hookup to the computer can also provide for credit authorization. After the sale with customer number has been recorded, the computer will consult the customer file showing whatever limitations have been placed, and report back the approval or rejection.

Cash Register (Class 5) with Automatic Drink Dispenser

The National Cash Register (Class 5) with automatic drink dispenser is a combined cash control and inventory control system. Figure 10-12 is an illustration of the register and the dispenser and Figure 10-13 is a diagrammatic sketch of the components of the system. The keyboard of the register includes selection keys of the most popular drinks. When the order is received, the drink is rung up on the register, which records and displays the standard price of the drink. At the same time, the dispenser mixes and dispenses the drink according to a standard formula. An inventory control operates on the basis of ounces in minus ounces dispensed equals ounces in inventory.

Internal Check in the Small Store

In designing a bookkeeping and cash control system for a small store, it is necessary to provide protection against errors and omissions in the original recording and against errors in posting to summaries and accounts. This is necessary even in the small business where the proprietor himself does much of the record work, since he may make errors just as the sales persons may make them. Where there are hired sales persons, it

Figure 10-12. Cash Register (Class 5) with Automatic Drink Dispenser

National Cash Register Company

NCR ELECTRA BAR

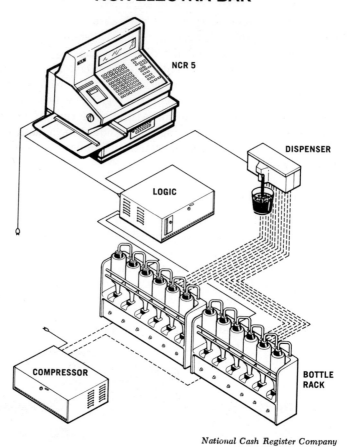

NCR 5

DISPENSER

LOGIC

COMPRESSOR

BOTTLE
RACK

National Cash Register Company

Figure 10-13. **Diagram: Cash Register (Class 5) with Automatic Drink Dispenser**

is also necessary to provide protection against deliberate manipulation of records and mishandling of merchandise and cash. The employer requires protection from the occasional dishonest employee, and the honest employees want assurance that a good system of accounting controls and internal checks will keep them clear of suspicion.

Figure 10-14 is a chart showing how various types of errors and manipulations in cash sales transactions would be discovered through the operation of internal check among customers, sales persons, and the proprietor. (The customer is not, strictly speaking, a part of the internal check system, but there are certain types of error that only he is likely to discover, and it is well for the systems man to consider those types.) Figure 10-14 deals with cash sales transactions in a system where sales slips are written in an autographic register. An audit copy is retained in the machine for the proprietor. The proprietor proves the cash and summarizes the transactions on the Summary of Sales, Cash Receipts, and Cash Paid Out at the end of the day.

The following general conclusions can be drawn from the internal check chart illustrated in Figure 10-14:

(1) The customers may provide a certain amount of detail-checking of the original recording, and they may or may not report their findings to the sales person or the proprietor. The proprietor can spot-check his audit copies, and he can check the recording of certain transactions on which he has detailed information.

(2) The proprietor has no formal detailed control over release of goods without recording the sale, unless an inventory procedure is tied to the sales recording procedure (which is unusual in small-item retail stores).

(3) A dishonest sales person may attempt to change the working copy of a sales slip after the customer has been given a correct sales slip and has left the premises, or he may destroy the working copy and keep the cash. Proper control over the audit copy makes it possible to detect destruction of working copies, and it provides the means of spot-check comparison of the working copies with the audit copies to determine whether the former have been changed after the original writing.

(4) There is no protection of the customer against short-changing, except the customer's own diligence. On the other hand, if the sales person has given the customer too much change and the customer has not reported the fact, the sales person's cash will not balance. Likewise if the sales person has misappropriated the cash in the till without manipulating the records, the daily cash report will not balance.

Figure 10-15 shows how various types of error and manipulation in handling charge sales would be discovered, and Figure 10-16 sets out the same information for receipts on account. It is assumed that an autographic register system is used, that the sales person handles these types of transactions, and that the proprietor summarizes the transactions at the end of the day.

Note that in recording cash sales by cash register, the machine itself provides features to support the internal check system. The reader is referred to the illustrations of cash registers and the descriptions of the features of the machines.

	Participant in detection		
Type of error or manipulation	Customer	Sales Person	Proprietor
ORIGINAL RECORDING (1) Multiple item sales: items were omitted in the recording of the sale	Customer inspects sales slip. May or may not report omissions.	Sales person should count number of items written; count number of items of merchandise; compare.	Proprietor has no formal detailed control unless an inventory control procedure is tied to the cash receipts procedure. (Not usual in small item retail stores.) (a)
(2) Incorrect prices were used in recording the sale	Customer inspects sales slip. May or may not report error. (b)	Sales person prices sales slip.	Proprietor can spot check sales slips if they are written in complete detail (which is often not feasible in small item retail stores).
(3) Incorrect extensions and totals were made		Sales person extends and foots sales slip.	Proprietor can spot check sales slips.
MERCHANDISE (4) Goods were released without recording a sale	(c)	To some extent sales persons observe each other and thus provide a deterrent to release of goods without sales slip.	Same as (1) above.
WORKING COPIES (5) Sales person makes out correct slip; destroys working copy and pockets the cash	Customer receives a correct sales slip.	Sales person could change the working copy of the sales slip but not the audit copy in the register. There is some possibility that a sales person who destroys a working copy or alters one after the customer has left will be observed by another sales person.	Proprietor leafs through working copies or sorts numerically to determine missing slips. Audit copy can be used to reconstruct information on missing slips.
(6) Sales person makes out a correct slip; changes the working copy to a reduced amount and pockets the difference			Proprietor can spot check working copies against audit copies to see if former have been changed.
(7) Sales person short changed the customer and pocketed the amount shorted	Only the customer (or an inspector posing as a customer) can detect and report short changing.		
MISHANDLING CASH (8) Sales person failed to put the cash in the till	Customer may or may not observe. May report.	A sales person who fails to put cash in till may be observed by another sales person.	Proprietor would discover shortages when proving out cash.
(9) Sales person takes cash out of the till, without manipulating any transaction records	Customer is not involved.	May be observed by another sales person.	

Figure 10-14. Internal Check in a Small Store: Cash Sales; Written Sales Slip Procedure

How various types of error and manipulation would be discovered.

(a) In some stores, sales, purchases, and inventory accounts are kept by *department or class of merchandise*. Any deviation from expected gross profit is investigated. Theft or losses of merchandise from other causes may be indicated.

(b) In some stores, all goods bear price tags, stickers, or marks (if nature of goods permits) to make it possible for the customer to determine whether he was charged the correct price.

(c) Where the customer pays the even amount of the sale and receives merchandise that does not have to be wrapped, there is no assurance that the customer will inspect the recording. He may leave the premises immediately. Some stores use outside shopping services which inspect sales person's handling of transactions on a spot basis.

Type of error	Person involved in detection — Customer	Sales Person	Proprietor
ORIGINAL RECORDING			
Multiple item sale: items omitted from total.	Customer inspects sales slip. May or may not report omissions.	Sales person should count number of items written; count number of items of merchandise; compare.	Proprietor has no formal detailed control unless an inventory control procedure is tied to the cash receipts procedure. (Not usual in small item retail stores.)
Customer charged for items not received.			
Items incorrectly priced.		Sales person prices sales ticket.	Proprietor can spot check sales slips if they are written in complete detail (which is often not feasible in small item retail stores).
Items incorrectly extended and totaled.	Customer inspects sales slip. May or may not report error.	Sales person extends and foots sales slip.	Proprietor can spot check sales slips.
Customer name incorrect.			
MERCHANDISE Goods released without recording sale.	Customer can report failure to write slip.	Sales persons can observe release of goods by other sales persons.	Proprietor can observe release of goods by sales persons.
MISSING SLIPS Sales slip (working copy) missing.		Sales person could destroy the working copy, but not the audit copy in the register.	Proprietor sorts slips numerically to determine that none are missing.
CONTROL SHEET Total of day's charge sales entered incorrectly on control sheet.			Proprietor takes total of slips and posts to control record. (Proprietor himself sets up Accounts Receivable control.)
CUSTOMERS' ACCOUNTS Item omitted from customer's account (slip not posted).	Customer can compare his copies of charge slips with statement at end of month; report differences.		If these errors are made, the customers' accounts will not balance with the control.
Item posted incorrectly.			An error of this kind will not be disclosed through balancing against control.
Item posted to wrong account.		Sales person is not involved.	
Balance computed incorrectly.			Customers' accounts will not balance with control.

Figure 10-15. Internal Check in a Small Store: Charge Sales

How various types of error and manipulation would be discovered.

(Sales person receives cash, makes change, writes receipt. Proprietor summarizes all transactions, proves cash)

Type of error or manipulation		Person involved in detection →		
		Customer	Sales Person	Proprietor
ORIGINAL RECORDING	Amount incorrect.	Customer receives his copy of receipt (which is incorrect) and his statement (which is incorrect) at end of month. Complains.		
	Customer's name incorrect.		No one checks the original writing except the customer.	
MANIPULATION OF THE WORKING COPIES (In each of these cases, customer has received a correct receipt)	Receipt (working copy) destroyed. Sales person keeps cash.	Customer receives statement (which is *correct*), at end of month.	There is some possibility that a sales person who destroys a receipt (working copy) or alters one after the customer has left will be observed by another sales person.	Proprietor sorts working copies numerically to determine that none are missing. Investigates missing copies.
	Receipt (working copy) altered: credit to customer's account correct, sales discount increased, cash debit decreased. (Sales person keeps difference between correct cash debit and adjusted cash debit.)	Customer receives statement (which is *correct*), at end of month.		Proprietor can re-compute discount. Can make spot comparisons of working copy with audit copy to determine whether former was changed.
	Receipt (working copy) altered: amount decreased. No discount involved. (Sales person keeps difference between correct amount and adjusted amount.)	Customer receives statement (which is *incorrect*), at end of month. Customer complains.		Proprietor can compare working copy with audit copy, if customer complains, to determine whether former was changed.
	Receipt (working copy) destroyed. (Sales person credits the customer with a fictitious allowance slip, and keeps the cash.)	Customer receives statement (which is *correct*), at end of month.		As noted above, proprietor sorts working copies numerically to determine that none are missing. Also examines *all* allowance slips.
MISHANDLING CASH	Receipt recorded properly; sales person failed to put cash in till.		A sales person who fails to put cash in till may be observed by another sales person.	Proprietor will discover shortage when proving out cash.
	Cash stolen from till: straight theft.		May be observed by another sales person.	
	Sales person short changes customer and keeps the amount of shortage.	No safeguard. Customer complains.		
CONTROL	Total of day's charge sales tickets entered incorrectly on control sheet.		Sales persons are not involved; proprietor prepares end-of-the-day summary entries.	Proprietor takes total of slips and posts to control record.

Figure 10-16. Internal Check in a Small Store: Cash Received on Account

How various types of error and manipulation would be discovered.

11

Order Procedures;
Billing Procedures—
Data-Processing Illustrated

The Order Function; the Billing Function

The order function in a jobbing, wholesaling, or manufacturing concern involves:

(1) Editing the order that the customer or the salesman has sent in, supplying any missing information with reference to product specifications and shipping routes which may be necessary for the shipping department to handle the order,

(2) Determining delivery date, and (in large organizations) determining plant from which to ship, and

(3) In many cases, writing a shipping order set
   (a) to put the information in the form best suited to the needs of the warehouse departments and the shipping departments, and
   (b) to provide copies to make it possible for several departments to work on the order at the same time.

In manufacturing concerns, it may also involve determining whether an order has to be manufactured or whether it can be shipped from stock. In some businesses where partial shipments are sometimes made against a single sales order, the order department (or the warehouse) must take care to release for shipment such quantities at one time as will comprise economical freight shipments.

The order function also involves (a) maintaining the unfilled order records from which the status of each order may be determined and (b) operating a follow-up on the warehouse and shipping departments to make certain that the orders are shipped on time. This function includes the control of back orders, that is, follow-up of the delayed portion of an order where only part of the customer's order can be shipped at one time.

In some businesses, contracts for blanket quantities of goods are made with customers. In such cases, the order function includes applying orders received against the contracts and thus keeping track of balances due customers on their contracts.

Customers' correspondence relating to cancellations, returns, claims for non-delivery, damage in transit, excess charges for freight because of failure to follow customers' instructions, and for faulty merchandise may be handled through operation of the order function. These matters may involve making entries in the unfilled order record as well as issuing journal vouchers to the Accounts Receivable department. The order function may involve record control of the price schedules and allowance schedules (advertising allowance, freight allowance, and so forth) negotiated by the Sales department with the customer. (In some cases, shipping orders may be priced in the Order department.) Likewise price claims by customers may be investigated and answered by the Order department. Finally, the order function may involve the control of shipping orders for samples to salemen and customers, movement of repair merchandise, and the like.

The billing function consists of supplying prices and extensions for invoice purposes, picking up the freight for which customers are to be billed and the various state sales taxes, and operating proofs of typing and mathematical operations. The billing function also involves providing necessary copies of the invoice for accounting purposes, such as accounts receivable, salesmen's commission, and sales distribution.

Organization

In some cases the order function as described above is carried out by clerks in the Sales department. In other cases it is performed by a separate order department. The order function as such does not include the production control function (which is dealt with in a later chapter), but in some smaller organizations the order function and the production control function are performed by a single set of clerks. Where this is the case, the so-called Order department would operate the production control records (raw materials ledger—quantities, finished goods ledger—quantities, and the production schedules) with which it is enabled to set delivery dates. Where the order function and the production control function are separate, as assumed in the present chapter, the Order department would communicate with the Production Control department to determine the delivery dates.

Managerial Information

The Order department makes reports of unfilled orders by product class and sometimes by promised month of delivery. Where there is a significant time lag between sales orders and invoices (that is, between the date of taking the order and the date of billing the customer), the Order department (or the Sales department) may analyze orders by salesman and by customer, making reports on orders to date for the sales management. Such reports would be more timely for close follow-up of sales performance than the sales reports based upon billing.

Shipping Order and Related Forms

In a small business, the shipping order proper is simply an order issued to the warehouse and shipping departments indicating (a) name and address of consignee and shipping instructions, and (b) quantities and descriptions of items to be shipped. In larger organizations various copies of the shipping order or related forms may be in use. (Figure 11-1 is the master for a shipping order set which comprises five copies and labels or tags. Other copies in general may be classified primarily according to what they are for and secondarily according to who gets them. Thus, one or more of the following forms or copies may be in use.

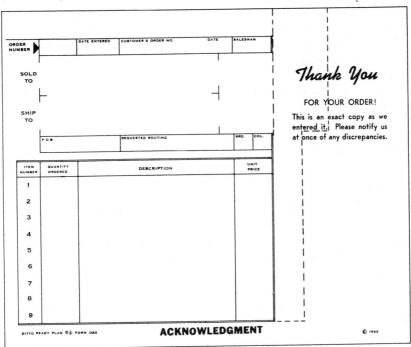

Ditto Division, Bell & Howell

Figure 11-1. Order and Invoice Master for Direct Process Duplicator

The dotted lines are shown on the shipping order form to outline the area of spot-carbon on the back of the form. Quantities shipped and other information entered on the shipping order by the shipping clerk can be carbonized onto the backing slip beneath.

Warehouse and shipping copies. In some cases, there is a copy of the order for each Warehouse department that is to fill any part of the order and a copy for the Shipping department to use in assembling the goods as they come from the warehouse departments. All affected departments can be working on the order at the same time. Use of such copies will save time in dispatching and in getting the order together for shipping.

Advice or acknowledgment copies. These copies indicate receipt of the order by the order department. Such copies are sometimes prepared for (1) customer, (2) Sales department, (3) salesman, and (4) Service department.

Journal or register. This may be a serial number list of shipping orders issued, with space for consignee's name, date issued, and date shipped. Such a register is a control over the shipping order proper until it comes back from the Shipping department and is used for seeing that the order is not delayed.

Unfilled order copies (or register copies). These are used for checking off the quantities actually shipped. These copies are filed by customer name. Such a copy may be needed in case of contract shipments where a customer's contract is shipped over some period of time.

Posting copies. Posting copies are provided for posting the stock records or the order statistics records.

Auxiliary forms. These include packing slips, labels, and bills of lading, which are sometimes produced by separate writing and sometimes produced as copies of the original shipping order.

Customer's Own Written Order as Shipping Order

Some small businesses use the customer's own written order as the shipping order, instead of writing a formal shipping order from it (as indicated in the previous section). The Order department simply assigns a serial number to the order when it comes in, enters customer's name and number in the order register, and sends the customer's order to the warehouse. Any instructions necessary for filling the order are written on a rider, which is pasted to the bottom of the customer's order. When the order comes back from the shipping room, it is priced, extended, and footed and the invoice is typed from it. This plan is often attractive, of course, because it eliminates writing and proofreading the shipping order forms.

In many manufacturing concerns, however, it is not feasible to send the customer's written order to the warehouse for one or more of a variety of reasons:

(1) Many of the sales orders are contract orders calling for shipping at various dates. It is necessary for the Order department to

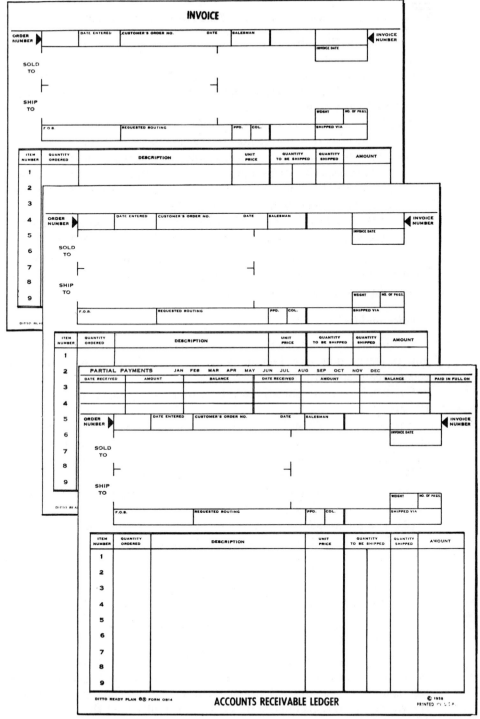

Ditto Division, Bell & Howell

Figure 11-2. Invoice and Copies

schedule the shipments and issue separate shipping orders according to schedule.

(2) Goods called for on sales orders frequently have to be manufactured. Often production control and shipping control cannot proceed from a single writing.

(3) Too many functions must be performed simultaneously (in different warehouse departments) to permit the use of a single order.

(4) The sales order (or customer's order) is usually incomplete as to technical specifications and various instructions to the departments which fill the order. Consequently it may be necessary to write a shipping order to supply missing details.

(5) If the customer's own order is sent to the warehouse and shipping departments, there is always the chance that it might get lost.

When it is not feasible or desirable to send the customer's own written order to the warehouse, the alternative, of course, is to write a shipping order with as many copies as are necessary.

Invoice and Related Forms

The invoice is an advice that is sent to the customer for shipment made and payment due (see Figure 11-2). Copies of the invoice that are sometimes prepared are:

Customer's copies. Sometimes the customer asks for several copies of the invoice.

Advice copies. These include the salesman's copy, which notifies him that the order has been billed. He may use this copy for computing his commission. Another example of an advice copy is the branch office copy.

Posting copies or accounting copies. These include:

(1) The accounts receivable copy, which is used to post the charge to the customer's account.

(2) The commission copy, which is used by the Accounting department for figuring the commission and crediting it to the salesman's account.

(3) The sales distribution copy, which is used for posting to the sales record or otherwise taking off a sales analysis.

(4) The cost copy, which may be used by the cost department for compiling the cost of goods shipped. Copies (3) and (4) are sometimes combined.

Note that it is sometimes not necessary that a separate posting copy be provided for each of the posting functions. Arguments in favor of providing separate copies are: (a) use of separate copies makes it possible for the various operations to be performed concurrently, and (b) in ledgerless bookkeeping the copies are filed instead of posted.

Journal or register copy. This copy is for serial number file.

COMBINATION OF ORDER PROCEDURES
AND BILLING PROCEDURES

Combinations Named

Sometimes the billing procedure is combined with the order procedure, and one set of forms serves the purposes of both procedures. Order and billing procedures may be classified as:

(1) Separate order procedure and billing procedure, in which the bill and its copies are not produced in the same writing as the order and its copies. The shipping order and its copies are, of course, written first, and the warehouse and shipping room copies are released. The bill and its copies are produced complete in a separate writing after the goods have been shipped.

(2) Complete pre-billing procedures, in which the bill or invoice and its copies are produced completely in the same writing as the shipping order and its copies. The invoice may be the original writing and the other forms carbon copies, or all copies of the forms may be produced from duplicating master. (Methods of writing and reproducing are illustrated in Chapter 6.) The shipping order and its copies are released immediately to the warehouse and other departments, and the invoice and its copies are released after the goods have been shipped.

(3) Incomplete pre-billing procedures, which are similar to complete pre-billing procedures except that the invoice is not written completely in the original writing. It may lack, for instance, shipping route, shipping weight, price, and extensions where that information cannot be determined until the goods are made ready for shipment. That information is entered on the invoice in a later writing (called a supplementary writing), after the goods have been shipped.

In general, the advantage of pre-billing procedures over separate order and billing procedure is saving in writing and proof of writing. Pre-billing cannot be used under all conditions, however, and the conditions for its use must be carefully studied.

(4) Unit shipping order procedures. This is not a distinct type of procedure but a modification of the conventional separate order and billing procedure. In a unit shipping order procedure, a separate shipping order is produced for each line item of the sales order. (Thus, if there are three line items in the sales order, there

will be three shipping orders or shipping tickets.) The unit tickets are dispatched to the warehouse immediately, or if goods cannot be shipped immediately, they are filed until goods are available. After the goods are shipped, an invoice is produced (as in a separate order and billing procedure) from the shipping orders.

Unit shipping order procedures are sometimes used where (a) numerous warehouse departments may be involved in filling a sales order, and it is not desired to send each department a copy of the entire order, and (b) the entire order cannot be shipped at once, and it is desired to release the unit shipping orders only as the goods are available for shipment.

Separate Order and Billing Procedure (Figure 11-3)

Figure 11-3 diagrams the main steps in a separate order and billing procedure. A shipping order and copies are written in the office and sent to the warehouse and shipping departments where the goods are picked, packed, and shipped. The packer writes the quantity shipped on his copy of the shipping order and sends it back to the office. The office prices and extends the shipping order, and types the invoice. In the case illustrated, only 15 units of Product A (of the 20 ordered) were shipped, and the office accordingly writes a new shipping order set (the back order) for the balance of five units not shipped.

Conditions for Use of Separate Order and Billing Procedure

In practice, there are reasons why it might be considered necessary to operate separate shipping order and billing procedures. In the first place, it may be necessary to supply a great deal of technical product information on the shipping order which it is unnecessary and undesirable to show on the invoice. In the second place, the company might have a difficult back-order situation because of which a single shipping order of, say, ten items may actually be shipped piece-meal in three or four lots. There might be, therefore, not one invoice for the one shipping order, but three or four. The company may desire to show only the items actually shipped on each invoice, with no indication of unshipped items. And in some lines of business (as in certain style lines), where the vendor is permitted certain latitude in the matter of sizes, colors, and shipping dates, it may be desired to show descriptions of goods actually shipped on invoices. (Note, however, that it is sometimes possible to solve some of these problems in a pre-billing procedure. Where direct process duplicating is used, for instance, a master writing may be used to produce invoices for a number of shipments on the same order. See Figure 6-7)

OFFICE

(1) Types shipping order and invoice set (original and 2 copies)
(2) Sends shipping order and packing slip to warehouse
(3) Files shipping order—office copy

WAREHOUSE AND SHIPPING

(4) Warehouse fills order and notes quantity shipped
(5) Shipping department checks and ships, enclosing packing slip in package

OFFICE

(6) Receives shipping order from shipping room
(7) Prices, extends quantities shipped, and foots

OFFICE

(8) Types invoice and office copy from file
(9) Sends invoice to customer
(10) Writes new shipping order (called the back order) for 5 units Product A not yet shipped (not illustrated).

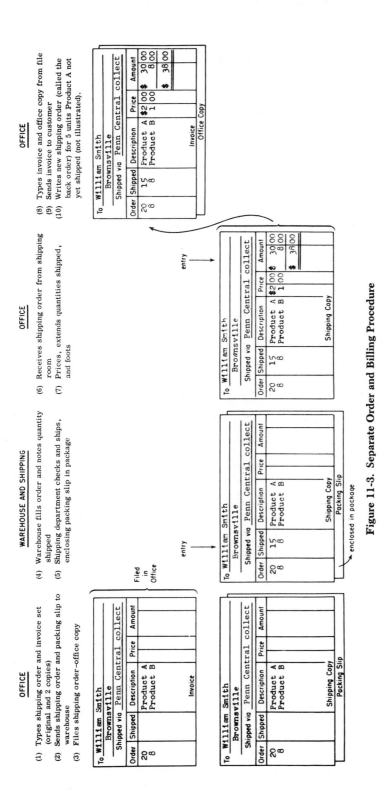

Figure 11-3. Separate Order and Billing Procedure

231

Illustration: Separate Order and Billing Procedures; Steel Warehousing

Figures 11-4 and 11-5 are illustrations of a shop order form and cost summary; Figure 11-6 is an invoice set for a steel warehousing company. The company stores a large inventory of sheet steel of various specifications in rolls and steel in other shapes and cuts them to customers' orders. It will be noted that the summary (Figure 11-5) contains a great deal of information which it is not necessary to show on the invoice, but which is used in producing the invoice set.

No. A 34274

TAKEN BY: J.E. TYPED: 2.40
CHECKED BY: J.O. NO. INVOICES REQUIRED
25 - 3%
SALESMAN
P.A. TEL.

SOLD TO: Smith Stamping & Mfg. Co.
1615 First Ave. So.
Bowmanville, Illinois
SHIP TO: Same
S O #

DATE 3-5-59 P.O. 207

PROMISED: 3-10-59 DATE OF SHIPMENT: 3-10-59 INVOICE NUMBER AND DATE: Mar. 10, 1959 20147

SHIP VIA: O K Trk. Line
TRUCK ☒ RAIL ☐ AIR P P ☐ AIR FRT ☐ COLLECT ☐ PPD & CHG ☒
PARCEL POST ☐ BY EXPRESS ☐ AIR EXPRESS ☐ SPEC DEL ☐ SD BL ☐ PPD ☐ INS'D ☐

WAREHOUSE USE	SPECIAL INSTRUCTIONS	TYPE OF MATERIAL	TEMPER	THICK	WIDTH	LENGTH	ID/OD	BO	QUANTITY	PRICE 100 #	EXTENSION
	38	302	Anld.	025	25/64	C	16		QO 230 QS 262	89.10 cwt. Less Scrap Allowance	

RATING 1☐ 2☐ 3☐ R☐
OWE P.D. SINCE
CREDIT AUTHORIZED

SKID
BOX
OTHER
PACKING INSTRUCTIONS

REMARKS: For Resale

C.A. REQ.
COPIES COMPLETED
BY
MAIL PKG SLIP

Figure 11-4. Order: Shop Copy

The invoice set (Figure 11-6) is an interesting one from a mechanical standpoint because of the specialized extensions that are made on the different copies. The following copies are prepared:

Original invoice ⎫
Duplicate invoice ⎬ shows quantities, selling prices, and sales value extensions.
Triplicate invoice ⎭

Salesman's copy — shows commission calculation at bottom.
Accounts receivable (2) — shows cost calculation at bottom.

Figure 11-5. Order: Cost Summary

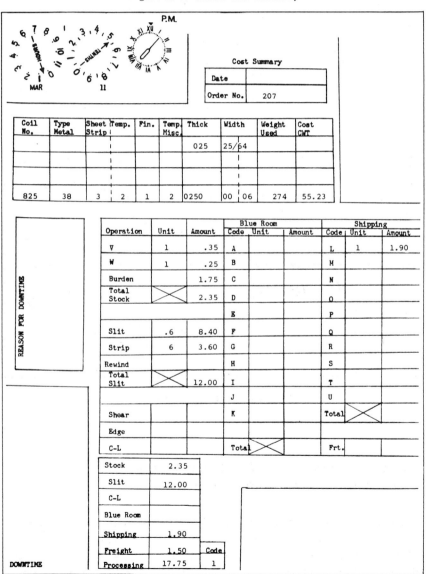

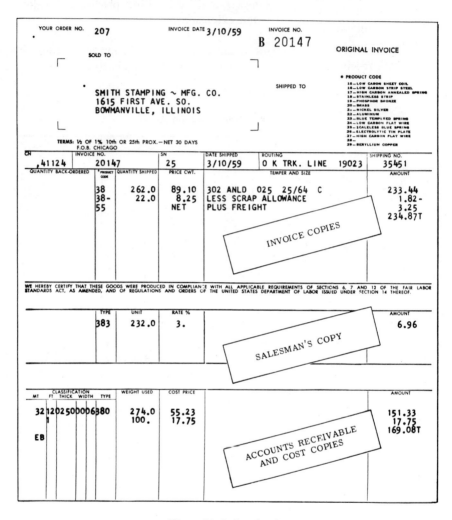

Figure 11-6. Invoice Set

Illustration: Invoices Prepared on Writing Machines with Arithmetic and Memory Capability

Figures 11-7 is an invoice prepared by writing machine with arithmetic and memory capability (pages 235-236), and Figure 11-8 is the accounts receivable ledger form which is posted in the same operation as the billing. Customers names and addresses (indexed by customer number)

Figure 11-7. Invoice Prepared by Writing Machine with
Arithmetic and Memory Capability

SOLD TO				SHIP TO				
SEATTLE DRUG STORE 4311 CRENSHAW ST. SEATTLE, WASHINGTON				-SAME-				

CUSTOMER DATE	CUSTOMER ORDER NUMBER	CUSTOMER NUMBER	INVOICE NUMBER	DATE	SALESMAN
4-30-70	10123	122	13458	4-30-70	MIKE BURN

QUANTITY ORDERED	QUANTITY SHIPPED	PRODUCT NUMBER	DESCRIPTION	PRICE	DISCOUNT	EXTENSION	COST	COST EXTENSION
10	10	264	MAPLE PIPE RACK	2.49	.10	22.41	1.98	19.80
12	12	312	DELUXE SHAMPOO	1.50	.03	17.46	1.00	12.00

			TAX	OTHER	FREIGHT	TOTAL INVOICE	GROSS PROFIT
361-457 (STD. 2)			2.39			42.26	COMMISSION 8.07
							.80

Victor

Figure 11-8. Accounts Receivable Ledger Posted in the
Same Operation as the Invoice Illustrated in Figure 11-7

Account Receivable

SOLD TO		CUSTOMER NUMBER
SEATTLE DRUG STORE 4311 CRENSHAW ST. SEATTLE, WASHINGTON		122
	LIMIT	10000.00

DATE	INV. NO.	SYM-BOL	DEBIT	CREDIT	BALANCE	SALES TO DATE	CK. DG.
4-30-70	13458	DB	42.26		42.26	39.87	4

Victor

and product descriptions with selling prices and cost prices (indexed by product number) for billing are both stored on-line in memory. The operator inserts the blank invoice form and the accounts receivable ledger form in the machine and indexes account number on the keyboard. The machine types customers name and address automatically. In the particulars section, she types quantity ordered, quantity shipped and product number for each product shipped. The machine types product descriptions automatically, and does all the calculations and footings illustrated automatically.

For the accounts receivable ledger operation, the operator picks up the old balance by keyboard operation before she inserts the ledger form in the chute. The machine is equipped for automatic line finding actuated through position perforations at the left edge of the form, made by the machine as it posts. The machine adds the sale to the old balance, computes the new balance, printing these items as shown and ejects the account.

The invoicing operation is performed on a computing billing machine and, as indicated above, it includes the complete package of mathematics: calculating the invoice proper (extensions, scrap allowance, freight, and net invoice), calculating commissions, and computing standard cost of sales for the shipment. Note that the cost and consequently the gross profit on each sale is known. This information is the basis for performance reports.

Integrated Data-Processing for Sales and Cash-Collecting

An integrated data-processing procedure for sales and cash-collecting used by the steel warehousing company mentioned above is diagrammed in skeleton form in Figure 11-9.[1] The procedure follows the basic principle that data be captured in the original writing if possible in form for subsequent use and that any re-writing be mechanical (that is, not by human application).

The current procedure starts with the typing of invoice and copies and the production of punched paper tape for use in a tape-to-card converter. The converter punches Accounts Receivable cards (one card for each invoice) and line item cards (one for each distributable item on each invoice). The Accounts Receivable cards (Step 3) are filed alphabetically for customer ledger purposes. (The file *is* the customers' ledger.) Cash receipts are applied (Step 5) by pulling the card to which a receipt applies and putting it in the paid file. Customers' statements are produced at the end of the month by processing the open Accounts Receivable file in a tabulator (ss Chapter 23).

---

[1] Punched-card tabulating procedures are explained in detail in Chapters 21 to 23. The purpose of the chart in Figure 11-9 is to explain what is done without explaining in detail how it is done.

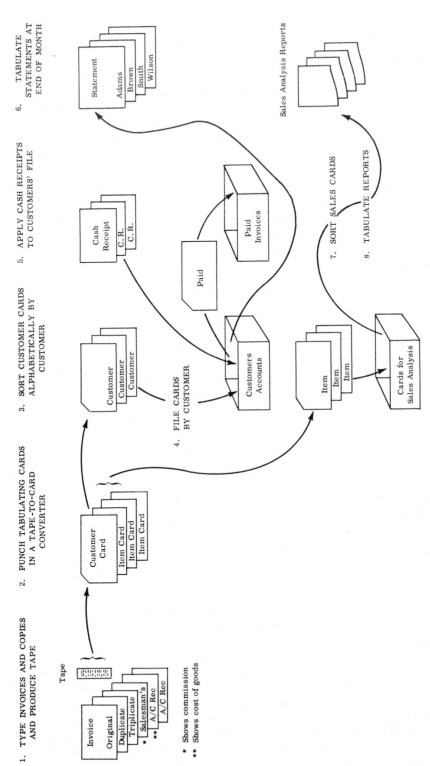

Figure 11-9. Integrated Data Processing: Invoice—Accounts Receivable—Sales Analysis

237

Complete Pre-Billing (Figure 11-10)

Figure 11-10 diagrams the writing of a shipping order and invoice set from a sales order. Note that after the sales order is received by the Order department, it is priced and extended; then it is used by the typist to type a shipping order and invoice set. In practice, a great deal of shipping information and technical information may be added before the shipping order and invoice are typed.

After being typed, the shipping order and packing slip are sent to the warehouse, and the invoice and office copy are kept in the office. The invoice is released after the goods have been shipped. Note that if the goods are not shipped as ordered, it is necessary to produce a new invoice for the goods shipped. It should be pointed out that complete pre-billing can be used under rather special conditions:

(1) Since both the shipping order and the invoice are written simultaneously (one as a copy of the other), all information that will have to appear on the invoice has to be known at the time the order is written. Such information includes shipping route, shipping weights, and prices.

(2) Inventory conditions must permit shipping most of the orders complete, and shipping them just as they are written.

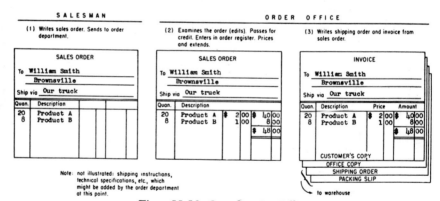

Figure 11-10. Complete Pre-Billing

Order department writes shipping order and invoices from sales order.

Incomplete Pre-Billing

Sometimes, whereas it is not possible to produce a complete invoice at the same time the shipping order is written, it is possible to produce most of the writing on the invoice at that time. Customer's name and address, product names, and certain other information on the invoice and the shipping order are identical. In that case, the systems man may desire to use an incomplete pre-billing procedure. In such procedure, the shipping order and the invoice, with their copies, are written as completely as possible (in a single writing) when the sales order is received. Then after the goods are shipped, the invoice and its copies are completed as to shipping weights, prices, extensions, and so forth.

Two illustrations of the use of incomplete pre-billing are presented in the following sections:

(1) Use of pre-billing where (a) actual weight shipped and (b) extensions have to be entered on the invoice after the goods are shipped. Shipping weights are not standardized; it is the custom of the industry to ship as nearly as possible the weight which the customer indicates in his order, and bill him accordingly.

(2) Use of pre-billing where (a) actual quantities shipped and extensions have to be entered on the invoice after the goods are shipped; either because of back order (out of stock) conditions or because certain items must be manufactured to order.

Note that the quantity which cannot be shipped on the original shipping order is shipped later on a separate shipping order called "the back order."

Incomplete Pre-Billing: Actual Weight for Billing Determined in Shipping Department

Figure 11-11 diagrams steps in pre-billing in a meat packing plant where the billing weight is determined in the Shipping department. In this procedure, the salesman or order clerk writes up the shipping order and invoice set (Figure 11-12), complete except for actual weights and extensions, and sends the shipping copy to the shipping room. At the shipping room the weights are entered when the goods are prepared for packing. Then the shipping order is returned to the office.

In the office, it is extended, footed, and used to complete the invoice and receipt copy. Note that the whole operation is done in pencil ("pencil billing").

In the office, the pounds shipped are copied from the shipping order to the invoice and receipt copies. (The carbon paper has remained intact.) Then the extensions are computed and entered, and the invoice and receipt copies are given to the truck driver. He gives the invoice to the customer along with the goods, and gets the customers to sign the receipt, which he returns to the office.

Incomplete Pre-Billing: Actual Shipping Quantities Determined in Shipping Room; Manufacturer of Medical and Dental Equipment

Figure 11-13 is a diagram of the flow of work in an order and invoice procedure in which a Computyper is used. The order set is produced from customer cards and item cards and two by-product tapes are produced:

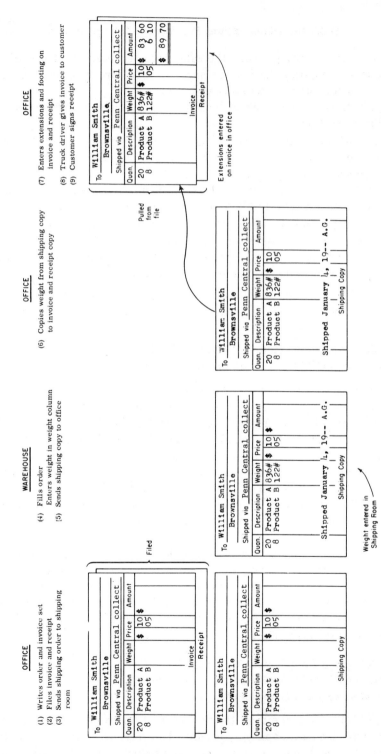

Figure 11-11. Incomplete Pre-Billing

Actual weight for billing entered after assembling the goods.

Figure 11-12. Invoice for Pencil Billing—Meat Packing

Invoice Date
Sold To
Address
S-man ___ Ship To

LOADING NO.

INVOICE
15587

Date Taken
Terms
When
Stop No.

QUAN.	I T E M	WEIGHT	PRICE	AMOUNT	QUAN.	I T E M	WEIGHT	PRICE	AMOUNT
	BNLS. R. & E. HAM					SMO. JOWL			
	BOILED HAM					CELLO SQR.			
	VA. CKD. HAM								
	CANNED HAM ( )					SLIC. BACON			
5#	( ) SAUS.								
	LIVER SAUS. ( )								
	BOLO. ( )					BX. w/H PK. SAUS. ( )			
						BX. 1 # CELLO SAUS.			
	PK. LOINS					BX. NO JAX BULK			
	B. BUTTS					BX. NO JAX CELLO			
	RIBS					BX. FRANKS			
	HOG LIVER								
	BNLS. BF. - PK. & BF. OFFAL					CHEESE · OLEO · FISH			
						LARD			
	SMO. HAM								
	FULLY CKD. HAM								
						BEEF · VEAL · HOGS			
	BACON								
	RTE. PIC.				EXTENDED BY	TOTAL WEIGHT	**TOTAL INVOICE**		
	SHKLS. HAM								

FOR CONDITIONS RESPECTING
WEIGHTS, ETC. - SEE REVERSE SIDE

INVOICE

a composite tape which is used later to type the invoice and a select tape which goes to the tabulating department for punching cards for the preparation of order reports.

When the shipping copy of the order comes back from the Shipping department, the composite tape of the order is pulled from file and used to type the invoice. The Computyper computes extensions, footings and

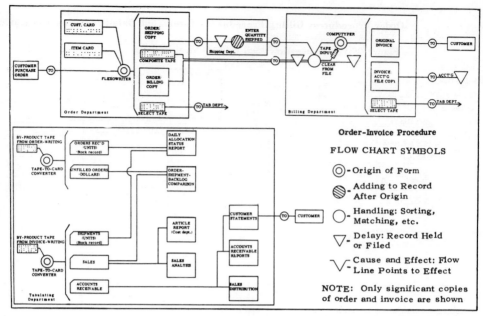

Figure 11-13. Integrated Data Processing: Order—Invoice—Accounts Receivable—Analysis

deductions automatically and produces a select tape which goes to the Tabulating department for punching cards for the preparation of sales distribution reports.

UNIT SHIPPING ORDER PROCEDURES

Unit Shipping Order Procedures in General

A unit ticket order procedure is one in which a separate order (a unit ticket) is issued for each line item on an order. Each ticket must bear, along with the product item, the name and address of the consignee or some other identification, and the order number. Unit tickets may be (1) partially pre-printed or (2) currently written.

Pre-Printed Unit Shipping Orders (Figure 11-14)

Where the number of products is not too great, it may be feasible to use partially pre-printed unit tickets with product names, sizes, and prices pre-printed, keeping them in files and pulling them as required to

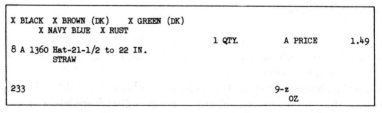

Figure 11-14. Unit Shipping Order

dispatch orders. These tickets become active when they are pulled from the files and stamped with the order number. Figure 11-14 illustrates a unit shipping order for a certain stock item carried in a number of sizes and colors. The order clerk checks color before releasing the ticket. Where the quantity is other than one, she also writes the quantity.

It is not desirable to use the original (multiple item) sales order as a warehouse and shipping order in this case because of the large number of items (and departments) on a typical order. The advantage of unit shipping orders is that they can be sorted and dispatched so that all the warehouse departments affected by an order can work on it at one time. Also, the unit orders received by a department can be sorted by product number to facilitate order picking.

Pre-printing, of course, saves current writing and proof of writing. Note, however, that where there is an extremely large number of products, it may not be desirable to use manually pulled pre-printed unit tickets because of the time taken to get them out of file.

The scheduling and dispatching procedure is interesting. Scheduling is accomplished by stamping (1) the sales order and (2) all the tickets for each order with the following information, all in large symbols:

(a) the time the order is scheduled to be filled,

(b) the number of the bin in which the order is to be assembled in the packing room, and

(c) the order number

The numbering operation (bin number) is done with a standard addressing machine loaded with one plate for each bin in the packing room. Each successive order is automatically stamped with a bin number until all the plates have been used. Then it is known that no bins are available until the next hour. The same plates are used over and over—once each hour. Note that the operation of warehouse and shipping rooms must be planned; warehouse labor capacity must be coordinated with bin capacity in the shipping room.

In dispatching, the unit orders are sent to the warehouse departments and the sales orders proper to the packing room. In the packing room, each order form is sent to the proper bin, to be used in checking the goods that come down from the warehouse departments.

Currently Written Unit Shipping Orders

In some organizations, unit shipping orders are currently written (instead of being pre-printed, as in the previous case). A certain mail-order house writes unit warehouse and shipping tickets from the customers' orders. In this case, the number of products is extremely large.

Unit Tickets Produced from Duplicating Master

Figure 6-12 is an illustration of unit tickets produced from a duplicating master. (Duplicating methods are explained in Chapter 6.) Figure 6-12a is the master which was typed for a three-item order. Figure 6-12b is a set of unit tickets which have been processed through the duplicating machine. Note that the sets of tickets are bound at the right; this binding can be detached to separate the tickets. On the set illustrated, the heading and one line item have been picked up on the top ticket, and one line item has been picked up on each of the next two tickets. These impressions were made by one pass through the duplicating machine. Figure 6-12c is the three tickets, separated. Note that the second and third tickets were each passed through the duplicating machine a second time to pick up the heading. The line items were masked off the master for this second run, leaving only the heading exposed on the master.

Uses of Unit Shipping Orders

Unit shipping orders can be used:

(1) Where it is desirable to provide each department with a separate shipping order covering only the items with which that department is concerned, rather than with a copy of the entire order.

(2) Where different items on the sales order have different promised delivery dates. When unit shipping orders are used, the items can be sorted and filed according to the promised delivery dates, and they can be released to the warehouse on the required dates.

(3) Where there is a difficult back order problem. Unit shipping orders can be released to the Shipping department, and if the goods are out of stock, the shipping orders can be filed by product number. When a product becomes available, the back orders are pulled from file and released to the warehouse for shipment.

(4) For analysis of orders received by product. In some businesses, orders are taken some time before promised delivery dates, or even before the goods are manufactured. It may be desired to write the shipping orders as the sales orders are received, produce unit shipping orders (as illustrated), and sort the unit shipping orders by product class to determine how many of each product have been sold.

Complete Procedures Outlined; Separate Order and Billing

The previous sections of this chapter have described basic order and billing procedures, and the descriptions have been restricted to major points. The present section describes all the steps in an actual separate order and billing situation, which is fairly typical. (It is not intended to be a model procedure. In fact, considerable clerical work could probably be saved by changing the procedure to incomplete pre-billing.) The purpose is to show all phases of the work of order and billing. The steps are as follows:

(1) Credit department receives either (a) the customer's purchase order or (b) the sales order written by the salesman, and reviews it for credit. If the order is approved, it is sent to the Order department. If the order is rejected, the Credit department corresponds with the customer accordingly.

(2) Order department reviews the order for completeness of detail necessary for filling it properly, adds such information relating to sizes, specifications, and routing as may be necessary, indicates whether the shipment is to be sent freight prepaid (charge selling expense), freight prepaid (charge customer), or freight collect, and writes a shipping order in three copies:
    (a) Shipping order proper.
    (b) Packing slip.
    (c) Office copy.

(3) Order department prices the order, files the customer's purchase order or the sales order alphabetically (after marking the shipping order number on it), sends the original shipping order and the packing slip to the Shipping department, and files the office copy numerically as an order register.

(4) In the warehouse and shipping departments, order pickers pull the goods from stock and assemble them, checkers recount the items and compare with the shipping order, and packers prepare the goods for shipment and pack them. The shipping clerk weighs the goods and writes the bills of lading in four copies:
    (a) Original for carrier.
    (b) Copy for carrier.
    (c) Copy for customer (with invoice).
    (d) Office copy.

Where the entire order was not shipped, due to out of stock conditions, the shipping clerk indicates the portions of the original order to be back-ordered, marks the shipping order "Shipped," and enters the date. He returns the original shipping order to the Order department, with copy (c) of bill of lading attached. He sends copy (d) of the bill of lading to the disbursement voucher clerk (who takes care of paying freight on f.o.b. destination shipments)

(5) Order department receives the shipping order from the Shipping department and copy (c) of the bill of lading, refers to the office (register) copy of the order, stamps it "Shipped," and enters the date. Where the entire order has not been shipped, the Order department writes a new shipping order (the back order) for the quantities yet to be shipped. The back order is in the same form as the original shipping order. It is cross-referenced to the

original shipping order by writing the number of the back order on the office copy of the original order. (The back order is sent through the same steps as the original shipping order.) Order department sends original shipping order with bill of lading attached to Billing department.

(6) Billing department receives the shipping order and copy (c) of the bill of lading. Billing department extends the quantities shipped on the shipping order, adds the freight (if the customer is to be billed) and sales tax, foots the order, and stamps an invoice number on the shipping order. It finally makes a listing machine tape of the amounts of the orders to provide a proof total for later accounting operations.

(7) The billing typist types the invoice and copies from the shipping order.

Typical copies are:

(a) Original to customer.

(b) Copy to customer.

(c) Journal copy for the Accounting department.

(8) Billing department proofreads the typing, recomputes the calculations, runs proof tape of totals, compares proof tape of invoices with proof tape of shipping orders (Step 6), and sends journal copy of invoices to Order department. Mails original invoice and copy to customer, with copy (c) of bill of lading.

Shipping order is filed alphabetically, behind customer's original order.

(9) Order department matches invoices (register copies) with register copies of shipping orders, writes invoice number and date on register copy of shipping order, and sends the journal copy of the invoice to the Accounts Receivable department

(10) Disbursement voucher clerk receives freight bill (copy b) from the carrier; matches with office copy of the bill of lading (Step 4); notes that the bill of lading was actually drawn "Prepaid"; marks the office copy of bill of lading "paid" and date; codes the day's freight bills by account to be charged. All shipments to customers are charged to Freight Out Expense.

(11) Cashier sends disbursement voucher to carrier with copy of freight bills covered by the voucher. Carrier stamps the freight bills "paid" and returns them. File with office copy of disbursement voucher.

(12) The Accounting department enters the journal copy of the invoice in the sales journal in serial number order, posts to the customer's accounts, takes off the sales distribution, and files the invoices by serial number. Note that in the sales distribution, the amounts of freight which were billed to customers will be credited to Freight Out Expense.

Order Processing and Inventory Control at Westinghouse[1]

This section describes the order processing and inventory control system at Westinghouse which is a part of the tele-computer system of that company. The purpose is to show how a very large and geographically extended system works. Although computers and data communication are involved, the discussion here is confined to features of the order processing and inventory control system as such. (Computers and data communication equipment are described in Chapter 24.)

Late in 1962, Westinghouse established a corporate, general purpose information processing center using a high-speed, real-time computer. This computer serves as the hub of a nationwide tele-printer network. The heart of the system is called the Tele-Computer Center . . .

The Tele-Computer Center serves approximately 300 locations throughout the United States and Canada. These include plants, administrative and sales offices, warehouses, repair centers, and distributors for the entire organization. The Tele-Computer Center has been designed to administer four major operations . . . (of which only the second will be described in this excerpt):

1. Message switching
2. Order processing and inventory control
3. Corporate accounting applications
4. Remote data processing . . .

Order Processing and Inventory Control. Any of the 117 industrial and utility sales offices served by the information system may originate an order message, using a teleprinter to prepare a message tape in a specified format. The address code of the message directs it automatically to the order processing program within the computer.

The computer performs certain checking and editing functions and then proceeds to locate the desired items in its file of inventory records. If an item is out of stock at the warehouse nearest the customer, the computer searches for the item at warehouse progressively nearer the factory, and finally at the factory itself, in order to minimize transportation costs.

Having located the required items, the computer generates a message, directing the warehouses to ship the items. It also prepares the shipping labels, bills of lading, and packing lists for those items on the receiving teleprinters at the warehouses. Meanwhile price extensions and sales taxes have been calculated for the periodic invoice printing run. Inventory records are updated as each order is processed, and examined for reordering points. If a reordering point is reached, the applicable formulas are automatically brought into play to determine the proper replenishment quantity. A requisition message is automatically produced and sent to the proper factory. Sales statistics are also accumulated during the processing or orders. The entire process takes less than three seconds after receipt of an order message.

The system provides as a by-product a high-speed, automatic stock inquiry service to sales offices . . . . Before installation of the system, information received by sales offices was often two to six weeks old.

[1] Edgar C. Gentle, Jr., *Data Communications in Business—An Introduction,* American Telephone and Telegraph Company (1965), pp. 32 ff.

12

Sales Distribution;
Principles of Distribution

Distribution Defined; Organization

Distribution is the procedure of abstracting details (dollars or quantities) from media (invoices in this case) and accumulating totals for report purposes. A distribution procedure includes (1) a journal entry for posting summary totals to the general ledger, (2) reports on which various class totals appear, and (3) worksheets, accounts, and other forms on which transactions are accumulated. A sales distribution procedure of the familiar columnar sales journal type accordingly includes (1) the journal entry for sales, (2) the sales reports, and (3) the sales journal proper.

The subject of sales distribution may be approached by considering (1) classifications and reports and (2) methods—manual and machine. It will be noted that the basic classifications and reports embrace not only sales, sales returns, sales allowances, and sales tax liabilities, but also (in manufacturing concerns) cost of sales and cost of returned sales. The media used in sales distributions are invoices and credit memos.

In small organizations, the sales distribution is operated as a part of the general accounting system. The columnar sales journal kept by the Bookkeeping department is an example. In the other cases where the volume is large, it may be operated by a separate set of clerks, who prove their reports against controls kept by the Bookkeeping department.

This chapter explains the principles of distribution and illustrates them by specific application to the field of sales distribution. The principles are the same for all distribution problems—sales, purchases, expenses, payroll, and any others. The applications of the principles are different, however, and separate sections are included in this book for purchase and expense distribution (Chapter 15), labor distribution (Chapter 17), and materials distribution (Chapter 18).

Note that the design of the distribution procedure is not a problem distinct from the other procedures to which the distribution is related. The sales distribution procedure and the billing procedure must be considered together. Likewise, the timekeeping procedure and the labor distribution procedure must be considered together. In fact, the requirements of labor distribution largely determine the requirements of job-time recording and how it shall be done.

Classifications

Some of the classifications used in sales distribution are:

(1) Product classifications.
(2) Salesman classifications.
(3) Customer classifications.
(4) Method of sale (direct sale by salesmen, mail order, and so on).
(5) Territory classifications (state and cities or other trading areas).
(6) Trade class (line of business or activity of the customer, such as schools, theatres, churches, merchants, manufacturers).
(7) Channel of distribution (jobber, wholesaler, retailer).

The first four classifications might be called the "primary classifications." If sales are distributed to each of these classifications, reports would be prepared to show (1) how much of each product was sold, (2) how much was sold by each salesman, (3) how much was sold to each customer, and (4) how much was sold by each method of sale (by mail, by direct solicitation, and so on).

The remaining three classifications might be called "special classifications," which apply to customer groups. They represent a formal identification of customer location and other characteristics. By distributing sales to these classifications, it is possible to determine:

(5) How much was sold in each territory.
(6) How much was sold to all customers in each line of business.
(7) How much was sold through jobbers, wholesalers, retailers, and the like.

Report Structure

Common reports are listed in the table in Figure 12-1. Note that all these reports or only some of them may be prepared in a particular organization.

(1) Monthly group totals of sales and cost of sales:
    (a) By product class (Figure 12-2).
    (b) By territory (Figure 12-3).

Note that the main statement of profits is likely to show the grand total of sales and cost of sales by product class (Figure 12-2) or by ter-

SALES CLASSIFICATIONS AND REPORTS				
	Product Groups and Products	Salesmen	Customers	Territorial Group Trading Areas
(1) Monthly Totals on Profit and Loss Statement	Total for each Product Group			Total for each Territory
(2) Daily, Weekly, or Monthly Totals	Total for each Product	Total for each Salesman	Total for each Customer	Total for each City
		Total for each Salesman and sub-total for each Product	Total for each Customer and sub-total for each Product	

Figure 12-1

JORDAN SCHOOL SUPPLY COMPANY

SCHEDULE OF GROSS PROFIT BY PRODUCT CLASS

FOR JANUARY, 19--

Particulars	Equipment	Supplies	Total
Sales	$ x x.xx	$ x x.xx	$ x x.xx
Less - Cost of Sales	x x.xx	x x.xx	x x.xx
Gross Profit	$ x x.xx	$ x x.xx	$ x x.xx

Figure 12-2. Statement of Profits: Distribution of Sales and Cost of Sales by Product Class

JORDAN SCHOOL SUPPLY COMPANY

SCHEDULE OF GROSS PROFIT BY TERRITORY

FOR JANUARY, 19--

Particulars	Eastern	Western	Total
Sales	$ x x.xx	$ x x.xx	$ x x.xx
Less - Cost of Sales	x x.xx	x x.xx	x x.xx
Gross Profit	$ x x.xx	$ x x.xx	$ x x.xx

Figure 12-3. Statement of Profits: Distribution of Sales and Cost of Sales by Territory

ritory (Figure 12-3), and this statement may be supported by one or more report(s) of the following types:

(2) Daily, weekly, or monthly totals (depending upon the use):
    (a) By product.
    (b) By salesmen.
    (c) By customer.
    (d) Total for each salesman, subtotal for each product (Figure 12-4).
    (e) Total for each customer, subtotal for each product (Figure 12-5).

Illustrative Product Classification

In the skeleton reports illustrated in the previous section, a two-account classification is used for the monthly distributions for the statement of profits—equipment and supplies—and a ten-account classification is used for the salesman by product class and the customer by product class breakdowns:

(1) Seating
(2) School equipment and furniture
(3) Science equipment
(4) Physical education equipment
(5) Visual equipment
(6) Miscellaneous equipment
(7) Classroom supplies
(8) Art supplies
(9) Duplicating equipment and supplies
(10) Janitor's supplies

Figure 12-4

SALES REPORT: SALESMAN BY PRODUCT CLASS			
Salesman _____ Jordan _____	Month of _____ Jan. , 19--		
No.	**Product Class**		**Total**
1	Seating		
2	School equipment and furniture		
3	Science equipment		
4	Physical education equipment		
5	Visual equipment		
6	Miscellaneous equipment		
7	Classroom supplies		
8	Art supplies		
9	Duplicating equipment and supplies		
10	Janitor's supplies		
	Total		

No.	Product Class	Total

SALES REPORT: CUSTOMER BY PRODUCT CLASS

Customer ___A. B. Jones___ Month of ___ Jan. ___, 19--

No.	Product Class	Total
1	Seating	
2	School equipment and furniture	
3	Science equipment	
4	Physical education equipment	
5	Visual equipment	
6	Miscellaneous equipment	
7	Classroom supplies	
8	Art supplies	
9	Duplicating equipment and supplies	
10	Janitor's supplies	
	Total	

Figure 12-5

The ten-account classification is a subdivision of the two-account classification. To illustrate the effect of the number of accounts upon the method of distribution (as one of the factors), these two classifications plus a third classification of 71 accounts are used in the following sections:

(1)	Seating	4 accounts
(2)	School equipment and furniture	18 accounts
(3)	Science equipment	5 accounts
(4)	Physical education equipment	3 accounts
(5)	Visual equipment	5 accounts
(6)	Miscellaneous equipment	12 accounts
(7)	Classroom supplies	10 accounts
(8)	Art supplies	6 accounts
(9)	Duplicating equipment and supplies	1 account
(10)	Janitor's supplies	7 accounts

Forms—Invoices and Credit Memos

The basic forms for distribution in a sales distribution procedure are sales invoices and credit memos (returns and allowances). From the standpoint of the sales account classification, the media are either mixed or unit. A mixed invoice is one that has to be credited to more than one sales account in the classification. A unit invoice is one that can be credited to a single account in the classification. Note that if there are only two accounts in the sales classification (equipment and supplies), it is possible that all the invoices are unit invoices. (A separate series of invoices could be used for each of the two classes of sales, if desired.) On the other hand, where the sales account classification is a long one, it is probable that the sales invoices are mixed invoices. As will be noted in the following sections, the method of distribution to be used in a given case depends partly upon whether the invoices are unit invoices or whether there are also mixed invoices that would have to be handled.

The nature of the forms other than the original media (invoices and credit memos) depends upon the method selected. Various forms are illustrated in the following sections.

THE METHODS OF DISTRIBUTION

Four of the main methods of distribution are explained and illustrated in detail on the following pages of this chapter. These methods may be grouped:

(1) Columnar methods (pages 253 to 261).

(2) Unit account and columnar account methods (pages 261 to 263).

(3) Summary strip and unit ticket methods (pages 263 to 281).

(4) Register method (pages 281 to 282).

Columnar Methods

As the name suggests, columnar method is an attempt to provide a column for each account in the classification, or a column for each group of accounts. The number of accounts in the classification and the activity of various accounts and groups are two of the determining factors in the use of columnar methods.

The types of columnar method include:

(1) Pen-kept columnar journals (diagrammed in Figure 12-7).

(2) Pen-kept worksheets (diagrammed in Figure 12-11).

(3) Machine-kept columnar journals, which are

(a) produced as a by-product of the account posting operation (Figure 7-16), or

(b) produced by a separate posting operation.

The first two types of columnar method are discussed in the following sections. The third type is discussed on pages 145-147

Pen-Kept Columnar Journals

To illustrate the use of a pen-kept columnar journal as a method of distribution, and some of the conditions for its use, assume that a sales distribution system is being designed for the small dealer in school equipment and supplies who desires to have a statement of profits which will show gross profit separately for equipment and for supplies (as indicated in Figure 12-6, column 1).

A columnar sales journal which provides two columns for sales is diagrammed in Figure 12-7, together with the procedures for recording sales invoices and accumulating the totals. Each invoice is entered in the sales journal and is spread into the distribution columns. At the end of the month, the journal is footed and cross-footed, and the totals are posted to the General ledger. The statement of profits is prepared from the General ledger trial balance.

FACTORS AFFECTING SELECTION OF METHOD OF DISTRIBUTION: FOUR SETS OF FACTORS AND METHODS OF DISTRIBUTION SELECTED

Factors in Selection of Method / Method Illustrated →	(1) Columnar Journal	(2) Either: Columnar Spread Sheets Register Method	(3) Columnar Spread Sheets	(4) Unit Tickets
(1) Number of classifications involved in the problem. Examples: product (salesmen groups (and salesmen) customer groups (and customers))	Product class	Product class	Product class Salesmen	Product class Salesmen Customer and others
(2) Number of accounts in each classification.	2 accounts (Equipment and Supplies)	Equipment 6 groups, 49 accounts in all Supplies 4 groups, 22 accounts in all	Product class: 10 accounts Salesmen: 15	Product: 10 groups comprising 150 accounts Salesmen: 15 Customers: 1000 accounts
(3) Activity of the accounts in a typical period. (What accounts or groups have high activity and what ones have low activity? Does the activity of accounts change from week to week, month to month, or season to season?	Both accounts are active every day.	16 supplies accounts active in every posting run; seating group high activity; school equipment groups low activity except in spring and summer.	Product class: high activity in supplies accounts, low activity in equipment (see previous column). Salesmen: practically 100% activity.	Product class: high activity in supplies accounts, low activity in equipment (see column 2) Salesmen: practically 100% activity. Customers: 7½% activity in each posting batch.
(4) What totals and sub-totals are desired in the monthly journal entry?	Total of each account and combined total.	Grand total sales.	Total sales for each of 10 product classes.	Total sales dollars for each of 10 product groups.
(5) What supporting reports? Frequency ⎫ Totals and ⎬ of each sub-totals ⎭ What information is shown: Quantity Cost value Sales value?	None	Monthly sales report showing: (a) grand total sales (b) total for each group (10 groups) (c) sub-total for each account in each group	Weekly sales report for each salesman showing: (a) total sales (b) total for each product class	(A) Daily for each product: Quantity shipped (for posting to perpetual inventory accounts) (B) Weekly for each salesman: (a) total sales dollars (b) total dollars for each product class (C) Monthly for each customer: (a) total sales dollars (b) total sales dollars for each product class

254

Question	Totals only are required in the monthly report.	Totals only are required in the monthly report.	Detail postings to salesmen's sheets are desired, since the amounts (for equipment) are considered significant.	Only totals are required on reports
(6) Are posted details of transactions required for current reference or are reports showing totals of accounts in the classification considered adequate by the manager?				
(7) What is the amount of the average transaction?	Equipment, $200.00 Supplies, $8.00	Equipment, $200.00 Supplies, $8.00	Equipment, $200.00 Supplies, $8.00	$2.00
(8) If detail posting is required, is any description required?	Question not applicable.	Question not applicable.	No; invoice number is considered sufficient reference.	Question not applicable.
(9) Frequency of posting required.				Daily for each product See (5)
(10) Are the media unit or mixed?	Mixed	Mixed	Mixed	Original invoices are mixed; unit media created.
(11) What is the quantity per day?	Average 10	Average 40	Average 20 per salesman per day	Average 20 per salesman per day
(12) If the media are mixed, what is the average number of postings per medium?	1½	3	2	5
(13) In what size batches do the media come for distribution? What is the frequency of the batches?	10, daily	40, daily	300, daily	300, daily
(14) What is the sorted arrangement of media when received for distribution? Is it possible to get the media grouped in such manner as to facilitate taking off certain totals?	Media received in serial number order.	Media received in serial number order.	Media received in serial number order.	See 10, above
(15) Is it possible to get the distribution at the source by arrangement of the original writing?	No	Not considered possible	Not considered possible	Not considered possible

Figure 12-6

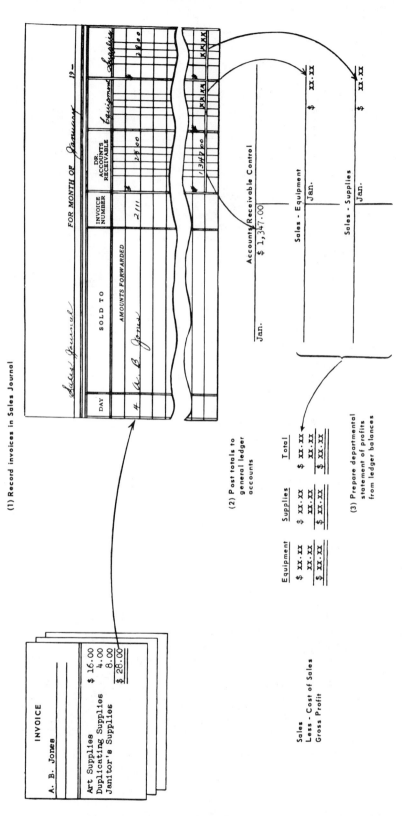

Figure 12-7. Distribution: Recording in Journal and Posting to Ledger
(a form of columnar distribution)

It should be noted that this simple plan illustrates the main elements of a complete distribution plan:

(1) Journal entry for posting summary totals to the General ledger.

(2) Sales report.

(3) Form (columnar) on which transactions are accumulated and classified.

Note that the invoices are mixed media, since a single invoice may comprise credits to more than one sales account. The invoices are entered at random in the journal, being recorded without preliminary sorting.

Note that in this example (and the following ones) the plan for recording and compiling credits to sales accounts is closely related to the plan for recording debits to accounts receivable. The sales journal is both (a) a columnar distribution of sales, and (b) a source of debit postings to accounts receivable. In many cases, however, the sales distribution plan in a business is separate from the accounts receivable plan. Illustrations of this situation appear in later sections.

Figure 12-8 is a sales journal with columns for freight-billed customers (credit Freight Out) and sales tax. This journal is similar to Figure 12-7 except for the addition of one column for freight-billed customers and two columns for sales tax (two states). Entries are made from sales invoices which show freight and sales tax as separate items at the bottom.

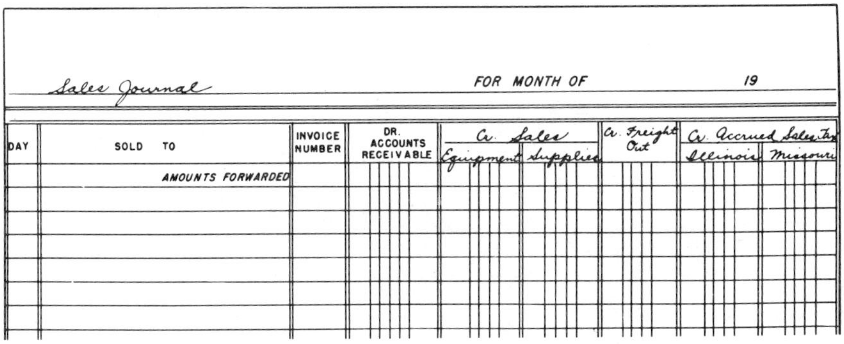

Figure 12-8. Sales Journal with Columns for Freight Billed Customers and Sales Tax

A sales journal similar to the above one could be designed to provide for a six-account sales classification. One could be set up to provide for the ten-account classification, or (by using a double-page spread) for a classification up to 20 or more accounts.

Figure 12-9 is a sales returns and allowances journal. The columns are the reverse of the ones in the sales journal illustrated in Figure 12-8. The original media from which entries are made are credit memos which show separately the sales value of the goods returned, the freight which is to be credited, and the sales tax on the sales value.

Sales, Returns and Allowance Journal

DAY	SOLD TO	CR. MEMO NUMBER	CR. ACCOUNTS RECEIVABLE	*Dr. Allowance*	*Dr. Sales Returns*		*Dr. Freight Out*	*Dr. Accrued Sales Tax*	
					Equipment	*Supplies*		*Illinois*	*Missouri*
	AMOUNTS FORWARDED								

Figure 12-9. Sales Returns and Allowance Journal

Columnar Spread Sheets

In some cases, the number of accounts in the desired sales classification is so large that it is not feasible to provide a column in the sales journal for each account (or even for each of the most active accounts). Assume that a distribution of sales to ten groups (71 accounts) is desired, as indicated in Figure 12-6, column 2.

Such a classification might be accommodated by a set of columnar spread sheets or worksheets, arranged with one or two sheets for each

Figure 12-10. Spread Sheet: Column for Each Product Class

Daily Distribution of Invoices, by Product

Major Division—Seating DATE 19

INVOICE NUMBER	*Total Seating*	*Steel Frame Classroom*	*Wood Frame Classroom*	*Auditorium Fixed*	*Auditorium Portable*

group of sales accounts. A spread sheet with columns headed for the four accounts in the seating group is illustrated in Figure 12-10. Note that the worksheet provides, among other features, a column for each of the classes of seating and one for the total. The total column is included to make the worksheet self-balancing (that is, to make it possible to foot and cross-foot the worksheet) and also, of course, because the group total is required for sales report purposes.

Note that when the worksheet is footed, two different classes of totals appear at the bottom of the columns. The total for all seating is described as a major total and the total for each of the four classes is described as a minor total.

Figure 12-11 illustrates how a set of worksheets is used as a sales journal. Although only three worksheets are indicated in this abbreviated diagram, there would be ten in the actual set—one for each group.

The procedure for operating these worksheets might be as follows: The invoices come to the distribution clerk in serial number order (average 40 per day) accompanied by pre-list tape. They are random-posted to the worksheets, and the invoices are kept in serial number order. The entry from the invoice onto each sheet affected by the invoice is invoice number, sales columns credits (one or more columns), and total of the items posted to that sheet from the invoice. An invoice may comprise items affecting several sheets. Periodically, say at the end of several days, sheets can be proved against the pre-list totals. Subtotals entered in the total columns of the ten sheets should agree with the totals of the pre-list tapes for the days posted.

Figure 12-11. Distribution: Recording on Spread Sheets
(a form of columnar method)

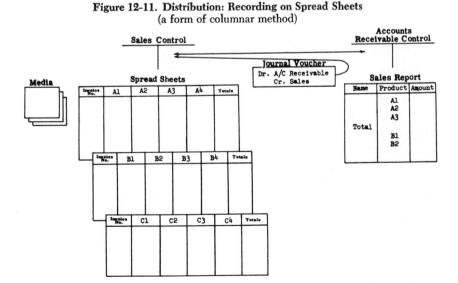

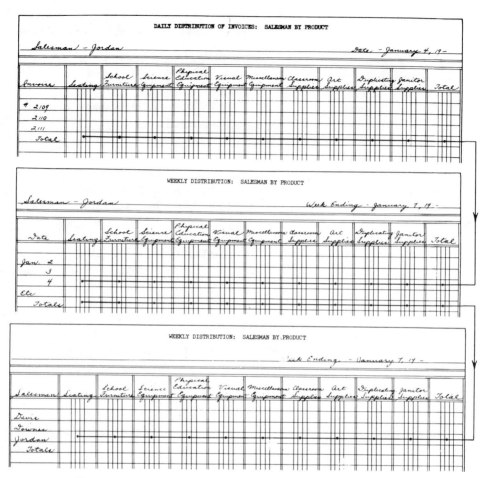

Figure 12-12. Arranging Spread Sheets to Compile Product Class Totals for Each Salesman

Note that in this case, the worksheets set up for supplies accounts will be uniformly active through the year, but the worksheets set up for equipment will be less active during the winter months than during the summer when heavy shipments are being made.

At the end of the month, only the grand total of sales is posted to the General ledger. This total is conveyed to the general ledger clerk by means of a journal voucher. The monthly sales report is prepared from the major totals of the worksheets.

Arranging Spread Sheets to Compile Product Class Totals for Each Salesman

In all previous illustrations, the media have been distributed to a single classification: products. Suppose, however, that the management desires to know (1) the monthly total of sales of each product class for the monthly statement of profits, and (2) the weekly total for each product for each salesman. There are fifteen salesmen, each of whom has an average of 20 invoices a day. Ten product classes will be recognized. In this case, if the spread sheet method is used, a spread sheet may be headed up for each salesman, each day's invoices sorted down to salesmen, and each salesman's invoices spread on the proper sheet.

This procedure is illustrated in Figure 12-12. Note the weekly summary sheet to which the daily totals are carried. Each day's postings are proved against the pre-list tape of invoices. In effect, the structure of worksheets resembles a pyramid with the daily worksheets for the various salesmen (15 each day) representing the base and the weekly summary sheet for all salesmen as the apex.

At the end of the month, the totals on the weekly summary sheet would be copied onto a monthly summary sheet. The monthly sales report and the monthly journal entry for sales would be made for this summary sheet.

Unit Account and Columnar Account Methods

Meaning of the Term "Unit Account Method";
Illustration of Unit Account

Unit account method involves setting up accounts (sales accounts in this case) according to the desired classification (product, customer, salesman, or territory), and charging or crediting each account with each transaction that affects the account.

Figure 12-13 is a unit account form designed for distribution of sales by product class. Note that an account form can be set up for each of the 71 accounts in the sales classification. Or if desired, unit accounts can be set up for the equipment groups only (leaving the supplies accounts to be distributed by some other method). The account form provides columns

Figure 12-13. Unit Account Form Designed for Distribution of Sales by Product Class

SALES DISTRIBUTION					
Account No._____					
Description _____					
DAY	SOLD TO	Invoice Number	ITEM AMOUNT	MONTH	YEAR TO DATE
	Amounts Forwarded				

for posting each invoice (date, sold to, invoice number, and item amount) and columns for month total and year-to-date total.

The methods of posting invoices to sales accounts have already been explained in connection with account posting in Chapter 7:

(a) If the invoices are unit invoices, random post, or sort according to the account classification and post in sequence. (Pre-sorting makes it possible to post all invoices which affect a particular account at one time, and reduces account locating time.)

(b) If the invoices are mixed, random post or exhaust.

Unit account method may be compared with columnar method in the following general terms:

(1) The unit account form provides for identification and description of the individual item. This provision is likely to be more important in the case of expense accounts than it is for sales accounts. Where the average sale is significant, as here assumed ($200.00 for equipment sales), the management may want to watch the sales of each product currently. In some cases, the management may want to know who is buying each product and the name of the customer may be entered in the particulars space of the account.

(2) Unit account method will accommodate a larger classification of accounts than columnar methods. Even when spread sheets are used, the number of columns that can be handled is relatively low.

(3) Unit account method provides readily for variation in activity among accounts in the classification within a period, and it provides for variation in activity in a given group of accounts from month to month or season to season. In unit account method, if an account has high activity, more account pages are added for it; if it has low activity, one account form may serve for the postings of a number of months. Columnar method (unless supplemented by some other method of distribution) is not well adapted to handling a large classification of accounts comprising a large percentage of relatively inactive accounts.

A variation of the unit account method occurs where an account form is set up for each account in the classification, but the accounts are total-posted periodically from a columnar journal or some other summary such as a register. Note that in the illustration at hand, it might be desired to detail-post the equipment accounts, as described above, and total-post the supplies accounts (whose transactions are more numerous and of smaller average amount).

Sales Accounts for Current Reference: Salesmen, Customers, Territories

In some cases, the sales management may desire unit accounts for salesmen and customers and summary accounts for territories. These accounts may provide comparison of sales during the current period with sales in previous periods or for comparisons with quotas. These accounts may be kept in the Sales department for current reference by the sales supervisors, and they may be housed in visible filing equipment to facilitate posting, reference, and follow-up. Illustrations of visible filing equipment appear in Chapter 8. None of these account forms are illustrated in this text. Sample forms may be obtained from any manufacturer of visible filing equipment.

Columnar Accounts for Sales

Columnar accounts for sales might be used, with an account for each of the ten groups described on page 251. These accounts would be similar to the worksheets in Figure 12-10 since each of them would provide a column for each account in the group. The columnar account forms would carry forward from week to week, showing periodic totals.

Summary Strip and Unit Ticket Methods

Use of Summary Strips in Distributing Sales Invoices; Totals by Product Class

In some cases, it is feasible to use summary strips to determine the total sales of each product class, instead of using the spread sheet method. A summary strip is illustrated in Figure 12-14. Note the product classification (ten accounts) on the left side of the strip and the amount column on the right side. One of these strips may be used each day, taking the place of a daily spread sheet.

Figure 12-14. Summary Strip

SALES BY PRODUCT CLASS

Product Class	Amount	
Seating		
School Furniture		
Science Equipment	952	00
Physical Ed. Equipment		
Visual Equipment		
Misc. Equipment	367	00
Classroom Supplies		
Art Supplies	16	00
Duplicating Mach. Supplies	4	00
Janitor's Supplies	1	00
Total	1,347	00

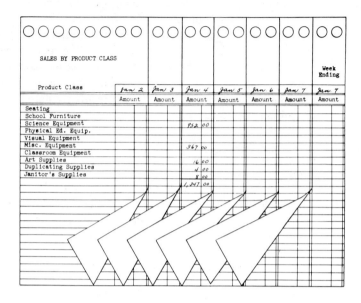

SALES BY PRODUCT CLASS							Week Ending
Product Class	Jan 2	Jan 3	Jan 4	Jan 5	Jan 6	Jan 7	Jan 7
	Amount	Amount	Amount	Amount	Amount	Amount	Amount
Seating							
School Furniture							
Science Equipment			952 00				
Physical Ed. Equip.							
Visual Equipment							
Misc. Equipment			367 00				
Classroom Equipment							
Art Supplies			16 00				
Duplicating Supplies			4 00				
Janitor's Supplies			8 00				
			1,347 00				

Figure 12-15. Shingling Daily Summary Strips to Build Weekly Strips

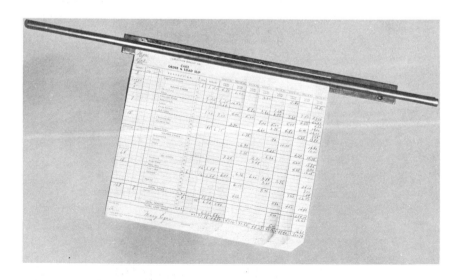

Figure 12-16. Peg Strip

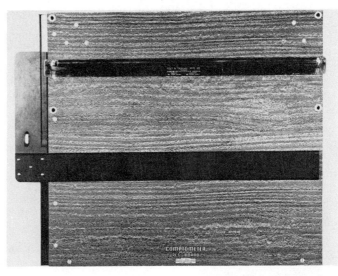

Figure 12-17. Peg Board

Comptometer Corporation

To build up weekly totals by product class, the daily summary strips would be shingled (placed side by side) as diagrammed in Figure 12-15. In that position, the six strips are added across, line by line, and the weekly totals are written on the strip at the extreme right. A peg strip (Figure 12-16) is used to hold the summary strips in alignment side by side. The holes on the summary strip are punched specifically to fit the pegs on the peg strip; the summary strips are thus quickly shingled by putting them on the pegs.

A peg board (Figure 12-17) is a board with a peg strip at the top, and a T-square parallel to the peg strip. The T-square slides horizontally over the summary strips on the board. Positioned just below a horizontal row of figures, it helps the operator to scan the row across and add it.

At the end of the month, the strip covering the month shows totals by product class. This summary strip is used as follows:

(1) As the basis for the journal voucher debiting Accounts Receivable Control and crediting Sales in the General ledger.

(2) As the sales report for the month, showing totals by product class. When summary strips are used as reports, they are sometimes filed in a ring binder. Note that for comparative purposes, "last month's" (or some other period's) sales strip can be filed beside that for the current month.

(3) As the Sales ledger.

Handling the Media

If the invoices are unit media, they are first sorted by product class (into ten piles in this case). Then each pile is totaled, using a listing machine or a key-driven calculator, and each total is entered in the summary strip for the day.

Where the invoices are mixed, it might be feasible to:

(1) Use the exhaust method. In this case, the operator would leaf through the batch of invoices ten times (using a listing machine or a calculator), beginning with the most active product class.

(2) Convert the mixed invoices to unit media. This might be done as explained on pages 270-274 of this chapter. When this is done, an invoice comprising, say, six product classes becomes six unit tickets. After the unit media have been created, they are sorted and totaled onto the summary strips as described in the previous section.

Note that from the standpoint of uses and limitations, the summary strip method is similar to the columnar methods. The advantage that summary strip method may have over conventional columnar methods in a given case lies in the fact that it substitutes sorting and total posting for the detail posting that is done in columnar methods. This advantage may be considerable from a clerical economy standpoint. The descriptive reference feature provided by columnar methods and unit accounting methods is eliminated through total posting. This elimination is not significant if the average amount of the invoices is small and may not be considered significant by the management even where the average amount of the invoices is large.

Salesman by Product; Daily Summary Strip for Each Salesman

As a second example of the use of summary strips, assume that it is desired to determine total sales of each product class by each salesman. (This is called a "salesman by product class" distribution.) The procedure would be fundamentally the same as the spread-sheet procedure illustrated in Figure 12-12, except that a summary strip, instead of a spread sheet, would be made out daily for each salesman. Thus, if there are ten salesmen, there will be ten summary strips each day. At the end of the week, each salesman's strips for the week will be shingled to produce a weekly summary strip for the salesman, and so on.

Designing Original Media for Shingling; Multiple Strip Form

In the previous illustrations, the summary strips were produced either from the original media (invoices) or from other summary strips. Sometimes it is possible to design original media for shingling. Figure 12-18 is a sales order in summary strip form. Note that the product classification is pre-printed on the sales order, and that the form is punched for

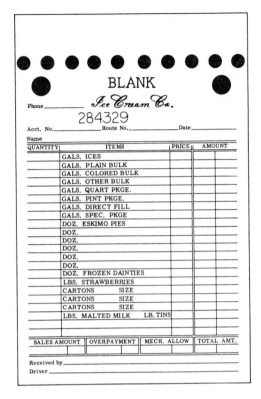

Figure 12-18. Designing Original
Media for Shingling: Sales Order

shingling on a peg board. When the salesman writes up the order, he simply enters the quantities on the appropriate product line.

When this type of sales order can be used, the order form itself is shingled on the peg board and added across; a copying step is eliminated. Of course, only a limited classification can be printed on such a sales order form; therefore the use of this type of peg strip is limited.

Note also that number of accounts in the classification and activity of the accounts is a factor in summary strip method, as it is in columnar methods in general. There is a mechanical limit to the number of accounts that can be accommodated on a summary strip (say 60 to a single strip), although multiple-fold strips may be used to increase the classification capacity. Likewise, it may not be desirable to use summary strips where the activity of the classification is very low, since most of each strip and most of the filing space in which the strips are filed would be wasted.

Figures 12-19 and 12-20 show a multiple-fold summary strip form. Figure 12-19 illustrates an unfolded form, and Figure 12-20 illustrates the same form folded and shingled. Once the folded forms are shingled, the folds may be "flipped out" for successive exposure of the columns.

FORM 6048 500 3-48 64786 ⊕

Figure 12-19. Multiple-Fold Summary Strip

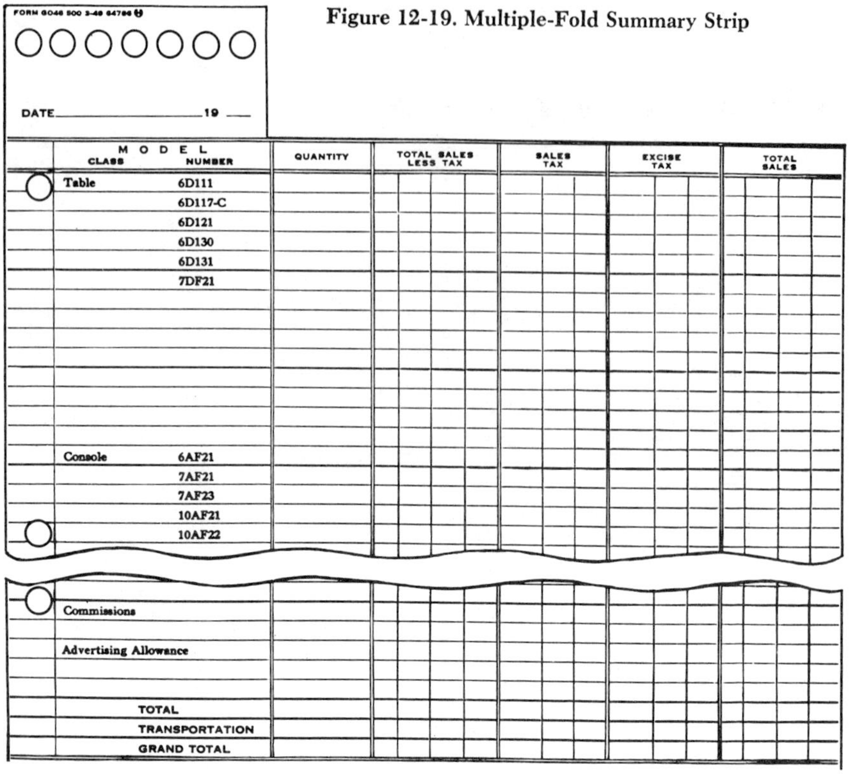

DATE_____19___

CLASS	MODEL NUMBER	QUANTITY	TOTAL SALES LESS TAX	SALES TAX	EXCISE TAX	TOTAL SALES
Table	6D111					
	6D117-C					
	6D121					
	6D130					
	6D131					
	7DF21					
Console	6AF21					
	7AF21					
	7AF23					
	10AF21					
	10AF22					
Commissions						
Advertising Allowance						
TOTAL						
TRANSPORTATION						
GRAND TOTAL						

Hautau & Otto

Unit Ticket Method in General

The term "unit medium" has been defined (in connection with account posting) as a paper which is to be posted to not more than one account in a classification in a single posting run. Invoices bearing a single-product item each are examples of unit media, as far as the product classification is concerned. Invoices bearing several product items would be mixed media.

Fundamentally, unit ticket method as a method involves (1) obtaining unit media (if the original media are not in unit form), (2) sorting the unit media to the account classification with which the report is concerned, (3) totaling the media by account, and (4) posting the totals to a report form, such as a conventional form or a summary strip, or to an account form which is to be used as a long-time summary. If several reports are to be prepared involving different classifications, the media can be re-sorted to the various classifications and the several reports prepared in succession. Naturally, the unit tickets must show all the classifications which are the basis for the desired reports.

The inherent advantages of unit ticket method are:

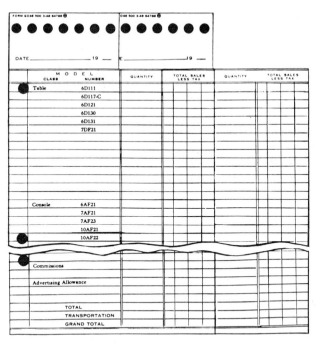

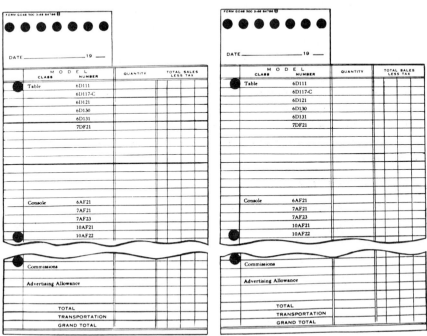

Figure 12-20. Multiple-Fold Summary Strip (folded, shingled above)

(1) Unit tickets, unlike mixed media, are sortable. They can be sorted to the account classification, thus bringing together in a batch all media that affect a given account. The sorting makes it possible to total all the media that affect one account at one time and post one total. Where the average number of postings per active account for a typical batch of media is large, sorting, totaling by account, and total posting to the account may be faster than random posting (posting each item on the media as it comes).

(2) Unit ticket method is ideally suited to redistribution. Where one batch of original media has to be used to prepare several reports involving different classifications, the unit media can be sorted and re-sorted as required.

There are other advantages which are not necessarily exclusive to unit ticket method. It can accommodate an unlimited number of accounts in the classification, and it can take care of any degree of activity of the accounts or variation in activity.

Probably the determining factors in the unit-ticket method are:

(1) How many classifications are involved in the various reports, and how many reports involving different classifications must be prepared?

(2) Are the original media unit media as far as the classifications involved in the reports are concerned, or, if not, how can unit media be obtained at reasonable cost?

The application of unit ticket method has to be studied carefully where the original media are not unit media; otherwise the cost of getting unit media may not be justified by the increased speed in getting the various distributions of the media.

The following sections illustrate some of the methods of obtaining unit media and the handling of unit media to obtain reports involving various classifications.

Methods of Obtaining Unit Media

Unit media may be obtained by:

(1) Requiring that original media be written as unit media, or in other words that multiple transactions be recorded in the original writing as unit documents. The extent to which this can be done in sales-distribution procedures is limited, although it sometimes happens that unit shipping orders are written (one product item on each order) and unit invoices reproduced from the original writing.

(2) Producing unit tickets from invoices by separate operation. A unit ticket is a unit medium that has been produced on a small piece of paper of a convenient size for sorting.

(3) Securing unit media as a by-product of producing the invoice.

Distribution to Products: Partially Pre-printed Biff Tickets

Assume that a daily distribution of sales to products is desired, and that the following quantitative data (as indicated in Figure 12-6, column 4) are available:

(1) There are 150 products in the classification in 10 product classes.
(2) The activity of the supplies accounts is high, but the activity of the equipment accounts varies considerably during the year, being highest in summer and lowest in spring.
(3) There are 300 invoices a day.
(4) The average amount of an invoice is $2.00.
(5) The invoices average 5 line items each.

No redistribution is involved.

Because of the large number of accounts in the classification and the low percentage of activity in certain seasons, it was decided not to use the columnar method or the summary strip method. Likewise, because of the low average invoice amount, it was decided not to use unit account method (which would be a permanent posting of the items). And because of the high average number of line items per invoice, it was decided not to use exhaust method as a means of producing the total of each product each day, since this would probably involve a great deal of invoice handling in getting all the active products off. It was decided to use biff tickets pre-printed with product names, as illustrated in Figure 12-21.

Class Room Supplies	No.	
Chalk, White	711	
Chalk, Colored	712	
Erasers, Blackboard	713	
Erasers, Pencil	714	
Ink	715	
Paper	715	
Pencils	717	
Pen Holders	718	
Pens	719	
Pointers	720	

Figure 12-21. Biff Ticket

Biff tickets are a form of unit ticket, written or filled in by hand. On the form illustrated, the product names are pre-printed, and the distribution clerk checks (√) the product name and enters the amount in the space at the lower right-hand corner of the ticket. A separate biff ticket is used for each line item on the invoice. Figure 12-22 diagrams the method of writing biff tickets from a batch of invoices and proving them after the writing. While writing the biff tickets, the distribution clerk has ten pigeonholes of biff ticket forms in front of her—one for each of the product classes—with the batch of invoices slightly to the left on the desk. She pulls the biff tickets from the pigeonholes as she actually needs them. (Actually the decision to use biff tickets was a decision to pull tickets and write amounts instead of either locating columns on spread sheets and posting or locating accounts and posting.)

While the clerk is writing the tickets, she keeps the written tickets in the same order as the invoices to make it possible to check the tickets back against the invoices if the proof tape (or total) does not agree with the pre-list tape. After proving the tickets, she sorts them by product, totals each product, and posts the product totals to summary accounts. Note that the tickets are printed for entry of amounts in the lower right hand corner. This permits the clerk to fan the tickets with her left hand, exposing the amounts of successive tickets, while she operates the calculator with her right hand.

Figure 12-22 illustrates a biff ticket form for one of the 15 product classes. Note that it comprises a pre-printed list of all the products in the class. Other similar forms are printed for the other classes. A supply of blank forms for each of the 15 classes is placed in pigeonholes in front of the distribution clerk. To produce the tickets required for the line items on an invoice, the clerk

(1) pulls a ticket of the appropriate class for the first item,
(2) checks (√) the product on the ticket,
(3) writes amount at the bottom of the ticket, and repeats the procedure for the other items on the invoice.

(1) Receive invoices, accompanied by pre-list tape

(2) Fill in a separate biff ticket for each product item on each invoice

(3) Run a proof tape of the amounts on biff tickets (or accumulate total on calculator)

Pre-list tape

*
28.00
952.00
367.00
1,347.00*

Invoices

INVOICE

A. B. Jones

Salesman   Jordan

Erasers, Blackboard	$ 16.00
Paper	4.00
Pointers	8.00
	$ 28.00

Class Room Supplies	No.	√
Chalk, White	711	
Chalk, Colored	712	
Erasers, Blackboard	713	√
Erasers, Pencil	714	
Ink.	715	
Paper	716	
Pencils	717	
Pen Holders	718	
Pens	719	
Pointers	720	

16.00

Proof tape

*
16.00
4.00
8.00
etc.
1,347.00*

Figure 12-22. Writing Biff Tickets from Invoices

The clerk proves the amounts on tickets by adding them and comparing the proof total with the pre-list total.

Note that the clerical work of creating tickets is comparable to the work, say, of locating columns on spread sheets and posting quantities and amounts to the columns. Creating biff tickets does, however, make possible the ready use of a larger classification of accounts than does posting to spread sheets.

Producing Unit Tickets with a Listing-Adding Machine

Unit tickets may be produced on a listing machine, as diagrammed in Figure 12-23. For this purpose packs of tickets similar to Figure 12-24 are used. Note that these tickets may be fed into the machine as a continuous strip. The operation resolves itself into spacing the tickets through the machine and striking the keys and the motor bar. To make this operation possible, of course, the original media from which unit tickets are prepared must be coded. In this case, a code number must be put on the invoice for customer, and one for salesman. The code numbers are listed non-add on the tickets, but amounts are accumulated in a register of the

Figure 12-23. Making Unit Tickets on a Listing-Adding Machine

(1) Receive invoices accompanied by pre-list tape

(2) Code the invoices: customers, salesmen, products

(3) Feed a roll of tickets into a listing-adding machine;

(4) Print a ticket for each item line on each invoice, code numbers non-add. Accumulate dollar amounts.

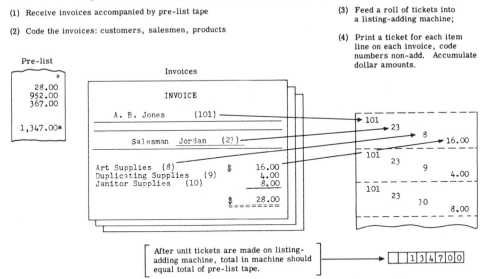

listing machine as the tickets are being produced. After the tickets are produced they are torn apart for sorting.

Two of the advantages of producing unit tickets with a listing machine are legibility of the tickets and speed in proving the media. The total of the dollars listed on the tickets is accumulated automatically in the listing machine as the tickets are produced; this total is proved against the pre-list total. The proof operation is a by-product of the production operation.

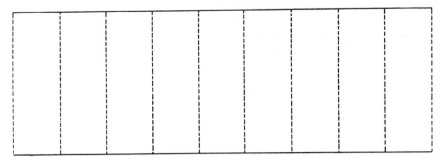

Figure 12-24. Strip of Unit Tickets

Unit Tickets as a By-Product of Writing the Invoice: Duplicating Machine

In the previous illustrations of unit tickets, the unit tickets were obtained by a separate operation—that is, by writing a separate biff ticket for each item line on the invoice. In some cases it is feasible to produce biff tickets either as (1) a duplicating machine copy of the original invoice or (2) a carbon copy of the original invoice. The special feature of making unit tickets by reproduction from the original invoice is that each unit ticket is basically a copy of one line of the invoice. The unit tickets have to be specially designed so that each ticket will show only what is wanted on it.

Figure 6-12 is an illustration of gang unit tickets reproduced by duplicating machine from an invoice master. Part (a) of the illustration is the invoice proper; part (b) is a set of gang unit tickets reproduced from the master that was used to reproduce the invoice; and part (c) is the set of unit tickets that was produced by breaking apart the gang illustrated in part (b). The gang proper is simply a set of unit tickets—one for each item of the invoice—with a detachable binding edge on each side. The method of producing unit tickets of this kind is described on pages 104 - 107.

Keysort Cards

Keysort cards are a form of unit ticket designed with a patented feature that facilitates rapid sorting. Figure 12-25 is a diagrammatic sketch illustrating the card, the punchings in the card, and the tumbler which is used for sorting. The punching is done at the edge of the cards, and each of the four edges can be used to accommodate the classifications. Figure 12-26 is a Keysort card that provides for the following classifications (among others): product, salesman, customer, territory (district), and trade class (customer class).

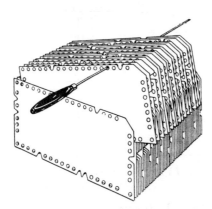

Figure 12-25. Keysort Cards and Tumbler

Note that four punching positions are provided for each digit in a classification:

7 4 2 1	7 4 2 1	7 4 2 1
hundreds	tens	units

customer number

Punching is done by notching out the number, as follows:

1 is punched 1	6 is punched 4 and 2
2 is punched 2	7 is punched 7
3 is punched 2 and 1	8 is punched 7 and 1
4 is punched 4	9 is punched 7 and 2
5 is punched 4 and 1	

In the sorting operation, which is illustrated in Figure 12-25, the tumbler is inserted in the 1 position of the deck, and the tumbler is lifted horizontally so that the cards punched in that position fall. The cards that

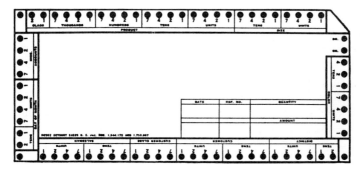

Figure 12-26. Keysort Card for Sales Distribution

fall are put in the back of the deck. The tumbler is then inserted in the 2 position, and the cards punched in that position are dropped out and put in the back of the deck. This operation is repeated for the 4 position and the 7 position.

The table below shows the successive rearrangement of the cards accomplished with each of the four sorts. Eleven cards are used as the basis for the illustration; they are punched in the unit position.

Where customer number is a three-digit number (as here assumed), the units field would be sorted (four positions) as above, and this would put the cards in order according to the reading of the units field. Then the cards would be sorted through the four positions of the tens field, and finally through the four positions of the hundreds field. The cards would now be in order by customer number from 1 to 999.

Table 12-1

SORTING KEYSORT CARDS

Before sorting	8	9	6	3	4	2	1	8	5	7	6
After first sort (1 position)	9	6	4	2	5	7	6	8	3	1	8
After second sort (2 position)	4	5	7	8	1	8	9	6	2	6	3
After third sort (4 position)	7	8	1	8	9	2	3	4	5	6	6
After fourth sort (7 position)	1	2	3	4	5	6	6	7	8	8	9

Sorting Keysort Cards. Eleven cards have been notched in the units field in the 1, 2, 4, and 7 positions as explained above. The eleven cards represent the values shown in the first line above ("before sorting"). When the 1 position was sorted, 8, 3, 1, and 8 (all of which included notching on the one position) dropped down and were put in the back of the deck. When the 2 position was sorted, 9, 6, 2, 6, and 3 dropped and were put in the back of the deck. When the 4 position was sorted, 4, 5, 6, and 6 dropped, and when the 7 position was sorted, 7, 8, 8, and 9 dropped. The cards were then in numerical sequence.

Where the batches to be sorted are relatively small, the sorting is done from units to hundreds, as explained in the previous paragraph. Where the batches are large, the operator may break them down into hundreds first to get manageable batches, sorting them in turn through the units and tens positions.

Note that an alternative to the above combinational punching would be a provision for *direct* punching and sorting. For direct punching and sorting, a position is provided for each account of the product class. This is sometimes done when the number of accounts is small. If the number of accounts is large, however, it is not possible to accommodate direct punching and sorting because of the space that would be required on the edge of the card and the amount of sorting time that would be needed.

Punches for Keysort Cards

Figure 12-27 is a key punch for individual punching of Keysort cards. This punch has a keyboard column of four keys (one, two, four, and seven) for each digit field (units, tens, hundreds, and so on). In the operation of the punch, the operator indexes the account number on the keyboard, striking the keys in combination where required as indicated above, and places the card in the feed at the top of the punch for the actual punching operation. The punching operation notches nine positions on one edge of a card at one time. The operation is performed separately for each edge of the card to be punched.

Figure 12-28 is a hand-operated groover. It can be used to groove common information in batches of about 50 cards at one time. The company also manufactures an electric groover which will groove 150 cards at one time. Either of these groovers might be used if it is desired to pre-punch product number in a quantity of cards for each product.

Figure 12-27. Key Punch

Figure 12-28. Hand-Operated Groover

Automated Business Systems
Division of Litton Industries

The cards for the various products would then be kept in a tub file, pulled as needed, and punched in the remaining fields from sales invoices.

Tabulating Punch

The tabulating punch (Figure 12-29) may be used to punch amounts (say quantities and dollars in a sales analysis application) in the body of the cards and at the same time to produce a tape of the amounts punched. It is basically a ten-key, single-register adding-listing machine with two feed slots—a punching slot and a reading slot. The first time the cards are to be added for any purpose, they may be inserted in the punching slot and punched by indexing the keys on the keyboard and depressing the motor bar. When the batch is completed, the total on the tape is compared with the pre-list total to prove the punching.

The tabulating punch may also be used to read amounts punched in cards and to list them automatically on a tape to produce a total. Thus, after the cards have been sorted (by means of the tumbler) into product order, the cards for a given product can be fed into the reading slot. The tabulating punch will list the amounts for the successive cards and total them. The total can be cleared into a summary card which would then represent a group total.

Figure 12-29. Tabulating Punch

McBee Card Converter

The card converter (Figure 12-30) may be used to read the edge matching on Keysort cards (source documents) and convert automatically to punched paper tape or tabulating cards for further electronic processing (Chapters 21-23).

Creating Keysort Cards

In the operation of an analysis procedure, how are the cards created in the first place? What is the source of the cards that are to be notched, sorted, and added? There are four common methods of creating cards for sales analysis:

(1) Pull tub method. Under this method a pull tub provides filing space for a quantity of cards for each product—pre-notched for product number. (A groover is used for the pre-notching operation.) Cards are then pulled from the tub, working from sales invoices, and new information from the invoices (salesman, customer, and so forth) is put on the face of the cards. (Note that some other factor than product might be used for pre-creation, and in this case the filing arrangement would change accordingly.) This method is said to be the most popular one for creating cards for sales analysis.

(2) Line picking. This method involves creating the cards as a by-product of a reproducing operation. A Keysort card for each line item on an invoice can be produced on a duplicating machine. Each card would show the quantity, product number, description,

price, and extension of one invoice item. (The illustration in Figure 6-10 shows the production of a unit ticket; a Keysort card can be produced by the same principle.)

(3) Creating a Keysort card as a carbon copy of an invoice. Cards created in this manner are not unit media if the invoices are mixed media.

(4) Using blank cards and writing them in the manner in which the biff tickets (Figure 12-21) were created.

Illustrative Application of Keysort Cards

Assume the same facts as on page 271, except that the management desires the following information:

(1) Daily distribution of sales by product (quantities) for use in crediting perpetual inventory accounts.

(2) Weekly report of sales by each salesman—dollars for each product class.

(3) Monthly report—total dollars for each product class to support the profits statement.

(4) Monthly report for each customer (equipment sales only)—by customer and product class.

The card form illustrated in Figure 12-26 is used. The procedure might be as follows:

Preparatory

(1) Groove product number in a quantity of cards for each product using the hand groover or the electric groover.

(2) File the cards for each product in a pull tub.

(3) Replenish the product file as required.

Daily

Daily batches of invoices are received from the Billing department. Each batch is accompanied by a pre-list tape of quantities and amounts. Each daily batch is processed as follows:

(1) Take the batch to the product-card file and for each invoice pull card for each line item on the invoice. Enter the customer and salesman code numbers and invoice number on the first card for each invoice. Put the cards for each invoice on top of the invoice so that invoices and cards are interspersed in a pack.

(2) Punch quantity and amount in the body of each card using the tabulating punch; at the same time prepare a proof tape of quantities and amounts. (Alternate method: Obtain a proof total with a desk calculator or adding-listing machine.) Check the cards back against the invoices if necessary to locate a difference.

(3) Using a key punch, notch salesman number and customer number in each card.

(4) Sort the day's cards by product number, total the cards for each product using the tabulating punch (reading slot), and enter the totals on the appropriate perpetual inventory accounts.

(5) Interfile this day's cards with the cards of the previous days of this week. (Alternate method: Hold each day's cards until the end of the week, then sort the week's cards by product class.)

Weekly

(6) Sort the week's cards by salesmen. (The cards for each salesman are now in order by product.)

(7) For each salesman, obtain total of each product class and post to summary strip for the salesman. File the summary strips in a binder which has a leaf for each salesman. (Shingle successive weeks so that each salesman will have four or five strips for the month, with the amount columns exposed.)

Monthly

(8) Put a blank summary strip for each salesman in the binder and add the product classes across to provide the total of each product class for each salesman. Enter totals on salesman's summary strip.

(9) Pull the salesmen's monthly summary strips (8) from the binder and shingle them to produce a summary for all salesmen. This summary strip provides the totals for the monthly statement of profits.

(10) Separate the equipment tickets from the supplies tickets. (Note: This separation can be facilitated by use of the "product class" field on the cards. Punch 1 for supplies and 2 for equipment.)

(11) Sort the equipment cards by product class and by customer.

(12) Prepare report for each customer showing total dollars for each product class for the customer.

Summary Cards

There are various summary forms that can be used to receive the totals taken off Keysort cards. In operation (4) above, the daily product totals are posted to account forms. In operation (7), each salesman's product class totals are posted to a summary strip for the salesman.

Note that summary cards can be used to record totals (operation 4). A summary card for products would be the same as Figure 12-26 except that on the face would be printed spaces for the daily posting of the totals taken off the detail cards (previously illustrated). The summary card is usually printed on a color of stock different from the detail cards so that it can be readily identified. Each day the summary cards would be sorted with the detail cards so that the summary card for each product would be behind its detail cards. In the totaling operation, the clerk would proceed through the deck taking off totals by machine until she reached the summary card for the product. Then she would write the total of that product on the summary card and proceed through the detail cards for the next product.

Register Method

General Description

As the name suggests, the register method is an analysis method that involves the use of a machine built to accumulate and print totals of amounts appearing in invoices or other media. One type of machine designed for distribution is the National Class 2000 distribution machine (not illustrated). These machines are no longer produced but there are numbers of them still in use. The NCR 2000 could be equipped with 27 registers. The amount keys are at the left of the keyboard, and the register control keys are at the right. In the operation of the machine, the operator depresses the amount keys to index the amount of the transaction and then depresses the appropriate register control key. This causes the machine to accumulate the amount in the register and print it on an audit tape. At the end of the distribution run, the grand total of the sum

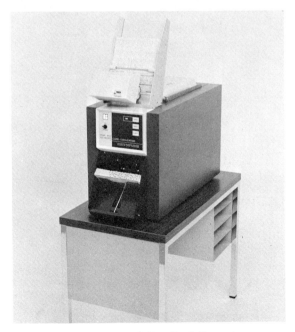

Figure 12-30. McBee Card Converter

is cleared onto the audit tape and compared with the pre-list tape. The National Cash Register Company produces a Class 41 Analysis machine (Figure 12-31) which will accumulate 6 to 18 separate totals. When coupled to a tape punch (illustrated), it accommodates a larger classification. The tapes can be used as input to a computer, either in-house or at an outside service bureau, to produce a variety of reports of the types illustrated earlier in this chapter.

Multiple-register distribution machines are probably most efficient for random posting of original *mixed* media. If the original media were in *unit* form they could be sorted to the account classification and the totals taken off one account after another with a single-register machine, and posted to a report, account, or summary strip form. Likewise if the media were mixed but the average number of accounts per medium were small enough to make exhaust method feasible, a single-register machine could be used.

National

Figure 12-31. Analysis Machine (Class 41) Coupled to Punched Paper Tape Recorder

SELECTION OF A DISTRIBUTION METHOD

Factors Discussed

The previous sections of this chapter have described the methods of distribution and, in connection with the descriptions, have indicated some of the factors that would lead to the selection of a particular method. It is now desirable to list the factors in summary, since the systems man may have to consider all of them before making a choice of method.

The factors actually involve two groups (which are not mutually exclusive):

(a) What information the management wants (what classifications, whether details or totals are required, what totals on reports, and what frequency). These factors can be discussed with the management. It may be pointed out that increases in number of accounts, number and frequency of reports, and the tendency to ask for detailed information rather than for summarized information (all of which are to some extent subject to the manager-user's decision) contribute to increased clerical cost.

(b) Quantitative factors, such as number of accounts in the classification, quantity of media, size of batches, and frequency of posting.

After the information phase has been resolved, the quantitative factors may be used as the basis for determining what machinery might be considered, how much clerical time will be required to operate a proposed new procedure, and the cost of printing and other elements. In some cases, the systems man may have several solutions to one distribution problem, and he may have to figure all of them to determine which one is the most economical.

The list of factors is:

Reports and Reference Information

(1) Number of classifications involved in the various reports. In some cases, a single classification is involved; for instance, the product classification. In other cases, two or more classifications may be involved in preparing a report, as, for example, salesmen and products or customers and products. In some cases, the entire report structure may involve *all* the classifications listed on page 249.

(2) What totals and sub-totals are desired in the monthly journal entry?

To produce the statement of profits in Figure 12-2, totals of two *product groups* are necessary. To produce the statement of profits in Figure 12-3, totals of two *territories* are necessary.

(3) What supporting reports are to be prepared? With what frequency?

It may be desired to prepare, in addition to the statement of profits which has a product breakdown, *salesman-by-product class* reports similar to Figure 12-4. Such reports might be prepared weekly and monthly. In some cases, a number of different reports involving *different classifications* and *different frequencies* (daily, weekly, monthly) might be desired.

(4) Are posted *details* of transactions required for current reference, or are reports showing *totals* of accounts in the classification considered sufficient by the manager?

(5) What is the amount of the average transaction?

This question should be asked in connection with Question (4). If the average amount is large, there is likely to be more reason for detail posting than if the average amount is small.

(6) If detail posting is required, what description is required?

If detail posting is required, usually some description is required to make the meaning of the posting clear without looking up the source documents.

(7) Frequency of posting required.

Is *daily posting* required, or is it feasible to accumulate media for a period of time and handle larger batches?

Number of Accounts in Each Classification; Activity

(8) Does the classification comprise two accounts, or 71 accounts, or 1,000 accounts, or 10,000 accounts?

This factor basically means how many columns, or accounts, or registers would have to be provided under particular methods.

(9) Activity of the accounts during a typical period.

The question is how many accounts of the whole classification will be posted during a typical day (or other period) or a typical posting batch. Obviously, a classification of 100 accounts that is 90 per cent active in a typical period is different from a classification of 100 accounts that is only 30 per cent active during a typical period, as far as selection of a distribution method is concerned. Sometimes it is possible to use certain distribution methods for a large classification having a low percentage activity that would not be used for large classifications having a high percentage activity. In the former case, separate columns or accounts or registers can be used for the active accounts, and "miscellaneous" columns or accounts or registers can be used for the inactive accounts.

In this connection, the question of whether the percentage of activity varies from season to season is important (for example, in the classification shown on page 252; it may be found that the supplies accounts are uniformly active the year around but that the equipment sales accounts are active mainly in the summer) since certain methods of distribution are better adapted to varying activity than others. The columnar methods, for instance, do not adapt themselves well to varying percentages of activity whereas the unit ticket method does.

The Media

(10) What are the media? Invoices? Credit memos? Are the media unit or mixed?

If the media are unit media, handling by sorting, accumulating totals, and posting totals to accounts, reports, or summary strips can be considered (instead of columnar methods) except where detail entries are actually desired. In general, the existence of unit media encourages consideration of methods that involve sorting and totaling.

(11) What is the quantity of media per day or other period? Does the load change from month to month?

This question is obviously fundamental, since some methods (such as the pen-and-ink journal) are not well adapted to handling large volumes.

(12) If the media are mixed, what is the average number of accounts represented by a single medium in the distribution contemplated?

The average number of accounts represented by a single medium will shed some light on volume of clerical work. Thus, 1,000 invoices having an average of three accounts each means 3,000 account items for which adding or posting or other clerical operations will have to be anticipated.

In making a survey for designing a distribution procedure, it is necessary to examine the source media; and if the media are mixed, it may be necessary to tally a typical batch by number of accounts per medium. Thus, the tally of a batch of 100 invoices might show five invoices of eight accounts each, four invoices of seven accounts each, and so forth.

Note also that the number of accounts per medium is also a factor in deciding whether to use exhaust method or to use an alternate method such as random posting or converting the mixed media to unit media. In the exhaust method, the larger the number of accounts per medium, the larger the average number of handlings per medium. Exhaust method works best where the average number of accounts per medium is small.

(13) In what size batches do the media come for distribution? How frequently?

Are each day's invoices handled separately a day at a time, for example, or are batches of, say, 100 papers dispatched?

(14) What is the sorted arrangement of the media when received for distribution? (Are the invoices in serial number order, or sorted?) Is it possible to have the media grouped in some manner in a previous operation to facilitate the taking of certain totals?

(15) Is it possible to get the distribution at the source by arrangement of the original writing?

Each of the above factors affects the selection of a distribution method. Some of the factors are interdependent, as indicated above. Some of them are determining factors in that they can eliminate a method. Thus, a large number of accounts in the classification, (8) above, and a high percentage of activity of those accounts (9) will eliminate pen-and-ink journals because of the limitation in number of columns it is possible to accommodate in such methods. A variety of reports involving redistribution of the same media may eliminate all methods except unit ticket. Posted details with description if a positive requirement (4) may eliminate or circumscribe the use of summary strips. And finally, a large quantity of media (11) combined with a low average transaction amount (5) promotes summary method and demotes detail entry methods.

13

Accounts Receivable; Cash Receipts

Function and Organization

The accounts receivable function keeps account of the amounts owed the business by customers and, in some businesses, includes producing and mailing statements of account at regular intervals. It also involves maintaining records to facilitate reference for credit purposes and collection follow-up. In small businesses, the credit functions may be performed through direct access to the customers' accounts. In larger organizations, separate records may be kept for the use of the credit department. From the organization standpoint, the Accounts Receivable ledger may be kept by the general ledger clerk (in small businesses) or by a separate department.

To the layman in methods work, the subject of accounts receivable usually appears to be a simple proposition of posting debits and credits. Actually, the design and installation of an accounts receivable procedure may turn out to be a considerable challenge. The systems man must be prepared to design a procedure for any type and size of business from an owner-operated corner grocery store to a department store with 50,000 or more accounts.

Forms Named

The principal forms with which the accounts receivable function is concerned are:

(1) Statements.
(2) Accounts forms.
(3) Credit history records and collection follow-up records. These records are discussed in connection with posting operations.

Posting media for accounts receivable are:

(1) Sales invoices, carrying charges for goods sold or services rendered.
(2) Credit memos, for goods returned by the customer or allowances made.
(3) Journal vouchers for write-offs. These are issued by the credit department to authorize write-offs of uncollectible accounts.

STATEMENT FORMS

Types

A statement of account is a form showing the amount that a customer owes at a particular date and (in some types of statement) supporting details. The following statement forms are explained in this chapter:

(1) Balance-end-of-month statement.
(2) Unit statement.
(3) Running balance statement with conventional account.
(4) Open item statement.

Balance End-of-Month Statement (Figure 13-1)

This form of statement shows simply the balance of the customer's account as it appears in the ledger at the end of the month.

It is easy to prepare, but of course it does not provide information with which the customer can reconcile any discrepancy between the statement and his own records.

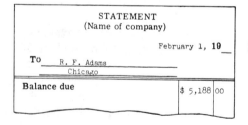

Figure 13-1. End-of-Month Balance Statement

Unit Statement (Figure 13-2)

This form, which is prepared in original and carbon copy, is intended to serve the function of account as well as statement. Figure 13-2 is an illustration. A unit statement shows (1) balance owed by the customer at the beginning of the month, (2) debits during the month (each posting comprises old balance, date, description, debit, and new balance), and (3) credits posted during the month.

A new set of statements is headed each month—one unit statement for each active customer—and the opening balance is posted as the first entry for the month. At the end of the month, the original copy is pulled and sent to the customer, and the carbon copy is kept as the house record of the account. Each month's set of unit statements is kept in a binder. This month's set will be kept in an active binder, and the previous months' sets in transfer binders.

Unit statements are well adapted to situations in which most customers pay their balances at the end of each month (as in retail stores). Often the top part of the customer's original is designed as a detachable portion which the customer may return with his remittance. Unit statements do not provide the same ease of reference as conventional accounts. Whereas a conventional account may carry the record of several months' business, a unit statement normally carries a single month's business with a specific customer. Thus, where it is desired to review the transactions of a customer for several months past, it is necessary in the latter case to refer to the duplicate statement for each of the several months. The credit department may keep a credit history for each customer (for credit reference purposes) showing balance at the beginning of each month and collection during the month. This record shows the long-time picture necessary for credit administration.

A variation of the type of unit statement described above is found in the meat packing business where statements are mailed weekly. In order

Figure 13-2 Unit Statement

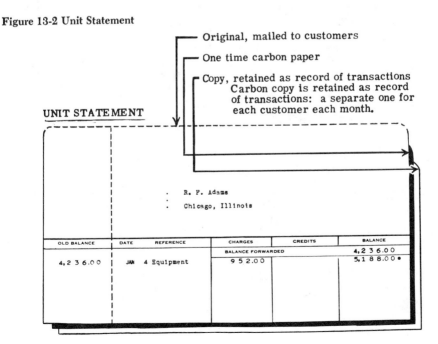

to eliminate the need for heading up new statements weekly, unit statements are provided with two extra copies—three copies in all. Such a set can be used for three weeks, and one copy is mailed each week. At the end of the first week, the statement shows one week's transactions; at the end of the second week, two weeks' transactions; and at the end of the third week, three weeks' transactions.

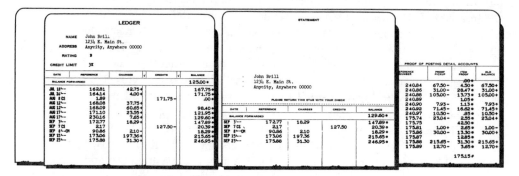

Figure 13-3. Running Balance Statement with Conventional Account

Running Balance Statement with Conventional Account (*Figure 13-3*)

A running balance statement with conventional account is illustrated in Figure 13-3. The statement itself shows the same information as a unit statement, and a new one is headed each month for each customer whose account had activity last month. Only the method of posting is different. In the form illustrated in Figure 13-3 the statement and the account are collated by hand by the operator. Carbon paper is inserted between statement and account. Note that the account form carries a number of months' transactions.

```
                    STATEMENT
                 (Name of company)
                             February 1, 19____
        To R. F. Adams
             Chicago
    ┌──────────────────────────────────────────┬───────────┐
    │ The following invoices for goods purchased│by         │
    │ you are unpaid as of the above date:      │           │
    │   Nov. 16, 19--                          $│   100 │00 │
    │   Dec. 10, 19--                           │   136 │00 │
    │        15, 19--                           │ 4,000 │00 │
    │   Jan.  4, 19--                           │   952 │00 │
    │        Total due                         $│ 5,188 │00 │
    └──────────────────────────────────────────┴───────────┘
```

Figure 13-4. Open Item Statement

Open Item Statement (*Figure 13-4*)

The open item statement contains a list of the specific invoices that the customer has not paid, together with the dates of those items and total amount due.

Use of this form is most likely when customers usually pay the amounts of specific invoices rather than round amounts on account. In some businesses, such as meat packing and wholesale groceries, vendors may *require* that customers pay the amounts of specific invoices. It is easily reconciled by the customer with his records, and when there are items past due (as in the above case) it is a reminder of the fact. It is sometimes prepared by first going through the ledger and checking off all related debits and credits in each account—that is, applying cash receipts to specific debits (Figure 13-5), and then typing the statements to include the open items and the total. This checking off is sometimes done as the remittances come in, as an operation preliminary to the actual posting, to determine that any discounts taken were proper. Items matched may be indicated by check marks as illustrated, or by letters of the alphabet.

Figure 13-5. Customer's Account: Cash Receipts Applied to Specific Debits
This is the account from which the statement above was prepared.

ACCOUNT						
R. F. Adams Chicago						
Old Balance	Date	Description	Debits	Credits	New Balance	
$	Nov. 2	785	$ ✓ 345 00	$	$ 345 00	
345 00	16	832	100 00		445 00	
445 00	Dec. 5	C 925		✓345 00	100 00	
100 00	10	1715	136 00		236 00	
236 00	15	1836	4,000 00		4,236 00	
4,236 00	Jan. 4	2112	952 00		5,188 00	

Why Prepare Statements?

In making a survey for an accounts receivable procedure, the systems man must consider whether statements are to be prepared for customers and if so, what kind of statement (as described above) is desired and how it shall be prepared. In some cases, the method of operating the accounts receivable procedure and the type of bookkeeping machine to be used depend upon the type of statement to be prepared. Often, a simplification of the statement will effect a considerable economy in the accounts receivable procedure.

Of course, the first question in this connection is whether the company needs to prepare statements at all. Some retailers feel that they must send statements to their customers, most of whom are householders rather than business people. They maintain that customers of retail stores depend upon the store to keep the accounts and notify them. Sometimes the retailer cannot eliminate the statement; the best he can do is to simplify it.

For jobbers and wholesalers whose customers are other businesses, the answer may be different than for retailers. There seems to be a trend in some lines among the former to cut out the statement and let the customer do his own accounting if he wants to earn the discount.

PEN AND INK ACCOUNT FORMS

Double Double Ledger (Figure 13-6)

The double double ledger (Figure 13-6) is designed on the same format as the familiar regular ledger, except that it is set up two on a page to increase the capacity of the page.

Regular Ledger with Balance Column at Right (Figure 13-7)

This form is the same as the standard ledger except that a balance column is added at the extreme right. When this form is used, the balance is always to be found in one place, and the latest figure in the column is the latest computed balance of the account. Sometimes the balance is entered on a separate line below the last debit or credit posting, together with the date of the balance. Since there is only one balance column, however, care must be taken to identify credit balances by entering them in red or by using an identifying symbol.

Regular Ledger with Center Balance Column (Figure 13-8)

This type of account was devised to provide a fixed column for the balance and to aid in computing the end-of-the-month balance. It is useful for accounts receivable and accounts payable where balances are normally paid monthly. Thus, at the end of the first month, the balance may be computed by simply adding the debits, as indicated in Figure 13-8. If, during the next month, the customer pays the balance, the credit is recorded on the line below the balance, as illustrated.

Sheet No. _____ Account No. _____

Terms   NAME

Rating   ADDRESS

Credit Limit

DATE	ITEMS	FOL	✓	DEBITS	DATE	ITEMS	FOL	✓	CREDITS	DATE	ITEMS	FOL	✓	DEBITS	DATE	ITEMS	FOL.	✓	CREDITS

National

Figure 13-6. Double Double Ledger

Sheet No. _____ Account No. _____

Terms   NAME

Rating   ADDRESS

Credit Limit

DATE	ITEMS	FOLIO	✓	DEBITS	DATE	ITEMS	FOLIO	✓	CREDITS	BALANCE

National

Figure 13-7. Regular Ledger with Balance Column at the Right

293

Sheet No. _____   Account No. _____

Terms   NAME _George Coombs_
Rating   ADDRESS
Credit Limit

DATE	ITEMS	FOLIO	✓	DEBITS	BALANCE	CREDITS	✓	FOLIO	ITEMS	DATE
19- Jan. 2				300						
4				500						
8				200						
31	Balance				1000					
						1000			Cash	Feb. 2

Figure 13-8. Regular Ledger with Center Balance Column

Sheet No. _____   Account No. _____

Terms   NAME
Rating   ADDRESS
Credit Limit

DATE	ITEMS	FOLIO	DEBITS	CREDITS	DR. OR CR.	BALANCE

Figure 13-9. Debit, Credit, and Balance Ledger

GENERAL LEDGER ACCOUNT

Sheet No. _____   Account No. _____

DATE	DESCRIPTION	POST. REF.	DEBITS	CREDITS	BALANCE	
					DEBIT	CREDIT

Figure 13-10. Debit, Credit, Debit Balance, and Credit Balance Ledger

294

Debit, Credit, and Balance Ledger Form (Figure 13-9)

This type of account form deviates from the basic principle of the T-account form to provide a single chronological list of transactions with a customer. The design of this form makes it easy to (1) compute running balances in the accounts and (2) analyze the account month by month, since it segregates the entries by month.

Debit, Credit, Debit Balance, and Credit Balance Ledger (Figure 13-10)

This form is the same as the previous one except that it includes two balance columns instead of one. Use of the two balance columns is intended to facilitate quick identification of the balance.

Basic Methods of Operating Accounts Receivable

The three basic methods of journalizing and posting transactions that were explained in Chapter 4 apply to accounts receivable. They are:

(1) Entering invoices in the sales journal and posting accounts receivable from the sales journal (described in the following section). This is the conventional pen-and-ink method.

(2) Posting charge sales direct to accounts or statements (pages 296 to 300).

(3) Ledgerless bookkeeping: filing copies of the invoices alphabetically by customer's name and pulling the invoices from file as specific items are paid (or applying payments to the invoices in file). The file of unpaid invoices comprises the Accounts Receivable ledger (pages 300 to 305).

ENTERING IN JOURNALS AND POSTING TO ACCOUNTS

Posting from the Sales Journal and Cash Receipts Journal

This method is the conventional pen-and-ink method of operating accounts receivable. The invoices are received in serial number order from the Billing department, entered in the sales journal in that order, and filed in serial number order. The customers' accounts (Figures 13-6 to 13-10) are random posted (presumably daily) from the sales journal.

Cash receipts are likewise recorded in the cash receipts journal, which is posted to the accounts.

Posting to the customers' accounts is proved by trial balance at the end of the month. An end-of-month balance statement may be prepared. Note that if more detail is desired on the statement, other forms of statement and account are likely to be used to avoid the double work of posting accounts and then preparing statements.

This method is used when the number of invoices per month is small (say, several hundred a month) and when no undue difficulty is expected in letting the proof of accounts receivable go until the end of the month.

POSTING DIRECT TO ACCOUNTS OR STATEMENTS

Outline of Illustrations

Following are examples of direct posting to accounts.
Current (Daily) Posting:
(1) Direct posting to accounts by pen and ink; journal shows daily totals only (no details).
(2) Direct posting to statement and account (collated).

Periodic Posting:
(3) Delayed posting (accumulating several days' media).
(4) Cycle billing (accumulating the media for a month, filed by customer name, with direct posting at the end of the month).

Direct Posting to Accounts by Pen and Ink: No Detail Journal

In some cases a considerable amount of clerical work can be saved by posting invoices directly to customers' accounts and using the sales journal simply as a means of compiling control totals for charging the Accounts Receivable Control account at the end of the month. Only daily totals or batch totals of sales are entered in the sales journal. Prelist totals are prepared of batches of invoices released by the Billing department, and these totals are recorded in the sales journal.

There are two methods of handling the media in direct posting:
(1) Sort the media alphabetically before posting, post the accounts, and take a proof tape of the postings to the accounts. To aid in finding the accounts readily when making the proof tape, offset or slug each account (put a piece of paper in front of it) when doing the posting.

When the total of the proof tape does not agree with the total of the pre-list tape, errors are located by comparing the proof tape with the sorted invoices, item for item. Note that if it is desired to prove old balance pick-ups, either long-run proof or old and new balance proof may be used (page 136). File the invoices alphabetically. (It is assumed that there is also a serial number file of invoices.)

(2) Retain the invoices in serial order number as they come from the Billing department. Random post the invoices to the accounts. Take a proof tape of postings and compare the total of the proof tape with the total of the pre-list tape. Note that in this case the items will not appear in the same sequence on the two tapes (because the invoices have not been pre-sorted alphabetically for pre-list, and the proof tape, on the other hand, will reflect alphabetical sequence of the accounts). File the media in serial number order.

Note: Direct posting to accounts by *machine* is explained in Chapter 7.

Direct Posting to Unit Statements: Descriptive Writing

Figure 13-11 illustrates postings of invoices direct to unit statements, using a bookkeeping machine equipped for descriptive writing. (Unit statements are explained in the first part of this chapter.) Figures 7-20 and 7-21 are machines built for descriptive writing. A sales journal (not illustrated) may be produced as a carbon copy. A similar operation may be performed manually, using a writing board. (See pages 201-205.)

Unit statements with descriptive writing are probably used more frequently by retailers than by manufacturers or wholesalers. The purpose of the description, of course, is to remind the customer what item was purchased.

Posting Invoices to Accounts or Statements by Machine; Delayed Posting

In some businesses, it is the practice to accumulate several days' batches of invoices for posting at one time. This procedure sometimes makes possible a more efficient posting operation by increasing the average number of postings per account. A high average tends to be more economical in posting than the low average because of the account-handling operations. For each account to be posted on a machine, a large number of operations has to be performed: the account has to be located, taken out of the binder, inserted in the machine and aligned, and the old balance has to be picked up. After the actual posting, the account has to

Figure 13-11. Posting Invoices Direct to Unit Statements: Descriptive Writing:
Running Balances

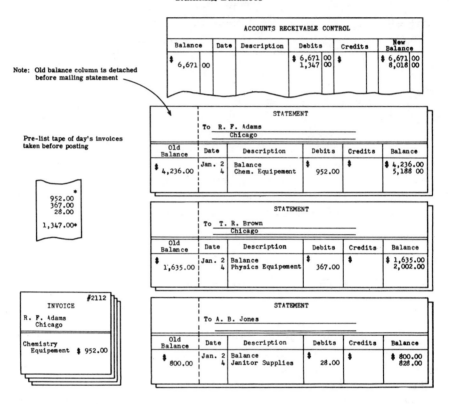

Note: Old balance column is detached
before mailing statement

Pre-list tape of day's invoices
taken before posting

be removed from the machine and returned to the binder. If three invoices can be posted to the account after it is put in the machine, the time of finding the account, putting it in the machine, and handling the old balance is spread over three invoices instead of one.

Media are handled as follows: the media are received in the serial number order from the Billing department, accompanied by the pre-list tape. The total of the tape is recorded in the sales journal and the day's media are sorted alphabetically and filed in a hold file. At intervals the media are pulled from the file and posted to the accounts. After posting, a proof tape is taken of the postings to accounts.

Note that the total of items on the proof tape agrees with the total of the sales journal, but that the items on the proof tape are not in the same order as the items on the pre-list tape. If the total of the proof tape does not agree with the pre-list total, compare the invoices with the items posted. File the invoices alphabetically.

Cycle Billing: Filing One Month's Invoices (Sales Checks) and Posting to Statements

A number of department stores have been extending the plan of accumulating sales media to the ultimate: accumulating a full month's invoices or sales checks for each customer and posting all of them to the statement at one time. During the month, the media are sorted and filed alphabetically by customer name. At the end of the period, the posting operation involves (1) posting the month's invoices (with no description) to the statement and (2) computing and entering the balance of the account. A photograph of the media is made on microfilm, and the media are mailed to the customer with the statement.

In most businesses it is necessary to use a *cycle billing plan*, according to which a certain number of statements are posted each day and mailed to the customers. It is usually not possible to send out all the statements on the last day of the month because of the peak load that would be created at the end of the month. The idea is to distribute the job of preparing statements over the working days of the month, and to this end a scheduled section of the alphabet is closed each day. Each customer receives his statement on the same working day of each month according to the schedule. Thus, customers whose last names begin with *A* would be billed on the first day of the month—say, on February 1 for sales made to them in January. Customers whose last names begin with *B* would be billed on the second day of the month—say, February 2 for sales made to them between January 2 and February 1. Customers whose last names begin with *C* would be billed on the third day of the month—say, on February 3 for sales made to them between January 3 and February 2. The machine(s) and the operator(s) would be used on the *A*'s the first day, the *B*'s the second day, and so on. This is unlike the large-volume current-posting plan in which a given operator posts the *A* ledger day by day as the sales checks come through.

Under this plan, customers have to be educated to pay their bills within a certain number of days after they are received and not to wait until the first of the next month. Electric light and gas companies in large cities have used cycle billing with success for some time, and a number of retail stores are likewise using it.

The steps in a cycle billing operation (in skeleton form) are:

(1) Receive the day's sales checks from sales audit.
(2) Sort by controls (separate control for each "billing day").
(3) Total the sales checks for each control and charge the control accounts for batch totals.
(4) File the sales checks alphabetically within each control.

(5) On the first billing day, take the file trays for the control (say, the A's) to the bookkeeping machine and post statements and customer history cards.

(6) After proving out the control, microfilm the statements and sales checks. Mail the original statements and the supporting sales checks to the customers.

The interval of proof of posting is longer (one month) in cycle billing than it is in conventional posting (possibly daily batches). In cycle billing, the sales checks are filed daily and posted monthly to the statements. If the total per the proof sheet does not agree with the balance of the control account for the billing day, the operator compares the sales checks (and other media) with the postings on the proof sheet. This comparison should show whether an item has been posted wrong. If no items have been posted wrong, and the total on the proof sheet is less than the balance of the control account, sales check(s) may be missing.

Points in favor of cycle billing from the methods standpoint are:

(1) It increases to the maximum possible the average number of postings that can be made at one time to an account.

(2) Since only date, reference, and amount are posted (with no description), the time required to post an item is reduced.

(3) The investment in bookkeeping machines is likely to be less than it would be if postings were to be made with descriptive writing.

(4) The filing space required for the microfilm of sales checks is very considerably less than the space that would be required to file those sales checks after the statements have been mailed.

LEDGERLESS BOOKKEEPING

Ledgerless Bookkeeping Principles

Ledgerless bookkeeping for accounts receivable involves filing copies of the sales invoices or sales checks alphabetically by customer name instead of posting them. The file of media constitutes the Accounts Receivable ledger. As cash is received on account, either of two procedures may be followed: Balances on account may be carried from one sales ticket to another, and when cash is received, a cash receipts ticket showing the amount of the receipt and the new balance may be filed. This procedure is explained in the following section. Or, if no balances are shown on the sales invoices in the file, cash receipts may be applied to them by pulling the invoices from file and stamping them "paid." This procedure is explained on pages 301-304.

Since ledgerless bookkeeping as a procedure does not produce statements (as do some of the posting methods), it is often used where either (a) no statement, or (b) a simple statement, such as end-of-month balance statement, is used.

Note that although posting to statements at the end of a cycle (cycle billing) involves filing the media during the month, it is not ledgerless bookkeeping. In the strict sense, ledgerless bookkeeping involves no posting.

Ledgerless Bookkeeping for the Small Retailer: Filing Sales Checks; Showing Balances to Date

Small retailers sometimes use a form of ledgerless bookkeeping for customers by filing copies of sales checks alphabetically by customer. One clip in a file is provided for each customer. In recording a sale, the old balance is picked up from the last previous sales check and carried to the new sales check. The sales slips are written by the sales person, who turns over the original and carbon copy to the bookkeeper, retaining a tissue copy of the slip. The bookkeeper picks up the old balance, computes the new balance, and then files one copy of the sales check and gives the other to the customer.

Figure 10-6 diagrams a method of summarizing sales checks and receipts on account to provide (a) a summary of transactions for the monthly statement of profits and (b) control figures for the accounts receivable control.

Ledgerless Bookkeeping for the Manufacturer or Wholesaler (Figure 13-12)

Figure 13-12 diagrams ledgerless bookkeeping of accounts receivable for a manufacturer or wholesaler. This method involves filing a copy of each invoice produced by the billing department, and it includes a control over the serial numbers of the invoices. The purpose of the serial number control is to assist in locating missing invoices or determining the amounts of missing invoices. Figure 11-2 includes an accounts receivable copy of the invoice, produced by duplicating machine.

The diagram (Figure 13-12) illustrates the procedure where it is feasible to use a single control account for the entire accounts receivable file. The procedure is as follows:

(1) Receive the invoices in serial number order, from the Billing Department.
(2) Sort the invoices alphabetically and file in the accounts receivable file. Enter the serial numbers (first number and last number in

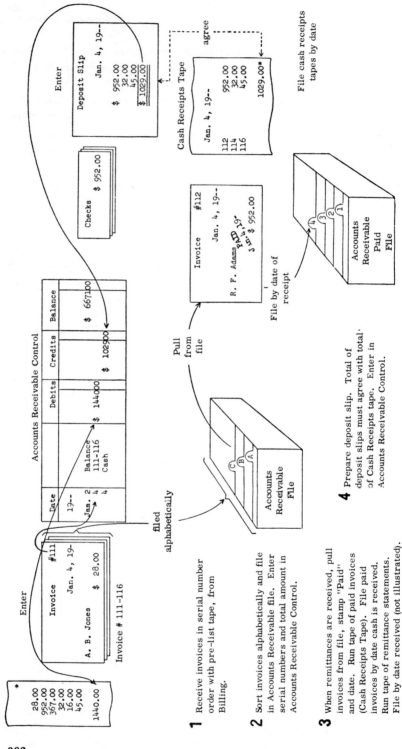

1 Receive invoices in serial number order with pre-list tape, from Billing.

2 Sort invoices alphabetically and file in Accounts Receivable file. Enter serial numbers and total amount in Accounts Receivable Control.

3 When remittances are received, pull invoices from file, stamp "Paid" and date. Run tape of paid invoices (Cash Receipts Tape). File paid invoices by date cash is received. Run tape of remittance statements. File by date received (not illustrated).

4 Prepare deposit slip. Total of deposit slips must agree with total of Cash Receipts tape. Enter in Accounts Receivable Control.

Figure 13-12. Ledgerless Bookkeeping: Accounts Receivable for Manufacturer or Wholesaler (Single Control Account)

the batch) and the total dollar amount in the accounts receivable control.

(3) When remittances are received, sort the remittance statements, or envelopes (with amounts written on them) or other evidence of the remittance, alphabetically and pull from file the invoices covered by the remittances. Stamp the invoices "paid" and the date. Run tape of the paid invoices (called the cash receipts tape) showing invoice numbers and amounts. Run tape of remittance statements or envelopes and compare total with total of invoice tape. File the remittance statements or envelopes by date cash is received. File the invoices by date cash received (as illustrated) or alphabetically. (Note the reason for filing the remittance statements or envelopes by date cash is received: If a customer complains that he was not given credit for the check he sent on, say, January 10, the accounts receivable clerk looks at the remittance file to see whether the amount was received, and then compares the remittances received that day with the invoices pulled, to determine whether the proper invoices were pulled.)

(3a) When a check is in partial payment of an invoice, stamp the invoice "Partial Payment" and the date. Enter the amount of the payment and the unpaid balance on the invoice. Write a dummy invoice showing the same information (including the entry for the partial payment) and file it in the paid invoice file.

(4) Prepare deposit slip from the checks. The total of the deposit slip must agree with the total of the cash receipts tape. Enter the total of the day's receipts in the Accounts Receivable Control.

At the end of the month, the total of the invoices in the accounts receivable file should agree with the balance of the Accounts Receivable Control account, and the file should be proved out to determine that the agreement does exist.

If the sum of the invoices does not agree with the balance of the control account, the following steps may be taken to determine the reason for the discrepancy:

(1) Count the number of items on the trial balance tape and count the number of invoices in the accounts receivable file. They should agree.

(2) Determine whether the file is greater than the control account, and if so by what amount. Look for "Paid" invoice of that amount in the accounts receivable file. It is possible that the invoice was put in the open file by mistake.

(3) If the accounts receivable file is less than the control account, an

unpaid invoice may have been removed from the open file. It may have been put in the paid file in error, or it may be on someone's desk. (This shouldn't happen, but it can.) Look in the paid invoice file for an unpaid invoice of that amount. This step may disclose that a particular invoice has been moved from the accounts receivable file to the paid invoice file. If it does not (and if the accounts receivable file is short, as here assumed) proceed with the next step.

(4) Determine that the credits to the accounts receivable control are actually the totals of the paid invoices pulled for a given day. Check out the days. It can usually be assumed that the debits to the control are correct if they agree with the credits provided by the sales distribution, but it may be necessary to check out daily credits to the Accounts Receivable Control.

(5) Check the serial numbers on the cash receipts tapes against the serial numbers put into the accounts receivable file. (The latter list is a straight sequence list.) The open numbers on the latter list are the invoices which should be in the accounts receivable file. Check the invoices in the file to determine whether they are in file.

(6) When the missing number is located, look up the invoice in the serial number file.

The above procedure seems to be (and is) a tedious one, but it is in the nature of an emergency procedure. Under proper care of the files, a user of ledgerless bookkeeping may seldom have the task of locating a missing invoice.

Note that it is possible that the accounts receivable clerk may pull the wrong invoice in applying cash receipts. He may, for instance, pull George Brown's invoice instead of Joe Brown's invoice. If the invoices are both for the same amount, the cash receipts tape will agree with the deposit slip. But Joe Brown will complain that he was not given credit for the payment he mailed on a specified date. Check the file of remittance slips or envelopes for the day against the file of pulled invoices to see whether (a) cash was received and (b) the wrong invoice was pulled.

Multiple Control Accounts

Where, because of the number of accounts, it seems desirable to set up a number of control accounts (say, one for each of four sections of the alphabet), the procedure is the same as diagrammed in Figure 13-12 except for the method of getting debits and credits to the controls. When the invoices are received from the Billing department, they are sorted by control, and an adding-machine list of invoice numbers and amounts is made of the items to be filed under each control. The dollars are, of course, charged to the proper control accounts.

When invoices are paid and pulled from the files, a tape showing invoice numbers and amounts is made of the invoices pulled from each control. With these tapes it is possible to locate the number of any invoice that is missing from the file for any control that happens to be out of balance.

Combined Credit Reference File and File for Unpaid Invoices: Ledgerless Bookkeeping

Figure 13-13 is a visible file which serves two purposes. It is, first of all, the accounts receivable open file, in which the invoices from the Billing department are held until paid. It is also the credit reference file. The signals on each pocket are used for showing the status of each account, identifying the ones that are overdue.

Figure 13-13. Credit Reference File and File for Unpaid Invoices

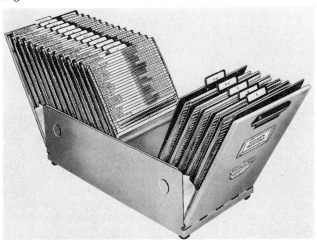

Remington Rand

CASH RECEIPTS PROCEDURE

The Cash Receipts Function

The function of cash receiving from a procedures standpoint includes:

(1) Physical handling and control
   (a) Receiving
   (b) Interim control and safeguarding
   (c) Depositing (own messenger or messenger service)

(2) Clerical handling and control
  (a) Originating the supporting data
  (b) Recording details of transaction to show:
  When received
  From whom received
  Amount received
  For what received (account distribution)
  (c) Posting to control and subsidiary ledger accounts

Basic Principles from an Internal Control Standpoint

In setting up the cash receipts procedure, the systems man keeps in mind certain basic principles from an internal control standpoint:

(1) The fixing of responsibility for physical handling and control.
(2) The daily deposit of current receipts intact.
(3) Segregation of physical handling from recording and accounting.
(4) Design and installation of records that can be easily audited for detection of fraud and error and which will deter any possibility of fraud and error. Such records make it possible to determine that all cash recorded as received is properly recorded and that cash recorded includes all cash that was received.

The degree of internal control prescribed in the system will depend upon available personnel, type of record keeping (manual or machine bookkeeping), volume of transactions, form of receipts (currency vs. checks), and method of receiving (whether largely through mail or largely through other methods). The above basic principles from internal control standpoint must always be instituted to the greatest degree possible.

Sources of Cash, Methods of Receiving, and Form of Receipt

The sources of cash, the methods of receiving, and form of receipt vary considerably among businesses. The following classifications are the more usual ones encountered:

Sources

(1) On account (credits to accounts receivable)
(2) Cash sales of merchandise
(3) On repayment of funds loaned or advanced as on notes receivable, travel advances, employee loans, and so on
(4) Collections on damages and refunds (from vendors, transportation claims, insurance proceeds, premium returns, and so on)
(5) Sale of capital assets

(6) Miscellaneous sales of supplies, waste, salvage, and the like

(7) Sundry income from rentals, vending machines, canteens, cafeterias, and so on

(8) Receipt of income on investments as interest or dividends

(9) Cash borrowed (short term and/or long term)

(10) Capital contributions

Method of Receiving

(1) By mail

(2) Directly from person making payment:
   (a) To accounts receivable cashier (house sales)
   (b) In "over-the-counter" sales
   (c) Purchases of tickets or payment of checks

(3) By collector (own salesmen, route supervisors, and so on, or by private collection agencies, banks, discount companies, and so forth)

Form of Receipt

(1) Coin or currency

(2) Checks, money orders, drafts

(3) Postage stamps, coupons, gift certificates, and so on

In designing a cash receipts procedure, the systems man determines the relative importance and volume of the various transactions. He then proceeds to (a) outline organization and methods for the physical handling and control of cash receipts, and (b) design and install records for clerical handling and control.

Organization

The internal organization pertaining to operation of an adequate cash receipts procedure is illustrated in Figure 13-14. The chart diagrams (a) the physical handling of cash and (b) the clerical handling of supporting data, by method of receiving. The organization includes:

(1) Mail opening to receive all incoming mail; to forward cash received direct to cashier; to forward supporting data received direct to accounting.

(2) Cashier to receive and assemble cash from various sources (from mail opening, direct from person making payment, and from own collectors); to safeguard cash held; to prepare and make deposit; to originate supporting data for direct receipts and to forward certain supporting data to accounting.

(3) Accounting to receive and assemble supporting data from various sources; to record entries in books of original entry and to post subsidiary ledgers.

(4) Files for all supporting data.

(5) Auditing, as a staff department to serve as an overseer over all other functions.

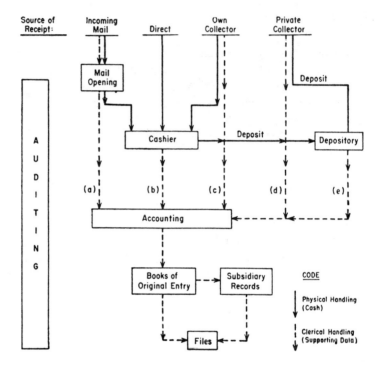

SUPPORTING DATA:

(a) Remittance advices and envelopes; daily cash receipts listings.

(b) Pre-numbered receipts originated by cashier; proof tapes, copy of deposit slips, etc.

(c) C.O.D. and collection advices; charge sheets; route books; pre-numbered receipts originated by own collectors, etc.

(d) Notices of collection.

(e) Bank stamped deposit slips, notices of bank collections, bank loan advices, etc.

Figure 13-14. Internal Organization for Cash Receipts

Note that the flow of cash is to the cashier and thence to the depository, whereas the flow of supporting data is to accounting. In the primary flow shown, no "supporting data lines" are shown to the cashier and, vice versa, no "physical handling cash lines" are shown to accounting.

In any particular organization, variation from the chart will be found depending upon local conditions. However the principle illustrated will always be found in any adequately organized cash receipts procedure. In larger companies, a separate department will be charged with responsibility to perform each of the tasks illustrated in the chart. In smaller companies, the segregation of tasks can be accomplished by spreading the above functions among various available personnel. For example, the office manager may perform auditing functions, the receptionist or telephone operator may perform mail opening, and a general clerk may be assigned cashier duties.

Managerial Information

Managerial information pertaining to cash receipts and the form of managerial reports are relatively simple as compared to information required in other procedures (as unfilled orders, sales analysis, production, costs, inventory control, and the like). Often the reports on cash receipts are a section of financial position reports which include other information.

In the simplest forms, cash recipts information furnished to management is intended to answer the following questions:

(1) How much do I have? (Cash receipts is part of the daily cash balance.)

(2) How much do others owe me? (Credit information for collections on accounts receivable balances.)

The first question is answered by a daily report of cash received together with cash disbursed and may be presented in a simple report as shown in Figure 13-15.

The second question is answered by a daily report of cash received on accounts receivable (gross amount), together with billings to customers, and may be presented in a single report shown in Figure 13-16.

REPORT OF DAILY ACCOUNTS RECEIVABLE BALANCE				
Form No. _____		Month of _____ 19 __		
Date	Previous Balance	Billed Today	Collected Today	Closing Balance
1				
2				
3				
etc.				

Figure 13-15. Report of Daily Cash Balance

Figure 13-16. Report of Daily Accounts Receivable Balance

REPORT OF DAILY CASH BALANCE				
Form No. _____			Bank _____	
		Month of _____ 19 __		
Date	Previous Balance	Received Today	Disbursed Today	Closing Balance
1				
2				
3				
etc.				

Variations from the above reports depend upon the desires of the particular management, type of business involved, business conditions, and so on. For example, under favorable business conditions, when management knows that ample cash balances are available and that collections on customers' accounts receivable are being made regularly, the need for the above reports may be somewhat less important. On the other hand, under unfavorable business conditions (when, for instance, the particular business is working on a close cash balance or when collections on receivable balances slow up), the above reports may become very important.

When several bank accounts are maintained, a report of daily cash balance may be required for each bank account, together with a summary to present the combined cash balance.

If prevailing conditions require management information of cash and receivable balances related to bank loans and payables, management may require still more detailed reports to include daily increases or decreases in bank loans and accounts payable. In a type of business engaged largely in cash sales (register sales) or comprising several departments or several retail stores, cash receipts reports may be designed to show amounts of cash received by department or by store, together with opening and closing register readings, actual cash count, and cash over and short columns. In these businesses, the cash over and short data may be of utmost importance from a cash control standpoint. See Figure 13-17.

SUMMARY OF CASH RECEIPTS

Date _____

Store No.	Register No.	Register Readings			Cash		
		Close Yesterday	Close Today	Register Sales	Count	Over	Short
1	A						
	B						
	C						
	Total						
2	A						
	B						
	C						
	Total						
etc Grand Total							

Figure 13-17

Forms

Forms used in clerical handling and control in a cash receipts system may be summarized as follows:

(1) Original data supporting each cash receipt:
    (a) Customer's check or money order.

(b) Customer's remittance memorandum or customer's envelope (used to support cash received through mail when no formal remittance memorandum is received with check).

(c) Pre-numbered cash receipts vouchers originated by cashier for direct sources of receipts.

(d) Cash sales register tapes.

(e) C.O.D. or collection advices, salesmen charge sheets, or route books.

(f) Bank advices for loans, collections made by banks, etc.

(2) Interim data accumulating or summarizing daily receipts:

(a) Bank deposit slips.

(b) Cashier cash remittance sheets; daily cash receipts listing sheets.

(c) Cash register summaries.

(d) Proof tapes.

(3) Books of original entry:

(a) Detailed cash receipts journal.

(b) Combined proof sheet and cash receipts journal.

(c) Daily cash receipts journal voucher.

(4) Subsidiary ledgers (Accounts Receivable ledgers).

(5) Books of final entry:

(a) Monthly cash receipts recapitulations.

(b) General ledger.

The basic form of original data supporting an entry for a cash receipt is the check, money order, or cash receipt itself. In very small and inadequately organized offices, entries in cash receipts journals are often made directly from the check itself. However, since no supporting data to the entry exists after the cash is deposited, it is often preferred that some other form of written data be retained.

For receipts received through mail, the customer will often send some form of remittance advice with the check or money order. The remittance memo may vary from a formal typed statement of invoice numbers, dates, discounts deducted, and amounts being paid, together with name, check number, date, and amount of the remittance, to an informal note or letter accompanying the remittance. In case only a check is enclosed in an envelope with no other supporting data, the customer's envelopes should be saved, showing customer's name, and writing thereon the date, amount, and number of check enclosed.

An important requisite in a cash receipts procedure is that all incoming mail be stamped with a receiving stamp showing date and time received. This stamp must be applied by mail opening to all remittance memoranda (or customer's envelopes) received to determine date of receipt from standpoint of cash discounts to be allowed and also as an internal check that cash received each day is being recorded and deposited intact daily.

Basic Plans of Journalizing and Posting Cash Receipts

The basic plans of journalizing and posting cash receipts are:

(1) Entering in journal and posting to ledgers:

    (a) Pen-and-ink ledger posted from detailed cash receipts journal.

    (b) Pen-and-ink ledger posted from daily cash receipts listing sheet, with daily summary cash receipts journal. This plan is described and illustrated in the following section of this chapter. The case illustrated applies to a medium-sized manufacturer whose receipts are largely received through mail and who allows cash discounts for prompt payment of specific invoices, billed through accounts receivable.

(2) Direct posting to accounts by machine-posted ledger with combined proof sheet and cash receipts journal posted from original data (customer's remittance memoranda or envelopes, own cash receipt vouchers, and so on).

(3) Ledgerless bookkeeping, illustrated in Figure 13-12.

The section titled "Illustrative Procedure: Cash Receipts on Account (Department Store)" of this chapter describes and illustrates a procedure for department stores or other types of businesses in which customers pay in full, or on account as of first of month, on a basis of monthly statements.

Illustrative Procedure: Cash Receipts Entered in Daily Cash Receipts Listing Sheet (Manufacturing Concern)

This procedure is illustrated in Figure 13-18. and is further explained below. As indicated above, the procedure was designed for a manufacturer whose receipts are largely received through the mail and who allows cash discounts for prompt payment of specific invoices.

Mail Opening

(1) Receives and opens all incoming mail, sorting out all incoming mail containing cash remittances from other mail (orders, quotations, correspondence, and so forth).

(2) Clips envelopes to related checks and remittance advices.

(3) Applies received stamp (showing date and time received) to each envelope, remittance advice, and so on, contained in mail received (exception of the check itself).

(4) Sorts remittances alphabetically by customer name.

(5) Compares check with remittance advice for customer name, amount, date, and check number. Completes any missing data on remittance advice.

(6) If no remittance advice is received, writes check data on envelope (which is then used as supporting data for that receipt).

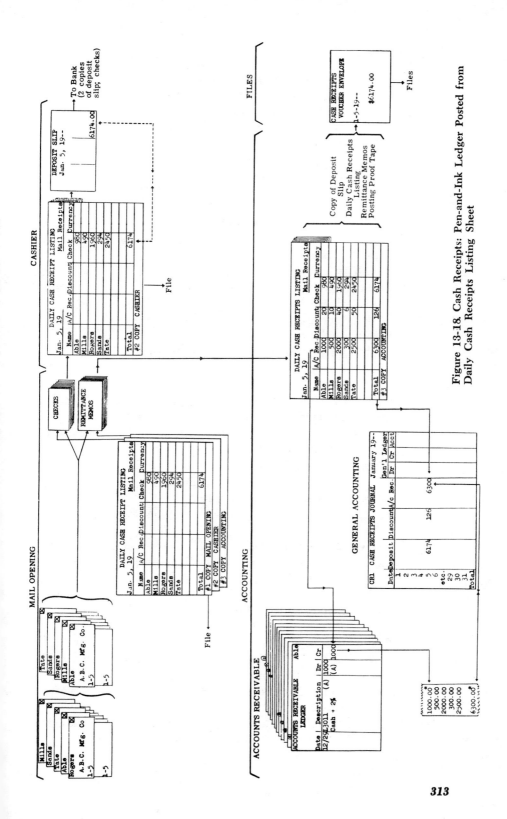

Figure 13-18. Cash Receipts: Pen-and-Ink Ledger Posted from Daily Cash Receipts Listing Sheet

(7) Destroys all unneeded envelopes, retaining checks with remittance advices attached (or envelopes, in lieu thereof).

(8) Separates checks from remittance advices.

(9) Prepares daily cash receipts listing sheet, in triplicate, from checks, showing:

    (a) Date (day cash received).

    (b) Department (Mail Receipts).

    (c) Name of customer making remittance.

    (d) Net amount of check.

(10) Totals column of check amounts.

(11) Attaches #2 copy (Cashier) to checks; attaches #3 copy (Accounting) to remittance memos.

(12) Forwards #2 copy with checks to Cashier; obtains Cashier's signature on #1 copy (Mail Opening) as receipt for checks turned over to Cashier.

(13) Files #1 copy in Mail Opening file under "Daily Cash Receipts Listing Sheets" by date of receipt.

(14) Forwards #3 copy with remittance memos to Accounting.

Cashier

(15) Receives #2 copy with checks from Mail Opening; compares name and amount listed with each check; signs #1 copy (Mail Opening) as receipt for checks received; holds checks aside pending preparation of deposit.

(16) Prepares daily deposit for day's accepted receipts:

    (a) Sorts checks in deposit slip arrangement.

    (b) Types deposit slip, in triplicate.

    (c) Applies company endorsement stamp on reverse side of each check.

(17) Forwards checks with original and one copy of deposit slip to bank (by own messenger or by private messenger service).

(18) Files #2 copy of daily cash receipts listing sheet in Cashier file, by date.

(19) Forwards copy of deposit slip to Accounting.

Accounting

(20) Receives #3 copy of daily cash receipts listing sheet with remittance memos directly from Mail Opening.

(21) Accounts receivable clerk pulls proper ledger cards from accounts receivable trays.

(22) Accounts receivable clerk compares remittance memos with debits charged to ledger card to determine:

    (a) Invoices being paid.

    (b) Payment received within discount period.

    (c) Discounts properly computed.

(23) Accounts receivable clerk completes entry on #3 copy of daily cash receipts listing sheet (for gross credit to accounts receivable and amount of discount).

(24) Accounts receivable clerk "red-lines" any entry on daily cash receipts listing sheet for checks to be rejected (improper discount taken, and so on.)

(25) Accounts receivable clerk totals all columns on daily cash receipts listing sheet:
(a) Total before "red-lined" entries.
(b) Total "red-lined" entries for rejected checks.
(c) Net total "accepted" receipts.

(26) Accounts receivable clerk notifies Cashier of "rejected checks" before deposit is prepared. Cashier withholds such checks from deposit, "red-lines" entries on #2 copy (Cashier) of daily cash receipts listing sheet; cashier forwards "rejected" checks to Credit Manager for letter to customer or other follow-up of rejected check.

(27) Accounts receivable clerk posts accounts receivable column per daily cash receipts listing sheet to proper ledger card, keying out credit against debits.

(28) Accounts receivable clerk prepares adding machine tape of credits posted to ledger cards.

(29) General bookkeeper enters daily totals per daily cash receipts listing sheet in cash receipts journal.

(30) General bookkeeper compares deposit column amount with copy of deposit slip (received from Cashier); compares accounts receivable credit total with posting proof tape (received from accounts receivable clerk).

Files

(31) Accounting forwards all supporting data (remittance memos, copy of deposit slip, proof tape) to files, enclosed in daily cash receipts envelope, showing date and amount of day's receipts on envelope.

(32) Cash receipts envelope filed by date in cash receipts file drawer.

Illustrative Procedure: Cash Receipts on Account (*Department Store*)

This procedure is used in a business in which charge sales are recorded in receivable ledgers of the unit statement type. As previously explained, the unit statement, prepared in original and duplicate, serves the function of account as well as statement, the account consisting of a carbon copy of the statement. A new unit statement is prepared for each active customer each month with the opening balance entered as the first item.

Debits and credits are posted during the month. At the end of the month, the original copy is pulled and sent to the customer and the carbon copy is permanently bound and filed by month.

The cash receipts procedures in this type of business are relatively simple because of the following features:

(1) No cash discounts are allowed for prompt payment. Credit terms are "cash" for amounts shown per monthly statement rendered, due upon receipt of statement.

(2) Top part of customer's statement is perforated and has instructions printed thereon for the customer to detach and remit with check in payment thereof. Thus, this stub accompanies check received and becomes a standardized remittance advice which shows pre-printed cash receipts data (customer's name, address, account code and number, month, and amount due).

The principles of cash receipts procedures are similar to those previously explained in this chapter, with the exception of the following possible variations:

(1) Cash receipt journals need not provide any cash discount column.

(2) Cash receipt procedures need not provide for checking remittances received to offsetting charges in customers' accounts to determine payment within discount period.

(3) Detailed individual cash receipts listings are not necessary in the cash receipts journal nor on daily cash receipts listing sheets.

The procedure is:

(1) Sort remittance advices (top stub of monthly statement) by Accounts Receivable ledger controls. (Often there are numerous accounts, segregated by alphabetical groupings in detail ledger trays with separate control accounts for each grouping.) Use of different colors on remittance advices by controls will facilitate sorting by detail ledger tray.

(2) Make totals of remittance advices received by ledger controls. These totals become the source of daily total entries in cash receipts journal.

(3) Post cash credits to unit statement directly from remittance stubs.

(4) File remittance stubs by day, by ledger tray control, as supporting data to cash receipts entry.

(5) Unpaid balances from previous month can be easily determined from file copies of unit statements after a specified number of days have elapsed. These delinquent accounts are listed on a collection sheet for overdue accounts receivable which is forwarded to Collection department for follow-up.

Note that where discount for payment of the end-of-month balance is allowed, a simple method may be used for checking the discounts on customers' remittances as they come in. At the end of the month after the customers' statements have been mailed out, the discounts allowable can be pre-figured and entered on the file copies of the unit statements. (Meantime a new set of unit statements for the new month has been started by the posting clerks.) As remittances are received they are (a) checked against the old statements in file to determine whether discount actually taken is proper, and (b) if proper, turned over to posting clerks who post them to the new statements.

Proofs and Internal Checks

Even with well-planned internal control over cash receipts handling, there is no substitute for honesty of all employees connected with each phase of the cash receipts procedure, especially for those employees handling currency receipts. This means careful selection of personnel assigned to these duties. Bonding of such employees is another precaution that must not be overlooked. Next to honesty of employees, adequate supervision, together with periodical audit by test checks of detailed transactions, is necessary to determine that procedures set up are actually being followed. Often cash defalcations occur when there exists a supposedly "airtight" cash receipts procedure with the most trusted employees.

The principles of cash procedure outlined in this chapter are designed to deter any possibility of fraud and defalcation, however, and minimize the time and effort required to record transactions. The segregation of physical handling from recording of cash necessitates that individually prepared totals be in agreement. The daily deposit prepared by Cashier must agree with entries for the day prepared from supporting data. The application of the time and date stamp to supporting data requires that all receipts for the day be deposited currently. The necessity of depositing receipts intact eliminates the possibility of substitution of one receipt for another. Retention of supporting data for each receipt makes entries subject to detailed audit to determine that cash receipts are properly recorded.

Other possible proofs and internal checks include:

(1) Proper equipment for registering and safeguarding cash by Cashier.

(2) Cashier not to have access to Accounts Receivable ledgers, and vice versa; Accounts Receivable ledger bookkeepers not to have access to cash or deposits.

(3) Monthly statements of customers' accounts be checked by Credit department after preparation and mailed directly by responsible person in that department.

(4) All customers' complaints pertaining to any particulars in their accounts, however small, be referred directly to a responsible person for adequate follow-up. Neither Cashier nor Accounting de-

partment should be allowed to handle any customer complaint pertaining to his account.

(5) All forms and/or original data to direct cash receipts be prenumbered and issued in adequate number of copies to allow as a minimum distribution (a) copy to person making remittance, (b) copy to person originating form, (c) bookkeeping copy, and (d) locked auditing copy.

14

Purchase Order and Receiving Report Procedures; Internal Check-Purchase and Payment

Purchasing and Receiving Functions

The purchasing function in industry is concerned with the purchase of machinery and equipment for the factory, materials for the manufacture of product, supplies and repair parts for maintenance of the factory, packing cases and shipping supplies for the shipping department, stationery and office supplies for the office, and various other goods and services. It involves, among other things, keeping in touch with sources of supply and obtaining current price information by correspondence and by interview, getting promises of delivery dates, executing purchase contracts for contract shipments, writing purchase orders, following up deliveries, examining purchase invoices to determine that prices are as agreed and that the quantities charged do not exceed the quantities ordered, and compiling reports on the status of unfilled purchase orders.

In case of contract purchases calling for a number of shipments, the purchase follow-up includes, as a matter of course, keeping track of the unfilled balances of the contracts. This follow-up puts the Purchasing department in position to certify, as invoices come up for approval, that no more goods have been received than were ordered. Ordinarily, the purchasing function operates on the basis of requests from other departments such as Planning or Production Control (particularly in case of direct materials) or from various supervisors, such as the office manager, for office supplies and services, and the maintenance foreman, for repair parts and supplies.

In the manufacture of styled merchandise, for instance garments, the purchasing function operates closely with the functions of planning the product ("merchandising") and selling it. In fact, the merchandise manager will make the decisions on what materials ("piece goods") are to be purchased for use in what styles and lot numbers and what quantities of materials shall be contracted for, for the coming style season. Here, the element of speculative profit or loss in inventories can be important.

The receiving function consists of receiving the goods, counting, weighing, or otherwise measuring the goods, examining them for general condition, signing carriers' receipts covering transportation of the goods, and writing receiving reports or approving the receiving copies of the purchase orders.

Organization

The question of organization of the purchasing function involves the two considerations of (a) carrying out the mechanics of purchasing from the moment the purchase is decided upon until the invoice is in and approved for payment, and (b) deciding what should be purchased, when, and at what price. In small concerns, the mechanics are likely to be performed by a clerk in the office who spends part time on that work acting upon oral or written requests from the Manufacturing department, the Sales department, and for some items, the office manager. In larger concerns, there may be a person who devotes full time to the function, or a purchasing department which operates for the purpose. In multiple-plant organizations, there may be administrative provision that a plant manager may issue local purchase orders for certain items (specified in instructions to the manager) provided that a purchase order may not exceed a specified amount. All other purchases would be made by the Central Purchasing department, one of whose functions would be to consolidate requests from the plants to make up larger quantity purchases.

The matter of deciding what shall be purchased and when is usually the responsibility of someone outside the Purchasing department who determines the need for the goods or services in the first place. Thus, requests for purchase of materials for production may come from the Planning and Production Control department; for repair parts, from the master mechanic; for advertising materials, from the sales manager; and for stationery, from the office manager. The question of what price shall be paid (particularly in the case of items that are bought repetitively) is the responsibility of the purchasing agent, although other executives may have the responsibility for approving or rejecting prices on special items.

The receiving function may be carried out by a receiving clerk or a receiving department that is located and equipped for the physical handling of the goods, which it turns over to the storekeeper or to the department making a request for direct delivery. In some cases, inspection is done by the Receiving department, and in other cases by a separate section.

Managerial Reports

The Purchasing department may make reports to the management on the current prices of important materials. Where purchase contracts represent significant commitments, the Purchasing department may make regular reports on the balances due on unfilled contracts.

Forms Classified

The following forms are typical in purchasing and receiving procedures and the related disbursing procedures:

(1) Purchase requisition or request for purchase is a form written by a department head or other authorized person to ask the Purchasing department to buy goods specified. The form may be written independently for each request, with two copies provided—original for the Purchasing department and a copy for the person who writes the request. Sometimes a third copy is provided for the Accounting department. Or it may be a *traveling* requisition—a separate requisition for each item for which a perpetual inventory account is maintained. Such requisitions are used repetitively, traveling back and forth between the inventory clerk and the Purchasing department. (See Figure 14-1)

(2) Request for quotation is a form written by the Purchasing department asking prospective suppliers to send price information about goods specified. (This may be an advance copy of a purchase order.)

(3) Purchase order, which is an order issued to an outside supplier requesting shipment of specified goods or supply of specified service. (See Figures 14-2, 14-3 and 14-4.) Common copies are:
   (a) Advice copies, such as one to the person who requested the purchasing department to order the goods, as notice that the goods have been ordered; also one to the receiving department as notice that goods have been ordered. (Note, however, that in "blind" receiving systems, the latter copy is omitted to encourage the Receiving department to perform an independent count and render an independent report.)
   (b) Unfilled order copies. These copies may be filed alphabetically by supplier in the Purchasing department, as a record of orders placed with each supplier.
   (c) Journal or register copy, filed by serial number for control of orders issued.

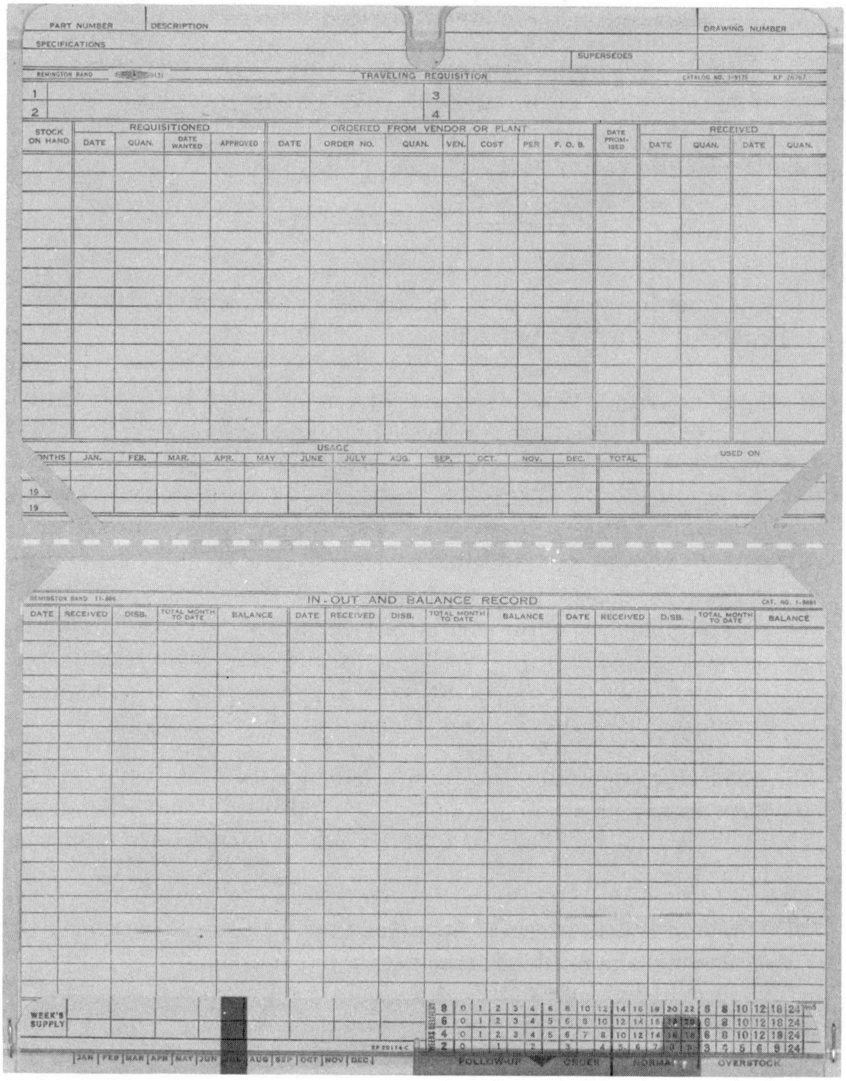

Remington Rand

Figure 14-1. Traveling Purchase Requisition.

This requisition fits in the pocket of a perpetual inventory account. When the re-order point has been reached, the perpetual inventory clerk pulls the requisition (top form in the illustration) from the pocket, enters the quantity to order, and sends it to the purchasing department. After ordering, the purchasing department returns the requisition to the ledger clerk who puts it back in the pocket. There is a requisition for each inventory account. Each requisition shows all of the specifications which the purchasing department needs to order the goods. Each requisition is used repetitively and re-writing of specifications each time a requisition is issued is eliminated.

(d) Posting or distribution copies. Copies may be provided for the Materials ledger clerk to post the "on order" section of the Materials ledger accounts or to a distribution clerk for taking off order statistics.

(4) Receiving report, which is notice written by the Receiving department that the goods have been received. (See Figure 14-5.) The original form may be issued to the Purchasing department to permit that department to perform its follow-up functions. There may also be:

(a) Advice copies to persons who are interested in the fact of receipt of the goods, such as the person who ordered the goods, Inspection department, and others.

(b) Journal or register copy, filed serially in the Receiving department as a control copy.

In some cases, a copy of the purchase order serves as a receiving report, as explained later in this chapter. (See Figure 14-2.)

Figure 14-2 Purchase Order Set (Carbon Interleaved).

This demonstrator set consists of the following copies: (1) Original. (2) Request for quotation (which may be detatched from the set and sent out in advance of releasing the purchase order). (3) Receiving report (illustrated). This copy is printed on translucent paper. After the receiving clerk has entered quantities received (R) and balance (B), copies can be made on a copying machine (Figure 6-8). (4) Other copies: quality control, purchasing file, accounts payable, and requisitioner.

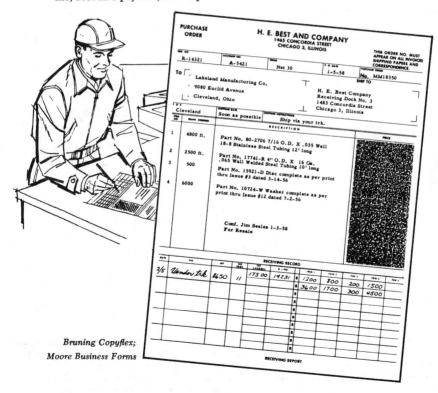

Bruning Copyflex;
Moore Business Forms

E

NUMBER EVERY PACKAGE AND MARK SHIPPER'S NAME

DEPARTMENT	CLASSIFICATION

CHICAGO__________________19 ___

TERMS__________ DATE OF SHIPMENT__________ DATE INVOICE IS TO BE DATED__________

THIS ORDER IS SUBJECT TO AND CONTINGENT UPON COMPLIANCE WITH INSTRUCTIONS AND CONDITIONS ON THE FACE AND BACK OF THIS ORDER.

NOTICE WE RESERVE THE RIGHT TO RETURN PART OR ALL OF THE GOODS CALLED FOR ON THIS ORDER IF FOR ANY REASON THEY ARE NOT IN EVERY RESPECT AS REPRESENTED.

WE FURTHER RESERVE THE RIGHT TO RETURN MERCHANDISE, AT YOUR EXPENSE, OR CANCEL THIS ORDER IF SHIPMENT IS NOT MADE UPON THE DATE OR IN THE MANNER SPECIFIED.

QUALITY	DESCRIPTION	QUANTITY	PRICE	AMOUNT

REQUISITION NUMBER	APPROPRIATION NUMBER	SPECIAL ORDER NUMBER	ESTIMATED TOTAL AMT.

SHIP BY__________

F. O. B.__________ SHIP FROM__________

IMPORTANT - SEE OTHER SIDE

ORDERED BY__________ DEPT. MGR. INC.

APPROVED FOR

MERCHANDISE MANAGER

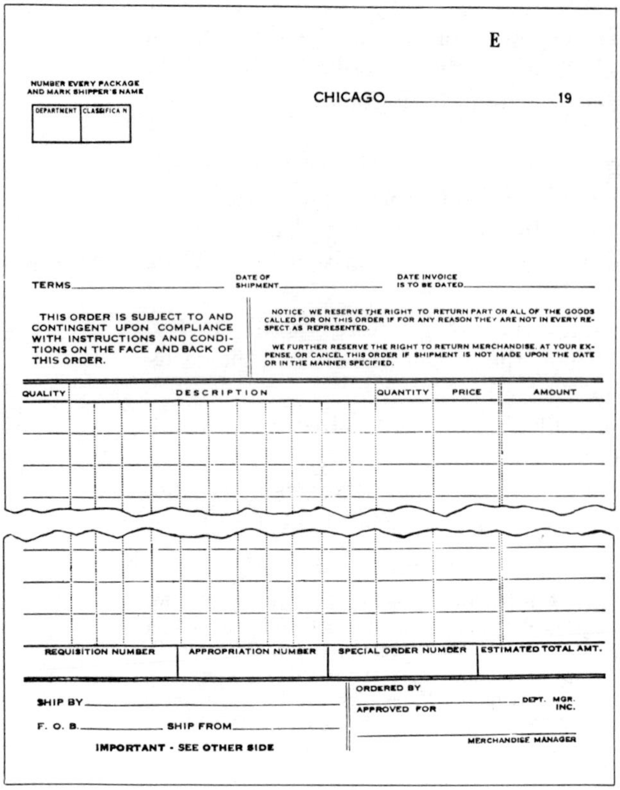

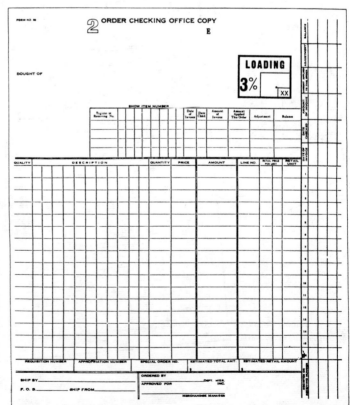

Figure 14-3. Purchase Order for Retail Store—Original

Moore Business Forms

FORM NO. 66

2 ORDER CHECKING OFFICE COPY

E

BOUGHT OF

LOADING 3% XX

SHOW ITEM NUMBER

Register or Receiving No.								Date of Invoice	Date Chkd.	Amount of Invoice	Amount Applied This Order	Adjustment	Balance

QUALITY	DESCRIPTION	QUANTITY	PRICE	AMOUNT	LINE NO.	RETAIL PRICE PER UNIT	RETAIL UNIT
					1		
					2		
					3		
					4		
					5		
					6		
					7		
					8		
					9		
					10		
					11		
					12		
					13		
					14		
					15		

REQUISITION NUMBER	APPROPRIATION NUMBER	SPECIAL ORDER NO.	ESTIMATED TOTAL AMT.	ESTIMATED RETAIL AMOUNT

SHIP BY__________

F. O. B.__________ SHIP FROM__________

ORDERED BY__________ DEPT. MGR. INC.

APPROVED FOR

MERCHANDISE MANAGER

BALANCE | ADJUSTMENT | AMOUNT APPLIED TO THIS ORDER | AMOUNT OF INVOICE | DATE CHECKED | DATE OF INVOICE | REGISTER OR RECEIVING NUMBER

Figure 14-4. Purchase Order—Office Copy.

Note spaces for retail prices and spaces at right for checking of successive receipts on the order. Used where successive receipts on one order are not numerous.

Where the arrangement of copies is as indicated above, the Purchasing department may approve quantities and prices before passing invoices to the Accounting department. In some cases, an Accounting department copy of the purchase order and one of the receiving report copies may be sent direct to the Accounting department. These copies may be used by that department to perform certain independent verification.

The vertical columns comprising the description section are used to record the dispersion of quantities ordered by size. Two horizontal lines would be used for each garment style purchased, the top for size and the bottom for quantity of the size.

(5) Purchase invoice apron (gummed sticker) or rubber stamp (Figure 14-6) for approvals. Either of these devices is used to provide spaces for entry of approvals for payment of the invoice with respect to quantities, prices, extensions, final approval of the invoice for payment, and the like.

Illustrations of purchase order and related forms appear in Figures 14-1 to 14-6.

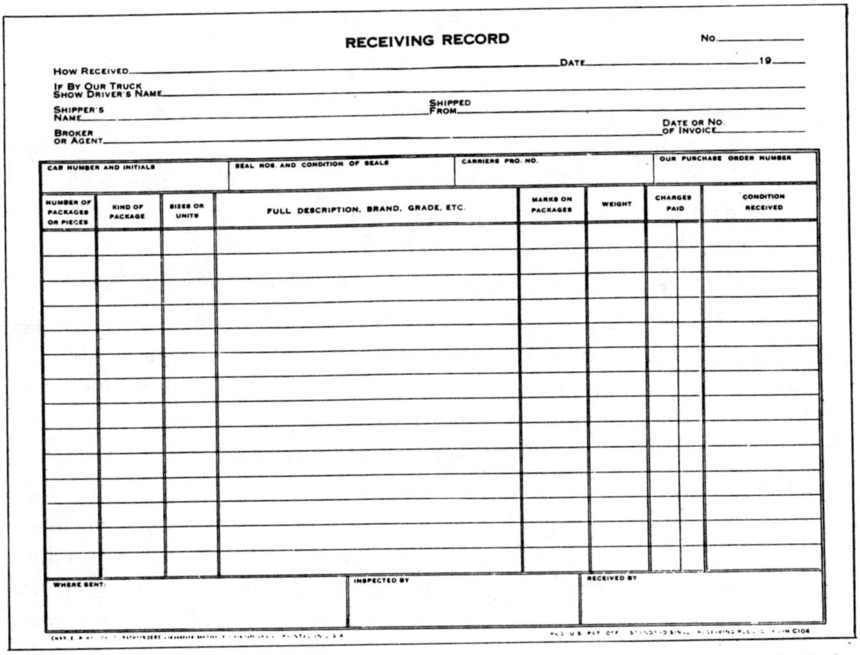
RECEIVING RECORD

No.

How Received

Date 19

If By Our Truck Show Driver's Name

Shipper's Name

Shipped From

Broker or Agent

Date or No. of Invoice

Car Number and Initials	Seal Nos. and Condition of Seals	Carriers Pro. No.	Our Purchase Order Number

Number of Packages or Pieces	Kind of Package	Sizes or Units	Full Description, Brand, Grade, Etc.	Marks on Packages	Weight	Charges Paid	Condition Received

Where Sent:	Inspected By	Received By

Pathfinder

Figure 14-5. Receiving Report

Invoice Rec'd_____
Mat'l Rec._____
Price O. K._____
Ext. O. K._____
Purchase Authorized by_____
O. K. for Payment_____
Voucher No._____
Check No._____
Date Paid_____
Charge to_____

Figure 14-6. Rubber Stamp Impression for Approval of Purchase Invoices

Illustrative Procedure Outlined

The steps in a typical purchasing and receiving procedure for a small manufacturing concern are:

Purchasing Department

(1) Receives requests for purchase from department heads. (Requests for purchase show, among other details, account number to be charged.)

(2) For some basic raw materials, executes contracts with suppliers covering expected requirements for several months, on basis of quantity schedule worked up by the Planning department. Original copy to supplier; copy filed alphabetically by supplier.

(3) Writes purchase order and four copies:
   (a) Original—to supplier.
   (b) Copy—for filing alphabetically by supplier (follow up).
   (c) Copy—for person requesting goods.
   (d) Copy—for filing by serial number.
   (e) Copy (on translucent paper)—for Receiving department.

Dispatches (a) and (c), after entering request number on copy (c). The account number appears on the purchase order and copies.

Note: Where the request has come originally from the materials ledger clerk, copy (c) of the purchase order is sent to that clerk, who enters it in the "On Order" section of the appropriate Raw Materials ledger account.

(4) Files copy (b) alphabetically by supplier. In case there is a purchase contract in file, posts the purchase order to the purchase contract copy, which provides spaces for quantities ordered and running balances due on contract. (Show date of purchase order, quantity ordered, and new balance due on contract.)

(5) Receives invoice from supplier. Checks the price against file copy of purchase contract or purchase order. If price is as agreed,

approves the invoice for price. Holds invoice for matching with receiving report (Step **7**).

Receiving Department

(6) Receives the materials, accompanied by (a) copy of supplier's shipping order or packing slip, and (b) carrier's freight notice. Gets the Receiving department copy of the purchase order from file. (If there is no copy, it is possible that the goods, though received, were not ordered.) Determines whether shipment is in good order. Counts, weighs, or measures the goods. Enters the receipt in the bottom section of the Receiving department copy of the purchase order (See Figure 14-2). As was stated above, this copy is printed on translucent paper. Produces three copies on the copying machine:

(a) Purchasing
(b) Purchasing
(c) To storekeeper with goods

If the order is complete, put the original Receiving department copy of the purchasing order in a completed order file. If it is not complete, return it to the open-order file in the Receiving department. Dispatch copies, which are called "receiving reports."

Enters receiving report number on the freight notice and sends it to the Accounting department. (The latter step assists the Accounting department in matching freight bills with receiving reports.)

Purchasing Department

(7) Matches one copy of the receiving report with invoice. If quantities agree, approves quantity on invoice for payment. Staples receiving report to invoice.
(8) Refers to alphabetic files of purchase orders, pulls the purchase order and discards it. If the order is complete, put the other copy of the receiving report in the completed-purchase-order file. If it is not complete, put it in the open-purchase-order file. Determines any unfilled balance on purchase order. Determines whether supplier has sent more goods than ordered.
(9) Sends invoice with receiving report attached to Accounting department.

Accounting Department

(10) Materials ledger clerk enters quantities and amounts (from invoices) in appropriate Materials ledger accounts and sends invoices and receiving reports to voucher clerk.

(11) Voucher clerk matches quantities on invoice with quantities on receiving report, verifies extensions, footings, discounts, and all other mathematical particulars on invoice, determines that all documents supporting the invoice are on hand and in order (so far as can be determined from the documents themselves), and determines that all documents are properly signed. Verifies account number to be charged, as entered on purchase order by Purchasing department. Enters voucher in voucher register. Cancels invoices and supporting documents by stamping them "paid" or by perforating them.

(12) General ledger clerk posts totals of voucher register to accounts in General ledger.

(13) Materials ledger clerk takes trial balance of Materials ledger, gives to General ledger clerk who compares total with balance of Materials ledger control account.

Physical Inventory Takers

(14) Physical inventory takers count goods on hand, report count to Accounting department. Accounting department compares physical count with book inventory.

Methods: Forms Illustrated

The principal methods problems that arise in connection with purchase order and receiving procedures relate to the writing and reproduction of forms. The reader is referred to Chapter 6 in which various carbon-paper and duplicating-machine methods of reproduction are described. Any of the methods of writing and reproduction used for billing procedures may be considered for purchase order and receiving procedures.

Accounting Control of Transactions: Internal Check

Figure 14-7 is a chart of the major features of accounting control of the purchasing and receiving procedure described on pages 326-328. The column at the left describes the major features of control, and the other columns show by descriptive entries what each person involved in the procedure does to contribute to the control. The numbers in parentheses refer to the steps of clerical procedure listed in the description. It will be noted that in some cases a single person is responsible for a particular control, and in other cases one or more persons check each other. (The procedures that were designed for the purpose of having one person check another person are internal check features.)

Following is a list of the various control features with a discussion of significant points and certain alternate methods:

(1) Goods ordered were actually required, in the quantity ordered.

(2) Goods were requested by someone who had authority to request.

(3) The purchase was made in good faith, and terms, prices, and conditions were in the apparent best interest of the company.

The department head issues a request for purchase to the purchasing agent, and the purchasing agent issues a purchasing order pursuant to that request, sending a copy of the purchase order back to the writer of the request for purchase. In this exchange of documents, the purchasing agent notes whether the person who wrote the request for purchase had authority to do so, and that person in his turn has the opportunity to see whether the purchase order is consistent with the request.

(4) Goods were actually received in the quantity invoiced.

(5) Goods received were actually ordered.

(6) Goods were in good condition when received.

(7) Goods were actually placed in stock or were received by the person who issued the request for purchase.

The goods were received by a receiving clerk who makes out a receiving report using a receiving copy of the purchase order. The fact that there is a copy on file indicates that the goods were actually ordered and protects the company against the nuisance of opening and inspecting goods that were shipped "on trial." Also, the purchasing agent checks the receiving report against the purchase order as a part of its function of following up on deliveries on purchase orders. Note that both the storekeeper and the receiving clerk examine the goods for general condition. The storekeeper receives a copy of the receiving report with the goods, and he is supposed to report any goods received in bad condition. In some cases, the storekeeper is required to sign for goods received.

Note that the operation of the perpetual inventory system is intended to place responsibility for custody of the goods upon the storekeeper until he receives a requisition giving him authority to release the goods. (See steps 10, 13, and 14 on the chart.)

(8) In case of partial shipments on contract, the aggregate quantity received does not exceed the contract.

The Purchasing department has the responsibility of following up deliveries to make sure that they arrive in time; in this case, it is also given the responsibility of approving invoices for payment with respect to total quantity received on the contract.

(9) Prices and terms on the invoice are consistent with agreement reached when the purchase order was accepted by the supplier.

(10) Correct account was charged (in the distribution of debits).

In the procedure diagrammed, request for purchase shows account

PURCHASE AND PAYMENT
ACCOUNTING CONTROL: INTERNAL CHECK

Control Feature / Persons Responsible	Department head or other person authorized to request	Purchasing agent or purchasing clerk	Receiving clerk	Storekeeper	Materials ledger clerk	Voucher clerk	General ledger
(a) Goods ordered were actually required in the quantity ordered.	(1) Writer assumes responsibility when he signs *request for purchase.*						
(b) Goods were requested by person who has authority.		(1) Determines that writer had authority to write *request for purchase.*					
(c) The purchase was made in good faith and prices, terms, and conditions were in the best apparent interest of the company.	(3) Receives copy of *purchase order* which he can compare with copy of *request for purchase.*	(2) Writes *purchase contract.* (3) Writes *purchase order.*				(11) Determines that *purchase order* was actually written and is apparently in proper order.	
(d) Goods were actually received, in the quantity ordered.		(7) Matches quantities on *receiving report* with *invoice.*	(6) Counts, weighs, or measures the goods. Writes *receiving report.*	(6) Receives copy of *receiving report* with goods.		(11) Matches quantities on *invoice* with quantities on *receiving report.*	
(e) Goods received were actually ordered.			(6) Determines whether there is a copy of the purchase order in the receiving department file.				
(f) Goods were in good condition when received.			(6) Examines for general condition. Notes condition on *receiving report.*	(6) Storekeeper observes whether goods are in good condition.			

Condition	Requisition	Purchasing	Receiving	Materials Ledger	Accounts Payable	Control
(g) Goods were actually placed in stock or actually received by department for which intended.			(6) Storekeeper (or other person requesting the purchase) checks goods against copy of *receiving report*.	(10) Enters quantities and amounts from invoice in appropriate materials ledger accounts (also enters requisitions). (13) Takes trial balance of materials ledger, sends to general ledger clerk. (14) Compares physical inventory sheets with materials ledger accounts.		(14) Compares trial balance of materials ledger with balance of Materials Ledger Control account.
(h) In case of partial shipments on contract, the aggregate quantity received does not exceed the contract.		(8) Compares quantities on *receiving reports* with *purchase contract* or *purchase order*. Keeps running balances.			(11) Compares quantities received on *receiving report* with quantities on *purchase order* (where entire *purchase order* is received at one time).	
(i) Prices and terms on the invoices are consistent with agreement reached when purchase order was accepted by supplier.		(5) Checks prices on invoice against file copy of *purchase order*.				
(j) Correct account was charged.	(1) Writes account to be charged on *Request*.	(3) Enters account number on *purchase order*.			(11) Verifies account number entered on invoice by Purchasing Agent.	
(k) Extensions, footings, discounts, and all other mathematical particulars on invoice are correct.					(11) Verifies extensions, footings, discounts, and all other mathematical particulars on invoices.	
(l) No payment for materials is made except on an invoice, and no invoice is paid twice.					(11) Matches *invoice* with *purchase order* and *receiving report*. Stamps *invoice* "Voucher No. ___."	

Note: Numbers in parentheses are clerical operations as listed in Section 311, "Illustrative Procedure Outlined."

Figure 14-7.

number to be charged, and the Purchasing department types account number on the purchase order. In other cases, the voucher clerk locates and enters the account number.

(11) Extensions, footings, discounts, and all other mathematical particulars on the invoice are correct.

(12) No payment for materials is made except on an invoice, and no invoice is paid twice.

The purchasing agent is responsible for determining that prices, and the like, are as agreed, and the Accounting department has responsibility for extensions, footings, discounts, and other mathematical particulars (and also for determining that all the documents that should support an invoice are actually on hand and appear to be in order). To guard against the possibility of an invoice getting into circulation and being presented for vouchering and payment a second time, the voucher clerk puts the voucher number and date on the invoice and supporting documents.

As an alternate to the above procedure, the Accounting department instead of the Purchasing department may match invoices with purchase orders to determine that (a) the prices, quantities, and conditions on the invoice agree with the purchase order, and (b) where the purchase order called for a series of shipments, the aggregate quantities received and invoiced agree with the purchase order. The Accounting department may also receive a copy of the receiving report direct from the Receiving department to permit it to verify quantities on invoices.

15

Accounts Payable;
Vouchers Payable; Cash Disbursements

Function and Organization

The function of the accounts payable or the vouchers payable procedure is to keep track of the amounts owed by the creditors of the business and to set up the proper forms for payment of the creditors when payment is due. The function always includes certain verification procedures intended to insure that the payments are correct. It also includes a determination that the steps which should have been performed (such as the approval of prices where it is done in the Purchasing department) apparently have been performed.

The function of the cash disbursements procedure is to issue checks to cover verified liabilities that have been approved for payment and to keep a record of such disbursements and a record of daily bank balances. (The reconciliation of bank statements is, strictly speaking, an internal audit function.)

In large organizations where the volume of clerical work permits, separate persons or groups are assigned to (a) verifying, approving, and recording the liabilities, (b) disbursing and recording disbursements, and (c) reconciling bank statements. In smaller concerns, the volume of clerical work may not permit the division of effort and responsibility that accomplishes internal check in a larger concern. In such cases the work may be divided between clerical employees and the proprietor or manager, with the latter person supervising the verification procedures, signing the checks, and possibly reconciling the bank statements.

The accounting control and internal check features of payables procedures are explained in Chapter 14. The present chapter explains and illustrates the operation of several types of accounts payable and vouchers payable procedures after the verification steps have been performed. In connection with these illustrations, it will be noted that an accounts payable procedure is one in which a posted account is kept for each creditor showing invoices, payments on account, and sometimes running balance due. A voucher procedure is one in which no posted accounts are kept with creditors, but copies of the disbursement voucher are used as a record of the liability.

ACCOUNTS PAYABLE PROCEDURES

Forms

The particular forms required vary as between accounts payable procedures and vouchers payable procedures. The following forms are typical:

(1) Creditor's account form.
(2) Purchase journal.
(3) Remittance advice, which is sent to the creditor with the check. It is a list of the items covered by the check.
(4) Check.

Accounts Payable Procedure: Pen and Ink

The steps in a typical accounts payable procedure by pen and ink are: When the invoice is approved for payment:

(1) Enter invoice in purchases journal.
(2) Post the amount of the invoice from the purchase journal to the creditor's account in the Accounts Payable ledger.

When an amount is paid on account:

(3) Enter the check in the cash payments journal.
(4) Post the amount of the payment from the cash payments journal to the creditor's account in the Accounts Payable ledger.

The invoices are entered in the purchase journal on date approved for payment (that is, as the matching of invoices with receiving reports and purchase order and other steps of verification and approval have been completed, as outlined in Chapter 14). As the invoices are entered, they are so marked to guard against the possibility of their being entered a second time by mistake. The invoices may then be filed alphabetically to provide a file of information on what was bought from each creditor.

Due date control can be provided by entering the discount terms in the particulars space of the journal or the account. In some cases, the invoices, after being entered in the purchases journal, are filed by due date instead of alphabetically in order to provide a due date control. In such cases, the invoices may be checked against the corresponding credit in the creditor's account at the time they are pulled from file for payment to provide additional verification of the posting operation. Invoices would then be filed alphabetically after checking against the creditor's account to provide a file of items purchased from each supplier and the prices paid. In some small businesses, no separate file is kept of prices paid for items purchased, and there is a certain amount of reference to the paid-invoice file to determine what prices have been paid for particular items.

This procedure provides a running record of the amount due each creditor and the total for all creditors. When statements are received from creditors at the end of the month, they are reconciled with the accounts in the Creditors' ledger.

The accounts payable procedure inherently requires more clerical work than the others explained in this chapter. When specific invoices are paid within their discount periods, considerable work may be involved in posting credits to creditors' accounts when invoices are approved, and then practically immediately posting debits for the cash payments. The Accounts Payable ledger may actually be considered unnecessary. The accounts payable plan is recommended, however, when there are frequent payments of round amounts on account, since the creditors' accounts provide a continuous basis for reconciling creditors' statements with the company records.

Remittance statements may be sent with checks, or the words "on account" or "balance end of month" may be written on the check or a stub attached thereto. If the check does cover specific items, they may be listed on the check or on the stub.

Accounts Payable: Machine Posting

In machine posting, the purchase invoice may be posted directly to the creditors' accounts, and the purchase journal obtained as a carbon copy by-product of the posting operation. Machine posting is illustrated and explained in Chapter 7.

VOUCHERS PAYABLE PROCEDURES

Forms

Forms used in vouchers payable procedures are:

(1) Voucher or voucher-check. This form is a statement sent to the creditor, but it is so designed that the copies retained by the issuer comprise the record of the liability with evidence of the authorization of the disbursement. It is the key form in what is commonly known as the voucher procedure. (Types of vouchers are explained in the following sections.)

(2) Voucher register.

(3) Cash disbursements journal or check register.

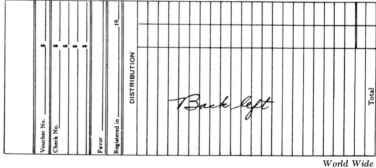

Figure 15.1. Voucher Form (Ready-Printed) for Internal Use

Vouchers: One-Time; Built-Up

The key form of the voucher procedure is the voucher proper, which shows, among other things, (a) the name and address of the vendor, (b) description or other identification and amount of each invoice covered by the voucher, (c) total or net amount due the creditor, and (d) account(s) to be charged. The voucher with its copies usually takes the place of the Accounts Payable ledger and the remittance advice of the accounts payable procedure.

A voucher with its copies is used as:

(1) Order to the cashier to pay the creditor.
(2) An advice to the creditor, to accompany the check.
(3) An accounting medium for recording:
    (a) the liability, and
    (b) the distribution.

A ready-printed voucher form is illustrated in Figure 15-1. Note the spaces for (a) a complete identification of the items covered, to eliminate question as to what the payment does cover, (b) spaces for authorization signatures or initials, and (c) spaces for names or numbers of accounts to be charged or credited. (The form illustrated is useful mainly as an internal form, since it provides space for information that would not ordinarily be sent to a creditor.) The forms illustrated are ready-printed, supplied in pads of fifty.

Figure 15-2 is a voucher form which is in the nature of a remittance statement. It is mainly a list of items covered by the check that accompanies the voucher.

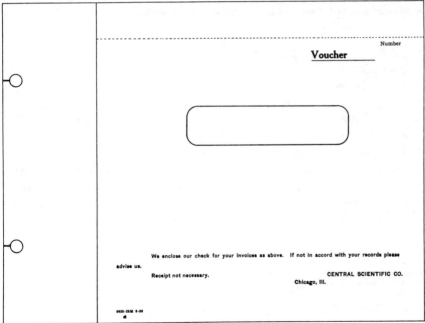

Number

Voucher

We enclose our check for your invoices as above. If not in accord with your records please advise us.

Receipt not necessary.

CENTRAL SCIENTIFIC CO.
Chicago, Ill.

Snapout

Figure 15-2. Voucher Form: Remittance Statement

Voucher-Checks

As the name indicates, a voucher-check is simply a combination of (a) voucher (as explained in the previous section) and (b) check with

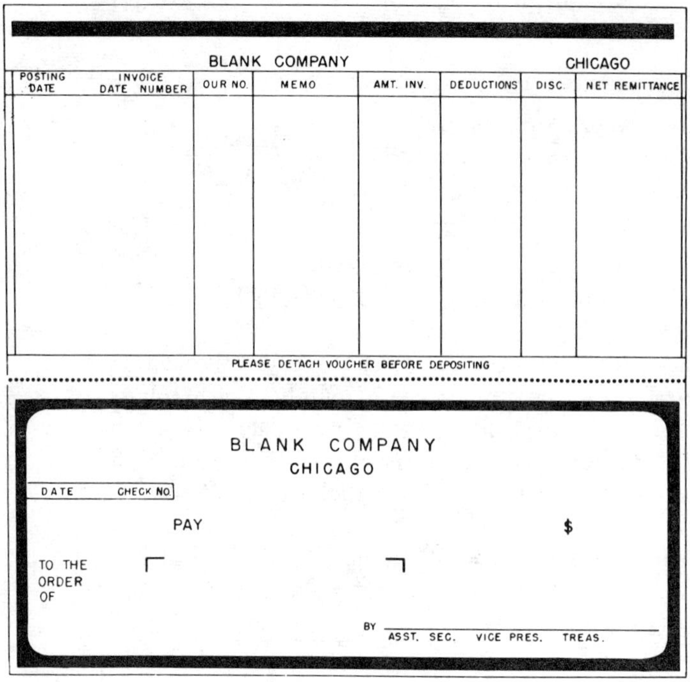

BLANK COMPANY   CHICAGO

POSTING DATE	INVOICE DATE NUMBER	OUR NO.	MEMO	AMT. INV.	DEDUCTIONS	DISC.	NET REMITTANCE

PLEASE DETACH VOUCHER BEFORE DEPOSITING

BLANK COMPANY
CHICAGO

DATE CHECK NO.

PAY $

TO THE
ORDER
OF

BY ――――――――――――――――
ASST. SEC. VICE PRES. TREAS.

Burroughs—Todd Division

Figure 15-3. Voucher-Check

which the creditor is paid. An illustration of a voucher-check appears in Figure 15-3. Note that the check portion is at the bottom of the form and the voucher portion at the top. Use of voucher-checks saves writing a check separate from the voucher, which is the case when the ordinary voucher form illustrated in Figure 15-2 is used. (The illustration is a sample form on which the name of the bank has not been printed.)

The form is drawn in three copies, which are used as follows:

(1) Original—when signed by the treasurer, it is sent to the creditor in payment of the invoices identified on the upper part of the form.
(2) Copy—filed alphabetically in the accounting department with invoices stapled to it to provide a unit record of business done with each creditor.
(3) Copy—filed numerically.

Basic Methods of Operating Vouchers Payable

The basic methods of operating vouchers payable procedures are:

(1) One-time voucher procedures (of which there are two variations):
 (a) Accumulating invoices until due date, posting to the voucher *on due date,* closing the voucher for payment, and entering the payment in the cash disbursements journal (pages 339-340). There is no formal record of *unpaid* invoices.

338

(b) Writing the voucher and closing it when invoice is *approved for payment* and entering it in the voucher register at that time; writing check on due date and entering it in the cash disbursements journal. (See pages 340-341.) Unlike (a), this is full-fledged voucher system. Note that there are only two basic steps (as compared to the four steps in an accounts payable procedure (page 334).

(2) Built-up voucher procedures (posting the invoices to open vouchers as the invoices are approved for payment—carrying running balances on the vouchers if desired—and closing each voucher for payment on due date). There are two variations:

(a) Posting by hand to open vouchers as the invoices are approved and entering closed vouchers on due date in the voucher register. Enter check in cash disbursements journal (page 341).

(b) Posting by machine (or by hand using a writing board) to open vouchers, obtaining a carbon copy voucher register as a by-product of the posting operation; when each voucher is closed for payment, entering it in the cash disbursements journal. This variation is not illustrated in this book.

One-Time Voucher-Check Procedure: Writing Voucher-Check on Date Invoice Is Due (Figure 15-4)

Under this procedure, the audited invoices are filed until due date, at which time a voucher-check is written and recorded in the cash payments journal which serves as the debit distribution of the vouchers as well as the serial list of voucher-checks issued.

Figure 15-4. One-Time Voucher-Check Procedure
(Writing voucher-check on date invoice is due)

1 File audited invoices until date due   2 Write voucher-check   3 Record in cash payments journal (and distribute debits)

CASH PAYMENTS JOURNAL

Date	Name	Voucher Check No.	Bank Credit	Merchandise Purchases Debit	Expense Purchases Debit

4 Send original voucher-check to creditor; file copy with invoice attached alphabetically; file second copy by serial number.

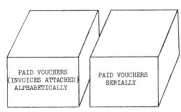

In small businesses, where no special due-date control is necessary, the unpaid invoices may be filed alphabetically and the bookkeeper may scan the file as often as necessary to bring the invoices up when due. If a due-date control is necessary, the invoices can be filed by due date.

The voucher-checks, which may be pre-numbered if desired, may be made in three copies:

(1) Original—for creditor.
(2) Copy—to be filed alphabetically with the invoices and other supporting documents attached.
(3) Copy—to be filed by serial number.

If the vouchers are filed in this manner, the alphabetical file constitutes a record of what has been purchased from the supplier and the prices paid. Some bookkeepers and auditors, however, prefer to attach the invoice and supporting copies of the serial number copy. Such a filing arrangement would facilitate audit of the invoices against the cash payments journal, but the file would not be as useful in looking up the transactions with a particular supplier.

The procedure as outlined above is actually accounting on the cash basis. It provides no record of amounts due creditors and it shows (in the expense columns of the cash disbursements journal) only the expenses paid in cash. This usually is not regarded as serious in a small business. At the end of the month (or other statement date) the General ledger accounts may be put on the accrual basis by recapping the unpaid invoices in the file and making a journal entry to record them, charging the appropriate asset, expense, and other accounts and crediting accounts payable. This entry would be reversed at the beginning of the next period.

It should be obvious that the reason for accumulating invoices until due date and then making out the voucher is to combine the maximum number of invoices from the same creditor in a single voucher. This practice reduces the amount of voucher writing and check writing to the minimum, although it can cause a peak load in writing if the payment dates are infrequent.

One-Time Voucher: Writing Voucher on Date Invoice Is Approved for Payment

In some cases, a typical disbursement may cover only one purchase invoice, and it may be desired to write each voucher immediately when the invoice is approved for payment and enter it in the voucher register. The voucher register would then be operated on the accrual basis. After the vouchers are entered in the voucher register, they are filed in an unpaid-voucher file until due date, at which time they are pulled for payment. Entry for payment is made in a check register for the bank on which the check is drawn. Separate sets of serial numbers would be used for the vouchers and the checks.

"Paid" columns can be provided in the voucher register in which to record date and check number when the voucher is paid. The voucher register of the Household Appliance Corporation (Figure 4-3) is an illustration.

Built-Up Voucher Procedure; Voucher Envelope Form
(*Figure 15-5*)

As explained above, a built-up voucher is one to which invoices from a particular creditor are posted in detail as they are approved for payment, and which is closed at the end of the month or other due date for payment. While open, a built-up voucher shows the total liability to date for the particular creditor. The file of open vouchers accordingly places the liability side of the purchase transaction on the accrual basis. The vouchers may be recorded in a voucher register when they are closed for payment. In that case, the debit distribution would be on the cash basis, but it could be put on the accrual basis by (a) making a journal entry for all unpaid vouchers at statement date, or (b) closing all vouchers and recording them at statement date.

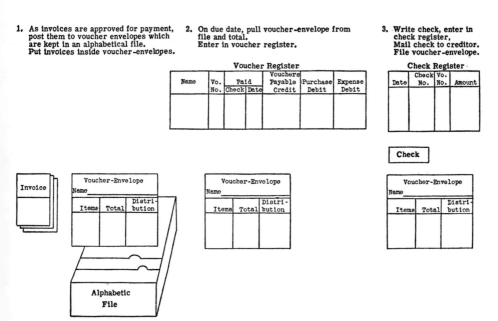

1. As invoices are approved for payment, post them to voucher envelopes which are kept in an alphabetical file. Put invoices inside voucher-envelopes.

2. On due date, pull voucher-envelope from file and total. Enter in voucher register.

3. Write check, enter in check register, Mail check to creditor. File voucher-envelope.

Figure 15-5. Built-Up Voucher Procedure (Voucher-Envelope Form)

Figure 15-5 diagrams the steps of procedure for a built-up voucher procedure in which a voucher envelope is used for each active creditor during the month. As invoices are approved for payment, they are recorded on the face of the appropriate voucher and filed in the envelope. When it is closed for payment, entry is made in the voucher register, the check is drawn on the desired bank account, entry is made in the appropriate check register, and the voucher envelope is filed alphabetically in the paid-voucher file.

Methods

In designing an accounts payable or vouchers payable procedure, it is necessary to consider some or all of the following factors:

(1) Writing and reproducing remittance statements or vouchers. (Carbon paper and duplicating methods are explained and illustrated in Chapter 6.)

(2) Checking calculations on invoices and making the computations on vouchers.

(3) Check protectors and check-signing machines. In this connection, note that bookkeeping machines can be equipped with check-protection features for writing checks.

(4) Bookkeeping machines and accounting boards. These devices may be used:

(a) On the liability side for posting invoices to creditors' accounts or disbursement vouchers and producing a purchase journal as a carbon copy by-product of the posting operation.

(b) On the payment side, for writing the checks or completing the vouchers and producing a cash disbursements journal as a carbon copy by-product of the posting operation.

Bookkeeping machines are explained in Chapter 7 and accounting boards are explained in Chapter 10.

DEBIT DISTRIBUTION FROM PAYMENTS AND GENERAL JOURNAL ENTRIES

Function

The debit distribution from payments involves abstracting the debits that arise from purchase and payment transactions and summarizing them for report and journal entry purposes. In small businesses, these debits may come exclusively from the cash payments journal. In larger businesses, they may come from the voucher register or purchase journal or from distribution of invoices separate from the journal procedure. Most of the debits are to asset, liability, and expense accounts; but it is possible to have debits to other groups of balance sheet or profit and loss accounts.

The debit distribution from journal entries is closely related to the debit distribution from payments, and it is also explained in this chapter. (The debit distribution for labor is explained in Chapter 17, and the debit distribution for indirect materials and supplies in Chapter 18.)

Classification and Reports

In manufacturing concerns, common classifications of debits arising from payments are:

(1) For direct materials:
  (a) Type of material (physical characteristics).
  (b) Product in which material is to be used.
  (c) Both (a) and (b).
(2) For expense materials and purchased services:
  (a) Object (nature of the goods or services bought).
  (b) Function or responsibility.
  (c) Both (a) and (b).

In mercantile concerns, common classifications are:

(1) For merchandise:
  (a) Type of merchandise (physical characteristics).
  (b) Organizational department.
  (c) Both (a) and (b).
(2) For expense materials and purchased services, same as for manufacturing concern.

An example of an expense classification for a distributing concern appears in Chapter 3, Table 3-1. This illustration is a General ledger classification including an object classification of expenses under the groupings Administrative, Selling, Receiving, Warehousing and Shipping, Occupancy, Service Department—Inside, and Service Department—Outside.

Standard journal entries for the Household Appliance Corporation (whose classifications and statements are referred to above) are illustrated on pages 68-74. The entries by which various expense debits would be recorded in the General ledger are:

J.E. No.   6   Debits arising directly from purchases (voucher register)
J.E. No.   7   F.I.C.A. Tax Expense (standard journal)
J.E. No.   8   Unemployment Insurance expense (standard journal)
J.E. No.   9   Depreciation (standard journal)
J.E. No. 10   Insurance (standard journal)
J.E. No. 11   Real Estate Taxes (standard journal)
J.E. No. 12   Personal Property Taxes (standard journal)
J.E. No. 13   Bad Debts (standard journal)

Forms

Typical forms (basic media) from which the debit distribution from payments and the related debit distribution from journal charges are made are:

(1) Invoices from suppliers. These may be rubber-stamped for re-

cording the steps of verification and coding, and the distribution may be made from the invoices.

(2) Disbursement vouchers. In a voucher procedure, the disbursement voucher form (office copy) may provide spaces for recording the distribution of the invoice(s) covered by the voucher. The debits may be summarized from the vouchers.

(3) Journal voucher or, if formal journal vouchers are not used, journal entries.

The summary forms vary according to method of distribution used. Various summary forms are illustrated in connection with the methods to which they are related.

Methods Classified

Methods frequently used for the distribution of debits from payments are:

(1) Columnar journal or spread sheet:
   (a) Cash payment journal.
   (b) Purchase journal.
   (c) Voucher register.
(2) Columnar account.
(3) Unit account.
(4) Unit ticket.
(5) Summary strip.

These methods are illustrated and described on the following pages. The following points of comparison of the various methods are tabulated in Figure 15-6:

(1) Type of purchases or expense classification (class of merchandise, object, function, function subdivided by object).
(2) What totals and subtotals are desired (and what frequency)?
(3) If detail posting is required for frequent reference, what description is required (vendor's name, date of invoice, description of items, etc.)?
(4) Number of accounts in classification accommodated by the method illustrated.
(5) Expense accounts operated on
   (a) Cash basis.
   (b) Cash basis adjusted to accrual basis at end of period, or
   (c) Accrual basis.
(6) Media used for distribution (vendor's invoice, copy of disbursement voucher). Are media unit or mixed?
(7) Relative quantity of media per day.
(8) Sorted arrangement of media received for distribution.

	Cash Payments Journal (account in general ledger for each object)	Purchases Journal (account in general ledger for each class of merchandise)	Voucher Register (account in general ledger for each object)	Voucher Register (columnar account in general ledger for each function)	Unit Account (account for each department, posted from invoices)	Unit Ticket; Summary Strip
Type of expense classification	One classification: object	One classification: class of merchandise	One classification: object	One compound classification: function subdivided by object	One classification: (sales) departments	One compound classification: function subdivided by object
What totals and sub-totals are desired (frequency)	Total of each object monthly	Total of each class of merchandise monthly	Total of each object monthly	Totals by department monthly; sub-totals by object	Totals by department monthly; current balances by department during the month	Totals by department monthly; sub-totals by object
If detail posting is required, what description is required	Journal shows name of payee and explanation	Journal shows name of payee and explanation	Journal shows name of payee and explanation	Journal shows name of payee and explanation	Detail posting to accounts shows amount, creditor's name and date of invoice	No detail posting; tickets are filed by account number
Number of accounts in the classification accommodated by the method		6 accounts; column for each account	6 groups of accounts; column for each group; column for miscellaneous	6 groups of accounts; column for each group; column for miscellaneous	60 departments; separate account for each department	About 30 possible object sub-accounts for each function; separate summary strip for each function
Expense accounts operated on cash basis or accrual basis	Cash basis, adjusted to accrual basis at end of month	Accrual basis	(a) Cash basis, adjusted to accrual basis or (b) accrual basis	Accrual basis	Accrual basis	Accrual basis
What media are used for distribution	Vendor's invoice	Vendor's invoice	Disbursement voucher	Disbursement voucher	Invoices	Copies of vouchers are used as unit media (or unit tickets are produced)
Are the media unit or mixed	Mixed	Mixed	Mixed	Mixed	Unit	Unit; copies of vouchers are used as unit media or unit tickets are created
What is the quantity per month assumed for illustration	80	150	150	150	1400	600
What is the sorted arrangement of media received for distribution	Unsorted	Unsorted	Unsorted	Unsorted	Invoices are received in batches, by department	Unsorted

Figure 15-6. Methods of Debit Distribution: Cash Disbursement Charges; Journal Charges

BANK FOR MONTH OF *January* 19 – SHEET NO.

DAY	IN FAVOR OF	CR. BANK CHECK NO.	CR. BANK AMOUNT	DAILY TOTAL (MEMO.)	CR. DISCOUNT	*Dr. Expense*	*Dr. Equipment*	*Dr. Merchandise Purchases*	*Sundry Accounts* ACCOUNT	*Sundry Accounts* ACCT. NO.	*Sundry Accounts* AMOUNT	✓
	AMOUNTS FORWARDED											
4	*T. S. Jordan*	704	$ 196 00		$ 4 00	$	$ 200 00				$	
	Fred Wilson	705	300 00			300 00						
	R. F. Jones	706	50 00					50 00				

Figure 15-7. Recording Invoices in Cash Payments Journal When Paid

Columnar Journals: Cash Payments Journal (Figure 15-7)

The cash payments journal provides a column for each of the most active accounts (object classification). The total of each object is desired at the end of each month on the monthly statement of profits. The number of accounts in the classification is small, and three of these accounts have sufficient activity to warrant providing a separate column for each account. The latter columns are posted in total to purchases and expense accounts in the General ledger. These accounts accordingly provide no details of transactions. Items in the miscellaneous column are posted in detail to accounts in the General ledger.

Invoices are entered in the cash payments journal as they are paid. Check number and date paid are entered on invoices as they are paid, and the invoices are filed alphabetically (by creditor's name) or numerically.

The cash disbursements journal shows the name of the person paid, and it can also show a brief description of the item, which probably is sufficient to answer most questions about charges to purchase and expense accounts. Since no entries are made for invoices until they are paid, the expense accounts are operated on the cash basis. They may be put on the accrual basis at the end of the month by recapping the unpaid invoices in file and making a general journal entry debiting the various purchase and expense accounts and crediting accounts payable. This entry is reversed at the beginning of the next period.

Purchase Journal with Distribution by Class of Merchandise (Figure 15-8)

The purchase journal provides a column for each of three classes of merchandise. The total of each class of merchandise is desired at the end

Figure 15-8. Purchases Journal with Distribution by Class of Merchandise

PURCHASES JOURNAL

January, 19—

	DATE	CREDITOR	F	ACCOUNTS PAYABLE CREDIT		PURCHASES APPLIANCES AND PARTS DEBIT		
				APPLIANCES	OTHER	KITCHEN	LAUNDRY	OTHER
1	Jan. 3	R. F. Jones		100 00		100 00		
2	3	A. B. Williams			300 00			300 00
3	4	T. F. Jordan		200 00			200 00	
4	5	L. C. Reese		200 00		200 00		
5				500 00	300 00	300 00	200 00	300 00
6								
7								
8								
9								
10								

of each month on the monthly statement of profits. This journal is operated in the same way (as far as the debit distribution is concerned) as the cash payments journal described in the previous section except that the invoices are entered in the purchase journal as they are approved for payment. The purchase journal is accordingly operated on the accrual basis.

Voucher Register: Debit Items Recapped at End of Month (Figure 15-9)

The voucher register for Household Appliance Corporation provides a column for purchases and one for freight, and one for each of six groups of expense accounts. Vouchers are entered in the register either (a) as they are written (one-time vouchers) or (b) as they are closed for payment (either one-time or built-up vouchers).

Note the method of recapping the debit items for posting to expense accounts at the end of the month. The accounts to be posted are indicated in the folio columns of the voucher register, and the charges to the accounts are recapped at the bottom of each column (after the voucher register has been footed and cross-footed). The recapped totals of the various accounts are posted to either (a) conventional T-accounts (Figure 15-11) or (b) columnar accounts (Figure 15-12). By this method, there is one posting to each active account (or each column of a columnar account) each month from the voucher register. The recapping method thus (a) provides a cross-footing proof of all postings from the voucher register and (b) reduces the number of postings to the ledger. These features may help to reduce trial balance trouble.

The voucher register can be designed to provide descriptive information as shown in the accounts.

Columnar Account Method (Figure 15-12)

Assume that it is decided to use columnar accounts instead of conventional T-accounts for the expense classification in the General ledger. The postings to columnar accounts (from the voucher register, Figure 15-9) are illustrated in Figure 15-12. A columnar account is provided for each group of expense accounts, and each account provides a column for each object sub-account.

The expense account classification comprises the following groups of accounts:

(1) Administrative Expenses, 18 accounts
(2) Selling Expenses, 18 accounts
(3) Receiving, Warehousing, and Shipping Expenses, 20 accounts
(4) Occupancy Expenses, 11 accounts
(5) Service Department—Inside Expenses, 11 accounts

VOUCHER REGISTER

DATE	ISSUED TO	VO. NO.	PAID DATE	PAID CHK.NO.	171 APPLIANCES	172 OTHER	911 PURCHASE DISCOUNT CREDIT	231-233 PURCHASES DEBIT ACCT.	AMOUNT	241-243 FREIGHT IN DEBIT ACCT.	AMOUNT	
Jan. 2	Edison Power Co.	101				23000						1
3	Mill Supply Co.	102				28000						2
5	Ellison Telephone Co.	103				12800						3
6	Gem Printing Co.	104				6500						4
8	Long and Newton	105				20000						5
12	Nash & Sons	106				43500						6
						133800						7

	300 ADMINISTRATIVE EXPENSE DEBIT ACCT.	AMOUNT	400 SELLING EXPENSE DEBIT ACCT.	AMOUNT	500 RECEIVING, WAREHOUSING AND SHIPPING ACCT.	AMOUNT	600 OCCUPANCY EXPENSE DEBIT ACCT.	AMOUNT	700 SERVICE DEPARTMENT -INSIDE DEBIT ACCT.	AMOUNT	800 SERVICE DEPARTMENT -OUTSIDE DEBIT ACCT.	AMOUNT	MISCELLANEOUS ACCOUNTS DEBIT NAME	NO.	AMOUNT
1									761	23000	830	13000			
2									780	15000					
3	362	12800													
4	331	3000	431	3500											
5					531	8000			730	9500	830	2500 842 20000			
6							661	23500			842	13500			
7		15800		3500		8000		23500	730	27500 761 47500	830	15500 842 20000			13500

Figure 15-9. Voucher Register: Debit Items Recapped at End of Month

GENERAL JOURNAL

DATE	DESCRIPTION OF ENTRY	GENERAL LEDGER DEBITS ACCT.	AMOUNT	GENERAL LEDGER CREDITS ACCT.	AMOUNT	300 ADMINISTRATIVE EXPENSE DEBIT ACCT.	AMOUNT	400 SELLING EXPENSE DEBIT ACCT.	AMOUNT	500 RECEIVING, WAREHOUSING & SHIPPING ACCT.	AMOUNT	600 OCCUPANCY EXPENSE DEBIT ACCT.	AMOUNT	700 SERVICE DEPARTMENT —INSIDE DEBIT ACCT.	AMOUNT	800 SERVICE DEPARTMENT —OUTSIDE DEBIT ACCT.	AMOUNT
Jan. 31	Administrative salaries:																
	Office Salaries					311✓	2,000 00										
	Total Supervising Salaries					312✓	2,800 00										
	Inside Salesmen							411✓	1,200 00								
	Outside Salesmen							412✓	1,500 00								
								413✓	2,200 00								
	Accrued Payroll			113✓	9,700 00												
	Administrative and office salaries for month.																
31	Supervising Salaries, Warehousemen									511✓	800 00	611✓	700 00	711✓	900 00		
	Truck Drivers and Helpers									512✓	1,400 00						
	Janitors and Watchmen									513✓	1,200 00	612✓	850 00				
	Repairmen													712✓	1,200 00		
	Service Men															811✓	900 00
	Accrued Payroll			113✓	7,950 00												
	Plant and service payroll.																
					17,650 00		4,500 00		4,900 00		3,400 00		1,550 00		2,100 00		900 00

Figure 15-10. General Journal

350

Service Department—Supervisory Salaries   No. 711

DATE	PARTICULARS	F	AMOUNT	DATE	PARTICULARS	F	AMOUNT
19— Jan. 31		GJ	# 900 00				

Service Department—Repairmen   No. 712

DATE	PARTICULARS	F	AMOUNT	DATE	PARTICULARS	F	AMOUNT
19— Jan. 31		GJ	# 1200 00				

Service Department—Operating Supplies   No. 730

DATE	PARTICULARS	F	AMOUNT	DATE	PARTICULARS	F	AMOUNT
19— Jan. 31		VR	# 245 00				

Service Department—Power   No. 761

DATE	PARTICULARS	F	AMOUNT	DATE	PARTICULARS	F	AMOUNT
19— Jan. 31		VR	# 230 00				

Figure 15-11. Expense Accounts: Conventional T Accounts

700 SERVICE DEPARTMENT – INSIDE

MONTH _January_ 19—

DATE	F	700 TOTAL DEPARTMENT	711 SUPERVISORY SALARIES	712 REPAIRMEN	719 OVERTIME PREMIUM	721 F.I.C.A. TAX EXPENSE	722 UNEMPLOYMENT INSURANCE EXPENSE	730 OPERATING SUPPLIES	761 POWER	791 DEPRECIATION	792 INSURANCE	799 LABOR USED ON CONTRACTS CR.
Jan. 31	VR	2475.00	900.00	1200.00				2415.00	230.00			
31	GJ	2100.00	900.00	1200.00				2415.00	230.00			
		2575.00										

800 SERVICE DEPARTMENT – OUTSIDE

MONTH _January_ 19—

DATE	F	800 TOTAL DEPARTMENT	811 SERVICE MEN	821 F.I.C.A. TAX EXPENSE	822 UNEMPLOYMENT INSURANCE EXPENSE	830 SUPPLIES	841 REPAIRS TO SERVICE TRUCKS	842 GAS AND OIL	880 UNCLASSIFIED	891 DEPRECIATION: TRUCKS	892 INSURANCE: TRUCKS	893 TAXES AND LICENSES: TRUCKS	899 LABOR USED ON CONTRACTS CR.
Jan. 31	VR	355.00	900.00			155.00		200.00					
31	GJ	900.00	900.00			155.00		200.00					
		1255.00											

Figure 15-12. Columnar Expense Accounts

(6) Service Department—Outside Expenses, 11 accounts

The first three accounts are double-page spreads. Note that by the use of columnar accounts, the number of accounts in the General ledger trial balance is reduced by 83 (89 − 6). Only the cross-footed total of each of the six columnar accounts is included in the General ledger trial balance.

Unit Account Method: Subsidiary Purchases Ledgers (*Figure 15-13*)

The procedure diagrammed provides a purchases account for each of 60 sales departments in a retail store (of which four accounts are shown in the diagram). These accounts are kept in a subsidiary ledger. They

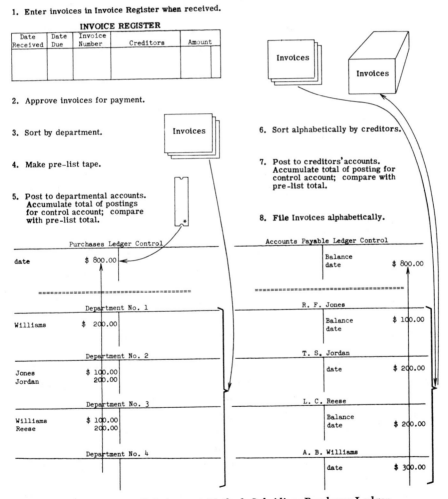

Figure 15-13. Unit Account Method: Subsidiary Purchases Ledger

are used to provide the purchase figures for the departmental statement of profits. They are posted in detail with description from the purchase invoices, and they show purchases to date for each of the departments. It is assumed for the purposes of this illustration that the amount of a typical invoice is significant for follow-up purposes and that the department heads require purchases to date.

The approved invoices are received in daily batches arranged by department (because they have been previously sent to department heads in departmental batches for approval). After a pre-list tape is made, the invoices are posted to the departmental purchase accounts, and the postings are proved against the control. The name of the creditor and the date of the invoice are posted to the account with the amount. The invoices are then sorted alphabetically, posted to creditors' accounts, and filed alphabetically by creditor.

A similar procedure can be used for expense accounts where (a) the number of accounts is large, and (b) detail posting with description is desired.

Unit Ticket Method: Summary Strip (Figure 15-14)

Figure 15-14 is a diagram of a procedure for unit ticket method of expense distribution. The distribution copies of vouchers are the unit tickets. The illustration is an example of ledgerless bookkeeping since it involves filing a unit ticket for each debit instead of posting it. The procedure was particularly designed for use when it is desired to operate a conventional pen-and-ink General ledger. After the tickets are recapped, a journal entry can be made to post expense control totals and other items into the General ledger.

Figure 15-15 is journal voucher by which unit tickets are produced as carbon copies. Such forms can be used to produce journal debits which can be sorted to the expense account classification. The journal voucher proper would be entered in the general journal and expense control totals would be posted to the General ledger.

Summary Strip: At the end of the month, after the unit tickets for disbursement vouchers and journal vouchers have been filed by account number, the monthly expense statement can be prepared, on a summary strip form if desired, by totaling the tickets for each account and recording the total on the report form. The total of expense per the report form must agree with the total shown by the Expense ledger control sheet.

Note that the reference information of the Expense ledger file is the same as that of a posted Expense ledger which shows the vendor's name beside each debit. Ease of reference, however, is not as great in a file as it is in a posted account.

After the month's expense statement has been prepared and proved, the

1 Obtain unit tickets from disbursement vouchers covering expenses.

2 Prove unit tickets against control total for disbursement vouchers.

3 File unit tickets by account number.

4 Make journal entry for total of expense vouchers.

5 Write journal vouchers and enter in general journal.

6 Obtain unit tickets from journal vouchers, and file by account number.

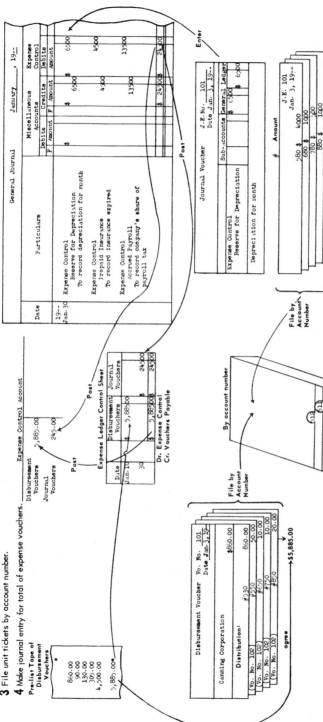

Figure 15-14. Debit Distribution: Unit Ticket Method

file can be microfilmed to provide a secondary reference medium in case of loss of any of the tickets. Sometime after the normal look-up period which follows the release of expense statements, the file may be destroyed and the microfilm kept as the record of debits to accounts.

In designing the procedure described above, provision could be made for debits from sources other than disbursement vouchers and journal vouchers. Payroll tickets, for instance, might be a separate source. Each separate set of documents should have its own control totals in the Expense ledger control sheet and in some cases its own serial numbers.

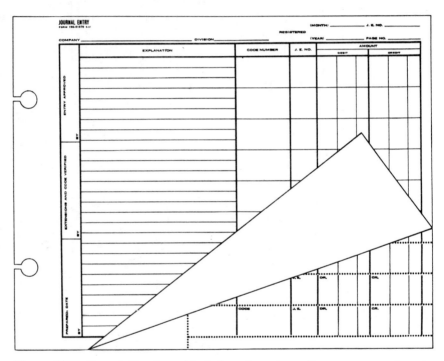

Figure 15-15. Journal Voucher with Carbon Copy Separable into Unit Tickets for Sorting

16

Employment and Timekeeping Procedures

EMPLOYMENT PROCEDURES

Function and Organization

The employment department performs the functions necessary for placing an employee on the payroll and also certain miscellaneous functions as follows:

(1) Recruiting, including:
   (a) Maintaining files to assist in locating laid-off employees and applicants for jobs.
   (b) Maintaining contact with employment agencies and services, schools, and other sources of employees.
   (c) Advertising.
(2) Interviewing.
(3) Processing, including:
   (a) Obtaining basic personnel data.
   (b) Obtaining W-4 forms (Employee's Withholding Exemption Certificate).
   (c) Arranging for medical examination.
   (d) Preparing authorization to place on payroll.
(4) Miscellaneous functions such as:
   (a) Handling of wage assignments and garnishments.
   (b) Maintaining employee location files.
   (c) Conducting termination interviews and records.
   (d) Maintaining employment history files.
   (e) Compiling vacation eligibility list.

In some cases, the employment function is a part-time function of some employee who has the ability and time to recruit and interview prospective employees. In large manufacturing plants, a separate employment department to hire plant employees is usually established under the jurisdiction of the chief production executive. In addition, office and accounting employees may be hired by an employment department under the jurisdiction of the controller.

Each of the above groups of functions is described in separate sections of this chapter. The description applies particularly to activities performed in a large company. Most of the activities described must also be performed in small companies.

Managerial Information

The employment department usually provides management with reports and statistical data on a variety of personnel subjects, such as the following:

(1) Turnover statistics.
(2) Termination statistics (quits, lay-offs, discharges).
(3) Industry wage rates.
(4) Local-area wage rates.
(5) Employee availability (by skill).

Forms

Basic forms used by the employment department are:

(1) Foreman's requisition for new employees (Figure 16-1): Prepared by the foreman to show number and skill of employees required, and when needed.
(2) Application for employment (Figure 16-2): Prepared by employee to show education, experience, references, personal data, and so on.
(3) Notice of employment or hiring ticket (Figure 16-5): Prepared by Employment department. When properly approved, this form is authority for payroll department and others concerned to place employee on payroll.
(4) Separation report or final payoff notice (Figure 16-6): Prepared by foreman as notification to drop employee from payroll and showing reason for industrial relations, personnel, and other purposes.

Recruiting

The foreman, or whoever is responsible for the addition of men to the payroll, notifies the Employment department of his needs. This may be done by telephone, in person, or by means of a foreman's requisition (Figure 16-1). Typical information shown on such a requisition would be the number of men, the type of skill, and the time when the men will

Form S. 87—40M—7-37

BLANK COMPANY

EMPLOYMENT DEPARTMENT

FOREMAN'S REQUISITION FOR NEW EMPLOYES

For Department_____Date_____19_____

NUMBER		POSITION	REQUIRED		REPL. ADD.	PART TIME REGULAR
F	M		DATE	HOUR		

APPROVALS:
FOREMAN_____ DIV. SUPT._____ SUPT._____

WHEN APPROVED SEND IMMEDIATELY TO EMPLOYMENT OFFICE
To obtain the best service have requisitions delivered to Employment Office at least 24 hours in advance.

Figure 16-1. Foreman's Requisition for New Employees

be required. The Employment department then locates the necessary prospective employees by:

(1) Referring to files of (a) current employees who might be promoted or raised to a better job, (b) ex-employees such as lay-offs, and (c) applicants.

(2) Contacting employment agencies and services, schools, and other sources of employees.

(3) Advertising in newspapers, in trade periodicals, on radio, and the like.

Interviewing

The applicant is interviewed to ascertain his experience, skill, education, age, and so on. If the preliminary interview indicates a reasonable possibility of employment, the applicant is asked to fill out an application blank showing previous employment, Social Security number, references, and such personal data as may be required (Figure 16-2). The application is then used to assist the interviewer in deciding whether the particular applicant should be employed. If the applicant does not meet specifications for the present opening, the application may be filed for future reference.

Processing

If the employee fits the needs as shown on the requisition, the following steps are taken:

THE STANDARD REGISTER COMPANY

Designers and manufacturers of business forms

APPLICATION FOR POSITION

DATE_____

NAME (PRINT) _____ FIRST _____ MIDDLE INITIAL _____ LAST _____ AGE_____

ADDRESS _____ NO. _____ STREET _____ CITY _____ STATE _____ TEL. NO. BUSINESS _____ HOME _____

POSITION APPLIED FOR? _____ EARNINGS EXPECTED $_____

PERSONAL

SEX ☐ M. ☐ F. DATE OF BIRTH _____ HEIGHT _____ WEIGHT _____ SOC. SEC. NO _____

MARITAL STATUS _____ NO. OF DEPENDENTS _____ AGES _____

DO YOU ☐ OWN YOUR HOME? ☐ RENT? ☐ LIVE WITH RELATIVES? OTHER _____ ARE YOU A U. S. CITIZEN ☐ YES. ☐ NO

ANY RELATIVES EMPLOYED HERE? _____ NAME _____ RELATIONSHIP _____

WHAT PHYSICAL DEFECTS, DISABILITIES OR WORK LIMITATIONS DO YOU HAVE? _____

FINAL EMPLOYMENT SUBJECT TO PHYSICAL EXAMINATION

EDUCATION

SCHOOL	NAME AND LOCATION	NO OF YRS COMPLETED	MAJOR	DEGREE	YEAR GRAD
ELEMENTARY			X X X	X X X	
HIGH			X X X	X X X	
COLLEGE					
COLLEGE					
OTHER					

SCHOLASTIC STANDING IN SCHOOL _____

EXTRACURRICULAR ACTIVITIES (SCHOOL, CLUBS, FRATERNITIES, ATHLETICS, ETC.) _____

CLUBS, CIVIC, BUSINESS OR PROFESSIONAL ORGANIZATIONS OF WHICH YOU ARE A MEMBER _____

MILITARY SERVICE

MILITARY SERVICE ☐ YES. ☐ NO _____ DATES OF ACTIVE DUTY FROM _____ TO _____

WHICH SERVICE? _____ SPECIALTY? _____ RANK AT DISCHARGE _____

CURRENT STATUS? _____

PREVIOUS EMPLOYMENT

FIRMS (BEGIN WITH MOST RECENT)	DATES	POSITION AND NATURE OF WORK	SALARY
1 NAME _____ ADDRESS NO. STREET CITY STATE _____ KIND OF BUSINESS _____ IMMEDIATE SUPERVISOR _____	FROM: TO:	REASON FOR LEAVING	STARTING: LEAVING:
2 NAME _____ ADDRESS NO. STREET CITY STATE _____ KIND OF BUSINESS _____ IMMEDIATE SUPERVISOR _____	FROM: TO:	REASON FOR LEAVING	STARTING: LEAVING:
3 NAME _____ ADDRESS NO. STREET CITY STATE _____ KIND OF BUSINESS _____ IMMEDIATE SUPERVISOR _____	FROM: TO:	REASON FOR LEAVING	STARTING: LEAVING:
4 NAME _____ ADDRESS NO. STREET CITY STATE _____ KIND OF BUSINESS _____ IMMEDIATE SUPERVISOR _____	FROM: TO:	REASON FOR LEAVING	STARTING: LEAVING:
5 NAME _____ ADDRESS NO. STREET CITY STATE _____ KIND OF BUSINESS _____ IMMEDIATE SUPERVISOR _____	FROM: TO:	REASON FOR LEAVING	STARTING: LEAVING:

MAY WE CONTACT YOUR PRESENT EMPLOYER FOR REFERENCE? ☐ YES. ☐ NO

IF ACCEPTED FOR A POSITION HOW SOON WOULD YOU BE AVAILABLE? _____

LIST ANY ADDITIONAL EXPERIENCES, SKILLS OR QUALIFICATIONS WHICH YOU FEEL WOULD BE APPLICABLE TO THE POSITION FOR WHICH YOU ARE APPLYING. _____

PERSONAL REFERENCES (NOT FORMER EMPLOYERS OR RELATIVES)

1 NAME	ADDRESS		TELEPHONE NO.
2 NAME	ADDRESS		TELEPHONE NO.

BE SURE THE ABOVE INFORMATION YOU GIVE US IS COMPLETE AND ACCURATE. THIS WILL ENABLE US TO GIVE YOUR APPLICATION PROMPT AND THOROUGH CONSIDERATION.

SIGNATURE _____

THANK YOU FOR YOUR COOPERATION

APPLICANT SHOULD NOT WRITE BELOW THIS LINE

INTERVIEWER _____

Figure 16-2. Application for Employment

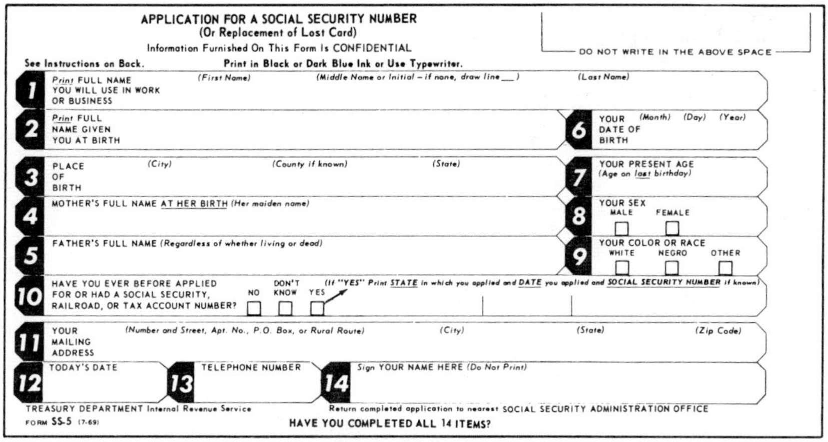

APPLICATION FOR A SOCIAL SECURITY NUMBER
(Or Replacement of Lost Card)
Information Furnished On This Form Is CONFIDENTIAL

DO NOT WRITE IN THE ABOVE SPACE

See Instructions on Back. Print in Black or Dark Blue Ink or Use Typewriter.

1 Print FULL NAME YOU WILL USE IN WORK OR BUSINESS (First Name) (Middle Name or Initial – if none, draw line __) (Last Name)

2 Print FULL NAME GIVEN YOU AT BIRTH

6 YOUR DATE OF BIRTH (Month) (Day) (Year)

3 PLACE OF BIRTH (City) (County if known) (State)

7 YOUR PRESENT AGE (Age on last birthday)

4 MOTHER'S FULL NAME AT HER BIRTH (Her maiden name)

8 YOUR SEX MALE FEMALE

5 FATHER'S FULL NAME (Regardless of whether living or dead)

9 YOUR COLOR OR RACE WHITE NEGRO OTHER

10 HAVE YOU EVER BEFORE APPLIED FOR OR HAD A SOCIAL SECURITY, RAILROAD, OR TAX ACCOUNT NUMBER? NO DON'T KNOW YES (If "YES" Print STATE in which you applied and DATE you applied and SOCIAL SECURITY NUMBER if known)

11 YOUR MAILING ADDRESS (Number and Street, Apt. No., P.O. Box, or Rural Route) (City) (State) (Zip Code)

12 TODAY'S DATE 13 TELEPHONE NUMBER 14 Sign YOUR NAME HERE (Do Not Print)

TREASURY DEPARTMENT Internal Revenue Service
FORM SS-5 (7-69)
Return completed application to nearest SOCIAL SECURITY ADMINISTRATION OFFICE
HAVE YOU COMPLETED ALL 14 ITEMS?

Figure 16-3. Form SS-5—Application for Social Security Number

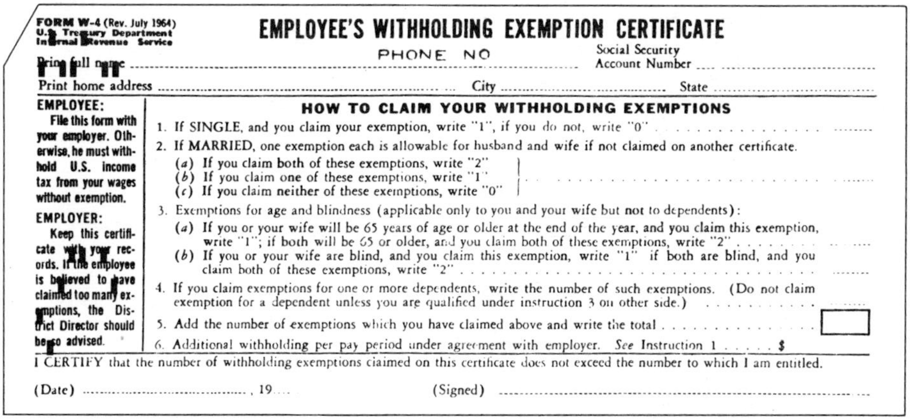

FORM W-4 (Rev. July 1964)
U.S. Treasury Department
Internal Revenue Service

EMPLOYEE'S WITHHOLDING EXEMPTION CERTIFICATE

PHONE NO

Print full name .... Social Security Account Number ....
Print home address .... City .... State ....

EMPLOYEE: File this form with your employer. Otherwise, he must withhold U.S. income tax from your wages without exemption.

EMPLOYER: Keep this certificate with your records. If the employee is believed to have claimed too many exemptions, the District Director should be so advised.

HOW TO CLAIM YOUR WITHHOLDING EXEMPTIONS

1. If SINGLE, and you claim your exemption, write "1", if you do not, write "0" . . . .
2. If MARRIED, one exemption each is allowable for husband and wife if not claimed on another certificate.
   (a) If you claim both of these exemptions, write "2"
   (b) If you claim one of these exemptions, write "1"
   (c) If you claim neither of these exemptions, write "0"
3. Exemptions for age and blindness (applicable only to you and your wife but not to dependents):
   (a) If you or your wife will be 65 years of age or older at the end of the year, and you claim this exemption, write "1"; if both will be 65 or older, and you claim both of these exemptions, write "2" . . . . . .
   (b) If you or your wife are blind, and you claim this exemption, write "1" if both are blind, and you claim both of these exemptions, write "2" . . . .
4. If you claim exemptions for one or more dependents, write the number of such exemptions. (Do not claim exemption for a dependent unless you are qualified under instruction 3 on other side.) . . . . . .
5. Add the number of exemptions which you have claimed above and write the total . . . . . .
6. Additional withholding per pay period under agreement with employer. See Instruction 1 . . . . . $

I CERTIFY that the number of withholding exemptions claimed on this certificate does not exceed the number to which I am entitled.

(Date) ...., 19.... (Signed) ....

Figure 16-4. Form W-4—Employee's Withholding Exemption Certificate

(1) The necessary personnel data are already on the application, and this is filed. If the applicant does not have a Social Security number, he must prepare form SS-5 (Application for Social Security Account Number, Figure 16-3).

(2) The employee must prepare form W-4 (Employee's Withholding Exemption Certificate, Figure 16-4), and he can usually do this most conveniently in the Employment office at the time he is hired. The number of dependents shown by the W-4 can be posted to the hiring ticket, and then the W-4's can be filed in the Employment office.

(3) Following the interview, the prospective employee is sent to the doctor's office with a Request for Medical Examination. After the examination, the doctor indicates the result and signs the form.

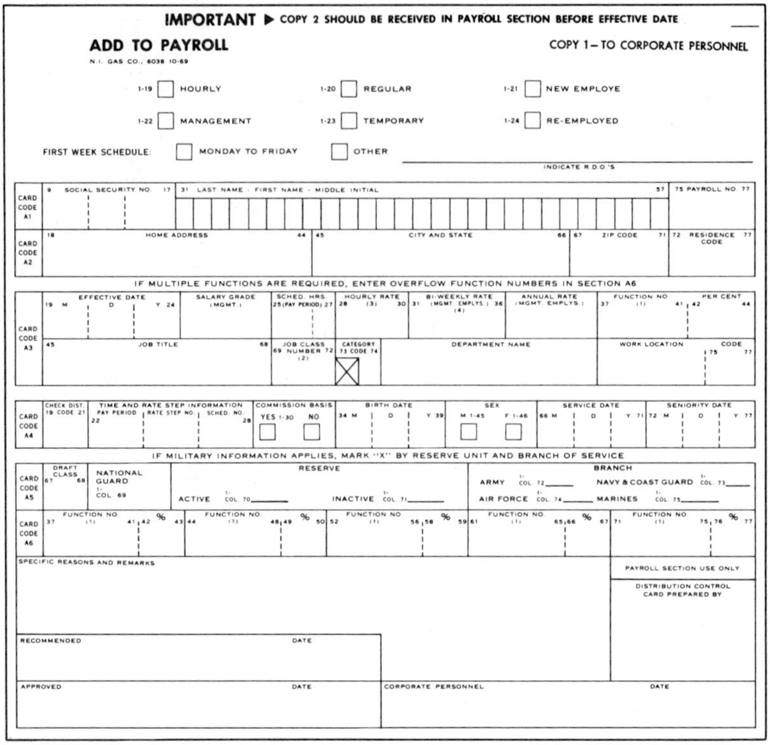

IMPORTANT ▶ COPY 2 SHOULD BE RECEIVED IN PAYROLL SECTION BEFORE EFFECTIVE DATE

ADD TO PAYROLL

COPY 1—TO CORPORATE PERSONNEL

N.I. GAS CO., 6038 10-69

1-19 ☐ HOURLY   1-20 ☐ REGULAR   1-21 ☐ NEW EMPLOYE

1-22 ☐ MANAGEMENT   1-23 ☐ TEMPORARY   1-24 ☐ RE-EMPLOYED

FIRST WEEK SCHEDULE: ☐ MONDAY TO FRIDAY ☐ OTHER ________ INDICATE R.D.O.'S

CARD CODE A1: 9 SOCIAL SECURITY NO. 17 | 31 LAST NAME - FIRST NAME - MIDDLE INITIAL 57 | 75 PAYROLL NO. 77

CARD CODE A2: 18 HOME ADDRESS 44 | 45 CITY AND STATE 66 | 67 ZIP CODE 71 | 72 RESIDENCE CODE 77

IF MULTIPLE FUNCTIONS ARE REQUIRED, ENTER OVERFLOW FUNCTION NUMBERS IN SECTION A6

CARD CODE A3: EFFECTIVE DATE 19 M D Y 24 | SALARY GRADE (MGMT.) | SCHED. HRS. 25 (PAY PERIOD) 27 | HOURLY RATE 28 (3) 30 | BI-WEEKLY RATE 31 (MGMT. EMPLYS.) 36 (4) | ANNUAL RATE (MGMT. EMPLYS.) | FUNCTION NO. 37 (1) 41 | PER CENT 42 44
45 JOB TITLE 68 | JOB CLASS 69 NUMBER 72 (2) | CATEGORY 73 CODE 74 | DEPARTMENT NAME | WORK LOCATION | CODE 75 77

CARD CODE A4: CHECK DIST. 19 CODE 21 | TIME AND RATE STEP INFORMATION PAY PERIOD 22 RATE STEP NO. SCHED. NO. 28 | COMMISSION BASIS YES 1-30 ☐ NO ☐ | BIRTH DATE 34 M D Y 39 | SEX M 1-45 ☐ F 1-46 ☐ | SERVICE DATE 66 M D Y 71 | SENIORITY DATE 72 M D Y 77

IF MILITARY INFORMATION APPLIES, MARK "X" BY RESERVE UNIT AND BRANCH OF SERVICE

CARD CODE A5: DRAFT CLASS 67 68 | NATIONAL GUARD 1- COL. 69 | RESERVE: ACTIVE 1- COL. 70____ INACTIVE 1- COL. 71____ | BRANCH: ARMY 1- COL. 72____ NAVY & COAST GUARD 1- COL. 73____ AIR FORCE 1- COL. 74____ MARINES 1- COL. 75____

CARD CODE A6: 37 FUNCTION NO. (1) 41 | 42 % 43 | 44 FUNCTION NO. (1) 48 | 49 % 50 | 52 FUNCTION NO. (1) 56 | 58 % 59 | 61 FUNCTION NO. (1) 65 | 66 % 67 | 71 FUNCTION NO. (1) 75 | 76 % 77

SPECIFIC REASONS AND REMARKS

PAYROLL SECTION USE ONLY

DISTRIBUTION CONTROL CARD PREPARED BY

RECOMMENDED DATE

APPROVED DATE CORPORATE PERSONNEL DATE

Figure 16-5. Notice of Employment

He returns it to the Employment office in a sealed envelope, via the prospective employee. The result of the doctor's examination is usually kept confidential.

(4) The Employment department then prepares the notice of employment (Figure 16-5). This notice will be used by the Payroll department and the Tabulating department, if there is one, to record the basic information needed for compiling the payroll, such as name, starting date, department number, clock number, Social Security number, occupation (and rate per hour) and so forth.

In some organizations, the "hiring ticket" is so designed that the foreman or shop clerk fills in the department data (which might include clock number, occupation, rate, and so on) and signs. One copy is then returned to the Employment office for file. The other copy is routed to the Payroll department or Tabulating department for making out a master card, or to the Addressing department to make a plate.

Miscellaneous

(1) Wage assignments and garnishments.

Amounts which employees owe their creditors, and for which wage assignments or garnishments are received, must be deducted from the payroll. This procedure may be handled by either the Payroll department or the Employment office; it is usually handled by the Employment office because:

  (a) It maintains complete files of all employees, whether on the payroll currently or not, and can therefore keep cumulative information on garnishments.

  (b) It is usually better set up for contact with outside parties, such as creditors. A record is made of the active wage assignments or garnishments for each employee, showing their priority position as to payment. Each week a list is made of employees and assignees and the amount to be withheld from each employee's pay. The Payroll department then fills in the gross earnings, net earnings, and the amount actually withheld. The amounts shown on the list are then turned over to the assignee via the Voucher department.

(2) Locator files.

The Employment department may keep active locator files showing in which department each employee is working and which jobs he is capable of filling. Also, since this department receives home addresses on application blanks, it can set up and maintain the addresses so that the company will know where to reach its employees, past and present.

(3) Termination reviews and records.

The Employment department may obtain this data from a separation report prepared by the foreman (Figure 16-6). This form may be used to:

  (a) Explain the reason for separation.

  (b) Grade the employee's past service and state special qualifications for future use. This information should be filed in the Employment office.

The Employment department may interview employees discharged or released for cause.

(4) Employment historical files including:

  (a) Record of employment, job, rate, and so on.

  (b) Separations. The Employment department obtains this data from a separation report prepared by the foreman (Figure 16-6).

PERSONNEL ACTION FORM THE STANDARD REGISTER CO.

(LOCATION)

☐ PERSONNEL REQUISITION ☐ PUT ON ☐ TRANSFER ☐ LEAVE OF ABSENCE ☐ SEPARATION ☐ VACATION ☐ PAY CHANGE

NAME	DATE ISSUED	EFFECTIVE DATE	
DEPT.	NEW DEPT.		T R A N S F E R
JOB TITLE	NEW JOB TITLE		
JOB NO.	RANGE	CLOCK NO.	PRESENT RATE	NEW RATE	NEW CLOCK NO.	NEW RANGE	NEW JOB NO.	

EMPLOYMENT DATA

ADDRESS	CITY, STATE & ZIP CODE	TELEPHONE NO.	BIRTHDATE
SOC. SEC. NO.	SEX	NEW	REHIRE	REINST.	TEMP.	PERM.	PART TIME	APPROVED PLAN YES NO	PLAN NUMBER	IN BUDGET YES NO

LEAVE OF ABSENCE

SICK	PERS.	ORIG.	EXTEN.	FROM	TO	DATE HIRED	INSURANCE INSTRUCTIONS
							PAYROLL DEDUCTIONS PAID IN ADVANCE NON-CONTRIB.

SEPARATION

LAST DAY WORKED	RESIGNATION	TERMINATION	DISCHARGE	MILITARY LEAVE	LAYOFF
LAST DAY PAID	WAGES / RESUME HOUSEHOLD DUTIES / ILL. HEALTH	PROB. PERIOD / NOT QUALIFIED FOR JOB	NOT DEPEND. ABLE / CHRONIC & EXCESS ABSENTEEISM	DRAFTED ENLISTED RESERVES	LACK OF WORK * OTHER *
ATTENDANCE GOOD FAIR POOR	DISSATIS-FIED WITH PROGRESS / MARRIED / TO SCHOOL	TERM OF TEMPORARY EMPLOYMENT / MISCELL-NEOUS *	VIOLATION OF POLICY / MISCELL-LANEOUS *	BRANCH OF ARMED SERVICES	INSURANCE INSTRUCTIONS PAYROLL DEDUCTION
REHIRE?	LEFT CITY / FAMILY CIRCUM-STANCES / DEATH OR RETIRE			DATE OF DISCHARGE	DISCONTINUE NON-CONTRIB.

REMARKS:
*

I HAVE READ AND AGREE TO THE ABOVE INCLUDING THE TERMS PRINTED ON THE REVERSE SIDE HEREOF.

EMPLOYEE'S SIGNATURE

APPROVALS:

859 REV. 4/69   ORIGINAL – EMPLOYEE RECORDS

Figure 16-6. Separation Report

(5) Vacation eligibility list.

Vacation service data may be obtained from either the Payroll department, the Employment office, or both. The best source of this information will depend on the vacation plan. Employees' earnings records are usually maintained by the Payroll department, but the Employment office usually maintains complete data on seniority. Furthermore, when the Employment office makes the eligibility list and the Payroll department calculates the amount and enters it on the payroll, there is better internal check than if the Payroll department did both the determination and the computation.

TIMEKEEPING PROCEDURES, INTERNAL
CHECK ON PAYROLLS

Function

The timekeeping function can be classified into two principal divisions, namely, attendance timekeeping and shop timekeeping. Attendance timekeeping is concerned with obtaining a record of (1) the total hours worked by the employee during the pay period, and sometimes (2) the pay rate for the job actually performed. Shop timekeeping refers to a second record of the employee's time obtained from the department in which the employee works. This record has the dual purpose of (a) improving the internal control by providing a record with which to check the attendance time record, and (b) obtaining production and job data required for incentive pay and cost accounting (payroll distribution).

Various miscellaneous duties related to preparing the payroll are frequently performed in connection with timekeeping. Examples are supervising the assignment of lockers to employees, replacing lost identification badges, and initiating advances to employees.

Organization

Attendance time records are usually the responsibility of a timekeeping department, which may be under the jurisdiction of either the controller or the chief production executive. Attendance timekeepers supervise the obtaining of attendance time, check rates to be paid for the work done, and perform various miscellaneous functions such as those cited in the preceding paragraph.

Shop time records are often supervised by the chief production executive through the foreman. Sometimes, however, these time records are placed under the jurisdiction of production control, the controller, or the chief cost accountant. Shop clerks obtain a department time record and gather the production and job data required for preparing the payroll and making the payroll distribution.

The combination of timekeeping department records and shop time records provides data necessary for controlling and accruing employees' pay and making payroll distributions. In addition, the timekeeping department may provide management with information such as the following: (a) the effectiveness of supervision in keeping employees on their jobs throughout the entire working day, and (b) incentive rates which have been rendered obsolete because of new equipment, changes in specifications, and so on, and, therefore, which require immediate cancellation and re-study by the Timestudy department.

Forms

Timekeeping forms may be classified as:
(1) Attendance time records.
(2) Shop time records.
(3) Combination attendance time and shop time records.

These records are explained and illustrated in the following paragraphs.
(1) Attendance time records may be obtained:
   (a) On a clock card designed for horizontal recording, that is, with "in" and "out" registrations for a particular day on one hori-

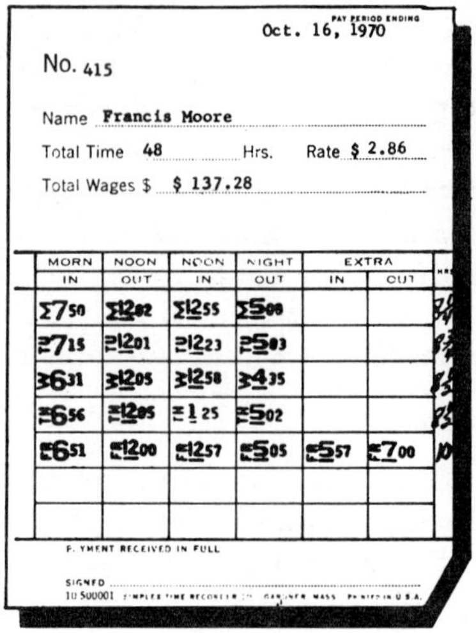

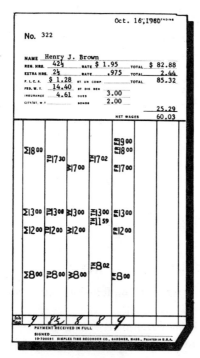

Figure 16-7. Clock Card Designed for Horizontal Recording

"In" and "out" registrations for a particular day appear on one horizontal line.

zontal line (Figure 16-7). Thus, four horizontal positions might be:

IN	OUT	IN	OUT
(8:00 AM)	(12:Noon)	(1:00 PM)	(5:00 PM)

Figure 16-8. Clock Card Designed for Vertical Recording

The registrations for a particular day appear in one column.

The clock card may have a stub attached to serve as a receipt to the paymaster for the check or cash. Some models of clocks are equipped with devices that change the ribbon color so that late or overtime recording is distinguished from regular recording. Where there is but one shift and each employee has a regular starting and finishing time, an irregularity such as a late or overtime recording is readily detectable through the color change. This feature facilitates the calculation of hours worked, since the regulars can be separated from the irregulars.

(b) On a clock card designed for vertical recording (Figure 16-8), in which a separate column is used for each day. There are no "in" and "out" positions. The clock automatically advances the punching position in the column at pre-selected times, so that the punchings for all regular employees working on the same shift will be on the same lines. Thus, the regular pattern in the card illustrated in Figure 16-8 comprises punchings on lines 2, 7, 8, and 12. If an employee punches early or late, the punching in question will be on some line other than the ones named. Payroll clerks can spot the irregulars by the off-line punching.

(c) On a card designed for optical scanning and vertical recording (Figure 16-9). Note the stylized type font used to record time. The left hand digit is day of week. Second and third digits are the hour (1 to 24) and the right hand digit is tenths of an hour. Seven two position blocks at the top are handprint code fields. The number 10 in this case means that the employee is authorized to work one hour overtime. The optical scanner reads all the recorded times and handprinted codes. Optical scanning equipment and its uses for computer input are explained on pages 589–595.

Cards designed for vertical punching are useful for staggered shifts. Where one shift punches at 8 A.M., 12 noon, 1 P.M., and 5 P.M., and an evening shift at 5 P.M., 9 P.M., 10 P.M., and 2 A.M., the punchings for the evening shift would appear at the top part of the card. In some companies, there are several shifts during the day and night, beginning with the employees who work in the bakery and restaurant (for example) and ending with the janitors and other service people. Time-clock manufacturers make a survey of the shift times to determine the punching positions desired.

Note that clock cards designed for vertical punching permit what the manufacturers call "direct subtraction," meaning subtraction of start time from finish time above by the payroll clerk. The manufacturers

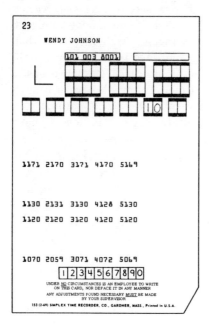

23

WENDY JOHNSON

101 003 8001

1171 2170 3171 4170 5169

1130 2131 3130 4128 5130
1120 2120 3120 4120 5120

1070 2059 3071 4072 5069

1 2 3 4 5 6 7 8 9 0

UNDER NO CIRCUMSTANCES IS AN EMPLOYEE TO WRITE
ON THIS CARD, NOR DEFACE IT IN ANY MANNER
ANY ADJUSTMENTS FOUND NECESSARY MUST BE MADE
BY YOUR SUPERVISOR
153 (2-69) SIMPLEX TIME RECORDER, CO., GARDNER, MASS., Printed in U.S.A.

Optical scanner will read the stylized numerals for day and time of day, and also the handprint codes in the Handprint Code fields at the top of the card. The optical scanner reads the cards and translates the reading into input for a computer.

**Figure 16-9.   Clock Card Designed
for Optical Scanning**

claim that most payroll clerks prefer this vertical subtraction to the cross subtraction necessary in clock cards designed for horizontal punching.

   (c) Time sheets which the employees sign daily—often one sheet or set of sheets for each department.

  (2) Shop time reports may be obtained by the shop clerk from:

   (a) Foreman's books or time cards.

   (b) Time sheets, job cards, or tickets prepared by the shop clerk or by the employee. Examples of these are:

    1. Daily time sheet. One sheet is prepared for each man each day. The sheet shows time spent on each job, and total time for the day.

    2. Job tickets in perforated strips (Figure 16-11). One strip is used for each man each day. Time for each job is entered on a separate ticket. After separation, tickets may be sorted and otherwise used on a unit basis.

    3. Unit job ticket (Figure 16-12). A separate ticket is used for each job. The card illustrated is a McBee Keysort card, which can be punched to facilitate payroll distribution.

	NO.	DESCRIPTION	MON.	TUE.	WED.	THU.	FRI.	SAT.	SUN.	HRS.	FUND	ACCOUNT			PROJ. NO.
WEEKLY PERSONNEL REPORT — Week of ___	1													1	
	2													1	
	3													1	
	4													1	
	5													1	
	6													1	
	7													1	
	8													1	
	9													1	
	10													1	
	11													1	
	12													1	
	13													1	
	14													1	
	15													1	
	16													1	
	17													1	
	Approved										REGULAR HRS.				
	Rate										OVERTIME	C	P		
	Absent Without Pay		Hrs.		Days			Comp. Time Used			Hrs.			
No. ___ Signature ___	Sick Leave							Comp. Time Earned							
	Industrial Inj.							Overtime Paid							
	Vacation Leave							Part Time							

Figure 16-10. Weekly Time Sheet

4. Multi-copy unit job ticket (not illustrated). Copies of job ticket are provided for any or all of the following: (a) payroll calculations, (b) cost distribution, (c) production control, and (d) employee's incentive production receipt.

(3) Combination attendance time and shop time records (not illustrated). A separate sheet is issued for each employee each day. It is basically a daily time sheet for recording time spent on each job during the day. It also provides spaces for recording attendance time for the day. Note that the combination of attendance time and job time on the same form facilitates checking job time against attendance time.

Production Counts

It is often necessary for the shop timekeepers or shop clerks to gather production counts for (a) incentive payment plans, (b) standard cost control calculations, and (c) payroll distribution. The timekeeper's job may then be a combination of clerk, checker, and inspector. Or the data

BLANK COMPANY

DAILY LABOR TICKET

NAME

CLOCK

WEEK ENDING

DEPT.	DATE		
JOB NO. (DIRECT)	LOT NO.	OPERATION	PART
ACCT. NO. (INDIRECT)	MACHINE NUMBER		

DEPT.	DATE		
JOB NO. (DIRECT)	LOT NO.	OPERATION	PART
ACCT. NO. (INDIRECT)	MACHINE NUMBER		

DEPT.	DATE		
JOB NO. (DIRECT)	LOT NO.	OPERATION	PART
ACCT. NO (INDIRECT)	MACHINE NUMBER		

DEPT.	DATE		
JOB NO. (DIRECT)	LOT NO.	OPERATION	PART
ACCT. NO (INDIRECT)	MACHINE NUMBER		

DEPT.	DATE		
JOB NO. (DIRECT)	LOT NO.	OPERATION	PART
ACCT. NO (INDIRECT)	MACHINE NUMBER		

BLANK COMPANY

DAILY LABOR TICKET

NAME

CLOCK NO.

WEEK ENDING

DEPT.

DEPT.	DATE	CLOCK NUMBER	HOURS	RATE	AMOUNT
JOB NO. (DIRECT) / LOT NO. / OPERATION / PART NO. / UNITS COMP					
ACCT. NO. (INDIRECT) / MACHINE NUMBER			O. T. EXC.		

DEPT.	DATE	CLOCK NUMBER	HOURS	RATE	AMOUNT
JOB NO. (DIRECT) / LOT NO. / OPERATION / PART NO. / UNITS COMP					
ACCT. NO. (INDIRECT) / MACHINE NUMBER			O. T. EXC.		

DEPT.	DATE	CLOCK NUMBER	HOURS	RATE	AMOUNT
JOB NO. (DIRECT) / LOT NO. / OPERATION / PART NO. / UNITS COMP					
ACCT. NO. (INDIRECT) / MACHINE NUMBER			O. T. EXC.		

DEPT.	DATE	CLOCK NUMBER	HOURS	RATE	AMOUNT
JOB NO. (DIRECT) / LOT NO. / OPERATION / PART NO. / UNITS COMP.					
ACCT. NO. (INDIRECT) / MACHINE NUMBER			O. T. EXC.		

DEPT.	DATE	CLOCK NUMBER	HOURS	RATE	AMOUNT
JOB NO. (DIRECT) / LOT NO. / OPERATION / PART NO. / UNITS COMP.					
ACCT. NO. (INDIRECT) / MACHINE NUMBER			O. T. EXC.		

	WEEKLY			DAILY		
	HOURS	RATE	AMOUNT	HOURS	RATE	AMOUNT
REGULAR						
OVERTIME						
TOTAL						

FOREMAN'S APPROVAL

Figure 16-11. Job Tickets on Perforated Strips

One strip is used for each man each day. Weekly strips may be provided if desired. Time for each job is entered on a separate ticket. After separation, tickets may be sorted and otherwise used on a unit basis.

may be gathered for the shop clerk by other persons, such as production checkers, inspectors, or stock clerks.

Where individual production data are required, it may be obtained by one of the methods listed below (there are many others):

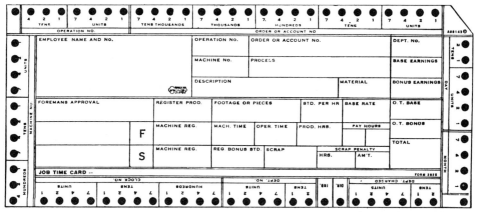

Automated Business Systems
Division of Litton Industries

Figure 16-12. Unit Job Ticket Designed for Needle Sorting

One ticket is written for each job on which each man works each day. The card form provides sorting positions for order number, operation number, and employee's number (among others). After punching, the tickets can be sorted by order number and summarized onto the Cost Summary Card. They can also be sorted by clock number and summarized onto the Payroll Summary Cards.

(1) Automatic counting devices.
(2) Inspector's count.
(3) Tags, tickets, coupons, and so on, placed on work by employee.
(4) Job cards (possibly originated by production control).

Typical Attendance Timekeeping Procedures

Described below are the steps in a typical timekeeping procedure, used in a large plant with several thousand employees:

(1) Racking cards. The timekeepers rack the attendance clock cards, which show name, clock number, and so on. The racking is usually done simultaneously with picking up the cards for the previous pay period.

(2) Supervising the clock punching. It may be that employees are punching out in their street clothes after taking shower, or they may be leaving a department early and lining up at the clock to punch out exactly at quitting time. There may be questions of industrial relations policy involved, and it is the duty of the timekeeper to report the condition so that proper action may be taken. Possibly an additional clock may be necessary. Poor supervision may be allowing the employees to leave the department ahead of time.

The importance of a minute here and a minute there may be better understood if such losses are converted into dollars. For example, assume that a company has 1,000 employees and one minute is wasted at the start and one minute at the end of the day. The four minutes a day for 300 working days in a year with employees paid $2.50 an hour would amount to $75,000.00 for the 1,000 employees. If this condition is multiplied by having losses of five minutes, ten minutes and more, it can be a very important item.

(3) Auditing. The timekeepers may function as auditors, checking the departments for the following:

(a) Padded payrolls. Timekeepers locate each man who has punched in on a clock card.

(b) Proper elapsed hours. Timekeepers spot check periodically, for example, just after starting time to make sure that all employees punched in are then present. This is a check against someone punching in for a late employee.

(c) Proper rates. Timekeepers may check the job each employee is working on and the rate of pay. If an employee has been hired as a machinist and is being paid that rate, he should not be working as a clerk.

(4) Computing hours and footing the clock cards. Timekeepers compute the elapsed hours and foot the clock card to arrive at the total hours worked for a week.

(5) In some cases, balancing attendance time with department time and adjusting differences between the attendance time record and the department time record obtained from job tickets. Differences may occur, for example, when it is unknown to the shop clerk that an employee punched in late. These should be checked and adjusted before all the payroll computations are made. It is usually not practical to wait for the auditor to do this because numerous differences would hamper getting out the final payroll. (In other cases it is the responsibility of the shop clerk to check with the clock card daily to insure balance.)

(6) Reporting time to Payroll department. Attendance time cards are the source record for calculating gross pay, and the timekeepers have the responsibility of collecting them and turning them over to the Payroll department.

(7) Obtaining pre-determined totals. The Payroll department's calculations are controlled by getting pre-determined totals of the straight time and overtime hours by departments. The timekeepers foot the clock cards and submit the totals to the control section.

(8) Supervision of lockers and badges. In some cases, the assignment of lockers to the employee and the maintenance of files on empty

lockers are handled by the timekeepers. (In other cases, lockers are controlled and assigned either at a central location for the entire plant or by the shop clerk. The procedure to be adopted will depend on whether there is a surplus or shortage of lockers and whether they are located in the departments, in the vestibules, or in centrally located locker rooms.)

Obtaining badges, assignment to employees, and taking care of lost badges are handled with the timekeepers as the liaison men between the employee and the issuing agency, which is the Payroll department.

Typical Shop Timekeeping Procedures

In the same plant cited in the preceding section, the following steps are used in department timekeeping:

(1) Issuing job tickets (where the employees do not write their own).

(2) Spotting visually each man on the job a certain number of times per day or per week, depending on the individual situation. This visual check verifies both actual attendance and performance of the particular job for which the employee is being paid.

(3) Balancing shop time against attendance record and making necessary adjustments (when this function has not been assigned to attendance timekeepers).

(4) Accumulating actual hours for each operation, which is compared with standard hours (where standard cost procedures are in use).

(5) Extending production figures by standard man-hour figures to obtain standard hours.

(6) Reporting piecework production by individuals (in departments on piece work). Procedures for obtaining these figures vary with the department.

(7) Preparing special reports for clothes-changing-time pay, clothes allowances, tool-sharpening pay, working through lunch hour, supper pay, and so on.

Timekeeping Equipment

In very small establishments or those in which employees work a standard working schedule on a salaried basis, attendance time may be obtained by:

(1) Securing the employee's signature on a time sheet or autograph time register.

(2) For salaried workers, using roll takers to check with each department and record working time (usually on the theory of excep-

Figure 16-13. Attendance Time Recorder

Figure 16-14. Time Job Recorder

tions; that is, absences, overtimes, and so on). The roll takers can also be used at the entrances to record tardiness.

In manufacturing concerns, however, attendance time is usually recorded by use of some form of time clock.

Types of recording time clocks are:

(1) Attendance time recorder (Figure 16-13), for recording daily in and out time on a clock card for the entire payroll period.

(2) Job time recorders (Figure 16-14), for recording time spent on jobs or operations. The worker, foreman, shop clerk, or other employee

Figure 16-16. Master Clock for Time Control

For keeping all clocks under control with accurate time. Each clock in the system is automatically brought into agreement with the master clock.

Figure 16-15. Time Stamp

assigning jobs creates a record by inserting the form into the job time recorder at the start and at the finish of each job, stamping the time in each case. The elapsed time on the job is computed as the difference between start and finish and is recorded on the job ticket.

(3) Time stamps (Figure 16-15), for recording date and time on rush orders, telegrams, telephone messages, packages, etc., when it is desirable to determine the time at which a paper, document or message was received so that responsibility for delays can be established.

(4) Master clocks for time control (Figure 16-16), for keeping all clocks under control with the accurate time. Each clock in the system is automatically brought into agreement with the master.

Note that time stamps and job-time recorders can be set up (by the manufacturer) to print:

(a) Hours and minutes. 1:15 P.M. (fifteen minutes after one) would be printed 1:15 P.

(b) Hours and hundredths. Fifteen minutes after one would be printed 1:25 P. The advantages are that it is easier to compute elapsed time in hundredths than in minutes (on the job tickets) and it is often easier to extend decimal hours into money than to extend hours and minutes.

(c) Continental time. The hours are recorded 1 to 24 beginning at midnight. 1 P.M. is recorded 1300.

Time elimination is a special feature used in some master clock installations for eliminating time off for lunch or regular rest periods. The regular starting time is sometimes printed at 0. Thus if starting time is 8 A.M., 11 A.M. would be printed 3:00. 2 P.M. would stamp 5:00. One hour for lunch would be automatically eliminated. Note that starting the day at zero and using time elimination facilitates computing elapsed time; such computing becomes straight subtraction of starting time from stopping time.

Location of Attendance Clocks

Attendance clocks may be located:

(1) At the entrance or entrances to the plant.

(2) In certain central locations such as dressing rooms, hallways, and the like.

(3) In the departments.

The best location in each case will depend on certain factors such as layout, size of plant, type of employees, standard control or incentives.

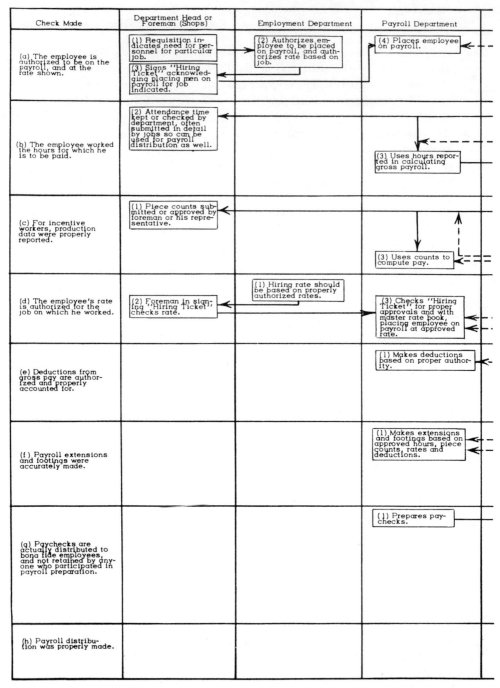

Check Made	Department Head or Foreman (Shops)	Employment Department	Payroll Department	
(a) The employee is authorized to be on the payroll, and at the rate shown.	(1) Requisition indicates need for personnel for particular job. (3) Signs "Hiring Ticket" acknowledging placing men on payroll for job indicated.	(2) Authorizes employee to be placed on payroll, and authorizes rate based on job.	(4) Places employee on payroll.	
(b) The employee worked the hours for which he is to be paid.	(2) Attendance time kept or checked by department, often submitted in detail by jobs so can be used for payroll distribution as well.		(3) Uses hours reported in calculating gross payroll.	
(c) For incentive workers, production data were properly reported.	(1) Piece counts submitted or approved by foreman or his representative.		(3) Uses counts to compute pay.	
(d) The employee's rate is authorized for the job on which he worked.	(2) Foreman in signing "Hiring Ticket" checks rate.	(1) Hiring rate should be based on properly authorized rates.	(3) Checks "Hiring Ticket" for proper approvals and with master rate book, placing employee on payroll at approved rate.	
(e) Deductions from gross pay are authorized and properly accounted for.			(1) Makes deductions based on proper authority.	
(f) Payroll extensions and footings were accurately made.			(1) Makes extensions and footings based on approved hours, piece counts, rates and deductions.	
(g) Paychecks are actually distributed to bona fide employees, and not retained by anyone who participated in payroll preparation.			(1) Prepares paychecks.	
(h) Payroll distribution was properly made.				

Figure 16-17. Payroll Procedures: Accounting Control (Internal Check)

376

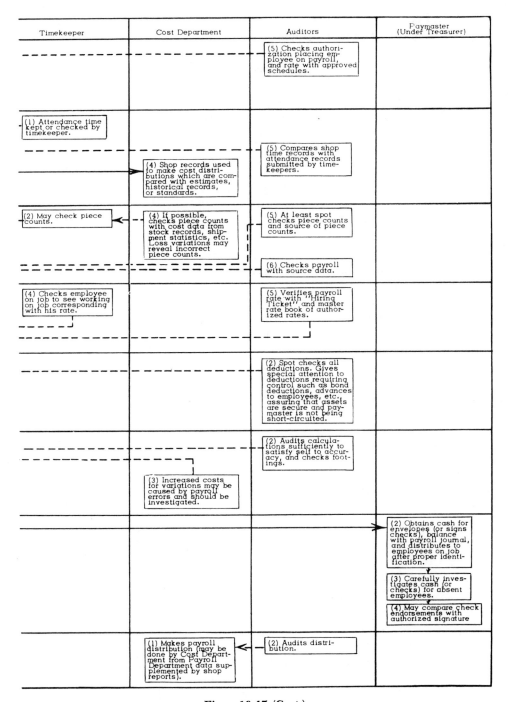

Timekeeper	Cost Department	Auditors	Paymaster (Under Treasurer)
		(5) Checks authorization placing employee on payroll, and rate with approved schedules.	
(1) Attendance time kept or checked by timekeeper.			
	(4) Shop records used to make cost distributions which are compared with estimates, historical records, or standards.	(5) Compares shop time records with attendance records submitted by timekeepers.	
(2) May check piece counts.	(4) If possible, checks piece counts with cost data from stock records, shipment statistics, etc. Loss variations may reveal incorrect piece counts.	(5) At least spot checks piece counts and source of piece counts.	
		(6) Checks payroll with source data.	
(4) Checks employee on job to see working on job corresponding with his rate.		(5) Verifies payroll rate with "Hiring Ticket" and master rate book of authorized rates.	
		(2) Spot checks all deductions. Gives special attention to deductions requiring control such as bond deductions, advances to employees, etc., assuring that assets are secure and paymaster is not being short-circuited.	
		(2) Audits calculations sufficiently to satisfy self to accuracy, and checks footings.	
	(3) Increased costs for variations may be caused by payroll errors and should be investigated.		
			(2) Obtains cash for envelopes (or signs checks), balance with payroll journal, and distributes to employees on job after proper identification.
			(3) Carefully investigates cash (or checks) for absent employees.
			(4) May compare check endorsements with authorized signature
	(1) Makes payroll distribution (may be done by Cost Department from Payroll Department data supplemented by shop reports).	(2) Audits distribution.	

Figure 16-17. (Cont.)

377

Human nature must always be taken into consideration. Location of attendance clocks away from the department has a tendency to cause employees to punch in on time but get to the department late and to punch out at or after quitting time but to leave the department early. Conditions such as lineups at the clock for punching, mediocre supervision, considerable clothes-changing time, and so on, tend to create a "lost time" problem. Time recorders are not of much help if the employee can punch in after the noon hour and then finish his lunch or visit.

Internal Check

Figure 16-17 is a chart of the major features of internal control that should be incorporated into timekeeping and payroll procedures. The column at the left describes the major features of control, and the other columns show by descriptive entries what each section or department involved in the procedure does to contribute to the control. The numbers in parentheses refer to the usual chronological order of the control steps shown.

Following is a list of the control features with a discussion of significant points not fully covered by the chart:

(1) The employee is authorized to be on the payroll and at the rate shown.

(2) The employee worked the hours for which he is to be paid.

(3) For incentive workers, production data were properly reported.

(4) The employee's rate is authorized for the job on which he worked.

(5) Deductions from gross pay are authorized and properly accounted for.[1]

On field-controlled deductions, a copy of the requisition or other authorization for the deduction is forwarded by the distributing agency to the Payroll department. The credits to stores or other accounts must equal the amount deducted from the various employees' gross pay.

Office-controlled deductions are of two types:

(a) Fixed: The amount of auditing required will vary, but where the amount deducted is turned over to another party, such as a trustee, insurance company, or union, the danger of fraud is slight and spot checks are usually sufficient. Bond deductions pose a special problem. Deductions must be properly accounted for and bonds must not be issued except to the proper employee on proper authorization.

---

[1] A discussion of deductions procedure and types of deduction appears on pages 383-387 of Chapter 17.

(b) Variable:
1. F.I.C.A. (Federal Insurance Contributions Act) deductions can be verified by those responsible for the employees' earnings records.
2. Withholding tax deductions need not be checked too closely as the deductions are merely payments to the government on account, and final settlement is made in any event. Spot checks to verify procedure and accuracy should suffice.
3. Advances should be very carefully scrutinized. Advances may be a device to pad the payroll by short-circuiting the paymaster. "Advance" authorizations not cashed should be thoroughly investigated. Vacation advances should be checked against an approved vacation list.

(6) Payroll extensions and footings were accurately made.
(7) Pay checks are actually distributed to bona fide employees and not retained by anyone who participated in payroll preparation.

Usually a paymaster is charged with the responsibility for distributing the pay check or pay envelope to the proper employee and obtaining a receipt therefor. Where cash is distributed, this function may be exercised by an outside firm. The paymaster is usually a separate department since internal check would be weakened if the pay check or pay envelope were distributed by the foreman, shop clerk, or timekeeper. An important check on padded payrolls would be lost if the persons responsible for reporting employees who worked also verified that there actually was such an employee by distributing the pay.

Additional precautions involve:
(a) Receipts: The clock card stub, signature on the payroll, and signed slip are some of the more common receipts.
(b) Rotation: For added protection, it is customary to rotate the employees distributing pay so that the same employee will not regularly distribute pay to the same department.

(8) Payroll distribution was properly made.

17

Payroll Department;
Payroll Procedures

Function and Organization

In general, the Payroll department calculates the net pay due each employee and makes the journal entry for the payroll accrual. It also prepares reports required by various laws concerning employees, and statistics and records concerning employees' pay. The department is usually under the jurisdiction of the controller, but in some cases it is under the chief production executive and closely audited by the controller's staff.

The work of the Payroll department may be outlined as follows:

(1) Calculating the payroll; including such steps as:
  (a) Gathering attendance time obtained by timekeepers.
  (b) Gathering data necessary to compute earnings of workers on piece work or other incentive basis.
  (c) Adding allowances for such items as sick pay, clothes, tools, and so on.
  (d) Extending attendance time by proper authorized rates.
  (e) Making necessary deductions from gross payroll for such items as the following:
    1. Withholding tax.
    2. F.I.C.A. (Federal Insurance Contributions Act) tax.
    3. Purchases from company for such items as tools, clothing, items sold by company made available to employees, and so forth.
    4. Insurance payments for group insurance, hospitalization, and the like.
    5. Bond installments.
    6. Union dues.
    7. Wage assignments and garnishments.

(2) Making the following statements and reports:
  (a) Payroll journal (and check register).
  (b) Pay check or envelope.
  (c) Pay stub or employee's earnings statement.
  (d) Employee's earnings record.
  (e) Forms and reports required of employers covering income tax withheld and tax due under the Federal Insurance Contributions Act.
(3) Keeping payroll statistics for such functions as personnel, industrial relations, and so on.
(4) Maintaining required files.

Legal Aspects of Payroll Procedures Design

With the passing of the Federal Social Security Act in 1935, it became necessary to:

(1) Make a 1 per cent deduction from each employee's gross taxable pay for the Federal government. (Current rates are stated later.)
(2) Compute gross taxable pay by deducting sick pay, allowances, supper pay, etc.
(3) Maintain an earnings record so that the 1 per cent deduction could be cut off after $3,000. (The current cut-off is stated later.)
(4) Give the employee a receipt for his Social Security deduction.
(5) Prepare quarterly reports on taxes withheld (described later).

In 1936, the Walsh-Healey Law was passed and in 1938, the Fair Labor Standards Act was passed. These require that overtime be paid weekly or, in some cases, daily, and provide a complicated set of exemptions as to which employees are excluded from these overtime provisions.

In 1943, the withholding tax was started. This required that a deduction be made for the Federal government from each employee's pay. The deduction depended on the gross pay and number of dependents. It extended the earnings record which was kept for each employee so that reports could be made to the employee and the government.

Meanwhile throughout these years, possibly starting with the Wagner Act in 1935, an increasing burden was thrown on the payroll department for such items as the deduction of union dues, allowances for such "fringe" payments as portal-to-portal pay, dressing and undressing time, clothing allowances, etc. Employers became more social-insurance conscious, and deductions were made for group insurance, pensions, hospitalization insurance, and the like.

With World War II came War Bonds and the resulting deductions and accounting problems in the Payroll department. State income and payroll taxes with payroll deduction and information returns became more and more widespread. Turnover increased, and hiring and separation records became a major clerical problem.

Because of this increased clerical load and also because clerical wage rates are constantly increasing, payroll mechanization and improved methods are worth more and more, and payroll procedures are a major problem for the systems man.

Gathering Attendance Time: Overtime Premium

The payroll department obtains attendance time from attendance clock cards, department time sheets or job tickets, which show the total hours worked for each employee, separated as to straight time and overtime. It may use either the attendance records or the department records as the source record for calculating gross payroll. Since one record is usually balanced against the other, either source may be used depending on the overall payroll procedure and the kind of payroll equipment.

The Fair Labor Standards Act sets the minimum wage rate at $1.60 per hour and provides for overtime premium for hours worked over 40 in one week. In an hourly wage rate plan the premium per hour of overtime work is, according to the Act, at least one half of the regular wage rate. (In an incentive pay plan, it is at least one half the earned rate per hour; earned rate per hour being total earnings for the week divided by total clock hours.) Under union contracts, however, higher overtime premium rates may be provided for Saturday work and Sunday work, and for many things in addition, such as holiday work and night shift work.

Gathering Incentive Pay Production Data

The required production information for calculation of gross payroll is usually obtained from some type of shop clerk. (The title given this employee may be clerk, checker, timekeeper, inspector, and so on.) Either the raw data or the completed gross earnings may be given to the Payroll department.

Allowances

Employees may be granted certain allowances in addition to the earnings based upon hours worked or production under incentive plans. Examples of allowances are:

(1) Sick pay. The employee may receive full pay or some percentage. Sometimes sick pay is given to salaried employees only. Such allowances may not be taxable under the Federal Insurance Contributions Act. Sick pay paid pursuant to a wage continuation plan

under Section 105(d) of Internal Revenue Code may be wholly or partly excludable from employee's gross income.

(2) Vacation pay and holiday pay (holidays not worked).

(3) Paid rest periods and lunch periods.

(4) "Portal-to-portal pay." The employee may be paid an allowance for (a) clothes changing time, (b) time inside the plant walking to the job, or (c) time spent on job preparation.

(5) Clothes, tools, and so on. If the employee purchases his own working clothes or tools, he may receive an allowance for reimbursement. The allowance for reimbursement is included in the employee's income, but his actual expense is deductible from gross income.

(6) Pieceworker's makeup allowance. Pieceworkers may be guaranteed a minimum hourly rate. The guaranteed rate may be the legal minimum of $1.60 per hour, or it may be a higher rate specified by the union contract. If their production times the rate does not equal this minimum, a makeup allowance is paid. There may also be other types of allowance in connection with incentive pay plans.

(7) Other allowances. (See Figure 17-1.)

Extending Attendance Time by Properly Authorized Rates

The Payroll Department usually has a rate book of authorized rates for each job. Customarily each employee has his base rate assigned to him and recorded on a master tabulating card, addressing machine plate or stencil, or other medium. The extension of hours and rate can be made using a calculating machine or calculator charts. The latter are prearranged tables of extensions for various amounts of hours at various rates, and can be purchased in well set-up form on tabbed cards (Figure 17-4, page 393).

Deductions: Types and Sources

Examples of deductions are:

(1) Withholding tax. Collection of income tax at the source on wages under the Internal Revenue Code may be made under either the percentage plan or the wagebracket method, at the election of the employer. Deductions vary with (a) the number of exemptions claimed by the employee and (b) earnings for the payroll period. Marital status is also a factor in determining the amount of the withholding. Deductions can be based on estimated itemized deductions and on agreement between employer and employee. Finally, the law now provides a withholding exemption for employees with no tax liability in the preceding tax year who an-

A. Premium for time worked
    1. Overtime premium, including premium for Saturday, Sunday, and holiday worked.
    2. Shift premiums, P.M. and night.

B. Pay for time not worked
    1. Sick pay (paid for by company)
    2. Vacation pay
    3. Holiday pay (holidays not worked)
    4. Paid rest period
    5. Lunch period
    6. Jury pay allowance
    7. Voting pay allowance
    8. Pay for military service

C. Employee benefits (employer's contribution)
    1. Old age and unemployment compensation
    2. Workmen's compensation
    3. Pension plan
    4. Profit sharing
    5. Christmas bonus
    6. Group life
    7. Hospitalization
    8. Health and accident
    9. Surgical
    10. Death benefits
    11. Food cost subsidy
    12. Work shoes and clothing cost
    13. Payments to union representatives for time in grievances, negotiations, etc.
    14. Administrative cost of benefits
    15. Separation pay allowance

D. Employees' activities
    1. Service awards
    2. Athletics recreation events
    3. Community activities, such as bowling, etc.

From Austin Fisher and John F. Chapman, "Big Costs of Little Fringes" (*Harvard Business Review,* Sept.-Oct. 1954), page 38.

Figure 17-1. Classification of Fringe Benefits

ticipate none in the current year. Wages for this purpose include sick pay, pensions and retirement pay, dismissal payments, fair value of lodging and meals furnished (except where they are for the "convenience of the employer," as with supper money), vacation pay, payments of stock, bonuses, and commissions. Wages subject to withholding also include reported tips where the tips received by the employee exceed $20.00 per month. After December 31, 1970, supplemental unemployment benefits will also be subject to withholding to the extent taxable to the employee. Amounts paid as advances or reimbursements for ordinary and necessary business expenses are not wages, but are subject to withholding unless the amounts are paid separately or clearly identified. Wages excluded for withholding tax purposes are: tips from customers where not accounted to employer, liquidated damages under the Wage and Hour Law, workmen's compensation, and group life insurance payments by employer. (Some states also have income taxes.) Other payments not included are amounts paid as reimbursements for medical care, or as payments for permanent injury or loss of bodily function. Reimbursements for ordinary and necessary business expenses, including direct moving expenses, are not subject to withholding if separately paid or clearly identified. Certain sickness and disability payments under wage continuation plans are not taxable to the employees, but an employer who *directly* makes such "loss of wage" has an election to withhold or not to withhold on the exempt portion of the payments. If the employer decides not to withhold, he must keep records which contain data supporting the employee's right to exemption and which separately show the amount of each payment and how much of it is not taxable. But if the payment is made by a third party in connection with the employee's sick pay plan, there is no withholding.

Errors of undercollection or overcollection may be adjusted with the employee later. However, if there is an undercollection and the employee is gone, the employer is responsible for the correct sum. [But see United States Internal Revenue Code, Section 1622(d) on reimbursement to employer where employee pays tax in final return.]

(2) F.I.C.A. tax
  (a) The Federal Insurance Contributions Act requires that a deduction of a stated percentage (5.2 per cent for 1971 and 1972) be made from each employee on the first $7,800 of wages paid. The stated percentage now includes so much for old age, survivors, and disability insurance, and, since 1965, so much for hospital insurance. The combined percentage will increase over the years from 5.2 per cent for 1971 and 1972 to 5.9 per cent in 1987. Generally, the same types of payment which are not subject to withholding for income tax are not subject to F.I.C.A. withholding either. Wages for this purpose include:
    1. Payments under employers' plans on account of retirement:

sickness or accident, disability; medical or hospitalization expenses; or death.

2. Retirement payments *not* under a plan or system.
3. Payments on account of sickness and accident disability, or medical and hospitalization expenses, made after expiration of six calendar months of employment.
4. Payments from or to certain tax exempt trusts or under certain annuity plans or bond purchase plans.
5. Payment by employer of *employee's* tax under F.I.C.A.
6. Payment for services which were not in the course of employer's trade or business, or for domestic service.

This deduction is designated in the text of this chapter as F.I.C.A tax. The designation OAB (for Old Age Benefit), which refers to the same deduction, frequently appears on standard printed forms, and it appears on some of the printed forms reproduced in this chapter. Sometimes the designation "Social Security tax" is used. As a general statement, the employer is liable for an amount identical to that which is deductible from the employee's pay. A qualification of this statement: The employer is not liable for amounts deducted from the employee's pay on account of taxable tips reported to the employer by the employee. Furthermore, tips are not counted in arriving at the $7,800 cut-off figure for purposes of the employer tax, although they are for purposes of employee's tax.

    (b) Some states require deduction from employees for unemployment insurance. No deduction is required by the Federal government.
(3) Deductions for purchases from the company are usually handled by having a copy of the requisition or sales ticket sent to the Payroll department.
(4) Insurance payments are usually made by posting from original authorizations to a posting medium used in making out this part of the payroll journal (that is, master tabulating card, Addressograph plate, earnings summary).
(5) Bond deductions have decreased in importance during recent years but are still a sizable factor in certain companies. The keeping of individual accounts for each employee, with the posting of deductions and bond payments, has been quite a job of record keeping.
(6) Union dues. Under some union contracts, the employer is required to deduct union dues from employees' pay and remit the total of such deductions to the union.
(7) Wage assignments and garnishments were previously discussed.

From the standpoint of payroll procedures design in general and the method of assembling deduction information in particular, deductions may be classified as:

(1) Field controlled or office controlled. Field controlled deductions (for example, purchases by an employee from the company store) are those which originate outside the Payroll department and for which the originating department or organization sets up the controls to which the Payroll department must prove. Office controlled deductions (for example, withholding tax) are those which originate within the Payroll department and for which the Payroll department sets up its own controls.

(2) Fixed or variable deductions. Fixed deductions (for instance, bond deductions and certain insurance deductions) are those made in a constant amount each pay or every other pay, so long as specified conditions for the deduction continue to exist. Variable deductions (for example, withholding tax and purchases from the company store) are those which are newly computed each time a deduction is to be made. Note that the Payroll department can handle fixed deductions from a list supplied by the source and kept up to date. Often the fixed deductions are posted to an information position on the employee's quarterly earnings record, where they are visible for use by the payroll clerk when he makes up the pay checks and other payroll forms.

Forms, Statements, and Reports

Common forms, statements and reports used in payroll procedures are illustrated in Figure 17-6, page 395, which is a collated set of forms:

(1) Payroll journal (and check register). This is a summary report listing the important factors that go to make up each employee's earnings for the payroll period. There is a horizontal line for each employee on which typical items shown are: employee's name and clock number, hours worked (by day: regular and overtime), hours for week, rate of pay, earnings at regular rate, excess for overtime, other earnings, gross earnings, various deductions, net pay and check number. Hours worked (by day) may be omitted where the weekly total hours are to be posted from the employee's weekly attendance card. Where there may be exempt earnings, a column may be provided for pay that is taxable under Federal Insurance Contributions Act.

(2) Pay check or envelope. The pay check or envelope, if payment is in cash, must have the employee's name and the amount of the net pay. It may have other identifying information, such as department, clock number, and Social Security number.

(3) Pay stub or employee's earnings statement. The law requires that each employee be given a receipt showing F.I.C.A. taxable wages and tax deducted. While this information may be rendered on an

annual basis, most employers give their employees a receipt each pay period and at the same time show the items that went to make up the net pay. A typical stub or earnings statement would include hours worked, F.I.C.A. taxable pay, gross payroll, withholding tax deduction, F.I.C.A. deduction, other deductions (listed in varying detail), and net pay. Frequently this detailed information is placed on the pay envelope itself.

(4) Employee's quarterly earnings record (Figure 17-3, page 392). This record is usually used to accumulate hours, regular earnings, overtime earnings, gross earnings, withholding tax, and F.I.C.A. deductions; however, it is also frequently used to assist in personnel matters, such as wage control, overtime control, and so on. Under some vacation plans, it is necessary to calculate average earnings for weeks where hours worked were not up to the desired minimum, etc. The earnings summary may be useful in obtaining this information. For any retroactive payments for wage adjustments, employees' earnings records may facilitate calculations. A column may be provided for earnings taxable under Federal Insurance Contributions Act, if necessary.

Statistics: Managerial Information

Compilation of statistics may be one of the major functions of the payroll department, or it may be relegated to a minor role. It is probably more important to have numerous statistics in very large companies where it is difficult to have the close personal touch than it is to have them in a relatively small concern where there is a personal touch between employer and employee. Wage statistics are also playing an increasingly important part in union negotiations. The types of data accumulated are as follows:

(1) Number of employees.
(2) Average hours worked.
(3) Average hourly earnings (male, female, skilled, unskilled).
(4) Straight time hourly earnings (male, female, skilled, unskilled).
(5) Average weekly earnings (male, female, skilled, unskilled).
(6) Straight time weekly earnings (male, female, skilled, unskilled).
(7) Turnover statistics (quits, lay-offs, discharges).
(8) Absenteeism data.
(9) Tardiness data.
(10) Average annual earnings.

Unemployment Insurance Taxes

The systems man should be familiar with the provisions of the Federal Unemployment Insurance program because it affects the type of payroll information the employer must keep as a basis for calculating the tax which the employer must pay. (The employee pays no tax under the Federal Unemployment Insurance program, although in a few states he may pay tax under a state Unemployment Insurance program.)

Under the Federal Unemployment Insurance program, any employer of four or more employees pays a tax of 3.1 per cent of the first $3,000 wages earned by each employee during the year. The employer must also pay state unemployment insurance taxes (since all states have unemployment taxes), the percentage amount of which may vary according to the employer's rating for providing steady employment. In Illinois, the state unemployment insurance tax rate during the first three years the employer is liable is 2.7 per cent of the first $3,000 of wages paid to each employee. After the first three years, an employer's rate varies depending upon employment experience. The rate may be as low as 0.01 per cent or as high as 4 per cent. The employer is entitled to credit his federal tax with state unemployment insurance taxes paid and certain rating adjustments up to 2.7 per cent of gross wages paid (of the first $3,000). Thus, in a typical situation, the employer pays 0.3 per cent for federal unemployment insurance and 2.7 per cent for state unemployment insurance.

The individual employee's earnings record (Figure 17-3) which is the record of an employee's earnings and deductions by pay period over a calendar period, shows the cumulative gross earnings for the employee. This cumulative figure is the basis for the $7,800 cut-off for F.I.C.A. tax and the $3,000 cut-off for federal and state unemployment insurance.

Reports Required by Law: Files

Certain reports are required of employers in the matter of (a) income tax withheld, (b) employers' tax and employees' tax under the Federal Insurance Contributions Act, and employers' tax under the Federal Unemployment Insurance tax.

Form 941 Employers' Quarterly Federal Tax Return is submitted to the Collector of Internal Revenue within a month after the close of each quarter. It covers income tax withheld and F.I.C.A. tax (both employer's and employee's share). Besides showing total amounts due, it shows a list of individual employee Social Security numbers and names, together with wages taxable under F.I.C.A. for each employee. The returns can now be filed on magnetic tapes.

An employer who has more than $2,500 of F.I.C.A. and/or withheld income taxes for any month of a calendar quarter must make semi-monthly deposits of the taxes in an authorized bank. An employer who has less than $100 of withholding per month need deposit only quarterly. All other employers must make deposits for each of the first two months of a quarter.

A W-2 Withholding Tax Statement is issued after the close of the year to each employee, with carbon copies to the Collector of Internal Revenue. It shows:

Social Security Information
   Total F.I.C.A. wages paid
   F.I.C.A. employee tax withheld
Income tax information
   Total wages paid in 19—
Federal income tax withheld

For Federal Unemployment Insurance tax, Form 940 Annual Return of Excise Tax on Employers of Four or More Individuals is filed before January 31, for the previous taxable year. This return shows among other things:

1. Total taxable wages paid during the year.
2. Gross Federal Tax (3 per cent of 1)
3. Less Credit for contributions paid into State funds
4. Remainder of tax

Forms for state unemployment insurance tax must likewise be filed.

Under the Fair Labor Standards Act (Wage and Hour Law), it is required that basic records be kept for four years. The pertinent statutes differ in the various states, and therefore it is necessary to check the specific law to determine how long to keep basic payroll data. The Illinois requirement of five years is based on the statute and regulations governing unemployment compensation.

Payroll Methods Named

Since the payroll is essentially a journal of labor transactions, the methods of producing a payroll and the related forms (pay checks, earnings statements, and employees' quarterly earnings statements) may be classified in the same way as other methods of journalizing:

(1) Conventional pen-and-ink methods.

Under these methods, the payroll is sometimes prepared first and the other forms produced from the payroll.

(2) Payroll board and machine methods (pages 394 to 405).

Under the payroll board and most of the accounting machine methods, payroll data are posted direct to the pay check and earnings statement, and some or all of the other forms are produced as carbon copies of the check posting or writing operation. Note, however, that under some machine procedures, the pay check and the other related forms are prepared simultaneously in the machine as originals.

(3) Ledgerless method (page 403).

Under this method, the pay check and earnings statements are written by pen and ink or by typewriter and two copies are filed: (1) by employee number, as the employee's quarterly earnings record and (2) by check number, as the check register.

PEN AND INK

Conventional Pen-and-Ink Payroll (Figure 17-2) and Employee's Quarterly Earnings Record (Figure 17-3); Calculator Chart (Figure 17-4)

Pre-payroll work: A weekly attendance time card is used for attendance time, and a job time recorder may be used to show start and stop time. A daily job card may be used by each employee to record the hours spent on each job. The hours as recorded on the weekly attendance time cards and the daily job cards are compared; the former will then be used for payroll purposes while the latter will be used for cost purposes.

Payroll work: Using pen and ink, enter names, clock numbers, and weekly hours separated into regular hours and overtime hours on a payroll journal (Figure 17-2) from the attendance time card. Enter rates on the journal from a book of authorized rates. (An addressing machine may be used to enter the employee's name, clock number, rate and Social Security number on the payroll journal and other records.) Make the extensions of hours and rates by use of a calculating machine or calculator charts (Figure 17-4).

List deductions such as the following on the payroll journal:

(1) F.I.C.A. deduction—calculated from gross payroll.
(2) Withholding tax—from tax charts based on payroll and exemptions.
(3) Fixed deductions such as bond deductions, insurance, and so on—from posting media such as employee's earnings record.
(4) Variable deductions such as company purchases, allowances, and so on—from source records such as individual tickets.

Obtain net pay by cross-footing. Total each column and balance each page. Obtain grand totals of each item.

From the completed payroll journal, prepare the following:

(1) The pay check or pay envelope, which requires copying name and net pay.
(2) The stub or employee's earnings statement, which requires copying such information as employee's name, clock number, regular hours, overtime hours, gross payroll, F.I.C.A. deduction, withholding tax, other deductions (in detail desired) and net pay.

Wilson-Jones

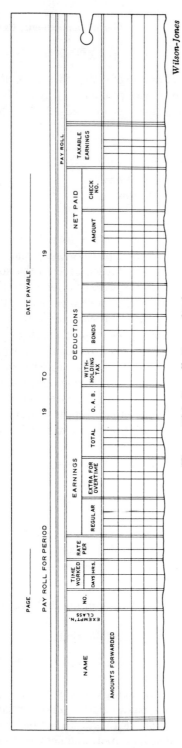

Figure 17-2. Payroll—Pen and Ink

Wilson-Jones

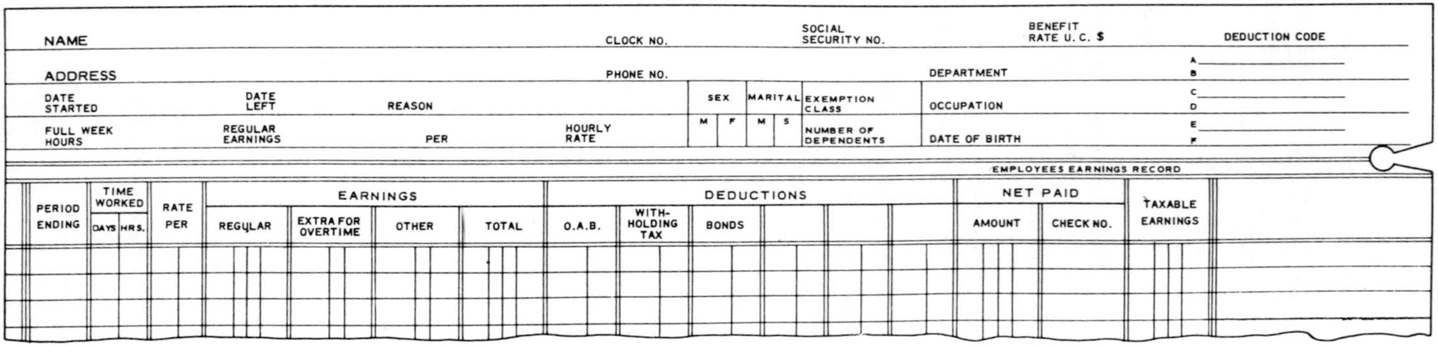

Figure 17-3. Employee's Quarterly Earnings Record—Pen and Ink

Per Hr. **2.10**
1½ Rate 3.15

HRS.	REGULAR 10	20	30	40	Reg.	1½	Total	50	Reg.	1½	Total	60
1-12	18	2100	4200	6300		8400		8400		8400	3150	11550	
1-4	53	2153	4253	6353	1-4	8400	79	8479	1-4	8400	3229	11629	1-4
1-2	105	2205	4305	6405	1-2	8400	158	8558	1-2	8400	3308	11708	1-2
3-4	158	2258	4358	6458	3-4	8400	236	8636	3-4	8400	3386	11786	3-4
1	210	2310	4410	6510	**1**	8400	315	8715	**1**	8400	3465	11865	**1**
1-4	263	2363	4463	6563	1-4	8400	394	8794	1-4	8400	3544	11944	1-4
1-2	315	2415	4515	6615	1-2	8400	473	8873	1-2	8400	3623	12023	1-2
3-4	368	2468	4568	6668	3-4	8400	551	8951	3-4	8400	3701	12101	3-4
2	420	2520	4620	6720	**2**	8400	630	9030	**2**	8400	3780	12180	**2**
1-4	473	2573	4673	6773	1-4	8400	709	9109	1-4	8400	3859	12259	1-4
1-2	525	2625	4725	6825	1-2	8400	788	9188	1-2	8400	3938	12338	1-2
3-4	578	2678	4778	6878	3-4	8400	866	9266	3-4	8400	4016	12416	3-4
3	630	2730	4830	6930	**3**	8400	945		**3**	8400	4095	12495	**3**
1-4	683	2783	4883	6983	1-4	8400		503	1-4	8400	4174	12574	1-4
1-2	735	2835	4935	7035	1-2	8400			1-2	8400	4253	12653	1-2
3-4	788	2888	4988	7088	3-4	8400		9581	3-4	8400	4331	12731	3-4
4	840	2940	5040	7140	**4**			9660	**4**	8400	4410	12810	**4**
1-4	893	2993	5093	7193	1-4		339	9739	1-4	8400	4489	12889	1-4
1-2	945	3045	5145	7245	1-2		1418	9818	1-2	8400	4568	12968	1-2
3-4	998	3098	5198	7298		8400	1496	9896	3-4	8400	4646	13046	3-4
5	1050	3150	5250	7350	**5**	8400	1575	9975	**5**	8400	4725	13125	**5**
1-4	1103	3203	5303	740?	1-4	8400	1654	10054	1-4	8400	4804	13204	1-4
1-2	1155	3255	5355	74??	1-2	8400	1733	10133	1-2	8400	4883	13283	1-2
3-4	1208	3308	5408	7???	3-4	8400	1811	10211	3-4	8400	4961	13361	3-4
6	1260	3360	5460	?60	**6**	8400	1890	10290	**6**	8400	5040	13440	**6**
1-4	1313	3413	5513	?13	1-4	8400	1969	10369	1-4	8400	5119	13519	1-4
1-2	1365	3465	5565	?65	1-2	8400	2048	10448	1-2	8400	5198	13598	1-2
3-4	1418	3518	5618	?18	3-4	8400	2126	10526	3-4	8400	5276	13676	3-4
7	1470	3570	5670	7??	**7**	8400	2205	10605	**7**	8400	5355	13755	**7**
1-4	1523	3623	5723	78?	1-4	8400	2284	10684	1-4	8400	5434	13834	1-4
1-2	1575	3675	5775	78?	1-2	8400	2363	10763	1-2	8400	5513	13913	1-2
3-4	1628	3728	5828	7928	3-4	8400	2441	10841	3-4	8400	5591	13991	3-4
8	1680	3780	5880	7980	**8**	8400	2520	10920	**8**	8400	5670	14070	**8**
1-4	1733	3833	5933	8033	1-4	8400	2599	10999	1-4	8400	5749	14149	1-4
1-2	1785	3885	5985	8085	1-2	8400	2678	11078	1-2	8400	5828	14228	1-2
3-4	1838	3938	6038	8138	3-4	8400	2756	11156	3-4	8400	5906	14306	3-4
9	1890	3990	6090	8190	**9**	8400	2835	11235	**9**	8400	5985	14385	**9**
1-4	1943	4043	6143	8243	1-4	8400	2914	11314	1-4	8400	6064	14464	1-4
1-2	1995	4095	6195	8295	1-2	8400	2993	11393	1-2	8400	6143	14543	1-2
3-4	2048	4148	6248	8348	3-4	8400	3071	11471	3-4	8400	6221	14621	3-4

(column group heading: TIME AND HALF AND TOTAL TIME PAY; arrow label: 47¾ HOURS AT 2.10)

Figure 17-4. Calculator Chart   *Meilicke*

(3) Employee's quarterly earnings record (Figure 17-3), which requires copying the hours, gross payroll, F.I.C.A. deduction, withholding tax, and other deductions (in detail desired).

(4) The journal entry:

Work in Process-Labor	xx
Indirect Labor	xx
F.I.C.A. Accrued	xx
Withholding Tax Accrued	xx
Group Insurance Accrued	xx
Accrued Payroll	xx

Note that in the above procedure the items listed below are copied the number of times indicated:

Name	4 (Weekly clock card, journal, pay check, stub)
Clock number	3 (Weekly clock card, journal, stub)
Hours worked	3 (Journal, stub, earnings record)
Gross payroll	3 (Journal, stub, earnings record)
Each deduction	3 (Journal, stub, earnings record)
Net pay	4 (Journal, pay check, stub, earnings record)

Naturally, writing each of these items the number of times enumerated, and checking and balancing to verify that the correct data have been written, takes considerable time. Mention was made of the use of addressing machines to do part of rewriting, but if much of the data varies from pay period to pay period there will still be much copying.

PAYROLL BOARDS; MACHINE METHODS

Payroll Board (Figure 17-5); Forms (Figure 17-6)

To eliminate the rewriting required by the handwritten procedure and still to avoid any sizable investment for a small concern, collated manual procedures have been devised. These procedures work on a payroll board, which is a type of peg board, illustrated in Figure 17-5. Use of this board makes it possible to obtain the payroll and the posting to employee's quarterly earnings record as carbon copy by-products of writing the earnings statement.

A typical set of forms is shown in Figure 17-6. The payroll journal is placed on the board and covered by carbon paper as diagrammed in Figure 17-6. Names are pre-written on payroll, and they are visible to the operator during the operation. The file of quarterly earnings records (bearing the postings of previous periods) and a quantity of blank employees' earnings-statements pay checks are within reach. The operator places an earnings record in position on the board, and places an earnings-statement pay check in position on the proper line of the earnings record.

Figure 17-5. Payroll Board

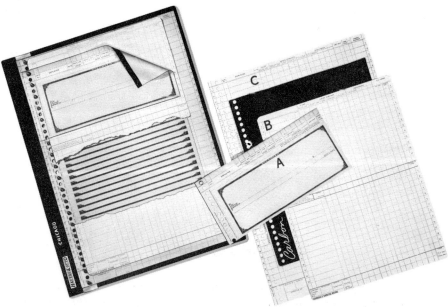

Hautau & Otto

As the following information is written on the earnings statement, carbon impressions are made on the proper line of the employee's earnings record and the journal: period ending, hours, rate, regular earnings, overtime earnings, total gross payroll, F.I.C.A. deduction, withholding tax, other deductions, and net pay. The body of the check proper is written by separate operation.

There is usually a nominal cost for the above devices except the cost of the forms. These procedures do eliminate the rewriting of the hand method. One complication is that the payroll journal cannot be audited before all the other forms are prepared.

Machine Methods: Posting or Writing Checks, Reproduction by Carbon Paper

Various bookkeeping machines in general and the use of registers and cross-footers in particular were explained in Chapter 7. Bookkeeping machines can be used to write or post pay checks and earnings statements and to obtain related payroll forms by use of carbon paper. The operation is similar to the accounting board described in the preceding section except that:

Figure 17-6. Forms Used on Payroll Board

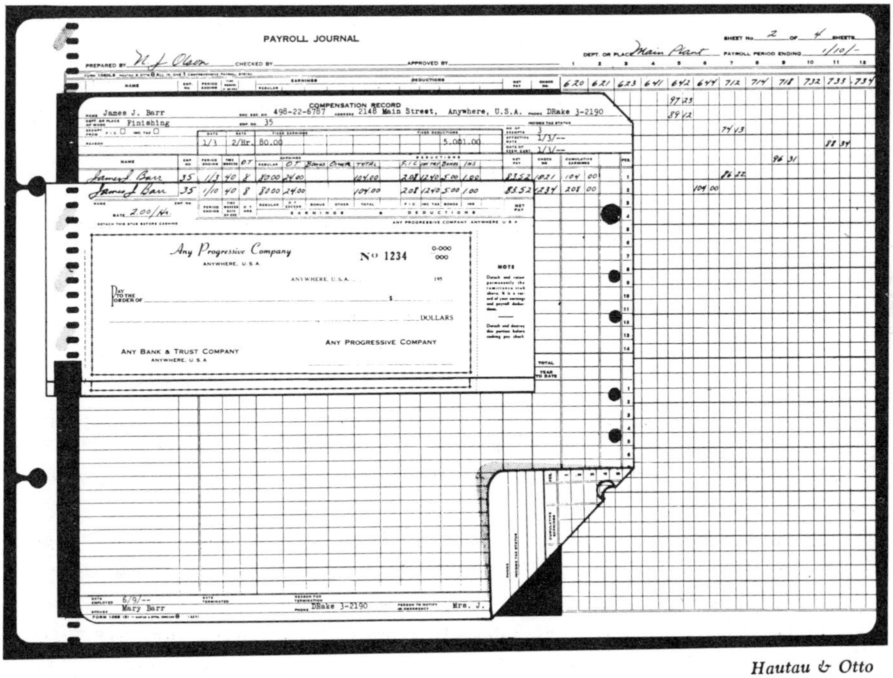

Hautau & Otto

(1) A platen with a front feed is used instead of pegs.

(2) Cross-footers and registers make it possible for the machine to do the required mathematics.

Figure 17-7 is a diagram of a typical payroll application, showing how a check and earnings statement may be produced and postings to (a) quarterly earnings records and (b) payroll obtained by carbon copy. The machine is numeric, and it comprises one cross-footer and four registers. The cross-footer is used to subtract deductions from gross earnings automatically to arrive at net earnings. The registers are used to accumulate separately the classes of deduction so that the totals by class can be proved against control totals. Note that in Figure 17-7 neither gross earnings nor F.I.C.A. tax is accumulated on the earnings records. These items are merely posted.

Types of Machines:

Types of bookkeeping machines and writing machines used for payroll applications are listed below. The figure numbers refer to several illustrations of each type.

(1) Machines with numeric keyboards (multiple register listing-adding machines, equipped with wide carriage and front feed).

(2) Machines with alphabetical keyboards and numeric keyboards (Figures 6-22 and 7-20).

(3) Machines with alphabetic keyboards and numeric keyboards, equipped with a multiplying mechanism (Figures 6-16, 6-19, and 7-22).

(4) Machines with alphabetic keyboards and numeric keyboards, also equipped with a multiplying mechanism and storage (memory). (Figures 6-24, 6-25, and 6-26.)

Machines used for payroll have, as a minimum, the capability to add and subtract, and to accumulate a number of totals during a posting run. The number of totals varies among models. Several of the above types of machines can be equipped for *automatic* writing (say, of employee names) by coupling to a punched-card/punched-paper-tape input unit (pages 112–116). Some others are equipped to handle magnetic strip ledgers (employees' quarterly earnings records); these machines have automatic writing capability.

The nature of the input media and the kind of pre-payroll preparation varies with the type of machine. For machines which do not have multiplying capability (1 and 2 above) pre-rated and extended attendance time cards (regular gross earnings separate from overtime earnings) are used. For types 3 and 4, attendance time cards not rated and extended may be used. Other types of input depend upon whether the machine has punched-

Payroll (Proof) Journal

```
101   Jan. 13, 19--    46.00    3.10    .69   15.00   27.21
102   Jan. 13, 19--    75.00    7.40   1.13   20.00   46.47
103   Jan. 13, 19--   125.00   15.20   1.88   40.00   69.72
```

Note: In the posting operation, the Earnings Statement is over the Employee's Quarterly Earnings Record, which in turn is over the Payroll.

Payroll (covered by carbon paper) remains in machine through the posting run or until filled with entries. It spaces automatically on the platen, so that it receives a carbon paper impression of each entry made on Earnings Statements and Quarterly Earnings Records.

The Earnings Statement and the Quarterly Earnings Record are dropped into place for posting, through a front feed chute. The latter drops to a fixed position which controls the line on which the entry will be reproduced.

→ indicates a single posting made on Earnings Statement and reproduced by carbon paper on Quarterly Earnings Record and Payroll.

(spot carbon on back of Earnings Statement)

EMPLOYEE'S QUARTERLY EARNINGS RETURN

Quarter Ending Mar. 31, 19___   Name George Calhoun   #103

Date	Gross Earnings	WH	OASI	Company Sales	Net Earnings
Jan. 6, 19--	125.00	15.20	1.88	25.00	82.92
Jan.13, 19--	125.00	15.20	1.88	40.00	67.92

EARNINGS STATEMENT

Name George Calhoun   #103   Check

Date This Pay	Gross Earnings	WH	OASI	Company Sales	Net Earnings
Jan.13, 19--	125.00	15.20	1.88	40.00	67.92

	(1)	(2)	(3)	(4)	(5)	(6)	(7)
Posting Cycle →							Not illustrated (Net earnings, on check)
Cross-Footer		Add	Subtract	Subtract	Subtract	Sub-total	Total
Registers		#1 Add	#2 Add	#3 Add	#4 Add		

Figure 17-7. Diagram: Payroll by Machine Posting (Pay Check and Earnings Statement, Employee's Quarterly Earnings Statement, and Payroll)

card/punched-paper-tape input and whether it handles magnetic ledgers (employees' earnings records) or only non-magnetic ledgers.

Payroll and Related Forms Produced on Alphanumeric Machine (Figure 17-8); Earnings, Withholding Tax, and F.I.C.A. All to Date: Package Proof

Figure 17-8 illustrates forms written on a National Class 36 bookkeeping machine, which is an alphanumeric machine. (The machine is illustrated in Figure 7-20.) The forms include:

(1) The payroll proper, which is placed on the platen of the machine and which remains there until the preparation of pay checks and earnings records is completed, or until it is filled with entries. It is covered with carbon paper, so that it receives a carbon impression of typing on earnings statements and pay checks.
(2) Employee's quarterly earnings record.
(3) Earnings statement and pay check.

The quarterly earnings record is placed in the machine first and the employee's earnings statement and check are placed in front of the quarterly earnings record. (The latter is spot-carboned on back.)

Note that in the posting operation, the operator picks up *old* balances (non-print) reading the *new* balances of the previous entries on the employee's quarterly earnings record:

Gross earnings to date ($1620.00)
Withholding tax to date ($172.80)
F.I.C.A. tax to date ($71.66)
State tax ($16.20)

She then indexes earnings (regular and overtime) which have been previously calculated and entered on the attendance time card. The machine prints these earnings, adds them, and prints gross earnings ($86.00). The operator indexes the various deductions, including F.I.C.A. ($4.13), withholding tax ($11.00), and state tax ($0.86). The machine prints net pay ($64.76) and new balances for gross earnings ($1706.00), F.I.C.A. tax ($75.41), and withholding tax ($183.80).

The operator types the employee's name on the check and the machine prints date and net pay on the check.

Package proof of old balance pickups: Note that in addition to picking up the three old balances indicated above, the operator also picks up the proof figure ($1502.66). If the operator has picked up the balances correctly the machine will clear 0.00 in the proof column.* If the operator has

---

* The formula for the proof total, automatically applied by the machine, is $1620.00 − $172.80 − $16.20 + $71.66 = $1502.66.

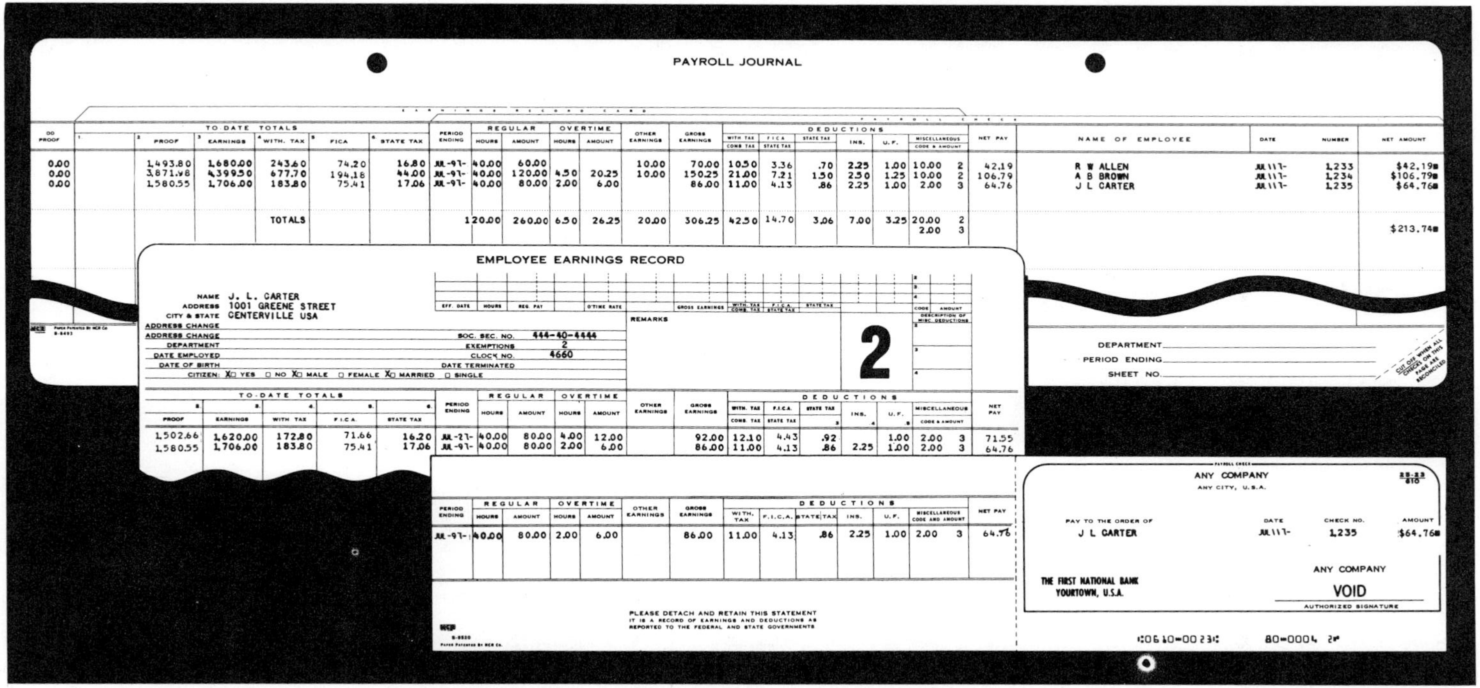

Figure 17-8. Payroll and Related Forms: Alphanumeric Machine (Class 36)

National

not picked up the balances correctly, the machine will fail to print, requiring the operator to re-do the pickups.

Magnetic Strip Employee's Quarterly Earnings Record and Related Forms on Computing Bookkeeping Machine

This section illustrates a magnetic strip employee's quarterly earnings record (Figure 17-9) prepared on a National Class 400 (Figure 7-22), which is an alpha-numeric machine with computing and memory capabilities. The pay check and employee's earnings statement, together with the payroll are produced concurrently with the postings to the quarterly earnings statement.

The computer makes the required calculations and prints on the employee's quarterly earnings record:

(1) Regular earnings ($130.00 in the illustration)
(2) Overtime earnings ($19.50)
(3) Gross earnings ($149.50)
(4) F.I.C.A. ($7.18)
(5) Whether F.I.C.A. has reached the limit
(6) Withholding tax ($19.04)
(7) Local tax ($1.50)
(8) Miscellaneous deductions (none for Jan. 16)
(9) Net pay ($121.78)

The "total fixed deductions $27.72," is actually total deductions; there were no miscellaneous deductions that week.

The computer updates the following totals, encoding them in the magnetic strips:

(1) Year-to-date gross earnings
(2) Quarter-to-date gross earnings
(3) Year-to-date F.I.C.A.
(4) Year-to-date income tax withheld
(5) Year-to-date state tax
(6) Year-to-date local tax

It accumulates the following totals in the memory of the computer (to be imprinted on the payroll at the end of the roll):

(1) Gross pay
(2) Withholding tax
(3) F.I.C.A.
(4) Net pay

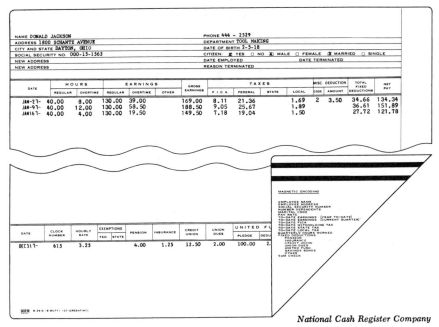

NAME DONALD JACKSON						PHONE 444 - 2529					
ADDRESS 1800 SCHANTZ AVENUE						DEPARTMENT TOOL MAKING					
CITY AND STATE DAYTON, OHIO						DATE OF BIRTH 2-5-18					
SOCIAL SECURITY NO. 000-15-1563						CITIZEN: X YES ☐ NO X MALE ☐ FEMALE X MARRIED ☐ SINGLE					
NEW ADDRESS						DATE EMPLOYED DATE TERMINATED					
NEW ADDRESS						REASON TERMINATED					

DATE	HOURS		EARNINGS			GROSS EARNINGS	TAXES				MISC. DEDUCTION		TOTAL FIXED DEDUCTIONS	NET PAY
	REGULAR	OVERTIME	REGULAR	OVERTIME	OTHER		F.I.C.A.	FEDERAL	STATE	LOCAL	CODE	AMOUNT		
JAN-27-	40.00	8.00	130.00	39.00		169.00	8.11	21.36		1.69	2	3.50	34.66	134.34
JAN-97-	40.00	12.00	130.00	58.50		188.50	9.05	25.67		1.89			36.61	151.89
JAN167-	40.00	4.00	130.00	19.50		149.50	7.18	19.04		1.50			27.72	121.78

MAGNETIC ENCODING

EMPLOYEE NAME
EMPLOYEE ADDRESS
SOCIAL SECURITY NUMBER
NUMBER DEPENDENTS
MARITAL CODE
PAY RATE
TO-DATE EARNINGS [YEAR TO-DATE]
TO-DATE EARNINGS [CURRENT QUARTER]
TO-DATE FICA
TO-DATE WITHHOLDING TAX
TO-DATE STATE TAX
TO-DATE LOCAL TAX
QUARTERLY HOURS WORKED
FIXED DEDUCTIONS
PENSION
INSURANCE
CREDIT UNION
UNION DUES
UNITED FUND
SAVINGS BONDS
OTHER
SUM CHECK

DATE	CLOCK NUMBER	HOURLY RATE	EXEMPTIONS		PENSION	INSURANCE	CREDIT UNION	UNION DUES	UNITED FU	
			FED.	STATE					PLEDGE	DEDU
DEC317-	615	3.25			4.00	1.25	12.50	2.00	100.00	2.

NCR 8-3012 -8-BUTF) -GT-GREENTINT)

National Cash Register Company

Figure 17-9.   Magnetic Strip Employee's Quarterly Earnings Record

In the machine operation, the payroll remains on the platen of the machine through the posting operation. The operator locates an employee's earnings record and drops it into the front feed of the machine. Line finding is automatic, and the machine is programmed to read employee's name, clock number, rates of pay and the previous year-to-date balances from the strips on the employee's earnings record into the memory unit in the processor. There is a package proof which will cause the machine to reject the account if these items are not picked up correctly.

The operator enters the clock number on the console from the clock card. The computer compares the clock number read from the strips on the employee's earnings record with the number entered on the console, and if they do not agree, rejects the account. If they do agree, the operator proceeds. She indexes hours worked on the console, and the computer performs the extensions and the other calculations.

Figure 17-10 is a composite illustration of pay check and statement of earnings and deductions, employee's earnings record and payroll transaction journal, prepared on a National Class 400. (This illustration is not related to Figure 17-9.)

The Automatic Ledger Reader Feeder (Figure 7-24 or Figure 7-25) can be used by the employer to prepare reports to the Social Security Administration. The reader reads the employees' quarterly earnings records and prepares the listing automatically.

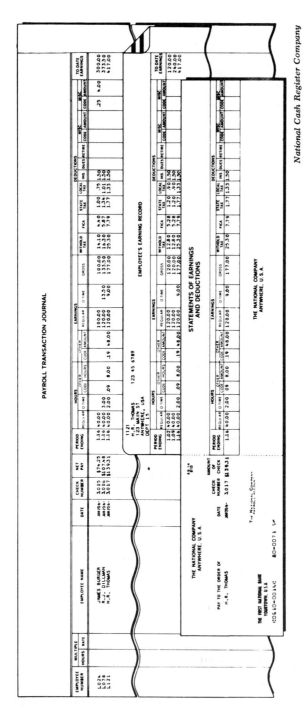

Figure 17-10. Pay Check and Statement of Earnings and Deductions, Employee's
Earnings Record and Payroll Transaction Journal (Class 400)

National Cash Register Company

Payroll and Related Forms: Terminal Computer (Victor)

The Victor terminal computer (illustrated in Figure 6-24 and described on pages 119–121) can be used as a stand-alone payroll writing machine or as a computer. As the former, it can post to non-magnetic quarterly earnings records, at the same time producing the paychecks and earnings statement and the payroll journal. In this operation, the 820 is a keyboard operated machine; the operator picks up the input (hours, rates, earnings to date, and so forth) from the employee's time cards and quarterly earnings records.

Alternatively, the 820 can post to magnetic ledgers (producing the paychecks and the journal in the same operation). In this case, the time cards and the magnetic ledgers are the input. Hours worked and certain other information are entered on the keyboard from the time card. To date balances, employee name, and fixed deductions are picked up automatically from the magnetic ledger cards.

The Victor 820, when equipped with a punched-card input and a punched-card output, can operate as a computer, either completely from cards or with variable data input on the keyboard. When operated from cards, input cards for each employee show (a) such fixed information as employee name and number, wage rates or salary, and fixed deductions, (b) such variable information as actual clock hours for the week—regular and overtime—and various variable deductions, and (c) earnings and F.I.C.A. year-to-date as of the beginning of the pay period. The machine would produce employees' pay checks and earnings statements and a payroll journal for the pay period, and it would update the individual year-to-date earnings and F.I.C.A. punching these data in a card for each employee (in the output punch). The latter cards, which become the employees' quarterly earnings records, are input cards for the next pay period.

The alternative to the above procedure is to input quarterly earnings and F.I.C.A. to date, through the punched-card input, manually enter current hours and variable deductions through the keyboard, and output the gross earnings and F.I.C.A. tax year-to-date and other fixed amounts through the punched-card output.

The terminal computer can be used to prepare the quarterly and annual reports on employees' earnings and F.I.C.A. tax, specifically the IRS Form 941a which is a list covering all employees and the IRS Form W-2 one of which (with copies) is prepared for each employee. Copies of the two forms are illustrated in Figure 17-11.

These forms can be prepared in any of three ways:

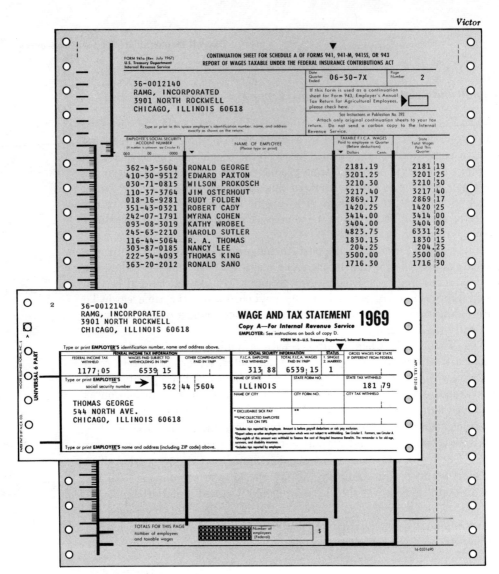

Figure 17-11. Quarterly and Annual IRS Reports Prepared on Terminal Computer

(1) If the employees' ledger is non-magnetic, use the to-date figures in that ledger to prepare the IRS reports manually by keyboard entry.

(2) If the employees' ledger is magnetic, prepare the IRS reports on the 820, using the magnetic accounts as input, or prepare them on a reader similar to Figure 7-24.

(3) If the employees' quarterly earnings records are kept on punched cards, the end-of-the-period file of cards can be used as input to the terminal computer to prepare the IRS forms as typewriter output.

Use of Addressograph Equipment in Payroll Work

Addressograph equipment is frequently used in payroll procedure for the repetitive writing of such standard data as name of employee, clock number, Social Security number, job description, and pay rate. It may be used to imprint employee's name and other information on time summary, payroll journal, work cards, pay envelopes, and earnings record.

Addressograph is also frequently used to write the employee's name and other information on the clock card, pay check, timekeeper's worksheet, and the like.

In some cases on salary payrolls, Addressograph may be used for writing such additional data as gross salary and fixed deductions. However, when accounting machines are also used, it is necessary to enter these amounts into registers and cross-footers to make it possible for the machine to compute net earnings.

Payroll Procedures with Ledgerless Bookkeeping

Ledgerless bookkeeping for payroll involves filing copies of pay checks for various purposes. After the payroll journal has been completed, with all computations made, the checks are typed with three carbons, showing name, date, pay period, hours worked, gross pay, F.I.C.A. deduction, withholding tax, other deductions, and net pay. Distribution and handling of the copies are as follows:

(1) Original—Pay check to the employee.
(2) Duplicate—"Stub" or employee's copy.
(3) Triplicate—Tax copy. Filed in individual envelope for each employee. Recapitulation made quarterly to obtain accumulations of F.I.C.A. pay or tax, withholding tax, and gross payroll.
(4) Quadruplicate—Serves as check register.

LABOR DISTRIBUTION

Functions: Organization

Payroll distribution is concerned with classifying and summarizing labor charges to produce (a) various operating reports and (b) the standard journal entries for recording labor in the General ledger. It also involves classifying and summarizing debits to various accounts for company's share of payroll taxes and insurance, and related charges.

In small organizations, payroll distribution usually is operated as part of payroll preparation in the payroll department. In such cases columnar distribution on the payroll journal may be used. In other cases where the volume is large, payroll distribution may be made by a separate set of clerks (such as the cost department), who prove their reports against controls established by the payroll department. In some manufacturing concerns, the labor distributions are made by the shop timekeepers of the several departments who send summaries to the cost department for consolidation and preparation of overall reports.

Classifications and Reports

In manufacturing concerns, common classifications of accounts for labor are:

(1) For direct labor:
   (a) Department
   (b) Operation
   (c) Job or production order
   (d) Production order by department, production order by operation
(2) For indirect labor:
   (a) Occupation (supervision, factory clerical, repairmen, and so on)
   (b) Department
   (c) Department by occupation

In mercantile concerns, common classifications of accounts are:

   (a) Function (administrative, buying, selling, and so on)
   (b) Department

Forms

Typical forms used in labor distribution are:

Original Media

(1) Departmental time sheets which the employees sign daily—one set of sheets for each department each day. These sheets are sometimes used in department stores and offices. Where the problem of employee transfers from department to department is not a difficult one, they may provide a satisfactory original record for distributing labor charges to departments.
(2) Shop time reports, described and illustrated in Chapter 16, often used to get a distribution of labor charges to expense accounts (indirect labor) or to jobs or production orders (direct labor):
   (a) Foreman's books or time cards.
   (b) Time sheets, job cards or tickets prepared by the shop clerk or by the employee.
(3) Combination attendance time and shop time records.

Summary Forms

These forms vary according to the method of distribution. Various summary forms are illustrated in the following sections.

Distribution as a By-Product of Payroll

Where the labor classification is simple (say, function or department) and where transfers of employees from department to department are not too numerous, it is often feasible to obtain the distribution of labor as a by-product of making the payroll. This may be done by (a) assigning clock numbers to employees by department and (b) setting up a separate payroll or set of payroll sheets for each department. The totals of the various payrolls provide the debits to labor in process account and other labor accounts in the journal entry for accrued payroll.

In some cases, a columnar distribution is combined with the payroll. The distribution section (right hand) provides a column for each department or other labor account. Entries can be made on the payroll proper (left hand sheet) from daily time reports and the earnings computed for each employee at the end of the week. Then the gross earnings record for each employee is distributed onto the columns on the right hand sheet. Where an employee spent his entire time in his home department, his gross earnings will be entered in one distribution column. Where he spent part of his time outside his home department, his gross earnings will be split between his home department and the other department, on the basis of hours shown on the daily time reports.

Methods of Distribution

Theoretically all of the basic methods of distribution (described in Chapter 12) may be used in connection with labor distribution. The following frequently used methods are illustrated in this chapter:

(1) Columnar account method.
(2) Summary strip-unit ticket method.
(3) Register method.

Columnar Account Method

Figures 17-12 through 17-14 illustrate a columnar account method of distribution of direct labor. A cost sheet (which is the columnar account form) is set up for each production order. The cost sheet, illustrated in Figure 17-13, comprises a column for each department, to provide the means for compiling the labor cost in each department on each production order.

The original media (not illustrated) are job tickets. One of these is written for each job on which each man works each day. The job tickets, which come to the distribution clerk in departmental batches, are sorted by production order number, totaled and posted to the cost sheets daily. The charge to Labor in Process for the total of direct labor comes from the payroll, via the General journal (page 409).

The total of indirect labor is charged to Account 510 through the General journal. A separate payroll is provided for employees working on indirect labor occupations. This illustration is based upon the assumption that indirect labor employees do in fact work on indirect labor operations exclusively, and do not work part of the time on indirect labor occupations and part of the time on direct labor occupations. Where employees work on both classes of labor, job tickets may be issued for indirect labor employees as well as for direct labor employees to provide for proper distribution, as described in the following section.

Summary Strip (Figure 17-15): Unit Tickets

Under this plan, job tickets (unit media) are provided for both direct labor and indirect labor. A separate job ticket is provided for each production order (if direct labor) or expense account (if indirect labor) on which each man works each day. The direct labor job tickets are sorted and filed by production order number, and these tickets are summarized periodically (say, weekly) onto summary cost sheets. The indirect labor job tickets are sorted by expense account and totaled onto summary strips which become the expense reports. A separate summary strip is provided for each department.

Illustrations of job tickets in unit form in this book are:

Figure 16-11.   Job tickets in perforated strips.
Figure 16-12.   Unit job tickets designed for needle sorting (Keysort: McBee Co.).

Register Method

Under this plan, the original media for distribution are daily time reports, one of which is written for each man each day. Each report shows the numbers of the accounts to be charged for the man's time, together with the hours and amount to be charged to each account.

It is assumed that a National Class 41 distribution machine similar to Figure 12-31 is used for the labor distribution. The machine illustrated is set up to provide a distribution to 6-18 accounts. In the operation of the machine, the distribution clerk handles the items "as they come" on the daily time reports (random posting method). The National Class 41 can be coupled to a tape punch to accommodate an extended classification of labor accounts. The tape can be processed in an in-house computer or a service bureau to produce labor reports.

GENERAL JOURNAL

FOR MONTH OF *January* 19___

DAY	DESCRIPTION OF ENTRY	GENERAL LEDGER DEBITS	√	Acct. No.	CREDITS	500 Manufacturing Exp. Acct. No.	AMOUNT	√	600 Administrative Exp. Acct. No.	AMOUNT	√	700 Selling Expense Acct. No.	AMOUNT	√	800 Shipping Exp. Acct. No.	AMOUNT	√
	AMOUNTS FORWARDED	$ 48000	√	142												$ 12000	√
13	Salary in Process																
	Expense					510	$ 24600	√							810	$	
	Accounts Accruable			120	$ 48000												
	Accrued OAB Tax—Employee's Share			231	1270												
	Withholding Tax Deducted			233	7650												
	Accrued Payroll			239	67400												
	Factory and shipping payroll for week.																
31	Expense					520	10890	√	610	$ 100000	√	710	$ 100000				
	Accrued OAB Tax—Employee's Share			231	3200												
	Withholding Tax Deducted			233	30000												
	Accrued Payroll			239	147000												
	Administrative Tax and office payroll for month.																
31	Old Age Benefit Tax																
	Accrued OAB Tax—Company's Share			232	7249	520	1089	√	620	1500	√	720	1500	√		1800	√
	To record company's share of OAB tax for month.																
31	Depreciation																
	Reserve for Depreciation					510	4000	√	610	1000	√	710	5700	√		1000	√
	To record depreciation for month.																
31	Insurance Expense																
	Prepaid Insurance					530	3200	√	630	500	√	710	500	√		500	√
	To record insurance expired.																
		$ 48000			$ 299869	510	32269		610	102500		710	102500		810	12500	
						520	24600		620	100000		720	100000		810	12000	
							1089		620	1500		720	1500		620	180	
							7000		630	1500		710	1500		620	500	
						530	32269			102500			102500			12500	

Figure 17-12.   Columnar Account Method of Labor Distribution

409

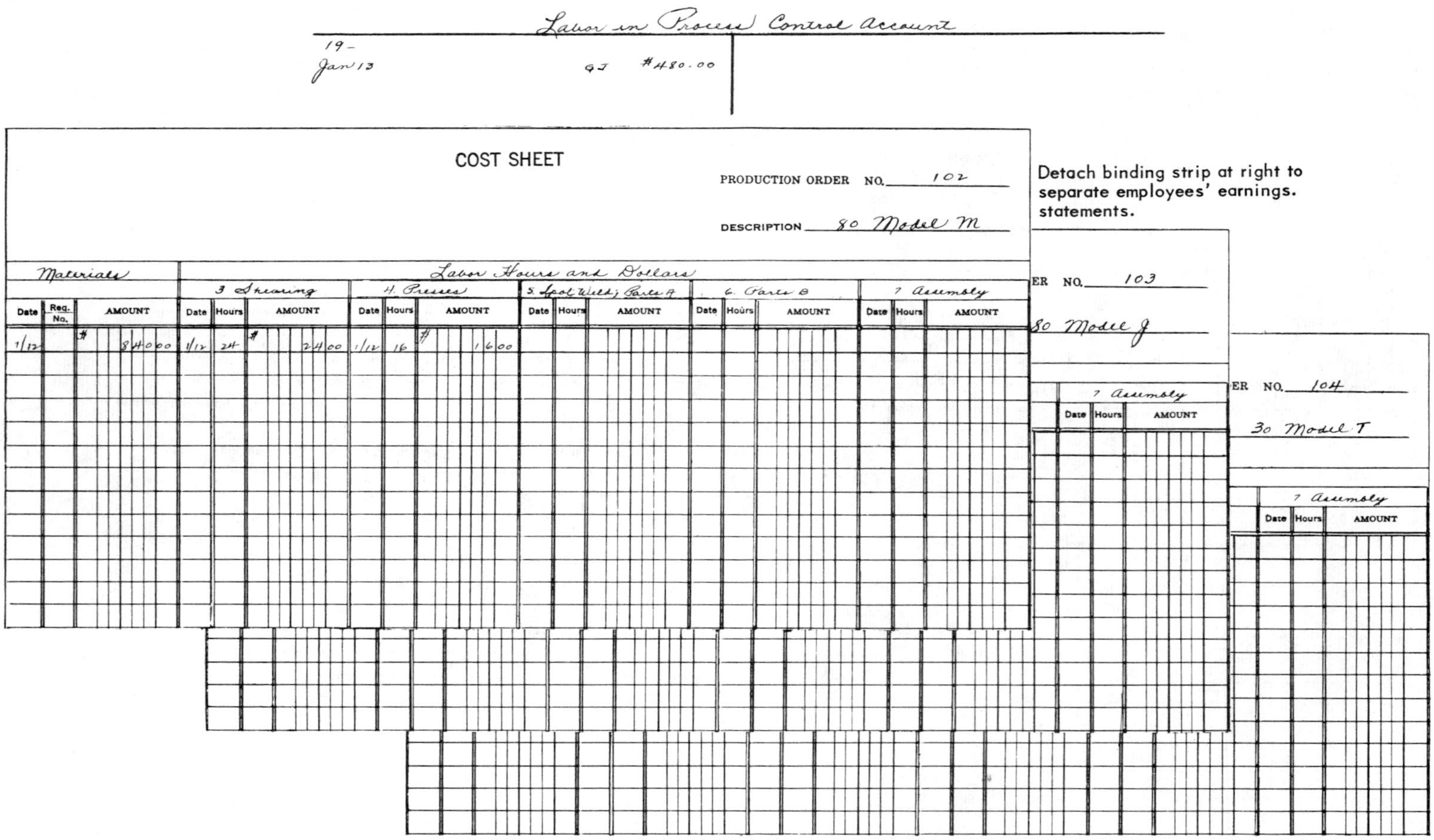

Labor in Process Control Account

19—
Jan 13   GJ $480.00

Detach binding strip at right to separate employees' earnings statements.

COST SHEET

PRODUCTION ORDER NO. _____ 102

DESCRIPTION _____ 80 Model M

Materials			3 Forming			4 Pressing			5 Spot Welding Bolts			6 Parts B			7 Assembly		
Date	Req. No.	AMOUNT	Date	Hours	AMOUNT	Date	Hours	AMOUNT	Date	Hours	AMOUNT	Date	Hours	AMOUNT	Date	Hours	AMOUNT
1/12		$4000.00	1/12	24	$240.00	1/12	16	$160.00									

ER NO. _____ 103

80 Model J

Date	Hours	AMOUNT

ER NO. _____ 104

30 Model T

Date	Hours	AMOUNT

Figure 17-13. Cost Sheet

ACCOUNT NO. 500 — ACCOUNT Manufacturing Expense Control

DATE 19__	POST. REF.	Control AMOUNT	510 Salaries	520 Payroll Taxes Insurance	530 Operating Supplies	540 Maintenance Supplies	550 Purchased Service	560 Travel	570 Unclassified	580 Fixed Charges
Jan 31	VR	110000			87000	2000	18000	3000		
31	GJ	32689	24600	1089						7000

ACCOUNT NO. 600 — ACCOUNT Administrative Expense Control

DATE 19__	POST. REF.	Control AMOUNT	610 Salaries	620 Payroll Taxes Insurance	630 Operating Supplies	640 Maintenance Supplies	650 Purchased Service	660 Travel	670 Unclassified	680 Fixed Charges
Jan 31	VR	7500			500	2000	1000	4000		
31	GJ	103000	100000	1500						1500

ACCOUNT NO. 700 — ACCOUNT Selling Expense Control

DATE 19__	POST. REF.	Control AMOUNT	710 Salaries	720 Payroll Taxes Insurance	730 Operating Supplies	740 Maintenance Supplies	750 Purchased Service	760 Travel	770 Unclassified	780 Fixed Charges
Jan 31	VR	13000			2000	4000	1000	4000		
31	GJ	102500	100000	1500						1000

ACCOUNT NO. 800 — ACCOUNT Shipping Expense Control

DATE 19__	POST. REF.	Control AMOUNT	810 Salaries	820 Payroll Taxes Insurance	830 Operating Supplies	840 Maintenance Supplies	850 Purchased Service	860 Travel	870 Unclassified	880 Fixed Charges
Jan 31	VR	8000			5000	1000	2000	3000		
31	GJ	13680	12000	180						1500

Figure 17-14. Columnar Expense Accounts

411

H R C FORM 27

MFG. EXPENSE REPORT

Dept.

Date

Hours	Acct. No.	Amount
	511	
	512	
	513	
	514	
	515	
	519	
	520	
	531	
	532	
	533	
	534	
	539	
	541	
	542	
	543	
	551	
	552	
	553	
	554	
	555	
	570	
	581	
	582	
	583	
	584	
	585	
	500A	
	Total	

FORM F-285

DEPARTMENTAL EXPENSE DISTRIBUTION

DEPT. NO.

MONTH

LABOR	MATERIALS AND POWER	MISCELLANEOUS	ACCOUNT No.	TOTAL
			511	
			512	
			513	
			514	
			515	
			519	
			520	
			531	
			532	
			533	
			534	
			539	
			541	
			542	
			543	
			551	
			552	
			553	
			554	
			555	
			570	
			581	
			582	
			583	
			584	
			585	
			500A	
			TOTAL	

Figure 17-15. Summary Strip Forms for Manufacturing Expense

18

Production Control Procedures;
Perpetual Inventory Procedures

Function

A production order is written instructions to a foreman or other responsible factory executive to produce goods specified according to the dates indicated in the order. Where the factory consists of a number of departments, which is usual except in the smallest organizations, production orders are issued to the various executives in such manner as to make possible the coordination of the operations of the various departments in matters of both time and quantity performance. A production order system is a set of procedures whereby production orders are issued in the first place in a manner which will coordinate sales, materials, plant facilities, and the available personnel, followed up to determine that the expected performance has been accomplished, and adjusted by the issue of changes in instructions if adjustment be necessary.

As will be indicated later under the heading of forms, the production order proper is sometimes accompanied by (a) a bill of material which is a complete list of materials and parts which shall be used in making the product named in the production order, and (b) an operations list which shows the operations required to produce the order, stated in the sequence of performance, and the machines or other facilities required to do the operations.

Organization

The production control procedure operates with direct reference to the sales order procedure, through which customers' orders are received, the purchase order procedure through which materials are ordered from suppliers, and the shipping order procedure, through which the shipment of goods to customers is effectuated. In some manufacturing organizations, the issue of production orders may be purely a factory clerical function, and the production orders may be issued from copies of sales orders which come from the sales department, or from month by month production schedules set up by the sales manager and the factory manager. In other cases, particularly where the short-run desires of the sales department and the factory are not consistent, production control may be the responsibility of a separate person or department, and top management will decide policy matters, such as the size and variety of inventories to be carried and the nature of delivery priorities to which the company can commit itself.

Types of Production Control Procedure

There are two basic types of production control procedure:

(1) Specific order production control procedure in which an order is issued to the factory to produce a specified lot of production, which lot is identified by the serial number of the production order as it moves through the factory. The application of a specific order production control procedure depends upon the possibility of identifying successive lots of production as they pass through the factory, as well as the desirability of identifying lots for control purposes. For example, specific order production control procedures are used:

(a) For custom jobs as in printing plants. The orders or jobs which pass through the plant are identified separately, and all scheduling of jobs and control of movement is done by reference to the number of the order. Control means getting the particular job done to meet a promised date.

(b) In assembly-type manufacture where
1. Parts are manufactured on parts-production orders,
2. Parts are assembled into subassemblies on subassembly orders, and
3. Subassemblies are assembled into final assemblies on final-assembly orders.

(c) In process type manufacture like paint and sausage and other food industries where product is made according to a formula or recipe. Batch orders are issued showing the quantities of product to be made, the formulas or recipes, and the quantities of materials to be used.

(2) Repetitive order production control procedure, in which an order is issued to the factory to produce specified goods during the coming period (say, one month). Identification of particular lots of production is either not possible or not desired. Production is controlled by simply issuing a schedule of quantities desired and then obtaining reports of quantities produced periodically (perhaps daily) to determine whether the schedules are being met.

Examples of repetitive order production control procedures are found in cement mills and in blast furnace departments where pig iron is produced. In these plants, it is not possible to identify successive lots of products because batches of input merge in process. Another example occurs in a certain camera factory where one model of camera is produced on an assembly line. Here it is possible to identify successive lots, but it is not desired to do so. The company simply budgets quantities to be produced period by period. Control in this case means getting a specified quantity of product completed in the time interval for which the repetitive orders or schedules are released.

Classifications: Managerial Information

The basic classification of the specific order production control procedures is the production order classification. This may be a sequence code (simple serial numbers) applied to the orders as they are issued, or it may be a block classification in which certain series of numbers are reserved for the orders issued to certain departments. Other classifications to be found in connection with specific order production control are the materials classification, the finished product classification, and the producing department classification.

The basic classification of the repetitive order production control procedure is the product classification (since orders are issued in terms of specified products for specified periods of time).

In connection with specific order production control procedures, the management wants to know:

(1) When a prospective job can be got through the factory. The answer to the question of completion is based upon the availability of machine capacity (as shown by the machine load file) and the availability of materials.

(2) Whether a job in process will be finished by the promised date. This information is provided through the procedures of follow-up.

In connection with repetitive order production control, the management wants to know what quantities (in units, dozens, pounds, and the like) of product were produced by each department in the sequence through which the product passes, and what quantities were finally finished for finished goods stores. This information is used to:

(1) Determine the rate of production in a department, and thus to apply physical measure of performance. The management of a plant in which repetitive production control is in use will likely receive a daily production report for each department. This report is significant to the experienced manager because he knows how many units each department should produce.

(2) Determine product costs if a process cost system is in use.

(3) Plan production of future periods, when used in connection with statistics on sales, unfilled orders, and inventories (materials, work in process, and finished goods).

Inventory position reports illustrated: Figure 18-1 is a report of sales, unfilled orders, and work in process used by a manufacturing company in working out the production plan for a coming period (say, one week). Note that the report shows not only what production is coming up but what production is likely to be needed to take care of unfilled sales orders. In addition, the sales figures are one guide for estimating future sales that will have to be provided for.

SALES AND INVENTORY POSITION REPORT

					Work in Progress					
Product No.	Sales to Date this Month	Sales Year to Date	Unfilled Sales Orders	Shearing	Punch Press; Drill Press	Spot Weld; Parts A	Parts B	Assembly	Unfilled Production Orders	Finished Goods Inventory
101										
102										
103										
etc.										

Figure 18-1. Sales and Inventory Position Report

Forms

Forms commonly used in specific order production control procedures are:

(1) Production order, which is an order issued to a foreman or other executive directing him to produce a specific product or to perform specified operations on the product. Usually the date when the product is to be delivered to the next department or to finished goods stores is shown. Where several departments are involved in getting out the goods, a copy of the production order may be provided for each department.

(2) Bill of materials, which is a list of the materials required for a production order. It shows the quantity of each material required for the quantity of finished product indicated on the production order to which it relates.

The basic bills of material for a product are made out by the planning department when the product is planned, and the quantities allowed for production orders are set out as the production orders are written.

(3) Requisition, which is a request for the storekeeper to issue specified materials. Where the materials are to be used for a particular production order, the number of the order is shown on the requisi-

tion. Requisitions may be issued by the planning clerk or by the foreman who needs the materials.

(4) Operation list, which is a list of operations necessary to be performed to produce a particular production order, stated in the order in which they are to be performed and showing the type of machine or other facilities to be used for the operation and in some cases, the particular machine to be used. Where a standard time has been set for each of the operations, the operation list may show the time allowed to perform each operation in the quantity shown by the production order.

The basic operation lists for a product are made out by the planning department when the product is planned, and the standard times allowed for production orders are set out as the production orders are written.

(5) A traveler or route card is an operation list set up on card stock and fastened to the materials or the tote box in which the materials are carried for the purpose of showing the shop people how the job is to be moved from work place to work place. As each operation is completed, the shop porter can refer to the route card to determine where to move the job for the next operation.

(6) Job tickets have been illustrated and described in connection with timekeeping (Figures 16-10 and 16-11). One of these tickets is issued for each operation to be performed on a job. Where job tickets are used mainly for payroll and cost accounting purposes, they may be issued by a dispatcher or timekeeper as the job is assigned to an operator for performance of a particular operation, and the starting time for the operation can be stamped on the job ticket at that moment. Where the job tickets are used for planning and production control purposes, the job tickets for a job (one for each operation to be performed) may be issued when the production order is issued. The job tickets may then be filed according to the machines or other work facilities to be used, in a machine load file, which would accordingly show the jobs ahead for each machine. As each operation is assigned for performance, the appropriate job ticket is pulled from the machine load file and stamped with the starting time for the operation. The job ticket is then used for payroll and cost accounting purposes as described in the chapters on timekeeping and payroll.

Note that where the job tickets in the machine load file show the standard time allowed for the operations, the machine load file for a particular operation will show (by adding the tickets) the total time the machine will be required for the jobs scheduled. Such a file is useful in the scheduling function because it can be used to show on what date a machine required for a certain operation will be available or, in some cases, what jobs must be re-scheduled to make it possible to move up a rush job.

In repetitive order production control the order proper and requisitions or other forms used to get materials into production are the basic forms.

Production Control Plans: Outline of Main Considerations

Four production control plans are described briefly in this chapter, making use of various combinations of the forms described in the previous section:

(1) Custom goods manufactured to the customer's order and entirely according to customer's specifications, for delivery immediately upon completion (no finished goods inventory carried).

(2) Style goods manufactured against customer's orders, mostly to company specifications but in some particulars according to customer's specifications, for delivery during a style season on delivery dates as promised by the sales department.

(3) Parts manufactured for stock and used out of stock to produce subassemblies or sold out of stock.

(4) Process manufacture: goods manufactured by formula or recipe.

Analysis of some of the main features of the first two production control plans named above appears in Figure 18-2 in which the following points are listed:

(1) Type of production order plan (specific order or repetitive order).

(2) On the basis of what records are delivery promises made to customers?

(3) Time interval between receipt of sales order and shipment of goods.

(4) Are materials ordered from suppliers
 (a) To cover specific customer's orders,
 (b) To keep inventories at prescribed levels, or
 (c) According to a production plan made for the season, which anticipates customers' orders?

(5) Are materials passed through perpetual materials inventory accounts?

(6) In writing production orders, what current records are consulted:
 (a) Sales order file?
 (b) Receiving reports?
 (c) Materials ledger?
 (d) Machine load file, showing for what jobs each machine is already scheduled?
 (e) Finished goods ledger?
 (f) Other records?

(7) Are all the materials required for a production order released

when the production order is issued or are the materials released piecemeal?

(8) On what form are materials released from store room to production: bill of materials or requisition?

(9) Is a machine load file maintained, and if so, how?

(10) Does the entire (specific) production order move intact from point to point (department, machine, or inspection point), or are there split production orders? If the entire order does not move intact, it may be necessary to keep track of the quantity on each job order which has passed through each department or operation.

(11) Is any formal method required to route an order from machine to machine?

(12) What check on quantities is operated as the order moves from point to point?

(13) Where the order moves intact, how is the progress of the order reported?

(14) Where the order does not move intact, how is the movement of quantities controlled and reported?

(15) Is an in-process record of quantities necessary for production control purposes or control of scrap or theft?

(16) Are there banks of processed materials between departments?

(17) What final check of quantities produced on a production order is made as the goods are delivered to finished goods warehouse?

(18) Is there a perpetual inventory of finished goods?

Illustrative Procedure: Custom Goods Manufactured to Customer's Order and Specifications for Immediate Delivery (Figure 18-2)

The diagram illustrates the main steps of paper work for a production order procedure of a small printing plant. The principal form is the production order proper, a copy of which is made out for each department (composing room, press room, bindery). Note that the planning clerk who writes the production orders also writes the purchase orders for outside purchases (paper and other materials not carried in stock, plates made outside, and so on).

The planning clerk sends the production order and departmental copies to the factory office where the copies are filed by department in a load file. The production order shows what equipment is to be used on the job (linotype or monotype, presses, bindery equipment), and the factory office is able to estimate the availability of any unit of equipment by scanning the load file. Since the plant is small, it is considered sufficient to file the production order copies by department rather than by individual machine to be used.

Items	Goods Manufactured to Customer's Order	
	For delivery as soon as completed (Pages 419-422)	*For production and delivery during a style season, according to promised delivery dates*
Type of production order plan.	Specific order: custom jobs.	Specific order; one order may be a combination of several customers' orders.
On basis of what records are delivery promises made to customers?	(a) Sales order file, showing orders received, not yet scheduled. (b) Inquiries made to prospective suppliers as to probable receiving dates of materials. (c) Machine load file showing what jobs each machine is already scheduled for.	Sales orders are tabulated by month of delivery promised. During the early part of the season, these quantities promised by months are compared with planned production. As the season gets under way, they are compared with quantities on production orders issued.
Time interval between receipt of sales order and shipment of goods.	Manufacturing time and in some cases time required to get materials.	Up to six months.
Materials ordered from suppliers: (a) to cover specific customers' orders, or (b) to keep inventories at prescribed levels, or (c) according to a production plan.	To cover specific customers' orders (most materials items).	According to a production plan (made for the season) which anticipates customers' orders.
Are materials passed through perpetual material inventory records?	No. (Exception: certain sundries.)	Yes.
In writing production orders, what current records are consulted?	(a) Sales order file, showing orders received, not yet scheduled. (b) Receiving reports and (for occasional items) materials ledger. (c) Machine load file showing for what jobs each machine is already scheduled.	(a) Sales orders accepted tabulated by promised month of delivery compared with (b) production orders issued tabulated by month of expected completion. Excess of (a) over (b) shows balance open to produce. This is checked against materials available and producing capacity available.
Are all the materials required for a production order released when that production order is issued, or are the materials released piece meal?	Materials are released piece meal.	All materials are released when the production order is issued.
On what form are materials released from store room to production?	Requisition written by superintendent's clerk.	Bill of materials written by production order clerk.
Is a machine load file maintained, and if so, how?	Yes; copy of production order for each department (or machine) concerned is filed in load file.	No; production orders are released with due regard to available capacity of departments (production plan, to date).
For control purposes, does the entire production order move intact from point to point (department, machine, or inspection point) or are there split (production) orders?	Entire job moves intact.	Entire job moves intact.

Table 18-1

PRODUCTION ORDER PROCEDURES: OUTLINE OF MAIN FEATURES

Is any formal method required to route an order from machine to machine?	Production order shows operation list which in turn shows machine number and name.	Route card showing operations in sequence accompanies the goods through the factory.
What check on quantities is operated as the order moves from point to point?	Inspectors check quantities against copies of production orders.	Inspectors check quantities against copies of production orders.
Where the order moves intact, how is progress of the order reported?	Inspector in a department gives completed production order to foreman who sends it to factory office.	Inspector in a department gives completed production order to foreman who sends it to planning clerk.
Where the entire order does not move intact, how is movement of quantities controlled and reported?	——	——
Is an in-process record of quantities necessary for production control purposes or control of scrap or theft?	None, except the inspector's copies of production orders.	None, except the inspector's copies of production orders.
Are there banks of processed materials between departments?	Yes; production orders intact.	Yes; production orders intact.
What final check on quantities produced on a production order is made as goods are delivered to finished goods warehouse?	There is no finished goods inventory; quantities shipped are checked against copy of production order by the shipping clerk.	Shipping clerk checks quantities received into shipping room against copy of production order.
Is there a perpetual inventory of finished goods?	No.	Portion of production order marked "reserve stock" is passed through perpetual inventory. Immediate shipments are not passed through perpetual inventory.

Table 18-1 (continued)

The factory office clerk files the production order copies for each department as nearly as possible in the order in which they are to be done. In case of jobs that cannot be run because certain outside materials have not been received, the production order copies are filed at the back of the file pocket for the department. When the factory office receives a receiving report showing that the materials in question have come in, the factory office clerk moves the appropriate production order into an active scheduling position in the file. Note that the load file is not designed to show when each job will be run in each department, but simply the order in which the jobs will be run in each department. The factory office clerk determines when a department is ready for another job by keeping in touch with the departments.

When a department is nearly ready for a new job, the clerk pulls the appropriate production order copy from the file pocket for the department and takes it to the foreman of the department, at the same time putting the "Factory" copy of the production order, a control copy, in the front position in the department file pocket. The control copy is pink, and its position indicates where the job is at any time.

When the job has passed through the last department, the shipping clerk prepares the job for shipping and checks the quantities against the "shipping" copy of the production order, marking that copy "shipped" and the date. The billing clerk bills from the shipping copy of the production order.

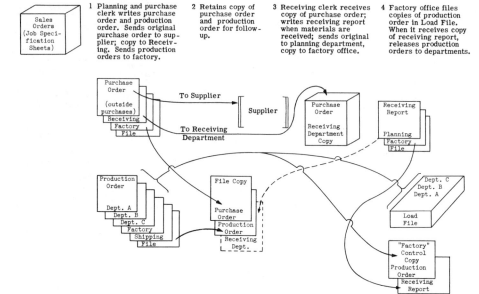

Figure 18-2. Production Order Procedure: Goods Manufactured to Customer's Order—Delivery as Completed

Style Goods Manufactured Against Customers' Orders for Future Delivery

In the manufacture and sales of seasonal style goods it is common for the manufacturer to set up a line of products each style season and to estimate the quantity of each style to be produced each month of the style season. There may be a Spring season and a Fall season. Sales estimates are matched with productive capacity and the production budget is set on the basis of productive capacities.

Purchase contracts are let for the materials that will be required, with the stipulation that materials will be called according to dates to be determined as the season gets under way. Samples of the styles are manufactured and the salesmen show the line to customers, taking orders for delivery in specified months. As orders are received by the manufacturer, they are sorted down by style number and month of promised delivery and tabulated so that the manufacturer knows what quantities of each product he has promised for delivery in each month of the style season.

The manufacturer schedules production orders month by month and product by product against the sales promises. He keeps a running tally according to month of delivery. The excess of production orders over sales orders accepted for any month and style is known as "stock" (this is really a future available balance open to sell; it is not stock in the sense that a perpetual inventory shows the balance on hand right now). Any excess of sales orders over production orders is known as "unfilled orders" (actually "uncovered" orders).

Note that, as was indicated in the chapter on order and billing procedures, the analysis of orders by promised month and style may be obtained by producing *unit* shipping orders, and sorting them down by month and style. The orders may be filed in the same way. The orders for any month can then be pulled from file at the appropriate time and sent to the warehouse for shipments.

Parts Manufactured for Stock and Sold or Used Out of Stock

Figure 18-3 is a master production order and operations card used for parts production.[1] The form illustrated is a translucent paper master designed for use with a copying machine. One of these forms is set up for each part to be manufactured. Each form is drawn for the specific quantity of parts to be produced in a lot.

The original paper master is filled out by a manufacturing process engineer at the time the part is designed and approved for production. It shows, among other things:

(1) Part Number.
(2) Part Description.
(3) List of materials and quantities of each allowed per hundred parts.
(4) List of labor operations with designation of machine to be used and standard set-up time for the operation and operating time (the latter in terms of quantity per hour).

The translucent paper master is kept in file and changed as and when the engineering details of the part are changed. The paper master is used only for making matte film masters which are tough stock on which variable information can be entered and wiped off as desired. The matte film master is produced on a copying machine directly from the translucent paper master (that is, a master is produced directly from a master).

The matte film master is used whenever production order copies are to be produced. Variable information such as work order number, quantity, date issued and date required and also materials quantities and labor time allowances are entered.

[1] The illustrated forms were supplied by Charles Bruning Company, and the information in this section was taken by permission from company bulletins.

SHEET 1 OF 1	PRODUCTION ORDER AND OPERATIONS CARD	PART NO. 30346

PART NO. 30346	W.O. NUMBER 5200	QUANTITY 1500	LOT	DATE ISSUED 5/15	DATE REQUIRED 6/25	AVERAGE RUN 5000	OPERATIONS RECORD

PREPARED 2/23/53 — BY L.Z. — PRINT ISSUE 4
REVISED 5/21/56 — BY L.Z. — REVISION ISSUE 1

DESCRIPTION: SWITCH FRAME

R.M. NO.	DESCRIPTION	QUANTITY PER C	UNIT COST	STANDARD COST PER C	TOTAL QUANTITY
885-5563	14 GA. (.064) 48 X 144 ALUMINUM	.044	.66		MODEL USED ON 3829 BRAZING MACHINE
	CUT 2304/SHEET				QUANTITY 1
88-1528	1/2 DIA. B1113 C.R.S.	2.9 FT.	44 FT.		SUB-ASSEMBLY USED IN 30350

DELIVER MATERIAL TO DEPT. _____ ON _____ TOTAL

OPER.	DEPT.	MACH.	DESCRIPTION	SPEED	FEED	TOOLS	LOC.	QTY. PER HR	SET UP HOURS	HOURS PER C	SET UP PER C / TOTAL TIME	LABOR RATE / WEEK SCH'D	LABOR COST / QTY COMPT.	BURDEN RATE / SCRAP	BURDEN / DATE COMPT.	BY WHOM
2	2	102	SHEAR TO 2 1/4" STRIPS					278 STRIPS		.02	.3	5/16				
4	4	1631	BLANK OUT PART			BLANKING TOOL	NS	714	1.0	.14	2.1	5/30				
6	4	1631	FORM			FORMING FIXTURE	R8	200	.6	.5	7.5	4/12				
8	10	2114	DRILL HOLE			DRILL JIG	P1	200	.5	.5	7.5	4/20				
10	10	2132	TAP			STD.	G5	200	.5	.5	7.5	4/22				
12	2	4401	C' DRILL	1100	H	E-1	AA1	41	.99	2.47	37.0	4/25				
			DRILL #9 (.196)	1100	.0025	STD	C3									
			TURN .311 +.000 -.002	1100	.0025	BOX TOOL	F6									
			CUT OFF TO 7/64 APPROX.	1100	H	1/2" WIDE	B84									
14			INSPECT													
16			STOCK													

FORM C 808

Bruning

Figure 18-3. Production Order and Operations Card

From this master, such copies as the following would be produced on the copying machine:

(1) Requisition for materials. The requisition form is a small one, copied from the upper left section of the master.

(2) Production order proper, called a shop scheduling copy. This form and the following ones, are copies of the entire master.

(3) Traveler, copied on heavy stock. It accompanies the goods through the operations. Each operator enters good quantity, scrap quantity and his initials on the appropriate line as he completes his operation.

(4) Time record copy. This copy can be produced on heavy stock providing spaces on the back for compiling job time.

(5) Cost copy. The right hand columns (which are dual purpose columns) are used by the cost department to compile the cost of the job when completed.

After the copies have been made, the variable information is erased or wiped (with a damp cloth) from the matte film master. New variable information can be entered on the master when it is desired to produce another parts order set.

Subassembly orders and *final-assembly* orders would be produced in the same way as parts orders described above.

Process Manufacture: Goods Manufactured by Formula or Recipe

Examples of one type of process production are paint manufacture and food manufacture. In this type of manufacture the operating people concerned with production must be notified not only what to produce and when it is required but also what materials and how much of each material to use. A large variety of products may be manufactured and formulas or recipes may change from time to time.

Figure 18-4 is an illustration of a master batch sheet for paint manufacture. The formula for a particular specification of product is recorded

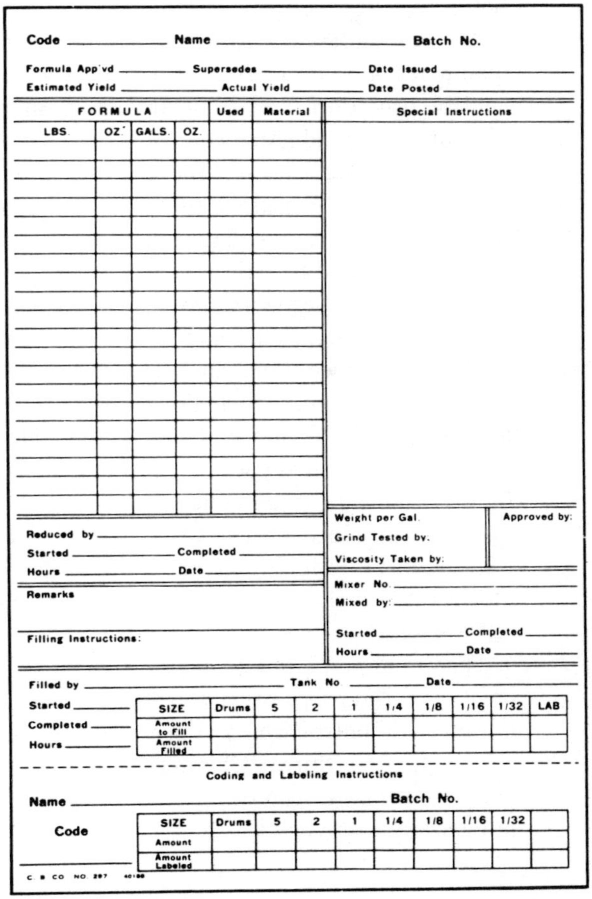

Figure 18-4. Batch and Formula Record: Process Manufacture

Bruning

on this sheet (which is a transluscent paper for use on a copying machine) and it is used to produce copies which are issued to operating people. Variable information is entered on the master as required for each production order, and removed after the copies are made.

PERPETUAL INVENTORIES

Function and Organization

A perpetual inventory procedure is a procedure whereby a card or account or other compiling mechanism is kept for each type or description of goods to show the quantity on hand. The cards or other forms are charged for acquisitions and credited for goods used or shipped out. The balance on hand is determined by the formula: previous balance on hand plus acquisitions minus used or shipped equals new balance on hand. The following sections illustrate and explain materials and finished goods inventory procedures and also quantity controls for work in process. The perpetual inventory records may be carried in quantities or values or both.

As was indicated earlier in this chapter, perpetual inventories in quantities are often an integral part of the planning and production control procedure and they are likely in that case to be kept by the planning and production control people. The major purpose of the records may be re-order control. Balances on hand shown by the materials accounts may be consulted to determine whether purchase orders should be issued, and both the materials accounts and the finished goods accounts may be consulted to determine whether production orders should be issued. In other cases, perpetual inventories in values or quantities and values may be an integral part of the cost accounting system, and they may be kept by the accounting or cost accounting department. These records may be used mainly to make it possible to obtain financial statements more frequently than would be possible under physical inventory methods.

Sometimes a single set of perpetual inventory records will serve both the requirements of planning and production control and those of financial and cost accounting. The feasibility of such combined usage should be considered in designing inventory procedures because of the possible (or at least theoretical) clerical economy in making a single set of records serve several purposes.

The use of perpetual inventory records as a control against waste, theft, or other misappropriation should be mentioned at this point. The chart on internal control which appears in the chapter on Purchase Order and Receiving Procedures (Chapter 14, Figure 14-7) illustrates how the perpetual inventory records are fitted into the plan of internal control of purchase and payment.

Materials Classifications: Managerial Information

The characteristics recognized in the materials classification depend upon the use to be made of the classification. Where the materials accounts are used for re-order control, the classification may incorporate even relatively minute physical specifications down to sizes and weights necessary for identifying the items to be ordered from suppliers.

Where the accounts are used mainly for financial or budget control, on the other hand, materials may be classified broadly according to balance sheet classification (raw materials, supplies, accessories, expense) or within these classes according to general physical types which correspond to or suggest particular uses (paints and varnishes, paper, and so on). The object of the classification is to make it possible for the management to judge the reasonableness of the current dollar investment in inventories by comparing the current balances with previous balances or by considering the investment in relationship to the current or expected volume of business, or other factors.

The control of inventories to the end of determining that the investment is not excessive is an essential element, along with the coordination of inventories with sales on the one hand and production capacity on the other hand. Various authorities estimate the cost of owning and maintaining an inventory in a manufacturing concern at from 20 per cent to 25 per cent of the investment in the inventories. It follows that excessive investment can become a considerable burden upon profits.

Forms

The following account forms are used in perpetual inventory procedures:

(1) Raw materials accounts; finished goods accounts. The function of these accounts is to show the quantities on hand. An account is set up for each type of materials or finished goods. The same basic forms may be used for both groups. The form comprises three sections. When used for materials the sections are headed "received," "issued," and "balance on hand." When used for finished goods they are headed "produced," "shipped," and "balance on hand." The forms may be set up for quantities, values, or both quantities and values.

The raw materials accounts may also have memorandum sections for materials on order (in which purchase orders issued are entered) and reserved or appropriated (in which the quantities required for production orders planned or written but not yet released are entered).

(2) Work in process accounts: quantities only (not illustrated). These accounts provide a control of quantities in process for purposes of

(a) production control, or (b) proof of quantities reported for piece rate wage payment, or (c) both. An account may be set up for each type of goods manufactured or each job order and the account may provide a column for each department or operation. Quantities produced in each department or operation would then be posted to the appropriate columns. A record of this kind will show (by subtraction of "quantity completed—this operation" from "quantity completed—previous department") how many units are in each department.

Note that a record of this kind is useful for control of quantities reported for piece work wage payment. In some plants this record is kept mainly for this purpose. If one department shows that 50 units were reported for piece work wage payment and the previous department shows only 40, there is evidence of possible over-reporting in the former department.

In job order cost systems, the Work in Process ledger may comprise a file of cost sheets of the open production orders. These cost sheets may either supplement or supplant the work in process quantity controls indicated in the previous paragraph.

(3) Posting media. The materials accounts may be debited from purchases invoices or receiving reports and credited from requisitions or bills of materials. The Work in Process accounts may receive entries from move tickets or job tickets. The Finished Goods accounts may be debited from move tickets written to cover movement of goods into the finished goods stores and credited from copies of shipping orders or sales invoices.

Requisition Forms

The following requisition forms are illustrative:

(1) Requisition form designed for needle sorting (Keysort—Figure 18–5).

Figure 18-5. Requisition Form for Needle Sorting (Keysort)

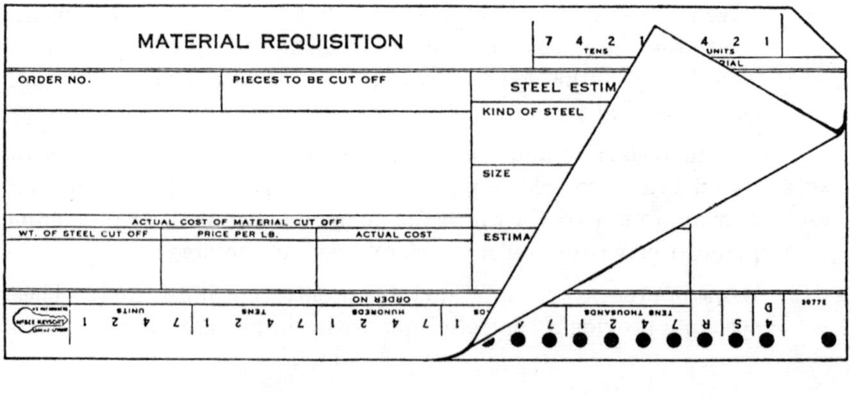

(2) Requisition form designed for ledgerless bookkeeping.

Methods of Operating Inventory Accounts

The three methods of operating perpetual inventory accounts are:

(1) Conventional pen-and-ink.
(2) Machine posting.
(3) Ledgerless.

These methods are explained in the following sections.

Conventional Pen-and-Ink Posted Inventory Accounts

Figure 5-4 (in Chapter 5) and Figure 18-6 are pen-and-ink forms of inventory accounts. Both of these forms provide sections for received, issued, and balance. Figure 5-4 is designed for quantities only and Figure 18-6 for both quantities and amounts. In addition to the basic information, the latter form provides spaces for quantities required and quantities ordered.

Posting media (invoices, requisitions, and the like) are usually posted directly to accounts of this type, and where dollar controls are maintained the daily totals or batch totals are entered in a requisition journal to build up the control total which is posted at desired intervals to the appropriate control accounts. Postings to the Materials ledger and the computation of balances in the accounts are proved at desired intervals by taking a trial balance of the accounts in the ledger and comparing the total with the balance of the control account.

Machine Posting: Crediting Materials Accounts
(Quantity and Value)

Machine posted accounts (not illustrated) are sometimes used to carry running balances of quantities and values. The posting operation is basically the one of picking up the old balance, posting the debit or credit, and printing the new balance, with which the reader is familiar. It involves, however, picking up two old balances (quantity and value). The requisitions are priced and extended before they come to the machine operation. Direct proof may be used. The amounts printed on the proof tape should be the same as the amounts of the requisitions. Proof totals shown by the proof tape should be the same as the pre-list totals of the media.

The proof sheet of this posting operation can be designed as a current report of materials balances (since it would show the new balance of each account posted during the posting run). The report can be used by the clerks responsible for re-order as notice of low balances on hand.

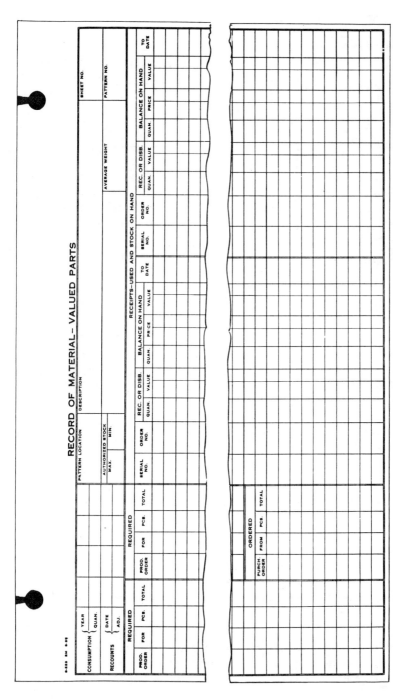

Figure 18-6. Stock Record (Special Form)

Sections for received or disbursed, and balance on hand. Quantities and values. Spaces for consumption by year (Quantity) and authorized stock; maximum and minimum. Spaces for entry of counts by physical inventory. Entries are made in the "Required" section for production orders as they are issued, and crossed off as the related requisitions come through, so that the materials ledger clerk can compare the requirements for production orders "to come" with the materials on hand and on order. Purchase orders are entered in the "Ordered" section as the copies of purchase orders come from the purchasing department, indicating that goods have been ordered. They are crossed off as goods are received, so that the materials ledger clerk can determine unfilled purchase orders at any time.

Ledgerless Bookkeeping

The equipment for ledgerless bookkeeping consists of a file which provides a clip for each materials account. The requisitions, which are designed to be filed in the clips, provide spaces for picking up the old balance, subtracting therefrom the quantity shown by the requisition, and bringing down a new balance.

A stock card provides space for entering successive materials prices, for use if the requisitions are to be priced and extended. The balances of the "accounts" can be proved by operating a Control account for the file and taking a trial balance of the accounts periodically for comparison with the balance of the Control account.

METHODS OF DISTRIBUTION: MATERIALS REQUISITIONS

Method Factor to to Considered	Unit Account Method	Summary Strip Method
Description of classification of accounts.	Production order cost sheets.	Expense account classification.
Number of accounts in classification.	200 production orders active at any one time.	7 departments × 10 objects accounts = 70 accounts.
Quantity of media.	100 requisitions per day.	140 requisitions per day.
Type of media.	Unit; one production order per requisition.	Unit; one expense account per requisition.
Average amount of debit per requisition.	$40.	$10.
Is detail posting with description desired?	Yes, detail posting with description of materials.	No.
Frequency of distributing debits.	Daily.	Weekly.
Method of distribution.	Unit account (production order cost sheet is the account form).	Summary strip.

Figure 18-7.

MATERIALS DISTRIBUTION

Methods; Factors in Selection

The distribution of debits from materials requisitions is often a simple problem because, as regards the debit accounts affected, the requisitions are often unit media. Requisitions for direct materials can often be drawn só that each requisition carries a charge to only one production order cost sheet. Likewise, requisitions for indirect materials or supplies can often be drawn so that each requisition carries a charge to only one expense account. This fact suggests that unit ticket method of distribution and summary strip method are likely to be popular.

Where the average amount of a requisition is large, however, and where detailed posting of individual requisitions with description I desired (as it may be in job order cost systems), the unit account method may be used.

In general, any of the standard methods of distribution (explained in Chapter 12) may be used for materials distribution, and the factors that affect the selection of a method are the same as for other distributions. Figure 18-7 is a list of factors to be considered in the selection of a distribution method together with (a) a set of factors which indicate unit account method, and (b) a set of factors which indicate summary strip method.

19

Cost Systems

Cost System and Procedures Which Comprise It: Organization

The cost accounting system proper in a small concern may comprise:

(1) Inventory and Cost ledgers: raw materials, work in process, and finished goods (Chapter 18).
(2) Purchase distribution (Chapter 15).
(3) Labor distribution (Chapter 17).
(4) Materials distribution (Chapter 18).
(5) Cost of sales distribution, which is related to sales distribution (Chapter 12).

The system may be operated by a separate department which proves its records against control accounts maintained in the General ledger. The various distributions may be made from the original media, dispatched to the Cost Accounting department, or they may be supplied in summary form by various sections of the Accounting department: the purchase distribution by the Vouchers Payable department, the labor distribution by the Payroll department, and the materials distribution by the Stores Accounting department.

The various inventory procedures and the various distribution procedures have been discussed individually in the previous chapters. The present chapter explains the design of a cost accounting system as an integrated set of perpetual inventories and distributions intended to provide specific types of management information.

Types of Cost Systems: Bases of Costing

The basic types of cost systems are:

(1) The *Job Order Cost System*, in which an account or a cost sheet is set up for each job or production order to be worked upon in the

factory. Materials used on the job are charged to the cost sheet through the medium of requisitions, and labor is charged through the medium of job tickets. When the job is completed, factory expense is applied to the cost sheet by means of rates. The total cost of the job is determined by adding the materials, labor, and factory expense elements, and product cost per unit is determined by dividing the total cost by the number of units produced on the job.

Job order cost systems are frequently used in conjunction with specific order production control procedures. In such cases a cost sheet may be set up for each production order issued by the planning and production control department.

(2) The *Process Cost System,* in which an account is set up for each process or operation through which the product passes. The labor and expense expended on each process is charged to the appropriate process account during the cost period (day, week, month), and at the end of the period the unit conversion cost for each process is determined by dividing the labor and expense for the process by the number of units produced. Note that in process costs, the focal point is the process or operation, whereas in the job order cost system the focal point is in the product cost, which is the result of keeping job costs. The unit conversion costs are reported to the management for use in the measure of performance currently. In a process cost system, product costs are determined by assembling the average cost of materials per unit of product and the appropriate unit conversion costs to determine an average cost per product unit for a particular period.

Process cost systems are frequently used in conjunction with repetitive order production control systems. In such cases, the periodic product reports issued for planning and production control purposes, which show the production of each operation, are used by the cost accounting clerks for computing unit conversion costs.

Bases of costing are:

(1) Historical basis, under which costing is done as and after the production has taken place. It reflects actual performance in the matter of prices, quantities, and level of operation.

(2) Predetermined basis, under which the costing is done before the production has taken place. It reflects estimated or expected performance in the matter of prices, quantities, and level of operation.

These types and bases are fundamental. Any cost procedure falls into some combination of the above types of cost system and bases of costing. The job order cost procedure may be either:

(1) Predetermined. The estimating procedures used by job printers and building contractors are a form of predetermined job order

costs. The estimators predetermine, on the basis of the best estimates, the cost of a prospective job.

(2) Historical. The cost procedures used by printers and building contractors to compile the cost of a job which is actually in production is an example of historical job order costing.

As indicated in the above examples, both bases of costing may be used in job shops—the predetermined basis by the estimator and the historical by the cost accountant.

Process costs, like other job costs, may be either predetermined or historical. Either historical costs or predetermined costs may be used by the accounting department for compiling current performance and inventory reports. (It may be noted in passing that many systems known as standard costs systems are really predetermined process cost systems.)

Uses of Manufacturing Costs

The uses of manufacturing costs may be classified as follows:

(1) Uses by or for the sales management. These may in turn be classified according to the nature of the business.

    (a) In what are known as "job" shops, costs are used as a direct factor in setting selling prices. The estimating department sets up an estimate of the cost of a prospective job, and the sales department sets the selling price through consideration of that cost and some other factors.

    (b) In mass production businesses, such as the manufacture of automobiles, clothing, and shoes, costs are likewise used as a direct factor in setting selling prices. In this case, the cost per unit of production for each model is determined at the beginning of the style season, and such costs are a factor in setting the prices for the coming season.

    (c) In staple production, where there are competitors who produce what is for all intents and purposes the same product, manufacturing costs per unit are used by the sales department, perhaps not to set selling prices, but to keep itself informed as to which products in the line are making a profit and conversely which ones are simply being carried by the profitable items.

(2) Uses in inventory control and valuation. These uses are indicated in Chapter 18 on Production Control and Inventories.

(3) Uses for the measurement of performance.

(4) Uses for business planning, including the solution of problems of alternative choice.

Recording Manufacturing Costs

Three methods for recording manufacturing costs either by jobs, process, standards, and so on, are used, namely:

(1) Memorandum cost records wherein cost records are not tied in with the General ledger accounts.

(2) Manufacturing cost is incorporated in the General ledger to reflect current inventory balances, cost of sales, variations from standard, and so on.

(3) Separate General ledger and Cost ledger wherein the Cost ledger, by use of "offset" accounts, is tied in with the General ledger accounts for purchases and manufacturing expenses, but current inventory balances, cost of sales, and so on, are carried in the Cost ledger.

The advantages of separate General ledger and Cost ledger may be outlined as follows:

(a) The Cost ledger serves as a private ledger so that certain income information is available to only those persons entitled thereto.

(b) The General ledger remains in a form suitable for easily preparing tax returns. Where material requisitions, costing of shipments, variations from standards are recorded in the General ledger, they usually are required to be eliminated in preparing tax returns.

Classifications and Managerial Reports in a Job Order
Cost System

The basic classifications and managerial reports in a job order cost system are:

(1) *General Ledger Classification* (Table 19-1). Note that the basic difference between this classification and the General ledger classification for a distributing concern (Chapter 3, Table 3-1) lies in the Factory Department Accounts in the present illustration. In this classification, the first two digits are department number:

20 Shear
21 Press
25 Material handling
29 General factory

The right hand (suffix) digits are *object* or *class of expense* digits, for example:

01 Clock time
03 Bonus
05 Overtime premium

Thus, the combined number is:

2001 Shearing clock time
2003 Shearing bonus
2005 Shearing overtime premium

Classification Plan of Central Manufacturing Company (Table 19-1)

First two digits of the four-digit account number refer to group or department; last two digits refer to nature of account.

(1) Group or Department (first two digits):

    10 Cash
    11 Receivables
    12 Inventories
    13 Prepaid expenses
    14 Plant property and equipment
    15 Liabilities
    16 Net worth
    17 Sales
    18 Miscellaneous income and expense
    19 Purchases
    20 to 29 Factory departments:
            20 Shear
            21 Press
            25 Material handling
            29 General factory
    30 Selling expense
    31 Administrative expense

(2) The last two digits (or suffix) indicate the nature of the item whether Balance Sheet, sales, income or expense, purchases, department of the factory, selling expense, or administrative expense.

Table 19-1

CENTRAL MANUFACTURING COMPANY

GENERAL LEDGER CLASSIFICATION

*Account
Number* *Name of Account*

Balance Sheet Accounts

Account Number	Name of Account
1001	Cash on deposit—regular account
1004	Cash on deposit—payroll account
1009	Petty cash fund
1101	Customers accounts
1102	Customers notes
1105	Employees loans
1119	Allowance for bad debts
1201	Inventory (at beginning of period)
1301	Prepaid insurance
1401	Machinery and equipment
1405	Office equipment
1419	Accumulated depreciation
1501	Bank loans
1505	Vouchers payable
1510	Accrued payroll

Table 19-1 (continued)

1511	Accrued compensation insurance
1512	Accrued group insurance
1515	Accrued commissions
1521	Accrued FICA and withholding taxes
1522	Accrued unemployment taxes
1524	Accrued property taxes
1526	Accrued income taxes
1601	Common stock
1603	Retained earnings
1605	Profit and loss (clearing account)

Sales Accounts

1701	Classification #1
1702	Classification #2
1703	Classification #3

Return Sales

1751	Classification #1
1752	Classification #2
1753	Classification #3

Miscellaneous Income

1801	Discount earned
1802	Interest income
1803	Gain or loss on fixed assets
1809	Sundry income

Miscellaneous Expense

1851	Discounts allowed
1852	Interest expense
1859	Sundry expense

Purchases

1901	Steel
1902	Freight on steel purchases
1903	Purchased parts
1904	Die repair material
1990	Scrap sales

Suffix Digits	FACTORY DEPARTMENTS	20	21	25	29
	Production Labor	*Shear*	*Press*	*Material Handling*	*General Factory*
01	Clock time	2001	2101	—	—
03	Bonus	2003	2103	—	—
05	Overtime premium	2005	2105	2505	2905
08	Vacation and holiday	2008	2108	2508	2908
	Indirect Payroll				
10	Supervision	2010	2110	2510	2910
11	Handling	2011	2111	2511	—
12	Rework	2012	2112	—	—
13	Inspection	—	—	—	2913
13–1	Idle time	2013–1	2113–1	—	—
14	Building maintenance	—	—	—	2914

Table 19-1 (continued)

15	Machinery maintenance	2015	2115	2515	2915
16	Die maintenance	—	2116	—	—
17	Production control	—	—	—	2917
18	Timekeeping	—	—	—	2918
19	Miscellaneous labor	2019	2119	2519	2919

Other Factory Expenses

20	Payroll taxes	2020	2120	2520	2920
21	Compensation insurance	2021	2121	2521	2921
22	Group insurance	2022	2122	2522	2922
23	Travel expense	—	—	—	2923
30	Supplies	2030	2130	2530	2930
31	Expendable tools	2031	2131	—	2931
32	Power	—	—	—	2932
33	Professional services	—	—	—	2933
39	Rent	—	—	—	2939
40	Maintenance and repair—building	—	—	—	2940
41	Machinery and equipment	2041	2141	2541	2941
42	Dies	—	2142	—	
44	Depreciation—machinery and equipment	2044	2144	2544	2944
48	Personal property taxes	—	—	—	2948
49	General insurance	—	—	—	2949
59	Miscellaneous factory expense	2059	2159	2559	2959

Selling Expenses

3001	Salaries—Executives
3003	Salaries—Salesmen
3005	Salaries—Sales office
3020	Payroll taxes
3021	Compensation insurance
3022	Group insurance
3023	Travel and entertainment
3035	Advertising
3036	Commissions
3037	Cartage, freight, etc. on shipments
3038	Bad debt provision
3059	Miscellaneous sales expenses

Administrative Expenses

3101	Salaries—Executives
3105	Salaries—Office and accounting
3120	Payroll taxes
3121	Compensation insurance
3122	Group insurance
3123	Travel expense
3130	Stationery and office supplies
3131	Postage
3132	Telephone and telegraph
3133	Legal and audit
3134	Dues and subscriptions
3148	Franchise taxes, etc.
3149	General insurance
3159	Miscellaneous adminstrative expense

(2) *Cost Ledger Classification* (Table 19-2). This classification includes inventory accounts (raw materials and work in process), cost of sales accounts, gain or loss accounts (explained on page 436) and offset accounts. The Cost ledger is self-balancing and the offset accounts are reciprocal accounts to comparable accounts in the General ledger:

Offset Accounts in Cost Ledger	*Accounts in General Ledger*
C–1201 Beginning inventory	1201 Inventory
C–1900 Purchases (in total)	1901–1904 Purchases
C–2000 Shearing labor and expense	2000 Shearing
C–2100 Press labor and expense	2100 Press
C–2500 Material handling labor and expense	2500 Material handling
C–2900 General factory labor and expense	2900 General factory

At the end of a period, the Cost ledger for the next period is set up by a debit to inventories (C-1251, and so on) and credit to inventory offsets (C-1201) for the amount of the closing inventories of the old period shown by the General ledger. To pick up purchases of steel in the Cost ledger during the new period, an entry is made debiting account C-1251 (Steel, including freight) and crediting account C-1900 (Purchases). To pick up labor and expense, the entry is debit work in process (C-1262) and credit offset accounts (C-2000 through C-2900) for the amounts of the balances in General ledger accounts (2000 through 2900). The complete set of standard journal entries for operating the Cost ledger appear on pages 442-443 and 447-449.

(3) *Balance Sheet* (Table 19-6).

(4) *Income and Expense Statement* (Table 19-7). This statement shows among other things, job gross profit by sales classification, gain or loss on factory departments, operating expense totals, financial income and expense, provision for income tax, and net income.

(5) *Statement of Factory Costs* (Table 19-8). This statement shows materials and machine cost (labor and expense) charged to jobs, work in process variation, and cost of sales.

(6) *Detailed Machine Cost* (Table 19-9). This statement shows the labor and expense cost of each department by object account, allocation of general factory expense to the other departments, machine cost charged to jobs, and gain or loss by departments.

Table 19-2

CENTRAL MANUFACTURING COMPANY

COST LEDGER CLASSIFICATION

Account Number	*Name of Account*
	Raw material Inventories (net debit balance):
C–1251	Steel, including freight
C–1252	Purchased parts
C–1253	Other materials

Work-in-Process Inventory (net debit balance):

C–1261	Materials charged	(debit)
C–1262	Machine cost charged	(debit)
C–1265	Handling cost	(debit)
C–1268	Cost of shipments	(credit)

Cost of Sales (all debits):

C–1901	Classification #1
C–1902	Classification #2
C–1903	Classification #3

Gain or Loss:

C–1920	Shear	
C–1921	Press	debit or credit
C–1925	Material handling	
C–1929	General factory (clearing)	

Offsets (all credits):

C–1201	Beginning inventory (raw materials and work-in-process)
C–1900	Purchases (in total)
	Factory payroll and expense (in total—per General ledger)
C–2000	Shear
C–2100	Press
C–2500	Material handling
C–2900	General factory

(7) *Statement of Selling and Administrative Expenses* (Table 19-10). This statement displays the object account balances for the selling expense group and the administrative expense group of accounts.

Standard Journal Entries and Journals: General Ledger

The standard monthly journal entries and journals for the General ledger appear in two groups:

Group I:

Table 19-3 *Standard General Ledger Summary Entries.* These entries exemplify the totals posted from journals to the General ledger. The journals designed from these entries are illustrated in Figures 19-1 to 19-4:

Figure 19-1 *Voucher Register*
Figure 19-2 *Check Register*
Figure 19-3 *Cash Receipts Journal*
Figure 19-4 *Sales Journal (Credit Memoranda)*

(All journal entries, forms, and statements in this chapter are filled in with illustrative amounts. These amounts are provided to make it possible for the reader to identify the source of all figures which appear on the statements, if he desires.)

Group II:

Table 19-4 Standard General Ledger Adjusting Entries. These are the end-of-the-month adjusting entries.

Standard Journal Entries and Journals: Cost Ledger

The standard journal entries for the Cost ledger appear in Table 19-5. The journals appear in the following illustrations:

Figure 19-5 *Machine Cost Journal.* This is a machine posted proof journal which receives a posting of each charge at the same time the item is charged to a job cost sheet. The charge for $6.00 (May 3) on the journal illustrated in Figure 19-5 is the same as the first charge (same date) on the job cost sheet (Figure 19-9).

Figure 19-6 *Materials Requisition Journal,* which is a listing of all materials requisitions posted to job cost sheets.

Figure 19-7 *Cost of Sales Journal* which is a summary of cost of shipments-out on jobs.

Table 19-3

CENTRAL MANUFACTURING COMPANY

STANDARD MONTHLY GENERAL LEDGER

SUMMARY ENTRIES, May 19___

Account Number		*Debit*	*Credit*
	VOUCHER REGISTER		
	Purchases—		
	Steel purchases—weight, 412,000 lbs.		
1901	Steel purchases—dollars	$31,000	
1902	Freight on steel purchases	520	

Table 19-3 (continued)

1903	Purchased parts	1,605	
1904	Other materials	—	
Suffix	Factory expenses—		
20 to 29	Account numbers*		
	Dollar amounts	3,446	
Prefix	Selling expenses—		
30	Account numbers*		
	Dollar amounts	265	
Prefix	Administrative expenses—		
31	Account numbers*		
	Dollar amounts	338	
	Sundry—		
Sundry	Account numbers*		
	Dollar amounts	380	
1505	Vouchers payable		$37,554

CHECK REGISTER

1505	Vouchers payable	32,608	
1902	Freight on steel purchases	500	
3037	Cartage, freight, etc., on shipments	182	
	Sundry—		
Various	Account numbers*		
	Dollar amounts	1,196	
1001	Cash on deposit—regular account		34,286
1801	Discounts earned		200

CASH RECEIPTS JOURNAL

1001	Cash on deposit—regular account	43,608	
1851	Discounts allowed	610	
1101	Customers accounts receivable		44,108
Various	Sundry—		
	Account numbers*		
	Dollar amounts		110

SALES JOURNAL

1101	Customers accounts	$45,550	
	Sales—		
1701	Classification #1		$19,500
1702	Classification #2		14,600
1703	Classification #3		10,300
1990	Scrap sales		1,050
Various	Sundry—		
	Account numbers		
	Dollar amounts		100

CREDIT MEMORANDUM JOURNAL

Entry is the same as the Sales Journal entry above
except the debits and credits are reversed.

None illustrated

* Detailed account numbers and dollar amounts are not shown in illustration. Cents omitted.

CENTRAL MANUFACTURING COMPANY
VOUCHER REGISTER

LEFT HAND PAGE

DATE 19__	CREDITOR	PAYMENT DATE	CHECK NO.	VOUCHERS PAYABLE NO.	AMOUNT	STEEL LBS.	AMOUNT	FREIGHT STEEL	PURCHASED PARTS	FACTORY EXPENSE A/C NO.	AMOUNT	
May 1	Johnson Corp.	3/6/59	1048	142	238.05				238.05			1
2	Metal Products Co.	3/3/59	1027	143	189.20					2130	189.20	2
3	Garry Mount	3/9/59	1107	144	82.50					2041	82.50	3
3	Steel Warehouse			145	96.50	1,064	96.50					4
4	Canada Steel			146	838.50	11,524	838.50					5
5	G. Berry			147	125.00							6
	Total for Month				36,987.00	412,000	31,000.00	520.00	1,605.00		1,836.00	

RIGHT HAND PAGE

SELLING EXPENSE A/C NO.	AMOUNT	ADMINISTRATIVE EXP. A/C NO.	AMOUNT	OTHER MATERIALS	SUNDRY A/C NO.	AMOUNT	
							1
							2
							3
							4
							5
3023	125.00						6
	1,160.00		486.00			380.00	

Figure 19-1. Voucher Register

CENTRAL MANUFACTURING COMPANY
CHECK REGISTER

	DATE 19__	CUSTOMER	CHECK NO.	CHECK AMOUNT	DISCOUNT EARNED	VOUCHERS PAYABLE	FREIGHT ON STEEL PUR.	FREIGHT ON SHIPMENTS	SUNDRY A/C NO.	SUNDRY AMOUNT	
1	May 1	United Express	1024	10.87				10.87			1
2	1	Penna. RR	1025	86.20			86.20				2
3	2	X&R Machinery	1026	236.80		236.80					3
4	3	Metal Products	1027	185.42	3.78	189.20					4
5	4	Payroll a/c	1028	1,196.00					1510	1,196.00	5
6	5	J. Berry	1029	125.00		125.00					6
		Totals for Month		34,286.00	200.00	32,608.00	500.00	182.00		1,196.00	

Figure 19-2. Check Register

CENTRAL MANUFACTURING COMPANY
CASH RECEIPTS JOURNAL

	DATE 19__	RECEIVED FROM		CASH DEPOSIT	CASH AMOUNT	DISCOUNTS ALLOWED	CUSTOMERS ACCOUNTS	SUNDRY A/C NO.	SUNDRY AMOUNT	
1	May 2	J. Burris Co.			246.00	—				1
2	2	Northlake Mfg.	5/2	890.84	644.84	13.16	658.00			2
3	3	Cole Corp.	5/3	346.00	346.00		346.00			3
4	4	Coleman, T.			26.40			1802	26.40	4
5	5				186.50		186.50			5
6	5		5/5	885.18	672.28	13.72	686.00			6
		Totals for Month			43,608.00	610.00	44,108.00		110.00	

Figure 19-3. Cash Receipts Journal

CENTRAL MANUFACTURING COMPANY
SALES JOURNAL *

	DATE 19__	CUSTOMER	INV. NO.	CUSTOMERS ACCOUNTS	SALES #1	SALES #2	SALES #3	SCRAP SALES	SUNDRY A/C NO.	SUNDRY AMOUNT	
1	May 1	Manderville Co.	2141	238.70		238.70					1
2	1	Motor Parts Co.	2142	181.55	181.55						2
3	2	Canton, Inc.	2143	634.20	634.20						3
4	2	Cartwell, Inc.	2144	86.50			86.50				4
5	4	Cole Corp.	2145	368.20		368.20					5
6	5	L. Smith	2146	41.50					1990	41.50	6
		Totals for Month		45,550.00	19,500.00	14,600.00	10,300.00	1,050.00		100.00	

*Same journal form is used for credit memorandums.

Figure 19-4. Sales Journal

Table 19-4

CENTRAL MANUFACTURING COMPANY
STANDARD MONTHLY GENERAL LEDGER
ADJUSTING ENTRIES, May 19___

Account Number	Particulars	Debit	Credit
	(1)		
Various*	Various factory payroll expense accounts (and subtotals by departments)	$11,422	
Various*	Various sales salary expense accounts	1,108	
Various*	Various administrative salary expense accounts	2,567	
1521	Accrued F.I.C.A. and withholding taxes		$ 1,280
1105	Employees loans		100
1510	Accrued payroll (amount of checks)		13,717
	Record payroll for month from company summary		
	(2)		
Various*	Vacation and holiday expense accounts	180	
Various*	Payroll tax expense accounts	745	
Various*	Compensation insurance expense accounts	154	
Various*	Group insurance expense accounts	126	
	Accrued taxes—		
1521	F.I.C.A. and withholding taxes		495
1522	Unemployment taxes		250
1511	Accrued compensation insurance		154
1512	Accrued group insurance		126
1510	Accrued payroll		180
	Accrue payroll tax expense, compensation insurance, group insurance, vacation and holiday pay for the month per summary		
	(3)		
	Depreciation—machinery and equipment		
2044	Shear	54	
2144	Press	280	
2544	Material handling	56	
2944	General factory	15	
1419	Accumulated depreciation		405
	Monthly provision for depreciation		
	(4)		
	Personal property taxes—		
2948	General factory	75	
1524	Accrued property taxes		75
	Monthly accrual of property taxes		
	(5)		
	General insurance—		
2949	General factory	200	
1301	Prepaid insurance		200
	Monthly write-off of prepaid insurance premiums		

Table 19-4 (continued)

(6)

3036	Commissions	962	
1515	Accrued commissions		962

Accrue commissions on sales for month

(7)

	Dies—		
2142	Press department	321	
1904	Die repair material		321

Record die repair materials used by Press department for the month (per requisition journal)

* Each of the above groups is recapitulated in the journal by the detailed departmental expense accounts.

Table 19-5

CENTRAL MANUFACTURING COMPANY

STANDARD MONTHLY COST LEDGER ENTRIES, May 19___

Account Number	Particulars	Debit	Credit
	(C-1)		
	Raw materials inventories:		
	Steel—weight, 412,000 Lbs.		
C-1251	Steel—dollar amount (including freight)	$32,020	
C-1252	Purchased parts	1,605	
C-1253	Other materials	—	
	Offset:		
C-1900	Purchases (total of A/C-1251 and 1252)		$33,625

Record purchases for the month per the General ledger.

Account Number	Particulars		Debit	Credit
	(C-2)			
	Work-in Process-Inventory:			
C-1262	Machine cost (charged to jobs per machine cost journal, (Figure 19-5)			
	Shear	$ 1,970		
	Press	12,315	14,285	
	Gain or Loss:			
C-1920	Shear (difference between C-2000 and C-1262S)			625
C-1921	Press (difference between C-2100 and C-1262P)			2,494
C-1925	Material handling (same as C-2500)		1,216	
C-1929	General factory (same as C-2900)		4,464	

Table 19-5 (continued)

Offsets:

Departmental totals of factory payroll and expenses (per General Ledger accounts)

C-2000	Shear	1,345
C-2100	Press	9,821
C-2500	Material handling	1,216
C-2900	General factory	4,464

Record (a) monthly summary of labor cost tickets charged to jobs, (b) actual payroll and other factory expenses per the General ledger, and (c) gross departmental gains and losses.

NOTE: Account C-1925 is charged for actual labor and expense of Handling department in this entry. Account C-1925 is credited for handling expense applied to work-in-process in Entry C-3. Account C-1929 is charged for actual labor and expense of general factory in this entry. It is credited for expense allocated to shear, press, and materials handling in Entry C-4. The balances of Accounts C-1925 and C-1929 then represent gains or losses.

(C-3)

Work-in-Process Inventory:

C-1261	Materials charged	20,675	
C-1265	Handling cost (a)	1,780	

Raw Materials Inventories:

Steel—pounds, 398,000

C-1251	Steel—dollar amount (including freight)		20,200
C-1252	Purchased parts		475
C-1253	Other materials		—

Gain or Loss:

C-1925	Handling materials—(a) above		1,780

Requisitions charged to jobs including handling charges per material requisition journal (Figure 19-6). Note the credit to C-1925 Handling for handling expense charged to Work-in-Process.

(C-4)

Gain or Loss:

C-1920	Shear	521	
C-1921	Press	3,456	
C-1925	Material handling	487	

Gain or Loss:

C-1929	General factory		4,464

Allocate total general factory expense for month based upon total payroll of shear, press and material handling departments.

(C-5)

Cost of Sales:

C-1901	Classification #1	15,000	
C-1902	Classification #2	12,800	
C-1903	Classification #3	8,700	

Table 19-5 (continued)

Work-in-Process Inventory:

C-1268   Cost of shipments   36,500

Record cost of sales for the month per cost of
sales journal (Figure 19-7).

Note that after the above entries have been posted, the following departmental balances (gains or losses) appear:

Particulars	Entry	Shear	Press	Material Handling	General Factory
Actual payroll and expense per General ledger	C-2	$1,345	$ 9,821	$1,216	$4,464
General factory expense allocated	C-4	521	3,456	487	4,464*
		$1,866	$13,277	$1,703	
Charged to Work-in-Process	C-2 and C-3	1,970	12,315	1,780	
Gains and losses		104*	962	77*	

* Gains

Department gains and losses are explained in the following section.

Machine Cost and Departmental Gain or Loss

In the Central Manufacturing Company, labor and factory expense together are charged to jobs by means of estimated or standard rates known as machine cost rates. These machine cost rates are computed and used as described in the following steps. Figure 19-8 illustrates the calculations of *departmental* rates. Machine rates are calculated in the same manner as departmental rates except that there are a number of machine rates in each department.

(1) Establish the capacity of each machine center or department in machine operating hours for the period.

(2) Determine the normal operating hours of each machine center or department for the period.

(3) Budget the total direct and indirect payroll and other factory expenses of each machine center or department.

(4) Budget the total indirect general factory payroll and other factory expenses and allocate total general factory expense to the various productive machine centers or departments based upon the direct and indirect payroll of the productive departments.

(5) Divide the sum of (3) and (4) of each machine center or department by the normal operating hours determined in (2) above. This is the standard machine cost rate.

CENTRAL MANUFACTURING COMPANY
MACHINE COST JOURNAL

	DATE 19___	CUSTOMER	DEPT. NO.	JOB NO.	MACH. NO.	OPER. NO.	TOTAL		SHEAR		PRESS		
							MACHINE HOURS	MACHINE COST	MACHINE HOURS	MACHINE COST	MACHINE HOURS	MACHINE COST	
1	May 1	Industrial Equip.	21	1173	21	2	2.49	7.47			2.49	7.47	1
2	1	Carey Corp.	21	1135	18	1	3.29	9.87			3.29	9.87	2
3	2	Manderville Co	21	1138	18	3	3.60	21.60			3.60	21.60	3
4	2	Cole Corp.	20	1122	21	6	2.00	10.00	2.00	10.00			4
5	2	Smith Corp.	21	1119	16	2	6.00	42.00			6.00	42.00	5
6	3	Cole Corp.*	20	1101	11	1	1.50	6.00	1.50	6.00			6
		Total for Month					2,996.00	14,285.00	576.00	1,970.00	2,420.00	12,315.00	

*See posting to Job Cost Sheet (Fig. 19-9).

Figure 19-5. Machine Cost Journal

CENTRAL MANUFACTURING COMPANY
MATERIAL REQUISITION JOURNAL

	DATE 19___	CUSTOMER	JOB NO.	TOTAL		STEEL		PURCHASED PARTS	HANDLING CHARGE	OTHER MATERIALS	SUNDRY		
				REQ. NO.	AMOUNT	LBS.	AMOUNT						
1	May 1	Manderville Co.	1138	486	532.05	7,050	496.80		35.25				1
2	2	Cole Corp.	1109	487	187.00			187.00					2
3	3	Cole Corp.*	1101	488	882.00	9200	836.00		46.00				3
4	3	G. N. Wells Co.	1108	RT168 †	(61.50)	760	(61.50)						4
5	4	Canton, Inc.	1122	489	1,968.45	20,600	1,619.45	246.00	103.00				5
		Total for Month			22,776.00	398,000	20,200.00	475.00	1,780.00	321.00			

*Job Cost Sheet (Fig. 19-9) shows this charge.   "RT" is returned material.

Figure 19-6. Materials Requisition Journal

CENTRAL MANUFACTURING COMPANY
COST OF SALES JOURNAL   Month of ___March___ 19___

	DATE 19___	CUSTOMER	JOB NO.	QUANTITY	CLASSIFICATION #1				CLASSIFICATION #2				
					BILLING		COST		BILLING		COST		
					PRICE	AMOUNT	PER UNIT	AMOUNT	PRICE	AMOUNT	PER UNIT	AMOUNT	
1	May 31	Cole Corp.	1102	21,000	1.00M	21.00		18.60					1
2	31	Smith Corp.	1135	1,000	12.00M	12.00		9.80					2
3	31	Burton Co.	1121	15,000					1.50C	225.00			3
4	31	Cole Corp.*	1101	1,000	1.50	1,500.00	1.068	1,068.00					4
		Total for Month				19,500.00		15,000.00		1,460.00		12,800.00	

*Job Cost Sheet shows this item.

Figure 19-7. Cost of Sales Journal

CENTRAL MANUFACTURING COMPANY

COMPUTATION OF BUDGETED HOURLY RATES OF FACTORY DEPARTMENTS

YEAR ENDED 5/31/19--

DEPARTMENT	MACHINE HOURS CAPACITY (1)	MACHINE HOURS NORMAL % (2)	NORMAL HOURS (3)	BUDGETED EXPENSES PAYROLL (4)	BUDGETED EXPENSES % TO TOTAL (5)	BUDGETED EXPENSES OTHER EXPENSE (6)	ALLOCATE GENERAL FACTORY EXP. (7)	TOTAL OF (4),(6) & (7) (8)	BUDGETED HOURLY RATE (8 ÷ 3)
SHEAR	6,800	75%	5,100	$13,500	12.0%	$3,000	$6,480	$22,980	$4.50
PRESS	40,000	80	32,000	87,500	77.4	30,000	41,796	159,296	4.98
SUB-TOTAL	46,800		37,100	$101,000	89.4%	$33,000	$48,276	$182,276	
MATERIAL HANDLING –									
TONS HANDLED	2,000 TONS			12,000	10.6	2,500	5,724	20,224	.005 per lb.
TOTAL PRODUCTIVE				$113,000	100.0%	$35,500	$54,000*	$202,500	
GENERAL FACTORY				27,000		27,000	54,000	—	
TOTAL FACTORY				$140,000		$62,500	$ —	$202,500	
SELLING				13,500		18,000			
ADMINISTRATIVE				30,800		5,700			
TOTAL BUDGET				$184,300		$86,200			

* Red figure

Figure 19-8. Computation of Budgeted Hourly Rates of Factory Departments

(6) Multiply the actual machine hours of each job by the machine cost rate (in (5) above). This is the "machine cost" charged to the job. The machine cost charged to the jobs is summarized for the period in the machine cost journal (Figure 19-5).

Machine cost charged to jobs is compared with the total of the actual expenditures for the machine center or department on Table 19-9 (detailed machine cost statement). This statement is set out in the same pattern as the budgeted figures in steps (3) and (4) above:

(a) Total direct and indirect payroll and other factory expenses, plus

(b) Share of total general factory payroll and other factory expenses allocated on the basis of the various direct and indirect payroll and other factory expenses of the productive departments.

The comparison for each machine center or department of the total actual direct and indirect expenditures with the total standard machine cost charged to jobs results in either gain or loss for the machine center or department. If the total actual expenditures exceed the total standard machine cost charged to jobs, there is a loss; if the total actual expenditures are less than the total standard machine cost, there is a gain.

Job Cost Sheet; Daily Time Card

Figure 19-9 is the *Job Cost Sheet*. One of these forms is set up for each job worked upon. It is charged for (a) materials, (b) materials handling expense, and (c) machine cost at standard rates (which, as explained in the previous section, are combined labor and factory expense). The record is machine posted and a running balance is kept for each element and for total cost. Each job cost sheet is also credited for billing (sales value) and cost of each shipment-out on the job. A work in process (cost) balance is carried. This is the difference between total cost debits to date and total cost of shipments to date.

The open job cost sheets comprise the Work in Process ledger and the sum of the open balances is proved against the balance of Cost ledger account C-1260 at the end of each month.

Figure 19-10 is the *Daily Time Card*. One of these is set up each day for each workman. The form is a strip of coupons or stubs, one of which is filled out for each job on which each man works. The top section, called the "employee record," is the summary for the day and week to date. It is used for preparing the payroll while the job stubs after separation are sorted to jobs and posted to the job cost sheets.

CENTRAL MANUFACTURING CO.
JOB COST SHEET

CUSTOMER _Cole Corporation_

JOB NO. 1101
DATE 4/24/7-
AUTHORIZED QUANTITY 1,000

SUMMARY	
MATERIALS	$ 836.00
HANDLING	46.00
MACHINE COST	186.00
TOTAL	1,068.00
SELLING PRICE	1,500.00
GROSS PROFIT	432.00

DATE	REF.	MATERIALS TODAY	MATERIALS TO DATE	HANDLING TODAY	HANDLING TO DATE	DEPT. NO.	OP. NO.	MACH. NO.	MACHINE HOURS TODAY	MACHINE HOURS TO DATE	MACHINE COST TODAY	MACHINE COST TO DATE	WORK IN PROCESS BALANCE
May 3	P.R					20	1	11	1.50	1.50	6.00	6.00	6.00
May 3	8024	836.00	836.00	46.00	46.00								888.00
May 4	P.R					21	2	24	3.00	4.50	18.00	24.00	906.00
May 5	P.R					21	2	24	4.00	8.50	24.00	48.00	930.00
May 5	P.R					21	3	28	4.00	12.50	48.00	96.00	978.00
May 6	P.R					21	3	28	7.50	20.00	90.00	186.00	1,068.00

SHIPMENTS

DATE	REF.	QUANTITIES TODAY	QUANTITIES TO DATE	BILLING TODAY	BILLING TO DATE	COST TODAY	COST TO DATE	WORK IN PROCESS BALANCE
May 6	INV 3042	500	500	750.00	750.00			
May 7	INV 3107	500	1,000	750.00	1,500.00			
May 31	COST OF SALES *					1,068.00	1,068.00	– 0 –

*Cost of jobs closed at end of month.

Figure 19-9. Job Cost Sheet

453

CENTRAL MANUFACTURING COMPANY

DAILY TIME CARD

SCHEDULED STARTING TIME
IS 7.00

72

HENRY WILSON

HOURLY RATE $ 2.00

	DAILY	
OUT	(A) MAY 4	16.50
IN	(A) MAY 4	6.48

EMPLOYEE RECORD

		HOURS						CLOCK HOURS
WEEK (B)	EARNED	HRS. ON STANDARD	BONUS	DAY WORK	WAITING	CLOCK	TOTAL HOURS (E)	9.00
	28.00	25.20	2.80	19.76	1.04	46.00	48.80	
	REGULAR (F)	O.T. HRS. (G)	O.T. RATE (H)	O.T. PREM. (I)	TOTAL $ EARNINGS	DEDUCTIONS TAX	INS.	O.T. HOURS
	$ 97.60	6.00	$ 2.12	$ 6.36	$ 103.96	$ 6.60	$ 1.00	1.00

DAY (C)	EARNED	HRS.-STD.	BONUS	DAY WORK	WAITING (D)	O.K.		WORKING TIME
	6.40	5.78	.62	3.08	.14	J.G.Roberts		8.86

JOB STUB SECTION

OUT	PRODUCED	CLOCK NO.	DEPT. NO.	MACHINE NO.	JOB OR ACCT. NO.	OP. NO.	OUT (A) MAY 4	9.55
	2,000	72	21	21	#1173	2		
IN	STD. HRS. PER M	PART NO.	DESCRIPTION				IN (A) MAY 4	7.06
	1.800	D11837	TRIM PANEL					
	EARNED	HRS.-STD.	BONUS	DAY WORK			WORKING TIME	2.49
	3.60	2.49	1.11	—				

OUT	PRODUCED	CLOCK NO.	DEPT. NO.	MACHINE NO.	JOB OR ACCT. NO.	OP. NO.	OUT (A) MAY 4	13.20
	—	72	21	18	A/C 2115			
IN	STD. HRS. PER M	PART NO.	DESCRIPTION	Repair Machine 18			IN (A) MAY 4	9.62
	—							
	EARNED	HRS.-STD.	BONUS	DAY WORK			WORKING TIME (J)	3.08
	—	—	—	3.08				

OUT	PRODUCED	CLOCK NO.	DEPT. NO.	MACHINE NO.	JOB OR ACCT. NO.	OP. NO.	OUT (A) MAY 4	16.50
	2,800	72	21	18	#1135	1		
IN	STD. HRS. PER M	PART NO.	DESCRIPTION				IN (A) MAY 4	13.21
	1.000	D11746	PIERCE BRACKET					
	EARNED	HRS.-STD.	BONUS	DAY WORK			WORKING TIME	3.29
	2.80	3.29	(49)	—				

OUT	PRODUCED	CLOCK NO.	DEPT. NO.	MACHINE NO.	JOB OR ACCT. NO.	OP. NO.	OUT
IN	STD. HRS. PER M	PART NO.	DESCRIPTION				IN
	EARNED	HRS.-STD.	BONUS	DAY WORK			WORKING TIME

OUT	PRODUCED	CLOCK NO.	DEPT. NO.	MACHINE NO.	JOB OR ACCT. NO.	OP. NO.	OUT
IN	STD. HRS. PER M	PART NO.	DESCRIPTION				IN
	EARNED	HRS.-STD.	BONUS	DAY WORK			WORKING TIME

EXPLANATIONS

(A) Job clock printing using 24.00 hours per day.

(B) Cumulative "Day" totals of 5 Daily Time Cards covering week.

(C) Daily total of job stub sections.

(D) "Waiting Time" is difference between "Clock Hours" for day and "Working Time" for day.

(E) "Total Hours" is sum of "Clock Hours" and "Bonus Hours" for week.

(F) "Regular Earnings" is "Total Hours" × "Hourly Rate" of $2.00.

(G) "Overtime Hours" is sum of daily "O.T. Hours" of the 5 days.

(H) "Overtime Rate" is "Regular Earnings" divided by "Clock Hours".

(I) "Overtime Premium" is ("O.T. Hours" × "O.T. Rate") ÷ 2.

(J) Subtract lunch period (from 12:00 to 12:50) from clock time to determine working time (3.08).

Figure 19-10. Daily Time Card

Statements Illustrated and Explained

The sources of information for the statements and the manner in which the statements tie together can be seen by starting with the last one and working forward.

(1) The *Statement of Selling and Administrative Expenses* (Table 19-10) is obtained directly from the selling and administrative expense accounts in the General ledger.

(2) The *Detailed Machine Cost Statement* (Table 19-9) is obtained in part from the departmental labor and expense accounts in the general ledger. The *totals* of payroll and expense per this statement agree with those picked up in the Cost ledger in Entry C-2:

Shear	$ 1,345
Press	9,821
Material handling	1,216
General factory	4,464
Total	$16,846

The machine cost charged to jobs comes from the following sources:

Shear, from machine cost journal (Figure 19-5)	$ 1,970
Press, from machine cost journal	12,315
Materials handling, from requisition journal (Figure 19-6)	1,780
Total	$16,065

The gains and losses on the last line are the differences between actual costs of the departments and machine costs charged to jobs:

Shear	$104*
Press	962
Material handling	77*
Total	$781

* Red figure.

(3) The *Statement of Factory Costs* (Table 19-8) is prepared from Cost ledger accounts. Note that the materials-charged-to-jobs-section of the statement can be matched with journal entry C-3 for materials used (page 448). Also the machine-cost-charged-to-jobs section of the statement can be matched with journal entry C-2 (Shear and Press) and journal entry C-3 (Handling).

(4) The *Income and Expense Statement* (Table 19-7) is prepared partly from the Cost ledger and partly from the General ledger. The job-costs-by-sales classification totaling $36,500 comes from the Cost ledger. (See journal entry C-5, page 448.) Gain or loss

of factory departments ($781) comes from Exhibit 4, Detailed Machine Cost (pages 458-459). Scrap sales ($1,050) and all other figures come from the General ledger.

(5) The *Balance Sheet* (Table 19-6) is prepared from the General ledger after the usual closing entries have been recorded. In these closing entries, the General ledger income and expense accounts and the opening inventory balance are closed to Profit and Loss account. The closing inventories (Materials, $96,436 and Work in Process, $22,880) are recorded by debits to inventories and a credit to Profit and Loss. These inventory balances are picked up from the Cost ledger and verified by the usual physical count. Note that, to all intents and purposes, the General ledger operates exactly as if no Cost ledger existed.

Exhibit 1

Table 19-6
CENTRAL MANUFACTURING COMPANY
BALANCE SHEET,
May 31, 19___

ASSETS

Current Assets:

Cash on deposit	$ 9,635	
Petty cash fund	100	$ 9,735
Customers accounts	$ 46,450	
Customers notes	2,050	
Employees loans	200	
Total	$ 48,700	
Less—Estimated uncollectibles	2,650	46,050
Inventories		
Raw materials	$ 96,436	
Work-in-process	22,880	
Supplies	400	119,716
Prepaid expenses		986
Total current assets		$176,487

Plant Property and Equipment:

Cost	$165,500	
Less—Accumulated depreciation	121,600	43,900
Total assets		$220,387

LIABILITIES AND STOCKHOLDERS' EQUITY

Current Liabilities:

Bank loans		$ 5,000
Vouchers payable		39,650
Accrued expenses		2,520
Accrued taxes—		
Income	$ 620	
Other	2,100	2,720
Total current liabilities		$ 49,890

Table 19-6 (continued)

Stockholders' Equity:
Common stock, $100 par—460 shares | | $ 46,000

Retained income
Balance May 1, 1959 | $123,053
Net income for one month ended
May 31, 1959 (Exhibit 2) | 1,444

Balance, May 31, 1959 | $124,497

Total stockholders' equity | 170,497

Total liabilities and stockholders' equity | $220,387

Exhibit 2

Table 19-7

CENTRAL MANUFACTURING COMPANY

INCOME AND EXPENSE STATEMENT

One Month Ended May 31, 19___

Particulars Sales and Gross Profit:	Sales	Job Cost	Gross Profit	Budget
Classification A	$19,500	$15,000	$4,500	
Classification B	14,600	12,800	1,800	
Classification C	10,300	8,700	1,600	
Total jobs	$44,400	$36,500	$7,900	
Add or Deduct:*				
Gain* or loss of factory departments (Exhibit 4)		781	781*	
Scrap sales*		1,050*	1,050	
Actual cost of sales		$36,231		
Actual gross profit			$8,169	
Deduct—Operating Expenses:				
Selling			$2,600	
Administrative			3,050	
Total operating expenses (Exhibit 5)			$5,650	
Operating profit			$2,519	
Add or Deduct:*				
Discounts earned			200	
Interest income			30	
Discounts allowed*			610*	
Interest expense*			35*	
Sundry expense*			40*	
Net income before taxes			$2,064	
Deduct—Provision for Income Taxes:			620	
Net income for period (Exhibit 1)			$1,444	

* Red figure.

Budget amounts omitted.

Exhibit 3

Table 19-8

CENTRAL MANUFACTURING COMPANY

STATEMENT OF FACTORY COSTS

One Month Ended May 31, 19___

Particulars			*Amount*
Materials Charged to Jobs:			
Purchases—			
Steel plus freight in		$32,020	
Purchased parts		1,605	
Other materials		—	
Total purchases			$33,625
Inventory of raw materials—			
At beginning		$83,486	
At end*		96,436*	12,950*
Materials charged to jobs			$20,675
Machine Cost Charged to Jobs:			
Shear		$ 1,970	
Press		12,315	
Material handling		1,780	
Total machine cost charged to jobs			
(Exhibit 4)			$16,065
Work-in-Process Inventory:			
Inventory at beginning			$22,640
Add—			
Materials charged to jobs (as above)		$20,675	
Machine cost charged to jobs (Exhibit 4)		16,065	36,740
			$59,380
Deduct—Job cost of sales (Exhibit 2)			36,500
Inventory at end (Exhibit 1)			$22,880

* Red figure.

Exhibit 4

Table 19-9

CENTRAL MANUFACTURING COMPANY

DETAILED MACHINE COST

One Month Ended May 31, 19___

Particulars	*Total*	*Shear*	*Press*	*Material Handling*	*General Factory*
Productive Labor:					
Clock time	$ 6,660	$ 772	$5,215	$ 673	—
Bonus	175	20	124	31	—
Overtime premium	70	13	40	17	—
Vacation and holiday	180	35	115	30	—
Total	$ 7,085	$ 840	$5,494	$ 751	—

Table 19-9 (continued)

Indirect Payroll:					
Supervision	$ 1,517	$ 200	$ 367	$ 200	$ 750
Handling	1,208	25	883	17	283
Rework	67	—	54	13	—
Inspection	350	—	—	—	350
Idle time	96	19	57	20	—
Building maintenance	100	—	—	—	100
Machine maintenance	113	13	71	21	8
Die maintenance	346	—	346	—	—
Production control	354	—	—	—	354
Timekeeping	354				354
Miscellaneous labor	12				12
Total indirect payroll	$ 4,517	$ 257	$1,778	$ 271	$2,211
Total*	$11,602	$1,097	$7,272	$1,022	$2,211
Other Factory Expenses:					
Payroll taxes	$ 571	$ 55	$ 373	$ 49	$ 94
Compensation insurance	122	10	82	10	20
Group insurance	104	10	69	9	16
Travel expense	52	—	—	—	52
Supplies	1,202	20	1,128	38	16
Expendable tools	96	30	66	—	—
Power	258	—	—	—	258
Professional services	70				70
Rent	1,334				1,334
Maintenance and repair—					
Building	80	—	—	—	80
Machinery	244	45	181	18	—
Dies	321	—	321	—	—
Depreciation—Machinery	405	54	280	56	15
Personal property taxes	75	—	—	—	75
General insurance	200	—	—	—	200
Miscellaneous	110	24	49	14	23
Total other factory expenses	$ 5,244	$ 248	$2,549	$ 194	$2,253
Total payroll and expense	$16,846	$1,345	$9,821	$1,216	$4,464
*Allocate General Factory Expense**		11.68%	77.43%	10.89%	
	—	521	3,456	487	4,464†
Total actual machine cost	$16,846	$1,866	$13,277	$1,703	
Machine Cost Charged to Jobs (Exhibit 3)	16,065	1,970	12,315	1,780	
Gain† or loss (Exhibit 2)	$ 781	$ 104†	$ 962	$ 77†	

* Allocated on basis of total payroll of shear, press, and material handling departments.
† Red figure.

Exhibit 5

Table 19-10
CENTRAL MANUFACTURING COMPANY
STATEMENT OF SELLING AND ADMINISTRATIVE EXPENSES

One Month Ended May 31, 19___

Particulars	*Amount*	*Budget*
Selling Expenses:		
Salaries—		
Executives	$ 500	
Salesmen	458	
Sales office	150	
Total payroll	$1,108	
Payroll taxes	52	
Compensation insurance	19	
Group insurance	12	
Travel and entertainment	32	
Advertising	97	
Commissions	962	
Cartage, freight, etc. on shipments	182	
Bad debts provision	104	
Miscellaneous sales expense	32	
Total selling expense (Exhibit 2)	$2,600	
Administrative Expenses:		
Salaries—		
Executives	$1,333	
Office and accounting	1,234	
Total payroll	$2,567	
Payroll taxes	122	
Compensation insurance	13	
Group insurance	10	
Travel expense	19	
Stationery and office supplies	30	
Postage	19	
Telephone and telegraph	24	
Legal and audit	50	
Dues and subscriptions	12	
Franchise taxes, etc.	20	
General insurance	10	
Miscellaneous administrative expense	154	
Total administrative expenses	$3,050	
Budget amounts omitted.		

PROCESS COSTS: OPERATION COSTS

In General

As was stated previously in this chapter, job order costing is a procedure whereby costs are distributed to jobs or production orders. Costs are compiled in job accounts or job cost sheets, from which the cost of each job can be determined when the job is finished. The focus of job order costing is upon the job, and the product cost determined under job costing is an average cost per unit for a particular job. The possibility of using job costing depends, of course, upon the possibility of identifying successive jobs as they pass through the factory. This fact suggests that a specific order production control system is a collateral requirement of the operation of a job order cost system.

Process costing, on the other hand, is a procedure whereby costs are distributed to process departments. Costs are compiled in process or department accounts by periods (day, week, or month), and at the end of each period, the cost of each process is divided by the units produced to determine the average cost per unit produced. Process cost systems are used where it is not possible (or not desired) to identify successive jobs or lots of production as they pass over the production floors. A classification of processes or departments may be set up for both cost distribution and production reporting purposes. This classification accordingly serves the purposes of process cost accounting and repetitive order production control.

Process Cost Accounting with Departmental Transfers of Inventory

The simplest type of process cost accounting is that in which an in-process inventory account is set up for each process or department, and the labor and expense of each process is compiled in the accounts during the period. Record is kept of the materials charged into each process and the quantities of processed materials transferred from one department to another and from the last department to finished goods inventory. At the end of each period, the *values* transferred are determined and recorded by transfer entries.*

Operation Costs (without Departmental Transfer Entries)

Operation costing is a form of process costing. Under operation costing, a classification of the direct labor operations being performed on the production floors is set up and direct labor is distributed to this classification. Thus, in a factory which assembles washing machines, the following classification (simplified for illustrative purposes) may be used:

---

* Illustrations of this type of costing appear in *Cost Accounting and Control* (Prentice-Hall, Inc., Englewood Cliffs, N.J.), Chapters 13 and 14, by the present author.

No.	*Description*
01	Attach main gear box to base
02	Attach tub, center post, and agitator to base
03	Attach motor, belt, and belt guard to base
04	Assemble wringer box and attach to wringer
05	Paint
06	Test
07	Pack

A unit operation cost would be determined at the end of each period by dividing the cost of each operation by the number of units of production run through the operation. A unit operation cost report is prepared weekly (or at other intervals) for the management.

In the simplest form of operation costs, product costs may not be prepared at all, except as and when required by the management. (This is unlike job order costs in which the product cost is necessarily a result of keeping job accounts or cost sheets.) Thus, product costs may be assembled when a manager asks for them by setting down the average cost per unit for materials and adding the unit operation costs for each of the operations required to turn out the product. Factory burden may be applied to the product cost by means of direct labor cost rate, direct labor hour rate (if hours as well as dollars are kept for each operation), or some other rate.

As was indicated above, departmental transfer entries are sometimes omitted in the interest of simplifying the clerical operations. When the balance sheet and the statement of profits are to be prepared, this can be done by arriving at cost of sales by deriving it from expenditures and inventories. Expenditures are charged to a production account during the period (to which is also charged the opening work-in-process inventory) and at the end of the period, the closing work-in-process inventory is estimated and deducted from expenditures to arrive at cost of goods completed. The inventories may be based upon book inventories (quantities) or physical inventories. In either case, the stage of completion would have to be estimated to determine the value of labor in process. It should be noted that any inventory discrepancies are lodged in cost of goods sold under this method. The method obviously lacks some of the controls of more formal cost accounting procedures, but it may sometimes be recommended from the standpoint of clerical economy.

20

Systems and Procedures Reports

Scope of this Chapter

This chapter explains and illustrates:

(1) A final report for a general assignment—a cost system designed "from the General ledger down" (pages 464–481).

(2) Departmental chart of accounts; departmental expense statements in manufacturing concerns (pages 481–485).

(3) Reports on comparative methods studies: some features (pages 485–487).

(4) Feasibility studies for computers—standards of presentation (pages 487–488).

Purposes of Final Report for a General Assignment

A general assignment has been described previously in this book as one involving the complete accounting system, as distinguished from an assignment involving some part of it, such as the order and billing procedure. The purposes of the final report of a general assignment are:

(1) To set out the coverage of the assignment and to state what has been accomplished.

(2) To explain how to operate the new system.

The present chapter describes the final report of a general assignment. The final report illustrated is presented to the client after the system has been in operation for one month and the first set of statements has been released to the client. The systems man has assisted the client's accounting personnel to get the new system started, and he has made such changes in the original design as were found to be necessary during the installation period. These changes are reflected in the final report.

The Parts of a Typical Final Report: Illustrations

The parts of a typical final report for a complete cost system are:

(1) Letter of transmittal.
(2) Statements.
(3) Classification of accounts.
(4) Description of debits and credits to accounts.
(5) Standard journal entries.
(6) Forms.

A general discussion of each part of a report is presented in the following sections.

Letter of Transmittal

The letter of transmittal (Figure 20-1) is a covering letter for submission of the operating manual to the client. It describes:

(1) The purposes of the new system with particular reference to (a) change in quality or quantity of information, (b) improvement of the clerical controls, or (c) clerical economies expected.
(2) The general features of the old system which were changed, and the reasons for the changes.
(3) A statement of final designing, installation work, or review work, if any, that remains to be done, and an indication of who will do the work and when it will be done. Rarely is a systems job "absolutely complete" even when the "final" report is presented. There are often good reasons why all of the contemplated changes cannot be made in a single assignment.
(4) Any necessary statement of qualifications placed upon the systems man's responsibility. In general, the systems man is responsible for the successful operation of the system, and he should not commit himself to an assignment that he cannot keep under control or on which he is not likely to receive cooperation of the client and his personnel. There are cases, however, in which the systems man is certain that the program as a whole will be successful and satisfactory to the client, although certain parts of it are not under his control. For instance, the structure of managerial information provided by a proposed system may be satisfactory, but the expense budget figures may have been compiled by client's personnel, who have accepted responsibility for them. This fact may be noted in the letter of transmittal.

JONES, WILSON & CO.
Accountants and Engineers
Chicago
(date)

Mr. John W. Hofstetter, President
Household Appliance Corporation
145 West 35th Street
Chicago, Illinois

Dear Mr. Hofstetter:

Pursuant to your instructions, we have prepared an
Accounting Manual for the Household Appliance Corporation to be
used by all subsidiaries of the Corporation and all franchise
dealers in Corporation products. A copy of the manual is submitted herewith.

The new accounting system set out in this manual provides:

(1) A complete set of financial and operating statements,
designed along the lines of organizational responsibility, by
which the management can effectively measure performance.

The income statement provides an anlysis of sales,
cost of sales, and gross profit by product class as well as net
income for outside service separate from inside service. This
analysis makes it possible to determine whether each product
class and service is profitable. Supporting expense schedules
are included for Administrative Expense; Selling Expense; Receiving, Warehousing, and Delivery Expense; Occupancy Expense;
Service Department--Inside; and Service Department--Outside.
Expense account classifications are organized upon a basic plan
which recognizes degrees of variability and types of remedial
action which are possible.

(2) A complete set of ledgers and journals, and all other
accounting forms and basic business papers, together with instructions for the operation of the system.

The classification of accounts and operating statements were
developed on the basis of a survey of the organization and plant
of the St. Louis subsidiary. St. Louis was selected because it
represented the median volume of the prospective users of the
manual and because its accounting problems were typical. We
visited a number of other distributors to test our hypothesis
that the selection of St. Louis for the basic survey and the
pilot installation was valid.

We have assisted the accounting staff of the St. Louis subsidiary of Household Appliance Corporation to install the system
in that subsidiary and to prepare the monthly statements. We
reviewed the set of statements for the month of January, 19--
with the supervisory staff of the subsidiary, interpreting the
results as shown by the statements and explaining management
uses of the statements.

Figure 20-1. Letter of Transmittal

It is customary to thank the client for the courtesies extended the systems man and his staff during the survey and installation. It may also be desirable to propose arrangements to the client for a periodic inspection of the operation of the system after it is installed (both for the benefit to the client and for the protection of the systems man), and such arrangements may be mentioned in the letter of transmittal.

Statements

A complete set of statements for the assumed Household Appliance Corporation is presented in this section of the report.

Figure 20-2.   Balance Sheet
Figure 20-3.   Income and Expense Statement
Figure 20-4.   Administrative Expense Schedule
Figure 20-5.   Selling Expense Schedule
Figure 20-6.   Receiving, Warehousing, and Shipping Expense Schedule
Figure 20-7.   Occupancy Expense Schedule
Figure 20-8.   Service Department—Inside Expense Schedule
Figure 20-9.   Service Department—Outside Expense Schedule
Figure 20-10.   Other Income and Expense Schedule

Classification of Accounts

The Classification of Accounts (Figure 20-11) is a list of all accounts in the General ledger, showing the new account numbers. It is provided for quick reference by the clerks who write accounting documents and those who code accounting documents, such as purchase invoices. (A Description of Charges and Credits to Accounts appears later in the report, to be used where the clerk must decide which of several likely accounts should be charged for the item at hand.) Where the new account coding is at all complicated, this section should contain an explanation of the coding scheme, perhaps with illustrative transactions coded, as illustrated and explained on page 476.

Description of Charges and Credits to Expense Accounts

This section of the report may cover all accounts in the General ledger or it may comprise simply the expense accounts. Figure 20-12 is a description of debits to an illustrative expense account. In some cases, the item description must be set out in great detail to guard against the possibility of an accounting clerk charging a particular item to one account

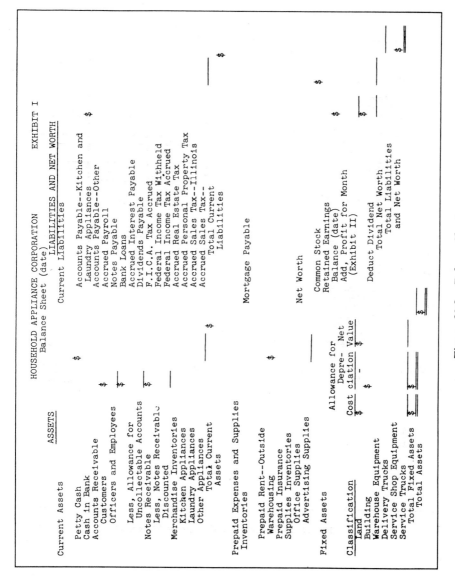

Figure 20-2. Balance Sheet

```
                    HOUSEHOLD APPLIANCE CORPORATION          EXHIBIT II
                        Income and Expense Statement
                         For the Month of (        )


                                Kitchen    Laundry    Other
                Particulars    Appliances Appliances Appliances   Total
    Sales                      $          $          $          $
        Less Returns and Allowances
            Net Sales          $          $          $          $

    Less Cost of Goods Sold

        Inventory (date)       $          $          $          $
        Purchases              $          $          $          $
        Add, Freight In
                               $          $          $          $
        Less, Returns and Allowances
            Net Purchases      $          $          $          $
            Goods Available    $          $          $          $
        Less, Inventory (date)
            Cost of Goods Sold $          $          $          $
    Gross Profit from Trading  $          $          $          $

    Add Profit from Service
                                Inside    Outside   Contracts
        Income                 $          $          $
        Expense (Schedules 5 and 6)
            Profit from Service $         $          $
    Gross Profit from Trading                                   $
    and Service

    Less Operating Expenses

        Administrative Expenses (Schedule 1)            $
        Selling Expenses (Schedule 2)
        Receiving, Warehousing and Shipping
         Expenses (Schedule 3)
        Occupance Expense (Schedule 4)
            Total Operating Expense
                Operating Net Income                    $

    Add, Other Income and Expense (Net) (Schedule 7)
            Net Profit (Exhibit I)                      $
```

Figure 20-3. Income and Expense Statement

```
                    HOUSEHOLD APPLIANCE CORPORATION
                    Administrative Expense Schedule
                         For the Month of (      )
                                                    Schedule 1

              Accounts                              Amounts

Salaries
   Administrative Salaries                    $
   Office Salaries
   Overtime Premium
      Total Salaries                          _____   $

Payroll Taxes and Insurance
   F.I.C.A. Tax                               $
   Unemployment Insurance
     Total Payroll Taxes And Insurance        _____

Stationery and Office Supplies

Repairs to Office Furniture and Equipment

Purchased Services
   Postage                                    $
   Telephone and Telegraph
   Association Dues
   Professional Services
   Donations
      Total Purchased Services                _____

Travel

Unclassified

Fixed Charges
   Rentals of Office Equipment                $
   Depreciation--Office Furniture and Equipment
   Insurance--Office Furniture and Equipment
   Taxes--Office Furniture and Equipment      _____
      Total Fixed Charges
         Total Administrative Expenses (Exhibit II)    $_____
```

Figure 20-4. Administrative Expense Schedule

at one time and to other accounts at other times. This section of the manual will be used by the accounting clerks as a constant reference as they code purchase invoices and other media. It will also be used by accounting executives when they explain the operating statements to the management, since there will be numerous questions as to what is in an account.

```
                    HOUSEHOLD APPLIANCE CORPORATION
                         Selling Expense Schedule
                         For the Month of (      )
                                                    Schedule 2

                    Accounts                                Amounts

    Salaries and Commissions
      Supervisory Salaries                        $
      Inside Salesmen
      Outside Salesmen
      Commissions
         Total Salaries and Commissions          _____    $

    Payroll Taxes and Insurance
      F.I.C.A. Tax                                $
      Unemployment Insurance
         Total Payroll Taxes and Insurance       _____

    Stationery and Office Supplies

    Advertising and Promotions
      Newspaper and Magazine Advertising          $
      Dealer Aids
      Convention Expense
      Advertising Allowances
         Total Advertising and Promotions        _____

    Purchased Services
      Association Dues                            $
      Professional Services
      Freight Out
         Total Purchased Services                _____

    Travel and Entertainment Expenses
      Automobile Expense                          $
      Travel and Entertainment
         Total Travel and Entertainment Expense  _____

    Unclassified
         Total Selling Expense (Exhibit II)                  $_____
```

Figure 20-5. Selling Expense Schedule

Standard Journal Entries

This section contains a transcript of all standard journal entries which were drawn in the design of the new system. Figure 20-13, comprising three of the 22 entries, illustrates the format of the section. (The entire

```
                    HOUSEHOLD APPLIANCE CORPORATION
           Receiving, Warehousing and Shipping Expense Schedule
                        For the Month of (      )
                                              Schedule 3

            Accounts                                    Amounts

  Salaries and Wages
    Supervisory Salaries                     $
    Warehousemen
    Truck Drivers and Helpers
    Overtime Premium
       Total Salaries and Wages              ─────────      $

  Payroll Taxes and Insurance
    F.I.C.A. Tax                             $
    Unemployment Insurance
       Total Payroll Taxes and Insurance     ─────────

  Packing Supplies

  Repairs to Warehouse Equipment

  Truck Expense (variable)
    Repairs to Trucks                        $
    Gasoline and Oil
       Total Truck Expense (variable)        ─────────

  Unclassified

  Fixed Expenses
    Depreciation--Warehouse Equipment        $
    Depreciation--Trucks
    Insurance--Warehouse Equipment
    Insurance--Inventories
    Insurance--Trucks
    Taxes--Warehouse Equipment
    Taxes--Inventories
    Taxes and Licenses--Trucks               ─────────
       Total Fixed Expenses                                ─────────
          Total Receiving, Warehousing and
          Shipping Expense (Exhibit II)                    $────────
                                                           ═════════
```

Figure 20-6. Receiving, Warehousing, and Shipping Expense Schedule

set of journal entries appears in the chapter on journals on pages 68–74.)
For each journal entry, the following information is shown:

(1) Number of the entry
(2) Summary from which the entry is drawn
(3) Frequency of the entry

(4) Complete list of debits and credits, if feasible

(5) Explanation

The standard journal entries have their roots in the systems man's worksheets. The systems man sets them up in the first place in the process of determining what journals will be provided and what columns will be

```
                        HOUSEHOLD APPLIANCE CORPORATION
                           Occupancy Expense Schedule
                            For the Month of (      )
                                                    Schedule 4

              Accounts                              Amounts


    Salaries and Wages
       Supervisory Salaries                  $
       Janitors and Watchmen
       Overtime Premium                      _____
          Total Salaries and Wages                    $

    Payroll Taxes and Insurance
       F.I.C.A. Taxes                        $
       Unemployment Insurance
          Total Payroll Taxes and Insurance  _____

    Supplies and Repairs
       Janitors' Supplies                    $
       Repairs to Building
          Total Supplies and Repairs         _____

    Heat, Light and Air Conditioning

    Fixed Charges
       Depreciation--Building                $
       Insurance--Building
       Taxes--Building                       _____
          Total Fixed Charges
          Total Occupancy Expenses (Exhibit II)      $_____
```

Figure 20-7. Occupancy Expense Schedule

```
                    HOUSEHOLD APPLIANCE CORPORATION
                 Service Department--Inside Expense Schedule
                        For the Month of (      )
                                              Schedule 5


            Accounts                                    Amounts

    Supervisory Salaries                                  $
    Repairmen
    Overtime Premium
    F.I.C.A. Tax
    Unemployment Insurance
    Operating Supplies
    Power
    Depreciation on Service Shop Equipment
    Insurance on Service Shop Equipment
    Taxes on Service Shop Equipment
        Total                                          $
    Labor Used on Service Contracts (credit)
          Net Service Department--Inside (Exhibit II)  $
```

Figure 20-8. Service Department—Inside Expense Schedule

required in each journal. They also include all of the end-of-the-month entries which the bookkeeper knows as "adjusting" entries. The standard journal entries for the special journals will show, for instance, whether the debit distribution from payments is intended to come through a pur-

```
                    HOUSEHOLD APPLIANCE CORPORATION
                Service Department--Outside Expense Schedule
                       For the Month of (        )
                                                    Schedule 6


                    Accounts                             Amounts

        Service Men                                       $
        F.I.C.A. Tax
        Unemployment Insurance
        Supplies
        Repairs to Service Trucks
        Gasoline and Oil--Service Trucks
        Unclassified
        Depreciation--Service Trucks
        Insurance--Service Trucks
        Taxes and Licenses--Service Trucks
          Total                                           $
        Labor Used on Service Contracts
            Net Service Department--Outside (Exhibit II)  $
```

Figure 20-9. Service Department—Outside Expense Schedule

chase journal, a voucher register, a cash payments journal, or through some combination of journals.

The standard journal entries also reflect the plan of accrual which the systems man has decided upon for each expense account and income account. Thus, Journal Entry No. 10 indicates that insurance expired will

```
                    HOUSEHOLD APPLIANCE CORPORATION
                    Other Income and Expense Schedule
                         For the Month of (      )
                                                    Schedule 7


              Accounts                               Amount

   Purchase Discounts
   Interest Income
   Sales Discounts
   Interest Expense
   Warranty Expense (Labor and Parts)
   Bad Debts
     Net Other Income and Expense--(Exhibit II)       $_____
```

Figure 20-10.   Other Income and Expense Schedule

be recorded monthly from the expiration columns of an insurance register
(insurance premiums paid being charged to the prepaid insurance expense account).

Where the system is a very simple one, it might not be necessary to
include the standard journal entries in the report, since the bookkeeper

HOUSEHOLD APPLIANCE CORPORATION

CLASSIFICATION OF GENERAL LEDGER ACCOUNTS

CLASSIFICATION PLAN: MAJOR GROUPS

```
100  Balance Sheet
200  Sales and Cost of Sales
300  Administrative Expenses
400  Selling Expense
500  Receiving, Warehousing, and Shipping Expense
600  Occupancy Expense
700  Service Department--Inside
800  Service Department--Outside
900  Other Income and Expenses
```

CLASSIFICATION PLAN: INTERMEDIATE GROUPS: EXPENSE ACCOUNTS
(Example: 300 Administrative Expenses)

```
310  Labor
320  Payroll Reserves
330  Supplies
340  Repairs
360  Purchased Services
370  Travel
380  Unclassified
390  Fixed Charges
```

CLASSIFICATION PLAN: MINOR GROUPS (OBJECTS): EXPENSE ACCOUNTS
(Example: 360 Purchased Services)

```
361  Postage
362  Telephone and Telegraph
363  Association Dues
364  Professional Services
```

Figure 20-11. Classification Plan: General Ledger Accounts

can determine from the journal forms (which are included in the report) what the end-of-the-month posting would be, and he can quickly work out the plan of accrual of expenses and incomes. Where the system is at all complex, however, as a standard cost system might be, it is necessary to include the standard journal entries to show how the entries tie together.

```
                    HOUSEHOLD APPLIANCE CORPORATION
                      CLASSIFICATION OF ACCOUNTS

                       BALANCE SHEET ACCOUNTS

          CURRENT ASSETS

     101    Petty Cash
     102    Cash in Bank
     111    Accounts Receivable--Customers
     111A   Allowance for Uncollectable Accounts
     112    Accounts Receivable--Officers and Employees
     113    Salesmen's Drawing Accounts
     114    Notes Receivable
     114P   Notes Receivable Discounted
     115    Accrued Interest Receivable
     120    Merchandise Inventories
     121        Kitchen Appliances
     122        Laundry Appliances
     123        Other Appliances

          PREPAID EXPENSES AND SUPPLIES INVENTORIES

     131    Prepaid Rent--Outside Warehousing
     132    Prepaid Insurance
     140    Supplies Inventories
     141        Office Supplies
     142        Warehouse and Shop Supplies
     143        Advertising Supplies

          FIXED ASSETS

     150    Land
     161    Building
     161A   Allowance for Depreciation--Building
     162    Warehouse Equipment
     162A   Allowance for Depreciation--Warehouse Equipment
     163    Delivery Trucks
     163A   Allowance for Depreciation--Delivery Trucks
     164    Service Shop Equipment
     164A   Allowance for Depreciation--Service Shop Equipment
     165    Service Trucks
     165A   Allowance for Depreciation--Service Trucks

          CURRENT LIABILITIES

     171    Vouchers Payable--Appliance Suppliers
     172    Vouchers Payable--Other
     173    Accrued Payroll
     175    Notes Payable
     176    Bank Loans
     177    Accrued Interest Payable
     178    Dividends Payable
     181    Accrued Payroll Taxes
     182    Withholding Tax Deducted
     183    Federal Income Tax Accrued
     184    Accrued Real Estate Tax
     185    Accrued Personal Property Taxes
     186    Accrued Sales Tax--Illinois
     187    Accrued Sales Tax
```

Figure 20-11 (Cont.)

It should be noted that in a large organization the procedure for closing the books at the end of each month requires a great deal of planning, since the various entries come from different parts of the Accounting department. In such cases, the systems report may show what section of the Accounting department will prepare each entry.

```
                    RESERVES

            189     Reserve for Warranty

                    LONG TERM LIABILITIES

            190     Mortgage Payable

                    NET WORTH

            195     Capital Stock
            196     Retained Earnings
            199     Profit and Loss

                         PROFIT AND LOSS ACCOUNTS


                    SALES AND PURCHASES

                    Sales and Service Income
            211         Sales of Kitchen Appliances and Parts
            212         Sales of Laundry Appliances and Parts
            213         Sales of Other Appliances
            214         Service Income--Inside
            215         Service Income--Outside
            216         Service Contracts
            217         Labor Used on Service Contracts (Debit)
                    Sales Returns and Allowances
            221         Kitchen Appliances and Parts
            222         Laundry Appliances and Parts
            223         Other Appliances
                    Purchases
            231         Kitchen Appliances and Parts
            232         Laundry Appliances and Parts
            233         Other Appliances
                    Freight In
            241         Kitchen Appliances and Parts
            242         Laundry Appliances and Parts
            243         Other Appliances
                    Purchase Returns and Allowances
            251         Kitchen Appliances and Parts
            252         Laundry Appliances and Parts
            253         Other Appliances
```

Figure 20-11 (Cont.)

Forms

This section comprises a copy of each form, and each form will be followed by a sheet explaining the use of the form. Such information as the following will be shown:

```
          ADMINISTRATIVE EXPENSES

     311  Administrative Salaries
     312  Office Salaries
     319  Overtime Premium
     321  F.I.C.A. Tax
     322  Unemployment Insurance
     331  Stationery and Office Supplies
     341  Repairs to Office Furniture and Equipment
     361  Postage
     362  Telephone and Telegraph
     363  Association Dues
     364  Professional Services
     365  Donations
     370  Travel
     380  Unclassified
     391  Rentals of Office Equipment
     392  Depreciation--Office Furniture and Equipment
     393  Insurance--Office Furniture and Equipment
     394  Taxes--Office Furniture and Equipment

          SELLING EXPENSES

     411  Sales Supervisory Salaries
     412  Inside Salesmen
     413  Outside Salesmen
     414  Commissions
     421  F.I.C.A. Tax Expense
     422  Unemployment Insurance Expense
     431  Stationery and Office Supplies
     451  Newspaper and Magazine Advertising
     452  Dealer Aids
     453  Convention Expense
     454  Advertising Allowances to Dealers
     461  Association Dues
     462  Professional Services
     463  Freight Out
     471  Automobile Expense
     472  Other Travel and Entertainment
     480  Unclassified Expense
     490  Warranty Expense
```

Figure 20-11 (Cont.)

Form number
Form name
Function of the form
Disposition of copies
Source of information for the form
Instructions on special points

RECEIVING, WAREHOUSING AND SHIPPING EXPENSE

511 Supervisory Salaries
512 Warehousemen
513 Truck Drivers and Helpers
519 Overtime Premium
521 F.I.C.A. Tax Expense
522 Unemployment Insurance Expense
531 Packing Supplies
541 Repairs to Warehouse Equipment
542 Repairs to Trucks
543 Gasoline and Oil
580 Unclassified
591 Rent--Outside Warehousing
592 Depreciation--Warehouse Equipment
593 Depreciation--Trucks
594 Insurance--Warehouse Equipment
595 Insurance--Inventories
596 Insurance--Trucks
597 Taxes--Warehouse Equipment
598 Taxes--Inventories
599 Taxes and Licenses--Trucks

OCCUPANCY EXPENSE

611 Supervisory Salaries
612 Janitors and Watchmen
619 Overtime Premium
621 F.I.C.A. Tax Expense
622 Unemployment Insurance Expense
641 Janitor Supplies
642 Repairs to Building
661 Heat, Light, and Air Conditioning
691 Depreciation--Building
692 Insurance--Building
693 Taxes--Building

Figure 20-11 (Cont.)

Journal forms for the Household Appliance Corporation are illustrated in Chapter 4. No basic papers, such as purchase orders and receiving reports (which would appear in the manual if they were a new part of the system), have been included in this illustration.

```
          SERVICE DEPARTMENT--INSIDE EXPENSE

    711   Supervisory Salaries
    712   Repairmen
    719   Overtime Premium
    721   F.I.C.A. Tax Expense
    722   Unemployment Insurance Expense
    730   Operating Supplies
    761   Power
    791   Depreciation--Service Shop Equipment
    792   Insurance--Service Shop Equipment
    793   Taxes--Service Shop Equipment
    799   Labor used on Service Contracts (Credit)


          SERVICE DEPARTMENT--OUTSIDE EXPENSE

    811   Service Men
    821   F.I.C.A. Tax
    822   Unemployment Insurance
    830   Supplies
    841   Repairs to Service Trucks
    842   Gasoline and Oil--Service Trucks
    880   Unclassified
    891   Depreciation--Service Trucks
    892   Insurance--Service Trucks
    893   Taxes and Licenses--Service Trucks
    899   Labor used on Service Contracts (Credit)


          OTHER INCOME AND EXPENSE

    911   Purchases Discounts
    912   Interest Income
    951   Sales Discounts
    952   Interest Expense
    953   Warranty Expense (Labor and Parts)
    954   Bad Debts
```

Figure 20-11 (Concluded)

Departmental Chart of Accounts: Departmental Expense Statements in Manufacturing Concerns

In manufacturing concerns where the object classification is supplemented by a departmental classification, it is useful to include in the report a chart that will show which of the theoretically possible combina-

DESCRIPTION OF CHARGES TO EXPENSE ACCOUNTS

600 Occupancy Expense

   611 Supervision:

      Wages and salaries of supervisors: superintendent,
      assistant superintendent, and foremen. (Straight
      time only; overtime premium is charged to Account
      519.) Summarized in General Journal, J. E. No. 4.

   641 Janitors' Supplies:

      Janitors' supplies, electric light bulbs,
      fluorescent tubes; lumber, paint, nails and
      other repair materials when used on a building
      repair order. Summarized in Voucher Register,
      J. E. No. 6.

Figure 20-12. Description of Charges to Expense Accounts

tions of objects and department account numbers will be used. Figure
20-14 illustrates such a chart. (This chart of accounts and the statements
in Figures 20-15 and 20-16 are related to the Central Manufacturing
Company, Chapter 19. They have no relationship to the Household Appliance Corporation, which is the basis for the previous illustrations in this
chapter.) On the chart shown in Figure 20-14, all of the accounts that

```
                         STANDARD JOURNAL ENTRIES


        Journal Entry No. 1        (Sales Journal)           Monthly

        111    Accounts Receivable--Customers
        112    Accounts Receivable--Officers and Employees
        186         Accrued Sales Tax--Illinois
        187         Accrued Sales Tax--
        211         Sales of Kitchen Appliances and Parts
        212         Sales of Laundry Appliances and Parts
        213         Sales of Other Appliances
        214         Service Income--Inside
        215         Service Income--Outside
        216         Income from Service Contracts
        463         Freight Out
                 To record sales for month, per sales invoices



        Journal Entry No. 2   (Sales Returns and Allowances Journal)  Monthly

        185    Accrued Sales Tax--Illinois
        186    Accrued Sales Tax--
        214    Service Income--Inside
        215    Service Income--Outside
        221    Sales Returns and Allowances--Kitchen Appliances and Parts
        222    Sales Returns and Allowances--Laundry Appliances and Parts
        223    Sales Returns and Allowances--Other Appliances
        454    Advertising Allowances to Dealers
        463    Freight Out
        111         Accounts Receivable--Customers
        112         Accounts Receivable--Officers and Employees
                 To record sales returns and allowances and advertising
                 allowances for month, per credit memoranda



        Journal Entry No. 3       (General Journal)           Monthly

        414    Commissions
        181         Accrued Payroll Taxes
        182         Withholding Taxes Deducted
        113         Salesmen's Drawing Accounts
                 To record commissions earned for month
```

Figure 20-13. Standard Journal Entries

will be used are listed in the left-hand column, and a separate column is provided for each department. The numbers in each department column indicate the accounts that are applicable to that department. The blank spaces in the department column, conversely, indicate either accounts that are (a) impossible in the nature of the activities of the department, or (b) not to be used. Some possible accounts will not be used because the

CENTRAL MANUFACTURING COMPANY
Labor and Manufacturing Expense Accounts
By Department

		20 Shear	21 Press	25 Material Handling	29 General Factory
	Productive Labor				
01	Clock Time	2001	2101		
03	Bonus	2003	2103		
05	Overtime Premium	2005	2105	2505	2905
08	Vacation and Holiday	2008	2108	2508	2908
	Indirect Payroll				
10	Supervision	2010	2110	2510	2910
11	Handling	2011	2111	2511	
12	Rework	2012	2112		
13	Inspection				2913
13-1	Idle Time	2013-1	2113-1		
14	Building Maintenance				2914
15	Machinery Maintenance	2015	2115	2515	2915
16	Die Maintenance		2116		
17	Production Control				2917
18	Timekeeping				2918
19	Miscellaneous Labor	2019	2119	2519	2919
	Other Factory Expenses				
20	Payroll Taxes	2020	2120	2520	2920
21	Compensation Insurance	2021	2121	2521	2921
22	Group Insurance	2022	2122	2522	2922
23	Travel Expense				2923
30	Supplies	2030	2130	2530	2930
31	Expendable Tools	2031	2131		2931
32	Power				2932
33	Professional Services				2933
39	Rent				2939
40	Maintenance and Repair--Building				2940
41	Maintenance and Repair--Machinery	2041	2141	2541	2941
42	Maintenance and Repair--Dies		2142		
44	Depreciation--Machinery and Equipment	2044	2144	2544	2944
48	Personal Property Taxes				2948
49	General Insurance				2949
59	Miscellaneous Factory Expense	2059	2159	2559	2959

Figure 20-14.   Manufacturing Expense Accounts by Department

amounts of likely charges to them is so small that it is not considered worthwhile to split invoices or otherwise break down the distribution so fine as to include charges to those accounts.

Illustrative departmental expense statements appear in Figures 20-15 and 20-16; Figure 20-15 is a report for a service department, and Figure 20-16 is a report for a producing department.

```
                   CENTRAL MANUFACTURING COMPANY
                  Schedule of Labor and Factory Expense

           General Factory Department - Month of _____ 19__

                                    Month          Year To Date
                                Budget  Actual    Budget   Actual
              Accounts

  INDIRECT PAYROLL
     Supervision                $        $        $         $
     Handling
     Inspection
     Building Maintenance
     Machine Maintenance
     Production Control
     Timekeeping
     Miscellaneous Labor
          Total-Indirect Payroll $      $        $         $

  OTHER FACTORY EXPENSES
     Payroll Taxes
     Compensation Insurance
     Group Insurance
     Travel Expense
     Supplies
     Power
     Professional Services
     Rent
     Maintenance and Repair--Building
     Depreciation--Machinery
     Personal Property Taxes
     General Insurance
     Miscellaneous
          Total-Other Factory Expenses $   $        $         $

     Total Payroll and Expenses  $        $        $         $

  Allocate General Factory Expenses
     Shear
     Press
     Material Handling
          Total                  $        $        $         $
```

Figure 20-15.   Schedule of Labor and Factory Expense: Service Department

Some Features of Reports on Comparative Methods Studies

Many procedure assignments involve comparative methods studies, usually for the purpose of determining cheaper ways to perform certain clerical operations. Sometimes a preliminary report on various possible

```
                    CENTRAL MANUFACTURING COMPANY
                   Schedule of Labor and Factory Expense

                  Shear Department - Month of _____ 19__
```

Accounts	Month		Year To Date	
	Budget	Actual	Budget	Actual
PRODUCTIVE LABOR				
Clock Time	$	$	$	$
Bonus				
Overtime Premium				
Vacation and Holiday				
Total Productive Labor	$	$	$	$
INDIRECT PAYROLL				
Supervision				
Handling				
Idle Time				
Machine Maintenance				
Total Indirect Payroll	$	$	$	$
OTHER FACTORY EXPENSES				
Payroll Taxes				
Compensation Insurance				
Group Insurance				
Supplies				
Expendable Tools				
Maintenance and Repairs-- Machinery				
Depreciation--Machinery				
Miscellaneous				
Total Other Factory Expenses	$	$	$	$
Total Payroll and Expenses	$			
GENERAL FACTORY EXPENSE CHARGES				
Total Department	$	$	$	$
MACHINE COST CHARGES TO JOBS				
Gain or Loss	$	$	$	$

Figure 20-16.   Schedule of Labor and Factory Expense: Producing Department

methods is presented to the management so that the systems man can get a decision on which method to work out in detail and install. Although clerical cost may be a major factor, the final selection by management may actually depend upon such factors as information provided by one or another method or proofs provided, or even upon personal prejudices among the management.

The preliminary report of a comparative methods study may comprise, among others, the following sections:

(1) Letter of transmittal, which explains the problem and states why several preliminary solutions are presented.

(2) Comparison of major features of the proposed methods, often in the form of a chart. Such a chart may comprise a list of questions for consideration, with a column for each of the methods. In the columns are brief answers to the questions. Sometimes a "yes" or "no" answer in each column is sufficient to point up an important element. Charts of this kind are useful in guiding the oral discussion when the report is presented.

(3) Comparative operation list in skeleton form. Often the management wishes to know the major changes in operations or flow of work, and comparative operation lists may be set out in sufficient detail (side by side) to show where the changes are.

(4) Comparative operation times and clerical costs.

Note that these comparisons may include information on the old procedure as well as the several new ones under consideration.

Feasibility Studies for Computers—Standards of Presentation

When a company management is considering the installation of computers, a feasibility study may be made to ascertain whether certain information systems and operating systems of the business should be put on computers and, if so, at what costs and with what advantages. Feasibility studies may be considered part of the broad area of methods studies. They are a special category, however, because they are likely to involve an expanded management information coverage and because of the probable size and extent of the proposed commitment. Usually the report on a computer feasibility study is presented to top management.

It is not possible to outline the report for such a study in this book, but it is useful to describe areas of interest to top management in such a report. These areas are excerpted from "Computer Feasibility Studies—Standards of Presentation," an article by J. E. Peffers.

1. The computer feasibility proposal must demonstrably be the work of company or company-oriented personnel.

2. The computer feasibility proposal must indicate which procedures and operations are to be computerized and demonstrate the physical feasibility of doing so.

3. The proposal must demonstrate the physical capability of the equipment selected to do the job asked of it.

4. The proposal must properly detail the physical facilities required to house the computer.
5. The proposal must adequately present the cost position of acquiring the computer.
6. The proposal must properly present the personnel problems of designing, implementing, and operating a computer system.
7. The proposal must properly present the personnel disruption problems of having a computer.
8. The proposal must demonstrate that the system and computer being selected are capable of absorbing expansion and change.
9. The proposal must frankly acknowledge that problems will occur during the installation period and give some indication of what these problems might be.
10. The proposal must give evidence of support from other functional areas.
11. The proposal must show evidence of solid planning for the computer installation.
12. The proposal must present, effectively, all the benefits to be derived from the computer installation.[1]

Each of these points is significant in itself and will be examined in detail. . . .

2. The Computer Feasibility Proposal Must Indicate Which Procedures and Operations Are to Be Computerized and Demonstrate the Physical Feasibility of Doing So.

This requirement is best fulfilled by including in the feasibility proposal a narrative summary describing each of the operations that will be computerized and exactly how the computer auxiliary systems will go about handling them. The narrative summary must then be backed up by solid documentary evidence in the form of systems flow charts, record designs, forms designs, sample reports, etc., which give ample evidence that the various routines were thoroughly analyzed and present graphically the manner in which a computer will handle them. The object is to present sufficient factual proof of the proposed applications having been thoroughly examined to remove management's doubts about the ability to achieve the defined goals.

---

[1] *Cost and Management,* October 1965, pages 387–393, reprinted in Bower and Welke, *Financial Information Systems* (Boston: Houghton Mifflin Company, 1968), pages 384–385.

21

Principles of
Punched-Card Accounting

Development of Punched-Card Accounting

The punched-card—or tabulator method of accounting, as it is some-times called—was originally invented for use in tabulating the United States census. A separate card was punched for each person reported by the census takers, and punched holes representing age, sex, and other significant details were accumulated for census purposes. These details were abstracted and summarized by placing the cards, one at a time, in the tabulator which read them electrically and accumulated the totals in registers.

Today, punched-card accounting is still based upon the principle of punching holes into cards to represent significant information. Equipment manufacturers have added many machines to the original punch and tabulator so that now the equipment can be used for all phases of an accounting system. Many types of businesses, both large and small, are now using punched-card equipment in varying degrees. Although analysis is still a major function, the applications now include billing, accounts payable, payroll, inventory control, and many other functions.

There are two principal manufacturers of tabulating equipment: The International Business Machines Corporation and The Remington Rand Division of Sperry Rand Corporation. Most tabulating machines are placed in customers' offices on a rental basis, although they can be purchased outright. Maintenance and obsolescence are two important factors to be considered when purchasing a machine.

Basic Units

The standard IBM (International Business Machines Corporation) tabulating card of 80 columns of punched information is a basic unit around which the entire processing revolves. It is described and illustrated below. The basic machines in a punched-card installation (that is, the ones to be found in practically every installation) are:

(1) Key Punch
(2) Sorter
(3) Tabulator

Descriptions of the above machines appear on the following pages. The three particular machines described were chosen because of their extensive use in tabulating-machine installations. The basic principles of these machines are also incorporated in later models. Most functions and features of these three machines are common in whole or in part to other machines of their group. Knowledge of these principles is necessary before attempting to cover the material in the next two chapters.

Representative types of distributions are described on pages 499–503 along with illustrations of the reports produced.

Tabulating Card (Figure 21-1)

The standard IBM punched card is $7\frac{3}{4}'' \times 3\frac{1}{4}''$, cut of rigid-stock paper. It has a capacity of 80 vertical columns of punched data. Any number of columns in any combination can be used for a particular application. Each column is made up of 12 punching positions, numbered from

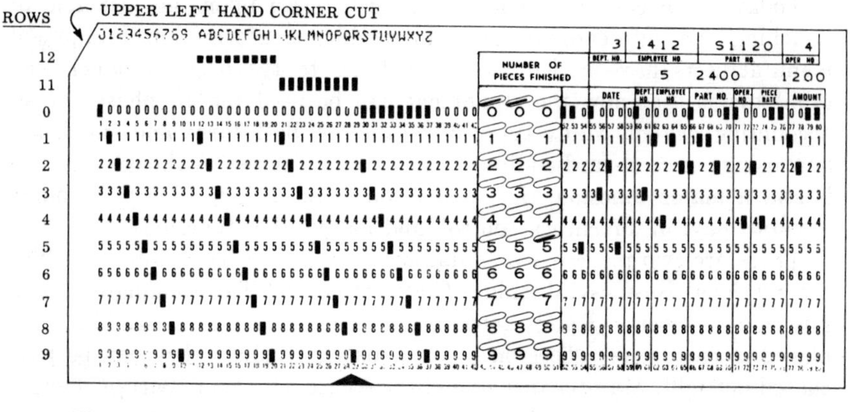

Figure 21-1.   Standard International Business Machines 80-Column Card

The above illustration shows the numerical and alphabetical punching used by the International Business Machines Corporation. The characters above columns 1-37 were printed on the 26 Printing Punch Machine (p. 505). The punching in columns 52-54 are from the mark sensed positions in columns 43-51, reproduced on the 519 Reproducing Punch (p. 509). The data in columns 52-80 was printed on the 557 Interpreter (p. 508).

top to bottom as positions 12, 11, 0 and 1 through 9. Thus the 80 columns of 12 positions each combine to offer 960 possible punching positions.

Normally only one punch per column for numerical characters and two punches per column for alphabetical characters are used, as shown in Figure 21-1. The numerical data is punched in positions 0 through 9. The 12, 11, and 0 punching positions are often referred to as zone positions. By combining a zone punch with any punch from 1 through 9 (in the same column), an alphabetical character is formed.

Most tabulators process the cards lengthwise, a row at a time (see Figure 21-1). By this method the cards enter the machine with 12 edge first and each of the rows (12) of 80 positions each, is read and registered a row at a time. Some other machines, such as the key punch (Figure 21-2) and the tape-to-card converter (Figure 22-20), process the cards a column at a time, reading from left to right. The tabulating machines read only the punched holes. The card format, color and corner cuts are optional, designed and used for ease in card identification and manual reading.

The term "field" is used extensively in punched-card tabulating. A field is the combination of one or more columns of a card to form a specific name or number. Columns 62 through 65 for instance, of the card in Figure 21-1 are combined to form the employee number field.

Punching: Type 24 Card Punch (Figure 21-2)

The Type 24 Card Punch—or key punch, as it is often called—is used to convert the written or typed data on a source document into punch card form. Both numerical and alphabetical punching is possible depending on the size keyboard used. The keyboard used with the Type 24 Key Punch in Figure 21-2 is for both numerical and alphabetical information. The alphabetical keys are in standard typewriter order. The numerical keys are to the right for ease and speed in punching numerical data.

The blank cards are placed in the card hopper by the operator. The machine feeds, positions, and ejects the cards automatically. The operator reads the source document and by depressing the keys of the key punch converts the written information into punched holes in the card, a column at a time. The operator's primary concern is to depress the keys in the proper sequence. When the source document is designed with key punching in mind, both speed and accuracy are increased.

The reading station on the left of the machine permits automatic duplicating of information into the following card. By the use of this feature, common information such as payroll number, department number, and date can be punched into the cards at a greater speed than if manually key punched for each individual card. This common information is punched into the first card. As this card is passing under the read-

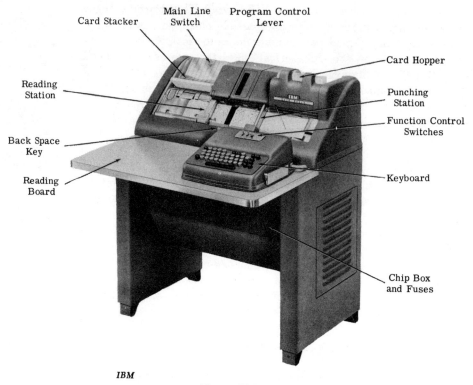

Figure 21-2.   Type 24 Card Punch

ing station, the following card is passing under the punching station in unison, a column at a time. The reading brushes sense the holes punched in the first card and by means of electrical current operate comparable punch dies at the punch station to duplicate the common information into the following card. This duplicating continues automatically for the remaining cards.

Sorting: Type 83 Sorter

Figure 21-3 is an illustration of the Type 83 Sorter. This machine automatically groups all cards of a similar accounting classification and at the same time arranges them in numerical sequence. Cards are fed into the card hopper at the upper-right side of the machine and they pass into the feed rolls past the sorter brush which is made of fine steel wires. Figure 21-4 is a close-up of the brush, feed rolls, and other operating parts of the sorter. The brush makes contact (through the hole punched in the card) with a brass cylinder causing an electrical circuit to actuate a mag-

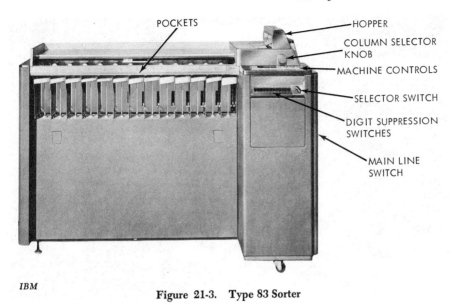

POCKETS

HOPPER

COLUMN SELECTOR
KNOB

MACHINE CONTROLS

SELECTOR SWITCH

DIGIT SUPPRESSION
SWITCHES

MAIN LINE
SWITCH

IBM

Figure 21-3.   Type 83 Sorter

net. This magnet causes a set of chute blades to drop, which, according to the position of the card when the contact is made, directs the card to the appropriate receiving pocket. The sorter normally reads only one column at a time; thus, if the field to be sorted consists of more than a single column, it is necessary to pass the cards through the machine once for each column of the field or fields being sorted.

The principle of sorting cards or tickets into numerical order by a common code is the same whether it is performed by a machine or by hand. The tickets are sorted on one digit of the control numbers at a time until the media are assembled according to number order. This is achieved by starting with the low order, or units digit, of the number, following with the tens digit, and continuing until all digits of the number have been sorted. A five-digit number would require each ticket to be sorted five times—once for each digit.

The manner in which the machine performs this operation is essentially the same as that used in a conventional box sort. Visualize a series of ten boxes placed on a table and numbered from 0 to 9. Take a packet of tickets numbered from 1 to 999, but in no numerical sequence. To arrange these tickets in order by means of a box sort, first sort these tickets into the boxes, placing the 0's in the front of the pack, the 1's behind them, and the balance of the cards through 9 in numerical sequence in the same manner. The tickets are now in consecutive order, but only by the units position of the numbers. Now take the tickets and repeat the same opera-

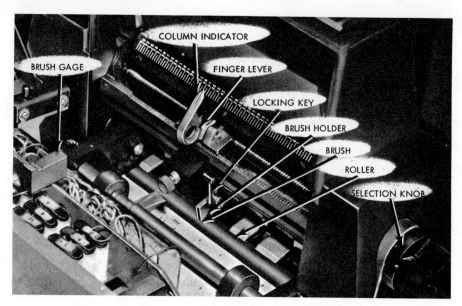

Figure 21-4. Operating Parts of a Type 83 Sorter

tion using the tens position instead of the units position. This sorting will put the cards in order numerically by the last two digits of the ticket number. A third sort, using the hundreds position of the ticket number, will then finally arrange the tickets in a strict numerical sequence from 1 to 999.

This same method of sorting is performed by the machine. The operator sets the column indicator (see Figure 21-4) on the units column of the control field. The cards fall in pockets 0-9. The cards in pocket 0 are first returned to the hopper, then the cards in pockets 1 thru 9 inclusive. The indicator is set on the next column to the left (tens position) and the process is repeated. This procedure continues for the remaining columns in the field. The Type 83 Sorter sorts cards at 1,000 cards per minute for each column.

By the use of a special switch, the sorting time of alphabetical information has been shortened. The alphabet is divided into three parts, A through I, J through R, and S through Z. As the cards pass through the sorter the first time the cards with A through I punched in them are sorted into pockets 1 through 9. The J through R cards are dropped into the 11 pocket and the S through Z cards dropped into pocket 0. These two groups are then sorted separately, with J through R cards sorted into pockets 1 through 9 and the S through Z cards sorted into pockets 2 through 9. Thus the number of passes required for alphabetical sorting has been cut to less than two passes per card, on an average. The basic principle of sorting from right to left on the particular field holds true for alphabetical as well as numerical information.

Principles of the Electric Tabulator (Figure 21-5)

The electric tabulator or accounting machine as it is often called, is basically a listing-adding machine. The operation of this machine is controlled by the punched holes in a tabulating card. As the punched card passes through the machine, a series of wire brushes makes contact with an electric roller through the holes in the card which actuates print bars and counters (registers) to print and accumulate the amounts being read. The Type 402 Accounting Machine will be used here to illustrate the principles of electric tabulators. The 402 Accounting Machine processes alphabetical as well as numerical punching. Negative as well as positive amounts can be accumulated and printed. The accumulation of minor, intermediate, and major totals is also possible on this machine.

All tabulators have the following common integral parts:

(1) Card feed, where the punched cards are fed from the hopper into the machine for processing.

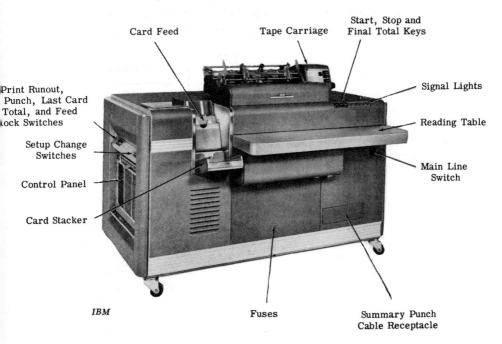

Figure 21-5. Type 402 Accounting Machine

(2) Reading stations, where the cards are positioned for processing (Figure 21-6). There are two reading stations in the 402 Tabulator, each station consisting of 80 wire brushes, one for each column of the card. The reading stations, although identical in appearance, perform different functions. At the first reading station, the functional or control punches are read. The 11 and 12 punches are normally used as control punches as explained in the following paragraph.

The "12" or "11" punch, as illustrated in Figure 21-1, are at the leading or top edge of the card. As the card is read into the machine, leading edge first, these two punches are read or sensed prior to the numerical punching. By the use of an early impulse from a control punch, the machine can be controlled to perform some predetermined function. For example, in the listing of amounts for one account, credit amounts are identified by a "CR" symbol. This symbol is printed under control of a "control punch" over the units column of the amount field. When using header cards for printing headings, titles, and other indicative information, the header cards are identified by a significant control punch in one of its columns.

(3) The comparing unit, which is used to set in motion a series of machine functions (program steps) when a change in the control

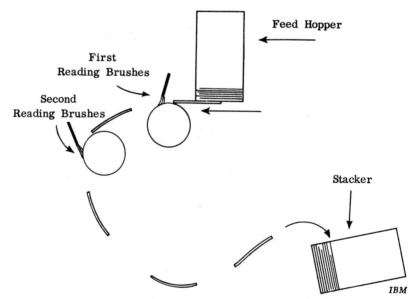

Figure 21-6. First and Second Reading Stations of the 402 Accounting Machine

number takes place. Each card has a control field (employee number and department number, for example) which is compared with the same control field of the card following it (see Figure 21-8, page 500). This method of comparing is made possible by using the two reading stations. The card being processed at the second reading station is compared with the card behind it at the first reading station. When a change in control number takes place, a set of electric contacts is made and an impulse is sent to the control panel. This impulse can be used to print out sub-totals and totals, cross-foot these totals to zero balance, print out headings, and so on. When a machine starts a series of program steps, card reading is momentarily discontinued.

Between the reading cycles the cards are advanced to the next location in the machine. Thus, the card at second read is sent out of the machine to the stacker, the card at first read is advanced to second read, and the next card in the hopper is positioned at first read. This comparing feature again takes place when the card at second read is compared with the card at first read on their control numbers. Thus, each card is compared with the card behind it to test for a change in control number.

(4) Counters, which consist of a number of single-digit accumulators. The maximum number of accumulators on a 402 Accounting Machine is 80. These 80 accumulators are associated in groups of two, four, six, or eight to form various size counters. The counters will accumulate both positive and negative amounts. By the use of a control punch (11 or 12) over a particular column of the amount field, the machine can be controlled to read the amount punched as a negative sum into the accumulator. One accumulator can accept both positive and negative amounts. By the same token, if a negative amount has been accumulated, a credit sign (CR) will automatically print after the total. It is possible to couple two or more counters together to form larger counters. An eight-position counter when coupled to a six-position counter forms a 14-position counter.

(5) Print units, which print out headings, accumulated totals, information directly from the card (listing), and special characters. The print unit consists of a number of print wheels or print bars depending on the type machine used. The 402 Accounting Machine has a maximum of 88 print bars. Of this number, 43 are alphameric and 45 are numeric. The alphameric bars are located on the left side of the print unit, the numeric bars on the right side. Because of this arrangement, alphabetical information can only be printed on the left hand side of the form when all print bars are

used. The alphameric bars print the 26 alphabetical characters, numbers 0 through 9 and a special character, the ampersand (&). The 43 numerical bars are divided into two sets, odd and even. The numerical bars contain the numbers 0 through 9 and a special character. The even-numbered bars contain the credit sign (CR), and the odd-numbered bars have the asterisk (*).

(6) Card stacker, which is directly below the card feed on the **402** Accounting Machine. The cards are advanced to the stacker and stacked automatically upon completion of processing.

(7) The Wiring panel, which controls the operations for the machine, is wired specially for each job. These control panels are removable, and easily inserted in the machine in a matter of seconds. By use of control panel wiring, the reading brushes are tied to the print bars, counters, and other machine parts to perform the desired function. Control panel wiring determines which columns of the card are processed and how. Because of the great flexibility in control panel wiring, many varied formats of printed information can be achieved.

(8) The Automatic carriages, which vary in types for different tabulators. The purpose of the carriage is to guide the form past the printing unit in such a manner as to insure maximum legibility as well as spacing and automatic skipping to various parts of the form. Some types of carriages will handle various size forms up to 22 inches in length and 19½ inches in width. A six-part form

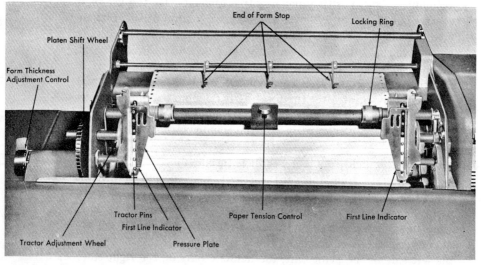

Figure 21-7. Automatic Carriage for Accounting Machine

IBM

(original and five copies) is standard, but forms with a greater number of parts can be run on most carriages. The continuous type form as illustrated in Figure 21-7 is used with the automatic carriages. The guide holes on either side of the form, which are used by the tractor to pull the form through the carriage, may be perforated and detached, if desired.

Tabulated Reports (*Distributions*)

Reports to Be Illustrated

It has been explained that the punched-card tabulating method is basically a unit-ticket method of distribution in which sorting is performed by machine, and in which totaling the sorted tickets and printing the totals on the report form are also performed by machine. The reports produced on a tabulator are columns of account numbers and quantity or money details and totals. Often they show the various totals of the sorted media, or, as they are called, major, intermediate, and minor totals. The number of classes of totals on a given report depends somewhat upon the counter capacity of the machine, as it does in a conventional listing-adding machine.

A number of reports are illustrated herewith, not with the idea of explaining all of the types that can be prepared on a tabulator, but to show the application of mechanical principles. They are based upon assumed 12 labor job tickets which have been punched for:

Transaction code number
Factory ledger account number
Department number
Employee number
Production order number
Hours
Rate
Amount

The tabulating card illustrated in Figure 21-8 shows the data as it is punched for the first of the 12 labor job tickets.

To illustrate the part that sorting plays in the production of tabulated reports, the reports are presented in the order in which they might be prepared:

(1) A listing of all 12 cards, showing employee number, hours, wages, and other information (Figure 21-9).
(2) Tabulated payroll (Figure 21-10).

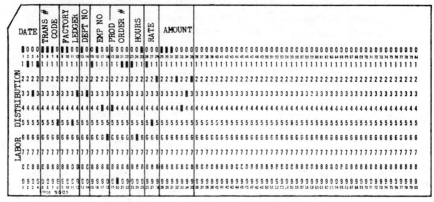

Figure 21-8. Labor Distribution Punch Card

IBM

IBM

(3) Department labor report. Labor totals by department (Figure 21-11).

(4) Production order cost report. Labor totals by production order (Figure 21-12).

(5) Analysis of labor costs. Job by department (major totals and minor totals) (Figure 21-13).

List (*Figure 21-9*)

Figure 21-9 is a list of 12 tabulating cards which were punched from employees' job tickets and sorted by employee number. Note that on a list, information from each card is printed on the paper. Hours and amount were being accumulated in counters in the tabulator and the totals printed by employee and department numbers. The major total was printed after the last card was run out of the machine.

Payroll: Control (*Figure 21-10*)

Figure 21-10 is a payroll prepared by tabulating the cards that have been sorted by employee number. The wiring panel is plugged to read transaction code number, employee number, hours, and wages. In the tabulating operation, as long as the employee number on successive cards is identical, the tabulator will accumulate hours and wages for that employee number. When the employee number changes, the machine stops reading cards, prints out the totals that stand in the counters, resets the counters to zero, and starts again. Thus, in the tabulating operation the

DATE	TRANS CODE NO	FACTORY LEDGER A/C NO	DEPT NO	EMPLOYEE NO	PROD ORDER NO	HOURS	RATE	AMOUNT
1-31	5	53	3	1046	4911	16.0	1.52	24.32
					(Minor Total)	16.0		24.32
1-31	5	53	3	1047	4911	12.0	1.32	18.24
1-31	5	53	3	1047	4232	16.0	1.32	24.32
1-31	5	53	3	1047	1197	8.0	1.52	12.16
						36.0		54.72
1-31	5	53	3	1051	4761	16.0	1.52	24.32
1-31	5	53	3	1051	4911	8.0	1.52	12.16
						24.0		36.48
					(Intermediate Total)	76.0*		115.52*
1-31	5	53	4	2001	1197	24.0	1.25	30.00
						24.0		30.00
1-31	5	53	4	2002	4911	40.0	1.25	50.00
						40.0		50.00
1-31	5	53	4	2003	4232	16.0	1.25	20.00
1-31	5	53	4	2003	4761	16.0	1.25	20.00
						32.0		40.00
1-31	5	53	4	2004	1197	35.5	1.25	44.37
1-31	5	53	4	2004	4761	4.5	1.25	5.63
						40.0		50.00
						136.0*		170.00*
					(Major Total)	212.0**		285.52**

Figure 21-9. List: Job Tickets—Direct Labor (all columns printed)

Trans. Code No.				Employee No.		Hours		Amount
5				1 0 4 6		1 6 0		2 4 3 2
5				1 0 4 7		3 6 0		5 4 7 2
5				1 0 5 1		2 4 0		3 6 4 8
5				2 0 0 1		2 4 0		3 0 0 0
5				2 0 0 2		4 0 0		5 0 0 0
5				2 0 0 3		3 2 0		4 0 0 0
5				2 0 0 4		4 0 0		5 0 0 0

Figure 21-10. Payroll

tabulator automatically senses a change in employee number. In this operation, the tabulator is said to control on employee number.

The transaction code number and employee number are printed from the first card of each group.

Departmental Labor Report (Figure 21-11)

The departmental labor report is prepared by tabulating the cards that have been sorted by department number. In this case, the wiring

Trans. Code No.			Dept. No.			Hours		Amount
5			3			7 6 0		1 1 5 5 2
5			4			1 3 6 0		1 7 0 0 0

Figure 21-11. Departmental Labor Report

panel is plugged to read transaction code number, department number, hours, and amount.

Production Order Cost Report (Figure 21-12)

The production order cost report is prepared by sorting the cards by production order number and tabulating them. In this case, the wiring panel is plugged to read transaction code number, production order number, hours, and amount.

Trans. Code No.					Production Order No.	Hours		Amount
5					1 1 9 7	6 7 5		8 6 5 3
5					4 2 3 2	3 2 0		4 4 3 2
5					4 7 6 1	3 6 5		4 9 9 5
5					4 9 1 1	7 6 0		1 0 4 7 2

Figure 21-12. Production Order Cost Report

Analysis of Labor Costs: Production Orders by Department (Figure 21-13)

Figure 21-13 is a tabulation showing hours and wages spent in each department on each production order. On this report, production order totals are an example.

Note that in tabulating the report, the tabulator is reading and controlling on production order number and department number. When department number changes, the accumulated hours and wages for the department are printed; when production order number changes, the accumulated hours and wages for the production order are printed.

Trans. Code No.			Dept. No.		Production Order No.	Hours		Amount
5			3		1 1 9 7	8 ¦ 0		1 2 1 6
5			4		1 1 9 7	5 9 ¦ 5		7 4 3 7
						6 7 ¦ 5*		8 6 5 3*
5			3		4 2 3 2	1 6 ¦ 0		2 4 3 2
5			4		4 2 3 2	1 6 ¦ 0		2 0 0 0
						3 2 ¦ 0*		4 4 3 2*
5			3		4 7 6 1	1 6 ¦ 0		2 4 3 2
5			4		4 7 6 1	2 0 ¦ 5		2 5 6 3
						3 6 ¦ 5*		4 9 9 5*
5			3		4 9 1 1	3 6 ¦ 0		5 4 7 2
5			4		4 9 1 1	4 0 ¦ 0		5 0 0 0
						7 6 ¦ 0*		1 0 4 7 2*

Figure 21-13. Labor Costs—Job by Department

Making One Sorting Operation Serve Two Reports

The series of reports illustrated shows that it is possible to make one sorting operation serve two reports. Figures 21-11, 21-12, and 21-13 were prepared in that order.

When a number of different reports are to be tabulated from the same cards, it is necessary to arrange the sequence of sorting and tabulating carefully. The object, of course, is to sort the cards the fewest number of times to produce the required reports.

22

Equipment for
Punched-Card Accounting

Machines Described in Chapter 21

In Chapter 21 the IBM (International Business Machines) standard 80-column tabulating card and three basic machines were described and illustrated. The following IBM machines were used for illustrative purposes:

(1) Type 24 Key Punch (Figure 21-2)
(2) Type 83 Sorter (Figure 21-3)
(3) Type 402 Tabulator (Figure 21-5)

In this chapter one or two types of each of the remaining punch-card machines will be described and illustrated.

The first part of this chapter is devoted to the IBM machines and the second part to the Sperry Rand Machines. The third part will briefly describe the principle of punched paper tape, machines producing these tapes, and how the paper tape is related to the punched card.

Chapter 21 was reduced to a minimum of detail to give the reader the general idea of punched-card tabulating. The present chapter contains detail necessary to a reasonably complete understanding. It is suggested that the reader cover this chapter rapidly the first time solely for the purpose of becoming familiar with the names of the various machines and in general what they will do. After reading the next chapter on machine applications, he may return to this chapter for a more thorough coverage of details.

When a demonstration of tabulating machines is contemplated, reading this chapter beforehand will make the demonstration more meaningful.

INTERNATIONAL BUSINESS MACHINES COMPANY EQUIPMENT

Card Punches and Verifiers

Type 26 Printing Punch (Figure 22-1). This punch has the same basic features as the Type 24 Key Punch covered on pages 491 and 492 of

Chapter 21. In addition to punching both alphabetical and numerical information, performing automatic duplication and skipping, this machine will also print the character directly above the column in which it is punched (see Figure 21-1). The latter feature is optional and is con-

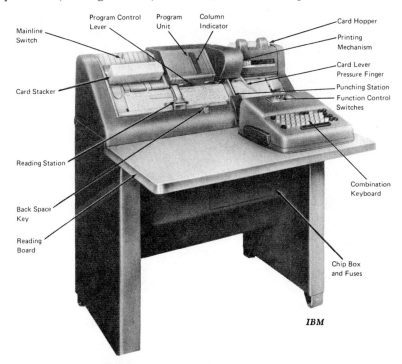

Figure 22-1. Type 26 Printing Card Punch

trolled by a switch on the keyboard. By printing directly above the column punched, 80 printed characters are possible across the top of the card. The processing time is the same whether the printing feature is used or not. This machine is popular in installations that do not have an interpreting machine.

Type 29 Card Punch (Figure 22-2). The Type 29 card punch is similar to the Type 26 except that the Type 29 has an expanded keyboard that allows this unit to be integrated with the IBM System 360.

Type 56 Verifier (not illustrated). This machine is identical in appearance to the Type 24 Key Punch. After the cards have been key punched, and if the checking for possible key punching errors is required, the 56 Verifier is used. Both the punched cards and the source document (from which they were punched) are forwarded to the verifying section. The verification of the data should be performed by a person other than the one who key punched the cards to eliminate repeating any incorrect inter-pretation that may have been committed in key punching.

The punched cards are placed in the hopper in the same order as they were when key punched. The operator reads the source document, de-presses the same keys that were depressed to punch the holes in the card. But, instead of punching holes, the keys set up comparing units that are comparing the punched characters in the card with the depressed keys of the verifier. When both the character in the card and the key depressed are the same, the card is automatically stepped to the next column. When an error is detected, either in the original punched data or in verifying, the machine stops. The operator is given a second chance to depress the key corresponding to the hole in the card. If on the second attempt, the key depressed is still different from the punched hole, a notch is made in the card directly above the column in error. The operator continues to verify the remaining columns of the card. After the entire deck has been verified, the error cards are removed and returned to the key punch sec-tion for correction. A card that is verified without error has an identifying notch made on the right hand edge of the card.

It is not always necessary to verify all the fields punched. Employee number, rate of pay, and hours worked are typical fields verified. Where the correct spelling of names, description of items and similar information

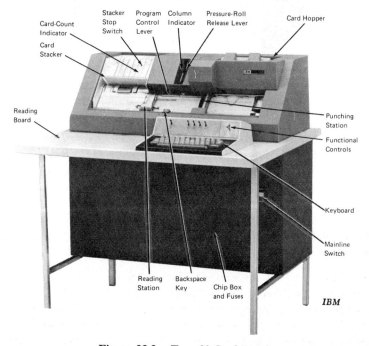

Figure 22-2. Type 29 Card Punch

need not be 100 per cent correct, these fields can be skipped when verifying the card.

Type 59 Verifier (Figure 22-3). This unit was designed for use in connection with the IBM System/360. The Type 59 verifier operates in a similar fashion to the Type 56 Verifier, except that the Type 59 combination keyboard can have the normal 48 characters or the expanded 64 characters compatible with the Type 59 card punch.

Type 557 Interpreter (Figure 22-4). Until recently the punched card was solely a medium or tool from which reports were printed. Today, as many of us know, tabulator cards are used for bills, checks, and income tax returns. To assist in the visual reading of the card, printing of the punched information on the card is necessary.

The interpreter is the machine used to print on the card the information punched in the card. As you can see in Figure 21-1, on page 490 the printing need not be directly related to the column or columns being interpreted. The printed characters are larger than those printed by the printing key punch machine, therefore, only 60 characters are possible across the card. When more than 60 characters are printed, two lines must be used. The 557 Interpreter will print both alphabetical and numerical information as well as a number of special characters. This machine will print on any of 25 lines across the card. Printing of data from a master

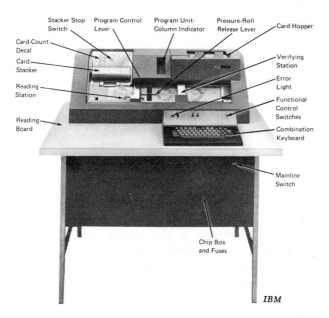

Figure 22-3. Type 59 Card Verifier

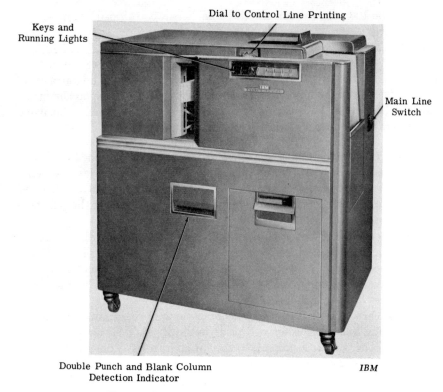

Dial to Control Line Printing

Keys and
Running Lights

Main Line
Switch

Double Punch and Blank Column
Detection Indicator

IBM

Figure 22-4.   Type 557 Alphabetical Interpreter

card onto the following detail cards is also possible. This machine operates at the speed of 100 cards per minute. A control panel is wired for each application of the 557 Interpreter.

Type 519 Reproducing Punch (Figure 22-5). Reproducing consists in reading certain information from one set of cards and punching it into another set of cards. Thus, in a salary payroll application where a card is punched each month for each salary employee, the constant information would include employee name, employee number, social security number, department number, and so forth. The common practice is to establish a "Master File" of all such constant information comprising a card for each employee carried on the payroll and bearing all such data for the employee. Such a file is kept currently up to date, and at the end of the payroll period, the entire file is reproduced into a new set of cards as a basis for the current month's classifications.

One of the machines in general use for such reproducing operations is the Type 519 Reproducing Punch (Figure 22-5). This machine actually

Read Feed Unit   Punch Feed Unit

Keys and Lights

Card Stackers

Comparing Indicator

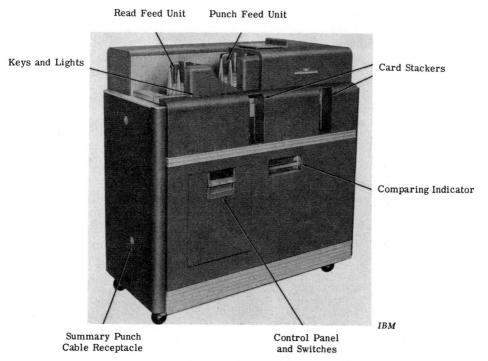

IBM

Summary Punch
Cable Receptacle

Control Panel
and Switches

Figure 22-5.   Type 519 Reproducing Punch

comprises two separate devices—a reading unit and a punching unit. The machine has two card feeds, one for each of the two units. The right-hand hopper is the feed for the punch unit of the machine and the left-hand hopper is the feed for the reading portion of the machine. In reproducing, the master file of original cards is fed into the left-hand hopper, and blank cards are placed in the right-hand hopper.

The machine has a wiring panel used to wire the various impulses which will cause the machine to read the original deck of cards and to punch the information into the blank cards. All or any portion of the cards may be reproduced, and the information may be punched into the same columns as in the original deck, or it may be punched into any other columns desired. The machine has a device known as a comparing unit which compares the result of the reproduced punching with the original punching. When an error or a failure to punch is detected, the machine stops and turns on a light. At the same time, a column signal device indicates the column or columns in which the punching failure has occurred.

The Type 519 Reproducing Punch will do the following operations in addition to the conventional reproducing operation described above:

(1) Mark Sensing
(2) Summary Punching
(3) Gang Punching
(4) End Printing

Mark Sensing

By means of the mark sensing feature, pen or pencil marks on cards are automatically converted to punched holes in any column of the card. A highly conductive lead or ink is used for marking the specially designed card (see Figure 21-1). This feature is made possible by the use of the wire brushes normally used to read the punched holes. As can be seen in Figure 21-1, the mark-sense position—or bubble, as it is often called—is approximately three columns wide. This means that three brushes are used to sense the pencil mark and operate a punch die. A maximum of 27 mark-sensed positions can be used when punching into the same card. When punching directly into a second card, leaving the mark-sensed card unpunched, 26 positions are possible. The 519 Reproducer reads and punches at the rate of 100 cards a minute.

Mark sensing is popular where information is gathered from various outlying points. Such constant information as month, year, warehouse number, item number and description can be pre-punched into the cards before they are forwarded to the warehouse for mark sensing. The variable data, such as quantity on hand, reordering point, and amount to be ordered, are mark-sensed, along with the day, on the card. The mark-sensed card becomes a source document thus eliminating key punching and key verifying—a saving in both machine and operator cost.

Summary Punching

The purpose of summary punching is to eliminate as many of the original detail cards as possible. This is made possible by punching the totals accumulated from a group of detail cards into one card in the summary punch. The summary punch is connected to a tabulating machine by means of a cable. Blank cards, ready to be punched, are placed in the punch hopper. The detail cards have been sorted on the control field and placed in the read hopper of the tabulating machine. The two machines work together in this process. When a change occurs in the control number, the tabulator reads the totals out of its counters and punches them into the summary card. On the next cycle, these same counters direct the print unit to print the same totals on the report. The counters are then reset to zero and are ready for the next group of cards.

Gang Punching

When the punching of common information is desired in a deck of cards, the gang punching feature is used. For this operation only the punch side of the 519 Reproducer is used. A header card, with the desired information (date and identifying code or account number, for example), is placed ahead of the detail cards in the punch hopper. As the header card moves under the gang punch brushes, the following detail card is moving under the punch dies. Those columns that are wired for gang punching on the control panel are sensed by the brushes and punched into the following card.

Thus, before punching the day's job tickets, it may be desired to gang punch the date, transaction code number, and factory ledger account number into a sufficient quantity of blank cards to take care of the day's requirement. This would be done to save the time of key punching or duplicating those fields. The 519 gang punches at the rate of 100 cards per minute.

End Printing

A feature of the 519 Reproducer not offered on other IBM Reproducers is end printing. The printing of eight digits is possible on either the right or left end of the card. Printing on two lines is possible by passing the cards through the machine a second time and positioning the printing unit to print on the second line (see Figure 22-6).

Sorters

In addition to the Type 83 Sorter described in Chapter 21, there are newer models having greater speed and flexibility:

Type 84 Sorter (Figure 22-7). The manufacturer, by the use of a photoelectric beam of light (Figure 22-8) instead of a wire brush to sense the punched hole, has increased the speed of sorting to 2,000 cards per minute on this machine. Because of this speed the capacity of the hopper and pockets has been increased accordingly. Radial stackers, each with a capacity of 1,650 cards, permit the removal of cards from the stacker while the machine is running. The file feed permits the loading of 3,600 cards at one time. Vacuum-assisted feeding of cards eliminates the card weight required on most other punched card machines.

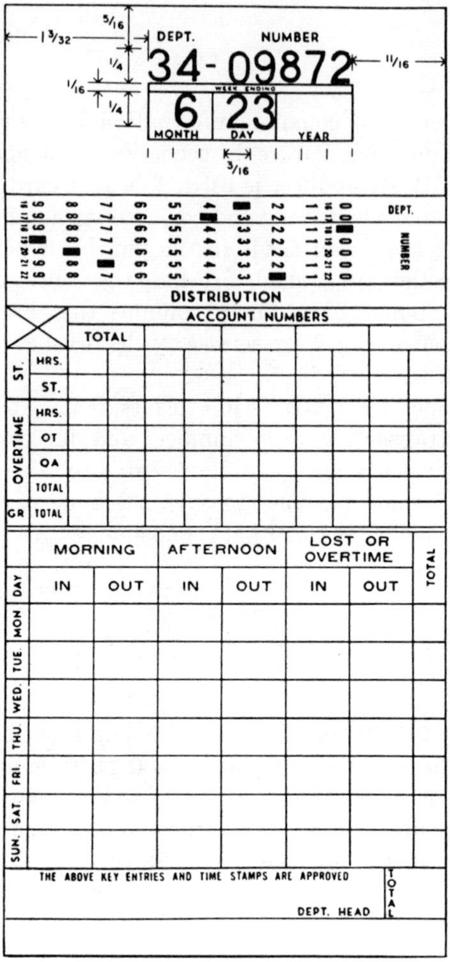

Figure 22-6.   End Printing

Type 101 Statistical Sorter (Figure 22-9). This sorter is used where the collection and tabulation of numerical information is desired. The 101 Sorter is an elaborate counting machine, capable of picking a varied number of items off a tabulator card, accumulating them in a like number of counters, balancing and editing these items (if desired), and printing out a report. The Statistical Sorter senses all 80 columns of the card on one pass through the machine. The basic sorters described above sense (read) only one column per pass. In statistical applications, various items punched in a card are counted and the sum of the times is printed out on a report. The total number of the combined items is also counted for

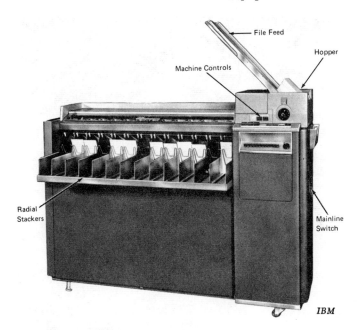

Figure 22-7. Type 84 Sorter

purposes of zero balancing. A cipher is printed on the right side of the report to signify that the items balanced.

The report illustrated in Figure 22-10 is a typical report run off on the 101 Sorter. A deck of 2,500 public health statistical cards were passed through the machine five times. On the first pass, the cards were counted for a total card count as well as by each age group as indicated. On the succeeding runs the cards are grouped according to classification. A total count by individual classification as well as by age group is printed out.

The editing feature of the 101 Statistical Sorter involves the reviewing, checking, and approval of a card before it is sorted or counted. Editing is made possible by control-panel wiring. The panel is wired to check for predetermined punches in certain columns of the card. For example, assume a study is made involving individuals with no more than an eighth-grade education, married, and earning between $2,000 and $3,999. The control panel would be wired to sort (select) only those cards with a "2" (married), "1" (1-8 year education) and "1" (earnings $2,000-$3,999) punched in the three appropriate columns (see Figure 22-10). These cards could be directed to any pocket desired, all other cards are dropped in the reject pocket. Thus the deck has been edited to insure that only those cards required for the study are used, all other cards are set aside.

Cards processed on costly computers should first be edited for proper

IBM

Figure 22-8. Sensing Mechanism Type 84 Sorter

punching. This procedure eliminates lost computer time because of incorrectly punched cards.

Accounting Machines

In addition to the 402 Accounting Machine described and illustrated in the previous chapter, IBM manufactures other tabulators, some very similar in operating features to the 402. The 407 Accounting Machine is the newest of the IBM tabulators, although the others are still widely used.

Type 403 Accounting Machine (not illustrated). This machine is very similar to the 402 in both appearance and function. In addition to the features of the 402 machine described on pages 495 to 499, the 403 machine also has the feature of printing three lines from one card. This feature permits the use of one card for printing the name, address, city, and state. Like the 402, this machine also incorporates the automatic-tape-controlled carriage. This carriage is controlled by holes in a narrow paper tape, the length of which exactly corresponds to the length of the form in

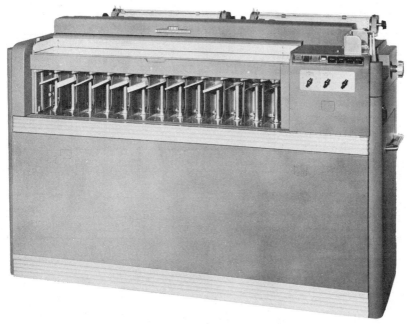

Figure 22-9. Type 101 Statistical Sorter   *IBM*

the carriage. In the operation of the machine, the tape is synchronized with the movement of the continuous form through the carriage. A special tape is prepared for each report form. The holes in the tape control skipping to predetermined locations on the form for printing out headings, first line of the body, various subtotals and totals and also controls skipping from one form to another.

Type 407 Accounting Machine (Figure 22-11). The printing unit consists of 120 print wheels, each wheel containing 47 characters (26 alphabetical, 10 numerical, and 11 special characters). This permits printing of alphabetical as well as numerical information any place across the form. The 120 print wheels are divided into 10 wheels per inch. This machine lists at 150 cards per minute, maintaining the same speed while adding, subtracting, comparing or selecting. The 28 counters are divided into three, four, six and eight position groups. Both negative and positive amounts can be added into the same counter. These counters may be coupled together to handle larger figures. In addition to the conventional major, intermediate and minor totals offered on most tabulators, this machine, by the use of a special programming feature, can expand the number of totals to greater than 20 and can cross-foot the same number of figures. The

Report - Totals by Age Group									
Run No.	Count Classification	G. I.	Tot 1	Age Groups				80-99	0 Check
				0-4	5-9	10-14	15-19		
				2	3	4	5	18	19
1	All Cards		2500	150	200	175	225	4	0
2.	Cause of Death								
	Infectious	1	275	1	4	12	9		0
	Respiratory	2	26		1		2	4	0
	Accident	3	112	40	18	16	7		0
	Other	4	2087	109	177	147	207		0
3.	Marital Status								
	Single	1	502	150	200	175	200	1	0
	Married	2	1117	•	•		24	1	0
	Other (3-5)	3	881	•	•		1	2	0
4.	Education								
	0 years		238	150	75	3	10		0
	1-8 years	1	316	•	125	79	104	2	0
	9-10 years	2	285	•	•	6	69		0
5.	Earnings								
	0-999		175	46	32	29	41		0
	1000-1999	1	108	28	12	6	3	4	0
	2000-2999	2	82	21	9	5	3		0
	etc.								

*Inconsistent Codes

IBM

Figure 22-10.   Report Produced on Type 101 Statistical Sorter

Feed Hopper   Stacker   Carriage   Operating Keys and Signal Lights

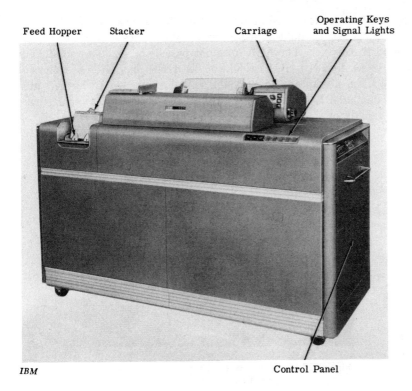

IBM   Control Panel

Figure 22-11. Type 407 Accounting Machine

number and size of the counters required for the particular application is the only limiting factor.

The 407 Accounting Machine also incorporates both the automatic tape controlled carriage and the multiple line read feature of reading and printing three lines from one card. Detail printing (printing of information from each card), group printing (printing indicative information from the first card and accumulating and printing out totals for the group), and summary punching, by coupling a reproducing punch to the 407, are all standard features of the 407. More than one particular job can be wired on a control panel by the use of four transfer switches or set-up change switches as they are called on the 402 and 403 machines. This feature permits the running of a daily zero balance sheet, a weekly listing as well as monthly report. Thus one control panel can handle a complete sales analysis, controlling first on salesmen, next territory, account number, and whatever other breakdown may be desired.

An optional feature of the Type 407 Accounting Machine is a calculating attachment, referred to as ACA (Advanced Computing Attachment). It (Figure 22-12) enables the 407 Accounting Machine to make calculations and to print extended amounts. When the 407 is used for billing, for instance, the ACA would multiply quantity by price and print the extensions on the invoice. The ACA does not punch the extended amount into the cards as does the IBM calculator described in a later section of this chapter. The advantage is that the calculations are performed at list speeds on the 407, which is faster than calculating and punching speeds on the calculator.

Figure 22-12. Advanced Computing Attachment for
Type 407 Accounting Machine

IBM 188 Collator

The IBM 188 Collator (Figure 22-13) is a transistorized high-speed collator that reads both numeric and alphabetic information. This machine is used to feed two sets of cards simultaneously, and to compare punching in both sets of cards for the purpose of either matching or merging. The machine has two card feeds for the separate feeding of two decks of cards. Five pockets are provided for distribution of the collated cards. This machine will process alphabetical as well as numerical information.

The five stackers or pockets (Figure 22-14) are designated 1 to 5 from right to left. Primary cards are stacked into Pocket 1 unless selected into Pocket 2 or 3. Secondary cards go into Pocket 5 unless selected into Pocket 4 or 3. Pocket 3 is the merge pocket. Each pocket holds approximately 1000 cards and when filled, card feeding stops. Cards stack on the column-80 end and can be removed without stopping the machine.

To select a certain type of card or cards out of a deck, cards are punched with the significant control information and placed in one feed of the collator. The deck of cards to be processed is placed in the other feed. Each card of the deck is compared with the key punched card on the control number. Those cards that match are directed to pocket two.

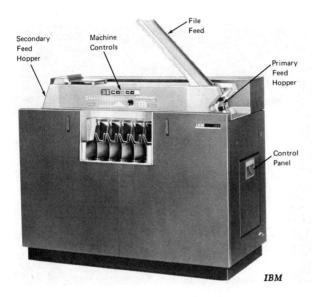

Figure 22-13. Type 188 Collator

The remaining cards are directed to pocket one. The deck is not disturbed in any way except for those matched cards removed from it.

The machine can also be used for comparing two sets of cards to ascertain that both decks are identical in certain matched columns. For instance, accounts receivable cards can be matched with cards representing cash receipts. The machine will compare the two decks and will separate those receivables for which no payment or part-payment only have been received. Those separated cards then become the outstanding accounts receivable file.

The machine feeds cards through each feed at the speed of 650 cards per minute. Depending upon the operation involved, the actual number of cards processed will vary from 650 to 1300 cards per minute. The machine is made to operate by a wiring panel located at the side of the machine.

Calculators

The Advanced Computing Attachment (pages 517–518) that can be coupled to the 407 Accounting Machine has replaced the calculator in those operations where the extended amount need not be punched into cards. However, there are still many operations that require the calculated amount to be punched in the card. Two calculators that provide this punching are explained in this chapter: the 602A Calculating Punch

IBM

Figure 22-14. Type 188 Collator

and the 607 Calculating Punch. These calculators can be used for complicated mathematical problems.

Note that the IBM 633 Electronic Typing Calculator and the IBM 6400 Accounting Machine System which are writing machines with computing capability, are described and illustrated in Chapter 6, Automatic Writing Equipment.

Type 602A Calculator (Figure 22-15). This machine is capable of solving many types of calculating problems that may be encountered in the punched card accounting system. Simple or complex mathematical problems involving addition, subtraction, multiplication, or division may be calculated by this punch either individually or in any combination. The wiring panel is so designed that it permits the simultaneous or successive use of all four basic mathematical processes for calculating and punching of results into the card as it passes through the machine a single time. The standard machine has a counter capacity of 20 positions arranged in six groups. Amounts can be added or subtracted directly into any or all counters of the machine and can be cross-added or cross-subtracted by total transfer from one counter to another.

In a multiplying operation, this machine has a capacity of eight positions in the multiplier, 22 positions in the multiplicand, and 30 positions in the product. Multiplying operations may be performed either by the individual or group multiplier method. In addition a factor may be taken

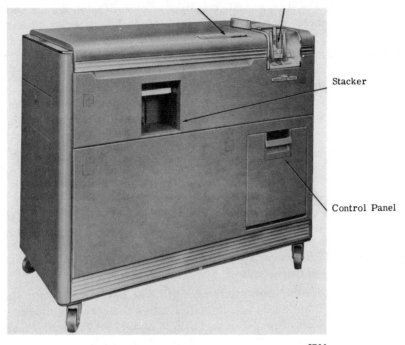

Operating Keys
and Signal Lights   Feed Hopper

Stacker

Control Panel

IBM

Figure 22-15.   Type 602A Calculating Punch

from one type of card for use either as a group multiplier or a group multiplicand. Factors may be computed by any of the four basic mathematical processes before being used as a multiplier or a multiplicand. Another distinctive feature of this machine is that a product can be calculated and then be further multiplied in the same operation by additional factors and the final result punched.

Multiplying speeds are contingent upon the number of digits in the multiplier and the number and location of the positions in the result punched. Speed varies from 521 to 3000 cards per hour depending upon the number of calculating cycles and the number of columns punched.

In performing division problems the machine has a capacity for a 15-position dividend, 8-position divisor and an 8-position quotient. The speed of the machine in dividing is dependent upon the number of digits in the quotient. The number of computations will range from 1100 to 2200 per hour based upon a one to eight digit quotient.

Type 607 Calculating Punch (Figure 22-16). This machine consists of two basic units—a punch unit and an electric calculating unit. Basic rate of speed for this machine is 100 cards per minute. The speed will vary with the number of program steps required to calculate the particular problem on the machine. The results can be punched into the same or different card. The standard 607 has 16 positions of factor storage and 32 positions of general storage. The basic machine has capacity to handle a problem involving a maximum of 40 different steps. In multiplication, an eight-digit multiplicand can be multiplied by a five-digit multiplier to produce a 13-digit product. In basic division a 13-digit dividend is divided by an eight-digit divisor to produce a five-digit quotient.

Like most calculators in its field, programming of the 607 is done by control panel wiring. Although there are 120 possible program steps, 40 program steps are basic. A wire connects each program step to the particular function to be performed at that step. Thus, step one would be wired to "read in a card"; step two—multiply a factor (a) in the card by a factor (b) previously placed in storage; step three—half adjust answer (if decimals are involved); step four—place results in storage for punching; step five—punch. This cycle would then be repeated for each card. Only five program steps would be required for this simple example.

Punched Card Equipment Produced by Univac Division of Sperry Rand Corporation

Three units of equipment produced by Univac Division of Sperry Rand Corporation are discussed and illustrated in this chapter on equipment for punched card accounting: Univac 1701VP and 1710VIP Card Punches and Univac 1720 Sorter. The two punches have capability not only for

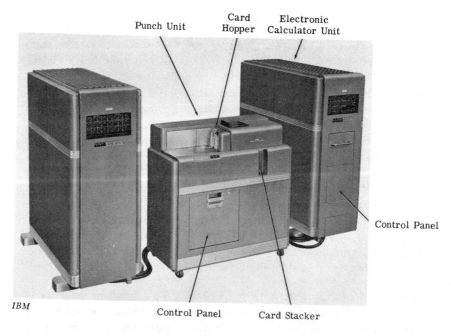

Figure 22-16. Type 607 Calculating Punch

key punching, but verifying, interpreting and printing punching. This equipment is also designed for use in Univac computer systems, and it comprises circuiting and memory which is computer oriented. This equipment is designed for use of 80 column cards (Figure 22-17). The cards used by the earlier Remington Rand equipment were 90 column.

Both punches look the same, as shown in Figure 22-18. The difference between them lies in the internal arrangement of the integrated circuitry. The Univac 1701VP is a punch-verifier, combining the functions of punch and verifier in a single unit. This unit can be used as (1) a punch *or* a verifier or (2) a punch *and* a verifier. When the machine is used as a punch and verifier by the same operator, the operator first reads the card from the source medium, depressing the keys on the keyboard to introduce a full recording for all columns to be affected. The card to be punched can be read in the visible station and a large digital indicator light shows the column next to be referenced. (The card is stationary while in the visible station; this is important when the card is the source document.) In the first time through, the machine is not punching the card; it is setting up the image of the punched card in a data storage area which provides storage for 80 columns of 12 core positions each. If the operator senses she has made an error, she backspaces and does the column over. Since no card has been punched, no card has been punched incorrectly.

In the verify operation, the operator proceeds immediately to re-read the source medium and to operate the keyboard. This time the machine is comparing the keyboard operation, column by column, with the image set up in the data storage area. If an error is detected, the operator is signaled and she re-examines the source medium and makes a new entry on the keyboard. This entry is accepted by the machine as the correct entry, and the corrected card image is used to punch a card.

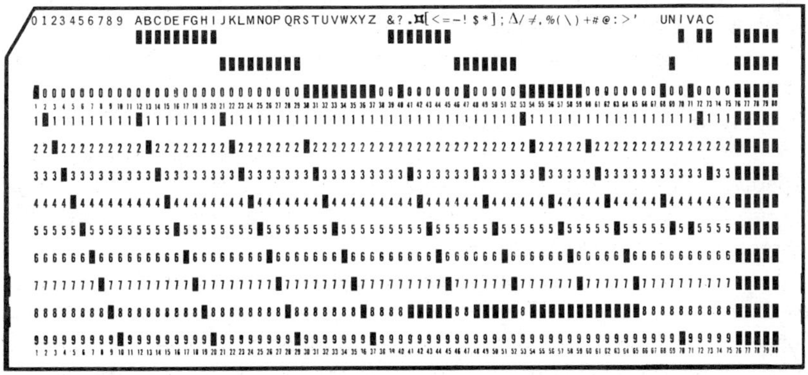

UNIVAC

Figure 22-17.   80 Column Tabulating Card

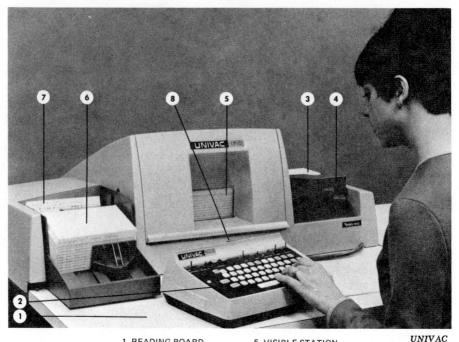

1. READING BOARD
2. KEYBOARD
3. INPUT MAGAZINE
4. AUXILIARY INPUT

5. VISIBLE STATION
6. OUTPUT STACKER
7. SELECT STACKER
8. COLUMN INDICATOR

UNIVAC

Figure 22-18. Type 1710 Card Punch

Program storage: As indicated before, a program in a card punch controls such factors as which columns to duplicate (date, department number, etc., repeated for a number of cards in sequence), which columns to punch with new data for each card, and which columns to skip. A program is controlled in the punch by feeding in a program card which is the prototype format of the detail cards to be produced from the source media. The program card is fed into an auxiliary input. In the 1701VP, programs (from program cards) are stored in magnetic core storage. Dual program capability is standard; the operator can switch-select either of two programs. Punching is thus controlled from the programs in storage rather than directly from program cards.

Data storage is used to store the image of the card as it is being created via the keyboard. There are two areas of card storage used for card image, input storage and output storage, and each of them has a capacity of eighty columns. The original image of the card is recorded in the input storage, where the image is verified. When verification is completed, the image is transferred to output storage. A card is punched from output storage while the input from a new reading is being recorded in the input storage.

The Univac 1710VIP operates on the same basic principles as the Univac 1701VP. All the features and capabilities of the 1701VP are combined with automatic card interpreting.

The Univac 1720 Sorter (Figure 22-19) performs the functions of sorting explained in the previous chapter (sensing and selecting). Sensing is photoelectric. The 1720 has 14 stackers to minimize alpha sort time. It can sort 1000 cards a minute.

PUNCHED PAPER TAPE

Use of Punched Paper Tape

Punched paper tape provides a means of transmitting information appearing on original documents at one location to another location where it is put into punched card form. Paper tape may be produced in five-, six-, seven-, or eight-channel form. The five- and eight-channel forms are the most commonly used. Machines processing these tapes will be

1. FILE FEED (Optional Feature)	4. CONNECTION PANEL (Beneath Cover)	*UNIVAC*
2. INDEX DIAL	5. OUTPUT STACKERS	
3. CONTROL PANEL	6. COUNTING UNIT (Optional Feature)	

Figure 22-19. Type 1720 Sorter

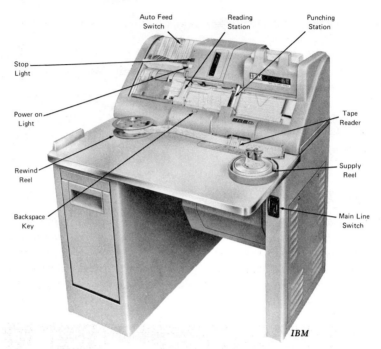

Figure 22-20.   Type 46 Tape-to-Card Punch

Figure 22-21.   Type 63 Card-Controlled Tape Punch

described here. The five-channel tape, often referred to as telegraphic tape, may be used to wire transmit the data punched in it. The eight-channel tape must be physically transported from one location to another. Many manufacturers of accounting and adding machines have developed equipment capable of producing a punched paper tape as well as the printed report.

IBM Tape Equipment

Type 46 Tape-to-Card Punch. The Type 46 Tape-to-Card Punch (Figure 22-20) will process either five- or eight-channel tape (Figure 6-21, page 115). The blank cards are placed in the hopper in the same manner as in 24 Key Punch (page 492). A control panel is wired for each job. Cards are positioned, read, and released automatically. Common information is punched into the first card from the tape and duplicated automatically into the following cards. Thus, indicative information such as date, branch office, and so forth, is punched only once into the paper tape. This data is reproduced into the first card and automatically duplicated into the following cards. Only the variable information (order number, part number, quantity, and so on) is punched from the tape into each of the following cards. Duplicating of common data minimizes the length of tape required, thereby cutting the time and cost of wire transmitting this data.

The Type 46 Tape-to-Card machine punches cards at the rate of 20 columns per second. There is an error device on the machine to insure correct punching. On the far right side of the card, a 1 is punched in the border (to the right of column 80) if a good card is processed. In case of an error card a 4 is punched instead of a 1. In this case the machine can be wired to stop. The only attention any of these tape processing machines require after the tape is started is to empty a full stacker or reload an empty hopper with blank cards. The machine stops automatically when either of these conditions exists.

Type 63 Card-Controlled Tape Punch (Figure 22-21). The 63 Card-to-Tape machine processes only the five-channel telegraphic tape. It also punches functional codes into the tape. Functional codes such as carriage return, line feed, and shift are the most common.

When data must be transmitted to a distant location and neither commercial wire transmitting nor forwarding the actual tabulating cards is desirable, the paper tape is used. Data is punched from the card to the tape, and the tape is mailed. When it is received at the distant location, the data is reconverted to card form for further processing. Information from five hundred 80-column cards (fully punched) can be converted to a tape that can be placed in a $4'' \times 4'' \times 1''$ paper container.

23

Punched-Card Applications

Subjects Discussed in This Chapter

Chapter 21 explained the basic principles of punched-card accounting. Chapter 22 described and illustrated the units of equipment which may be incorporated, in various combinations, into a system of punched-card accounting. The present chapter describes some typical applications of punched-card accounting:

Order and billing
Perpetual inventory on cards
Accounts receivable
Sales analysis
Accounts payable
Purchase distribution
Payroll

These applications are presented as a means of illustrating how punched-card machines are used and not as an exhaustive and detailed coverage of technical machine operations. The payroll application, which involves the use of six different machines, is charted and explained in some detail.

Billing

Billing, in principle, is one of the simplest applications of tabulating and fundamentally involves punching a series of cards and feeding them through a tabulator to print a bill. In most cases, sorting is not involved. The cards are punched, or pulled from files, in the order in which they are to be fed into the tabulator to print the invoices.

Five types of cards are generally used in billing. They are:

    (1) Name and address cards. These cards contain the name and address to be billed. The IBM 403 accounting machine and others

are capable of printing three lines of information from a single card. This feature permits the merging of headings of three lines on a single card, thus materially reducing the number of cards punched.

(2) "Ship to" name and address, used where the goods are to be shipped to a name and address different from the billing name and address.

(3) Shipping instructions cards and terms cards, to print information on the bill.

(4) Detail commodity cards, each of which contains a description of the item being billed, size, weight, price, extension, and so on.

(5) Parcel post, freight, sales tax cards for information shown at the end of the invoice.

Bills are usually printed on continuous feed forms, and a form-feeding device is usually employed to space automatically between the heading and the body of the form, and between one invoice and the next, keeping the forms in perfect register.

Punching the Cards

Name and address cards for billing may be (1) completely pre-punched or (2) currently punched. Where there are customers who regularly receive bills, it is often feasible to pre-punch heading cards and retain them in the files from one billing period to another. Where there are few customers who regularly receive bills, it may not be feasible to pre-punch the heading cards. It is necessary, in such cases, to punch up the heading cards at the time of billing.

Commodity cards, showing a description of the items being billed, and the like may be (1) completely pre-punched, (2) partially pre-punched, or (3) currently punched, as explained in the following paragraphs.

(1) Completely pre-punched detail cards are used in commodity billing where product names, specifications, sizes, and prices are standardized, and where there is fairly high activity in a relatively limited product list. Quantities of each specific card are punched at one time in a gang punch or reproduced to eliminate key punch time that would otherwise be required to punch them individually. Such cards are generally kept in tub files until they are used.

A certain manufacturer uses completely pre-punched cards, filing them by product name (and under each product, by representative order quantities, such as one box, two boxes, five boxes, ten boxes and twenty boxes) and pulling them from files as required. There are about 50 products in the line at any time, all standard. Although only three of them are perennial sellers, it is not a difficult task to punch new cards as new products are added to the line and to discard old ones as products are discontinued.

(2) Partially pre-punched cards are used where some of the particulars are standardized (such as names and prices) but where some of the information is variable. Cards are made up for the standardized classifications. These partially pre-punched cards are pulled from the file as needed, and the variable information is punched by one of the various punches.

(3) Currently punched cards are used where there is no appreciable degree of constancy of information or where the information is too varied to maintain practical tub files. Currently punched cards need not, of course, be entirely key punched. The term "currently punched" means that they are punched as required for active tabulation. They may be duplicated, reproduced, and so on.

Commodity Billing Using Completely Pre-Punched Cards

An illustration of a hypothetical commodity bill appears in Figure 23-1. This bill was produced on an alphameric tabulator. The steps consist simply in pulling pre-punched billing name and address cards and commodity cards from their respective files, punching cards for "ship to" name and address, shipping route, terms and customer number, and feeding them through the tabulator, which prints the finished bill.

Two of the four types of cards used in preparing the bill are illustrated herewith: (a) heading cards, containing name, street address, city and state, and shipping route, in Figure 23-2, and (b) commodity cards, in Figure 23-3.

Sets of billing name and address cards are maintained in the tub files for each regularly billed customer, being separated by clips or a distinct marker card. In some installations, only one set is maintained for each customer, and it is pulled for the listing of the bill and returned to file after use.

The commodity cards show, among other data, the name of the commodity (punched alphabetically), quantity, weight, unit price, and extension. There are separate sets of commodity cards maintained for each commodity and for the prevailing usual quantities ordered. Accordingly, if a certain product were customarily ordered in one, two, five, ten, or twenty box lots, there would be five sets of cards for that commodity. Any variation from the usual ordering amount would be provided for by pulling a combination of these cards; for instance, were a quantity of 13 ordered, the clerk would pull one 1, one 2, and one 10 card.

In preparing the bill, the tabulator is set to tabulate with a minor control on product numbers, so that quantities and values of each commodity would be accumulated and printed on the bill. Thus, in the

INVOICE

SQUARE DEAL OIL CO
255 ESSEX STREET
CLEVELAND OHIO

SOLD TO

BRANCH	CUSTOMER'S NO.
7	62

SHIP TO

ARNOLD SIMPSON
1487 SMITH ST
CLEVELAND OHIO

MAKE ALL CHECKS PAYABLE TO
AND FORWARD REMITTANCE
DIRECTLY TO

SHIPPED VIA: TRUCK PREPAID

TERMS: 2 PCT 10 DAYS NET 30

INVOICE

CUSTOMER'S ORDER NO.	SALESMANS NAME	SALESMANS NO	DATE	NUMBER
1472A1	WEBER	8	63058	12348

DESCRIPTION	COMMODITY NO.	QUANTITY	UNIT PRICE	AMOUNT
SQ SHANK RIGID	21103	25	177	4425
ADJ ADAPTER SQUARE	23703	35	222	7770
SQ SOCKET RIGID	26104	2	244	488
FLAT TOP SWIVEL	33202	35	279	9765
SQ SHANK RIGID	51105	20	411	8220
FLAT TOP SWIVEL	53209	5	505	2525
ROUND SOCKET SWIVL	55706	3	651	1953
FREIGHT				117
				35263*

029.01.006

IBM

Figure 23-1. Invoice Printed on Tabulator

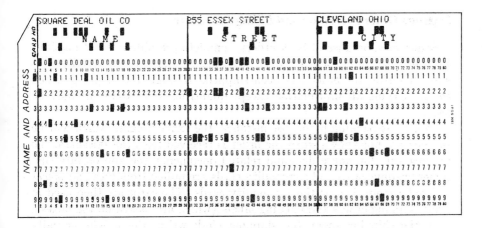

Figure 23-2. Name-and-Address Card Used in Order and Billing

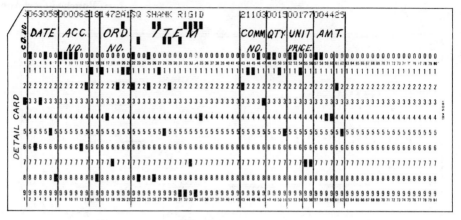

Figure 23-3. Commodity Card Used in Order and Billing

instance cited in the previous paragraph, the machine would add the multiple cards and print only a single line, with the quantities and amounts accumulated from the three cards.

The bills are made in three copies: one for the customer, one for the Customer's Ledger department, and one (order copy) for the Shipping department. For "special" bills, such as ones that show shipping addresses different from the billing address, the "ship to" name and address card is punched specially and inserted in the deck after billing name and address, before tabulating.

The card for freight is punched after the order has been assembled for shipping and the freight has been calculated.

At the completion of the billing operation, cards are used for production control and sales analysis. For production control the cards are sorted by commodity, and quantity reports are prepared.

Separate Order Procedure and Billing Procedure

Sometimes, because of back orders, complete pre-billing is not possible. In this case, order writing may be done at one time and billing at another—after the order has been shipped. A single file of pre-punched cards carrying all information except quantities and extensions may be used.

In a meat packing plant, for instance, the exact weights which will be shipped are not known when the order is received from the salesman. To produce the shipping orders and related documents, the appropriate customer heading cards and commodity cards are pulled from files and *pieces ordered* are punched on the commodity cards. The cards are then used to print shipping orders and packing labels (which are pasted on the boxes).

In the shipping room, the shipping clerk writes the weight actually shipped on the billing copy of the shipping order. If an item cannot be

532

shipped, he marks the item "back order." He then sends the office copy back to the Tabulating department.

In the Tabulating department, the back order cards are separated from the others and used when goods are available to produce a new order set. The cards representing goods shipped are key punched for weights actually shipped, extended in a calculating punch, and printed on an invoice in a tabulator.

IBM 6400

The IBM 6400 is explained on pages 112–116. When this machine is used, pre-punched heading cards and partially pre-punched commodity cards may be placed as input to produce an order set on the typewriter, which is part of the machine. Quantities and any other variable information may be typed by the operator using the keyboard.

Likewise, the cards may be put into the machine to produce an invoice. The operator may type quantities actually shipped and other variable information. The 6400 can compute extensions and footings automatically. The reader is referred to pages 112–116 for further details.

Tabulating Cards Used as Perpetual Inventory; Inventory Tub Files

Pre-punched commodity cards may be used as media for perpetual inventory. Sets of tabulating cards are filed on end in tub files, separated by fiber or metal dividers, permitting the reading of the description shown on the end of the card or on the separators. The cards are filed in sequence in the tub, either alphabetically or in product number sequence. This arrangement makes it possible for the clerks to acquire a high degree of speed in pulling cards.

When goods are received by the warehouse, cards are punched representing the quantities received and are placed in file. When goods are shipped out of the warehouse, cards are taken out for the quantities involved. Use of such an inventory file is, of course, most practical where goods are to be shipped in the original packages. A separate tabulating card is punched for each item received.

The following features of tub-file indexing can be used:

(1) "Warning" signals can be set in the tub files so that as the low point in stock is approached, various order routines can be set in motion.

(2) A card for "order" can be placed at order point. When that card is reached, the clerk will send it to the Purchasing department as their notice that the order point has been reached.

(3) A "danger" card can be placed at that point in quantity which

normally allows the Purchasing department time to replenish before the stock runs out.

(4) An "out" card can be placed after the last commodity card in the file.

Tabulating Applications Related to Billing

It should be obvious that cards created for use in billing may, under some conditions, be used for other applications, or at least card punching done primarily for billing may be utilized in related applications. Some applications related to billing are (1) inventory control (as indicated in the previous section) (2) accounts receivable (described in the following section), and (3) sales analysis (described on pages 538–540).

Accounts Receivable Principles

In principle, accounts receivable by tabulator method is ledgerless bookkeeping, since the Accounts Receivable ledger is a file of tabulating cards. In addition to comprising the ledger, however, the cards are used to tabulate a cash receipts journal (Figure 23-4) and aged trial balances (Figure 23-5) at the end of the month. This method is subject to the disadvantages of ledgerless bookkeeping in general, but it overcomes certain disadvantages by the use of machine methods of handling and proof.

Punching and Filing Debit Cards

Under the tabulator procedure, a tabulator card may be key punched for each invoice sent the customer, showing, among other details, the customer's number, date, invoice number, and amount of the invoice. The customer's number is duplicated from a master customer's card in order to insure the accuracy of punching in detail cards. The detail cards are then tabulated immediately to determine whether the total of amounts punched agrees with the prelist total. If the cards prove by this procedure, they are filed in the customers' active file (which is the Customers' ledger).

In some cases, the debit cards (one for each invoice) may be secured as a by-product of some other tabulating card application. Thus, if the billing is done on tabulators, a debit card for each invoice may be produced on a summary punch connected with the tabulator. Also, where sales analysis is being done on tabulator, a debit card for each invoice may be an integral part of the sales analysis procedure.

Applying Credits for Cash Received from Customers

The procedure of applying credits for cash received may be very simple if customers pay the amounts of specific invoices, for then the appropriate debit cards can be pulled from the files as cash comes in from the customers. In the simplest possible situation—where each amount of cash received covers one invoice (that is, one card in the debit files), it is only necessary to pull the card, punch the date of the receipt, and file it in the paid file. Something close to this situation exists in utility accounts receivable, the method of applying cas described illustrates the basic principle of operating accounts receivable files.

A more difficult situation arises where many round amounts are received on account. To illustrate this situation, assume that a check for $100 is received from the customer and that the following debit cards are found in the accounts receivable file:

November 2	$40
6	50
December 3	30

Under one method of handling the credit, the operator would punch a credit card for $90 and one (covering the unapplied portion) for $10. She will then file the debit card for $40 and the debit card for $50 in a paid file with the credit card for $90. And finally, she will file the unapplied balance card for $10 in the open accounts receivable file.

Cash Receipts Journal

A cash receipts journal is prepared by punching a cash-received card for each check received. These cards show:

Date check received
Payor
Check number
Amount of check
Discount
Gross credit
Bank account number (for deposit)

The total of cash receipts cards punched must balance with the total of the accounts receivable cards pulled (plus the unapplied cash cards) as explained in the previous section.

Cash receipts cards are used to prepare a cash receipts journal, as illustrated in Figure 23-4.

(COMPANY NAME)

CASH RECEIPTS

DATE

DATE NO.	DAY	TR.	PAYOR	CHECK NO.	AMOUNT OF CHECK	DISCOUNT	GROSS CREDIT	ACCOUNT NO.	SUFF.
9 2	3	5	ATCHISON TOPEKA / SANTE FE	20646	2429		2429	1000	
9 2	3	5	BUCYRUS ERIE COMPANY	77607	145		145	1000	
9 2	3	5	CHICAGO & NORTHWESTERN RR	86346	380		380	1000	
9 2	3	5	CONTRACTORS SUPPLY	5389	621		621	1000	
9 2	3	5	CORNELL UNIVERSITY	234911	1831		1831	1000	
9 2	3	5	GENERAL FOODS BIRDS EYE	17091	11390		11390	1000	
9 2	3	5	GRINNELL CO OF THE PACIFIC	52425	11153		11153	1000	
9 2	3	5	GRINNELL CORPORATION	49861	5764		5764	1000	
9 2	3	5	KIMBERLY CLARK CORPORATION	41540	309		309	1000	
9 2	3	5	KOONTZ EQUIPMENT	21999	1000		1000	1000	
9 2	3	5	LOVELAND EQUIPMENT CO	1769	12754		12754	1000	
9 2	3	5	MIDCO SUPPLY	10513	3658		3658	1000	
9 2	3	5	MISSOURI PACIFIC RR	1225	14411		14411	1000	
9 2	3	5	L E MYERS COMPANY	43652	9050		9050	1000	
9 2	3	5	REPUBLIC SUPPLY	8504	780		780	1000	
9 2	3	5	RUCKMAN & HANSEN	1030	573		573	1000	
9 2	3	5	SUNDSTRAND MACHINE	73377	1785		1785	1000	
9 2	3	5	TEXAS & NEW ORLEANS R R	472022	19832		19832	1000	
9 2	3	5	UNION PACIFIC R R	250767	8094		8094	1000	
9 2	3	5	UNION PACIFIC RAILROAD	250665	2841		2841	1000	
9 2	3	5	URANIA LUMBER COMPANY	158826	1768		1768	1000	
9 2	3	5	WEST VIRGINIA TRACTOR	3528	43843		43843	1000	
9 2	3	5	HAJOCA CORPORATION	32789	145125		145125	1000	
9 2	3	5	MONTREAL LOCOMOTIVE WORKS	9279	134400		134400	1000	
9 2	3	5	STATE OF NY FINGER LAKES	2267114	2403		2403	1000	
9 2	3	5	DEWEY AND ALMY			131 CR	131 CR	1000	
					436339	131 CR	436208		

Figure 23-4. Cash Receipts Journal

The Open-Item Statement

At the end of the month, open-item statements (not illustrated) may be tabulated by (a) matching and merging the debit and credit cards in the accounts receivable file at the end of the month with the file of customer name and address cards and (b) running the merged set through the tabulator to print the statements. The merging operation is done on a collator. The master name and address file is put into one input feed and the detail credit cards are put into the other input feed. Both sets are in customer number order. As the collator operates, the matched and merged name and address cards and detail cards are discharged into one pocket. The name and address cards for which there are no detail cards are discharged into another pocket. These are presumably the customers whose accounts were inactive during the period. The detail cards for which there are no name and address cards are discharged into a third pocket. These are presumably the transactions of new customers for whom no name and address cards have been punched.

The statements (produced on continuous forms) show the unpaid items and the unapplied cash items, also the final balance due. At the same time the machine accumulates the total of debits and the total of credits for proof against the Control account.

The customer's number, which appears on each card, is listed on a column to the extreme left of the form, and detached on a perforated line before mailing the main statement. This listing makes possible a visual check of the statements to ascertain that all the items belong on the same statement and were not misfiled in the active files.

Aged Trial Balance

An aged trial balance (Figure 23-5) is prepared by the use of what is called "x-punching." When the debit cards are punched an x is punched in the proper month space in the eleventh position. Thus when the cards are punched for January's billing, January will be x-punched; when the cards are punched for February's billing, that month will be x-punched; and so on. Now, suppose an aged trial balance is to be prepared at the end of March. The trial balance form shows columns for:

90 days and older
60 days
30 days
current

The tabulator will be wired so that all cards bearing the x-punch for February will register in the 30-day column and all cards bearing the x-punch for January will register in the 60-day column, and so on. If the Credit department desires additional information regarding the composition of any of the balances shown on the aged trial balance, the office copies of the open-item statement can be furnished.

MONTH OF ______

Name of Customer	Div.	Plant No.	Commodity	Terms	Date Mo.	Date Day	Preference Number	Kind of Entry	90 Days and Older	60 Days	90 Days	Current	Balance
Dubuque 2503							2883	00					
	1	0	4	3	7	18	3243	10	6349				
	1	0	4	2	8	26	5340	10		2118			
	1	0	4	3	10	19	2783	10				6083	
									6349•	2118•	•	6083•	14847•
2505							2888	00					
	1	0	4	1	8	05	0130	10		8628			
	1	0	4	1	9	15	2956	10			19843		
	1	3	3	1	9	29	6840	12			366		
	1	0	4	1	10	01	0095	10				52185	
	1	0	4	1	10	03	0148	10				8790	
	1	3	8	1	10	06	0270	10				38688	
	1	0	4	1	10	08	0456	10				10320	
	1	0	4	1	10	11	1047	10				9545	
	1	0	4	1	10	17	1793	10				62781	
	1	3	8	1	10	20	2140	10				32132	
	1	0	4	1	10	22	2688	10				4860	
					10	23	0444	22				99999675	
	1	0	4	1	10	24	3016	10				72184	
	1	0	4	1	10	28	3830	10				22633	
	1	0	4	1	10	26	4218	10				10150	
	1	3	8	1	10	26	4219	10				21012	
	1	0	4	1	10	29	6734	10				14034	
									•	8628•	19898•	388658•	384181•
[illegible]							2647	00					
	1	0	3	1	3	18	2430	10	12960				
	1	0	3	1	6	20	3827	10	13840				
	1	0	4	2	7	18	3320	10	6097				
	1	0	8	1	8	20	3930	10		7810			
	1	0	7	1	9	26	5332	10			19820		
	1	0	8	1	9	27	3993	10			32840		
									32897•	7810•	52660•	•	92467•
8836							2838	00					
	2	6	4	1	6	06	3885	10	3248				
	2	6	4	1	7	12	3341	10	16272				
	2	6	7	1	7	26	3362	10	1664				
	2	2	8	1	8	19	3916	10		8417			
	2	2	8	1	8	20	3906	10		20226			
	2	6	8	1	9	02	2905	10			2918		
	2	2	4	1	9	11	2914	10			44008		
	2	8	4	1	9	29	2909	12			942		
	2	8	4	1	10	06	2714	10				46486	
	2	6	4	1	10	06	2644	12				1642	
	2	6	3	1	10	10	2661	12				2880	
	2	4	8	1	10	14	4216	10				26260	
	2	6	4	1	10	17	4234	10				1910	
	2	2	4	1	10	21	4442	12				34664	
	2	2	3	1	10	21	4203	10				11094	
	2	2	3	1	10	29	4201	10				17686	
	2	2	8	1	10	30	4209	10				8730	
									21181•	28642•	47862•	150992•	248677•
9216							3216	00					
	1	0	4	0	9	16	2834	10			6484		
	1	0	3	5	10	04	4344	10				60678	
	1	0	3	5	10	04	4349	10				2528	
	1	4	3	5	10	10	4366	10				8640	
	1	0	8	5	10	17	4222	10				10592	
	1	4	5	5	10	17	3806	10				25757	
	1	4	8	5	10	21	4378	10				88850	
	1	1	8	5	10	24	4388	10				8686	
	1	1	8	5	10	30	4267	10				1112	
									•	•	6484•	173537•	180021•

Figure 23-5. Aged Trial Balance

History of the Customer's Account

An additional record that is kept for the Credit department (along with the copies of the open-item statement and the aged trial balance) is the history of the customer's account. This record (not illustrated) shows the sales to each customer, the collections by month, and the balance at the end of each month. This record supplements the other two in that it shows the story for a period of time. It is brought up to date at the end of the month by running the cards for the month through the print unit of the tabulator.

Sales Analysis

Sales analysis usually involves punching a card for each item line on each invoice and then sorting the cards a number of times to produce a series of reports. The sales analysis cards are sometimes obtained as a by-product of some other tabulating machine application, such as billing. If the tabulating machine installation is used exclusively for sales analysis, the cards would be punched for the one purpose. Tabulating cards may then be (a) currently punched or (b) pre-punched. Sales analysis applications based upon each of those methods of originating the cards are discussed in the following sections.

Sales Analysis Using Currently Punched Cards

Under this method, one card is punched for each item line on the invoice, as explained above, and each card is punched for such information as:

Columns	Descriptions
1- 6	Date
7- 8	Transaction code number (10)
9-10	(Skip)
11-14	Invoice number
15-16	Salesman number
17-20	Customer number
21-24	Product number
25-27	Quantity
28-30	Unit cost
31-36	Cost total (quantity × unit cost)
37-42	Sales value

Note that the information in columns 1-20 is common to all item-line cards on an invoice. If there are three cards on an invoice this information can be *duplicated* from the first card to the second card and thence to the third card. The operator key-punches columns 21-42 on each card.

Sales Analysis Using Pre-Punched Cards in the Reproducing Punch

Under this method, customer master cards are used for customer number and salesman number, and pre-punched product-item cards are used for the item lines on the invoices. The former are punched for customer number and salesman number and the latter are punched for product number, quantity, and amount. (In the actual situation on which this description is based, the company has a very limited product list.) Thus, there are two files of cards:

(1) The file of master customer-code cards, which comprises several cards for each customer.
(2) The file of product-item cards, which is similar to the file of pre-punched cards used for commodity billing (page 530).

The latter file comprises a quantity of pre-punched cards for each of the common ordering quantities of each product, as is sometimes done in billing applications (page 530). In the operation of the sales analysis, the file clerk pulls one customer master card from the file for each invoice and one or more product-item cards for each product on the invoice. The product-item cards, when pulled from file, do not show customer number, salesman number, date, or invoice number.

The reproducing punch is used to reproduce customer number and salesman number from the customer master card into the product-item cards. This is done simply by feeding the master card into the punch unit of the reproducing punch, followed immediately by the item cards for that invoice.

The reproducing punch is also used to reproduce the date and invoice number into the detail cards. The date and invoice number are punched in the first item card for each invoice. Actually, that first detail card then becomes the master card, which causes date and invoice number to be punched in the detail cards which follow it.

Reports

Some of the sales distribution reports prepared by a steel warehousing company are illustrated herewith. (Certain reports are printed directly by the tabulator from punched cards and others are prepared from tabulations of the current cards plus other information.) The reports are:

Figure 23-6. Salesman's Commission Statement, which shows invoice number, salesman number, and amount due.

Figure 23-7. Salesmen Performance Report, a comparison of actual sales with forecast sales, both month and cumulative, for each salesman.

Figure 23-8. Sales by Product Class Report.

Figure 23-9. Sales Performance Report of High-Volume Customers.

Of special interest is the fact that the company also prepares a Statement of Profit Contribution by Sales Territory showing the *net* profit of each territory. This report involves a considerable amount of cost accounting, but the basis for the report is sales, cost of sales, gross profit, and commission which come from the punched cards. There is also a similar Statement of Sales and Cost of Sales by Product Line which shows net profit by product line. These management tools are made possible by modern methods of data-processing.

Accounts Payable: *Principles*

Tabulating equipment may be used for any of the accounts payable functions—writing the voucher and the invoice register or the voucher register, distributing the purchase debits, writing expense reports, posting expense accounts, writing journal vouchers for the control entries to be made in the Factory ledger and the General ledger, and writing checks and the check register.

In addition to the operations on the machines proper, the function of due-date control is sometimes served by a file of tabulator cards, comprising one card for each invoice or voucher to be paid. When these cards are punched for due date, it is a simple matter of sorting by due date to segregate the items due on each payment date.

SALESMAN'S COMMISSION STATEMENT   ORIGINAL

2 2 7 3 2 2 3	.75
2 2 8 5 1 2 3	1 0.30
2 2 8 5 4 2 3	3.40
2 2 8 6 5 2 3	.30
2 2 8 7 7 2 3	4.10
2 2 8 8 8 2 3	2.96
2 2 8 9 1 2 3	1 8.39
2 2 8 9 2 2 3	3.00
2 2 9 0 7 2 3	.50
2 2 9 1 0 2 3	3.95
2 2 9 3 2 2 3	1 1.82
2 2 9 5 5 2 3	3.30
2 3 0 3 4 2 3	3.00
2 3 0 4 7 2 3	2 1.48
2 3 0 6 9 2 3	1.98
2 3 0 7 1 2 3	.46
2 3 0 7 5 2 3	7 4.50
2 3 0 7 8 2 3	.19
2 3 0 9 4 2 3	.60
2 3 1 1 1 2 3	4.30
2 3 1 1 5 2 3	5.07
2 3 1 1 9 2 3	.74
2 3 1 3 5 2 3	4.59
2 3 1 3 9 2 3	1.75
2 3 1 7 0 2 3	2 4.60
2 3 1 7 7 2 3	6.90
2 3 1 8 0 2 3	2.90
2 3 1 8 1 2 3	.75
2 3 1 9 5 2 3	1.77
2 3 2 4 0 2 3	3.15
2 3 2 5 5 2 3	.30
2 3 2 6 2 2 3	1.35
2 3 2 9 1 2 3	2.30
2 3 3 3 3 2 3	4.80
2 3 3 5 1 2 3	1 5.90
2 3 3 6 2 2 3	.70
2 3 3 7 2 2 3	.69
2 3 3 7 4 2 3	1.62
2 3 4 0 3 2 3	1.20
2 3 4 0 3 2 3	1.05
2 3 4 1 6 2 3	.61
2 3 4 3 4 2 3	.90
2 3 4 7 0 2 3	3.50
2 3 4 8 2 2 3	1 4.19
2 3 4 9 7 2 3	2.75
2 3 4 9 7 2 3	2.75 -

Figure 23-6. Salesman's Commission Statement

It should be noted that, although the term "accounts payable" is applied to tabulating procedures, the plan illustrated is essentially a voucher plan rather than an accounts payable plan. The plan systematically records and provides for the payment of specific invoices or groups of invoices.

Types of Cards

The types of cards may be classified as follows:

(1) Debit cards, which would be used for a distribution of debits represented by the invoices. One or more of these cards is punched for each invoice, depending upon how many debit accounts are affected by the invoice.

(2) Credit cards, which would be filed as the record of amounts due creditors or used to write various records for liabilities. One of these would be punched for each invoice.

Date __January 31, 1960__

13 - Gielow   **PERFORMANCE REPORT**

PRODUCT GROUP	MONTH			CUMULATIVE TO DATE		
	ACTUAL	FORECAST	INDEX	ACTUAL	FORECAST	INDEX
I. LOW CARBON STEEL						
A. (15) C. R. Sheet Coil	3,753	2,045	184	24,807	14,315	173
soft & deep draw only						
B. (35) C. R. Sheet, all c. lgths & coil in int.	1,672	125	1338	4,432	875	507
temps & F. H.						
C. (16) C. R. Strip & Shim	6,253	6,000	104	41,659	42,000	99
D. (24) C. R. Flat Wire	621	500	124	3,031	3,500	87
E. (26) Electrolytic Tin Plate	5,598	5,250	107	28,118	36,750	77
F. (36) Electro Galvanized	33		100	33		100
G. (46) Special Alloy Strip						
TOTAL	17,930	13,920	129	102,080	97,440	105
II. HIGH CARBON STEEL						
A. (17) Annealed Spring Steel	2,424	2,670	91	20,395	18,690	109
B. (27) H. C. Annealed Flat Wire	68		100	179		100
C. (23) Blue Tempered & Polished	1,760	3,085	57	13,591	21,595	63
D. (25) Blue Tempered Scaleless	759	1,125	67	9,641	7,875	122
E. (37) Spec. Temper S. P. 37	194		100	295		100
TOTAL	5,205	6,880	76	44,101	48,160	92
III. STAINLESS STEELS						
A. (18) T301 & T302 other than soft	5,465	5,170	106	33,322	36,190	92
B. (38) T302 Soft	1,497	835	179	8,577	5,845	147
C. (48) T430	1,105	835	132	6,014	5,845	103
TOTAL	8,067	6,840	118	47,913	47,880	100
IV. ALUMINUM						
A. (42) Flat	623		100	1,144		100
B. (22) Coiled Sheet	477	50	954	1,264	350	361
TOTAL	1,100	50	2200	2,408	350	688
V. COPPER BASE ALLOYS						
A. (20) Brass	2,394	250	958	4,399	1,750	251
B. (19) Phosphor Bronze	97	75	129	571	525	109
C. (29) Beryllium Copper	9	50	18	448	350	128
TOTAL	2,500	375	667	5,418	2,625	206
VI. SLITTING & SHEARING						
A. (88) Slitting	210		100	1,155		100
B. (99) Shearing						
TOTAL	210		100	1,155		100
GRAND TOTAL	35,012	28,065	125	203,075	196,455	103

FORM SA-2 8/58

Figure 23-7. Salesman's Performance Report

Name	Spring Manufacturing Co.				Acct. & Territory No.	6306011	
	SALES TO DATE				FORECAST	ACTUAL	ACTUAL
PRODUCT	J.A.S. 1st Quarter	O.N.D. 2nd Quarter	J.F.M. 3rd Quarter	A.M.J. 4th Quarter	19 59-60	19 58-59	19 57-58
(15)	452	1033	2454	2941	2000	3073	
(35)							
(16)	166	808	1321	1863	2500	2243	3565
(24)							38
(26)							
(36)							
Total Low Carbon							3603
(17)	1706	4145	6019	6575	12000	13692	10512
(27)					250	367	
(23)					500	556	431
(25)	96	95	201	1115	800	718	688
(37)							
Total High Carbon							11631
(18)	788	1274	2611	4021	5000	8459	4755
(38)							
(48)		328	328	328	750	629	
Total Stainless							4755
(42)							
(22)							
Total Aluminum							
(20)							34
(19)	114	114	114	114	3000	3176	2758
(29)							
Total Cop. Base Al.							2792
(87)							
(88)	79	111	111	111			17
Total Slitting & Shearing							17
GRAND TOTAL Form SA50 Rev. 5/59	3400	7909	13159	17067	26800	32912	22798

Figure 23-8. Sales by Product Class Report

(3) Debit and credit combination cards. In some cases, the same cards
are used to record both the debits and credits represented by invoices. In punching the cards one card would be punched for each
debit on an invoice, and the first card for each invoice would also
be punched with the total credit. For distribution of debits, all
the cards would be used; for recording credits, only the "first"
cards would be used. Figures 23-10, 23-11, and 23-12 illustrate
combination cards used for both debits and credits.

Date February 28, 1960

PRECISION STEEL WAREHOUSE, INC.

SALES PERFORMANCE REPORT
of High Volume Customers

CUSTOMER	MONTH OF FEBRUARY			JULY TO DATE		
	ACTUAL	FORECAST	INDEX	ACTUAL	FORECAST	INDEX
22 Plate Supply	2,232	1,542	145	15,258	15,205	100
23 Johnson Manufacturing	911	1,604	57	12,753	12,833	99
27 Timmon's Spring Mfg.	710	2,083	34	16,199	16,665	97
26 Bock & Bock	725	1,388	52	14,909	11,103	134
23 Micro Din Company	4,486	567	791	17,245	4,535	380
27 Washer Manufacturing Co.	3,819	1,275	300	14,134	10,200	139
11 Avondale Manufacturing Co.	450	1,433	31	11,115	11,465	97
28 G.M.C., Inc.	288	1,667	17	4,237	13,335	32
24 Crown Tool & Manufacturing	4,457	1,275	350	19,538	10,200	192
26 American Wire & Mfg.	1,273	1,200	106	10,073	9,600	105
44 Textile Manufacturing Co.	751	1,292	58	4,742	10,335	46
22 Method Manufacturing	-----	1,250	---	5,973	10,000	60
22 Lock Mfg. & Plating	26	1,604	2	3,656	12,833	28
24 Chicago Mfg. & Plating	3,698	1,333	202	14,381	10,664	135
25 Lendo Mfg. Co.	-----	1,042	---	8,018	8,335	96
23 William Mfg. Co.	1,079	980	110	8,947	7,838	114
44 General Mfg. Co.	105	1,217	9	16,278	9,735	167
98 Castle & Company	804	-----	100	11,123	------	100
11 Ames Die Mfg.	-----	1,017	---	4,319	8,135	53
24 Molder Tool & Die	2,038	1,667	122	10,448	13,335	78
24 Indiana Products Mfg.	503	1,000	50	9,771	8,000	122
27 New York Spring	2,066	965	214	8,922	7,719	116
22 A B Tool Products	556	967	57	4,589	7,735	59
22 Harco Electronics	1,554	975	159	10,164	7,800	130
22 Drum Manufacturing Co.	2,034	1,075	180	8,908	8,600	104

Figure 23-9. Sales Performance Report of High-Volume Customers

Accounts Payable Distribution; Writing Vouchers for Creditors

In this application, one card is punched for each debit on each purchase invoice and each card is punched for the following information:

Columns	Description
1- 4	Voucher number
5-10	Date
11-15	Vendor number ⎫ from a master file of
16-38	Vendor name ⎭ name and address cards

39-45	Vendor invoice number
46-49	General ledger account number
50-51	Expense account
52-59	Amount of the debit
80	Card code

Figure 23-11 and Figure 23-12 illustrate two debit cards (one for $260.00 and one for $7.35) prepared from one invoice which totals $267.35.

One credit card form is punched for the total of the voucher. The information is similar to that punched for debits, except that columns 52-58 are punched for the gross amount of the invoice. The remaining columns are punched as follows:

Columns	Description
59-64	Discount
65-71	Net amount
72-75	Date due
76-79	Date paid
80	Card code

Figure 23-10 is a credit card for an invoice for $267.35.

The credit cards are listed to produce an invoice register, and the debit totals are proved against the credit totals. The debit cards are sorted by expense account number and listed to obtain a distribution of charges to expense accounts.

The "credit" cards—one for each invoice—are filed in an "accounts payable" file, and pulled, or sorted out, to tabulate vouchers as the items become due. The cards are then punched with date paid and used to tabulate a cash payments journal.

Figure 23-10. Accounts Payable Credit Card

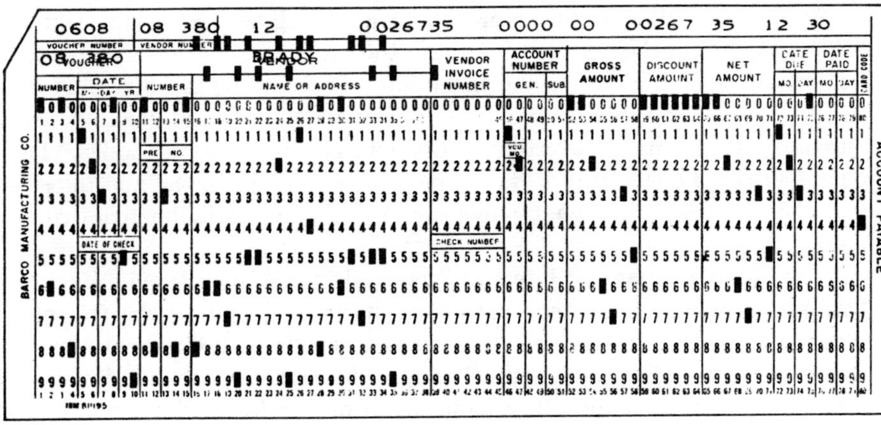

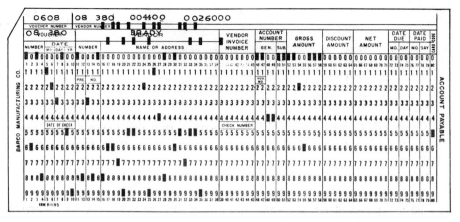

Figure 23-11. Accounts Payable Debit Card

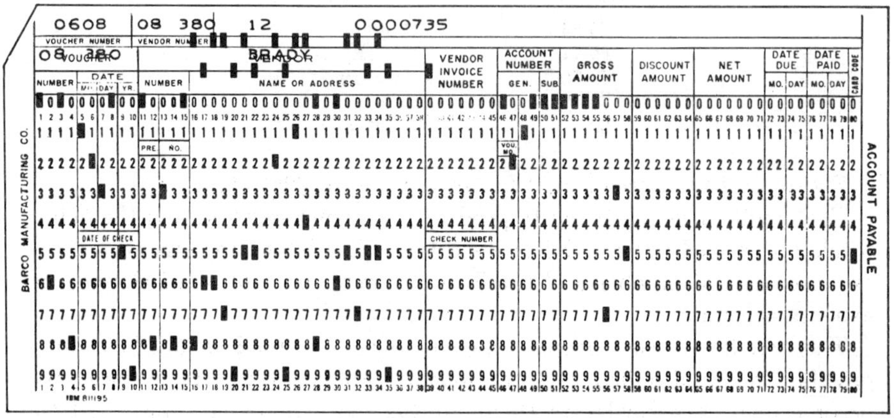

Figure 23-12. Accounts Payable Debit Card

Payroll

In Chapter 21 a simple approach to a payroll register is illustrated. The payroll punched cards containing the basic information were sorted in employee number order and listed on the accounting machine showing hours worked and amount paid. To this simple application, taxes, deductions, employee name, overtime hours, and net pay must be added. The number of different factors (taxes, deductions, and so forth) and the size of the roll determine what punched-card machines will be required to process the payroll.

Payrolls are separated into two types, salary and hourly paid (factory rolls). Generally the salary payroll is the more simple of the two procedures. The reason for this is that the salary rolls are not normally based on hours worked, thus overtime and premium hours are not involved. In factory rolls, on the other hand, overtime work, holidays, and piece work must be taken into consideration when establishing a punch-card procedure. Two typical payroll applications will be described here, one illustrating a salary roll, the other a factory roll.

Types of Cards

The following types of cards are used in all payroll applications, in either individual forms as described below or in combined forms:

1. Name Cards—The name card has punched on it the employee's name, employee number, department, and department number.
2. Earnings Card—The earnings card contains the employee number, rate of pay, overtime rate, F.W.T. (Federal Withholding Tax) deduction, and F.I.C.A. (Federal Insurance Compensation Act) deduction. In applications where space on the card permits, the name and earnings cards are combined into one card. This is generally the case in salary rolls where information is more constant and overtime differential is not involved.
3. Deduction Cards—The deduction cards contain the employee number, name, or description of deduction, numeric code if one is used, and the amount of each deduction. Deduction cards vary in number. Often the description of the deduction is pre-printed on the check stub (statement of earnings); thus only the amount is printed from the card. In applications where only codes and amounts are punched, one card may be used for all deductions.

The above types of cards are identified by a significant punch in column one. The employee number is punched in the same columns of all cards to permit sorting, matching, or merging one type of card with another, say deductions cards with earnings cards.

Salary Rolls

In a salary payroll application, it is possible to keep key-punching to a minimum by the use of file cards which are up-dated as necessary. After the manual procedure has been converted to machines, little additional key-punching is necessary. In cases where salaried employees receive overtime pay, an additional earnings card is key-punched and placed with the file of earnings cards just prior to processing. A significant punch in column one identifies this card in processing and permits removal of these cards at the end of processing when they are no longer needed. In the following application, completely pre-punched cards are used.

Two files of cards will be considered, the name-earnings cards and the deduction cards. Because cards are being added, removed, or corrected during the pay period, maintaining order in these files is not always possible. Thus at the end of the pay period, the two files of cards are removed and sorted on employee number. The name-earnings cards are placed in the sorter first, followed by the deduction cards. By sorting the decks together in this order, the various deduction cards for an employee are placed directly in back of their respective earnings cards. In some applications where the maintenance of the files permits, the two decks are matched and merged together by collating machine instead of by sorting. Unmatched name-earnings cards and deduction cards are selected out of the decks for purposes of investigation. The matched cards are in order by employee number.

The merged decks are next processed on the accounting machine. The control panel is wired to print the name, employee number, and date on the check while at the same time (and on the same line) the employee number, gross pay, F.W.T., and F.I.C.A. are printed on the statement of earnings. The gross pay is entered into a register as a plus amount. The control panel is wired to read the earnings card three times before reading another card. The second and third reading cycles permit the F.W.T. and the F.I.C.A. to be printed on the statement of earnings and also entered into the same counter as the gross pay, but as negative amounts. This multiple-read line feature is common to most accounting machines today. After processing the name-earnings card, the check is skipped to the next lines. The associated deduction cards are next processed. At the same time that the deduction is printed on the statement of earnings, it is also subtracted from the "gross pay" registered. The accounting machine is continuously comparing employee number in the cards at its first and second reading stations. After the last deduction card is processed for the particular employee, the gross pay counter has the net pay remaining in it. The net pay is then printed on both the check and the statement of earnings. The registers are set to zero for the next group of cards.

When year-to-date information is desired, a summary punch is included in the above application. (The summary punch operation is described in the following "hourly-paid" application. The procedure would be the same for salary payrolls.) After the tabulating and summary-punching operation, the merged decks are separated on the sorter by sorting on column one. This column identifies the type of card. The sorter is used in preference to the collator because of its speed, approximately five to one. This ratio quickly changes with an increase in the number of columns to be sorted. The cards must be passed through the sorter once for each column, whereas they must be passed through the collator only once to compare and separate on 20 columns or more, depending on the type machine.

Factory Rolls (Hourly Paid)

The hourly paid rolls are also produced from name/earnings and deduction cards. In addition to these cards daily time cards are used. They contain the employee's number, hours worked, job number, and the code for the particular work performed (punch press, lathe, drill press, and so on). An employee may work on several jobs during a day. In such cases, a card is punched for each job worked on.

Overtime paid for work over 40 hours does not require a special code unless desired for cost studies. But, when overtime is paid after eight hours, a different code is required for reporting this time. A prefix is used, say 09 for straight time and 19 for overtime for a particular operation. This identification is necessary for computing gross pay as described later.

The source documents, either time sheets or time cards, are sent daily to the key-punch unit. (See Figure 23-13.) They arrive in batches, in department and section number order. When time sheets are used, the key-punch operator punches the necessary data into a time card for each employee. Common data such as date, department, and section number is duplicated to minimize both time and errors. When the cards in the form of tabulating cards are used, the common information is pre-punched (by gang punching) into the card before it is given to the employee. The employee enters his employee number, hours worked, and code or job number involved. Only that information entered by the employee need be key-punched. Each batch of source documents has a control sheet showing the necessary indicative information and the number of items. A control card is punched from this sheet.

The daily time cards are sent to the tabulating section where they are "zero balanced" on the accounting machine. This operation involves nothing more than counting the cards and comparing the count with the total in the control card. It insures that all the cards are accounted for. The time cards are then sent to file until the end of the payroll period. At the end of the payroll period they are pulled from file and sorted on employee number. The earnings cards (already in employee number order) contain the employee number, rate of pay, overtime rate, F.W.T., F.I.C.A., and year-to-date gross pay and taxes. The time cards and earnings cards are merged together on the collator. The earnings cards fall in back of the time cards when they match on the employee number. The unmatched cards are dropped into separate pockets from which they can be removed and investigated. Incorrectly punched employee number, vacations, leave of absence, and similar situations account for many of these unmatched earning cards.

The merged deck is then processed on the calculating punch where the gross pay is computed. The hours worked are first accumulated in a register. Regular hours are separated from overtime hours when paid overtime after eight hours. When paid overtime after 40 hours, all the hours are stored in one register from which a constant of 40 (previously

HOURLY PAID PAYROLL
PUNCH CARD PROCEDURE

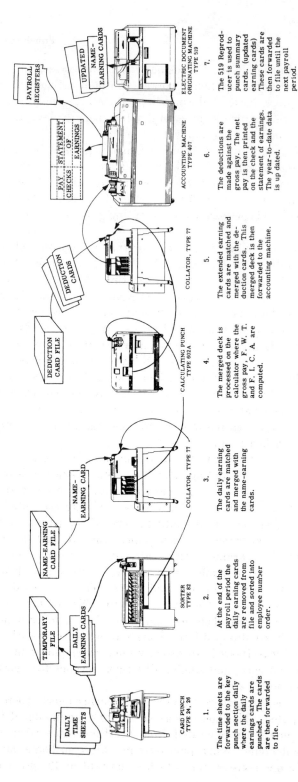

DAILY TIME SHEETS

CARD PUNCH TYPE 24, 26

1.

The time sheets are forwarded to the key punch section where the daily earnings cards are punched. The cards are then forwarded to file.

TEMPORARY FILE

DAILY EARNING CARDS

SORTER TYPE 82

2.

At the end of the payroll period the daily earning cards are removed from file and sorted into employee number order.

NAME-EARNING CARD FILE

NAME-EARNING CARD

COLLATOR, TYPE 77

3.

The daily earning cards are matched and merged with the name-earning cards.

CALCULATING PUNCH TYPE 602A

4.

The merged deck is processed on the calculator where the gross pay, F. W. T. and F. I. C. A. are computed.

DEDUCTION CARD FILE

DEDUCTION CARDS

COLLATOR, TYPE 77

5.

The extended earning cards are matched and merged with the deduction cards. This merged deck is then forwarded to the accounting machine.

PAY CHECKS | STATEMENT OF EARNINGS

PAYROLL REGISTERS

ACCOUNTING MACHINE TYPE 407

6.

The deductions are made against the gross pay. The net pay is then printed on the check and the statement of earnings. The year-to-date data is up dated.

UPDATED NAME-EARNING CARDS

ELECTRIC DOCUMENT ORIGINATING MACHINE TYPE 519

7.

The 519 Reproducer is used to punch summary cards. (updated earning cards) These cards are then forwarded to file until the next payroll period.

Figure 23-13. Hourly Paid Payroll—Procedure

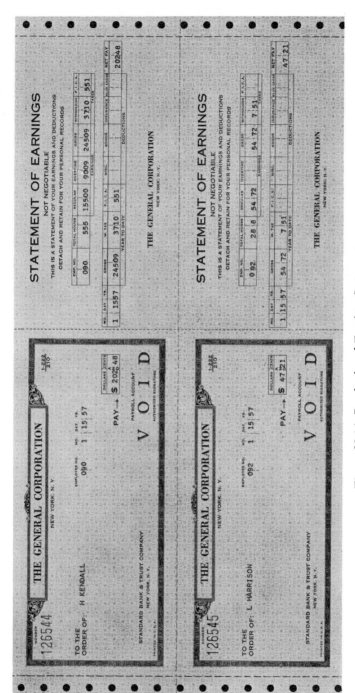

Figure 23-14. Paycheck and Earnings Statement

551

PAYROLL REGISTER

| Year-to-Date | | Employee | | Employee Name | | | Hours | | | Rate | Earnings | | | Deductions | | | Net Pay |
Earnings	Withholding Tax	Dept.	No.	1st	2nd	Surname	Regular	O.T.	Total		Regular	Overtime	Gross	Withholding Tax	F.I.C.A.	Other	
245 09	37 10	05	090	H	L	KENDALL	40 0	15 5	55 5	3 875	155 00	90 09	245 09	37 10	5 51		202 48
54 72	7 51	05	092	L		HARRISON	28 8		28 8	1 900	54 72		54 72	7 51			47 21
45 32	3 48	05	093	P	P	PALMER	22 0		22 0	2 060	45 32		45 32	3 48	1 02		40 82
45 50	3 51	05	094	J	R	AXTELL	33 7		33 7	1 350	45 50		45 50	3 51			41 99
77 81	9 33	05	095	P	E	HAIDT	37 5		37 5	2 075	77 81		77 81	9 33	1 75		66 73
116 11	16 22	05	096	E		SCHLEGEL	40 0	11 0	51 0	2 025	82 20	33 91	116 11	16 22	2 61		97 28
64 98	9 36	05	098	H		WOLFF	22 8		22 8	2 850	64 98		64 98	9 36	1 46		54 16
118 25	18 95	05	099	S		LEENHOXTS	40 0	10 0	50 0	2 150	86 00	32 25	118 25	18 95	2 66		96 64
58 23	5 80	05	100	C		DIEHL	28 2		28 2	2 065	58 23		58 23	5 80	1 31		51 12
										Totals →			826 01	111 26	16 32		698 43
													Gross	W. Tax	F.I.C.A.	Other Deducts	Net Pay

Figure 23-15. Payroll Register

stored in calculator) is subtracted from the total hours to determine amount of overtime worked, if any. After the gross pay is calculated, the year-to-date F.I.C.A. is read from the card and tested to determine if the maximum amount has been reached. If not, this tax is computed and stored for punch. The F.W.T. is also computed based on the gross pay multiplied by the percentage factor in the card. Thus the gross pay, current F.I.C.A., and F.W.T. are computed and ready for punch. When all the necessary calculations are computed for the particular earnings card, it is moved to the punch position in the calculator where the stored data is punched into it.

The earnings cards are then merged with the deductions cards and processed on the accounting machine. The year-to-date data is read into registers on the accounting machine, to which the current gross pay and taxes are added. The name and employee number are also read from the earnings card and printed on the paycheck (Figure 24-14). The employee number, gross pay and current F.I.C.A. and F.W.T. are also printed on the attached statement of earnings. The earnings card then moves out of the machine, and the deduction cards are processed. Each deduction is subtracted from the gross pay register and also printed on the paycheck. After all deductions have been read, the net pay is printed on both the paycheck and the statement of earnings. A summary card or year-to-date earnings card is also punched at this time. The necessary information is punched into the card just prior to its printing on the check or statement of earnings.

The new, updated earnings cards are next listed on the accounting machine to produce current payroll register (Figure 23-15). The deduction cards are separated from the previous earnings cards and sent to file. The previous earnings cards are stored for a period of time and then destroyed. The printing of year-to-date data on the statement of earnings, if not desired, may be suppressed during processing. The time cards (one for each job on which each man worked) can be used for labor distribution reports.

24

Electronic Data Processing

Fundamentals

Electronic data processing is the collection of any form of data, manipulation of the data, and output by electronic as distinguished from mechanical means. For our purposes "any form of data" can be considered as digital information or analogue information. Digital information is described as discrete units of alphabetic or numeric characters. ("A digital computer counts.") Analogue information is described as a continuous flow of information under some unit of measure of flow. (An analogue computer measures "like a meter.") Collection may involve the use of terminal(s) at the computer site or at some distant site, and data *transmission* is involved. Manipulation may include recognizing and storing (source) information, performing arithmetical and logical operations, and rearranging (editing) information.

Output may involve writing the manipulated data on continuous forms (producing hard copy) say on a high-speed printer, or transferring it to a repository called an external memory for later use by the computer or some other unit of the data-processing system. Operation at "electronic speed" can mean performance at extremely high speeds not possible under mechanical methods and certainly not under human manipulation. An electronic calculator can do in a few seconds or minutes calculations that would take men with mechanical calculators weeks or months.

What is meant by programs and stored program computer should be considered along with the above definition of electronic data processing. The stored program is a basic feature of electronic data processing which distinguishes it from punched-card accounting (Chapters 21-23). A program is a formal list of instructions that tells the computer what to do. There might be a separate program, for instance, for payroll, for sales and accounts receivable and for the solution of some problem such as a linear programming problem. Since a computer is built to accept and respond to a specific set of commands (sometimes a small number, sometimes a large number depending upon the computer), the program must be set up on the basis of those commands. The final program which controls the computer must be in machine-readable language. In the early days of computers, the programs were written by the programmer in machine-readable language. Now most programs are written by the programmer in a programmer-oriented language, such as Fortran or Cobol, and this program is converted by the computer into machine-readable language.[1]

A stored program is one which resides in the computer and which controls the performance of the series of operations covered by the program. Whereas in punched-card accounting, human control is required in the movement of cards from machine to machine, and wired panels control the operations within each machine, in electronic data-processing the stored program may control the whole system. Use of stored programs is one of the fundamental features of electronic data-processing systems. In operating procedures such as payroll, it harnesses the great speed of the computer by eliminating most of the delay between operations.

An important feature of the stored program principle is that, in the process of operating the program, the computer can modify the program:

> Almost concurrently with the use of electronics came another major development that was to widen the capabilities of data-processing systems and expand their opportunities for application. . . .
>
> It soon became apparent that . . . programming techniques inhibit the performance of the computer. To give the computer greater latitude in working problems without operator assistance, scientists proposed that the computer store its program in a high-speed internal memory or storage unit. . . . It could even be made to modify its own instructions as dictated by developing stages of the work.
>
> Because the computer is capable of making simple decisions and because it is capable of modifying instructions, the user is relieved of a vast amount of costly and repetitive programming.[2]

Historical Background

The earliest of the big computers (1944 and later) were laboratory models designed by university scientists for use in solving scientific problems. The design of these computers provided for extensive mathematical manipulation of a relatively small input. These computers were process bound rather than input bound. The design of some of the later com-

---

[1] Computer languages are discussed on pages 595–597.

[2] *Introduction to IBM Data Processing Systems—Student Text* (Second Edition; International Business Machines Corporation, 1968), page 4.

puters (1954 and later) was aimed at business use. In a typical operating procedure in business, relatively large amounts of data input require relatively small amounts of mathematical manipulation in the computer. This situation would obviously hold in the case of payroll data from which pay checks, employees' earnings records and the other output of a payroll procedure are produced, and similarly for other business procedures. Early business-oriented computers were input bound rather than process bound. As will be seen later, getting the data into the computer in a business system is an important design problem. It should be noted, however, that today the difference between scientific computers and business computers is less marked than it once was. To the extent that a "business computer" is used for management problem solving, it takes on the nature of a scientific computer.

The first of the so-called "giant brains" was the Harvard Mark I (the IBM Automatic Sequence Controlled Calculator). It was huge in size, 51 feet long, 12 feet deep, and 8 feet high. The computer had a memory capacity of sixty 23-decimal digit words. It could add or subtract two of these words in 3/10 of 1 second. This machine was basically a relay machine and used punched cards and paper tape for its input and output. Its major feature was sequential control of operation.

The next important advance was the ENIAC (Electronic Numerical Integrator and Computer) built for Army Ordnance at the Moore School of Electrical Engineering of the University of Pennsylvania under the direction of Dr. John Mauchley and J. Presper Eckert. It also was a very large machine containing some 1,500 relays and 18,000 electron tubes. It could add 5,000 ten-digit numbers in 1 second. This was the first of the "electronic brains" and its big feature was its speed.

In July of 1946 the Bell Telephone Laboratory brought out its General Purpose Relay Calculator. This machine weighed ten tons and it could add ten-digit words in 3/10 of 1 second. Its outstanding feature was its tremendous reliability, due to a great extent to its self-checking design in which one half of the machine was a duplicate of the other.

There followed a series of "brains" each showing some advance in the state of the art. The Harvard Mark II (July 1947) was twelve times as powerful as the Mark I. In January 1948 the IBM Selective Sequence Electronic Calculator made its appearance. It had 12,500 tubes and 21,500 relays and could add or subtract nineteen-digit words in ten milli-seconds (1/1000 of one second). In September of 1949, the Harvard Mark III, an electronic machine, appeared with a magnetic drum memory. Other machines developed about this time include MIT's Whirlwind, the Moore School's EDVAC, the Institute for Advanced Study's machine, Engineering Research Associates' 1101, the National Bureau of Standards' machines, and many others.

In March 1951 the UNIVAC appeared—the most significant step in the field of data-processing. This machine, developed by the Eckert–Mauchley Computer Corp. for the Bureau of Census, can be considered the first commercial electronic data-processor. It featured speed, reliability, memory capacity, and an ability to handle alphanumeric characters. It also had magnetic tape units as input and output devices.

From that time on developments in the field came rapidly. Computers that were introduced up until about 1959 are now generally referred to as "first generation computers." For the most part, these were all vacuum tube computers. Transistors characterized the computers of the second generation which lasted from about 1959 to 1964. Integrated circuits distinguished the third generation which started in 1964. Most computers in use today are of the third generation.

Classification of Computers

Computers are generally classified in three ways:

(1) By purpose
   (a) General purpose—those systems of equipment designed to solve many different kinds of problems.
   (b) Special purpose—those systems of equipment designed to perform basically one type of operation. A good example is the Sabre system, the American Airlines Reservation system.[3] There are many other examples of special purpose computer systems.
(2) By type
   (a) Digital—those systems that operate on discrete bits of alphabetic or numeric information. The computer that the telephone company uses to produce monthly bills to subscribers is a digital computer, actuated by the dialing of alphabetic and numeric information. Digital computers dominate the business field.
   (b) Analogue—those systems of equipment which operate on information supplied in a continuous flow measured in units such as gallons, pounds, volts and so forth. Analogue computers are used to monitor and control process industries such as oil refineries, blast furnaces (iron), and certain types of steel rolling mills.

---

[3] According to Wayne S. Boutell (*Computer Oriented Business Systems*, Prentice-Hall, 1968, pp. 192–3), the Sabre System (Semi-Automatic Business Research) was developed by American Airlines at a cost of approximately $30 million. It handles (1968) approximately 40,000 reservations, 30,000 seat availability requests, and 20,000 ticket sales daily. . . . There are a total of 600,000 reservations records.

(c) Hybrid—These systems are computer systems which combine the features of analogue computers for certain phases of the total computer operation and digital computers for other phases. Brightman et al., point out that each of the above types of computer has its place in industry and that they were designed to supplement each other.[4]

(3) By capacity (referring to the volume of work which the computer can handle, rather than to the physical size of the computer)

(a) Small

(b) Medium

(c) Large

In the early stages of electronic computer development, capacity was sometimes gauged in terms of physical size. Today, however, physical size is not a good measure of capacity, because of the compactness of technical features found in late models. Examples of these features are small magnetic cores in memory packages, transistorized circuitry (replacing relatively bulky tubes), and advanced packaging design applied to equipment housing.

Components of a Computer System

The components of a computer system (Figure 24-1) are

(1) Input unit

(2) Central processing unit, consisting in turn of
Arithmetic–logic unit
Control unit
Main memory

(3) Output unit

(4) Program and built in instructions

(5) Data transmission units

Figure 24-1 is a photograph of the units of a large electronic data-processing installation. It shows the input and output unit and the processing unit, which in turn contains the control unit, a storage unit (memory), and an arithmetic unit. The following paragraphs of this section explain the functions of each of the units. Later sections describe and illustrate various types of input–output units, memory, and so forth. It will be apparent from the description of components in the following sections that electronic computers are put together in different assemblies of the components.

---

[4] Richard W. Brightman, Bernard J. Luskin, and Theodore Tilton, *Data Processing for Decision Making* (New York: The Macmillan Company, 1968), page 176.

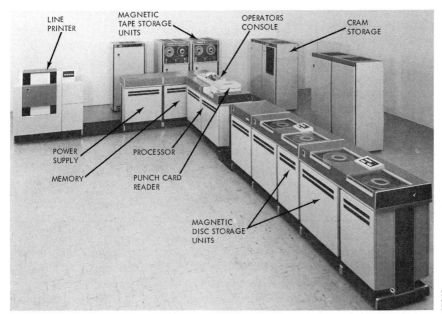

Figure 24-1.   Units in a Large Electronic Data-Processing Installation

The *input units* perform the obvious function of getting data into the central processing unit. There are many types of input units (some are listed in Table 24-1), but the one most familiar is the punched-card reader. In the use of this type of input, 80-column cards are punched as previously described (pages 490–491) and loaded into a punched-card reader, which reads them and may, according to the configuration of the system, transfer information into the main memory of the central processing unit.

Output units read processed data out of the central processing unit and either store it (in this case the output unit is also a type of external memory), put it on a transmission line to another location, or print it as hard copy. A computer system may have a number of input and output units.

Various types of input–output units are described on pages 561–572. Some units (the card reader, for instance) are input only; other units (the card punch) are output only; still others (magnetic tape transport) are used for both input and output. *Optical character recognition* is a system of reading typed or manually written characters on paper and converting them to machine language for input into a computer. The author regards OCR as a system rather than a simple input unit. OCR is discussed and illustrated at the end of this chapter.

Table 24-1

Input–Output Units Described in This Chapter

Card reader
Card read–punch
Magnetic-tape writer
Magnetic-tape transport
Paper-tape reader
Console typewriter
Magnetic-ink-character readers
Data collection units
Visual display units
High-speed printers

The *central processing unit* is the aggregation of sub-units that does the work of the computer. It is sometimes called the main frame. As indicated above, it consists of three sub-units.

The *arithmetic–logic unit* performs addition, subtraction, multiplication, division, square root, rounding, shifting, and setting the sign, together with certain logical operations. In a large computer (IBM 360-40 for instance) it consists of thousands of transistors, resistors, and diodes which can perform additions at a rate of 100,000 a second.[5] An example of a common logical operation is the comparison of two numbers to determine whether one is greater than, less than or equal to the other. The outcome of this operation determines what the computer will do next. For example, it may determine whether the computer will continue to the next operation in sequence in the program or *branch* to some other later (or earlier) operation in the program. This operation is very frequently used in computer practice.[6]

The *control unit* causes the computer to perform the operations called for by the program. Its operation is similar to that of a switchboard. It connects the input unit called for by the program to main memory, activates the arithmetic logic operations called for, storing the processed data in main memory, and finally causes the processed data to be transferred to the output unit called for in the program. Related to the control unit is a control panel which enables the operator to initiate a program, alter

---

[5] Life Educational Reprint 33, *How the Computer Gets the Answer,* Life Educational Reprint 33, *Life Atlantic,* November 27, 1967.

[6] In the calculation of the social security deduction in a payroll application, for instance, if the gross earnings to date for an individual is less than $7,800, the computer takes 10.4 per cent of gross earnings for this period. If it is equal to or more than $7,800, the computer proceeds with the next step in the program. (10.4 per cent is the combined rate for employer and employee as this book goes to press.)

the program, interrupt the computer if need be, or request progress reports. The typewriter console can print out such reports and provide additional access to the computer.[7]

The *main memory* stores the active program, the data being used, and also processed data pending transfer to an output unit. The main memory is contained in the central processing unit, in distinction to auxiliary memory which is outside the main frame. Various types of memory are described on pages 572–577. In a computer, information or data input including letters of the alphabet is resolved into the specific format of a number system to accommodate (a) storage in memory and (b) mathematical manipulation. Computers are designed to accommodate particular number system(s). Several types of number systems are described on pages 577–581, following the discussion of memory.

As stated earlier in this chapter, a *program* is a formal set of instructions designed to tell the computer what to do, step by step. It is nonpermanent and specially written for, say, sales accounting, or payroll, or the solution of a particular engineering problem. To get a program into the computer initially, a tabulating card (Figure 21-1) may be punched for each line of the program, and the cards read into the computer by a card reader. Programs can also be read into the computer from magnetic tapes and discs as well as from cards.

INPUT–OUTPUT UNITS

Card Reader: Card Read–Punch

Punched cards are a popular data *source* for business oriented computer systems. According to Sanders:

> Punched cards are the most familiar medium. They are easily understood, and they possess advantages because of their fixed length and unit record nature, e.g., some cards can be deleted, added to, sorted, etc., without disturbing the others. However, their data density is low, they are bulky, and they represent a slow means of input and output.[8]

The card reader (Figure 24-2) can be used to read 80-column cards (Chapter 21) to provide input to the computer. The cards pass through the computer one by one and the reader operates automatically under program control, continuing until the file is completed. The reader reads the holes and transmits electric impulses to the main memory of the computer. Unlike the reader in punched-card accounting, this reader reads

---

[7] Life, op. cit., page 8.

[8] Donald H. Sanders, *Computers in Business—An Introduction* (New York: McGraw-Hill Book Company, 1968), page 92.

Control Data

Figure 24-2.   Card Reader Type 405

the entire card in one pass. There may be several input units in the system and the program indicates what unit is activated and to what storage area the data is to be transferred.

In the card reader, cards are read under either of two principles, depending upon the design of the reader. One principle involves electrical contact, suggested by the diagram in Figure 21-6. Cards pass between a roller and a set of 13 brushes, one for each position in a column. When a brush senses a punched hole, an electric circuit is completed between the roller and a brush. A counter accordingly registers the number which represents the position of the hole in the column.

The other principle is photoelectric. In this case, light passes through the hole and is picked up by a light-sensitive cell. Each cell—one for each digit position in a column—allows an electric current to pass when the light strikes it. Card reading speeds vary from 12 cards to 1,000 cards a minute, depending upon the type of card reader.[9]

Card punches are used to punch information from the memory into tabulating cards. Card read–punches are built to do either reading (input to the computer) or punching (output from the computer). In a card read–punch, the cards pass through both the reading and punch units.

9 IBM, op. cit., page 49.

Either the read unit or the punch unit is activated in a pass, depending on how the controls are set. The IBM 2,520 card read–punch unit can read or punch 500 cards per minute.[10]

Card readers are much slower than the computer, i.e., the computer can process information much faster than the reader can feed it. To take up the difference in speed between the card read–punch and the computer, any of several devices can be used. A buffer, which is a form of memory, may be used between the card read–punch and the computer. On the read operation, the buffer will receive the data at reader speed, accumulate it, and, when the program says the computer is ready for it, transfer it to the computer at electronic speed. On the output side, the reverse process would take place. Another plan is to use a card to magnetic tape reader. Use of the magnetic tape method suggests itself because of the great speed of the tape method.

Magnetic-Tape Writer: Magnetic-Tape Transport

Magnetic tape used in computer systems is similar to the tape used in the familiar tape recorders. Tape is ½″ wide and a reel is 2,400 feet long. The tape can be visualized as a reproduction of a string of punched cards, so that the data in a column of the card is deposited across the width of the tape. One side of the tape is coated with an iron oxide compound and this side receives a magnetic coding in the process of writing data onto the tape. The other side has a protective coating. Magnetic tape can be read into a computer much faster than punched tabulating cards can be read. Input/output data rates in the range of 20,000 to 100,000 numeric characters a second are prevalent.[11]

Magnetic tape can be created:

(1) by a magnetic-tape writer which is equipped with a keyboard. An operator reads source documents and produces magnetic tape via the keyboard.

(2) by a punched card to magnetic tape converter. Punched cards produced in some previous operation can be read into a converter which produces magnetic tape.

(3) as output of the computer. In certain applications, this month's magnetic tape output is stored off-line and next month used as input to the computer for updating with next month's transactions. The magnetic tapes would be updated each month.

Note that when the tape is stored off-line as indicated in the previous paragraph, it is a form of auxiliary memory to the computer. The author

---

10 Brightman et al., op. cit., page 219.
11 IBM, op. cit., page 27.

thinks of a sales, accounts receivable, cash receipts system in which 7,000 reels of magnetic tape are stored off-line (as external memory) from which selected reels are put on-line each day. Putting the reels "on-line" is done by an operator who takes the reel from external file and places it in a tape transport unit.

A magnetic tape writer (Figure 24-3) can be used to write information

NCR

Figure 24-3.   Magnetic Tape Writer

onto a tape, and by a second operation, to verify what was written on the tape in the first operation. It is equipped with a keyboard similar to a typewriter keyboard and a device for handling the tape. The operator types from transaction media of some sort. To verify, the operator rewinds the tape to the start positon, sets the writing machine to *verify* and repeats the writing operation. If the machine detects any difference between the first operation and the second, the machine signals the operator, who then determines the correct entry and puts it on the tape over the previous entry. The NCR tape writer can also be used in data transmission systems. A tape writer in one office can be connected by telephone line to a tape writer in another office, possibly in another city. Data can be transmitted from the keyboard in the first city to the tape in the second city. The tape would then be used in the computer system in the second city.

The magnetic-tape transport (Figure 24-4) is the machine unit used either for reading from the tape (input to the computer or input to a printer), or writing onto the tape (computer output). The tape transport has two spindles and in the operation of the transport, the tape moves from one spindle onto the other. The unit includes a read head and a write head, side by side between the spindles. The tape moves past these heads when the machine is in operation.

Sperry Rand Univac Division

Figure 24-4. Magnetic Tape Transport (Uniservo 2)

There is a vacuum column below each spindle which is used to provide slack in the tape between spindle and reading head on the one side and between spindle and writing head on the other side. If this slack were not provided in threading the tape in the machine, the sudden stops required to position the tape might break the tape. For some models of tape transport, tape cartridges are provided for threading the transport automatically after the cartridge is placed in the tape transport by the operator. Use of these cartridges eliminates the manual threading operation.

In the writing operation, a magnetic field set up by the read head energizes the iron oxide coating on the tape and in the reading operation, the read head picks up the magnetic field from the tape. The reading operation is non-destructive, i.e., the tape can be read a number of times without destroying the information on the tape. On the other hand, the writing (onto the tape) operation is destructive, which means that the new information is put right on top of the old information, obliterating the old information. It is obvious that controls must be operated to guard against writing on the wrong tape.

Punched-Paper-Tape Readers

A discussion of punched-paper tape in connection with punched-card accounting machines appears on pages 525–527. Punched-paper tape may also be used as a means of input to a computer by means of a punched-paper-tape reader (not illustrated). Sanders points out:[12]

> Punched paper tape is a popular means of capturing data as a byproduct of another processing activity. . . . Certain advantages accrue to paper tape because of its continuous length. There is no upper-limit restriction on the length of records and no wasted space when records are short. Paper tape is also more economical than is the case with cards. And, like cards, paper tape is a relatively slow I/O medium.

Console Typewriter

The console typewriter is used to transmit data directly to the internal memory of the computer, simultaneously producing hard copy of the data transmitted, and also to get data out of memory, making hard copy. Figure 24-5 is an illustration of a console typewriter. Sanders lists the uses of the console typewriter as (1) modify a portion of the program instructions, (2) test the program of instructions, (3) inquire about the contents of certain storage areas, (4) alter the data content of specific storage locations, (5) determine intermediate computing results and (6) receive and type output information. Console typewriters, because of the slowness of their I/O operations, are seldom used if the volume is significant.[13]

Magnetic-Ink-Character Inscribers and Readers

Magnetic-ink characters are characters printed or inscribed in magnetic ink in a highly stylized standard font which can be read by a magnetic-ink-character reader. Magnetic-ink characters are used on bank checks to accommodate bank clearing and proof processes. A bank's *clearing account number* is printed by the manufacturer of the check in mag-

---

12 Sanders, op. cit., page 85.
13 Ibid., pages 106–7.

RCA

Figure 24-5.   Console Typewriter Type 70/90

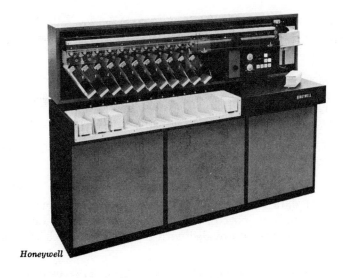

Honeywell

Figure 24-6.   Magnetic-Ink-Character Reader-Sorter (Type 232)

netic ink on the bottom edge of the check. Standardization was sponsored by the American Bankers Association. The *dollar amount* of a check is inscribed in magnetic ink after the check has been deposited, ordinarily by the bank in which the check is deposited. Some large bank customers who issue large numbers of checks do some of their own reading and sorting for clearing. The object is to save some banking service charges.

Two machines basic to the process are the magnetic-ink inscriber (not illustrated) and the magnetic-ink-character reader-sorter (Figure 24-6). The Honeywell Magnetic Ink Character Reader-Sorter illustrated reads the magnetic-ink characters on checks, converting the characters into machine language which it transmits directly to a computer. It also sorts the checks for subsequent clearing operation. The reader is built to handle checks of various sizes in one run.

An interesting explanation of MICR scanning appears in the Honeywell bulletin:

> In the Magnetic Ink Character Readers, the method of scanning differs from optical devices in that it does not view the character "visually," but "feels" it through electronic impulses. The MICR units are limited to reading highly stylized magnetic fonts and each character in a particular font generates a signal with a unique wave form. As characters move past the read head, the magnetic scanner compares their wave forms with reference wave forms stored in the recognition unit. . . .[14]

Data Collection Units

Data collection units are remote terminals used for collecting transactions at the source. In-plant data collection systems have been designed to carry out three basic functions:

> 1. To record data automatically
> 2. To automatically transmit this data to a control point—usually the data processing center, and
> 3. To record the data in a machine processable medium, such as punched cards or perforated paper tape . . .
> Recording is usually accomplished through a combination of prepunched cards or tags and the manual insertion of variable data through a keyboard attached to the recorder.[15]

One make of data collection units is used to collect time and cost information, specifically job cost information, in factories. Each workman who works on jobs is provided with a job ticket which is punched

---

[14] Honeywell, *Introduction to Optical Character Recognition* (1969), pages 2–3.
[15] *Data Collection and Transmission—The Next Important Step in Business Data Processing* (Arthur Andersen & Co., 1962), page 28.

with job number and an identification ticket which is punched with his own number. When a workman clocks in one job, he inserts the job ticket and his own identification ticket in the terminal, causing it to transmit to the computer. He performs a similar recording operation when he clocks the job out.

Visual Display Units

Visual display units are output units which include tubes or panels or a screen on which the output is projected for direct readng. According to Howard:

> The common element is some sort of image forming device to convert data from an electronic form to optical form for direct viewing or projection on a screen. In computer generated displays, the digital computer controls the display as well as providing data and information . . .
> The cathode ray tube is probably the most flexible, and next to printed outputs, the most common of computer generated output displays.[16]

In some models a keyboard and the tube are built into the same console (Figure 24-7). In others, the tube is in a cabinet which is separate from the keyboard. With the latter arrangement, the operator can be located

IBM

Figure 24-7.   Visual Display Unit with Light Pen

---

[16] James H. Howard, *Electronic Information Displays for Management* (American Data Processing, Inc., 1966), page 33.

at a little distance from the tube, which in turn can be located for easy viewing by a group of people. The keyboard provides one source of input to the computer and the input is shown in image form on the tube where the operator can read it before transmitting it to the computer. Errors can be erased or they can be corrected by typing over them.

For some engineering problems, the solution is desired in the form of a set of curves on a chart. All of the curves in the set relate to one basic problem, and each curve illustrates the effect of a change in input variables. By studying the family of curves on the display, the analyst can immediately see the effect of changes in particular variables.

A light pen can be used for input to the memory of the computer, in conjunction with the display unit. The light pen is a cylindrical tube with a light on the end. The operator uses it by pointing it to the tube in the visual display unit. The mathematical position of the point is picked up in memory. A straight line can be defined in memory by positioning two points on the screen.

Computer output on the tube gives a faster readout than a typewriter; the system can be so programmed that entire "pages" of information can be put on the screen at one time. Tabular material and graphic material such as charts, diagrams, drawings of machine parts, and architectural drawings, can also be called out of memory and put on the screen exhibit by exhibit. Visual display (CRT) can be photographed and captured on microfilm at high speed for permanent low cost storage or for subsequent reproduction in hard copy. (See pages 181–186.)

The terminal can be designed to accommodate mathematical calculations. Special keys are provided to control performance of mathematical functions. Thus, a SIN key would be provided to initiate the calculation of a sine, using data input by the operator. There would be a special key for each function that the computer is programmed to calculate.

High-Speed Printer

The high-speed printer is used to produce hard copy, printing a line at a time. The major printing devices consist of the print wheel printer, wire matrix printer, chain printer, and incremental bar printer. In high-speed printers, characters are printed 120 to the line, at a rate of 500 or 1,000 lines a minute, depending upon the device model.[17]

Figure 24-8 is a high-speed printer and Figure 24-9 a picture of the train printer used in this printer. The train printer is stationed in front of the paper, and a series of hammers, one for each printing position on the entire line, is located behind the paper. The train moves at high speed,

---

[17] IBM, op. cit., page 58.

Control Data

Figure 24-8.   Printer Type 512

Control Data

Figure 24-9.   Print Train for High-Speed Printer (Figure 24-8)

and the hammers strike at the proper time to print a required letter when the letter is in position for printing.

A drum printer (not illustrated) is a cylinder on which there is a series of bands of type. Each band of type comprises a complete alphabet, the numbers 0 to 9 and special characters. The cylinder is positioned behind the paper in the printer and the bands are so positioned that all of the A's are in one line, likewise all the B's, and so forth. The drum makes one complete revolution for each line to be printed on the paper. While the paper is positioned momentarily for printing a line, the hammers strike all the A's which appear in the line, then all the B's, and so forth.

STORAGE

Storage and Access to Storage

Storage, sometimes called memory, in a computer system is the equipment used to hold addressable information in coded form. The information can be held either as a file (for example, inventory balances, customers account balances) or as a program and data for operation by the computer. Storage is *on-line* when it is connected electrically to the central processor, *off-line* when it is not connected electrically to the central processor. Magnetic tape is on-line when it is in the tape transport. It is off-line when the reels of tape are stored in a file to be taken from file and put into the tape transport by the operator when needed for a particular application of the computer. (Magnetic tape is accordingly both an input–output device and a storage device.)

Some storage is designed for on-line use, for direct or random access, and for random inquiry. Storage designed for random access and random inquiries will receive and process transactions as they occur and will also handle questions as to the current contents of specific accounts as these questions occur. Canning pointed out that random access memory would allow the processing machine to locate any one unit record in memory as quickly as it can find any other.[18] The processing of transactions indicated here is known as real time processing. Gregory pointed out that "real-time control requires that information become available soon enough to permit control of the operation while it is being carried on."[19]

Other storage (magnetic tape) is designed for sequential access, which means that it is necessary for the computer to examine the items on a tape in order to locate a specific account. Sequential access involves

---

[18] Richard G. Canning, *Electronic Data Processing for Business and Industry* (New York: John Wiley & Sons, Inc., 1955), page 57.

[19] Robert H. Gregory, "Computers and Accounting Systems" (*Accounting Research,* Volume 6, no. 1, 1955).

processing in periodic batches. This processing was described by Canning as delayed central processing. The input, the accounts in memory, and the output are all in order according to a common classification. If the data to be input is not in this order, it must be sorted, either before reading it into the computer or by computer operation.

The delayed central processing or batching concept, as it is often called, is familiar in punched-card installations, where cards are punched from basic documents which have been batched and then sorted and tabulated in certain time intervals to produce periodic reports. An example found in electronic computer practice occurs where punched cards for this period's employees' gross earnings and deductions are input to the computer together with tape containing employees' quarterly earnings records as of the end of last pay period. The output is new updated tapes of employees' earnings records.[20]

Some Factors in Comparison of Storage Units

There are a number of types of storage units. They differ in the principles by which they operate, their capacity (in units of information), access time (time required to get information out of storage), and cost of the memory unit in terms of capacity. The type of memory selected depends upon the application(s) for which the computer system is set up. Some electronic computer systems have several types of memory. A number of types of storage are described in the following sections.

Magnetic Tape

A description of magnetic tape as an input–output device appears on pages 563–566. It was pointed out that magnetic tape has a considerable advantage in speed over, say, punched cards. According to Sanders (1968), "magnetic tape is the most popular I/O medium being used today for high speed, large volume applications [and] it is the most widely used off-line storage medium."

As a storage medium the advantages are reduction in storage space required and relatively low cost of tape as a storage device. A disadvantage is that access to tape is sequential, as distinguished from random. Another disadvantage is that tape must be read by machine; it is not possible to read tape directly as it is to read punched cards.[21]

---

[20] The terms *delayed central processing* and *real time central processing* and an excellent discussion of these concepts appear in Canning's *Electronic Data Processing in Business and Industry* (pages 49–66), under the general heading "Patterns for Posting Transactions." The present author uses these terms by permission.

[21] Sanders, op. cit., page 86.

Core Storage

A magnetic core is a minute doughnut-shaped piece of ferromagnetic material. Magnetic core storage consists of a series of frames on each of which rows of cores have been strung by passing two wires at right angles through the hole in each core. A single frame is illustrated in Figure 24-10. In one computer model (IBM 360-40) there are 33,280 cores in a frame, each of which has its own "address," determined by the two wires that intersect it like coordinates on a map.[22] Ferromagnetic material is used because of its magnetic response to current which is passed through the wires. The two wires, capable of carrying an electric current, pass through the hole in the core as shown in the upper part of Figure 24-11.[23] When the current is in one direction, the magnetic field moves clockwise, and when it is in the other direction, the field moves counter clockwise. Thus the magnetic state of a core indicates whether the core is read as a 1 or a 0. In addition to the two wires that turn the core on or off, a set of sense wires are strung through the holes, and the purpose of these sense wires is to read the cores.

When the coding system is binary coded decimal (BCD), explained

Figure 24-10. Magnetic Core Storage (A Single Frame)

---

[22] Life, op. cit., page 8.

[23] *The Bell System's Approach to Business Information Systems* (American Telephone and Telegraph Company, 1965), page 32.

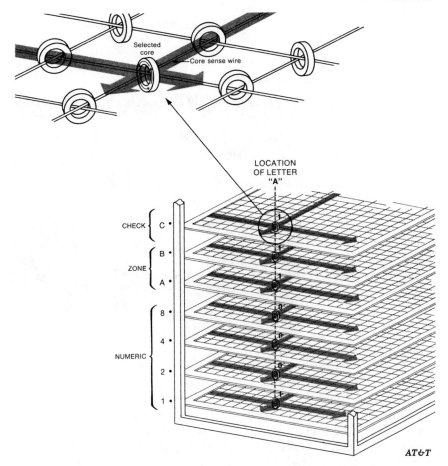

Figure 24-11.   Column of Seven Magnetic Cores

on pages 580–581, seven cores are required for one digit position. The seven positions will provide for the arabic numerals 0 to 9 and the letters of the alphabet, together with punctuation. These cores are arranged in a vertical column, like Figure 24-11 (lower part). The cores shown in Figure 24-11 read the letter "A," and, in a read-out to printer operation, that number would be read, converted to a letter of the alphabet, and printed. Core storage is said to be the fastest access and the most expensive storage.

Magnetic Drum

A cross-section diagram of a magnetic drum, together with the read–write head, appears in Figure 24-12. The drum of one model (IBM

**Figure 24-12.   Cross Section
of Magnetic Drum**

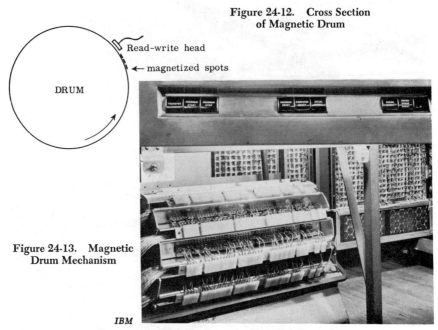

Read-write head

← magnetized spots

DRUM

**Figure 24-13.   Magnetic
Drum Mechanism**

IBM

2303) has addressable tracks around its periphery, as well as some spare
tracks which can be put into use in case one of the 800 is disabled. The
drum rotates at a constant speed of 3500 revolutions per minute. Positioned above the drum are the stationary read–write heads (diagrammed). There are 40 rows, each row comprising 20 heads. The heads
are positioned a slight space above the track. During the operation of
storage, the magnetically sensitive coating on the outer surface of a
rotating drum is covered with groups of magnetic spots arranged according to the code. In the operation of reading data out of memory, the
read–write head reads data from a specific address as the surface of the
drum goes past. Figure 24-13 is a photograph of a magnetic drum
mechanism.[24]

Discs

Discs used for storage are somewhat similar to phonograph records
except that the former have concentric tracks. They have a magnetically
sensitive coating on each side and as many as 500 tracks on each side.
They are mounted in stacks on a single vertical drive shaft in the on-line
disc storage drive.

---

[24] IBM, op. cit., page 36.

In one model of disc storage there are 25 discs in a set. They are positioned about ½″ apart, are accessed by read–write heads which move horizontally. A single read–write head accesses the bottom surface of one disc and the top surface of the disc below locating a track by its address, according to the program.

There are also disc packs (Figure 24-15) which are removable from the storage unit, and replaceable by another disc pack. Thus, disc packs can be used for off-line storage, in the same way as magnetic tape is used. There are six discs in a pack, and a pack can store up to 7.25 million characters of information. Figure 24-14 is a disc storage drive and Figure 24-15 is a disc pack.

IBM

Figure 24-14.   Disc Storage Drive

NUMBER SYSTEMS

Decimal

Computers are designed to accommodate specific number system(s). It is useful therefore to consider the attributes of numbering systems in general and the attributes of certain number systems used in computers.

The basic attributes of a number system are *absolute value* and *position value*. Absolute values are the values attaching to any digit position. In the decimal numbering system, there are ten possible ab-

Control Data

Figure 24-15.   Disc Pack

solute values in a single position, and they are 0, 1, 2, 3, 4, 5, 6, 7, 8, and 9. If a number comprises only one digit position, the number can have any one of these ten values. Position value is the value attaching to a number by reason of the number of digits to the right or left of the decimal point. In a decimal numbering system, the position value of each digit to the left of the decimal point is ten times that of the next previous position.

The decimal numbering system is used in the familiar electro-mechanical desk adding machine. Each of the digit positions in such a machine comprises a wheel bearing the decimal numbers 0 to 9 equally spaced on the rim. The wheel revolves through ten places in all, depending upon the place value of the number indicated on the keyboard. When the tenth position is passed, there is a carryover to the next digit wheel, advancing it one place.

No computers are built to use decimal number systems in the arithmetic units. A computer intended for business application is built to receive decimal numbers at the input unit, then automatically convert to (usually) binary or binary coded decimal (BCD) for storage in memory and used by the arithmetic unit. After processing, it converts the numbers back to decimal for output. The printer in a computer designed for U.S. dollars prints decimal numbers.

Binary numbering and BCD numbering systems are explained in the following sections. Binary numbering systems are used in some computers designed for scientific applications, and BCD systems in some computers designed for business applications. There are other numbering systems in use in computers, but they are not explained in this book.

Binary Number System

The storage units or memories of computers explained in the previous sections are designed to handle a one or a zero in each position (core, for instance), "one" being a magnetized core and "zero" being a non-magnetized core. In a pure binary system, each digit position has an absolute value of one or zero and each digit position has a position value of twice the value of the position to the right. Thus:

Binary number   1 = the decimal number 1
Binary number   10 = the decimal number 2
Binary number   100 = the decimal number 4
Binary number 1000 = the decimal number 8

In the binary system four positions are used to express the decimal numbers 0 through 9, as follows:

Decimal number	Binary number
0	0000
1	0001
2	0010
3	0011
4	0100
5	0101
6	0110
7	0111
8	1000
9	1001

In a pure binary system, the same four positions have the capacity to express the additional decimal numbers 10 through 15, as follows:

Decimal number	Binary number
10	1010
11	1011
12	1100
13	1101
14	1110
15	1111

Note that the decimal number is the sum of the decimal value of all of the digits in the binary number. Decimal 8 = binary 1000; decimal 2 = binary 0010; decimal 10 = binary 1010.

Binary addition is accomplished by the application of four rules: 0 plus 0 = 0; 0 plus 1 = 1; 1 plus 0 = 1; 1 plus 1 = 10 (1 plus 1 produces a carryover). As stated above, the arithmetic section of a computer is built to handle binary numbers, i.e., to do binary arithmetic. Thus, the sum of 0001 and 0001 is 0010:

Binary	Decimal equivalent
0001	1
0001	1
0010	2

The sum of 0101 and 0011 is 1000:

Binary	Decimal equivalent
0101	5
0011	3
1000	8

Binary Coded Decimal

The binary coded decimal system is a combination of binary system and decimal system. In this combination, four binary positions are provided for units 0 to 9, but although the same four positions would accommodate 10 to 15, as illustrated above, the full binary potential is not needed or utilized. Four more binary positions are provided for tens, four for hundreds, and so forth. Thus the conventional decimal number 265,498 would be expressed:

Decimal Digits	2	6	5	4	9	8
Binary Value	0 0 1 0	0 1 1 0	0 1 0 1	0 1 0 0	1 0 0 1	1 0 0 0
Place Value	8 4 2 1	8 4 2 1	8 4 2 1	8 4 2 1	8 4 2 1	8 4 2 1

IBM

Figure 24-16. Binary coded decimal representation of decimal number 265,498

In order to represent alphabetic information it is necessary to use two additional positions per character. These two extra positions are called "zone positions." With two positions there are four possible zone combinations (00, 01, 10, 11) as shown in Table 24-2. This code plan provides for all the letters of the alphabet and all the decimal numbers. Zone 00 is used for decimal numbers 0 to 1 respectively (00 − 0001 = one), zone 01 is used for letters A to I respectively (01 − 0001 = A) zone 10 is used for letters J to R (J = 10 − 0001), and zone 11 is used for letters S to Z respectively (11 − 0010 = S).

The blank or unused combinations are usually coded for special characters such as %, #, &, and so forth.

Thus the word COMPUTER could be represented by eight vertical stacks of cores, each of the eight contiguous stacks representing one letter:

C	01–0011
O	10–0110
M	10–0100
P	10–0111
U	11–0100
T	11–0011
E	01–0101
R	10–1001

A stack of cores energized for the letter A is diagrammed in Figure 24-11. This stack includes seven cores, the seventh core being a "parity-check" core provided for proof purposes.

Table 24-2

CODE FOR NUMERIC AND ALPHABETIC INFORMATION

Binary	Zone 00	Zone 01	Zone 10	Zone 11
0000	zero	—	—	—
0001	one	A	J	—
0010	two	B	K	S
0011	three	C	L	T
0100	four	D	M	U
0101	five	E	N	V
0110	six	F	O	W
0111	seven	G	P	X
1000	eight	H	Q	Y
1001	nine	I	R	Z
1010	—	—	—	—
1011	—	—	—	—
1100	—	—	—	—
1001	—	—	—	—
1110	—	—	—	—
1111	—	—	—	—

Third-Generation Computers

Concerning third-generation computers, Brightman, Luskin, and Tilton say:

Third-generation computers such as IBM's System 360 are characterized by multiprogramming capability, time sharing terminals, and increased main memory size. The 360, for example, is supposed to cover the "full circle" of needs of all users. It is appropriate for both business and scientific processing. Real time processing is characteristic of third generation computers. The necessity for batch processing has been significantly reduced. . . .

The general trend, then, is toward a single family line of hardware and away from the multitypes of similar systems of the second generation. Industry will probably continue to evolve and develop toward the total information system and information science will come to play an increasingly important role at all levels within the business organization.[25]

Figure 24-17a is a picture of the central processing unit and the typewriter console of an International Business Machines Corporation System 360/40 computer.[26] The CPU is opened to show the complete set of components, the functions of which have been explained previously in this chapter. The control unit is at the left and the arithmetic (logic) unit at the lower left. The memory (magnetic core), which contains special instructions in the form of programs and data, is at the right. The plastic tape cartridges which house the mechanism for special instructions are at the lower right.

Multi-programming and time-sharing are explained in the following chapter, and information systems in Chapter 26.

Hardware configurations of other computer systems illustrated in this chapter are:

Henry Groskinsky LIFE Magazine © Time, Inc.

Figure 24-17a.   System 360/40

---

[25] Richard Brightman et al., op. cit., page 101.
[26] Life, op. cit., pages 8–9.

Figure 24-1 National Cash Register Company
24-17b System 370 International Business Machines Corporation
24-17c System 9400 Sperry Rand Univac Division
24-17d System 70/60-61 Radio Corporation of America
24-17e System 6600 Control Data

Figure 24-17b.   System 370

Sperry Rand Univac Division

Figure 24-17c.   System 9400

RCA

Figure 24-17d.   System 70/60-61

Control Data

Figure 24-17e.   System 6600

DATA TRANSMISSION

DATA-Phone

Data transmission is defined in the Arthur Anderson & Co. brochure on the subject as follows:

Data transmission can be considered as that part of data processing which provides the link between the devices used in the original recording of data in a machine processable form, and the machine which is to carry out the actual processing—that is, the computer, punched card or other mechanical equipment . . . Communications techniques are being used for the automatic transmission of the great quantities of the *raw data* and processed *information* necessary in the operation of the business.[27]

A large number of companies use A.T. & T. toll telephone facilities or Western Union lines on a message basis or employ leased lines from those utilities. Some have their own private lines. Some of them use networks of lines which cover large geographic areas. These networks are sometimes established for message switching among administrative offices, sales offices, manufacturing plants, and warehouses and for transmitting sales orders, manufacturing orders, and shipping orders, as well as for data transmission. This section of the chapter is concerned with the latter and specifically with the communication service as such and several of the available units of terminal equipment.

The A.T. & T. brochure *Machine Talk* says:

> Actually, telephone dial pulses are a form of machine talk that have been sent over telephone lines since 1896, when the first rotary dial system went into operation. This is because telephone connections are set up by data-processing machines which are commonly called central offices or telephone switching centers. . . .
>
> The Bell System—having triggered much of the computer technology—now (by the 1950's) developed the data set for sending computer information over the regular telephone network from punched cards, magnetic tape, paper tape, handwriting, and pictures. Today DATA-Phone[28] [Figure 24-18] data sets are installed as part of a customer's telephone system to send and receive machine talk in addition to voice.
>
> Since the telephone network is tailored to transmit past the range of frequencies of the human voice, the data set [left side of Figure 24-18] converts signals into tones within this range. . . .
>
> A variety of data sets and associated services are offered today by the telephone companies to meet customer's needs for translating various kinds of analog and digital information into machine talk that can be sent over telephone lines. . . . On an ordinary dialed telephone call, DATA-Phone service can transmit machine talk at speeds as high as 2,500 words a minute. (Higher-speed systems are planned for the future.)
>
> For greater speeds, the telephone companies provide users with specially arranged "pipelines"—equivalent to various numbers of voice circuits—comprising one big channel. Using these larger pipe lines and associated data terminals, computers talk back and forth more rapidly.
>
> In the space program, for example, aerospace designers send rocket-test data on three large channels . . . at a rate equivalent to 200,000 words per minute.

The DATA-Phone 100 Series bulletin further describes the data-*set* as follows:

---

[27] Arthur Andersen & Co., op. cit., pages 5 and 7.
[28] Trademark.

DATA-Phone [Figure 24-18] makes it possible for business machines to "talk" *to each other* [italics ours] over regular telephone circuits. Its function is to accept binary digital information from customer's data equipment and convert the information to suitable frequency modulated tones for transmission over telephone circuits. At the receiving station, the binary digital signals are recovered and passed on to the receiving data equipment. . . .

Many new circuits for handling communications signals use binary numbers.[29]

Picture Phone

Figure 24-20 is a Picture Phone. In this illustration, the picture of the person at the other end of the line is shown. According to a press release dated June 30, 1970, it is intended that

these units will make it possible to dial a computer from the picture phone and have displayed on the screen any kind of information for which the company has programmed its computer, such as balance sheets, stock market reports, inventory lists or pending airplane reservations.

Conference calls by picture phone can be set up, with executives displaying and reacting to information retrieved from computers.[30]

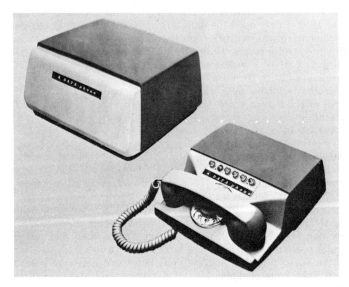

AT&T

Figure 24-18. DATA-Phone

---

[29] "Transmission" (Bell Telephone Laboratories, Information Monograph No. 4).
[30] Chicago *Tribune*, July 1, 1970.

Teletypewriter

Figure 24-19 is a Teletype Model 35 Teletypewriter. This familiar type of terminal is keyboard operated, and it produces hard copy both in transmitting and receiving. The Teletype Model 35 can print 10 characters a second.[31]

Teletype Corporation

Figure 24-19.   Teletypewriter Model 35

Terminal Computer; Data Transmission and Control Unit

As indicated in Chapter 6, the Victor Terminal Computer (Figure 6-25) is a unit which combines the features and capabilities of (1) an input–output terminal for a computer system and (2) a computer. The 820/03 can be programmed to operate

(1) Off-line as a stand-alone writing machine (as noted in Chapter 6), or
(2) As a stand-alone computer, or
(3) As a terminal interactive with a main frame, or
(4) As a terminal on line as a batch processor

The main features of the 820/03 by which it operates as a stand-alone writing machine are explained in Chapter 6 (pages 119–121). In this

---

[31] *The Bell System's Approach to Business Information Systems,* page 75.

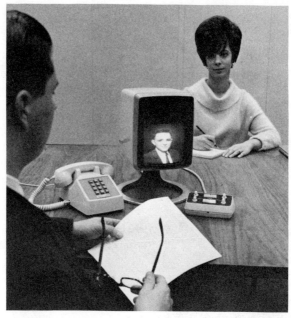

AT&T

Figure 24-20.   Picture Phone

chapter, it is appropriate to discuss the 820/03 as a stand-alone computer and as a terminal with telecommunication capabilities.

The 820/03 is designed on a modularity principle. Any component,
for instance, typewriter, keyboards, central processing unit and certain
program panels, are removable. Application of the modularity principle
makes it possible to upgrade or expand the computer system easily and
it facilitates maintenance. Some features of the 820/03 as a desk size
computer are discussed in the following paragraphs.

The 820/03 is built for manual input through an alphabetic keyboard,
a numeric ten-key keyboard, and up to 29 additional function keys.
Automatic input can be provided by a card reader (120 to 150 cards per
minute), paper-tape reader (200 characters per second), and magnetic-
tape cassette. Output is through the writing head in the typewriter,
punched cards, punched-paper tape, and magnetic tape.

The central processor performs the typical functions: analyzes and
executes individual instructions, monitors and coordinates all functional
units, and performs all arithmetic, logical and transfer operations.

The 820/03 has two types of memory: magnetic core, described and
illustrated on pages 574–575, and magnetic rod (not illustrated in this
book). Victor literature states that "rod cell memory provides an
extremely fast storage medium that is only one tenth the cost of core

memory." The rod cell memory is used for the micro-program (4096 instructions), which supervises the user's program, and for the user's program and data (4096 words). The magnetic core memory is used for storage and manipulation of data.

Telecommunication capabilities. One 820/03 can communicate with other computers directly or with the Victor Transmission and Control Unit via direct cable or telephone/telegraph lines. Up to sixteen terminal computers can be connected with the communication control unit with a maximum cable length of 600 feet. The communications control unit contains its own micro-program and its own magnetic core memory. The micro-program is a communications controller and multiplier. It provides dynamic memory allocation and buffering. The 820/03 terminal can operate on a polling mode (in which the central computer or the control unit is programmed to ask the terminals, "Do you have anything to send?") or the contention mode (in which each of the terminal computers is trying to get into the main computer).

OPTICAL CHARACTER RECOGNITION

General Description

Optical character recognition is the reading by machine of typed characters, computer printout and, under some important limitations, hand lettering. The purpose is usually to provide computer input directly or to produce punched cards, magnetic tape, or punched-paper tape. It is an alternative to card punching and card reading as an input to the computer. The purpose is usually cost savings, although some users state that, since they find key punch operators in shorter supply than typists, they would use OCR even though it were more expensive. In the matter of cost savings, it is pointed out that the rate of pay for a typist (who produces the original document for OCR) is 20 per cent less than the rate for a key punch operator, her production is on the average 30 to 35 per cent greater than that of the key punch operator, she is easier to train and the typist can correct errors more readily than the key punch operator can correct her errors.[32]

The first large-scale OCR system was installed in the oil industry, as a means of coping with the millions of charge tickets which came in from the service stations. By the end of the fifties, most of the major oil companies were using reading machines to read and punch imprinted account numbers into the tab card charge tickets.[33]

---

[32] *Introduction to Optical Character Recognition* (Wellesley Hills, Massachusetts: Honeywell, Inc., 1969), pages 1–4.

[33] "Where Is OCR Going"? an address by P. F. McCloskey, Data Processing Supplies Association (Stamford, Connecticut) Fall Meeting, New York City, October 27, 1969, page 3.

Although the growth of the OCR industry was not rapid in the early fifties and sixties, sales of OCR equipment are increasing at the present time. Deliveries of OCR equipment in 1968 were an estimated 70 million dollars compared with 45 million dollars in 1967. A conservative estimate of growth is 400 to 500 million dollars by 1975.[34]

Components of the Reader

Most types of reader consist of (1) document transport, (2) scanning unit, and (3) recognition unit. The document transport moves each paper from the intake hopper into position for scanning, holds it during the scanning process, and then moves it from the scanning position to the output position.

The scanning unit and the recognition unit are described in Honeywell's Introduction as follows:

Scanning Unit

The scanning unit, which functions as the "eye" of the reader, scans each document as it is positioned by the transport. Although the methods of scanning vary widely, the documents and the characters they contain must always be scanned by some kind of photoelectric device. These optical systems are the most salient feature of any OCR device. Not only do they determine the flexibility of the reader, but also the types of inks and paper surface qualities necessary for efficient operation.

Recognition Unit

The recognition unit, called the brain of the optical character reader, takes the signals derived by the scanner and analyzes them to determine what character the pattern of signals represents. . . .[35]

The configurations of readers varied considerably (during the sixties) and still do from single line, single font, stylized numeric to multiple line, multiple font, unstylized upper and lower case alphameric, and hand printed characters. There are on-line readers, off-line readers, and remote readers. Reading rates range from 10 characters per second to 14,000 characters per second. Processing rates range from 6 documents per minute to 1,500 documents per minute. Prices range from $5,000 to well over $1,000,000 per reading system.[36]

Basic Types of Optical Readers

The basic types of true optical readers are:

(1) Document readers (Figure 24-21). The machine illustrated handles documents of varying sizes for 2.62 inches to 8.5 inches in

---

[34] Honeywell, op. cit., page 5.
[35] Honeywell, pages 1–2.
[36] McCloskey, pages 3–4.

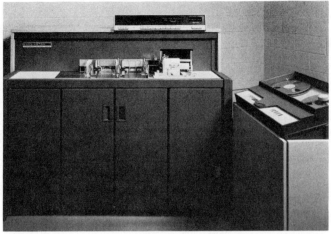

Farrington

Figure 24-21.   Document Reader (Model 3010)

width and from 2.75 inches to 6.0 inches in height. The reading capability of the machine illustrated is one or two lines (at a single pass) on documents prepared with high-speed computer printers, electric typewriters, adding machines, cash registers, and imprinters equipped with one or two optical typefonts. One line must be directly above the other, and the zone read may be located in either the upper or lower portion of the document. The optical typefonts may be composed of the numeric characters 0 through 9, the 26 alphabetic characters, special symbols and punctuation marks. The output units selected for the system by the user can produce magnetic tape or column punched cards. Or the reader illustrated can be connected directly on-line to the computer. Figure 24-22 is a turnaround document. Applications are discussed on page 594.

(2) Page readers (Figure 24-23) are designed for capability to read the whole page, not just one or two lines on the paper. The machine illustrated handles pages from 4.5 to 8.5 inches wide and from 5.6 inches to 14 inches in length. It can read pages prepared on most electric typewriters available today. It accepts both in-house typing (white paper) forms and preprinted source documents. The system comes with a computer which controls the system and which can be used for functions normally performed by a company's big computer. Choice of output is magnetic tape, punched cards, or punched-paper tape. Or the machine can be connected direct on-line to the computer. Figure 24-24 is an in-house typed form for a page reader. See discussion on page 594.

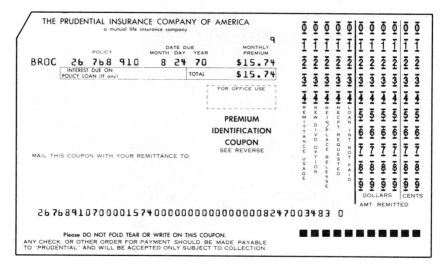

Figure 24-22.   Turnaround Form

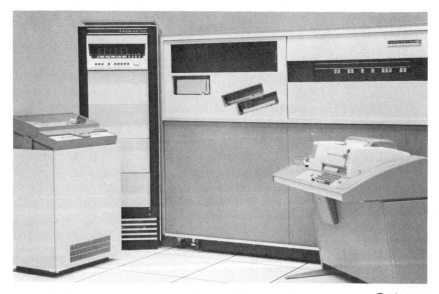

Farrington

Figure 24-23.   Page Reader Model 3030

(3) Reader–sorters and sales check for use in the reader–sorter (not illustrated). The sales check form is designed for filling in by hand by the sales person. The reader sorts the sales checks for some later operation and at the same time reads the hand written

```
9483726|MRS VE ROEPKE|2534 BROOKLINE DR|HUNTSVILLE AL|10
7654567|MRS ROBT O JENSEN|3125 LEWISBURG DR|HUNTSVILLE AL|10
9352678|MRS GENICE GILL|3609 BLUE SPRING RD|HUNTSVILLE AL|10
6342345|MRS SARA MOTE|2602 FIELDCREST DR|HUNTSVILLE AL|10
8765432|MRS HELEN DRUM|6015 SANDIA BLVD|HUNTSVILLE AL|10
8765678|MRS FRANK W SIMS|2419 ESTHER AVE|HUNTSVILLE AL|10
2345678|MRS JB STANLEY|608 MURRA RD|HUNTSVILLE AL|1■1
8765432|MRS CLIFFORD CURLEY|5001 STAG RUN CR|HUNTSVILLE AL|10
8765432|MRS JD MOORMAN|PO BX 1047|HUNTSVILLE AL|01
2389054|MRS WH ESSLINGER JR|R■T 1 BX 656|HUNTSVILLE AL|10
0989787|MRS BF WARD|PO BX 453|HUNTSVILLE AL|06
7465736|MRS EARNEST LEES|PO BX 24|NORMAL AL|62
8765432|MRS JERRY DAVIS|1007 PULASKI PIKE|HUNTSVILLE AL|05
9876567|MRS TOM SEATON|1409 RANDOLPH AVE|HUNTSVILLE AL|02
8754345|MRS JACK USELTON|2618 VENETIAN WAY|HUNTSVILLE AL|02
8765654|MRS FRANK PRESTON|806 MCKINELY AVE|HUNTSVILLE AL|02
0987890|MRS PAT COLLINSWORTH|3602 LAKEWOOD DR|HUNTSVILLE AL|20
```

Figure 24-24.   Typed Input Form for Page Reader

Farrington

Figure 24-25.   Journal Roll Reader (Model 4040)

characters and transmits them to the computer in machine-readable language. As this chapter is being written, at least one manufacturer has these items in the laboratory.

(4) Journal roll readers (Figure 24-25) are designed to read tapes produced by cash registers and other accounting machines. The machine can read a variety of type faces. The system has a

built-in computer, and it can operate off-line as a self contained input unit or on-line to the company's main computer.[37]

Types of Applications

There are three types of applications for optical character readers: turnaround paper applications, in-house paper applications, and field applications which are those originated in the field on forms and format acceptable to OCR readers. In this connection in-house would mean one within the control of the Data Processing Department, and "field" would mean a source outside the control of the Data Processing Department.

An example of a turnaround document is the stub which is sent out to the customer with his bill. It is detached by the customer and sent back to the company with the remittance. Since the stub was produced by the company in the first place, it can obviously be set up in a form which is readable by the optical reader.

> Typical applications of turnaround documents are processing billings of public utilities and insurance companies. The font style is usually numeric only, and because they are limited to one or two lines of information, document readers offer very high processing speeds.[38]

In regard to in-house applications, McCloskey says that file conversion and file maintenance are typical in-house applications.[39]

McCloskey comments on the savings possible in the first two types of application where optical character recognition replaces key punching:

> The savings realized are the salary differential of a typist and a key punch operator, plus the substantial difference in cost of a typewriter and key punch machine offset by the cost of a page reader. In this type application, the economic justification of a page reading system renting at $2500 a month may come at about ten key punch machines.[40]

According to McCloskey, the more dramatic savings are to be found in the third type of application, the adoption of optical scanning for source forms outside the data-processing department. This involves the basic systems design principle of capturing all of the data that is possible in the original form. It also involves designing the form to accommodate the use of optical character reading. For instance, the original form created by the personnel department when a man is hired should capture not only the information needed for the personnel files but also for the payroll department files. He cites not only Farrington's own ex-

---

37 Honeywell, op. cit., pages 2–5.
38 Honeywell, op. cit., pages 2–5.
39 McCloskey, op. cit., page 5.
40 Ibid., page 6.

perience but also that of the United States Marine Corps in the operation of its personnel records.[41]

An Estimate of the Future of OCR

McCloskey is of the opinion that the trend of application and developments in OCR will continue to be toward the comprehensive collection of data at the source in form for use of OCR, as indicated above. He says further:

> There are machines under development that read characters at phenomenal rates and the typical rate on machines now being installed is steadily increasing. It is easy to see a time in the very near future when the limitation on throughput on all readers will be the speed at which paper can be handled rather than the speed of scanning or the recognition logic.
>
> . . . The ensuing years will see data processed remotely, formatted, edited and transmitted in processable form to central locations for merging, filing and batch processing. These self contained satellite systems are available now and teleprocessing of processed data is inevitable. . . .
>
> Another application of OCR in the 70's may well be its use in information retrieval. Microfilm copy can be easily stored, indexed and recovered. By combining such a system with OCR, you will have a massive, inexpensive data bank directly accessible by a computer capable of replacing magnetic tape as a long term permanent storage.[42]

Computer output microfilming is explained on pages 181–186.

APPENDIX
ILLUSTRATION OF A COMPUTER PROGRAM IN
FORTRAN LANGUAGE COMMANDS[43]

In FORTRAN and other programming languages the basic functional unit is the COMMAND. A COMMAND is, as its name implies, an instruction to the computer to perform the indicated function. Some typical FORTRAN commands are:

READ — This command causes the computer to go to the designated INPUT file and input the contents to a designated location in memory. Companion to this statement is a statement called FORMAT, which tells the computer the position of the data on the input medium and what type of data to expect (either alphabetic or numeric).

[41] Ibid., page 7.
[42] Ibid., page 9.
[43] The reader desiring to acquire a working knowledge of programming in Fortran is referred to *A FORTRAN Primer with Business Administration Exercises* (International Business Machines Company, 1964), 125 pages, and Daniel D. McCracken, *A Guide to Fortran Programming* (New York: John Wiley & Sons, Inc., various editions).

IF

This command causes the computer to perform testing of variable values and—depending on the results of its tests—to perform other programmed instructions. For example, IF(X.EQ.1) 1,2 will test the value of X, and, if its value equals 1, it will go to the statement numbered 1 and perform the functions indicated. If it is not equal to 1, then it will go to statement numbered 2 and perform the functions indicated there.

DO 1
.
.
1 CONTINUE

This DO command causes the program to perform the operations contained between the DO and the CONTINUE (called a "DO LOOP"). It will perform these functions a number of times, the number of times being controlled by an index contained on the original DO statement. For example, DO 1 I = 1,6 will perform the instructions in the "DO LOOP" six times, starting off with I = 1 and incrementing I by one each time until I = 6.

PRINT

This command takes the contents of a designated location in memory and puts it on the designated output medium (TAPE, DISK, DRUM, or PRINTED OUTPUT). Again a FORMAT card is used to designate the form which the output will take on the output medium.

ARITHMETIC STATEMENTS

These commands permit the user to mathematically manipulate the variables in his program. For example X = Y*Z instructs the computer to take the value of the variable Y and multiply it by the value of the variable Z and store the resulting answer in the location reserved for variable X.

While the above statements do not represent the full range of FORTRAN commands they do point out how close the commands correspond to the English language and simple algebra equations. The following excerpts from a FORTRAN program serve to illustrate the commands discussed above.

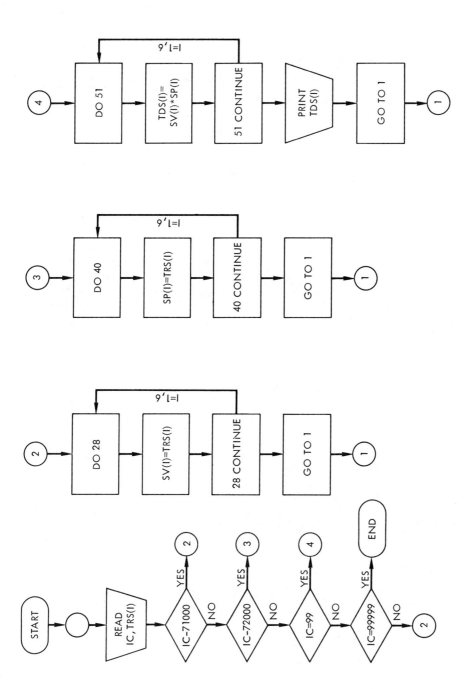

```
      PROGRAM PLANSIM (INPUT,OUTPUT)
      DIMENSION SV(6), SP(6), TRS(6), . . . .
C THE ABOVE CARDS SERVE TO BEGIN THE PROGRAM BY INFORMING THE COMPUTER
C SYSTEM WHAT HARDWARE FUNCTIONS ARE TO BE USED AND HOW MUCH CENTRAL
C MEMORY IS TO BE RESERVED FOR THE VARIOUS ITEMS OF DATA
      .      .      .      .      .      .      .      .      .
      .      .      .      .      .      .      .      .      .
    1 READ 2, IC,(TRS(I),I=1,6)
    2 FORMAT (I5,4X,6(F9.2,X))
C THE ABOVE CARDS READ IN A DATA CARD CONTAINING AN INPUT CODE (IC)
C AND SIX ITEMS OF DATA TO BE STORED IN A TEMPORARY READ-IN SECTION
C (TRS). THE NATURE OF THE DATA IS CONTAINED IN THE INPUT CODE.
      .      .      .      .      .      ,      .      .      .
      .      .      .      .      .      .      .      .      .
   13 IF (IC.EQ.71000) 27,14
   14 IF (IC.EQ.72000) 39,15
   15 IF (IC.EQ.00099) 50,16
   16 IF (IC.EQ.99999) GO TO 60
C THE ABOVE CARDS DETERMINE THE NATURE OF THE DATA ON THE CARDS BY
C TESTING THE INPUT CODE. IF IC EQUALS 71000, THEN CONTROL IS TRANS-
C FERRED TO A SECTION OF THE PROGRAM WHICH STORES THE DATA IN THE
C LOCATION SET ASIDE FOR THE SALES VOLUME (SV) DATA. SIMILARLY IF
C IC EQUALS 72000, THEN DATA IS STORED IN THE SECTION RESERVED FOR
C THE DELLING PRICE (SP) DATA. IF IC EQUALS 00099, THIS IS THE PRO-
C GRAMS INDICATION THAT NO FURTHER DATA IS TO BE ENTERED AND IT CAN
C PROCEED WITH THE CALCULATION AND PRINTOUT OF THE DATA. IF IC EQUALS
C 99999 THEN THE PROGRAM WILL TERMINATE.
      .      .      .      .      .      .      .      .      .
      .      .      .      .      .      .      .      .      .
   27 DO 28 I=1,6
      SV(I) = TRS (I)
   28 CONTINUE
      GO TO 1
      .      .      .      .      .      .      .      .      .
      .      .      .      .      .      .      .      .      .
   39 DO 40 I=1,6
      SP(I) = TRS(I)
   40 CONTINUE
      GO TO 1
C THE ABOVE CARDS TRANSFER DATA FROM TRS(I) INTO THE SECTIONS
C RESERVED FOR  SELLING PRICE AND SALES VOLUME DATA. THE DATA
C IS KEPT BY YEAR HENCE THE ABOVE IS THE DATA FOR YEARS 1 THROUGH
C 6.
      .      .      .      .      .      .      .      .      .
      .      .      .      .      .      .      .      .      .
   50 DO 51 I=1,6
      TDS(I) = SV(I) * SP(I)
   51 CONTINUE
C THE ABOVE CARDS CALCULATE THE TOTAL DOLLAR SALES
   52 PRINT 53,(TDS(I),I=1,6)
   53 FORMAT (/X,18HTOTAL DOLLAR SALES,6X,6(F15.0,X))
      GO TO 1
C THE ABOVE CARDS PRINT OUT THE TOTAL DOLLAR SALES AND THEN TRANSFERS
C CONTROL BACK TO THE READ FOR MORE DATA.
C THE FOLLOWING CARDS WILL TERMINATE THE PROGRAM
   60 CONTINUE
      END
```

25

Time Sharing

Definition and Scope

Time sharing is a technique for using electronic computers which permits several users working simultaneously at remote terminals to utilize programs and to process data. Through fast computer response each of the users has the illusion that the central computer is serving him exclusively and immediately. In reality the computer is alternating between jobs and serving many users who have different requirements, programs and data, and are in different locations.

Time sharing is important because it extends the capabilities of the computer to many companies, organizations, and individuals that could not previously afford acquisition of on-site computer processing. In addition, for many applications time sharing offers a better way of processing the data than would be possible with a small on-site computer having more limited input/output devices.

The central computer is often provided by a service-bureau type company that is in the business of selling computer time to its subscribers. The subscriber may be a company that has several terminals and several computer applications but does not necessarily have its own computer. The following discussion is from the point of view of the user or subscriber, rather than the provider, of time sharing services.

This chapter describes the principal features of time sharing and how it applies to accounting. Advantages and disadvantages of the time-sharing technique are discussed for each of the systems and procedures areas covered in earlier chapters.

The Important Elements of Time Sharing

Time sharing is used in a variety of ways, but most of these ways have in common the following elements:

1. *Immediate availability of the computer.* With time sharing it is not necessary to wait until all other users are finished or until the work can be fitted into the computer schedule. The user can have access to the computer when he wishes and as frequently as he wishes. He pays only for the time used.

2. *Time slicing.* The method that the computer uses to alternate between jobs is controlled by software programs in the central computer and usually is not of interest to a particular operator. He is satisfied if he receives a sufficiently fast response from the computer. However, the software principles are not complicated and involve little more than a basic understanding of multiprogramming explained below.

   Although it seems that the computer is doing several things at once, it can really only process one instruction such as add, subtract, or compare at a time. It can, however, perform these instructions while it is waiting for completion of an input or output operation, such as reading a card or typing a line. Since these input and output operations generally are at least partly mechanical and slower than the electronic speeds at which internal instructions can be executed, computers often have idle time available for other processing. One way to make use of this available processing time is multiprogramming. Multiprogramming is the simultaneous processing of two or more programs in one computer.

   If the multiprogramming is accomplished through a time clock that apportions a certain amount of the total time to each user, time sharing or time slicing is being employed. When referring to the use of an electronic timer and the software method to alternate processing among computer users, the terms *time sharing* and *time slicing* are synonymous. Often the term *time slicing* is used when referring to the software technique because *time sharing* is also used in a broader sense as a technique for using computers or to refer to the industry that provides the time and services.

   Thus, in time slicing a user may be assured of receiving several fractions of each minute of the processing time of the central computer. The illusion that the computer is exclusively available to a particular computer operator or terminal operator results because the alternating between jobs is so fast and because the computer can accomplish sufficient work in the short periods of service.

3. *Interaction between computer and terminal operator.* Through interaction or conversational ability, a computer is able to respond quickly to the input provided by a human operator so that the operator can benefit from the computer responses while he is still working on the same data or problem. This response makes it pos-

PROG: DRATE

DISCOUNTED RATE OF RETURN PROGRAM

INSTRUCTIONS?YES

THIS PROGRAM CALCULATES DISCOUNTED RATES
OF RETURN (PERIOD AND CONTINUOUS), THE
DOUBLE-LIFE, AND THE PAYBACK PERIOD FOR
A SEQUENCE OF CASH FLOWS.

ENTER DATA IN THE FOLLOWING FORMAT
LINE 1...NUMBER OF CASH FLOWS(N)
LINE 2...FLOW(1), FLOW(2),......FLOW(N)

N=10
-668,-470,300,410,415,421,407,413,450,780

DISCOUNTED CASH FLOW CALCULATION

FOR   TIME-VALUE-OF-MONEY = 0.0
      THE PAYBACK PERIOD = 4.03088

PERIODS	THIS PERIODS NET .FLOW	CUMULATIVE FLOWS END OF PERIOD
0	-668.0000	-668.0000
1	-470.0000	-1138.0000
2	300.0000	-838.0000
3	410.0000	-428.0000
4	415.0000	-13.0000
5	421.0000	408.0000
6	407.0000	815.0000
7	413.0000	1228.0000
8	450.0000	1678.0000
9	780.0000	2458.0000

THE DISCOUNTED RATE OF RETURN(PERCENT)
ON A PERIOD BASIS = 26.0561

Figure 25-1.   Printout on a Teletype Terminal

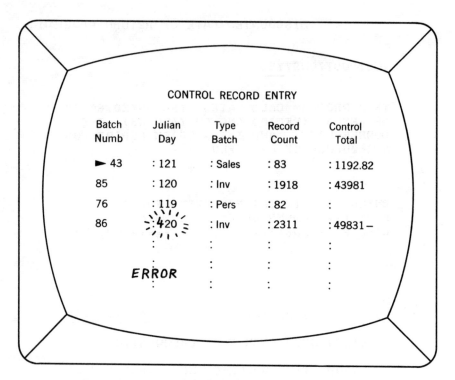

Figure 25-1.   Cont.

sible for the computer to reply to questions from the operator, make suggestions to the operator for his next step, indicate invalid input from the operator, or provide more information on request from the operator. Figure 25-1 shows the printout on a teletype terminal of a program that calculates a discounted rate of return. The lines typed in by the terminal operator are underlined for this example to distinguish them from those emitted by the computer. The following entries were required of the operator:

—Initial entries to request the program

        BUS

        DRATE

—YES to request instructions for entering the data. If the operator had used the program previously and was familiar with it, he might skip the instructions to save time.

—Data entries, in this case a series of periodic net costs or income from a potential capital investment.

—NO to terminate the program after the solution for the first set of data. If the operator had other data, he could have continued.

One of the most significant advantages of this time sharing conversational feature is in the ability to thoroughly edit and validate input data. The system can instantaneously notify the operator at the terminal of an error condition, prompting immediate correction. Some of the errors the computer can detect are: an invalid code, a field that should be numeric but is not, an impossible date such as month 13, a formula with incorrect notations, an unplanned answer to a question from the computer, or a part number that does not match the master file.

Figure 25.2 shows an example of a cathode ray tube (CRT) terminal screen that is displaying an error on some input data entered by the terminal operator. In this case, the terminal operator had entered certain information from a source document by means of the CRT keyboard. After the operator transmitted the data to the computer, the computer detected the error and returned the data to the operator for correction, indicating the incorrect field by flashing it on and off. The operator can easily check the source document again, correct the field, retransmit, and move on to the next document.

Naturally, the responses and error detection capabilities of the computer are limited to those planned in the system design and included in the computer program. For example, if the computer program provides for a YES or NO answer from the operator and he replies MAYBE, the computer can only indicate the reply was invalid and request another reply.

The superiority of this conversational mode of processing makes it possible to reduce training time, to simplify and eliminate coding catalogs or input preparation procedure manuals, and to provide the satisfaction that the input data was entered correctly and can go on to further processing.

4. *On-line program entry.* The normal way to activate a program in time sharing is to call the program from a program library disk or drum located within the central computer. To do this, the operator identifies himself and types in the program number desired. In other cases, if the program is not already located on the program library, a user will want to enter the program through the terminal. A third possibility is that the program has already been entered either from the library or from the terminal, and many different operators are making use of it. In this case only the first operator has to be concerned with calling in the program. A computer program is always necessary whether it comes from the library, the

PRESENT WORTH OF CASH FLOWS AT ABOVE RATE

PERIOD	PRESENT WORTH THIS PERIODS NET FLOW	CUMULATIVE PRESENT WORTH END OF PERIOD
0	-668.0000	-668.0000
1	-372.8498	-1040.8498
2	188.7962	-852.0535
3	204.6877	-647.3658
4	164.3585	-483.0073
5	132.2702	-350.7371
6	101.4403	-249.2968
7	81.6586	-167.6382
8	70.5831	-97.0552
9	97.0552	0.0000

THE DISCOUNTED RATE OF RETURN (PERCENT)
ON A CONTINUOUS BASIS = 23.1557

THE DOUBLE-LIFE = 2.9934 PERIODS

CONTINUE? (YES OR NO) YES   NO

Figure 25-2.   CRT Terminal Screen

important features of time sharing is that the user can process his program at once without waiting for completion of other programs.

Programs can also be developed at a terminal, instruction by instruction. In this case, the computer can help the operator-programmer by means of some software routines that tell him if the instructions in his program are valid and help him to test the program.

5. *On-line data entry.* In addition to a program, input data is necessary. The data can be transactions entered currently such as for a calculation program or can be master file data which had previously been entered into the system and is now available for use, such as an inventory stock status file. Programs using master file data usually have some sort of limited volume input transactions also. For example, a small number of inquiry transactions might be used to obtain selected information from a large volume inventory file.

In time sharing the input data can be transmitted to the computer whenever the terminal operator wishes, but the input/output transaction volume is usually limited because of terminal speeds and costs of telephone lines. Time-sharing applications are most frequently those with low-volume input or output. For higher volume computer applications many time-sharing companies offer a different technique called remote batch processing or remote job entry.

In remote batch processing, card readers, magnetic tapes, or other high speed terminals are available at the user location. The input data is transmitted to the central computer, stored temporarily on a disk or drum, and processed at a later time. Output results can be transmitted back to the user's high speed printer or other terminal or may be mailed or otherwise delivered to the user.

The following table compares regular time sharing with remote batch processing:

Time Sharing	*Remote Batch*
On-line data entry.	On-line data entry.
Interactive communication usually on each input record.	Transmission of all input for subsequent processing.
Interactive program execution.	Processing uninterrupted by user.
Low-speed keyboard terminals.	High-speed terminals such as card readers, line printers, magnetic tapes and disks.
Input/output limited because of terminal speed.	High volume input and output.

The difference then between regular time sharing and remote batch processing is that remote batch processing can handle higher volume data through higher speed terminals. Only the original input and final output are done on an on-line basis. The job itself is done in a service bureau type operation without interaction or on-line communications with the user.

Personnel Who May Operate a Time-Sharing Terminal

One of the striking features of time sharing is the wide variety of people and occupation classifications that it concerns. The following paragraphs show some examples:

Computer programmers. Programmers can use terminals to develop their programs and to test new time-sharing systems. If the programmer has access to a terminal he can test his program immediately. When he encounters errors he can see the results and ask for additional information. He can correct his program or his test data or alter the path of a particular test. Most important, he can make on-the-spot decisions that can avoid extensive delays.

Full-time terminal operators. Just as key-punch operators are full-time personnel in data preparation work, time-sharing terminal operators may be employed on a full-time basis for certain applications. The high speed and accuracy that a full-time operator can achieve, together with the conversational advantages of the time-sharing terminal, can provide a very effective method of data preparation.

Operating personnel. Salesmen, stockbrokers, bank tellers, and many other employees whose primary job is in company operations can use time-sharing terminals on a part-time basis. The salesmen can check credit or inventory availability. The stockbroker can obtain quotations. The bank teller can obtain current balances and update savings accounts.

Accountants and administrative personnel. Certain accounting and financial calculations or reports may require time of company personnel only at certain periods during the month. These requirements may occur in only one or two departments and involve only a few employees, but time sharing may aid these employees in performing their functions.

Students, housewives, customers, the public. A student working on a business mathematics course might use a time-sharing terminal to solve an operations research problem. The student would not have to be a computer programmer. He would not even have to know how to calculate the solution to the simplest type of operations research problem. All he would have to know is how to define the problem and set it up for the computer to solve.

The customer could obtain information on the status of his orders through a time-sharing service. Public utilities and many other companies have found it possible through time sharing to extend their services in the way of customer information. Normally a company employee obtains this information from the time-sharing terminal and reports it to the customer, but in some cases the customer or the person who needs the information could use the time-sharing terminal.

The technology exists that a housewife could do her shopping and plan menus through a terminal in her home.

In summary, operating a time-sharing terminal does not require data processing experience, programming ability, or extensive training. The determination of who the operator should be is based not so much on the data processing background or dexterity of the potential operator as on who needs the information, what employees are available at the terminal location, and what the volume requirements are.

Note that although the personnel who operate the terminal do not have to be specialists, there can be a danger in underspecialization. For example, a company would not want an experienced programmer to spend a large portion of his time working like a key-punch operator. Similarly, a skilled engineer should not have to spend a large amount of his time working like a typist. For these reasons and others, the top executives of companies usually do not have their own time-sharing terminals nor do they operate time-sharing terminals even if their company has several available. Top management decisions are often strategic and involve policy decisions; these cannot be predefined into computer programs that require known data requirements and bases for decision making. Many top management decisions can, however, be aided by information obtained from middle managers working through a time-sharing system.

Selection of a Time-Sharing Service

Once an organization decides that it has a need for the processing capabilities of time sharing, it must decide either to develop these capabilities in an on-site computer or to select a time-sharing vendor. By purchasing time from a vendor, the user avoids developing and training a large data processing staff, saves space requirements and site preparation effort, does not have to keep abreast of the software, and avoids concern about underutilization or obsolescence of an on-site computer.

Time-sharing vendors, or computer utilities as they are sometimes called, do not all offer the same type of service. Some specialize in providing information from central files that they maintain such as for legal research or real estate listings. Others emphasize mathematical and engineering work or commercial data processing primarily.

The cost usually consists of three main elements: (1) connect time for each hour the terminal is in use on-line with the computer, (2) central processor time for the actual minutes and seconds used, and (3) mass storage rental for the use of central location devices for constant storage of programs and master files. Additional costs may be incurred for special handling costs or use of extra devices or extra main memory. The monthly cost, depending on the type of processing and data volumes, can range from less than the cost of the lowest paid clerk to more than the rental of a medium-size computer.

A summary of selection criteria includes the following:

Cost
Equipment—
    Availability (hours of day, days of week)
    Response time
    Terminal capability
    Mass storage
    Communications (long-distance or local)
Support—
    Local personnel
    Program library
    Programming languages
    Data base
    Operating efficiency
    Standardization
Other—
    Financial stability
    Contractual negotiations
    Administration capabilities

Input and Output Devices

The most common terminals are the teletype and the cathode ray tube (which were discussed in Chapter 24). Each can be thought of as both an input and output device. The teletype has a keyboard for input and a low-speed printer for output; the cathode ray tube has a keyboard or light pen for input and a video screen for output.

Almost any other device that can be used for input or output on the computer can also be used as a time-sharing terminal. Figures 25-3 and 25-4 illustrate some of these other input and output devices. The higher speed devices would more likely be used for remote batch processing.

Capabilities of Special Interest to Accountants

Time sharing may be the most economical way to meet the company's overall data processing needs. A controller or chief accountant in his function of conserving the company's assets, may wish to point out the time sharing alternative if his company is faced with a decision as to whether to obtain its own computer. He might also point out the alternative of service bureau processing without time sharing or remote batch processing if immediate access, fast response, or conversational abilities were not required.

For strictly accounting-type applications, an on-site computer might not be justified. For example, most general accounting work is done

INPUT TYPES

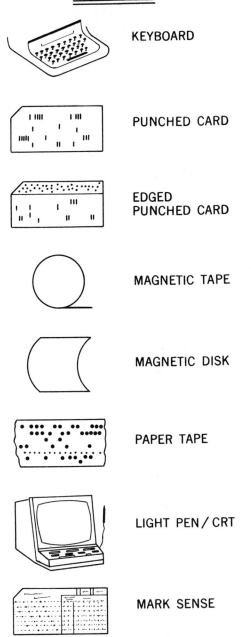

KEYBOARD

PUNCHED CARD

EDGED
PUNCHED CARD

MAGNETIC TAPE

MAGNETIC DISK

PAPER TAPE

LIGHT PEN / CRT

MARK SENSE

ETC.

Figure 25-3.   Input Types

OUTPUT TYPES

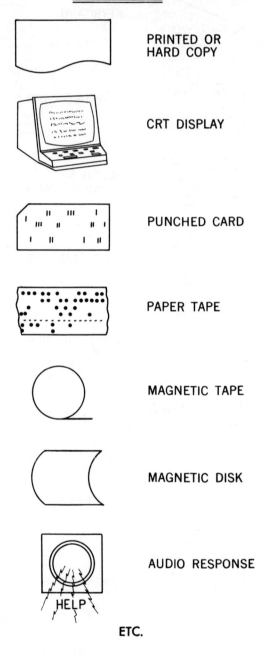

PRINTED OR
HARD COPY

CRT DISPLAY

PUNCHED CARD

PAPER TAPE

MAGNETIC TAPE

MAGNETIC DISK

AUDIO RESPONSE

ETC.

Figure 25-4.   Output Types

monthly and much budgeting work is done annually; these alone would not be sufficient to justify the day-to-day rental of an on-site computer. Thus, time sharing might be the only technique by which a particular company could economically obtain the benefits of computer processing for its accounting work.

Time sharing can also aid in many other financial calculations that could be desired by the accounting department. For example, many time-sharing services have standard calculation programs in the following areas:

Actuarial Calculations
Amortization
Capital Investment
Cash Flow
Consolidated Statements
Critical Path Methods
Depletion
Depreciation
Discounted Rate of Return
Economic Order Quantities
Exponential Smoothing
Financial Models
Financial Ratios
Financial Statements
Graphs
Income Tax Calculation
Interest Computation
Linear Programming
Present Value Computation
Random Number Generation
Scheduling
Simulation
Statistics

Systems and Procedures

Chapters 11 to 19 explain the principles involved in various accounting subsystems. Some of these subsystems provide good time-sharing applications; others do not. For a particular company a subsystem may be so important or may provide such valuable information that rapid response or quick turn-around may make it an unusual but good time-sharing application. The discussion below, however, applies to the most commonly found situations and refers to on-line time sharing rather than remote batch processing.

Order Procedures. Time sharing could be used effectively for scheduling orders and/or obtaining fast information about the status of any order. Like any status information, order status might be difficult to keep current and might be better provided on an exception basis. For example, a good manual system to report the orders behind schedule could be much more effective than a time-sharing system providing the status for all orders. Nevertheless, good order status information can be of great value to customers, sales, purchasing, operations, and other departments.

The billing portion of the order procedures would probably be a less desirable time-sharing application. Here a delay of a few hours in the preparation of the bill would not be crucial and it would probably be more economical to have billing specialists prepare the bills when time permits.

Sales Distribution. Sales distribution also does not require the fast turn-around of time sharing. The sales analysis reports are often prepared on a monthly basis, and a short delay is not critical. The volume in this application may also be somewhat high for time sharing. However, some low volume charts and graphs could be prepared on time-sharing terminals.

Accounts Receivable. Point of sale credit information and information on the status of the account receivable could be useful through time sharing. Preparation of monthly statements and processing of daily cash receipts, however, are higher volume applications that generally do not require quick turn-around.

Purchase Orders and Receiving Reports. Although this application sometimes lends itself to on-line real-time processing and on-line data collection or inquiries, the high volumes would usually rule out contracted time-sharing services for purchasing. Inquiries about purchase order status and processing of intracompany orders could be done through time sharing.

Accounts Payable. This is probably one of the poorer possibilities for time sharing. The account distribution and check preparation work are not urgent and do not provide especially valuable information compared to other applications.

Employment and Time Keeping Procedures. Time reporting by employee and by job can be effective through time-sharing terminals as a data collection technique. In the area of personnel records, however, rapid response is unnecessary for many companies, who find it satisfactory to use the manual personnel files for any status information.

Payroll Procedures. The areas of account distribution and check preparation are most often ill suited for time sharing.

Production Control/Inventory Control. Time sharing has many uses in production control and inventory control, including machine loading, machine shop scheduling, economic order quantity, production efficiency reporting, production reporting, scrap reporting, production scheduling, and part availability. Again, the time sharing would be useful where rapid access to information, fast turnaround, or on-the-spot data collection or inquiries are useful and would not be applicable in high-volume processing of routine transactions such as high-volume inventory usage.

Cost Systems. Most cost systems would not require time-sharing capability, except in small specific categories such as calculation of variances, or scheduling of projects.

General Accounting and Budgeting. Although the high-volume data might be better processed in another way, accounting report preparation, consolidation, or adjustments, budgeting comparisons, and budget estimating and revisions could become time-sharing applications. Also, some companies find the data collection and validation capabilities of time sharing useful in their accounting.

Conclusion

In the development of the computer for business processing, time sharing has been a break-through in cost, in capabilities, and most important in bringing the services of the computer to those who previously could not afford it, or lacked the technical ability to use it effectively. Time sharing ordinarily will not be selected to process the majority of the company's accounting. Many companies' accounting systems, though, include specific areas that can be done better by time sharing.

26

Management Information Systems

Definition

A management information system is a system for collecting, storing (in some situations), manipulating, and reporting as required the information needed for making programmed management decisions. It is concerned with day to day operating decisions and with short and long term planning decisions as distinguished from decisions for strategic planning (which may be short term or long term).

The complete management information system includes internal information and external information relating to the environment in which the business operates. The latter information may in turn include information on economic resources and transportation, competitive activity, sociological and technological factors, and the political situation and government regulations, all as they affect management decisions.

The Information System and the Decision Structure

As stated above, the structure of the information system depends upon the types of decisions to be made. Operating decisions are short run decisions having to do with the operating system, i.e., with the day to day operation of the business. They are repetitive, and a decision once made may be later modified on the basis of feedback which is the control mechanism. The same people make these decisions in the same areas more or less continuously. Examples of this type of decision are credit decisions affecting customers and prospective customers and production order decisions involving when and for what products and in what quantities shall production orders be issued. These decisions may be made by middle and lower management, often according to programmed decision rules.[1] When the information system is computerized, some of the decision rules may be incorporated in the computer program, and the computer makes the decisions on the basis of data input.

Short run planning decisions are those decisions required to set up the operating and financial plan for a coming year, or shorter period, such as a quarter, or a month. The decisions are made with the aim of meeting the financial and other objectives of the business. The financial plan is the basis for the budget.

Strategic planning decisions are decisions on the nature, form and size of the business. They can be concerned with the on-going business, or with a proposed business or segment. They involve such factors as what business to be in (what products or services), basic promotion and logistics, organization, plant, and manpower. Allocation of resources is fundamental. When strategic planning decisions are concerned with an on-going business, they may follow what is called the inside-out approach, which means finding out what things the business does best and emphasizing them; or the outside-in approach, which means finding out where the opportunities are and going after them.

Note that management information systems are designed to collect information for *programmed* decisions. Such decisions include operating decisions and short term planning decisions. They do not include strategic planning decisions, since these decisions are not programmed, but ad hoc. This chapter includes some discussion of information required for strategic planning as well as that required for short term planning and operations to put all of the information gathering areas in perspective.

The Information System Approach: The Total Information System

The information system approach involves determining (1) the types of decisions being made, (2) the information required to make those decisions, and (3) the sources from which the information can best be obtained. This approach (an output approach) to systems design is relatively new, and it is contrasted with the procedures approach, which has

---

[1] According to Wayne S. Boutell, *Computer Oriented Business Systems* (Englewood Cliffs, N.J.: Prentice-Hall, Inc., 1968), pages 155–56, "The concept of a business information system has been structured on certain concepts of organization theory." One of the primary exponents of the decision making approach has been Professor H. A. Simon of Carnegie-Mellon Institute of Technology. As a result of his research in the area of decision making, Simon was able to categorize decisions in two general classifications: programmed and non-programmed. In Simon's *The New Science of Management Decision* (New York: Harper and Row, publishers, 1960), page 8, he describes programmed and non-programmed decisions and lists decision making techniques, both traditional and modern, applicable to each type.

to do with the most economical processing of input. Typically under the latter approach, the existing flow of paper work is studied and charted, and the new forms and flow are designed from the charts of that study.

A *total* management information system (still largely in the conceptual stages) is one which is designed to provide for the information requirements of all the decision makers of the business except the strategic planners. Such a system would be based upon a master classification of data for the company, without regard for organizational lines, which would be used for coding all input. It would also comprise a data base which is the repository or memory containing the accumulated information. A further principle, long recognized by systems men, is that data for the information system would be captured complete in the original recording in the most minute particulars required for the data base and it would be summarized in various ways for various users. Subsequent processing would require no new segmentation or disaggregation of data, although it could of course involve aggregation.

Accounting for Decision Making

Davidson and Trueblood say that, in applying the decision making view to information systems design, the designer must consider the following list of questions:[2]

1. What is the decision that needs to be made?
2. What is the best rule for making the decision?
3. What information is required in making the decision?
4. How accurate must the information be?
5. How frequently must the information be supplied?
6. How can the information best be obtained and transmitted to the user?

Table 26-1 sets out typical questions and answers involved in an MIS survey. (Jordan Printing Company described in Gillespie, Accounting Systems: Procedures and Methods, First Edition, pages 741–748, is the basis for the questions. Whereas the assignment on the pages indicated is for a job order cost system, the present concern is an MIS aimed at management planning and control.)

The table provides columns for the answers to four major questions which constitute an abbreviation of Davidson and Trueblood's list above.

   I What major decisions are being (or should be) made?
  II What information is required to make those decisions?

---

[2] H. Justin Davidson and Robert M. Trueblood, "Accounting for Decision Making" (*Accounting Review,* October 1961), page 122.

III What are the existing information sources?

IV What redesign of (or change in or additions to) the present system is necessary?

The first (pair of) questions are "Is the business profitable?" and "What kinds of press work are profitable?" The information required to answer these questions includes internal information: the monthly profit and loss statement, job cost sheets, and job estimates, to determine what are the most profitable customers and classes of work, together with press time summaries showing hours, profits (total and per running hour), profit breakeven point, and cash breakeven point for each press (or group of identical presses).

The next question is "Should we buy new presses to stay competitive"? The decision implied here is an ad hoc decision. The answer to this question involves internal information as to what presses are operating at capacity, what presses have substantial idle time, and what presses are not used. It involves external information in the way of statistics published by trade associations, discussions with manufacturers of printing plant equipment, and market research on magazine and catalog business available. Finally it involves information on financing any new presses.

The third question is what selling price (bid) should we (can we) set for a job. This involves internal information on costs from the company's cost system and external information (probably guesses) on competitor's bids. The fourth question is "Should more salesmen be hired"? This question is particularly pertinent if it is found that there appears to be business available that the company is not presently getting. It is also concerned with the profitability of the sales turned in by the present salesmen.

The Accounting System and the Operating System as Parts of the MIS

The accounting system and the operating system are parts of the MIS, although they do not comprise the whole system. Figure 26-1 is a chart titled "The Accounting System and the Operating System" (providing information for the Information System). It is a rearrangement of Figure 1-1 intended to point up information sources. The upper part of Figure 26-1 is the Accounting System and Supporting Systems:

Sales and cash collecting
Purchase and payment
Labor
Production order and cost accounting

Table 26-1
JORDAN PRINTING COMPANY

(1) What major decisions are being (or should be) made?	(2) What information is required to make those decisions?	(3) What are the existing information sources?	(4) What redesign of (or change in, or addition to) the present system is necessary?
I Is the business profitable? What kinds of press work are profitable?	(1) Monthly profit or loss	Monthly income statement.	Monthly income statement is out of bookkeeping control, and is too late (20 days) for decision making. Apparently these have not been explored.
	(a) Inside-out approach	Trade association statistics on expense and profit percentages.	
	Fully allocated costs (long run)		
	(2) What contracts (jobs) show a profit of X% or more of sales? What contracts (jobs) show a loss? (What customers and classes of work should we sell? What types of jobs should we reject?)	Cost sheets showing cost, billing, and gross profit. Makeready separate from operating cost.	Job cost sheets must be put under bookkeeping control—present costs are not reliable. Job costs should preferably be ready immediately after the job is finished. Press rates will have to be audited.
	(3) How many hours per month is each press operated? What gross profit per running hour does each type of press make?	Press time summary. Job cost sheets.	

| (4) | Does there appear to be any trading profit (labor, ink, outside purchases)? (Do some customers supply their own paper?) | Job estimates (compare prices used by estimators with prices paid). Presumably estimators use current replacement prices. | |
| (5) | How do our billing prices compare with prices of outside sources:
Composition
Press time
Bindery? | Job estimates for our billing prices. Quotation for type-setting, and bindery work sub-let. | Overhead rates must be separated into variable and fixed portions per hour. |

Variable manufacturing costs
(short run costs)

(6)	What profit contribution per press hour does each type of press make? Do some jobs and presses show an out-of-pocket loss?	Same as (3) except press overhead is re-stated at variable costs only.	Fixed overhead ÷ (Average dollars billed per press hour – average variable cost per hour.)
(7)	What is the breakeven point in dollars of sales for the business (assuming that the present mix of press time remains constant)?		
(8)	What is the cash breakeven point in terms of current production mix in the press room? How much cash per press hour is generated above the cash breakeven point?		Same as (7) except that depreciation is not included in "fixed overhead".

Table 26-1. Cont'd

JORDAN PRINTING COMPANY

(1) What major decisions are being (or should be) made?	(2) What information is required to make those decisions?	(3) What are the existing information sources?	(4) What redesign of (or change in, or addition to) the present system is necessary?
	(9) What is the present and expected future debt situation?	Balance sheet.	Projected cash flow.
II Should we buy new presses to stay competitive?	(b) *Outside-in approach*		
	(1) Which presses are working to capacity? Which presses have substantial idle time, and what presses are not used?	Press time summary	
	(2) What kinds of press work can be sold and in what amounts (hours of press time)?	Explore statistics published by printing trade associations. Discussions with manufacturers of printing plant equipment. Market research on magazine and catalog business available. Manufacturers.	
	(3) Cost of new press(es).		
	(4) Can we generate enough cash internally? (See 8 above)		
	(5) Can we handle additional debt? (See 9 above)		

III What selling price (bid) should I set for a job?

(1) Out-of-pocket cost of the job (this is the floor).
(2) Long run = fully allocated cost plus return on investment in facilities used.
(3) Best guess as to what competitor(s) would charge.

Job estimates by the estimators. These are presumably based upon sound engineering standards for composing, press work, and bindery.

There is no comparison of actual job costs. Comparison must be made on a regular basis. Any differences between actual and estimated cost could mean either that the standards are not good or that performance was unsatisfactory. (Note that comparison does not yield automatic solutions.)

IV Should more salesmen be hired? (Should some salesmen be released?)

(1) What is the total sales by each salesman?
(2) How profitable is the business supplied by each salesman? ("Anybody can give printing away!")

Job cost sheets. (These show salesmen name and profit on job.)

These supporting systems, representing the basic functions of a business, produce respectively the

Sales distribution
Purchase and expense distribution
Labor distribution
Cost distribution

which flow into the general ledger, from which the balance sheet and the income statement are produced. This historical information is a basic part of the MIS since planning and control decisions must be made within the framework of the balance sheet and the income statement. It should

THE ACCOUNTING SYSTEM AND THE OPERATING SYSTEM
(PROVIDING INFORMATION FOR THE INFORMATION SYSTEM)

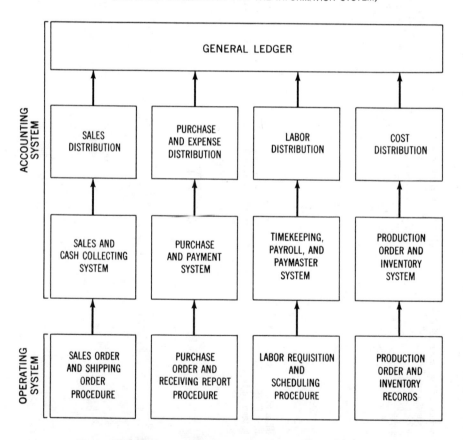

Figure 26-1. The Accounting System and the Operating System

be noted, however, that the conventional accounting system without change will not produce information in a form most suitable for a *management* accounting system. The conventional financial accounting system is likely to be designed to meet SEC, Internal Revenue, and other statutory requirements—requirements that more often than not, fail to correspond to management information needs.[3] (Figure 26-2, pages 625–632, is a set of financial statements designed especially to provide for management information needs.)

The bottom part of Figure 26-1 is the operating system of the business. The operating system is a part of the management information system. As shown in the illustration, it includes the purchase order and receiving report procedure, the production order and inventory procedure, the labor requisition and scheduling procedure, and the sales order and shipping order procedure. Each of these procedures conveys orders to someone to do something and likewise conveys the feedback indicating when and to what extent the orders were carried out. Collectively, they are the network for day to day decisions on logistics and of short run planning and control. As indicated above, the program for the operating system may convey information to a decision maker who makes the decision or it may have designed into it certain decision rules which are applied to the system without specific recourse to human decision makers.

Classification of Management Information Systems

Management information systems may be classified according to the *type* of system, meaning nature and stage of development for decision making purposes, or by *function,* such as financial, marketing, production, and personnel.[4] Information systems by type are discussed below

---

[3] W. Thomas Porter and Dennis E. Mulvihill, "Organization for Effective Information Flow" (*Management Science,* November/December 1965).

[4] Various authors classify management information systems by function in different ways. Thomas R. Prince, authority on management information systems, in his *Information Systems for Management Planning and Control* Second Edition, Homewood, Illinois: Richard D. Irwin, Inc., 1970), names the modules (the term is the present author's) as follows, devoting one or more chapters to each:

Traditional information systems
  Responsibility accounting systems
  Profitability accounting systems
  Critical path planning and scheduling information systems
Production and operation information systems
Marketing information systems
(Movement toward a) total information system

George A. Steiner in his *Top Management Planning* (New York: The Macmillan Company, 1969), names the major information systems as accounting, personnel, material flows, periodic planning information, special reports, the grapeview ("it exists in every enterprise. . . . By any standard it is a major information system") and scanning ("scanning involves simply an exposure to and perception of information").

and information systems classified by function on pages 625–636. A brief discussion of program budgeting and the relationship of the information system to a program budgeting system appears on pages 637–638.

Information Systems by Type

The types of system as defined by Massy are:[5]

Type 1: the Librarian
Type 2: the Predictor
Type 3: the Searcher

These types are described as follows:

The Type 1 Librarian is essentially a storage and retrieval system. It involves coding the documents which are the input of the system according to the master classification mentioned above, in descriptors acceptable to the computer, storing the data in computer memory (this file is the data bank) and finally calling information out of memory on demand, again according to the master classification. The data file is updated perpetually from the basic sources as new information becomes available. Descriptors for a marketing oriented system could include (for example) the type of data (sales, costs, etc.), time period, product, geographic area or branch and salesman number.

The Type 2 Predictor system would be designed to answer "what if" questions. The data bank would comprise updated information in a master classification as in Type 1 and the computer program would include the instructions for answering specific questions. Thus, recognizing that there are certain identifiable controllable variables affecting sales (or expenses), what would be the sales (or expense) for the coming period if the controllable variables behave in manner now being specified? The basic constraint of the Type 2 system is the formal models of behavior that are designed into the program. This would mean that the models and the programs would be designed to answer questions that arise frequently enough to justify the expense of designing the model and the program.

The Type 3 Searcher is designed to assist the manager in searching among various alternatives. "The important point is not that these models allow the decision maker to achieve an optimum solution, but that rather that they extend his ability to make a search for good solutions. . . ."

---

[5] This section is paraphrased from William F. Massy, "Information and the Marketing Manager: Systems Analysis" (*Computer Operations,* October 1968), pages 10–12.

MANAGEMENT INFORMATION SYSTEMS CLASSIFIED BY FUNCTION

Financial Management Information Systems

The financial management information system is a system for collecting, storing, manipulating, and reporting as required the information needed for making financial management decisions.

In respect to short term planning, the financial management information system provides basic internal information regarding what activities (manufacture and sale of what products, for instance) does the firm do best and what activities does it do least well? This information comes from the profitability accounting reports described and illustrated below. Profitability accounting reports are focused upon products and product lines, and they are organized on a profit contribution basis.[6] The financial management information system is also designed to provide external information for financial planners on such matters as sources of short term financing and current rates of interest.

In respect to short term control, the financial management information system provides information on who is responsible for what activity and how well did he perform? The classification of accounts for responsibility measurement is designed to fit the organization chart, so that each supervisor who has profit responsibility can receive an income statement covering the sales, expenses, and profit for which he is responsible. Likewise, each supervisor who has plant operating responsibility receives an expense report covering the expenses for which he is responsible.

Profitability Accounting Statements

Figure 26-2 comprises a complete set of profitability accounting statements based upon profit contribution accounting including standard costs:

Schedule	Title
1	Summary of Operations and Variances from Plan
2	Income and Expense Statement
3	Report on Sales By Products: Units and Amounts
4	Direct Margin Per Unit, By Product
5	Summary of Manufacturing Cost Variances
6	Materials Price Variances, By Class of Materials
7	Materials Quantity Variances, By Product
8	Variable Manufacturing Expense Statement
9	Programmed Expense and Fixed Property Expense Statement
10	Balance Sheet, with ROI and Turnover Comparisons

---

[6] Robert Beyer, "Profitability Accounting: The Challenge and the Opportunity" (*The Journal of Accountancy,* June 1964), page 33. According to Beyer, standard costs, budgetary control, costs for pricing, product line accounting, return on capital employed, make or buy accounting, management reports and many other tools have been in use for many years; what is new is their integration into one package.

These statements are intended for top management. Schedules 1, 2 and 3 provide analysis of the business as a whole, and the others provide analysis of segments of the information shown on Schedule 2.

On Schedule 1, Analysis of Differences Between Budget and Actual Profits shows five major indicators, of which the first four concern profit contribution:[7]

Quantity: change in profit contribution due to selling more or less than budget quantity of goods

Mix: change in profit contribution due to selling more or less of the higher profit items than budgeted

Selling price: Change in profit contribution due to not selling goods at the budget selling prices

Cost: Change in profit contribution due to producing at more or less than standard variable costs.

The fifth variance on Schedule 1 is difference between actual and budget costs for programmed expenses and fixed property expenses.

Only the top level reports are illustrated in Figure 26-2. The report structure in a complete responsibility accounting system is a pyramid which would incorporate the layers of responsibility of the supervisors from the president at the top of the pyramid (profit responsibility) to the foreman at the bottom of the pyramid (cost responsibility). All of these reports show actual results compared with budget, with variances

Schedule 1

INLAND COMPANY

Summary of Operations and Variances from Plan
Month of January, 19—

	Schedule	Amount
Budget Profit	2	$ 3375
Actual Profit	3	3106
Loss		$ 269
Gain in Profit Contribution		
Quantity (gain)		$ 1586
Mix (loss)		149*
Selling Price (loss)		322*
Cost (loss)		834*
Total Gain		$ 281
Budget Variances on Programmed Expense and Fixed Property Expense (loss)		550*
Total Loss in Budget Profit		$ 269*

Figure 26-2. Profitability Accounting Statements

---

[7] For the formulas for the profit contribution variances, see *Standard and Direct Costing,* Third Edition, Prentice-Hall (1962), Chapter 10, by the present author.

Schedule 2

INLAND COMPANY

Income and Expense Statement
Month of January, 19—

Particulars	Sched-ules	Budget Amount	Percent To Sales	Actual Amount	Percent To Sales	Increase (Decrease)
Sales	3 & 4	$50,325	100.00%	$53,650	100.00%	$3,335
Less Variable Cost of Sales						
Materials		13,500		14,490		990
Labor		12,000		12,840		840
Variable Factory Expense		5,000		5,380		380
Total at Standard		$30,500	60.61%	$32,710	60.97%	$2,210
Manufacturing Variances				834	1.55	834
Total		$30,500	60.61%	$33,544	62.52%	$3,044
Profit Contribution		$19,825	39.39%	$20,106	37.48%	$ 281
Less Programmed and Fixed Property Expense	9	16,450	32.68	17,000	31.69	550
Net Profit		$ 3,375	6.7064%	$ 3,106	5.789%	$ 269*

BREAKEVEN POINT

$$\frac{\text{Fixed and Programmed Expense}}{\text{Profit Contribution \%}} = \frac{\$16,450}{.3939} = \$41,762 \qquad \frac{\$17,000}{.3748} = \$45,357$$

Margin of Safety
(Percent net profits to profit contribution)   17.03%   15.45%

Schedule 3

INLAND COMPANY

Report on Sales By Products: Units and Amounts
Month of January, 19—

Product	Budget Units	Amount	Actual Units	Amount	Variation (Amount)
Product A	500	$12,375	550	$13,750	$1,375
Product B	500	14,850	550	16,500	1,650
Product C	500	23,100	520	23,400	300
Total	1,500	$50,325	1,620	$53,650	$3,325

Figure 26-2. Cont.   Profitability Accounting Statements

Schedule 4

INLAND COMPANY

Direct Margin Per Unit, By Product
Month of January, 19—

Particulars	Product A		Product B		Product C	
	Standard	*Actual*	*Standard*	*Actual*	*Standard*	*Actual*
Selling Price	$24.75	$25.00	$29.70	$30.00	$46.20	$45.00
Variable Cost	15.00	15.91	18.00	19.24	28.00	30.43
Direct Margin	$ 9.75	$ 9.09	$11.70	$10.76	$18.20	$14.57
Percent Margin to Sales	39.39%	36.36%	39.39%	35.86%	39.39%	32.38%

Schedule 5

INLAND COMPANY

Summary of Manufacturing Cost Variances
Month of January, 19—

Particulars	Schedule	Amount
Materials Price Variance	6	$113
Materials Quantity Variance	7	160
Labor Rate Variance		331
Labor Efficiency Variance		120
Variable Factory Expense Spending Variance		60
Variable Factory Expense Efficiency Variance		50
Total		$834

Schedule 6

INLAND COMPANY

Materials Price Variances, By Class of Materials
Month of January, 19—

Material	Amount
Material X	$ 46
Material Y	47
Material Z	20
Total	$113

Figure 26-2. Cont.   Profitability Accounting Statements

Schedule **7**

INLAND COMPANY

Materials Quantity Variances, By Product
Month of January, 19—

Product	Amount
Product A	$ 20
Product B	60
Product C	80
Total	$160

Schedule **8**

INLAND COMPANY

Variable Manufacturing Expense Statement
Month of January, 19—

	Adjusted Budget			
	Rate		Actual	Budget
Account	Per Hour	Amount	Expense	Variance
Actual hours		3,310		
Indirect labor	$ .60	$1,986	$2,000	$14
Operating supplies	.20	662	685	13
Maintenance supplies	.10	331	340	19
Power	.10	331	345	14
Totals	$1.00	$3,310	$3,370	$60

Schedule **9**

INLAND COMPANY

Programmed Expense and Fixed Property Expense Statement
Month of January, 19—

Accounts	Budget Amount	Actual Expense	Variance
Administrative salaries	$ 3,000	$ 3,200	$200
Marketing salaries	2,000	2,100	100
Factory supervision and staff salaries	2,500	2,600	100
Office salaries	4,000	4,100	100
Stationary and office supplies	600	620	20
Office expense	120	130	10
Telephone and telegraph	230	250	20
Depreciation	2,000	2,000	0
Property insurance	500	500	0
Property taxes	1,500	1,500	0
Total	$16,450	$17,000	$550

Figure 26-2. Cont.   **Profitability Accounting Statements**

INLAND COMPANY

Balance Sheet   January 31, 19—

Assets

Assets	Budget	Actual	Increase or Decrease*
Current Assets			
Cash	$ 38,567	$ 24,041	$14,526*
Accounts receivable	50,325	73,000	22,675
Materials-raw, in process, and finished goods	40,500	28,980	11,520*
Labor in process and finished goods	18,000	12,840	5,160*
Variable factory expense in process and finished goods	7,500	5,380	2,120*
Factory supplies inventory	500	450	50*
Prepaid insurance	3,000	3,000	0
Total current assets	$158,392	$147,691	$10,701*
Plant and Machinery (net)	240,000	240,000	0
Total assets	$398,392	$387,691	$10,701*

Liabilities and Net Worth

Liabilities and Net Worth	Budget	Actual	Increase or Decrease
Current Liabilities			
Accounts payable-materials and supplies	$ 14,000	$ 4,268	$ 9,732*
Accrued wages	3,750	2,533	1,217*
Accrued salaries	11,500	12,000	500
Accrued expense	317	334	17
Accrued property taxes	9,000	9,000	0
Total current liabilities	$ 38,567	$ 28,135	$10,432*
Net Worth			
Capital January 1, 19—	$356,450	$356,450	$ 0
Add Profit for month (Schedule 2)	3,375	3,106	269*
Total net worth	$359,825	$359,556	$ 269*
Total liability and net worth	$398,392	$387,691	$10,701*

	Budget	Actual
Return on Investment (annualized)		
Percent profit to net sales (Schedule 2)	6.7064 %	5.7894 %
Turnover	1.7688 times	1.6603 times
Return on investment (net assets)	10.166 %	9.611 %
Return on investment (net worth)	11.26 %	10.37 %
Turnovers		
Cash (sales ÷ cash)	1.30 times	2.23 times
Accounts receivable (sales ÷ accounts receivable)	1.00 times	.73 times
Inventory (variable cost of sales ÷ inventories)	.46 times	.69 times

Percent profit to net sales × Turnover

$$\text{ROI} = \frac{\text{Profit}}{\text{Sales}} \times \frac{\text{Sales}}{\text{Net Assets}}$$

Figure 26-2. Profitability Accounting Statements, Concluded

between actual and budget. We may assume for purposes of discussion that there are three levels of responsibility: Major (president), intermediate (executives who report to the president and to whom the foreman, marketing managers, and others report) and minor (foreman and others). The president's reports show intermediate totals, with which he can judge the performance of supervisors who report to him. The intermediate supervisors' reports show minor totals with which they in turn can judge the performance of foremen who report to them. And finally the foremen's reports show the breakdown of expenses for which they are responsible.

Marketing Information System

A marketing information system is a system for collecting information, both external and internal, for making marketing decisions.[8] Marketing decisions may be grouped strategic and short term planning and budgeting. Strategic planning decisions relate to such questions as what products should we be selling?; in what territories should we be operating?; what channels of distribution (distribution through jobbers, wholesalers, retailers, industrial outlets) should we be using?; and what methods of sale (selling by house salesmen, city salesmen, traveling salesmen; direct mail selling) should we be using? These questions are not mutually exclusive. The question of what territories to exploit, for instance, immediately raises the question of method of sale (salesmen? mail order promotions?) as indicated above. Planning includes the projection of alternatives as a part of the decision making process. This generalization is especially true of marketing planning, where typically a number of alternative methods, and so forth, are available.

Internal information for strategic planning includes analyses of current operations to determine in what areas (referring to the question

---

[8] Professor Thomas Prince, *Information Systems for Planning and Control,* Revised Edition (Homewood, Illinois: Richard D. Irwin, Inc., 1970), page 261, says that because of the high interface required between the marketing information system and other operating and information systems, it is rare (1969) to find a complete marketing information system. He made the statement on the basis of his in-depth study of thirty-four corporations. Professor Prince says that in three years, there will be a number of full fledged marketing information systems.

Professor Philip Kotler, "A Design for the Firm's Marketing Information Center" (*Business Horizons,* Fall 1966), page 64 says that "where the firm does not have a complete marketing information system, the marketing information for planning is likely to come from the market research department, the controller, the research and development department, the long range corporate planning department, the legal department, the economic research department and other departments of the company." A formal marketing information system would integrate the information now obtained from various sources.

above) the company performs best. External information includes economic, industry, technological, sociological and competition conditions and areas.

Short term planning and budgeting involves the decisions necessary to implement the strategic plan. Once the strategic planning decisions have been made to establish new territories by using traveling salesmen, for example, operating decisions must be made as to hiring, training and deploying the salesmen, and the types of promotion to support them. These decisions require their own information inputs.

Budgeting is an instrument of control of operating decisions, supported by more or less elaborate quantitative controls which themselves require the collection of information. Control in the marketing function is concerned with income and expense, and with assets committed. (Examples of assets committed are owned sales office quarters, finished goods warehouses and inventories, and the fleets of trucks and ships used to deliver finished goods.) In the operations planning phase, the planners set up budgets, one for each territory for example, to show where the firm will "come out" if the plans are carried out as formulated. For a new territory the managers may have to decide how much of a net loss to underwrite to get the territory opened. After the budget is approved by management, it becomes a measuring stick for actual performance for the period to which the budget relates. The marketing information system collects actual sales, expense, and asset data for making comparison of actual results with budget.

Check List of Information Areas for Business Planning and Decision Making[9]

William F. Christopher describes situation analysis for marketing and discusses a check list of information areas for business planning and decision making which his company uses. The form illustrated in Figure 26-3 is a matrix: market data by market sector and competitive data by competitor. "It can be used as a review check list, without putting anything in writing, or a more detailed report, or for programming information into a computer data bank." The check list is the second part of a two step development, being used in connection with and support for written business definitions and goals, a two to four page written document prepared by each division manager for his division.

---

[9] This section is based upon William F. Christopher, "Marketing Planning That Gets Things Done" (*Harvard Business Review,* September-October 1970), pages 57–62.

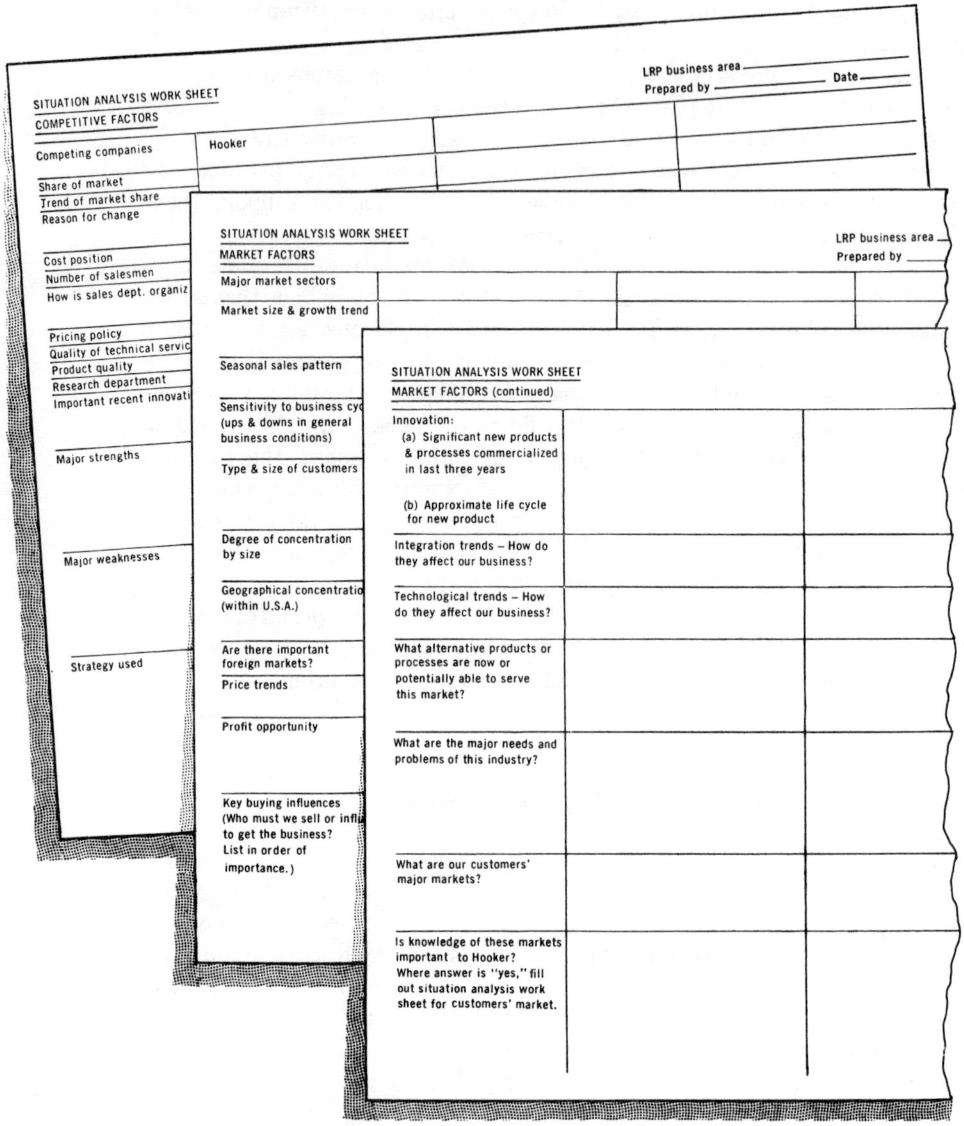

LRP business area _____ Date _____
Prepared by _____

SITUATION ANALYSIS WORK SHEET

COMPETITIVE FACTORS

Competing companies | Hooker

Share of market
Trend of market share
Reason for change

Cost position
Number of salesmen
How is sales dept. organiz

Pricing policy
Quality of technical servic
Product quality
Research department
Important recent innovati

Major strengths

Major weaknesses

Strategy used

SITUATION ANALYSIS WORK SHEET

MARKET FACTORS

LRP business area __
Prepared by __

Major market sectors

Market size & growth trend

Seasonal sales pattern

Sensitivity to business cyc
(ups & downs in general
business conditions)

Type & size of customers

Degree of concentration
by size

Geographical concentratio
(within U.S.A.)

Are there important
foreign markets?

Price trends

Profit opportunity

Key buying influences
(Who must we sell or infl
to get the business?
List in order of
importance.)

SITUATION ANALYSIS WORK SHEET

MARKET FACTORS (continued)

Innovation:
(a) Significant new products
& processes commercialized
in last three years

(b) Approximate life cycle
for new product

Integration trends – How do
they affect our business?

Technological trends – How
do they affect our business?

What alternative products or
processes are now or
potentially able to serve
this market?

What are the major needs and
problems of this industry?

What are our customers'
major markets?

Is knowledge of these markets
important to Hooker?
Where answer is "yes," fill
out situation analysis work
sheet for customers' market.

**Figure 26-3. Checklist for Information Areas for Business Planning
and Decision Making**

*Source: William F. Christopher, Marketing Planning that Gets Things Done, Harvard Business
Review, September-October, 1970, page 58.*

Production and Operations Information System

The production and operations information system is concerned with collecting information, both internal and external, required for making decisions with reference to planning the purchase of materials and services and the production of goods and services for customers. It also includes feedback and control.

Information for strategic planning for production and operations includes product requirements, plant processing and capacity, and plant locations (all of which are directly related to strategic marketing planning), sources of materials, supplies and services, and transportation of materials and supplies. It includes information relating to such questions as what products should be manufactured at what times of the year, what plant capacities should be provided, the cost of plant capacity and the cost of product turned out by the plant. Allocation of resources to plant is involved. Information on the cost of product involves the cost of materials, supplies, and services, and the transportation of materials and supplies to the plant.

Information for short term budgeting (months, quarters, year) refers to the determination of products and quantities to be manufactured, together with completion dates, and the expected cost of processes and products. In a multiple plant operation, the information is by plant. Where alternative processes are possible, information in the data bank may provide for the calculation of costs of alternative processing. Some of the information required for production and operations decisions is external information, collected in the operation of the marketing information system.

Information for control is concerned with actual products produced and processes used, together with the actual costs. This information is internal information, collected from the operating system (Figure 26-1) and it is integrated with the financial information system which produces the departmental and company balance sheet and income statements.

Information for (day to day) operational planning is provided by the short term planning system and the operating system including the inventory procedures. The various orders in the operating system (purchase orders, production orders and shipping orders) are written in the pattern of the short term planning system. Feedback upon actual performance, from the operating system and inventory procedure, is used to apply adjustments in operations to keep inventories at the desired levels.

Under the heading of Production and Operations Information systems it should be pointed out that in some industries the computer system not only reports production; it reads the relevant variables of the physical production process, applies programmed decisions rules, and controls the physical processes.

Diebold says:[10]

> "As a result of such developments, management will never be the same again. The ADP system will gradually encompass more and more of the business structure. The distinction between the control system of the plant—where over all "on-line" computer control is already a reality in electric utilities, steel rolling mills, and petroleum refineries—and the ADP system in the office will disappear. One information system will feed the entire business. This system will be the arteries through which will flow the life stream of the business: market intelligence, control information, strategic decisions, feedback for change. . . ."

Personnel Management Information System

The personnel management information system is concerned with collecting information, both external and internal, on manufacturing labor, office personnel, and administrative and sales personnel. It is involved with sources of these classes of personnel and with the current training, scheduling, skills inventory, and performance measures for personnel.

For strategic planning of products, manufacturing plants, and distribution systems, information on labor sources geographically, skills, and prevailing rates of pay is required. Strategic planning for personnel parallels strategic planning for marketing and for production.

For short term planning, the personnel information system provides information on staffing the short term marketing and production plans. In many cases, the existing labor force and staffing will continue with some change for planned growth or contraction. The historical data bank provides the basic information for labor cost in terms of production units, and staffing for the administrative and sales activities. The plans are crystallized into a budget which becomes the basis for measuring performance. Variances between actual and budget are determined on the basis of feedback from the accounting systems and the operating system.

Day to day operational planning is based upon the daily production plan; in other words the daily operation plan for production is the information input for operational planning for personnel. This involves making up the daily labor assignment. The information feedback is the daily production report.

---

[10] John Diebold, "ADP—the Still Sleeping Giant" (*Harvard Business Review*, October 1964), page 241.

PROGRAM BUDGETING

Organic Budgeting vs. Program Budgeting and the Information System

It was stated before that the accounting system supplies part of the internal information required for the firm's information system. The traditional internal information system may include a responsibility reporting system in which the income and expense reports are built upon the lines of the organization chart and a profitability accounting system which is designed to ferret out weak points and strong points. The responsibility accounting system, if fully developed, has a built-in budget system which fits the organization chart perfectly. The budget system provides the measuring stick by which the actual performance can be judged. This type of budget system is known as an *organic budget* system. Shillinglaw states that "in organization-based, or organic budgeting, primary responsibility for planning is vested in line executives who supervise the personnel who will implement the plan."[11] The management information system including the general ledger is designed to fit the organic budgeting system.

A *program* is a set of activities directly related to a *defined objective* which has been approved by management and for the fulfillment of which the necessary resources of the firm have been allocated by the management. Examples of programs that readily come to mind are styling of automobiles by an automobile manufacturer, advertising programs (which may involve millions of dollars), and research and development of product and manufacturing methods. Programs are likely to cut across departmental lines, and furthermore, time periods vary among programs. Some programs may be completed in a year, others may take four or five, or even ten years. *Program budgeting* is the formal process of defining objectives and programs, evaluating alternative ways to carry out a program for a specific set of objectives, setting up the allocation of resources, identifying responsibility for the program, and comparing performance on the programs with plans. In a full fledged program budgeting system *all* "overhead" activities of the company would be covered either by formal programs or by fixed property expense accounts. One automobile manufacturing company which operates a complete program budgeting system operates about 600 programs in the system at any one time.

Comments on program budgeting from recent literature follow:

---

[11] Gordon Shillinglaw, *Cost Accounting Analysis and Control* (Homewood, Illinois: Richard D. Irwin, Inc., 1967), page 747. References 8–11 inc. are from an unpublished paper by John Steel, used by permission.

Shillinglaw says, "in program budgeting, the focus is on individual product lines or customer groups, with a separate plan for each as responsibility of a program executive."[12] Under the heading "Approaches Used in Structuring the Program Budget," Steiner says, "The budget is end product oriented, the programs are functional, and they are organized in mission-identifiable terms."[13] Donald J. Smalter in his excellent papers on this subject uses the term *mission* instead of *program*, presumably as being more meaningful and descriptive.[14]

Hitch says, "The program extends far enough into the future to show to the extent practical and necessary the full resource requirements and financial implications of the programming outputs. The traditional (organic) budget usually included only one year and did not indicate the implications of a project." New programs are being added as the need arises. Whereas organic budgeting is built on the traditional class of expense and responsibility classification, program budgeting is built upon class of expense, subresponsibility, and program classification.

"*Information system* considerations (in program budgeting) are aimed at the support of (the structural aspects and the analytical aspects of program budgeting). There are several senses in which this is important, the primary ones being (1) progress reporting and control, to give an indication of how well (or poorly) major program decisions are being carried out in the process of implementation, and (2) providing data and information to serve as a basis for the analytical process—especially to facilitate the development of estimating relationships and analytical models which will permit making estimates of benefits and costs of future alternative courses of action."[15]

---

[12] Shillinglaw, *op. cit.* p. 747.

[13] George A. Steiner, "Program Budgeting, Business Contribution to Government Management" (*Business Horizons,* Spring 1965), page 43.

[14] Donald Smalter, Charles J. Hitch, "Program Budgeting" (*Datamation,* September, 1967), page 37.

[15] G. H. Fisher, *The World of Program Budgeting* (Santa Monica, California: The Rand Corporation, May 1966), page 9.

Problems and Questions

I. General Assignments: Design of a complete system "from the general ledger down." (Term assignments.) These assignments cover all the major phases of design in typical systems jobs: University Bookstore: Problems 3-1, 4-1, 20-1. Universal Electronics Company: Problems 3-2, 4-2, 13-1, 15-1, 17-1, 20-2. Metropolitan Manufacturing Co.: Problem 19-1.

II. Procedures assignments, problems, and questions (grouped by chapter).

III. Notebook: Field trips and demonstrations.

Note: The general assignments and all procedures assignments are adaptations of actual professional and private assignments. Only such changes have been made in the actual facts and conditions as were necessary to keep the material here presented within manageable limits.

Chapter 1

Question 1-1

"Definitions of systems and procedures vary from those which emphasize managerial aspects to those which emphasize technical aspects." Discuss.

Question 1-2

(a) What are the basic systems of a personal service business? A retail or wholesale business? A manufacturing business?

(b) What are the usual procedures found in each basic system of a manufacturing business?

Question 1-3

(a) What is an operation?

(b) Name some "do" operations. Why do systems men distinguish "do" operations from other operations?

Question 1-4

What is a process?

Question 1-5

What are the general aims of systems work?

Question 1-6

(a) What is a "general assignment"?

(b) What are the main features of a typical report covering a general assignment?

Question 1-7

(a) What is a comparative procedures and methods assignment?

(b) What are the main features of a typical report covering a comparative procedures and methods assignment?

Question 1-8

(a) What is a clerical work loading assignment?

(b) What are the main features of a typical report covering a clerical work loading assignment?

Question 1-9

What are feasibility studies for office automation?

Question 1-10

Discuss the private and professional organizations that do systems work and the areas in which each of them might operate.

Question 1-11

What are the major findings of the *Profile of a Systems Man* by the Systems and Procedures Association which are reported in Chapter 1?

Chapter 2

Question 2-1

It is said that systems notes, charts, and worksheets have particular uses for various persons concerned with a systems assignment. What persons are concerned with a typical systems assignment, and what use does each of them make of the records of the survey?

Question 2-2

Comment on the statements made by Schlosser, as reported in Chapter 2.

Question 2-3

Name the types of charts and worksheets that may be used in procedures assignments where the main purpose is likely to be cost reduction of cost control.

Question 2-4

Why is it often necessary to use operation times in systems survey and design assignments?

Question 2-5

What are the purposes of using formal operation symbols in preparing flow charts?

Chapter 3

Problem 3-1

THE UNIVERSITY BOOKSTORE

The University Bookstore sells the following classes of merchandise:

(1) Textbooks: Textbooks, course outlines, laboratory manuals, practice sets, and books of readings for particular courses.
(2) Other books: Trade, fiction, reference, adventure.
(3) Stationery: Notebooks and blank books, writing and typewriter paper in sheets, typewriter ribbons, carbon paper, tablets and writing pads, graph paper, columnar analysis paper, fountain pens, penholders and pens, ink, pencils, rulers, erasers, post cards and greeting cards, and so forth.
(4) Art paper and art supplies.
(5) Drafting equipment and slide rules.
(6) Typewriters and desk furnishings: Typewriters, desk sets, table lamps, and so forth.
(7) Cameras: Cameras and auxiliary equipment, photograph albums, and film.

The company occupies rented quarters under a lease which covers heat and water but no other utilities. The staff includes a manager, two office employees who handle all the purchasing paper work and accounting work, four regular full-time sales clerks, a part-time janitor, and extra sales clerks who work during peak seasons. The manager is paid monthly, the office employees and full-time sales clerks on the first and fifteenth of each month, and the janitor and the part-time sales clerks are paid weekly. Deductions are made for withholding tax and Social Security tax. Sales persons are paid commissions on all sales of merchandise in Class 6 and Class 7 above. The commissions are calculated monthly and paid within a few days after the end of each month.

The company buys merchandise on account, borrowing on short-term bank loans to carry early first-semester and second-semester business. It sells for cash. Cash sales are rung up on cash registers, of which there are two. These registers are used to analyze sales by class, but not by sales person. The company collects states sales tax. Cash payments ("paid-outs") are made from one of the registers, which has a "paid-out key" and an accumulator for such items. A paid-out slip is written for each such payment, and the slips are kept in the drawer of the register until the cash is balanced at the end of the day. Each register is provided with a change fund of $300 during the peak seasons when textbooks are being sold and $50 at other times. The Bookstore maintains a checking account at the local bank. Gross cash receipts less paid-outs are deposited intact daily. Payroll checks as well as checks for merchandise and service suppliers are drawn on this account.

The Bookstore canvasses teachers at the University before each semester and summer session to obtain lists of books and supplies that will be required for classes. Records of textbooks used in each course from semester to semester are carried for follow-up purposes in case replies from teachers are late. Textbooks are ordered from publishers under certain return privileges which protect the store in case the estimated course registration does not materialize in sales by the Bookstore. Merchandise is bought subject to a 2 per cent discount for payment within 30 days. Services bought outside are paid within their discount periods. Supplies used in the office are mostly taken from stock, but some store supplies, such as wrapping paper and janitors supplies, are bought outside and paid within the discount period. There are about 200 merchandise suppliers.

Physical inventories are taken at the calendar year-end and at the end of June. A Balance Sheet and an income statement for six months are prepared as of each of the inventory dates. The income statement for the first six months covers second-semester business and most of the summer-session book business. The income statement for the second six months covers first-semester business. The manager desires an analysis of sales by merchandise class, but he says he does not desire gross profit by merchandise class, stating that he knows what gross profit percentage he is making on each class.

The manager asks you to design a classification of accounts which will give him proper financial and operating statements, and a set of books in which to collect information. You tell him that such a project involves:

(1) Designing the formal classification of accounts, which the bookkeeper can use to determine which accounts to use in making entries.
(2) Designing a Balance Sheet, together with income and expense statement.
(3) Designing a set of model journal entries (called "standard journal entries") which the bookkeeper can use to guide her in making entries. This set of entries will show end-of-the-month adjustments separately from the entries for daily transactions, and it will show what journal is used to record each type of transaction.
(4) Designing a set of journals. This involves making drawings of the forms to scale for use by the printer.

The manager authorizes you to proceed. For the present assignment, design the classification of accounts and the statements. Assignments (3) and (4) will be made after Chapter 3.

Problem 3-2

UNIVERSAL ELECTRONICS COMPANY

The Universal Electronics Company operates a wholesale business to sell to new car dealers, garages, and radio repair shops radios designed for each make of car.

The company has been in operation for about five years. It is a very profitable, small company. The company buys all its radios from one manufacturing company. Other small items, such as antennas, may be purchased from any company. The company's business is based on selling car radios to dealers at a lower price than the dealer can get from the auto manufacturer.

The company has monthly sales of from $50,000 to $70,000. There are about 200 customers. Each customer buys once or twice a month.

There are five employees and the owner; three salesmen, a delivery man, the owner, R. Olsen, and a girl who does all office work and keeps the books.

Mr. Olsen supervises the office, manages the salesmen, and sells as a fourth salesman. He signs all checks and orders all merchandise. An individual payroll record is kept for each employee and the owner. Each payroll check is entered in the cash disbursements journal.

The books are kept on a partial cash basis:

1. Depreciation is recorded on an accrual basis.
2. Inventories are taken once a month.
3. Accounts payable are listed each month from unpaid bills and debited to purchases and credited to accounts payable. The beginning balance in accounts payable is reversed: Debit Accounts Payable; credit Purchases.
4. All other expenses are kept on a cash basis.
5. (a) The building was rented for three years. The first and last two months' rent were paid in advance.
   (b) The following items are prepaid in part: Insurance, interest, and advertising.
   (c) The following are accrued: all taxes, salaries, commissions, utilities, and interest.

The present books:

Cash receipts—all sales entered as collected.
Cash disbursements—all purchases entered here when paid.
General journal
General ledger
Customers' ledger
  These ledger accounts are not tied into an accounts receivable control. Debits are posted from charge invoices. The date each item is paid is entered on the credit side.

Mr. Olsen wants the books changed to the accrual basis of accounting.

The Universal Electronics Company has a credit limit of $25,000 with the manufacturer of the only brand of radio sold. It purchases $30,000 to $50,000 worth of radios a month. In order not to exceed the credit limit, it must order for weekly delivery and make weekly paymnts.

Sales and purchases have not been broken down by models. This year the models are as follows: 601, 602, 603, 604, 605, 606, 607, and parts. Next year, starting in October, the models will be 611, 612, 613, 614, 615, 616, 617, and parts. Mr. Olsen wants to know the amount of sales, purchases, and inventory of each model and parts.

Accounts payable have been entered in the Cash Disbursements journal as the invoices are paid. Each check pays at least one invoice. Mr. Olsen thinks a simple voucher system should be installed.

Account Classification

Accumulated Depreciation—Delivery Truck
Accumulated Depreciation—Furniture and Fixtures
Accumulated Depreciation—Sales Cars
Accounts Payable
Advertising
Bank Loans
Cars for Salesmen
Cash in Bank
Commission to Salesmen
Delivery Truck
Delivery Truck Expense
Depreciation on Delivery Truck
Depreciation on Furniture and Fixtures
Depreciation on Sales Cars
Freight-in on Air Shipments
Freight-in on Regular Purchases
Furniture and Fixtures
Insurance
Interest Expense
Inventory
Leasehold Expense
Leasehold Improvements
Legal and Auditing Expense
Mortgage Payable—Cars
Notes Payable
R. Olsen, Capital
R. Olsen, Drawing
Sales
Sales Car Expense
Rent Expense
Purchases
Taxes—Old Age Benefit
Taxes—Unemployment
Taxes—Personal Property
Utilities

Required:

(1) Make a list of additional accounts necessary to put the company's books on the accrual basis; also the additional accounts necessary to have a Sales and Purchases account for each model and for parts.

(2) Rearrange the accounts in the order they should appear on the Balance Sheet and on the income statement.

(3) Make up a form for a Balance Sheet and an income statement. Separate expenses into selling, general, and financial. Also design schedules showing the gross profit on each model of radio and on parts.

Question 3-1

Outline the steps in a general systems assignment.

Question 3-2

In the survey for a general systems assignment, is it better to proceed "from the top down" or otherwise? Why?

Question 3-3

Why is it necessary for the systems man to get approval of the statements before completing the classification of accounts and the formal manual of accounts?

Question 3-4

What are the main features of the account numbering plan used for the Household Appliance Corporation in Chapter 3?

Question 3-5

(a) In connection with accounting systems work, what is a code?

(b) Why might it be desirable (or necessary) to use codes in connection with classifications?

(c) Name several coding plans and give the characteristics of each.

Question 3-6

Discuss the reasons for a formal accounting manual.

Chapter 4

Problem 4-1

THE UNIVERSITY BOOKSTORE
(Survey information on pages 641-642)

(1) Referring to the classification of accounts which you designed for Problem 3-1, design a set of standard journal entries which the bookkeeper can use to guide her in making entries. This set of entries should show end-of-the-month adjustments separately from the entries for daily transactions, and it should show what journals are used to record each type of transaction.

(2) Design a set of pen-and-ink journals.

Problem 4-2

UNIVERSITY ELECTRONICS SALES COMPANY
(Survey information on pages 643-644)

(1) Referring to the classification of accounts which you designed for Problem 3-2, design a complete set of standard journal entries for the company.

(2) Design the necessary pen-and-ink journals.

Question 4-1

What are the uses of standard journal entries?

Question 4-2

Discuss the factors to consider in selecting a plan of journalizing.

Question 4-3

The standard journal entries illustrated in Table 4-2 (page 66) are based upon a particular plan of recording accruals and deferrals. Describe an alternate plan briefly, illustrating your description with appropriate standard journal entries relating to fire insurance and property taxes. (The entries may be skeletonized.)

Question 4-4

The owner of a medium-sized company calls you to see if you can help with the following situation. His financial statements are reaching him about the middle of the month. He would like to get them as early as possible. He has talked this matter over with his bookkeeper who tells him that the books of original entry are for the most part closed about the seventh of the month and that it is impractical to close certain of them much earlier, a conclusion with which, upon investigation, you agree.

The bookkeeper states that he regularly has about thirty general journal entries for depreciation, insurance, accrued payroll, and so forth, which he makes first on his working papers and then on the books, and that the General ledger contains over 300 accounts. Making these journal entries, posting the General ledger, and taking the trial balance is a difficult, time-consuming task.

What do you suggest?

Question 4-5

(a) What are the advantages and disadvantages of the cash journal?

(b) What are the advantages and disadvantages of the three-journal set operating on a current-cash basis with periodic adjustment to accrual basis?

Chapter 5

Problem 5-1

What ready-printed account forms would you recommend for the accounting system which you designed for the University Bookstore (Problem 3-1)?

Problem 5-2

What ready-printed account forms would you recommend for the accounting system which you have designed for the Universal Electronics Company (Problem 3-2)?

Question 5-1

What are the advantages and disadvantages of the T-account ledger (Figure 5-1) over the Debit, Credit, Balance ledger (Figure 5-3)?

Question 5-2

What are the principal physical characteristics (such as weight of paper) that you would consider in the design of a form? What are the considerations governing each characteristic?

Question 5-3

It is said that writing, reproducing, sorting, and filing operations must be anticipated in designing printed forms. Explain what is meant by this statement. Give illustrations.

Question 5-4

(a) What is a form layout?

(b) In making a form layout, what difference, if any, does it make whether a form is a source form or an end-purpose form?

Question 5-5

(a) What is meant by "forms standardization"?

(b) How may economies in the design of printed forms be achieved through forms standardization?

Chapter 6

Question 6-1

Name some of the structual types of continuous forms.

Question 6-2

Name some of the types of writing machines and registers that may be used for handling continuous forms.

Question 6-3

(a) Name some of the basic duplicating methods and state the essential differences among them from the standpoint of design of shipping order and billing procedures and other order procedures.

(b) Explain briefly the uses of fixed masters and variable masters in connection with duplicating methods.

Question 6-4

(a) What is meant by "line-picking" in connection with duplicating methods?

(b) Give an illustration of its use in systems work.

Question 6-5

(a) What is the basic difference between duplicating and copying?

(b) What is the basic difference between diazo process and xerography?

Question 6-6

(a) What is "addressing," as it is considered in connection with systems work?

(b) Discuss, in general, the use of addressing machines in systems work.

Question 6-7

(a) What types of equipment are considered in Chapter 6 under the heading of "Automatic Writing Equipment"?

(b) Discuss some of the uses of card or tape input, card or tape output, arithmetic and logic capability, and memory capability.

Question 6-8

How are the various automatic writing machines described in this chapter programmed?

Chapter 7

Problem 7-1

Following is a list of (a) old balances and (b) charges posted to Accounts Receivable during a single posting run:

Name	Old Balance	Charges Posted
Brown	$2,835	$283
Smith	4,762	478
Williams	3,829	695
Johnson	782	43
Wilson	6,384	286
Meyers	295	795

Using the above information, diagram:

(1) a pre-list tape.
(2) a proof tape—old and new balance proof—and show how the proof operates.
(3) a proof tape—long-run proof—and show how the proof operates.
(4) a proof tape for direct proof on a single-register machine and show how the proof operates.
(5) a proof tape for direct proof on a two-register machine and show how the proof operates.

Question 7-1

What is meant by the following terms used in connection with listing-adding machines?

(1) total	(6) split platen
(2) subtotal	(7) proof tape
(3) non-add	(8) proof sheet
(4) register	(9) posting cycle
(5) cross-footer	

Question 7-2

What are the old and new balance proof and the long-run proof intended to prove? What do they fail to prove?

Question 7-3

How does the number of accounts that are active each day affect the usefulness of the old and new balance proof as compared with the long-run proof?

Question 7-4

When direct proof was invented, what was it intended to do that was not already done by the old and new balance proof and the long-run proof?

Question 7-5

State the relative advantages of (1) proof tape and (2) proof sheet.

Question 7-6

(a) For what types of applications are "window machines" used?

(b) For what types of applications are alpha-numeric machines used?

Question 7-7

In what essential respects is posting by machine likely to be different from posting by pen-and-ink methods?

Question 7-8

Define or explain briefly the following terms as they relate to machine posting of accounts:

(1) media	(4) random posting
(2) sorting	(5) exhaust method
(3) stuffing	(6) stuff and exhaust

Question 7-9

Is it feasible to post debits to accounts without carrying running balances on the accounts as illustrated in the text? If it is feasible, what would be gained by this method over the method illustrated in the text? What would be lost?

Question 7-10

It is said that when a bookkeeping machine is used for posting, it is easier to locate errors than when the posting is done by pen-and-ink methods. Discuss.

Question 7-11

Sometimes the auditor recommends a bookkeeping machine over pen-and-ink posting because use of the former makes it possible for him to enforce internal check. Discuss.

Question 7-12

State briefly several reasons why the method of proof used in machine posting affects the clerical economy of the installation.

Question 7-13

It is said that, in accounts receivable posting by machine method, there is a tendency away from the use of proofs which involve second pickups of old balances and a tendency toward reducing the number of accounts under each control account. Without passing upon the validity of this statement, explain what can be said in favor of this practice. What can be said against it?

Question 7-14

How is automatic pickup of old balances accomplished in a machine-posting operation?

Question 7-15

How does use of magnetic strip accounts operate to produce a proof of posting to right account?

Question 7-16

Discuss card or tape output in relationship to bookkeeping machines. What might be the uses of such output?

Question 7-17

What machines illustrated in Chapters 6 and 7 are examples of the application of the common-language principle?

Question 7-18

In handling the media in a machine-posting operation, does it make any difference whether the media are unit or mixed? Discuss.

Chapter 8

Question 8-1

(a) What is meant by "records management"?
(b) Discuss some of the phases or areas of records management.

Question 8-2

Name and describe briefly the basic types of sorting equipment.

Question 8-3

Distinguish visible record equipment, visible margin equipment and visible index reference equipment.

Question 8-4

(a) Discuss the uses of microfilming in accounting systems work.
(b) Discuss computer output microfilming (COM) in accounting systems work.

Chapter 9

Question 9-1

What is a "system of internal check"?

Question 9-2

Name some of the details of protection which may be provided by internal check and accounting control.

Question 9-3

Name some of the control devices and methods used in internal check and accounting control.

Chapter 10

Problem 10-1

The Regal Restaurant, a single proprietorship, is open to the general public from 6:00 A.M. to 9:00 P.M. daily, except Sundays.

The proprietor uses a simple "guest check" and rings up all sales in a cash register. The cash register is of the non-resetting variety which provides a tape and cumulative totals at the close of business each day.

The business was acquired by William Johnson on January 1, 19___ and at the end of the month you are called upon to set up the books and assist in keeping them thereafter in order to provide a monthly profit and loss statement. You arrange a meeting with the proprietor to obtain the necessary financial details to enable you to make the opening entries and, in the course of the discussions, discover nothing in the form of an adequate system to provide for continuing the bookkeeping operation even after it is installed. You are able to obtain from the proprietor an agreement permitting you to design a system that will provide for the minimum requirements and the instructions necessary to obtain the daily records. You are instructed to "'make it simple" and keep in mind that "we are not bookkeepers; serving our customers must come first."

Purchase Facts: Purchase of the Business

		Estimated Life
Total paid for business............	$10,000	
Values assigned by proprietor		
Silverware, glassware, china.......	400	Replacement basis
Dining room fixtures..............	1,600	15 years
Kitchen equipment................	1,500	10 years
Fountain equipment...............	3,500	10 years
Leasehold improvements...........	1,000	Life of asset
Food inventory...................	500	

Lease assigned to new owner originally was for 5 years with 4 years to run at monthly rental of $150; last three months' rent was paid by the former owner at the time of signing the lease.

Change fund for cash register......	$ 40
Cash in bank.....................	200

Operating Facts

The proprietor plans to spend most of his time waiting on trade and acting as his own cashier. There will be the following employees:

Cooks

M. Lucas—$1.25 per hour—8 hours daily
J. Ronald—$1.15 per hour—8 hours daily

Waitresses

Sue Miller   —full time (8 hours) $.75 per hour and 2 meals daily
Mae Johnson —full time (8 hours) .75 per hour and 3 meals daily
Sally Erickson—part time (4 hours) .75 per hour and 2 meals daily
Mae Martin   —part time (4 hours) .75 per hour and 2 meals daily

Mr. Johnson wants a salary of $200 per month to be recorded for him for accounting purposes. He plans to draw cash only as he needs it.
The restaurant is closed on Sundays.

Records for January

The records delivered to you for the month of January consist of a bundle of paid invoices for food and various other supplies which include cash paid-outs as well as those paid by check. There is no separation by days for January.

A bundle of "guest checks" and the cash-register readings are also delivered. Not all cash receipts are recorded on "guest checks," and they are not dated. The cash-register readings were kept by the proprietor by days so that the only dependable record of receipts available is that of the cash register. Daily amounts may be obtained, but since the number of servings is not available and other records were not kept by days in the month of January, daily totals are meaningless. Statements for the month of January will have to be prepared from totals, but the daily requirements of the future and necessary instructions, based on the forms and procedures to be designed, must be started at once. This is necessary so that facts will be available for:

(1) Statistics to assist the proprietor.

(2) Check on cash discrepancies daily.

Daily Cash Control

After considering all the factors, and keeping in mind the proprietor's admonition, it is decided to design and install a system based primarily on two main subdivisions, namely:

(1) A daily cash record for all receipts and cash payments.

(2) All other credit transactions, including payroll, to be paid by check.

The Daily Cash Record

It is decided to design an envelope in which will be put all guest checks for receipts and all suppliers' (vendors') invoices and any other "payment" vouchers for cash actually paid out during the day. Printed on the outside of the envelope will be a simple form for summarizing the facts to be recorded in the Summary of Cash Receipts and Paid-Outs.

Credit Transactions and Payrolls

It is decided not to keep any Accounts Payable ledger. However, as each invoice is approved for payment by the proprietor, it will be filed in a "Bills Payable" file folder. When the proprietor pays any of the bills, he will enter a brief description on check stub, enter on the paid invoice the check number with which paid, prefixed by "Pd. 1-27" (paid in January with check #27), and file them in a temporary file folder labeled "Bills Paid by Check." Any invoices remaining in the "Bills Payable" file folder at the end of every month will be listed on a work paper and classified as to "Food by Type or Expenses" for use as a ten-column work paper adjusting entry—debiting Food by Type or Expenses and crediting Accounts Payable. No entry to the ledger is necessary from month to month except at year-end for tax purposes and then a post closing reversal will be made for the next year's interim statements.

The bills paid are used in connection with the check stubs when entering to check register (purchase and disbursements journal) for verifying classification in case the description shown on the stub is not clear or has been omitted. When all entries have been made, the paid bills are returned to the proprietor to file alphabetically for future reference.

Payrolls

Payroll payments will be made by check with the meals allowances, withholding tax, and O.A.B. deductions shown in the "Items" section of the check.

For a small business with few employees, say six to ten, much time can be saved by using *individual payroll sheets*. These sheets are similar or identical to employees' quarterly earnings records (Figure 17-4). One form is set up for each employee; it is the record of original entry for wages earned, deductions, and net pay. Pay checks are written on regular bank checks which are entered in the cash disbursements journal. A separate payroll *journal* is not kept.

The individual payroll sheets will be kept in the same binder as the General ledger. Two tabs will be provided which read:

PAYROLL—ACTIVE

PAYROLL—INACTIVE

The active section will include the sheets for employees regularly on the current payroll. The inactive section will include the sheets for employees whose services have been terminated but who have been paid some wages during the current accounting period or the current year.

Final Month-End Data

After you have selected, or designed, the forms to be used, and the form of profit and loss statement, you proceed to enter all the checks and summarize the cash receipts and paid-outs for the month. The totals obtained are as follows:

Cash receipts		
Food sales	$3,440.50	State sales tax of 2% included in sales.
Deposits made per pass book		
1/ 4	$ 125.00	
1/ 5	200.00	
1/ 8	175.00	
1/11	135.00	
1/13	205.00	
1/15	165.00	
1/19	250.00	
1/22	180.00	
1/24	170.00	
1/27	180.00	
1/29	250.00	
	$2,035.00	
Cash on hand not deposited until 2/1	$ 300.00	
Change fund	40.00	

Cash Paid-outs after separating them from the bills paid by check are summarized as follows:

Meat and fish	$ 175.00
Groceries	225.00
Eggs and dairy products	115.00
Bread and pastries	225.00
Vegetables and fruits	195.00
Stationery and menus	12.50
Operating supplies	65.00
Renewals and replacements	15.00
Advertising	18.00
Donations	5.00
William Johnson, drawing	40.00
	$1,090.50

After all checks are entered in the purchase and disbursements journal and it is totaled and balanced, the totals to be posted to the General ledger are as follows:

	Dr.	Cr.
Meat and fish	$ 300.00	$
Groceries	225.00	
Eggs and dairy products (milk)	75.00	
Wages—waitresses	443.00	
Wages—kitchen	455.20	
Prepaid insurance—general	180.00	(12 mos.)
Gas and light	75.00	
Telephone	12.50	
Laundry and cleaning	18.50	
Rent	150.00	
Cash discounts taken		12.00
Federal O.A.B. deducted		8.99
Income tax withheld		59.30
Meals allowance included in wages		93.00
Net checks issued		1,760.91
	$1,934.20	$1,934.20

The bank has been reconciled and no discrepancies found. Therefore, the cash as shown per books will stand as correct.

Inventory

In small restaurants such as this, the turnover is almost complete from day to day. Therefore the beginning inventory will remain a fixed amount until year-end inventory at which time an actual inventory will be taken and set up to remain unchanged for the next year.

Unpaid Suppliers' Invoices as of January 31, 19___

A-1 Ice Cream Co.	$ 45.00
Fresh Meat Supply Co.	115.00
National Restaurant Supply Co. (china)	32.00

Required

(1) Design a classification of accounts. Under cost of sales, provide accounts for meat and fish, groceries, eggs and dairy products, bread and pastries, vegetables and fruits, and employees' meals (credit). Analyze the expenditures of the past month to obtain a guide for setting up expense accounts. Include accounts for taxes—general, taxes—payroll, insurance—general, and insurance—compensation.

(2) Design Balance Sheet and Statement of Profits. Show how statistics on average cost of meals will be presented on the statement of profits. Provide for month- and year-to-date presentation of amounts and also significant percentages.

(3) Design an envelope to contain meal checks and the evidences of paid-outs for one day, with a summary of receipts and paid-outs on the front.

(4) Design a Summary of Cash Receipts and Paid-Outs, providing (among others) columns for analysis of debits to be posted to the General ledger. (Use columnar analysis paper to save drafting time.)

(5) Design a Check Register and Disbursements Journal providing (among others) columns for analysis of debits to be posted to the General ledger. (Use columnar analysis paper.)

(6) Design a general journal. (Use columnar analysis paper.)

(7) Prepare an opening entry in general journal form.

(8) Prepare, in simple debit and credit form, summaries of the month's transactions for recording in the journal which you have designed.

(9) Prepare Balance Sheet as of the end of the first month and Statement of Profits for the first month's operations, omitting (because of lack of information) statistics on average cost of meals.

(10) Describe the method used to properly reflect unpaid suppliers' invoices for interim statements when no accounts payable entries are made or Accounts Payable ledger kept.

Question 10-1

(a) What do you consider the main protective features of autographic registers from an internal-check standpoint?

(b) What do you consider the main protective features of cash registers?

Question 10-2

(a) Name the special features of the source record punch used to record transactions as they occur in a manufacturing plant.

(b) What information does it collect, typically?

Question 10-3

What do forms and equipment manufacturers mean by the term "one-writing systems"? Discuss the use of writing boards in this connection.

Question 10-4

(a) Name some of the control totals that may be accumulated in cash registers.

(b) Name some of the statistics that may be accumulated in cash registers.

Question 10-5

(a) Name the special features of the retail on-line electronic terminal used as a point-of-transaction recorder in retail stores.

(b) What information does it collect, typically?

Chapter 11

Problem 11-1

HOLTON, INC.

Order-Billing Procedure

All orders are received in the morning mail delivery. The orders are sorted from other correspondence and sent to Clerk #1. The orders are always written on the customer's purchase order form for there are no salesmen in the field.

Clerk #1 reviews and edits the order, corrects any incorrect parts numbers, and generally improves the legibility of the order. If the name of the customer is unfamiliar to the clerk, the credit rating of the customer is checked by reference to a credit rating book. If the customer's name is familiar to the clerk, she checks the master customer file to see what terms are allowed the customer and whether or not the customer is on C.O.D. This information is penciled in on the customer's original order. The order is then sent to Clerk #2.

Clerk #2 maintains the perpetual inventory file. The perpetual inventory cards are filed by part number. The list price of each item is shown on these cards. Clerk #2 prices each line item and relieves the inventory of the items on the orders. If the inventory cards show that there are none of a certain item available, the clerk indicates this on the order. The order is then sent to the order typist, Clerk #3. Clerk #2 also attaches a note to the inventory card indicating what customer had ordered the part. When a stock of the item is received, the back order of the customer indicated on the card is pulled from the file and sent to the Shipping department.

Clerk #3 refers to the master customer cards for information as to routing and any special handling. The clerk then types the order in triplicate: the shipping copy, the packing slip, and the order control copy. The customer's original order is attached to the control copy, which is filed numerically in the Order-Billing department. The other two copies of the order are sent to the Shipping department. Clerk #3 also creates a back order which is filed by customer's name.

In the Shipping department, order fillers pull the items from stock and assemble them on the shipping table where they are checked by the Shipping department assistant foreman. If an item is not in stock, it is so indicated on the two copies of the shipping order. If the shipment is to go out parcel post, the postage is computed after the order is packed, and the amount is entered on the two copies of the shipping order. If the order is to go out by truck, the Shipping department prepares four copies of the bill of lading. The original and first copy go to the carrier. The other two copies are clipped to the order. When the shipment has been completed, the order is marked "shipped," and the two copies of the order and the two copies of the bill of lading are sent to the Order-Billing department.

In the Order-Billing department, one copy of the bill of lading is removed and sent to the vouchers payable section. The matching control copy and the customer's original order are pulled from the file and clipped to the documents received from the Shipping department and sent to the billing clerk.

The billing clerk refers to the master customer deck to get the coding for the invoice and pencils this on the order. The code indicates the sales district and distribution channel of the order.

The billing clerk types the invoice from the shipping order. The line items are extended, the postage and freight added, and the invoice is complete. The billing clerk types a back order for those items which the Shipping department indicated were not in stock. The back order is sent to Clerk #2 who corrects the perpetual inventory cards and attaches a note to the inventory card indicating which customer has the item on order. The back order is then filed by customer name.

The extensions and additions on the invoice are checked by Clerk #1. A control tape of the invoices is taken by Clerk #1. The original invoice and two copies along with a copy of the bill of lading are sent to the customer. The fourth copy of the invoice along with the control tape is sent to the Accounting department. This copy is used as a basis for posting to the Accounts Receivable ledger and is then filed by day. The fifth copy of the invoice is attached to the original copy of the shipping order, and filed by invoice number. The third copy of the shipping order is destroyed. The customer's original order and order copy #2 are filed by customer's name if it has been completed. If some items are back-ordered, it is filed in another file by customer's name until such time as all items on the order have been shipped.

Required

Prepare a process chart and forms distribution chart. Revise the system, if necessary, and set up the forms that are needed.

Problem 11-2

MORTON MANUFACTURING COMPANY

Order-Billing Procedure

The Morton Manufacturing Company is a supply house for the electronics market. Most of its business is done with television, radio, and phonograph repairmen throughout the Midwest. Over the past ten years, the order billing procedure has undergone several major revisions as the firm has attempted to improve the procedure. The procedure now followed is outlined below.

The customers' orders are sorted from the incoming mail and passed to the office manager. He edits the order and approves the order for credit and passes it to a pricing clerk.

The pricing clerk prices all items on the order and completes all extensions and additions in pencil on the customer's order. The order is then passed to the order typist.

The order typist types the complete invoice-order set, including extensions and additions. The invoice-order set is composed of five copies. Two of the copies are for the customer and one copy each for the salesman, Accounting department, and Billing department. The typist records the numbers of the invoices typed and sends all five copies to the Shipping department.

The Shipping department pulls from stock all the items listed on the order-invoice. A packing slip and label is prepared after all the available items have been assembled. If the quantity shipped does not agree with the quantity on the order, the shipping clerk pencils in the quantity shipped on the first copy of the invoice-order. The items are then packed and shipped with the packing slip enclosed. The first copy of the invoice-order is stamped and dated as shipped, and all copies are returned to the Order-Billing department.

The order typist checks off on her control list all invoice-orders returned by shipping. The typist retypes all invoice-orders on which changes in the quantity shipped have been made. She also types back orders on the special back-order form for all items ordered but not shipped. The original copy of the back order is sent to the customer. The duplicate is sent to shipping, and the triplicate is filed in the Billing department by customer name. The retyped invoice-orders are extended and footed, and a control is taken of all shipments for the day.

The customer's copies are then mailed; the salesman's copy is sent to the Sales department, the accounting copy to the Accounting department, and the billing copy is filed numerically. The Accounting department uses its copy as follows: posts to Accounts Receivable ledger; enters in sales book for calculating commission; performs sales distribution, including standard journal entry for sales.

Over the past few years, the increase in business and the introduction of many different types of television, radio, and phonograph models has made it difficult to maintain a complete inventory of parts. This inventory problem has created the situation where in approximately 30 per cent of the orders received have items to be back-ordered.

In the past, all orders have been shipped prepaid, freight or postage allowed. A change in policy to bill all shipping charges for orders of less than $75 is to go into effect. Shipping charges will be calculated by the Shipping department after the order is processed.

You are to revise the order billing procedure. If changes are necessary, you are to present your new procedure along with any revised forms.

Forms used by the company appear in Figures 1 through 4.

Question 11-1

In what factors do the savings in complete pre-billing over separate order system and billing procedures lie? Explain the significance of each factor.

Question 11-2

What are some of the factors that limit the application of complete pre-billing, incomplete pre-billing? Explain the significance of each factor.

Question 11-3

(a) Name the clerical operations in an order and billing procedure.

(b) Indicate which clerical operations have to be proved, and state how you might prove each such operation.

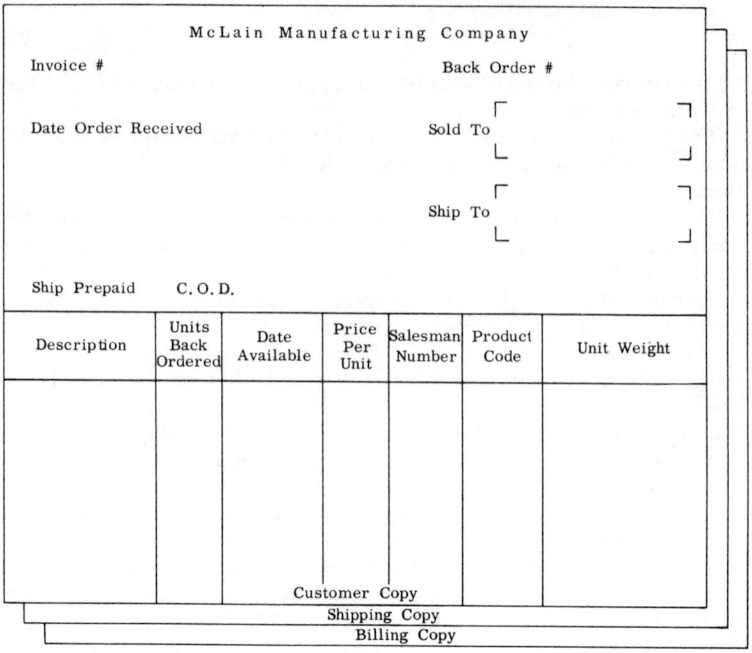

McLain Manufacturing Company

Invoice #   Back Order #

Date Order Received   Sold To

Ship To

Ship Prepaid   C. O. D.

Description	Units Back Ordered	Date Available	Price Per Unit	Salesman Number	Product Code	Unit Weight

Customer Copy
Shipping Copy
Billing Copy

Figure 1. Back Order

Figure 2. Invoice Order

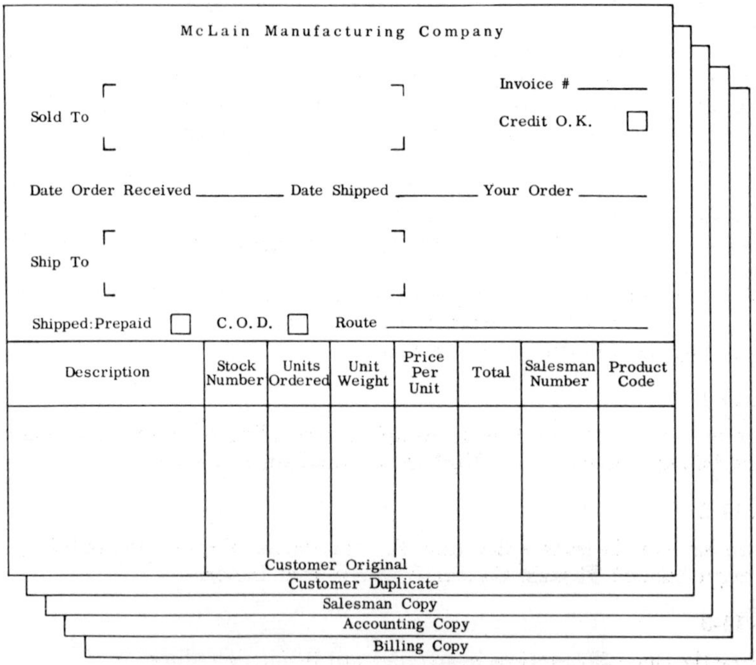

McLain Manufacturing Company

Sold To   Invoice # _____

Credit O. K. ☐

Date Order Received _____ Date Shipped _____ Your Order _____

Ship To

Shipped: Prepaid ☐   C. O. D. ☐   Route _____

Description	Stock Number	Units Ordered	Unit Weight	Price Per Unit	Total	Salesman Number	Product Code

Customer Original
Customer Duplicate
Salesman Copy
Accounting Copy
Billing Copy

McLain Manufacturing Company

Ship To　　　　　　　　Sold To

Route ______________________　Date Shipped ______________

Description	Units	Unit Weight	Unit Price	Total	Product Code

Packing Slip

Figure 3. Packing Slip

SHIP TO

SHIPPED FROM

Figure 4. Label

Question 11-4

Note the following two definitions:

A *contract order* is a type of blanket order covering the customer's requirements for a period of time. It specifies or is based upon an understanding as to delivery dates. If it is a mixed order (calling for a variety of items), different dates may apply to different items on the order.

A *back order* is a shipping order covering a portion of a previous shipping order that could not be shipped because of lack of stock. In many cases, the back-order situation is wholly undesirable as far as both the customer and the management are concerned. If a back-order condition exists, however, the order (and billing) procedure must obviously provide for the paper work.

Explain what differences you would expect to find between an order and billing procedure designed for contract shipments and one designed for simple back orders, where the great majority of orders are shipped complete immediately.

Question 11-5

In some companies, it is not possible to use a shipping order set of a fixed number of copies because of varying numbers of copies required for (a) goods manufactured to order and goods shipped from stock, (b) different shipping points for different products, and (c) possibly, differences between "at once" shipments and future shipments. Likewise, it is not possible to use an invoice set of a fixed number of copies because of different customer requirements. Some customers want one copy, some two, and so on. (Also some customers want extra copies sent to special addresses, such as home office.)

Explain how varying copy requirements are provided for in (1) carbon paper and (2) duplicating methods of reproduction.

Question 11-6

Discuss the main features of order and billing by integrated data processing as explained in Chapter 11.

Question 11-7

(a) What are some of the factors that might be stored in the memory of an automatic writing machine used in an order and billing system application?

(b) How would the existence of each of these factors in memory affect the billing operation?

Chapter 12

Problem 12-1

Using the survey data in the following table:

(1) State what basic plan or combination of plans you would use for the distribution of sales.
(2) Design any forms that you would use.
(3) Write an operations list, showing separately (a) daily, (b) weekly, and (c) monthly operations necessary to produce the desired reports.
(4) List the several plans that you did not use in your solution, and explain why you did not use each plan. In each case, state the factors in the survey data that caused you to eliminate the plan.
(5) If you believe that an alternate plan should be presented to your client for his consideration, describe the plan and state why you believe it worthy of consideration.

Survey Data for Sales Distribution

(1) Number of classifications involved in the problem.	Product, channel of distribution.
(2) Number of accounts in each classification.	Three products, seven channels.
(3) Activity of the accounts in a typical period.	Activity in each of the 21 accounts each day; 90 per cent of the activity is confined to four channels in each product classification.
(4) What totals and subtotals are desired in the monthly journal entry?	Grand totals, product totals.
(5) What supporting records are required. Frequency, totals and subtotals. What information is shown?	Daily sales of each product in dollars and sales of each product through the seven channels in dollars.
(6) Are posted details required for current reference, or are reports showing totals of accounts in the classification considered adequate by management?	Totals only are required.

(7) What is the amount of the average transaction?	Average $24.00 per invoice.
(8) If detail posting is required, is any description required?	Question not applicable.
(9) Frequency of posting media.	Daily.
(10) Are the media unit or mixed?	Two of the products are shown on one invoice. The third type of product is shown on separate invoices.
(11) What is the quantity per day?	95 invoices a day.
(12) If the media are mixed, what is the average number of postings per medium?	1⅓
(13) Are the media coded when received for distribution?	Yes
(14) In what size batches do the media come for distribution? What is the frequency of the batches?	One batch per day.
(15) What is the sorted arrangement of media when received for distribution?	Invoices are sorted by product: either product 1 and 2 or product 2. Pre-list tape accompanies each batch.

Question 12-1

A janitors' supply concern handles 150 items. Analysis of its sales indicates that 95 per cent are in some 45 items. The other 5 per cent are necessary to the line to service the customers completely. The company has 150 salesmen, each of whom averages 10 orders a day. There are generally only one or two slow items on an order. It is vital that a quick, inexpensive method of entry on the stock control be developed.

What would you suggest?

Question 12-2

Name all the methods of distribution discussed in Chapter 12.

Question 12-3

Name all the factors affecting the selection of a distribution method discussed in Chapter 12.

Question 12-4

Explain how certain factors in the selection of a distribution method for a particular problem can eliminate one or more of the methods of distribution, and consequently how consideration of all the factors is likely to eliminate all the methods except one or two. In answering this question, discuss each of the factors in order, taking the whole list, and be as specific as possible.

Question 12-5

(a) Name the methods of handling mixed media in connection with the various distribution methods.

(b) Which methods of handling mixed media are likely to be used with each distribution method?

Question 12-6

What is the purpose of the converter used in connection with edge punched cards?

Question 12-7

(a) In a certain company, one executive insists that the sales report showing totals by product should be prepared week by week. Another executive says that once a month is often enough. In general, how does frequency of distribution affect the clerical cost of the distribution?

(b) Name other quantitative factors that affect the clerical cost of a distribution procedure.

Question 12-8

Assume that the average sales transaction is of significant amount and that the management desires a record of individual transactions by salesmen with a one- or two-word description of the item sold. A transaction-by-transaction follow-up of the salesmen is desired by the sales manager. Which of the methods of distribution provides such reference possibility?

Question 12-9

It is sometimes said that mixed media should always be reduced to unit media in order to facilitate distribution. Does this statement hold true for all the basic methods of distribution? Explain.

Question 12-10

(a) It is said that in designing a sales distribution (or any other type of distribution), the entire procedure for recording sales from the moment the original record is produced must be studied. Explain how a step that is preliminary to the actual distribution procedure can affect the method of distribution itself.

(b) In connection with sales distribution, what do you think is meant by distribution at the source? Give an example.

Question 12-11

It is said that some of the basic methods of distribution yield a report directly without copying, or at least a record that can be referred to directly by the interested user of the statistics. Discuss this point, with specific reference to the various basic methods of distribution.

Chapter 13

Problem 13-1

UNIVERSAL ELECTRONICS COMPANY

(Survey information on pages 587-588)

Write instructions stating changes that are necessary to control accounts receivable. Include instructions on how to make the monthly proof.

Problem 13-2

The Roycemore Publishing Company operates a file of 500,000 subscribers' cards against which it checks subscription orders as they come in to determine whether a subscription is new or a renewal and, if the latter, to verify names and addresses, expiration dates, duplications, and so on. The file is strictly alphabetical by subscriber's name.

The peak season for new subscriptions is November and December, since at that time the company makes a special price for orders on which there are three or more subscriptions. Most of the orders that are received are multiple orders (since no one would send in a single order if it were at all feasible to send in a multiple order and get the advantage of the reduced price). The average order calls for three subscriptions.

The fact that the media are mixed makes it difficult for the file girls to locate cards. The files are being used for what amounts to random posting. Each girl takes a few orders and goes through them one name after the other. This makes it necessary for the girl to roam over the entire file of 500,000 cards. In the peak season, 15 girls are required to operate the files. (On a Monday, there will be 14,000 subscriptions.) Because of the random-posting method which each girl uses, a number of them might have to check the same drawer at the same time. In fact, the girls do waste a great deal of time lining up at the same drawer.

You are required to devise a remedy for this situation.

Problem 13-3

The Martin Publishing Company publishes a monthly magazine with a circulation of about 400,000. The company takes subscriptions on a credit basis and operates the accounts receivable by ledgerless bookkeeping by filing copies of invoices alphabetically.

The invoices are typed on a seven-part continuous form. The original copy is the usual invoice to the customer; one carbon copy is the file copy, and the remaining five copies are follow-up copies. Serial numbers are pre-printed on the forms. The stencils which are used to address mailings of the magazine are cut from the original invoice before it is sent to the customer. The stencils, which show the invoice number, are filed by state, city, and customer. The alphabetical sorting and filing of follow-up copies requires considerable time in the busy season when there are as many as 1,500 invoice sets a day.

The credit follow-up must be very strict in this business, otherwise subscribers would receive a number of issues of the magazine without having made any payment to the company. The follow-up days are the first and fifteenth of each month, but no follow-up is made on a new customer until the second regular follow-up date after the receipt of his subscription. (In other words, if a subscription is received on the tenth of the month, no follow-up is mailed him on the fifteenth. Thus, a number of days of grace in which to pay are given the customer without bothering him with a follow-up.)

The operation of pulling the follow-up copies of the statements and mailing them is a time-consuming one, since there are sometimes as many as 60,000 sets of statements in the active files at one time. On each follow-up date, the file clerks pull each statement set out of the file, examine the date of billing, and if the billing date is more than fifteen days old, tear off a copy of the statement and put it in one or another file, depending upon whether it is a first statement, a second, or a third, and so on.

A series of collection letters is sent out with the statements. Each first statement receives a friendly letter, and each fifth statement receives a letter which threatens cancellation. Before mailing the statements, they are sorted into piles: firsts, seconds, thirds, and so on, so that they can be matched with the appropriate collection letter for mailing.

Most customers pay in full in a single payment, and they send in a statement top, showing name and invoice number, with the remittance. After the cash is separated from the statement tops in the mail room, the statements tops are sent to the Accounts Receivable department. Here they are sorted alphabetically and used to pull the appropriate sets of statements out of file. Each fully paid statement is then stamped "paid" and put in the paid file. Ninety-five per cent of the remittances are accompanied by statement tops.

You are asked to design a simpler method of:

(1) Putting new invoice sets into the file.

(2) Applying cash receipts to the invoice sets.

(3) Pulling statement copies for follow-up.

Write your answers in the form of a formal report, addressed to your client. Explain the handling of remittances received not accompanied by statement tops.

Problem 13-4

A four-part invoice is used by the Cranston Bookstore for charge sales. The four copies all have distinctive colors and are used as follows:

Copy	Use
Original	Accounts receivable
1st copy	Sales copy
2nd copy	Statement
3rd copy	To customer at time of sale

There are approximately 125 charge sales a day. The accounts receivable copy and statement copy are filed by customer at the end of day. At the end of the month, the sales copies are totaled and a journal entry made as follows:

Accounts receivable	$xx	
Sales		$xx

The statement copy is taken out of the customer's file at the end of the month, adding machine statement in duplicate is prepared to which the statement copy is attached, and the statement is forwarded to the customer.

Since most accounts are paid within the the month, it is necessary to prepare only a few statements for past-due accounts, and this presents very little difficulty.

The clerks prepare the original invoice and copies in one writing at the time of sale.

The store owner is very happy with his system, except for two particulars, and will not permit major changes. His objections are:

(1) The accounts receivable control is regularly out of balance.

(2) Statements are not ready for customers until about the middle of the succeeding month.

What improvements can you suggest in the present methods to help overcome the objections?

Problem 13-5

A company makes most of its sales on the installment plan. When an installment sale is made, a customer's payment card is set up, a portion of which is shown below:

Installment due: 15th of month Amount $25.00			
Payment Record			
Instal. No.	Due Date	Date Paid	Balance
	Initial loan		$500.00
1	Oct. 15	Oct. 15, 19—	475.00
2	Nov. 15	Nov. 12, 19—	450.00
3	Dec. 15	Dec. 18, 19—	425.00
4	Jan. 15	Dec. 18, 19—	400.00
5	Feb. 15	Jan. 15, 19—	375.00

Because of the setup on its customer cards, the company will accept no irregular payments in excess of a full installment (*e.g.,* $35.00) or less than an installment (*e.g.,* $15). Excess amounts (the $10.00) are refunded by check, and under payments (the $15.00) are either held by the cashier without entry until a full payment is received or returned to the customer with a demand for full payment. About 99 per cent of the customers pay one or more full installments at a time.

The company likes its customers' card system very much because it can very readily determine past-due and advance payments. Do you have any suggestion for handling the irregular payment situation?

Question 13-1

Name and distinguish the types of statement used in customer accounting.

Question 13-2

Name the basic methods of posting customers' accounts.

Question 13-3

(a) What is meant by the statement that, in machine bookkeeping, the sales journal can be prepared as a by-product of posting the customers' accounts?

(b) What is meant by the statement that the cash receipts journal can be prepared as a by-product of posting cash receipts to the customers' accounts?

Question 13-4

Explain fully why preparation of media for posting to *Accounts Receivable ledger* (debits) may be simpler than preparation for machine posting to the *Expense ledger.*

Question 13-5

In connection with machine posting of customers' accounts, name the book-keeping machine proofs with which you are familiar.

Question 13-6

Set up an operations list for a large-volume Accounts Receivable department, showing all steps in the movement of batches of sales invoices or sales tickets. Assume that a large number of ledgers is maintained and that the ledgers are machine posted on a daily basis with running balances carried in the accounts.

Question 13-7

(a) Set up an operations list for a large-volume cycle billing operation, showing all the steps in the movement of batches of sales invoices through mailing the statements.

(b) Discuss the reasons for including microfilming in the system.

Question 13-8

Referring to Question 13-7, upon what factors does the clerical economy of cycle billing depend?

Problem 13-9

The Houghton Company operates a wholesaling business. Accounts receivable are posted by machine, and the functions of the receiving cashier and the accounts receivable bookkeeper are separate. The management believes that the procedure for receiving cash and crediting customers accounts comprises more steps than are actually necessary for the control of incoming cash. You are called in to examine the procedure and outline a new one that will be simpler to operate.

The steps in the existing procedure are:

(1) The mail clerk opens the mail and writes a blotter, listing the amounts of cash and the names of customers to be credited. Sends the cash, in the original envelopes, to the receiving cashier. Sends the blotter to the treasurer.

(2) The receiving cashier takes the cash out of the envelopes and makes unit posting media out of the envelopes. Since the envelopes already bear the name and address of the customer (return name and address), it is only necessary to write the amount of the remittance on the outside of the envelope. The receiving cashier balances the cash against the envelopes, sends the envelopes to the Accounts Receivable department, and keeps the cash.

(3) In the Accounts Receivable department, the cash application clerk applies each remittance by (a) locating the customer's account and (b) checking off the invoices which the remittance covers evenly. He computes the discount and enters it on the envelope. Where it appears that the customer has taken allowances or discounts to which he is not entitled or where the check is obviously in error, the cash application clerk indicates the fact on the envelope. He sends all envelopes back to the receiving cashier.

(4) The receiving cashier types up a posting medium for each account to be credited (*i.e.*, for each envelope), except for the ones that are in error. (He prepares a cash receipts record as a carbon copy of the posting media.) He sends posting tickets to the Accounts Receivable department, and the incorrect remittances to the Credit department (where the credit manager writes to the customer, returning the check).

(5) The accounts receivable ledger operator posts the media to the customers accounts and proves against the cashier's total.

Required:

(a) Outline the new procedure.
(b) Name the steps in the old procedure that you consider unnecessary.

Question 13-10

Name the basic methods of recording credits to customers' accounts for cash received.

Question 13-11

Explain the types of records that a receiving cashier may keep for (1) getting a record of individual amounts to be credited to customers' accounts and (2) compiling control totals for the daily journal entry covering cash receipts on accounts.

Question 13-12

Some concerns believe it necessary to verify each discount at the time the remittance is received and to return the check to the customer immediately if he has taken an improper discount. Explain the steps by which the check is determined incorrect and returned to the customer.

Question 13-13

Explain the basic differences in procedure for receiving cash on customers' accounts as between (a) a manufacturing concern and (b) a retail department store.

Chapter 14

Question 14-1

What are the usual follow-up functions performed by the Purchasing department?

Question 14-2

Internal check in a purchase and payment procedure should establish for each purchase that the goods were requested by a person who has authority to request, and certain other particulars. Name as many of the other particulars as you can.

Question 14-3

It has been stated that the Purchasing department is the logical department to certify on purchase invoices that the quantities shown by the invoices were actually ordered and were actually received. It is contended that the Purchasing department must receive a copy of the receiving report and match it with the purchase order to perform its normal function of following up purchase orders, and that the Purchasing department might as well certify the invoices (for quantities received) at the same time.

Comment upon this statement.

Question 14-4

(a) What is meant by a "blind check" of quantities in the Receiving department?

(b) How does the fact that a blind check is desired affect the design of forms used by the Purchasing department and the Receiving department?

(c) Discuss the pros and cons of blind check.

Question 14-5

(a) What would be gained by combining the purchase-order set with the receiving-report set?

(b) How would the combining be accomplished under carbon paper methods? Under duplicating methods?

(c) What limitations are there upon such combining?

Chapter 15

Problem 15-1

UNIVERSAL ELECTRONICS COMPANY

(*Survey information on pages 643-644*)

(a) Outline the procedure for a simple voucher system. Take details of handling it away from the owner. He still should approve all purchases and payments.

(b) Design a statistical record showing the running balances daily of vouchers payable to the manufacturer of the radios, and the orders that have been placed but not received. Total these two balances in an additional column. Show cash payments and balances. Illustrate, by making up your own figures, how Mr. Olsen can easily see his credit limit and payments that must be made in order to make future purchases.

Problem 15-2

The Jordan Printing Company operates a plant for printing catalogs and magazines. It employs about 400 men in the factory and office and clears about 200 purchase and expense invoices a month. The following departments are maintained:

Administrative and accounting	Press room
Sales (10 salesmen)	Bindery
Composing room	Shipping room

The company has been in existence for about forty years. In the early years, during the active managment of the founder, profits were high. Recently, however, large dividends were drawn out of the business, and no purchases of new presses have been made to keep the company in a competitive position. Sales have shrunk from over a million dollars a year to less than half a million dollars. Currently, the company shows a small profit or a small loss each month.

The same bookkeeper has kept the books for the last thirty years. There has been almost no change in the accounting system in that period. All the expense accounts are kept in the General ledger and conventional T-account forms are used. The accounts are arranged in alphabetical order in the ledger, and the bookkeeper has difficulty making it balance. Operating statements come out about 20 days after the close of the month. The expense statement is simply a list of the balances of the expense accounts for the month.

The company does about 80 jobs a month. Actual job order costs are kept on the jobs, and as each job is finished the bookkeeper makes a report to the manager of cost, selling price, and profit or loss. The job order costs are not tied to the general books, however, and the profit or loss on the statement of profits for a month never agrees with the profit or loss figure obtained from the cost sheets. This always upsets the manager, who keeps his own record of profit or loss on the jobs closed as shown him by the bookkeeper, and who therefore has his own idea of what the statement of profits should show.

The company has several estimators who set up estimates for all jobs on which the company bids. The president of the company is the head salesman, and he sets the selling price on the basis of the estimate, shading it as much as he thinks is necessary to get the business. Estimates cover the following elements separately:

Paper	Cylinder press labor and press
Ink	Bindery labor and expense
Composing labor and expense	Total labor and expense
Job press labor and expense	Outside purchases

No comparison of actual costs by elements with estimate costs by element is made.

Perpetual inventories are kept for paper and ink, but, as indicated previously, the charges to job cost sheets are not controlled by the General ledger. On the monthly statement of profits, an adjustment is made to the cost of production for the cost of jobs in process at the beginning and end of the month as shown by the job costs sheets.

Required:

(1) Design general journal, voucher register, and a set of expense accounts to reduce the length of the General ledger trial balance. Provide such object ac-

counts for each department as you deem appropriate. Explain why your forms and the procedure for their use will help to eliminate trial balance trouble.

(2) Explain how you propose to put the job costs under control.

(3) Design a job cost sheet.

(4) Design a finished goods journal which will serve: (a) to compile credits to Work in Process, and (b) as a list of completed jobs showing the profit or loss on each job. This list will take the place of the informal list which the manager keeps in his desk.

Problem 15-3

(a) Using the survey data in the accompanying table, select a method of distributing purchase and expense invoices. Design the necessary distribution forms and describe the method of handling the media through the distribution procedure.

(b) Name the methods you have eliminated and state why you eliminated them. In each case, refer to the factors in the survey data that were controlling factors in your decision.

Factor	*Data for Problem*
(1) Type of expense or procedure classification.	Compound classification, function subdivided by object.
(2) What totals and subtotals are desired (frequency)?	Total of each function, subtotals of each object—monthly.
(3) If detail posting is required, what description is required?	Date and name of vendor.
(4) Number of accounts in the classification.	12 functions—40 accounts.
(5) Are expense accounts operated on a cash basis or accrual basis?	Accrual basis.
(6) What media are used for distribution?	Purchase invoices.
(7) Are the media unit or mixed?	Invoices are mixed; $1\frac{1}{2}$ debits each.
(8) What is the quantity of media per month?	800.
(9) What is the sorted arrangement of media received for distribution?	Invoices received in serial number order with control tape.
(10) What percentage of the accounts in the classification have low enough activity to justify putting them in the "miscellaneous" group?	5 per cent.

Question 15-1

What are the advantages of operating a one-time voucher system as against a built-up voucher system? What are the disadvantages?

Question 15-2

What are the advantages of operating a one-time voucher system as against an accounts payable system? What are the disadvantages?

Question 15-3

Why does the treasurer stamp the invoices "paid" before he returns them to the Accounting department?

Question 15-4

What are the advantages of operating a separate check and voucher system as against a combined voucher-check? What are the disadvantages?

Question 15-5

(a) Name classifications frequently used in expense distribution in manufacturing concerns.

(b) Name classifications frequently used in the distribution of merchandise purchases and expense purchases in retail stores.

Chapter 16

Problem 16-1

The manager of the Jordan Printing Company asks your advice on controls for indirect labor in the composing room. He feels that the company is making a small profit on all elements of cost except composing room labor. That the composing room is losing money is confirmed by the fact that although the current billing rate for hand composition is $4.50 an hour, the actual cost to the company (determined by simply dividing composing room payroll by direct labor hours) is $5.87. The Jordan Printing Company sells composition to other printers as well to its own customers.

The manager says that due to the difficulty of getting customers to submit their copy when promised the composing room foreman often calls out more compositors than are actually needed. He assigns them to do indirect labor work instead of sending them home (which is not permitted by the union). Examples of such work are as follows:

Supervision	Handling copy
Handling plates	Oiling
Handling cuts	Changing bad letters or
Proof press	characters
Melting metal	Idle time
Receiving instructions	Repairs
Distribution (returning	Errands
type to cases)	Miscellaneous

Workmen doing indirect labor in the composing room indicate the classification on their job tickets, but no record is made of it in the Bookkeeping department. All composing room labor, both direct and indirect, is charged to a single account in the General ledger.

Required:

(1) Design the control report which you would recommend to the manager. Explain how the manager would know whether the expenditure for indirect labor is excessive.
(2) Design the timekeeping forms required to produce the control report.
(3) Explain the labor distribution procedure.

Question 16-1

A large company with about 5,000 widely scattered employees frequently needs certain of its qualified employees for special jobs. Generally, these people must be located very quickly. The company does not wish to use its mechanical accounting equipment for this purpose as it would involve upsetting the accounting functions often. Have you any suggestions?

Question 16-2

Why are timekeeping records frequently obtained from two different sources; that is, from the Timekeeping department and from the "Shop" department?

Question 16-3

The ABC Company operates on a standard one-shift basis, all employees starting at 9 A.M. and finishing at 5 P.M. Would you recommend a horizontal or a vertical clock card? Why?

Chapter 17

Problem 17-1

UNIVERSAL ELECTRONICS COMPANY

(Survey information on pages 643–644)

Outline a procedure for payroll. Make the payroll record a journal. Salesmen are paid a commission based upon the dollar value of each week's sales. Payrolls are paid weekly.

Problem 17-2

The Rashel Supply Company is a wholesale supply firm. In the past five years, the number of hourly employees increased from 35 to 110.

The operation at Rashel has been divided into four departments by type of product handled. Each hourly employee is assigned to one of the four departments. Because of various amounts of activity, an employee may be used in two, three, or even four departments during any given day.

Each employee punches in and out each day on the weekly time card. (See Figure 16-7). Each day he records the time he spends in the various departments on the daily time sheet.

At the end of each day, the employee submits his daily time sheet to the foreman of his regular department for approval. The foreman reviews the time sheet, signs it, and sends it to the Payroll department.

At the end of the week, the Payroll department sorts all the daily time sheets by employee. The number of hours on each line and for each day are computed for each employee. All the time sheets for a given employee are clipped together and the number of hours worked during the week is written on the last sheet. The total is compared to the total hours worked as shown by the time card. Any discrepancies are reconciled by the Payroll department and the Operating department foreman.

After the time sheets and the time cards are in agreement, the time sheets are sent to another payroll clerk. The payroll clerk prepares the payroll register. In preparing the register he uses the time cards for the hours worked, the pay rate cards to obtain the employee's hourly rate, the deduction card showing all the standard deductions and exemptions for the employee, and any other miscellaneous deduction cards for purchases and donations by the employee.

When the register is completed, it is sent to Payroll Clerk #3, who manually prepares the earnings statement, the quarterly earnings record, and the pay check. Each document is an original document. After these documents have been prepared, a tape is taken of the earnings statement, the pay checks, and the payroll register to see if the totals agree. When all totals are in agreement, the payroll check numbers for each employee are entered in the appropriate column on the payroll register. The checks are then taken to the proper officials for signature and distribution.

The time sheets are used in the Cost department to get the labor distribution. The time sheets are divided between two clerks in this department, each of whom handles the distribution for two of the operating departments. Division of the time sheets is based on the employee's regular department.

There is a distribution sheet for each department. The clerk enters the employee's name and the hours he worked in this department during each of the five or six days in the week. The clerks usually post all the hours for one department before posting the hours for the second department. After completely posting their respective batches, the clerks exchange batches and repeat the procedure.

When all the hours have been posted and cross-footed, the clerks obtain the hourly rate of each employee from his pay-rate card. The clerk extends and foots the dollar charges to get the total labor charge for the department.

The total of the labor charges for all four departments is then proved against the total of the gross pay column on the payroll register. Usually the clerks spend several hours bringing these figures into agreement.

Forms used in the present payroll system are illustrated in Figures 5 through 9.

Describe the new forms, equipment, and procedures you would use to improve the payroll and labor distribution procedures.

Problem 17-3

(a) Using the survey data in the following table, select a method of distributing labor charges. Design the necessary distribution forms and describe the method of handling the media through the distribution procedure.

(b) Name the methods you have eliminated and state why you eliminated them. In each case, refer to the factors in the survey data that were controlling factors in your decision.

Daily Time Sheet					
Date	Name	Department	In	Out	Hours

Foreman Approval _____ Total Hours _____

Rate   Total Dollars _____

Figure 5. Daily Time Sheet

Statement of Earnings					

Employee _____ Date _____

Gross Pay	Federal OAB	Withholding Tax	Insurance	Miscellaneous	Net Pay

Figure 6. Statement of Earnings

Individual Wage Record						
Employee _____						
Date	Federal OAB	Withholding Tax	Insurance	Misc.	Gross	Net

Figure 7. Individual Wage Record

Payroll Register							
Date	Check #	Name	Gross Pay	Fed. OAB	Withholding Tax	Ins.	Misc.	Net.

Figure 8. Payroll Register

Distribution Sheet		Department							
Date (Week Ending)	Name	Hours							
		Mon	Tues	Wed	Thurs	Fri	Sat	Total Hrs.	Total $

Figure 9. Distribution Sheet

Problem 17-3–Survey Data

Factor	Direct Labor	Indirect Labor
(1) Type of classification of labor accounts.	Production Order department.	Department; operation.
(2) Number of accounts in each classification.	300 production orders per month—10 labor operations.	6 departments—6 operations. No one department has more than five operations.
(3) Activity of the classifications.	About 50 production orders are active at any one time. A typical order takes from three to seven days. It is very seldom that any order will require more than eight labor operations.	Usually there is activity in every existing account each week.
(4) What totals and subtotals are desired and with what frequency?	Monthly total of direct labor is required for monthly standard journal entry. Monthly total of labor in each department. Weekly total of labor in each department. Total labor on each order on the week end after completion of the order.	Monthly total of indirect labor for standard journal entry. Monthly total of indirect labor in each department and each operation. Weekly total of indirect labor in each department.
(5) Media used for distribution.	Daily time report for each employee for each job he may work on during the day. Average number of jobs is 1½.	Weekly time sheet for each employee in each department.
(6) Sorted arrangement of media received for distribution.	Cost clerk receives daily time cards daily in employee number order.	Cost clerk receives weekly time sheet in employee number order.

Question 17-1

A particular bookkeeping machine or writing machine to be considered for preparation of paychecks and related forms (employees quarterly earnings records and payroll) may comprise some combination of the following features:

Punched card/punched paper tape input
Punched card/punched paper tape output
Numeric keyboard
Alpha-numeric keyboard
Add-subtract capability
Calculating (add-subtract-multiply-divide) capability
Non-magnetic ledger (employees quarterly earnings records)
Magnetic ledger (employees quarterly earnings records)
Storage (memory) for storing programs and accumulating totals

There are a number of bookkeeping machines and writing machines illustrated in this book that can be considered for payroll work. Name some of the machines and state some one combination of the above features that can be incorporated in each machine. (It is recognized that there might be several possible combinations for one particular machine. You are asked to name one combination for each machine.)

Question 17-2

Does the combination of features (in Question 17-1) in a particular bookkeeping or writing machine affect the type(s) of input forms for the machine and the pre-payroll processing necessary for those forms? Explain, giving several specific examples.

Question 17-3

Some machines on the market are designed for use as a writing machine or a computer. They are desk size, and they have keyboard(s), computing and logical capabilities, and memory.

Assuming that you intended to use such a machine as a computer with punched card input and punched card output, how would you produce the weekly pay checks and payroll? How would you produce the annual IRS forms 941a and W-2?

Chapter 18

Question 18-1

(a) Describe the basic types of production control procedures.
(b) What managerial information is required for each type of production control procedure.

Question 18-2

Outline the main considerations in the design of a production control procedure.

Question 18-3

(a) Discuss the use of duplicating methods in connection with the reproduction of copies of the production order and related forms.

(b) What types of equipment would you consider for use where scheduling and follow-up of production orders is one of the main problems in the operation of the production control procedure?

Question 18-4

Name the types of filing equipment you might consider for housing perpetual inventory accounts in a new procedure that you are designing for a manufacturing company.

Question 18-5

(a) Name some methods of pricing requisitions that you might consider in connection with a perpetual inventory procedure for a manufacturing company.

(b) Discuss the procedures design features that would have to be incorporated in a perpetual inventory procedure to facilitate pricing according to one of the pricing methods that you named in your answer to part (a).

Chapter 19*

Problem 19-1

Cost Ledger: Metropolitan Manufacturing Company

I. *Information about the Business—Nature of the Assignment*

The Lake Shore Manufacturing Company operates a metal stamping plant. It employs about 150 men and women in the factory who operate shears, punch presses, rollers, brake presses, welding equipment, etc. The following departments are maintained:

Shear
Punch press (including brake presses)
Die shop
Assembly (including rollers, welding equipment, etc.)
Finishing room (painting, etc.)
Material handling
General factory
Selling and Administrative

The company was incorporated in 1920 and had accumulated a substantial earned surplus through 1952, due primarily to operations during the period from 1941 through 1949, but since 1952 the profits have been good in one year and poor in other years depending upon the kind of jobs performed during the period. In the past two years the company operations reflected small losses.

A double-entry set of books is maintained by the bookkeeper; the accounts are arranged in alphabetical order, and operating statements are prepared quarterly based upon an estimated inventory submitted by the plant superintendent. Once each year, a physical inventory is taken and the books are closed based upon such inventory.

* The requirements of the cost system problem in this chapter are divided into parts which can be handled as a series of separate assignments. See the requirements for Problem 19-1 on pages 625-628. Background chapters for the solution of these problems are Chapters 1, 2, 3, 4, 5, 18 and 19; consequently, if it is desired to present a cost accounting problem early in the course, Chapters 6 through 17 can be deferred until after Chapters 18 and 19 have been assigned.

The factory completes about 200 jobs per month and usually has about 60 jobs in operation at one time. Jobs average four operations, and a memorandum record of each job is maintained by the office showing:

(a) Material cost of steel, component parts (manufactured by the company) and purchased parts.
(b) Productive labor hours and cost.

As each job is completed, the above data is summarized by the office, and the unit cost of material and productive labor is compared with the selling price per unit to determine the prime gross profit dollar amount per unit and the ratio to the selling price. These job costs are not reconciled with the General ledger material and labor costs.

The company has two estimators who prepare estimates for all jobs on which the selling price is computed by them as follows:

(1) Material cost of steel, purchased parts, etc., plus 5 per cent scrap allowance.
(2) Material handling charge based upon $.005 per lb. of steel used on the job.
(3) Productive labor based upon estimated labor hours at a standard rate of $1.75 per hour.
(4) Factory burden at 175 per cent of productive labor dollars in (3) above.
(5) Total factory cost is the sum of items (1) through (4) above.
(6) Selling price is 125 per cent of total factory cost to cover selling and administrative expenses, cash discount, and profit.

With the foregoing information, management establishes quoted selling prices based upon their experience with competition. In some instances where customers supply the material, selling price is based upon cost items (2) through (4) plus 160 per cent of total factory cost.

The management believes that the foregoing method of computing factory cost and selling prices is unsatisfactory since the company is obtaining jobs using the larger presses but is losing the small press jobs. In addition assembly jobs including welding are being lost to competitors because of the high factory burden rate. Hence the small presses are having more and more idle time, whereas the large presses cannot handle the volume.

The management requests that your study should observe the following objectives:

(a) Recognize the variation in factory burden expense applicable to each size of press or other machine.
(b) Establish a job cost system which can be reconciled with the General ledger.
(c) Provide daily reconcilement of machine labor hours by jobs with daily hours shown on the payroll records.
(d) Provide for monthly financial statements which will incorporate the job cost system and departmental operations.
(e) Establish machine hourly cost rates by departments which combine productive labor and factory burden.

II. *System Man's Notes on the Present Procedure*

(1) The old accounts used are shown on page 624. The names of the departments responsible for each type of expense are noted in this list on the right.

Note that if no specific department (factory) is responsible, the list indicates "general factory."

(2) Establish General ledger account numbers by using 2-digit prefix for departments, etc. and 2 digit-suffix for kind of item. For example:

Prefix numbers suggested:

10 to 14 for asset accounts
15 to 16 for liability and net worth accounts
17 for sales and purchase accounts
18 for miscellaneous income and miscellaneous expense accounts
20 to 29 for factory labor and expense accounts
30 for sales expenses and 31 for administrative expenses

Suggested examples:

1001 would be Cash on Deposit; 1101 for Customers Accounts Receivable; 1401 for Machinery and Equipment; 1501 would Bank Loan; 1701 for Sales —Stampings; 1751 for Steel Purchases; 2001 for Shear Department Productive Labor, etc.

(3) Factory and office budget estimates for the ensuing year:

			Machine Hours	
Departments	Payroll	Other Expense	Capacity (hours)	Normal (per cent)
Shear	$ 12,000	$ 8,000	6,000	80
Press—				
Large	120,000	72,000	20,000	80
Small	60,000	40,000	30,000	60
Die shop	24,000	18,000	18,000	60
Assembly	100,000	40,000	80,000	80
Finishing	40,000	24,000	20,000	75
Material handling—	40,000	12,000		
Estimated weight of				
steel—6,000 tons				
General factory	30,000	90,000		
Total factory	$426,000	304,000		
Selling	24,000	60,000		
Administrative	30,000	16,000		
Total budget	$480,000	$380,000		

(4) The following journals are to be established:

For the General Ledger

(a) Voucher register to record—
Steel purchases—showing weight and amount
Purchased parts—dollar amount
Factory supplies
Factory expenses
Selling expenses   } showing account number and dollar
Administrative expenses   amount
Other items

(b) Check register showing date issued, check number, payee, amount of check, voucher number, vouchers payable amount, discounts earned, and sundry account number and amount.

(c) Payroll journal showing date of check, check number, payee, check amount, F.I.C.A. and withholding tax deduction, group insurance deduction, etc., suffix account number, and dollar amount of each labor account to be charged. Note that employees are to be listed in departmental groups.

This weekly payroll journal will be summarized for the month (four- or five-week period) and is the basis for standard monthly journal entry #1.

(d) Sales journal showing invoice date, invoice number, name of customer, invoice amount, column for the four classifications of sales, namely: stampings, dies, assembly, and miscellaneous; and sundry columns for account number and dollar amount.

(e) Credit memo journal, showing information similar to sales journal.

(f) Cash receipts journal showing date of deposit, payor, amount received, discount allowed, credit to customer's account, and sundry columns for account number and dollar amount.

(g) Standard monthly general journal, including the following monthly entries:

#1 Payroll accruals from monthly labor or payroll summary indicated in (c) above

#2 Vacation and holiday pay, payroll taxes, compensation insurance, group insurance based upon payroll in entry #1 above

#3 Depreciation

#4 Personal property tax accrual

#5 Prepaid insurance writeoffs based upon estimates

#6 Sales commissions based upon commission statements to agents

#7 Material requisitions charging die repair materials to large and small press departments and crediting Purchase account.

(h) Special general journal to provide for non-recurring entries.

For the Cost Ledger

(i) Material requisition journal showing date, requisition number, dollar amount of requisition, job number, steel weight, steel dollar amount, handling charge, component part job number and dollar amount, purchased parts dollar amount, and sundry columns for account number and dollar amount.

(j) Machine cost journal showing date, job number, operation number, hours and machine cost by departments as summarized from the daily labor cost tickets.

(k) Cost of sales journal showing date, job number, dollar amount credited to job cost record for units shipped and billed for the month. To the right, columns classifying the shipments as to stampings, dies, assemblies and miscellaneous should be included in this journal.

(l) Standard cost ledger journal containing the following monthly entries:

(C-1) Record actual purchases per the General ledger by charging the Cost Ledger Raw Material Inventory accounts and crediting the Cost Ledger Purchase-Offset accounts.

(C-2) Record monthly labor cost summary in (g), #1 above and machine cost to jobs in (j) above by charging Work-in-Process Inventory Machine Cost, charging or crediting Gain or Loss by departments and crediting the Cost Ledger Productive Labor and Factory Expense-Offset accounts for the actual expense increase during the month.

(C-3) Record the material requisitions for the month by charging Work-in-Process Inventory Material Cost and Handling Cost and crediting Work-in-Process Inventory for Component Parts Used and crediting Raw Materials Inventory accounts for raw materials used and crediting Gain or Loss-Handling account for handling charged on the requisitions.

(C-4) Allocate the total general factory department expense for the month (from C-2) to the other factory departments based upon the total payroll expended by the productive factory departments. This entry should charge Gain or Loss by Departments and credit Gain or Loss—General Factory.

(C-5) Record cost of sales journal by charging classified Cost of Sales accounts and crediting Work-in-Process Inventory Cost of Sales.

(5) Expense bills to be charged as follows:

(a) General Factory expense
Power and light
Rent (Company rents building)
Janitors and cleaning (charged to Building maintenance labor)
Fire and general liability insurance
Personal property taxes
Building maintenance and repairs

(b) Departmental expenses

Supplies	—charged directly to departments
Depreciation	—per company schedule
Payroll taxes	—$5\frac{1}{2}\%$ of payroll
Compensation insurance	—$1\frac{1}{2}\%$ of payroll
Group insurance	—1% of payroll
Vacation and holiday pay	—4% of payroll
Professional services	
Legal and audit	—Administrative expense
Engineering fees	—Specific factory department or General factory expense
Dues and subscriptions	—General factory or administrative
Telephone and telegraph	—Administrative
Advertising	—Selling expense
Commissions on sales	—Selling expense
Travel and entertainment	—Selling expense

(6) Monthly depreciation provision—

Fixed Amount

Shear	$ 300
Large press	1,100
Small press	600
Die shop	100
Assembly	150
Finishing	150
Material handling	150
General factory	250
Total factory	$2,800

Autos
    Selling 300
    Administrative 100
Office equipment (Administrative) 100

    Total $3,300

Chart of Old General Ledger Accounts in Use

                                      Department

Accounts payable	
Accounts receivable	
Accrued payroll	
Accrued F.I.C.A. and withholding taxes	
Accrued unemployment taxes	
Accrued compensation insurance	
Administrative and accounting salaries	Administrative
Administrative and accounting expenses—miscellaneous	Administrative
Advertising	Selling
Autos and automotive equipment	
Bad debts	Selling
Cartage, freight, and express (on shipments)	Selling
Cash in bank	
Commissions on sales	Selling
Common stock	
Depreciation expense	All departments
Electric light and power	General factory
Engineering fees	All factory departments
Insurance expense—fire, general liability, etc.	General factory
Insurance expense—compensation	All factory departments
Interest expense	Miscellaneous expense
Inventory and material purchases	
Legal and audit fees	Administrative
Machinery and equipment	
Maintenance and repair (other than payroll)	All factory departments
Notes payable	
Notes receivable	
Payroll—productive	All productive factory departments
Payroll—factory indirect	All factory departments
Petty cash	
Postage expense	Administrative
Profit and loss	
Purchase discount	Miscellaneous income
Rent expense	General factory
Reserve for bad debts	
Sales	
Sales discount	Miscellaneous expense
Sales expense—miscellaneous	Selling expense
Sales salaries	Selling expense
Salaries—factory supervision, etc.	All factory departments
Stationery and office supplies	Administrative
Surplus	
Taxes—payroll	All departments
Taxes—property and other	General factory and administrative
Telephone and telegraph	Administrative
Travel and entertainment	Selling and administrative

Required:

Part 1

(1) Prepare a new chart of General ledger accounts in duplicate, using a four-digit account number system. In setting up this chart, follow the suggested prefix digits in the Notes. The departmental expense suffix numbers should follow in this sequence:

(a) Productive labor group, consisting of clock time, overtime, premium, vacation and holiday pay.

(b) Indirect payroll accounts, such as supervision, handling, idle time, etc.

(c) Payroll taxes, compensation insurance and group insurance.

(d) Supplies, expendable tools, power, etc.

(e) Professional services.

(f) Maintenance and repair accounts (other than payroll).

(g) Fixed expenses such as rent, depreciation, general insurance, property taxes, etc.

Note that the Balance Sheet accounts should be listed in detail; sales and cost of sales accounts should provide separate classifications for stampings, dies, assemblies, and miscellaneous products. Purchase accounts should provide for steel, purchased parts, die materials and finishing materials. Section covering departmental payroll and expenses of the factory should show opposite each suffix number the departmental prefix number applicable to the specific expense (see page 407). Separate listing in detail covering selling, administrative and miscellaneous expenses, and miscellaneous income should be submitted. Scrap sales should be included in the purchase account group as #1790 and handled as a credit to cost of sales.

(2) Prepare a new chart of Cost ledger accounts reflecting:

(a) Raw material inventories of steel, purchased parts, etc.

(b) Work-in-process inventories classified as to materials, handling cost, machine cost, and cost of sales (credit).

(c) Cost of sales accounts classified as to stampings, dies, assemblies, and miscellaneous products.

(d) Gain or loss by departments.

(e) "Offset" expenditures accounts classified by the various purchase accounts in the General ledger, departmental expense accounts (in total for each department) from the General ledger and the opening raw material and work-in-process inventories at the beginning of the fiscal period. Note that departmental expense totals include direct and indirect labor.

(3) Based upon the budget estimates of the factory department payroll and other expenses, normal machine hours and estimated steel weight handled (submitted in Notes), submit schedule showing computation of budgeted hourly machine rates by departments and material handling rate per pound which would be used in company quotation estimates and in charging the various jobs. In this schedule allocate the general factory expenses to the productive departments based upon the labor expended by the productive departments.

Part 2

(1) Prepare specimen standard monthly General ledger entries with adequate explanations covering the various journals and data outlined in the Notes. Use X's ("XXXXX") to illustrate debits and credits in the respective debit and credit columns. On the depreciation entry, use the dollar amounts shown in the Notes.

(2) Prepare standard monthly Cost ledger entries with adequate explanations covering the various journals and data outlined in the Notes. Use X's ("XX-XXX") to illustrate debits and credits in the respective debit and credit columns.

(3) Prepare specimen journals for each of the General ledger journals outlined in the Notes (i.e., voucher register, check register, cash receipts, sales and credit memos). Have these specimen journals illustrate several typical entries.

(4) Prepare specimen journals for the following Cost ledger journals—
  (a) Material requisitions
  (b) Machine cost charges to jobs (from the job cost sections on the daily time cards).
  (c) Cost of sales journal
Have these specimen journals illustrate several typical entries.

(5) Prepare specimen Payroll recap for a month to support the General ledger journal entries #1 and #2. This recap should provide for five weekly entries of the gross payroll and a total for the month and four columns for computation of vacation pay, payroll taxes, compensation insurance, and group insurance. Only the Shear department and the General Factory sections need be shown since the other productive departments will follow the Shear department listing of labor account classifications on the left side.

Part 3

Prepare specimen job cost sheet which would provide for:
  (a) Date of entry
  (b) Reference
  (c) Materials cost—today and to date
  (d) Handling cost—today and to date
  (e) Department number, operation number, and machine number
  (f) Machine hours—today and to date
  (g) Machine cost—today and to date
  (h) Quantities shipped—today and to date
  (i) Billing amount of shipments—today and to date
  (j) Cost of shipments—today and to date (Cost of shipment entries are made once each month—all the other entries are made daily)
  (k) Work-in-process inventory balance which is the net balance of job charges (c), (d), (g), less cost of shipments in (j)

Make specimen entries.

(2) Prepare specimen daily time card which combines the functions of the regular clock card and the separate labor cost ticket.

Use the specimen daily time card (Figure 19-10) as a model. Enter the following data on your specimen daily time card and complete the card:

  (a) Data for entry by Payroll department and employee:

1. Clock number	36	
2. Employee's name	Joseph Black	
3. Date of shift	July 6	
4. Department number of employee	21	
5. Job clock punches by employee	*Continental Time*	
	In	*Out*
Reported at beginning of shift	6:54	
Scheduled start of shift	7:00	

Job stubs		
First	7:10	10:25
Second	10:30	14:60
Third	14:70	15:50
Fourth	15:50	16:50
Lunch period (no punching required)	12:00	12:50
Scheduled end of shift		15:50
Employee checked out		16:50

(b) Job stub data entered by timekeeper:

	1st Stub	2nd Stub	3rd Stub	4th Stub
Machine number	28	16	25	–
Job number	1143	1136	1092	–
Account number				2115
Operation number	2	3	4	–
Part number	D–10734	D–11962	M–8472	
Description	Form panel	Trim angle	Draw cup	Repair mach. #25
Quantity produced	350	2,180	250	–
Standard rate per M per hr.	10.00	1.500	.750	–

(c) Weekly data entered by Payroll department for Joseph Black:

1. Earned hours (on rated jobs)		22.50
2. Actual hours on standard		18.00
3. Bonus hours (1 minus 2)		4.50
4. Daywork hours		26.50
5. Waiting time		1.50
6. Overtime hours		6.00
7. Employee's hourly rate, $2.00		
8. Deductions		
Withholding and F.I.C.A. taxes	$8.69	
Group insurance	3.00	

Part 4

Prepare specimen monthly financial statements which should include:

Exhibit

1   Balance Sheet

2   Income and Expense

3   Factory Costs—this statement would include material costs, departmental totals of machine costs charged to jobs and work in process inventories at beginning and end of period.

4   Detailed Machine Costs—this statement would detail factory payroll and other factory expenses by departments, allocate the general factory expenses to the productive departments, and compare the result with the machine cost charged to jobs to reflect the gain or loss by factory departments.

5   Selling and Administrative Expenses

In preparing these statements, use the General ledger and Cost ledger chart of accounts.

Question 19-1

(a) Name and describe the basic types of cost system.
(b) Name and describe the bases of costing.

Question 19-2

Name and discuss the uses of cost accounting.

Chapter 20

Problem 20-1

THE UNIVERSITY BOOKSTORE

(*Survey information on pages 641–642*)

Assemble your solutions for the assignments on The Campus Bookstore to make a formal report. Write a letter of transmittal, and put the whole report in a cover.

Problem 20-2

UNIVERSAL ELECTRONICS COMPANY

(*Survey information on pages 643–644*)

Assemble your solutions for the assignments on Car Radio Sales Company. Write a letter of transmittal, and put the whole report in a cover.

Question 20-1

Name typical parts of a final report for a general systems assignment and explain the purpose and content of each part.

Question 20-2

Name parts of a preliminary report on a comparative methods study, and explain the purpose and content of each part.

Question 20-3

Discuss the types of information that should be included in a feasibility study for a computer installation.

Chapter 21

Question 21-1

Describe briefly the uses of the basic units of the punched card method: (1) card, (2) punch, (3) sorter, and (4) tabulator.

Question 21-2

Name the main parts of the electric tabulator and explain the function(s) of each part.

Question 21-3

Name typical labor distribution reports that might be produced on a tabulator.

Chapter 22

Question 22-1

a) Name the IBM punches available and describe the uses of each punch.
b) Name the Sperry Rand punches available and describe the uses of each punch.

Note that several of the punches have more than one basic use. For each punch, name all the basic uses.

Question 22-2

Describe briefly the uses of the following auxiliary units: (1) verifier, (2) interpreter, and (3) collator.

Question 22-3

Name some particulars in which various models of tabulators differ.

Question 22-4

(a) What special capability does the IBM 407 Accounting Machine have when an Advanced Computing Attachment is coupled to it?

(b) What basic principle of machine operation distinguishes the ACA from the Type 602A Calculating Punch?

Chapter 23

Question 23-1

(a) Name a punched card application in which pre-punched cards are used.
(b) What is the advantage of using pre-punched cards?
(c) Is there a possible disadvantage? Discuss.

Question 23-2

(a) Name a punched card application in which several punches may be used in processing a packet of cards.
(b) Name the card concerned and explain the use of each punch in processing the cards.

Chapter 24

Question 24-1

(a) What is meant by "electronic data processing"?
(b) What is meant by the terms "analogue computer" and "digital computer"?

Question 24-2

(a) What is a program?
(b) What is the meaning and significance of the stored program concept?

Question 24-3

What is the meaning and significance of the statement that the computer is capable of making simple decisions?

Question 24-4

Name three ways of classifying computers in general.

Question 24-5

Name the components of a computer system and describe briefly the function of each component.

Question 24-6

(a) What is the difference between a program and a built-in set of special instructions?
(b) What is the purpose of each?

Question 24-7

How does a card reader read cards?

Question 24-8

In general, what are the methods of creating magnetic tape?

Question 24-9

What is the function of the tape transport?

Question 24-10

Name some of the uses of the console typewriter.

Question 24-11

(a) What is a data collection unit?
(b) What is the function of a data collection unit?

Question 24-12

(a) What are visual display units?
(b) Name several types of visual display units.
(c) What comparison can you make of a cathode ray tube with a teletype as an output unit in a computer system?

Question 24-13

What are the major types of printing mechanisms in high speed printers?

Question 24-14

What is the meaning and significance of the terms storage, on-line, off-line, random access and random inquiry, sequstial access, real time, delayed central processing?

Question 24-15

What are a few of the factors pertinent in the comparison of types of storage units?

Question 24-16

Name and describe briefly several types of storage.

Question 24-17

(a) What are the basic attributes of a number system?
(b) What are the specific attributes of decimal, binary, and binary coded decimal number systems?

Question 24-18

What is the relationship between the on-and-off principle of electronic circuitry and the binary number system?

Question 24-19

What is the binary coded decimal representation of the decimal number 2805?

Question 24-20

What are some of the features of third generation computers?

Question 24-21

(a) What is data transmission?
(b) What are some of the units that might be included in a data transmission system?

Question 24-22

(a) What is a terminal computer?
(b) What are some of its functions?

Question 24-23

(a) What is optical character reading?
(b) What are the components of the reader?
(c) What is a document reader? a page reader?

Question 24-24

Describe briefly the types of applications of optical character reading.

Question 24-25

How does optical character reading (OCR) differ from magnetic ink character reading (MICR)?

Chapter 25

Question 25–1

What is time sharing?

Question 25–2

(a) What is meant by time-slicing?
(b) What is meant by interaction between computer and terminal operation? Give examples.

Question 25–3:

What is the difference between time-sharing and remote batch processing?

Question 25–4:

Who are the personnel who may operate a time-sharing terminal? With what activity may each person be concerned?

Question 25–5:

What are the three main elements in the cost of time-sharing service?

Question 25–6:

What are some of the criteria to be considered in the selection of a time-sharing service?

Question 25–7:

What are some of the types of input devices for time-sharing?

Question 25–8:

What are some of the types of output devices for time-sharing?

Question 25–9:

What are some of the capabilities of time-sharing which have special interest to accountants?

Question 25–10:

Name some of the procedures described in this book to which the use of time-sharing lends itself. Describe each use briefly.

Chapter 26

Problem 26-1

WILSON BAKING COMPANY*

The Wilson Baking Company manufactures a line of cookies in band ovens through which the cookies pass under precisely controlled speed and temperature. Each oven is about 60 feet long and 10 feet wide and the "band" is a continuously moving belt of sheet metal which comprises the floor of the oven on which the baking is done. The batter is dropped onto the band at one end of the oven and the finished cookies are discharged from the other end, ready for packaging.

The line of cookies includes about twenty styles, which are produced at varying rates in pounds per oven hour. There are three ovens. One is used exclusively for saltines, one for both grahams and sweet cookies, and one for sweet cookies.

The company sells to retailers in six states. The business is seasonal—sales are low in the summer and high in the winter. All ovens operate at capacity in December.

---

* Wilson Baking Company (fictitious name) is an actual case, adapted from Cecil Gillespie, *Standard and Direct Costing,* Third Edition, Prentice-Hall (1962), p. 303.

The chief accounting officer uses conventional absorption cost accounting for costing production. He calculates gross profit percentage for each style and he includes both fixed and variable manufacturing costs in inventories on the balance sheet. He maintains that the sales department should push the products that carry the highest gross profit percentage.

The vice president in charge of marketing uses the gross profit percentages issued by the chief accounting officer. He states, however, that a salesman never sells a single style of cookie to a customer but gets the best combination of styles he can. The salesmen are paid straight commission (the same rate for all products) plus traveling expenses, and they accordingly attempt to sell dollar volume without regard to style composition. Each salesman regularly travels by automobile a route laid out by the marketing vice president. Some salesmen are based in the headquarters city and some in a territory city.

The executive vice president engaged a systems man, requesting him to survey the existing information procedures and make a recommendation. The systems man reported that (1) the manufacturing accounting system in operation does not provide sound information for the decisions to be made (it will produce the wrong decisions) and (2) marketing decisions are being made intuitively rather than with the aid of solid information.

Write a report on (a) decisions, (b) information requirements, and (c) information sources for the Wilson Baking Company. Cover both manufacturing and marketing.

To keep your report within time limits, do not consider advertising and delivery to customers.

The following questions are independent of Problem 26-1, except as noted.

Question 26-1

What is a management information system?

Question 26-2

What distinctions can you draw among a management information system, an accounting system, and an operating system?

Question 26-3

Discuss in general terms the structure of the decision system on which the operating system and the management information system, respectively, are based.

Question 26-4

Discuss the role of internal information and external information in the management information system.

Question 26-5 (Related to Problem 26-1)

Assume that a complete sales distribution (in the accounting system sense) procedure has to be designed for Wilson Baking Company to set up the internal information sources. It is anticipated that computers will not be used. You have been given the assignment to design the distribution procedure and you begin by separating the unlikely methods from the likely methods.

Required:

(1) Name all the methods of distribution (except computers).
(2) Name the quantitative and time factors influencing the selection of a distribution method.

Question 26-6

Discuss the evolution and objectives of the total systems concept.

Question 26-7

In applying the decision making view to the design of information systems, what is the list of questions that should be considered?

Question 26-8

Referring to the Jordan Printing Company case (Table 26-1), comment on the general applicability of the questions relating to strategic planning decisions.

Question 26-9

What purpose is served by the profitability accounting sub-system in the financial information system? by the responsibility accounting sub-system?

Question 26-10

Comment on the following statement with reference to marketing information systems:

"The planning decisions that the marketing manager must make will require information variously on products, territories, channels of distribution, and methods of sale."

Question 26-11

What are the functions of the production management information system?

Question 26-12

What are the functions of the personnel management information system?

Question 26-13

A giant steel manufacturing company designed and installed an information system-personnel in the mid 1930's. (This was a unit of what might eventually include financial, marketing, manufacturing, and total.)

Using the information system-personnel as a basis for discussion:
(a) What is meant by a common data base?
(b) Give a few examples of the kinds of information that would be collected in the data base.
(c) What are the inherent payoffs (anticipated) of a common data base in a large company?

Question 26-14 (Related to Problem 26-1)

The management of the Wilson Baking Company does not wish to begin the development of a strategic planning model for the firm but desires to start with model(s) for short term planning that could be developed readily and integrated with the information system you worked out in the problem.

Answer the following questions concisely:

(a) What kind of model do you propose? For what purpose?

(b) Name some of the input variables for your model.

(c) What generalizations can you state about the nature of the decision process and the nature of the input variables for strategic planning models as distinguished from operational planning models (short term)?

Question 26-15

(a) What is a program as considered in connection with program budgeting?

(b) What is the relationship between the decision making process (for major decisions) and the formulation, justification and approval of programs?

Question 26-16

(a) Program budgeting is integrated with the management information system in the decision making process at the top level, and also in the feedback from the financial accounting system. True or false? Explain concisely.

(b) Proponents of program budgeting state that one advantage is that unlike conventional financial accounting, program budgeting accommodates itself to differing time cycles. They say that a consistent monthly or annual time span is not necessarily desirable in a management information system. True or false? Comment.

Index

Optical character recognition (OCR), 589–595
defined, 559
Order procedures, 223–247
combination of billing procedures and, 229–236
function described, 223–224
time-sharing and, 612
Order systems, codes in, 48
Organization charts
for internal control, 189–192
as survey tools, 22
Output in automatic writing and calculating equipment, 109
Output units (*see also* Input-output units)
in computer system, 559
shipping order sets, invoice sets and IBM 6400, 116
Overtime premiums, 382

Package proofs, 147–148
alphanumeric machine, 398–400
Padded multiple copy forms, 91–94
Paper
buying own, 89
standardization of form, 88–89
"Paper Roll Machine," 208
Parts manufactured for stock, 423–425
Payroll boards, 394–395
Payroll department, 380–412
function and organization of, 380–381
Payroll forms produced on alphanumeric machines, 398–400
Payroll journals, 287
Payroll and labor cost analysis procedures in manual of accounts, 10
Payroll procedures, 378–403
forms, statements and reports for, 387–388
internal check on, 378–379
in ledgerless bookkeeping, 405
legal aspects of design of, 381–382
methods used in, 390–403
punched-card accounting and, 546–547
payroll control and, 500–501
time-sharing and, 612
Pen-and-ink account forms, 292–295
Pen-and-ink accounts payable procedures, 334–335
Pen-and-ink journals, 55–74
Pen-and-ink payroll, 391–394
Pen-and-ink posting
differences between machine-posting and, 158–159
direct posting to accounts by, 296–297
Pen-kept columnar journals in sales distribution, 253–258
Perforators, 193
Perpetual inventory procedures, 426–432
forms for, 427–429
requisition forms, 428–429
function and organization of, 426
materials classification in, 427
punched-card accounting and, 533–534

Personnel management information system, 636
Picture phone, 586
Pigeon hole sort, defined, 167
Planning, accounting forms, papers and, 2
Plant layouts, as survey tools, 22
Portal-to-portal pay, 383
Posting
to accounts, for accounts receivable, 295–296
of business papers, 55
of cash receipts, 312
delayed, 297–298
direct, 296–298
as "do" operation, 6
machine (*see* Machine-posting)
payroll, 395–396
pen-and-ink
differences between machine-posting and, 158–159
direct-posting to accounts by, 296–297
perpetual inventory accounts, 429–431
random, 162
to statements, cycle billing and, 299–300
visible record equipment for, 170–175
Posting copies (accounting copies), 226, 228
Posting cycle, defined, 132
Posting media in machine-posting application, 158–164
Power files, 177–178
Pre-billing, 238–242
Preliminary work in general assignments, 36–37
Pre-printed unit shipping orders, 242–243
"Press-Down-Key" cash registers, 209
Prices, internal check and verified, 196
Print keys for salesmen or department identification, 212
Printed forms, 62–90
layout, 81–82, 84
ordering and inventory control of, 89–90
paper for, 88–89
ready-printed
accounts forms, 75–79
journal forms, 62–65
rules for spacing, for typewriter use, 83
standardized, 84–89
Printing calculators, ten-key, 129–130
Procedure, defined, 2, 4
Procedures staffs, organization of, 17–19
Process, defined, 7
Process charts, 22–27
Process cost accounting with departmental transfer, 461
Process cost system, defined, 434, 435
Process costs, defined, 460–461
Process manufacture, 425–426
Processing of employee, 359–364
Product classifications in sales distribution, 251–252
Product lists as survey tools, 22
Production control procedures, 413–426
classifications of, 415–416